John MacEvilly

An Exposition of the Gospel of St. John

John MacEvilly

An Exposition of the Gospel of St. John

ISBN/EAN: 9783744659307

Printed in Europe, USA, Canada, Australia, Japan

Cover: Foto ©Thomas Meinert / pixelio.de

More available books at **www.hansebooks.com**

AN EXPOSITION

OF

THE GOSPEL OF ST. JOHN,

CONSISTING OF

AN ANALYSIS OF EACH CHAPTER,

AND OF A

COMMENTARY,

CRITICAL, EXEGETICAL, DOCTRINAL, AND MORAL,

HAVING THE TEXT, ENGLISH AND LATIN, PREFIXED IN
FULL TO EACH CHAPTER;

ALSO,

THE VERSES IN EACH CHAPTER MARGINALLY ARRANGED,
SIDE BY SIDE WITH THE COMMENTARY.

BY HIS GRACE
THE MOST REV. DR. MacEVILLY,
Archbishop of Tuam.

DUBLIN:
M. H. GILL & SON, 50 UPPER O'CONNELL STREET.

NEW YORK:
BENZIGER BROTHERS, 113 BROADWAY.

1889.

Works by the same Author.

AN EXPOSITION
OF
THE GOSPELS OF MATTHEW AND MARK.
THIRD Edition, enlarged.

OF LUKE.
SECOND Edition, enlarged.

AN EXPOSITION OF ALL THE EPISTLES,
PAULINE AND CATHOLIC.
In 2 Vols.
THIRD Edition, enlarged.

DUBLIN: PRINTED BY SEALY, BRYERS AND WALKER, 94, 95 AND 96 MIDDLE ABBEY STREET.

GENERAL INTRODUCTION.

As the General Introduction prefixed to the first edition of our Commentary on the Gospel of St. Matthew was meant for the three other Gospels also, which we contemplated expounding in course of time, we shall not trespass on the patience of the reader by travelling over the same ground once more.

But as one portion of that Introduction is peculiarly suited to the circumstances of the present time, we may be allowed to reproduce it, and prefix it to this our Commentary on the Gospel of St. John :—

"In addition to the foregoing reasons, the character of the age on which we have fallen, considerably influenced me in publishing a Commentary on the Gospels at the present time. Was it ever more necessary, at any period in the history of Christianity, than it is at this day, to place before the world, in as clear a light as possible, an exposition in accordance with the unerring teachings of the Catholic Church, of the fundamental principles of faith and morals, with which the Son of God came down to enlighten a world He found sitting in darkness and in the shadow of death? Does the condition into which many parts of the world are at this moment relapsing, promise to be an improvement on that state of Paganism in which He found it when He came to proclaim glory to God and peace to men? Has not His spouse and representative, the Catholic Church, with whom He deposited the fulness of truth, and to whom He bequeathed the plenitude of His authority, as fierce a struggle before her, enemies as embittered to encounter, as she had when she was forced to seek shelter for a time in the bowels of the earth, and the Flavian Amphitheatre re-echoed to the savage yells of, '*Christianos ad leones?*' Are the principles of Atheism, Materialism, total negation of all future sanction, which even the very fables of Paganism dimly shadowed forth, less deadly or noxious in their consequences, both as regards here and hereafter, than the principles of Polytheism she succeeded in extirpating? As regards public authority, was the all-absorbing power of Pagan rulers more crushing that the iron-despotism which men would now fain establish in the most powerful kingdoms under the specious name of Liberty? Liberty—that name, like religion itself, so often injuriously invoked, as if it could be ever found dissociated from the holy influences of God's Spirit, for, '*Where the Spirit of the Lord is, there* (and there only) *is liberty*' (2 Cor. iii. 17).

"Do we not see every day, unholy efforts persistently made and unjustly enforced, even at the risk of Anarchy, to render to Cæsar, not only what belongs to Cæsar, but also to concentrate in him all rights, human and divine; to constitute him the sole guardian, depositary and dispenser of what belongs to God, and this in defiance of all the principles of true liberty, despite solemn treaties, and in violation of guaranteed rights of conscience? Does not this all absorbing power of the State, resting solely on brute force, entering into an unholy league with condemned Secret Societies, which embrace both hemispheres, unjustly invade and trample under foot the sacred rights of parents, forcing them to have their children, destined one day to fill those seats vacated by the fallen angels, brought up in schools, where the sacred name of God is utterly ignored, and their tender minds indoctrinated in the soul-destroying principles of Materialism?

"What is this but a persistent attempt at the revival of Paganism, making might or the law of the strongest, the sole standard of right? What is it but the substitution of brute force for the abiding blessings of moral influences. What is it but a rapid approach to that sad state of spiritual decay, of which our Redeemer Himself forewarns us, '*Think you when the Son of Man cometh, shall He find faith on earth?*' (Luke xviii. 8.)

"As the Son of God came down from heaven, not only to be our Redeemer, but our teacher; not only to ransom us with the effusion of His precious blood, but to enlighten us with these saving truths, the knowledge of which, joined to firm and unhesitating faith, He has made an indispensable condition of salvation, it must be ever a subject of the deepest spiritual interest, to place these truths in as clear a light as possible. Whether this Commentary may serve in any way to advance this end, must be left to others to decide."

✠ JOHN MacEVILLY,

Archbishop of Tuam.

Tuam, *February* 21*st*, 1889.

PREFACE
TO
GOSPEL OF ST. JOHN.

St. John, the Apostle, the inspired author of this fourth Gospel, was son of Zebedee and Salome. He, as well as all the other Apostles, if we except the Traitor Judas, were natives of Galilee. He followed his father's humble occupation of fisherman on the lake of Galilee. Zebedee, it would seem, was possessed of some means, as he had in his employment hired servants (Mark i. 20). John himself, it would appear, was also possessed of some means. For, we find, he took into his own house in Jerusalem, the Blessed Mother of God, who had been confided to his filial care by her dying Son and Saviour (xix. 27).

His mother Salome was nearly related to the Blessed Virgin (xix. 26). The Evangelist was, therefore, closely connected with our Blessed Lord, by ties of kindred. This circumstance, perhaps, might have influenced Salome in preferring her request to our Lord to assign a place of pre-eminence in His kingdom to both her sons, James and John (Matthew xx. 20, 21). This Salome is reckoned among the pious women, who accompanied our Lord in His mission, and ministered to Him out of their substance (Mark xx. 40, 41; Matthew xxvii. 55, 56). She faithfully followed Him to the foot of the cross (Matthew xxvii. 56). Nor did she leave Him until He was placed in His sepulchre (Mark xvi. 1).

It is said that John was one of the two disciples of the Baptist, who attached themselves, in the first instance, for a short time, to our Blessed Lord (John i. 37). Likely, he was among the few disciples who were present at the Marriage Feast of Cana (chap. ii.), which, as an eye-witness, he so graphically and minutely describes. Having returned, for a time, to his ordinary occupation of fisherman, he was permanently called by our Lord, while engaged with his father Zebedee, and his elder brother James, afterwards called "James the Greater," in mending their nets on the shore of the sea of Tiberias or lake of Galilee (Matthew iv. 21, 22).

He is known, as *the beloved disciple*, "the disciple whom Jesus loved." (xiii. 23, etc.) No doubt, he made a grateful return, from all his heart, for the singular love which his Divine Master had shown him on several occasions. By the constant repetition of the holy name of Jesus, throughout his Gospel and Epistles, he shows how this adorable name was uppermost in his mind, engraven on his heart, and the chief absorbing thought of his inmost soul.

On several occasions, our Lord had selected him as the object of special favour. He was chosen to be present at the raising of Jairus's daughter from the dead

(Mark v. 41); also at our Lord's glorious Transfiguration. (Matthew xvii. 1, etc.) To him was granted the singular privilege of leaning on our Lord's bosom (John xiii. 23) at the Last Supper, when he was instituting the adorable Eucharist. It was in reply to his question, proposed on that occasion, at the request of Peter, our Lord made known who the traitor was. Finally, our Lord gave him the crowning proof of His singular love, by committing to him from the lofty summit of His cross, the care of His beloved Mother, whom He bequeathed to him, and to us all, as the last precious legacy of His dying love (xix. 26, 27). He was specially favoured in being among the first of the Apostles to whom was communicated the earliest tidings of our Lord's Resurrection. He was also privileged to be the first to recognise our Lord at the miraculous draught of fishes after the Resurrection (xxi. 7).

After our Lord's Ascension, he remained some time in Jerusalem (Acts i. 13; iii. 1; iv. 13). Charged by her divine Son with the filial care of His beloved Mother, (xix. 27), it can hardly be supposed, he left Jerusalem till after her death and Assumption into heaven. Indeed, Nicephorus (Hist. Eccles. Lib. 2, c. 42), and St. Epiphanius expressly assures us, that this was the case. He was at Jerusalem on the occasion of St. Paul's visit there, in the year 52 (Gal. ii. 3–9). When St. Paul visited Ephesus in the year 58, St. John was not there. It was only after St. Paul's martyrdom, that St. John fixed his permanent abode at Ephesus, with the view of counteracting the efforts of the false teachers, who had made their appearance there after St. Paul's departure (Acts xx. 29).

While displaying his wonted Apostolic zeal, thundering against Heresy and Infidelity, and especially against the worship of the great Diana of the Ephesians, he was denounced, as a dangerous character, to the tyrant Domitian, who had raised a second furious persecution against the Church. Having been sent to Rome, and confronted with the jealous Emperor Domitian, this cruel persecutor of the Christians, he was condemned to an extraordinary kind of punishment. He was sentenced, as we are told by Tertullian (de Presc. 36) to be thrown into a cauldron of boiling oil, whence he came forth, as St. Jerome assures us (Contra Iovin.) quite uninjured, thus earning for himself the glorious title of Martyr, as the punishment inflicted would have caused his death, were he not miraculously preserved. Domitian fearing that any further attempts on his life might prove abortive, had him banished to the little island of Patmos, one of the Sporades in the Ægean sea. It is commonly held, that it was here, he wrote the Apocalypse. The acts of Domitian, so remarkable for cruelty, having been, on that account, cancelled under his successor, the Emperor Nerva, St. John was permitted to return to Ephesus, where he died in peace, after having reached an extreme old age. The precise year of his death cannot be exactly determined; it must have closely bordered on the 100th year of our Æra.

This disciple of love, which he is never tired of inculcating in all his writings, was particularly distinguished for his horror of Heresiarchs, the founders of pernicious sects and propagators of false doctrines. We can have no doubt, that in his charity he was tolerant towards those who, having the misfortune of drinking in false doctrines with their mother's milk, were educated and brought up in the bosom of heresy. He would surely extend the greatest consideration towards those who, brought up from infancy in the profession of false doctrines, may, it is to be hoped, be more or less excused on account of their sincerity and good faith. He surely, would inculcate the same charitable feelings in regard to all future generations. But for the wicked propagators of false doctrines, the founder of Heretical sects, he had no toleration. It is of such, whom he frequently designates as "Antichrists," he says, notwithstanding the great charity he taught and practised, "If any man come to you and brings not this doctrine, receive him not into the house, or say to him, 'God speed you,' for he that saith to him, 'God speed you,' communicates with his wicked works" (2 John 10, 11).

Of this he gave a practical example. On one occasion, hearing that Cerinthus was in the same bath with him, he cried out, "*Fugiamus ne cadat et opprimat nos balneum in quo lavatur Cerinthus, inimicus veritatis*" (Irœneus iii. 4). A similar incident is recorded of St. Polycarp, a disciple of St. John, in relation to the Heretic, Marcion, whose salutation the Saint returned, by saying, "*Cognosco primogenitum Diaboli.*" Such conduct, far from being uncharitable, is the perfection of the charity we owe our own souls and those of our brethren.

HIS GOSPEL, OBJECT AND DESIGN OF.

THE Evangelist himself assures us, that his chief object in writing this Gospel was to prove our Lord's Divinity and Humanity as well, and thus beget faith in this fundamental article of Christian truth, as a necessary means for securing salvation (see page 5). By establishing this fundamental article of faith, the Evangelist fully refutes all the errors, past, present or future, regarding our Lord's Divinity and His Incarnation. Whether he had also directly intended to refute the errors that sprang up in his own time, is questioned by some. It is, however, generally asserted by ancient ecclesiastical writers, that he had specially in view to meet the errors of Ebion and Cerinthus, who propagated pernicious doctrines even in the Apostle's lifetime regarding our Lord's Divinity and Humanity. St. Jerome tells us (Proæm. in Mattheum), he did so, at the earnest entreaty of the Bishops and faithful of Asia, and that he consented, on condition, that a general fast would be proclaimed and fervent prayers offered up to God to enlighten him. After this, eagle-like, gazing steadily on the Son of Justice, transcending all creatures, all space and time, he burst forth into the sublime words, "*In principio erat verbum*," etc.

WHEN WRITTEN, DATE OF.

IT is commonly held, that it was written at Ephesus, after the Epistles and Apocalypse, towards the close of the Apostle's life, shortly before the 100th year of our Æra.

THE HOLY GOSPEL OF JESUS CHRIST,

ACCORDING TO ST. JOHN.

CHAPTER I.

1 In the beginning was the Word, and the Word was with God, and the Word was God.

2 The same was in the beginning with God.

3 All things were made by him: and without him was made nothing that was made.

4 In him was life, and the life was the light of men:

5 And the light shineth in darkness, and the darkness did not comprehend it.

6 There was a man sent from God, whose name was John.

7 This man came for a witness, to give testimony of the light, that all men might believe through him.

8 He was not the light, but was to give testimony of the light.

9 That was the true light, which enlighteneth every man that cometh into this world.

10 He was in the world, and the world was made by him, and the world knew him not.

11 He came unto his own, and his own received him not.

12 But as many as received him, he gave them power to be made the sons of God, to them that believe in his name.

13 Who are born, not of blood, nor of the will of the flesh, nor of the will of man, but of God.

14 And the Word was made flesh, and dwelt amongst us (and we saw his glory, the glory as it were of the only-begotten of the Father) full of grace and truth.

15 John beareth witness of him, and crieth out, saying: This was he of whom I spoke: He that shall come after me, is preferred before me: because he was before me

16 And of his fulness we all have received, and grace for grace.

17 For the law was given by Moses, grace and truth came by Jesus Christ.

18 No man hath seen God at any time: the only begotten Son who is in the bosom of the Father, he hath declared him.

19 And this is the testimony of John, when the Jews sent from Jerusalem priests and levites to him, to ask him: Who art thou?

20 And he confessed, and did not deny, and he confessed: I am not the Christ.

21 And they asked him: What then? Art thou Elias? And he said: I am not. Art thou the prophet? And he answered: No.

22 They said therefore unto him: Who art thou, that we may give an answer to them that sent us? what sayest thou of thyself?

A

23 *He said:* I am the voice of one crying in the wilderness, Make straight the way of the Lord, *as said the prophet Isaias.*

24 *And they that were sent, were of the Pharisees.*

25 *And they asked him, and said to him:* Why then dost thou baptize, if thou be not Christ, nor Elias, nor the prophet?

26 *John answered them, saying:* I baptize with water; but there hath stood one in the midst of you, whom you know not.

27 *The same is he that shall come after me, who is preferred before me: the latchet of whose shoe I am not worthy to loose.*

28 *These things were done in Bethania beyond the Jordan, where John was baptizing.*

29 *The next day John saw Jesus coming to him, and he saith:* Behold the lamb of God, behold him who taketh away the sin of the world.

30 *This is he of whom I said: After me there cometh a man, who is preferred before me: because he was before me.*

31 *And I knew him not, but that he may be made manifest in Israel, therefore am I come baptizing with water.*

32 *And John gave testimony, saying:* I saw the Spirit coming down as a dove from heaven, and he remained upon him.

33 *And I knew him not: but he, who sent me to baptize with water, said to me:* He upon whom thou shalt see the Spirit descending and remaining upon him, he it is that baptizeth with the Holy Ghost.

34 *And I saw; and I gave testimony, that this is the Son of God.*

35 *The next day again John stood, and two of his disciples.*

36 *And beholding Jesus walking, he saith:* Behold the lamb of God.

37 *And the two disciples heard him speak, and they followed Jesus.*

38 *And Jesus turning, and seeing them following him, saith to them:* What seek you? *Who said to him:* Rabbi (which is to say, being interpreted, Master), where dwellest thou?

39 *He saith to them:* Come and see. *They came, and saw where he abode, and they staid with him that day: now it was about the tenth hour.*

40 *And Andrew the brother of Simon Peter was one of the two who had heard from John, and followed him.*

41 *He findeth first his brother Simon, and saith to him:* We have found the Messias, which is, being interpreted, the Christ.

42 *And he brought him to Jesus. And Jesus looking upon him, said:* Thou art Simon the son of Jona: thou shalt be called Cephas, which is interpreted, Peter.

43 *On the following day he would go forth into Galilee, and he findeth Philip. And Jesus saith to him:* Follow me.

44 *Now Philip was of Bethsaida, the city of Andrew and Peter.*

45 *Philip findeth Nathanael, and saith to him:* We have found him of whom Moses in the law, and the prophets did write, Jesus the son of Joseph of Nazareth.

46 *And Nathanael said to him:* Can anything of good come from Nazareth? *Philip saith to him:* Come and see.

47 *Jesus saw Nathanael coming to him, and he saith of him:* Behold an Israelite indeed, in whom there is no guile.

48 *Nathanael saith to him:* Whence knowest thou me? *Jesus answered and saith to him:* Before that Philip called thee, when thou wast under the fig-tree, I saw thee.

49 Nathanael answered him, and saith: Rabbi, thou art the Son of God, thou art the king of Israel.

50 Jesus answered, and said to him: Because I said unto thee, I saw thee under the fig-tree, thou believest: greater things than these shalt thou see.

51 And he saith to him: Amen, amen I say to you, you shall see the heaven opened, and the Angels of God ascending and descending upon the son of man.

SANCTUM JESU CHRISTI EVANGELIUM SECUNDUM JOANNEM.

CAPUT PRIMUM.

1 *In principio erat verbum, et verbum erat apud Deum, et Deus erat verbum.*

2 *Hoc erat in principio apud Deum.*

3 *Omnia per ipsum facta sunt: et sine ipso factum est nihil, quod factum est,*

4 *In ipso vita erat, et vita erat lux hominum:*

5 *Et lux in tenebris lucet, et tenebræ eam non comprehenderunt.*

6 *Fuit homo missus à Deo, cui nomen erat Joannes.*

7 *Hic venit in testimonium, ut testimonium perhiberet de lumine, ut omnes crederent per illum.*

8 *Non erat ille lux, sed ut testimonium perhiberet de lumine.*

9 *Erat lux vera, quæ illuminat omnem hominem venientem in hunc mundum.*

10 *In mundo erat, et mundus per ipsum factus est, et mundus eum non cognovit.*

11 *In propria venit, et sui eum non receperunt.*

12 *Quotquot autem receperunt eum, dedit eis potestatem filios Dei fieri, his qui credunt in nomine ejus:*

13 *Qui non ex sanguinibus, neque ex voluntate carnis, neque ex voluntate viri, sed ex Deo nati sunt.*

14 *Et verbum caro factum est, et habitavit in nobis, et vidimus gloriam ejus, gloriam quasi unigeniti à patre, plenum gratiæ et veritatis.*

15 *Joannes testimonium perhibet de ipso, et clamat, dicens: Hic erat, quem dixi: Qui post me venturus est, ante me factus est, quia prior me erat.*

16 *Et de plenitudine ejus nos omnes accepimus, et gratiam pro gratia.*

17 *Quia lex per Moysen data est, gratia et veritas per Jesum Christum facta est.*

18 *Deum nemo vidit umquam: unigenitus filius, qui est in sinu patris, ipse enarravit.*

19 *Et hoc est testimonium Joannis, quando miserunt Judæi ab Jerosolymis sacerdotes et Levitas ad eum ut interrogarent eum: Tu quis es?*

20 *Et confessus est, et non negavit: et confessus est: Quia non sum ego Christus.*

21 *Et interrogaverunt eum: Quid ergo? Elias es tu? Et dixit: Non sum. Propheta es tu? Et respondit: Non.*

22 *Dixerunt ergo ei: Quis es, ut responsum demus his, qui miserunt nos? quid dicis de teipso?*

23 *Ait: Ego vox clamantis in deserto: Dirigite viam Domini, sicut dixit Isaias Propheta.*

24 *Et qui missi fuerant, erant ex Pharisæis.*

25 *Et interrogaverunt eum, et dixerunt ei : Quid ergo baptizas, si tu non es Christus, neque Elias, neque Propheta?*

26 *Respondit Joannes, dicens eis : Ego baptizo in aqua : medius autem vestrûm stetit, quem vos nescitis.*

27 *Ipse est, qui post me venturus est, qui ante me factus est : cujus ego non sum dignus ut solvam ejus corrigiam calceamenti.*

28 *Hæc in Bethania facta sunt trans Jordanem, ubi erat Joannes baptizans.*

29 *Alterâ die vidit Joannes Jesum venientem ad se, et ait : Ecce agnus Dei, ecce qui tollit peccatum mundi.*

30 *Hic est, de quo dixi : Post me venit vir, qui ante me factus est : quia prior me erat.*

31 *Et ego nesciebam eum, sed ut manifestetur in Israel, proptereà veni ego in aqua baptizans.*

32 *Et testimonium perhibuit Joannes, dicens : Quia vidi Spiritum descendentem quasi columbam de cœlo, et mansit super eum.*

33 *Et ego nesciebam eum : sed qui misit me baptizare in aqua, ille mihi dixit : Super quem videris Spiritum descendentem, et manentem super eum, hic est, qui baptizat in Spiritu Sancto.*

34 *Et ego vidi : et testimonium perhibui quia hic est Filius Dei.*

35 *Alterâ die iterùm stabat Joannes, et ex discipulis ejus duo.*

36 *Et respiciens Jesum ambulantem, dicit : Ecce agnus Dei.*

37 *Et audierunt eum duo discipuli loquentem, et secuti sunt Jesum.*

38 *Conversus autem Jesus, et videns eos sequentes se, dicit eis : Quid quæritis? Qui dixerunt ei : Rabbi, (quod dicitur interpretatum Magister) ubi habitas?*

39 *Dicit eis : Venite, et videte. Venerunt, et viderunt ubi maneret, et apud eum manserunt die illo : hora autem erat quasi decima.*

40 *Erat autem Andreas frater Simonis Petri unus ex duobus, qui audierant à Joanne, et secuti fuerant eum.*

41 *Invenit hic primùm fratrem suum Simonem, et dicit ei : Invenimus Messiam. (Quod est interpretatum Christus.)*

42 *Et adduxit eum ad Jesum. Intuitus autem eum Jesus, dixit : Tu es Simon filius Jona : tu vocaberis Cephas, quod interpretatur Petrus.*

43 *In crastinum voluit exire in Galilæam, et invenit Philippum. Et dicit ei Jesus : Sequere me.*

44 *Erat autem Philippus à Bethsaida, civitate Andreæ et Petri.*

45 *Invenit Philippus Nathanael, et dicit ei : Quem scripsit Moyses in lege, et Prophetæ invenimus Jesum filium Joseph à Nazareth.*

46 *Et dixit ei Nathanael : A Nazareth potest aliquid boni esse? Dicit ei Philippus : Veni, et vide.*

47 *Vidit Jesus Nathanael venientem ad se, et dicit de eo : Ecce verè Israelita, in quo dolus non est.*

48 *Dicit ei Nathanael : Unde me nosti? Respondit Jesus, et dixit ei : Priusquam te Philippus vocaret, cùm esses sub ficu, vidi te.*

49 *Respondit ei Nathanael, et ait : Rabbi, tu es Filius Dei, tu es Rex Israel :*

50 *Respondit Jesus, et dixit ei : Quia dixi tibi : Vidi te sub ficu, credis : majus his videbis.*

51 *Et dicit ei : Amen, amen dico vobis, videbitis cœlum apertum, et Angelos Dei ascendentes, et descendentes supra Filium hominis.*

THE chief object the Evangelist had in view, as he himself expressly assures us, in writing this Gospel was to prove our Lord's Divinity and beget faith in this fundamental article of Christian truth, as a necessary means for securing eternal life (c. xx., v. 31). He, therefore, enters on his sublime Preface to his Gospel by proclaiming our Lord's Divinity, His distinct, Divine Personality, His consubstantiality with the Father together with His Omnipotence shown in His having educed out of nothing every thing created (vv. 1–3). Whether, in doing this, the Evangelist had also in view to confound the false notions of the Pagan Philosophers and the blasphemous errors regarding our Lord's Divinity broached by Heretics, of whom some, such as Ebion and Cerinthus, etc., appeared in his own day to trouble the peace of the Church, others, in the near future, bearing the imposing title of Gnostics, of whose errors he may possibly have been divinely gifted with a clear foresight, is a subject of dispute among the learned. One thing, however, is quite certain, that all these errors, past, present, or future on the subject of our Lord's Divinity and Attributes are completely refuted in the sublime Preface of this Gospel (v. 1–18). How unfathomable, how far transcending all human understanding is this fundamental truth of our Lord's eternal existence. It is hard to see, with what consistency some men, glorying in the name of Christian, reject mysteries, while they admit our Lord's Divinity and Eternity, the foundation of all Christian belief. Will they explain *how* God existed from Eternity?

ANALYSIS.

In the sublime Preface of this Gospel (v. 1–18), St. John declares the Eternity, Personality, and Divinity of the Son of God (1–2). His Omnipotence, as Creator of all things, visible and invisible, material and spiritual (3–5). He adduces in confirmation the testimony of the Baptist (6–7). He removes the erroneous opinions entertained of the Baptist himself (8). The advent of the WORD among men—the cause and success of His advent, His incarnation (9–14). He adduces as witnesses, those, who like himself, beheld His glory (14), the Baptist. (15). He points out the blessings we derived from the Word (16). How far superior to those of preceding dispensations (v. 17). He corroborates all, by the testimony of the Word Himself, the Source of all truth (v. 18).

19—In this and the following verses is fully described in detail the splendid testimony rendered by the Baptist to our Lord's Divinity, when in reply to the solemn embassy sent from Jerusalem to question him on the subject, he proclaims his own nothingness and our Lord's infinite superiority over himself (19–29). Further testimony of the Baptist addressed to his own disciples in favour of our Lord's Divinity (29–35). Repetition, for greater emphasis sake, of the same testimony by John (35–38). The call by our Lord of His first disciples, Andrew, Peter, Philip, Nathanael (38–48). Our Lord proves Himself to be the searcher of hearts, and displays a knowledge of future events (48–51).

Commentary.	Text.
1. "*In the beginning was the Word.*" St. Cyril, by, *beginning*, understands, the Principle of the Word, God the Father, of whom the Son was begotten by an eternal generation. The meaning, according to him, would be ; the Word abode in the Father, as the Principle, of whom He was begotten, just as it is said of Him "*he is in the bosom of the Father*" (v. 18). This, although quite orthodox is, however, a very improbable interpretation.	1. *In the beginning was the Word, and the Word was with God, and the Word was God.* 1. *In principio erat Verbum, et Verbum erat apud Deum, et Deus erat Verbum.*

Commentary.

For, the term, "BEGINNING," has here the same signification as in v. 2, which is but a summary of the three clauses of this v. 1, and in v. 2 it could not designate any of the Divine Persons without a manifest absurdity.

The term, then, denotes *duration* thus; *In the beginning* of every thing else that had a beginning—thus are excluded the Father and Holy Ghost, who had no beginning; or, when everything else began to be; before any time, actual or imaginary "*the Word* WAS." He must, therefore, have no beginning; since, He was, when everything else began; and, consequently, must be Eternal. The *existence* of the Word before all creation is here *directly* proved. His *Eternity, indirectly*, in accordance with Scriptural usage (Isai. xlii. 13; John xviii. 5; Ephes. i. 4; Col. i. 7). Jansenius and others found the proof of the Eternity of the Son of God in this passage on the two words taken conjointly, v. 2 ("*erat*," "he was") and, (*in principio*, "*in the beginning*"). The Word WAS already in existence in the beginning of all things created, before everything else began; and so, if He had a beginning or began to exist, He would have been before Himself—a manifest absurdity. Unlike the commencement of the Genesis of creation (Genesis i.) to which this is allusive, described by Moses, who denotes the first dawn of creation thus, "*In the beginning, God created the heavens,*" etc.; here, in the eternal Genesis of the Word described by St. John, there is no allusion whatever to the act or process of creation. He *was* before the beginning—"*before the world was*" (John xvii. 5). continued up to the beginning; and continues to the present and all future periods.

The imperfect *erat* (*was*) is used preferably to *fuit*, as this latter might be taken to denote a cessation of existence; while, *erat*, denotes, unceasing, endless continuity.

Some commentators say the "*beginning*" directly denotes eternity, which was a beginning without a beginning. Hence, St. John (1 Ep. i. 1) says, "*that which was from the beginning,*" or eternity, termed "*beginning,*" to suit the weak conceptions of our limited understandings.

"*The Word*" (ὁ λόγος). The Second Person of the Blessed Trinity. The term clearly refers not to any Attribute or Attributes of God; but, to a person, personal actions being ascribed to Him, throughout the entire chapter. Moreover, He is here called "*God*." He is distinguished from God, "*with God*," and in v. 14, he is identified with the Person of our Lord Himself, assuming human nature here on earth.

WHY called λόγος? The reason generally given by theologians, apart from the revelation of the term by the Holy Ghost to St. John, who alone of all the sacred writers of the New Testament employs it in a personal sense, if we except St. Paul to the

Commentary.

Hebrews (c. iv. 12, 13), is, that as our thought or the internal word of our mind generated in our intellect remains in the mind, even after it is externally expressed by the voice; so, as far as human and Divine things admit of comparison, the Son of God begotten of the Father by an eternal generation through the Divine intellect, the substantial expression of the Divine mind, is one, consubstantial with Him, yet still existing in Him, as a distinct Divine Person. This and other comparisons whereby it is attempted to illustrate the eternal generation of the Son of God, His identity of nature and distinction of Person with the Father, His birth in the flesh, are so imperfect and obscure, that it is for us to believe and adore, rather than too curiously investigate, lest we be "*overwhelmed by the Majesty of Glory*" (Proverbs xxv. 27).

It is rendered in the Vulgate, *verbum*, which implies unity and identity with the mind that produces it, preferably to *Sermo*, which would seem to imply composition, multiplicity and distinction.

WHENCE, did St. John derive this term, as expressive of his doctrine regarding the Personality and Divine attributes of the Son of God?

Not from Plato, who never ascribes to the λογος θεου either in his *Timeus* or *de Republica* (c. vii.), where he treats of this subject, distinct personality or supreme creative power, or the other attributes predicated of him here by the Evangelist.

Not from Philo, whose notions concerning the "*Word of God*," to which he frequently refers, are so contradictory, confused and unintelligible; and, as far as they are intelligible, clearly erroneous on the Attributes of the Word. For, among other points, Philo maintained the Eternity of matter.

Nor, from the Alexandrian schools, whose notions on these subjects are clearly conjectural.

Patrizzi observes, that one could hold, without censure of any kind, that St. John might have derived the *term* λογος, abstracting from false doctrines, from the Oriental Philosophy, in which it denotes some Divine reason or Emanation, just as the word, θεος, whereby the Pagans denoted a false Divinity, was employed by the Apostles and the Jews before them, to designate the only true God. Nay, the same author observes that the Evangelist may have been divinely inspired to use the word in opposition to the ETERNAL SILENCE propounded by the Gnostics.

It is most likely, the Apostle derived the *term* itself and the full doctrinal truths it conveys from the Old Testament, as well as from Jewish tradition; from the teachings of our Lord and the full insight into the meaning of the SS. Scripture, which He was pleased to impart to him (Luke xxiv. 45).

In the Old Testament, we have clear and frequent allusions to the Creative Power of the "*Word of God*" (Psa. xxxii. 6). "*By* THE WORD *of God the heavens were established*" (v. 9).

Commentary.

"For He *spoke* and they *were made*" (Wisdom xviii. 15), etc. In these and several other passages of SS. Scripture, a creative power is attributed to the *Word* of God. The same idea is expressed here by St. John (*v.* 3), "*Omnia per ipsum facta sunt.*"

"*And the Word was with God.*" This is a reply to the latent question suggested in the first clause, viz.:—If the Word was before everything created, before time, place, heaven, earth, from Eternity, *where* was He? He "*was with God*" the Father. Προς (*apud*) conveys, that the "*Word*" was not a mere accident subsisting in God; that He had a peculiar, individual subsistence, a Personality of His own, distinct from the Father, with whom He always was, never divided or separated from Him. No one could be said to be *with himself*.

"*And the Word was God*," και θεος ην ὁ λογος.—The term "*Word*," having the definite article prefixed is the *subject* of this, as of the two preceding propositions. The sense is, that Word, already spoken of, is God. The preceding propositions, while declaring the Eternity of the Word, His Personality, distinct from the Father, do not enunciate the nature or essence of the *Word itself*. In this clause is declared His essence, viz., identity of nature with the Father. This was necessary to prevent men from fancying that because God was one, and the Word distinct from Him, the Word could not, therefore, be God. Here, is declared His identity of Divine Nature with the Father.

The article is prefixed to "God" in the words "with God," προς τον θεον—and denotes a Person, the Person of God the Father. Here, it is omitted before "God," και θεος ην ὁ λογος— "*and the Word was God*," because having, in the preceding clause, denoted the *Person* of God the Father, if repeated here, it would refer to the same Person and denote that the "*Word*" was the Person of God the Father, as if to say, "and the Word was God," ὁ θεος, or the Person above referred to, which St. John could not mean.

The word, θεος, without the article, far from denoting a Divine Person inferior to God, as the Arians would have it, denotes one possessing the nature of the Supreme Being, as in *vv.* 6-12, 13-18 of this chapter. Whenever in SS. Scriptures, it is employed to denote creatures; then, there is always some qualifying epithet or circumstance to determine this latter meaning, as in Exodus vii. "*Te constitui Deum Pharaonis.*" Psa. "*Ego dixi, dii estis,*" etc.

The Socinians, by placing a comma after *erat*, in the sentence, "*Deus erat verbum,*" and joining "*verbum*" with the following, thus: "*Verbum hoc erat in principio,*" etc., *v.* 2, employ an arbitrary and erroneous punctuation, opposed to all MSS. and copies of the Gospel, and fall into a manifest absurdity, as if St. John only meant to tell us, *Deus erat. God existed.*

Commentary.

2. The words of this verse are a mere emphatic summary of the three clauses of the preceding.

"*This*" Word who was God, was all that has been stated regarding Him, viz : "He *was in the beginning*" from Eternity, enjoying Co-eternity "*with God*" the Father; distinct from Him, while possessing the same Divine nature with Him.

"This" is almost universally understood of the Word or λογος, who is manifestly the subject, having the definite article prefixed, of whom all that is said in the preceding clauses is predicated.

Whether St. John had in view, besides directly affirming our Lord's Divinity (c. xxi. 31), to refute the blasphemous teachings of Ebion and Cerinthus, as is asserted by many ancient writers, and to guard against the errors of the Gnostics, which he may have foreseen in the near future; one thing is quite certain, viz., that his teachings regarding our Lord's Eternity, His distinct, Divine Personality, identity with the Father, as in *vv.* 1, 2 ; His omnipotence, as displayed in the educing out of nothing every thing created, as in *v.* 3, completely refutes all the errors of the Pagan philosophers before his time, and, by anticipation, all the blasphemous doctrines regarding our Blessed Lord, that were to spring forth afterwards. He refutes the absurd notions or systems of the Gnostics relative to their Æons or inferior Divinities, to whom, according to their absurd notions, the Supreme Deity confided the work of creation. The system regarding these fabulous Æons was chiefly formulated by Valentinus, who gives a long and imaginary history of their number, their genealogy, and other frivolous unmeaning accounts of them.

3. Having described the eternal relations of the Word with the other Persons of the Godhead, the Evangelist now proceeds to point out the *works* of the Word, his external relations in time with creatures. He describes, in the briefest form, the great work of creation, the different parts of which embracing times, days and seasons, are so circumstantially described by Moses (Genesis i).

These he divides into the *Natural*, as in this verse, and the *Supernatural*, as in the following verse :—

The truth regarding creation is announced affirmatively in the clause, "*All things were made by Him*," time among the rest ; therefore, He preceded all times and was eternal. If the Word Himself were made, He should have been made by Himself and preceded Himself ; and *negatively*, in the clause, "*and without Him*," etc. Hence, if the Word were made, He could not have been made without His own active agency, in His own creation—a manifest absurdity. The negative clause is very emphatic in the Greek, "*without him*

Text.

2. *The same was in the beginning with God.*

2. *Hoc erat in principio apud Deum.*

3. *All things were made by him: and without him was made nothing that was made.*

3. *Omnia per ipsum facta sunt, et sine ipso factum est nihil quod factum est.*

Text.	Commentary.

was made not ONE THING (οὐδὲ ἕν) *that was made."* The creative power of the Word being confined to things that were created, could not extend to the Father or the Holy Ghost, who were not created.

The words of this verse, combined with the following verse, are differently punctuated in different versions.

(*a*) As in our Vulgate and most Greek copies, "*et sine ipso factum est nihil quod factum est.*"

(*b*) The Vulgate of Sixtus V. (A.D. 1590), runs thus, "*et sine ipso factum est* nihil; *quod factum est, in ipso vita erat,*" signifying either, that all things had their principle of life in Him; or, that they LIVED and existed, from Eternity, in the Divine mind.

(*c*) The Bibles of Clement VIII. (1592–1598), place no full stop at all, and we are free to connect the words, "*quod factum est*," with either the preceding words, *factum est nihil quod factum est;* or with the following, thus "*quod factum est, in ipso vita erat.*" The first reading, as in our Vulgate, is the one commonly followed.

4. *In him was life, and the life was the light of men:*

4. *In ipso vita erat, et vita erat lux hominum.*

4. "*In Him was life,*" etc. Having referred in the preceding verse to the *Natural* order, and affirmed that all created beings, whether in heaven or on earth, visible or invisible (Col. i. 16, 17), whether merely existing, sentient, or rational were brought into existence by the power of the Word,—for, by Him, God created all things, and their very providential conservation in existence (Col. i. 17), is implied here—the Evangelist in this verse proceeds to the *Supernatural* order, and refers, in a special way, to the work of Redemption, the second creation, whereby He gave back to man, dead in his sins, the spiritual life of grace (Ephes. ii. 1). In this sense, St. John often refers to our Lord as *life* (v. 21; vi. 33; xi. 25, etc.).

"*In Him,*" essentially, of Himself, as *effect* in its *cause*, and not by mere external delegation.

"*Was life,*" of which He was the EXEMPLARY cause; also the EFFICIENT cause, being the source of life which He gave to all, "*In Te est fons vitæ*" (Ps. xxxv. 10); the MERITORIOUS cause. From Eternity He might be said to be the MERITORIOUS cause, since, the fall and reparation of man were foreseen from Eternity (Ephes. i. 4, 5), and the word to be incarnated in time was, from Eternity, the *meritorious* cause of spiritual and eternal life, "*Agnus occisus ab origine Mundi*" (Apoc. xiii. 8).

"*And the life was the light of men*" It was, inasmuch as He enlightens men through revelation with the supernatural light of faith enlivened by charity, here, and by His Divine essence with the life of glory, hereafter, that He is the source of life to them. "*Light*" means the illumination communicated by God to man.

Commentary.

At all times, even before His Incarnation, He "*was the light,*" etc. For, it was in view of the future merits of Christ, that men from the beginning of time, enjoyed the light of faith, the supernatural life, by which the just man lives (Rom. i.).

In the preceding clause, "*in Him was life,*" the term "*life*" denotes the *effect* produced in us by the "WORD." In the latter, "*and the life was the light of men,*" "*life,*" having the definite article prefixed, ἡ ζωη, means the Word Himself, or *cause* of light in men. Hence, in several passages of SS. Scriptures, especially in the writings of St. John, it is said, "*He is life,*" "*the way of life,*" etc. If many, after His coming, remain in darkness; this, is owing to their own perversity, as in *v.* 5.

5. "*And the light shineth in darkness.*" "*Light*" refers to the Word, which was the light of men unto life.

"*Shineth,*" without intermission, both through the light of faith and the light of reason. This same light, which heretofore was invisible, has now, in the flesh, become visible to our corporal senses by His words and the external works of His power enlightening mankind with the supernatural light of faith (1 John, i. 2), "*quæ erat apud Patrem et apparuit nobis.*"

"*Darkness*" is taken in a metaphorical and moral sense, to denote men sunk in spiritual misery, shut up in the prison of infidelity and sunk in depravity. To this, the Apostle refers (Ephes. v. 8), "*but you were heretofore darkness.*" He uses "*shineth*" in the present tense, to convey, that even now after His Ascension, our Lord does not cease through His Church to enlighten the world.

As our Lord, "*the light,*" existed from Eternity, and, at all times from creation, shone through the light of reason to men, it is not unlikely, that "*shineth*" denotes also the light of reason through which man from the beginning received the knowledge of God and of His leading attributes. "*Because, that which is known of God is manifest in them. For, God manifested it to them . . . His eternal power also and divinity*" (Rom. i. 19, 20). This is "*the light shining*" to them. This knowledge they abused, having transferred the worship of God to senseless idols (Rom. i. 23).

"*And the darkness,*" that is to say, *most* of those whom He found in unbelief and sin. For, that there were exceptions is clear from *v.* 12, "*but as many as received Him.*"

"*Comprehended it not,*" believed *not* in Him. There is question here of faith in the light (*v.* 7). They received it not, admitted it not. They continued voluntarily in a state of incredulity. The light shone. They obstinately refused to open their eyes, and would not admit it (Rom. ix).

When the sun shines on the earth, those who close their eyes cannot perceive it. The shades of darkness in which they volun-

Text.

5. And the light shineth in darkness, and the darkness did not comprehend it.

5. Et lux in tenebris lucet, et tenebræ eam non comprehenderunt.

Text	Commentary
	tarily shut themselves up, are so thick, that the light could not penetrate them. So ignorant, so debased were men, that far from valuing His teachings, they, as a body, rejected them.

Some Commentators not taking into account, that here, there is question of *moral* darkness, or rather men enclosed in darkness, seem perplexed as to how the light could shine in darkness without enlightening and dissipating it, understand the word "*shineth*" to mean, is capable of producing the effect of enlightening, even when through the fault of others, that effect, as here, may not follow.

It is to be borne in mind, that "*darkness*" here denotes men, free agents, who are at liberty to receive or reject the light of reason or faith offered to them.

6. There was a man sent from God, whose name was John.

6. *Fuit Homo missus a Deo, cui nomen erat Joannes.*

6. "*There was*," etc. The object of the Evangelist here may be to correct an error which seemed to prevail, that the Baptist was the Messiah (Luke iii. 15; John i. 19). While correcting this error, the Evangelist adduces John, who was commonly supposed to be a Prophet (Matthew xxi. 26), as an important witness to prove that Jesus was the Christ, "*the Son of God*," which was the chief design of this gospel (John xx. 31).

The Evangelist may also have in view to show that, while obstinate unbelievers rejected our Lord, God had employed, on His part, the most effectual means to dispose men to receive Him; among the rest, He employed the ministry and testimony of the Baptist, so much prized and valued by the Jews. The Evangelist commends his ministry and testimony by saying he "*was sent from God*" divinely commissioned.

7. This man came for a witness, to give testimony of the light, that all men might believe through him.

7. *Hic venit in testimonium, ut testimonium perhiberet de lumine, ut omnes crederent per illum.*

7. "*He came for a witness*," etc. In preceding verse, he points out John's Divine mission; in this, the object of that Divine mission, which was to give testimony regarding our Lord ("*of the light*") as the long expected Messiah, thus to prepare the people to receive Him (Matthew iii). He also pointed Him out after He had come. "*Ecce agnus Dei*," etc. (John i. 31). He extols John's character and Divine mission, beyond others who were not selected by God for so high an office.

"*Light*" refers to the person of our Lord, "*through Him*," through John's testimony and preaching.

While extolling John in the preceding verse, he here lowers him in comparison with the Word, whose herald he was.

8. He was not the light, but was to give testimony of the light.

8. *Non erat ille lux, sed ut testimonium perhiberet de lumine.*

8. "*He was not the light.*" Although, in some finite respect, a light, the Baptist was not the immense, increated light of which we speak, but the herald and witness of the light, not the sun, but the precursor of the Sun of Justice, "*a burning and shining light*," enkindled by the great increated light and true lamp of

Commentary.

creation. The Evangelist thus removes any false opinions which the people or the disciples might entertain regarding John as the long expected promised Messiah.

9. After stating that John was *not* the true light, the Evangelist now states who was the light, viz., the Word Himself, who was different from John; and he enumerates the works of this true light, that is, of the Word, hereafter.

"*True light*" may metaphorically signify, that He really produces the same effects spiritually in our minds, that the sun produces in enlightening our corporal senses, just as He is termed "*true food*" (vi. 32), "*the true vine*" (xvi.), or "*true*" may mean essential light. Others have all their enlightening powers communicated from without; but He is essential, unchangeable, permanent light, such as John or any other creature could not be. John's light was temporary and precursory.

"*Which enlighteneth*," as far as he is concerned, "*every man*," of whatever nationality, without distinction of Jew or Gentile. "*Enlightens*" may refer to the light of reason; but, more probably, to the light of grace and faith. All who are enlightened are enlightened by Him, and if any man is not enlightened, it is his own fault, since the light is offered to all and provided for all.

"*That cometh into this world.*" In the Greek, the construction is doubtful. According to it "*coming*,"—ἐρχομενον—may be joined to "*light*," thus: He was the light, that coming into this world enlighteneth every one, or, to "*every man*," as in our Vulgate. The former construction seems more in accordance with Scriptural usage, which represents our Lord as the light that enlightens mankind (John iii. 19; xii. 46). The expression, in this connexion, would imply our Lord's pre-existence before His Incarnation. The word too may have a future or past signification.

It is in favour of the Vulgate reading which connects "*coming*" with "*every man*," "*omnem hominem venientem in hunc mundum*," that, whether we understand, "*enlightens*" of the light of reason, or the light of faith, or both, our Lord, before He came in the flesh, enlightened mankind with the light of reason and of faith. Moreover, the position of "*coming*," ερχομενον, in the sentence, is such as to connect it with "*every man*" "*cometh into this world*," is same as, every man born of woman.

10. "*He*," the λογος or "*Verbum*," not "*lux*," as is clear from the Greek ουχ εγνω αυτον—"*was in the world*" from its very foundation, upholding it by His conservative providence, "*omnia portans verbo virtutis suæ*" (Heb. i.), "*and the world was made by Him*" (v. 3), "*and the world knew Him not.*" From the visible works of creation, man might have known God, and thus be stimulated to glorify and worship Him as the fountain of all good. "*But, the*

Text.

9. That was the true light, which enlighteneth every man that cometh into this world.

9. Erat lux vera, quæ illuminat omnem hominem venientem in hunc mundum.

10. He was in the world, and the world was made by him, and the world knew him not.

10. In mundo erat et mundus per ipsum factus est; et mundas eum non cognovit.

Text.	Commentary.
	world," meaning wicked and perverse men, "*knew Him not.*" They altogether rejected Him, and transferred the worship due to Him, to dumb, senseless idols (Rom. i.) The term, "*world*," has a two-fold signification in this verse. In the words, "*was in the world*," it denotes visible creation. The words "*the world knew Him not*," mankind. There is question here, of the period before our Lord's Incarnation, when in virtue of His Divine omnipresence, He filled all creation, and unceasingly bestowed benefits on mankind (v. 3) *erat*, at all times. In the next verse there is allusion, by anticipation, to His Incarnation among His own people. St. John, as disciple of love, burning with love for his Divine Master, indignantly notes the ungrateful treatment our Lord met with at the hands of men, who received so many signal benefits from Him. This world that "*was made by Him*," "*knew Him not*," rejected and despised Him. Could there be greater ingratitude?
11. *He came unto his own, and his own received him not.* 11. *In propria venit, et sui eum non receperunt.*	11. In the preceding verse there is question of His Divinity at all times filling the universe; here there is question of His assumed humanity in time; "*into His own*"—εις τα ιδία—His own country, His own house, and "*His own*" (οἱ ἰδίοι). The change in the original Greek is deserving of observation. He came into His own land, and His own chosen people, specially beloved by Him, to whom He was sent to preach, in the first place, among whom and of whom He was born, "*received Him not*," as their long expected Messiah, their future deliverer. Far from it, they rejected, repudiated Him, "*nec reputavimus cum*" (Isaias liii. 1–6), nay, persecuted Him, and subjected Him to the ignominious death of the cross. Our Lord reproaches the Jews for having, as a body, rejected Him, although some few among them received Him, and believed in Him.
12. *But as many as received him, he gave them power to be made the sons of God, to them that believe in his name.* 12. *Quotquot autem receperunt cum, dedit eis potestatem filios Dei fieri, his qui credunt in nomine ejus.*	12. The Evangelist in this verse conveys that our Lord was not rejected by all; and he shows the benefits conferred on such as received Him. It may also be intended to convey that His rejection by His own people did not cause Him to change His beneficent designs, "*as many as received Him*," whether from among the Jews or Gentiles. The phrase is explained in the words, "*that believed in His name*," believed in Him, as their God, Creator, and Author of their salvation. "*Name*" often signifies the Person Himself. To them, He transferred the Divine Sonship, taken from the Jews, who, as a body, rejected Him. "*He gave power to become sons of God*" (εξουσίαν); "*power*" may mean, He gave them the privilege to become His adopted children, or the *actual right* to become sons of God in His own Kingdom of Glory, if they believe in Him and obey Him in this life.

Commentary.

13. He points out that the exalted Sonship of God referred to does not come from carnal generation or human descent, thus correcting the erroneous ideas which the Jews attached to their carnal descent from Abraham. "*Not of blood, nor of the will of the flesh,*" whether sinful, which this phrase means; "*nor of the will of man,*" or lawful. The above words express the natural mode of human carnal generation. "*But of God,*" by a spiritual generation, opposed to the carnal generation referred to. This spiritual generation, by which we become sons of God, is effected in Baptism, whereby we are born again of water and the Holy Ghost, and as sons of God fitted for His kingdom. This is accomplished through grace and faith. Sanctifying grace conferred on us in Baptism, the laver of regeneration and renovation (Titus iii. 5), makes us partakers of the Divine nature" (2 Peter i. 4).

14. "*And the Word,*" etc. Some understand "*and*" to mean *for*, as if the Evangelist were assigning a reason, why they were made sons of God. It arose from this, that the Word assumed human nature and merited this great privilege for us. The term, "*Word,*" has the definite article before it to show it refers to the same "*Word*" mentioned in *v*. 1. Some Commentators connect this with *v*. 4. These regard the intervening portion as parenthetical.

"*Flesh*" denotes *man*, human nature, a signification it has in several passages of SS. Scripture. The term, "*soul,*" too, is employed to designate the same. The word "*flesh*" is used preferably to the word, man, to show more clearly the great contrast between Infinite Power,—the "*Word*" being the creator of the universe—and the greatest weakness and debasement—flesh being the weaker part of human nature. It may also be that "*flesh*" is used to confound the error of the Docetæ, and such others as denied that our Lord assumed human flesh.

"*Was made.*" Not by any change in the Divine nature, which could not be; but by assuming human nature, under the Personality of the Word, the human nature of the "WORD" being full and entire, composed of a created soul and body without any distinct human Personality of its own, having for Person, the Divine Person of the Word. The Word had two distinct natures, the Divine and human; and only one Person, the Person of the Son of God. Some Expositors say that St. John's object here is to show that we need not be surprised at men becoming by adoption and through a spiritual birth, sons of God, when the Eternal Son of God Himself became, what is more surprising still, man, and really assumed human nature so intimately that Christ-man could be truly termed the Son of God. The real union of the two natures was so perfect, that God is man and man is God.

Text.

13. *Who are born, not of blood, nor of the will of the flesh, nor of the will of man, but of God.*

13. *Qui non ex sanguinibus, neque ex voluntate carnis, neque ex voluntate viri, sed ex Deo nati sunt.*

14. *And the Word was made flesh, and dwelt among us (and was his glory, the glory as it were of the only begotten of the Father), full of grace and truth.*

14. *Et verbum caro factum est, et habitavit in nobis, et vidimus gloriam ejus, gloriam quasi unigeniti a Patre, plenum gratiæ et veritatis.*

Commentary.

"*And dwelt amongst us,*" conversed familiarly, sojourned with men, as a member of a family, as a friend, He ate, drank, slept, etc. (1 John i.) They had full opportunity of a familiar acquaintance with Him, so as not to be mistaken, that He was really man. "*He came in and went out among them*" (Acts i. 21). "*Afterwards He was seen upon earth and conversed with men*" (Baruch iii. 38). The Greek word for "*dwelt,*" εσκηνωσεν (*Tabernacled*) denotes temporary dwelling, not making this earth His permanent habitation; dwelt for a time, like those who dwell in tents, which are not their permanent home.

"*And we saw His glory,*" etc. The Evangelist said, in proof of the Word becoming *flesh*, that so far as His *humanity* was concerned, they had ample opportunity of witnessing it since He sojourned as man among them for a time, and he says, as to His *Divinity*, they had several proofs of it in "*seeing His glory,*" the splendour of His majesty, at His Transfiguration, of which St. John was one of the witnesses—to this St. Peter also refers—(i. 16), at His Resurrection, His Ascension, and in the splendid miracles wrought by Him. "*The glory as it were of the only begotten of the Father,*" a glory suited to the only begotten Son of God. They did not see the Word in Himself. But, from His glory; they saw it was He, just as one seeing the splendour of the sun knows it is over the horizon. "*As it were,*" signifies reality, here, as in many other passages of SS. Scripture, "*the glory as it were,*" suited to or becoming Him alone and no other, who was "*the only begotten of the Father,*" the Eternal, consubstantial Son of the Father, equal with Him in all things. These words are read within a parenthesis, and the following words spoken of the Word made flesh, are to be joined immediately with the words, "*and the Word was made flesh* (. . .) *full of grace and truth.*" The words, "*of the Father,*" may also be joined, according to some, with "*glory,*" as if to say, the glory which He received from the Father, such glory as the Father would bestow on the beloved object of His eternal complacency.

"*Full of grace and truth.*" While dwelling amongst us, the Word, as man, had not His hands empty. He was distinguished for two qualities, "*grace and truth;*" of these He was "*full,*" not only in *Himself*, in whom "*dwelt the whole plenitude of the Divinity*" (Col. ii. 9), but also, since He went about doing good, "*full,*" in reference *to us*, so that we could communicate from this inexhaustible fulness to others; and we did so, for we received of it. The Evangelist wishes to show what the Word did while dwelling with us. He communicated to us the abundance of grace and truth. *Grace and truth* correspond with *life and light*. *Grace* gave life; *light*, the knowledge of truth.

"*Full of grace,*" in bestowing all the blessings of Redemption, and liberation from the slavery of the devil, opposed to the weak

Commentary.

and needy elements of the Old Law; "*and truth,*" as the true teacher of mankind. Everything He revealed and taught was free from error of any sort.

"*Truth*" may be understood not only as opposed to error and falsehood, but also to the types and figures of the Old Law, He being their fulfilment—"*finis legis, Christus*" (Rom. x. 4). He verified all the promises made regarding Him. The *Law*, from Moses; *truth*, from Jesus Christ.

15. The Evangelist adduces in corroboration of his own testimony regarding the "*Word*" having become man, "*full of grace and truth,*" etc., the testimony of the Baptist, which was of the greatest weight, among the Jews, "*John beareth witness of Him,*" as the Word made flesh, "*and crieth out, saying,*" publicly, fearlessly, acting the part of herald as well as of witness. The Evangelist having already referred, in general terms, to the testimony of John (*vv.* 7, 8), now specifically states what that testimony was. "*Crieth out,*" in allusion to the words of Isaias regarding the Baptist, "*vox clamantis in deserto.*"

"*This was He*" (or, *is* He) "*of whom I spoke*" before I saw Him in person. The Evangelist mentions by *anticipation* what he describes (*v.* 29, etc.) when John pointed out our Lord as present.

"*He that shall come after me,*" in the public exercise of his ministry, of whom I am the mere precursor, "*is preferred before me,*" shall be regarded as far superior to me in dignity and excellence. The past is used, in prophetic style, for the future, or, it may mean, has been preferred, in the predestination of God. If these words were spoken after our Lord's Baptism, then, the past form, "*has been preferred before me,*" "*ante me factus est,*" would be verified in the preference shown our Lord in the words of the Heavenly Father, "*This is my beloved Son,*" etc., or, if spoken *before* His Baptism, before the words were uttered by the Heavenly Father, they would be verified in His miraculous birth, the adoration of the Magi, His sanctity of life, and even these signs, apart, in the designs of the Eternal Father in His regard. Hence, He was made preferable by repeated and successive manifestations on the part of God and man.

"*Because He was,*" in existence, "*before me,*" being from eternity; and He was essentially, of His own nature, more exalted in dignity. The phrase chiefly signifies the pre-existence of the Word before John, having been from the beginning, from Eternity.

16 "*And of His fulness we all,*" etc. This is said of Christ as man God, "*in whom dwelleth all the fulness of the Godhead corporally*" (Coll. ii. 9). By some, these are understood to be the words of the Baptist. But, they are more commonly said to be the words

Text.

15. *John beareth witness of him, and crieth out, saying: This was he of whom I spoke: He that shall come after me, is preferred before me: because he was before me.*

15. *Joannes testimonium perhibet de ipso, et clamat dicens: Hic erat, quem dixi: Qui post me venturus est, ante me factus est quia prior me erat.*

16. *And of his fulness we all have received, and grace for grace.*

B

Text.

16 *Et de plenitudine eius nos omnes accepimus, et gratiam, pro gratia.*

Commentary.

of the Evangelist, resuming his narrative from *v.* 14, *"full of grace,"* etc., the verse 15 being parenthetical. For, as regards the Baptist, he could hardly say in the past tense, *"we all have received,"* etc., as it should then be confined to himself and the Prophets of the Old Law, whereas these words are clearly meant to extol the beneficence of our Lord who extended to all His followers in the New Law, the abundant participation of the grace and truth which emanated from Him as their inexhaustible fountain.

In our Lord, was that plenitude of grace, which St. Bonaventure terms, the *plenitudo superabundantiæ*, which He, the great inexhaustible fountain, communicated to others. In the Blessed Virgin, was the *plenitudo prærogativæ;* and in all the other saints, the *plenitudo sufficientiæ.* Every word in this clause is emphatic. The words *"of His fulness,"* convey, that this fulness which resides in Him, as intrinsically His own, properly belongs to Him alone, of which all others, the Apostles included, shared, according to measure, which limited measure in them is implied in the words, *" His fulness "*—the fulness of the Great fountain which continues inexhaustible; they also convey, that no one received grace except through Him.

"And grace for grace." By some *"and"* is understood to be explicative *namely, that is.* By others, *emphatic*, signifying, we received not only the Gospel Law, and doctrine from Christ, *but also* grace. By others, *adversative*, received of His fulness, but grace for grace.

There is a great diversity of opinion regarding the meaning of the words, *"grace for grace."* According to some Expositors, they mean an accumulation of graces, grace upon grace, one grace upon another (Beelen. Grammatica Grecitatis). There are several other interpretations given, but the more probable seems to be that of Patrizzi and others, who, giving the Greek word, αντι, *pro*, *"for,"* its natural meaning, explain the words thus, *"grace"* or the abundant effusion of grace furnished in the New Law, *"for,"* in place of, the scanty measure of grace given under the Old Law. This we derived from the fulness of Christ, the inexhaustible source of grace. In reply to the objection that the Old Law is never called a grace, these say, that it is not of the Old Law directly there is question here; but, of the grace so scantily bestowed on those who lived under the Old Law, and even this small measure of grace came from the New Law, and the retrospective merits of Christ, *" the lamb slain from the beginning of the world "* (Apoc. xiii. 8). Owing to this plenitude of Christ, of which we have all partaken, instead of the scanty measure of grace bestowed in the Old Law, we have received the abundant effusion of grace in the New Law.

The context favours this interpretation, as this *v.* 16, seems to be more fully explained and developed in next *v.* 17.

Commentary.

17. "*For the law*," which, of itself, did not confer grace, and under which but a very small measure of grace at best was dispensed, "*was given*," merely promulgated to one nation or one people only, in its several parts, moral and ceremonial, "*by Moses*," who could give no grace. "*But grace*," in all its abundance, whereby men can observe the *moral* precepts of the law, "*and truth*," whereby all the ceremonies and figures of the Old Law are fulfilled, "*came*," or, as the Greek has it, *were made*, or brought about, "*by Jesus Christ*," the great fountain of grace, who purchased it by the death of the Cross, and confined it to no one people; but, extended it to all mankind.

Those who understand "*grace for grace*," of the accumulated plenitude of grace in the New Law, say, the words of this verse are introduced to show that this was peculiar to the New Law, that this plenitude comes from Christ alone. For, as to Moses, he merely promulgated the Old Law, but could give no grace to fulfil it. Not so with Christ, He gave grace to observe His law, and brought about truth to fulfil its ceremonial and typical precepts. The Evangelist here points out to the Jews the superior excellence of Christ and the dispensation established by Him over Moses and the dispensation he promulgated.

18. "*No man*" in this life "*hath seen God at any time*," with the eyes of the body. Those who are said to have seen Him in this life—(it is only of testimony rendered by mortal man there is question)—Job, Moses, Jacob, Isaias, Elias, etc, only saw some luminous body assumed by an angel representing in some way the glory of God (A. Lapide). In the next life, the angels and saints see God intuitively by a clear vision, in which vision consists their sovereign happiness. They see Him in His essence, as far as God enables them. For this the Blessed require the *lumen gloriæ*. But, no mere creature, whether in this or the world to come, could see Him *comprehensively*, by a *comprehensive vision*, or comprehend the entire Divine essence, which, being infinite, could not be comprehended by any finite being. In this latter sense, God alone has a comprehensive vision. He alone can comprehend Himself.

"*The only begotten Son*," dearly beloved. The article, for greater emphasis sake, is prefixed to this word. "*Who is in the bosom of the Father*," who fully shares in the Father's most profound secrets, alone fully comprehends Him. The words, "*in the bosom*," according to the Holy Fathers, refer to the Divinity and consubstantiality of the Son; they signify His eternal generation of the same substance, having identity of nature with Him. These words also convey full and intimate acquaintance, in a way not communicated to any creature, with all the secrets of God.

Text.

17. *For the law was given by Moses, grace and truth came by Jesus Christ.*

17. *Quia lex per Moysen data est, gratia et veritas per Jesum Christum facta est.*

18. *No man hath seen God at any time: the only begotten Son who is in the bosom of the Father, he hath declared him.*

18. *Deum nemo vidit unquam; unigenitus Filius, qui est in sinu Patris, ipse enarravit.*

| Text. | Commentary. |

"*Is,*" conveys that He has been there from Eternity and continues there unchangeably.

He then who alone fully comprehends, fully knows the secrets of God, "*hath declared.*" What had He declared or revealed? All these sublime truths and divine mysteries, already referred to in the preceding part of the chapter, regarding the "WORD," as He is in Himself and in relation to creatures.

The Evangelist uses these words as an overwhelming corroboration of his own testimony and that of the Baptist regarding the Divinity and Incarnation of the WORD, and the other mysteries connected with Him.

The testimony of the Eternal Word Himself—the source of all truth and knowledge—exceeds all other testimony; since He, the God of all truth, testifies to what He alone fully knows, regarding the Divine nature and all mysteries. For, He alone possesses the same Divine nature and is intimately conversant with the deep counsels of God.

19 *And this is the testimony of John, when the Jews sent from Jerusalem priests and levites to him, to ask him: Who art thou?*

19. *Et hoc est testimonium Joannis, quando miserunt Judæi ab Jerosolymis sacerdotes et Levitas ad eum ut interrogarent eum: Tu quis es?*

19. "*And this is the testimony,*" etc. Some Commentators hold that the testimony spoken of Him was given after the Baptism of our Lord by the Baptist. The testimony given before His Baptism, is, according to them, recorded by the other Evangelists; and hence, not referred to, by St. John, in this Gospel.

The words of this verse are connected by some Expositors with vv. 7 and 15, where there is made a general allusion to John's testimony regarding our Lord's Divinity. These say, we have here a more definite and specific description of John's testimony borne by him on the occasion of the deputation referred to.

Others connect the words with the foregoing verse, thus: He alone who was in the bosom of the Father, could disclose all regarding Him. For, as regards John, He disclaimed all pretensions to superior excellence on this occasion.

Others say, there is question of a new testimony borne by John.

"*The Jews . . . from Jerusalem*"—the most distinguished men of the nation—"*sent Priests and Levites.*" The highest ecclesiastical representatives. The object of this embassy was "*to ask Him who art thou?*" "*Who,*" what quality or character dost thou bear or assume? This deputation, no doubt, represented, or were sent by, the Sanhedrim, the Supreme Jewish Council, to whom it belonged to judge of true or false prophets, and in general, of all things appertaining to religion. Some say, they were influenced by jealousy towards John, whose sanctity of life and preaching seemed to lower them in public estimation. Others say, the jealousy was towards our Redeemer, to whose superiority John had so openly testified. It was a subject of doubt, all things considered, if John were not the Messiah, at least, in the minds of the people (Luke iii. 15), whether reason-

Commentary.

ably or not, whether in accordance with the ancient prophecies or not, is another question. But, the fact is recorded by St. Luke, as above; and in this state of doubt, they send forward this solemn embassy to inquire into John's claims to be considered their long-expected Messiah, the term of whose coming was now accomplished. John's manner of life and preaching created this doubt, and, likely, it was to clear it up—all feelings of jealousy apart—they deputed these men to make inquiry. This was a very solemn embassy considering all its circumstances. The *persons* sent, Priests and Levites. The *authority* by whom sent, the Sanhedrim, *from Jerusalem*. The *grave subject* of inquiry, John's office and authority.

John's evidence was given publicly and openly to this embassy, of select ecclesiastical personages, who were well able to judge, and not before the crowd, who might misunderstand it. Hence, the Evangelist minutely details every circumstance of it.

The *Priests and Levites* were taken from the Tribe of Juda. The Priests, from the family of *Aaron* alone.

These latter were consecrated by a more solemn rite, and exercised more exalted functions in connexion with the service of the Temple and the offering of sacrifice. The Levites were taken from the other families of the Tribe of Juda, consecrated in a less solemn manner, and told off for the inferior functions in the Temple.

20. The question which they were deputed to ask him was, "*Who art thou?*" From the first reply which he gave them, "*I am not the Christ,*" it seems clear, that after asking him, in a general way who he was, they at once ask him, "*Art thou the Christ?*" For, otherwise, the Baptist could not, with any sense of propriety say, unasked, "*I am not the Christ,*" as if the people could have so exalted an idea of him, or he could himself have imagined it.

"*And he confessed and denied not,*" a Hebrew form of conveying most emphatically, as well positively as negatively, a full explicit reply to a question, and of conveying a full, open declaration. "*He confessed*" the truth, "*and denied not,*" that he was not the Christ.

21. "*Art thou Elias?*" In the Prophecy of Malachias (c. iv. 5, 6), it is stated that Elias, who had been taken up into heaven, is to precede the coming of our Redeemer. In this passage of Malachias, there is question of his coming at the end of time in glory and majesty. But, he was also to come before this last coming in meekness and humility (Malachias iii. 1 ; Zacharias ix. 9). The Jews made no distinction between his *first* and *second* coming. They ignored this first coming; and hence, they supposed, that Elias, who was taken up into heaven (4 Kings ii. 11), would precede our

Text.

20. And he confessed, and did not deny: and he confessed: I am not the Christ.

20. Et confessus est, et non negavit: et confessus est: Quia non sum ego Christus.

21. And they asked him: What then? Art thou Elias? And he said: I am not. Art thou the prophet? And he answered: No.

21. Et interrogaverunt eum: Quid ergo? Elias es tu? Et dixit: Non sum Propheta es tu? Et respondit: Non.

Text.

22. *They said therefore unto him ; Who art thou, that we may give an answer to them that sent us? what sayest thou of thyself.*

22. *Dixerunt ergo ei : Quis es ut responsum demus his, qui miserunt nos? quid dicis de teipso?*

23. *He said: I am the voice of one crying in the wilderness, make straight the way of the Lord, as said the prophet Isaias.*

23. *Ait : Ego vox clamantis in deserto: Dirigite viam Domini, sicut dixit Isaias propheta.*

24. *And they that were sent, were of the Pharisees.*

24. *Et qui missi fuerant, erant ex Pharisæis.*

Commentary.

Redeemer whenever He came. This gave rise to the question, "*Art thou Elias?*"

"*I am not.*" True, he was not Elias, the Thesbite, in person, to whom their question had reference, although, he came in the spirit and power of Elias (Luke i. 17), to discharge the same office of precursor at our Lord's *first* coming, that Elias is to discharge at His second (see Matthew xvii. 11 ; Mark x. 9, Commentary on).

"*The Prophet*" (ὁ προφητης) whom the Jews, from an erroneous interpretation of Deuteronomy (xviii. 15), supposed to precede as well as Elias, the coming of our Lord, or rather accompany Him. The passage in Deuteronomy referred, no doubt, to our Lord Himself (Acts iii. 23 ; vii. 37). But, the Jews understood it otherwise ; and hence, John though a Prophet, and more than a Prophet, denies that he was "THE *Prophet*" they referred to, or the Prophet in the sense of their question (see Matthew xi. 9, Commentary on).

22. Their opinion of the Baptist was so exalted as to make them fancy that if he were not the Messiah, he must be one of the two great Prophets who were expected about the time of the Messiah's coming. Finding he was neither, they content themselves with a general question, as to who he was. With what authority or power was he invested? What mission did he receive, to be exercised? This they want to know, in order to bring back word or return a satisfactory answer to the Sanhedrim, by whom, they were deputed to wait on the Baptist.

23. See Matthew iii. 3, Commentary on. Having already declared what he *was not*, he now declares in very distinct terms, what *he was*, thus meaning to show the nothingness of his origin, compared with the Messiah.

24. Those sent were of the *sect* of the Pharisees, while in *dignity* Priests and Levites. Who the Pharisees were (see Matthew iii. 7). The reason why the Evangelist makes special mention of them here was, that besides being the most powerful party in the Sanhedrim, they were overbearing and haughty ; glorying in their knowledge of the law and affected sanctity of life, which will account for their captious questioning, recorded in next verse. Likely, they were not commissioned by those who sent them to question the Baptist further than was necessary to know *who he was, by what authority* he acted ; or if he was the Christ, as the people generally thought in their hearts regarding him (Luke iii. 15).

Commentary.

25. "*Why therefore,*" etc. ? By what authority, then, dost thou baptize publicly and with a show of authority, the people flocking to you in crowds, whom you wish to subject to the Baptism of Penance? This they regard as audacious on the part of John, after the declarations elicited from him. The Prophets foretold that at the coming of Christ, Baptism was to be administered to the people (Ezech. xxxvi. 25 ; Zach. xiii. 1). The Pharisees learned in the law knew this. They thought, however, that it was only by the Messiah or His accompanying Prophet this could lawfully be done.

26. "*I baptize in water.*" I am commissioned and sent by God —the Jews themselves would not deny that John's Baptism was from heaven—to "*baptize in water*" only, as a preparation for the Baptism of the Messiah. Hence, I don't assume the office which He is to discharge. For, His Baptism will be quite different both in itself and in its effects. Most likely, the Baptist added, "*He shall baptize you in the Holy Ghost and in fire.*" The Evangelist omits this part as it was fully given by the other Evangelists. The effects and the end of both Baptisms are quite different.

He is not far off from you, whose precursor I am, whose Baptism will perfect mine, He is "*in your midst, whom you know not,*" whose exalted dignity you are ignorant of. Hence, their culpability in not finding Him and not believing in Him.

27. (See *v.* 15, also Matthew iii. 2). "*He shall come after me*" in his public manifestation, when I shall have discharged the office of precursor. But, "*He is preferred before Me*" in dignity, a dignity so great, that "*I,*"—whom you seem to esteem so much—"*am not worthy to loose the latchet of His shoe,*" unworthy to discharge in His regard the most menial and servile offices, the distance between us being infinite. He, true God ; I, a creature.

28. For "*Bethania,*" several writers, Origen, Chrysostom, etc., read "*Bethabara.*" But "*Bethania*" is the more common reading of MSS. Both words, probably, refer to the same place. *Bethabara* signifying *the house or place of passage*, as it was there, the Hebrews first crossed the Jordan on coming up from Egypt, and it was a place for crossing the Jordan from Perea into Judea. "*Bethania*" signifies a ferry passage, or *house of boats*, which were always kept in readiness there, for ferrying passengers across the Jordan. If the words do not denote the same place, the places were quite close to one another on the banks of the Jordan. This "*Bethania*" is by no means to be confounded with the dwelling-place of Mary and Martha, near Jerusalem. John selected this place for his Baptism, as crowds used to resort to it, when crossing

Text.

25. *And they asked him, and said to him: Why then dost thou baptize, if thou be not Christ, nor Elias, nor the prophet?*

25. *Et interrogaverunt eum, et dixerunt ei: Quid ergo baptizas, si tu non es Christus, neque Elias, neque Propheta?*

26. *John answered them saying: I baptize with water; but there hath stood one in the midst of you, whom you know not,*

26. *Respondit eis Joannes, dicens: Ego baptizo in aqua: medius autem vestrum stetit, quem vos nescitis.*

27. *The same is he that shall come after me, who is preferred before me; the latchet of whose shoe I am not worthy to loose.*

27. *Ipse est, qui post me venturus est, qui ante me factus est: cujus ego non sum dignus ut solvam ejus corrigiam calceamenti.*

28. *These things were done in Bethania beyond the Jordan, where John was baptizing.*

28. *Hæc in Bethania facta sunt trans Jordanem, ubi erat Joannes baptizans.*

Text.

29. *The next day John saw Jesus coming to him and he saith: Behold the lamb of God, behold him who taketh away the sin of the world.*

29. *Altera die vidit Joannes Jesum venientem ad se, et ait: Ecce agnus Dei, ecce qui tollit peccatum mundi.*

Commentary.

the Jordan. The Evangelist refers to this place of public resort to show, that the testimony of John was publicly given so as to leave no room for afterwards questioning it.

29. "*The next day*," immediately following that, on which the foregoing testimony was rendered by the Baptist, to the deputation spoken of in the preceding verses.

"*John saw Jesus coming to him.*" Our Redeemer retired into the desert, immediately after His Baptism by John (Mark i. 12), where He, probably, was, when the Baptist gave the testimony of Him above recorded. Now, He comes forth from the desert, to give the Baptist an opportunity of bearing the testimony referred to here. This was *after* His Baptism. For, John says he saw "*the Spirit descending on Him*," etc. (*v.* 32). Now, this occurred at His Baptism. "*Behold*," which points to a determinate, distinct Person, "*the Lamb of God.*" This is allusive to the passage of Isaias (liii. 7) and Jeremias (xi. 19) in which our Lord is called a lamb. There is also allusion to the typical signification of the Paschal lamb, whose qualities, as described in the Old Testament, typified the character of our Lord. He was also prefigured by the lamb offered up in daily sacrifices by the Jews, and by the other legal oblations. "*Of God*," offered up by God the Son, to His Father, as a victim of full atonement. Thus we say, the sacrifice "of Abraham," offered up by Abraham—"*Lamb of God*," the Divine Lamb, begotten of God the Father, marked out by Him as the true victim, alone adequate to make full atonement for all sin, "*the sin of the world*," and utterly destroy it. It is worthy of remark, that whenever our Lord is called a lamb in SS. Scripture, it is always in connexion with His sacrificial character, as a victim of atonement for sin. It is so here, as appears from the words, "*taketh away the sin of the world.*" "*Sin*," in the singular, embraces all the sins of all mankind, "*the world;*" "*taketh away*" (Isaias liii. 6-12; 1 Peter ii. 24, 25); taking on Himself the imputability of *all* sins, and the voluntary obligation of making full atonement for them, He utterly effaces by His blood, so far as He is concerned, unless obstacles on the part of creatures mar it, all the guilt and punishment of sin. Unlike the Paschal Lamb and other victims among the Jews, which had only a passing effect and were offered for only one people, the oblation of this Lamb had a permanent, abiding effect, in regard to the sins of all mankind.

John then, tells them, that his own Baptism can have no effect compared with His, who alone can remit and atone for all sin. To Him, therefore, they should go for the means of salvation.

ST. JOHN, CHAP. I.

Commentary.

30. (See v. 27).

31. Far from being influenced by any private or personal motives in bearing testimony.

"*I knew Him not,*" in person, till He came to my Baptism, although I knew He had come and I had saluted Him even from my mother's womb. From my knowledge that He was born and conversing among His people in an unknown capacity.

"*I came,*" commissioned by God, "*baptizing in water,*" which, of itself could not remit sin, this being reserved for His Baptism, whose precursor I was—in order "*that He may be made manifest in Israel,*" when amidst the great concourse of people flocking to my Baptism, I could bear testimony to Him and make Him known, as He was made known to me; first, by revelation, on His coming to be baptized; and again by the voice of the Eternal Father at His Baptism, when I saw the Holy Ghost descending on Him.

32. "*And John gave testimony, saying:*" These are the words of the Evangelist. They are interposed between the preceding and following words, conveying the Baptist's testimony.

"*I saw the Spirit,*" etc. at our Lord's Baptism (Matthew iii. 16, 17, see Commentary).

33. "*I knew Him not,*" personally and externally. For, it was from the desert I came, being sent to baptize. But God, by whom I was sent, gave me this corroborative, undoubted sign for knowing Him personally and distinguishing Him from the crowds of those flocking to my Baptism. John knew Him by revelation in his mother's womb. He had also a revelation regarding Him before Baptism, on which account, he said, "*ego debeo a Te baptizari*" (Matthew iii. 14).

"*This is He that Baptizeth with the Holy Ghost,*" of whom I spoke to you already. John added this, as is recorded by the other Evanglists, when he said, "*I baptize in water*" (v. 26). If, then, you believe in my baptism, and receive it as from God (Matthew xxi. 25), know, that He, who sent me, gave me this sign for knowing

Text.

30. This is he of whom I said: After me, there cometh a man who is preferred before me: because he was before me.

30. Hic est, de quo dixi: Post me venit vir, qui ante me factus est: quia prior me erat.

31. And I knew him not, but that he may be made manifest in Israel, therefore am I come baptizing with water.

31. Et ego nesciebam eum, sed ut manifestetur in Israel, propterea veni ego in aqua baptizans.

32. And John gave testimony, saying: I saw the Spirit coming down as a dove from heaven, and he remained upon him.

32. Et testimonium perhibuit Joannes, dicens: Quia vidi Spiritum descendentem quasi columbam de cælo, et mansit super eum.

33. And I knew him not: but he, who sent me to baptize with water, said to me: He upon whom thou shalt see the Spirit descending and remaining upon him, he it is that baptizeth with the Holy Ghost.

33. Et ego nesciebam eum: sed qui misit me baptizare in aqua, ille mihi dixit: Super quem videris Spiritum descendentem et manentem super eum, hic est, qui baptizat in Spiritu sancto.

Text.	Commentary.
	the Messiah. If then, you believe in me when baptizing, you should believe in me also when testifying regarding the Messiah, of whose exalted dignity and my own unworthiness I have already spoken.
34. *And I saw; and I gave testimony, that this is the Son of God.* 34. *Et ego vidi: et testimonium perhibui quia hic est Filius Dei.*	34. When did John bear testimony that "*this is the Son of God*," ὁ υἱὸς, *the* Son, the only begotten, natural, consubstantial Son of God, Himself God? This is not distinctly seen in the Gospel. But it may be among the several parts relating to our Lord's acts, not recorded in the Gospel. It may also be said, that John declared this implicitly, when speaking of His exalted dignity, His "*taking away*"—remitting—"*the sins of the world.*" For, the Jews themselves held, that no one but God could remit sin. It would be blasphemy, according to them, to say otherwise. "*I saw,*" the sign given of His Divinity; and as it was given, not for myself;—as I knew Him already—but for the people; hence, I bore testimony of His Divinity, as was declared by the Eternal Father at His baptism. "*Hic est filius meus dilectus,*" etc. (Matthew iii. 17.)
35. *The next day again. John stood, and two of his disciples.* 35. *Altera die iterum stabat Joannes, et ex discipulis ejus duo.*	35. "*The next day again*" immediately succeeding that on which John gave the testimony referred to in *v.* 29. He bore testimony before the Jewish deputation in *v.* 27. Secondly, in *v.* 29. Thirdly, here. "*John stood,*" engaged in the ministry of baptizing and preaching to the multitudes. "*And two of his disciples,*" among the crowd. These are specially mentioned on account of their faithful correspondence with John's exhortations.
36. *And beholding Jesus walking he saith: Behold the lamb of God.* 36. *Et respiciens Jesum ambulantem dicit: Ecce agnus Dei.*	36. "*And beholding Jesus walking,*" it would seem towards home, as appears from what follows. Our Lord was among the hearers of John, and now, towards evening, returns home "*the Lamb of God,*" the Divine Victim, the Saviour of men, alone capable of atoning for sin and of appeasing the Divine anger. John said this in the presence of all. He repeats this testimony for greater emphasis sake.
37. *And the two disciples heard him speak, and they followed Jesus.* 37. *Et audierunt eum duo discipuli loquentem et secuti sunt Jesum.*	37. "*And the two disciples,*" who are specially noted, on account of their prompt correspondence with grace, "*heard Him speak,*" repeating the testimony rendered by Him on the preceding day. "*And they followed Jesus,*" on His way home, with a view to more familiar intercourse, and greater instruction.
38. *And Jesus turning, and seeing them following him, saith to them: What seek you? Who said to him: Rabbi, (which is to say being interpreted, master) where dwellest thou?*	38. "*And Jesus turning, and seeing them following Him.*" Anticipating their wishes, He, in the fulness of His mercy, and wishing to free them from embarrassment, asks them, "*What seek ye?*" What do you want with Me? This He well knew. But, He wishes to give them a full opportunity of accosting Him. "*Rabbi,*" etc. "*Rabbi,*" a title of honour and distinction, which

Commentary

the Evangelist interprets for his Greek readers. By using the word "*Rabbi*," they conveyed that they wanted instruction.

"*Where dwellest Thou?*" meaning where did He lodge, or where had He taken up His temporary abode? Being a Galilean, He was not supposed to have a house or permanent abode in that district. Likely, the day being now far advanced, they only wished to know where they could find Him on the morrow, in order to converse fully with Him on the subject of His Divine mission.

Our Lord, who did not regard the hour as inopportune—for no time would be considered by Him inopportune for promoting the work of salvation—instead of putting them off to the following day, as probably they expected, blandly and kindly invited them to His place of abode. "*Come and see.*" He graciously asks them to follow Him, in order to inspire them with courage to question Him.

"*They stayed with Him that day,*" and as St. Augustine probably conjectures, the whole of that night, as the business was too great to be disposed of in two short hours.

"*Now, it was about the tenth hour,*" from sunrise, and only two hours of day time remained. For the Jews, divided their days into twelve hours and their nights into twelve hours. The hours varied in length, at different seasons of the year.

Who can imagine the spiritual joy and heavenly light with which these favoured disciples were blessed by our Lord, on this, the first occasion of His making disciples? Likely, He fully satisfied their questions, as to His Divinity and mission of Salvation referred to by the Baptist, when speaking of the Lamb of God, who was to make atonement for sin and to ransom mankind. The result would indicate this. For, they were not only themselves convinced, that He was the Son of God, the expected Messiah (*v.* 41). They also zealously exerted themselves to share their happiness with others.

40. "*Andrew, the brother of Simon Peter,*" etc. The Evangelist gives the name of one of the two disciples, *Andrew*, on account of the part he had in the introduction of his brother Peter to our Lord. He is here by anticipation called "*Simon Peter,*" which name our Lord promised him (*v.* 42).

41. "*He findeth his brother Simon,*" having sought him, in the first place, to share with him the heavenly treasure he found. The Greek for "*first,*" πρωτος, "*primus invenit,*" etc., would signify that he was the first after leaving our Lord's lodging, on the following morning, to find Simon, for whom the two disciples were searching in different directions, vieing with each other to find him.

Text

38. *Conversus autem Jesus, et videns eos sequentes se, dicit eis: Quid quæritis? Qui dixerunt ei: Rabbi, (quod dicitur interpretatum Magister) ubi habitas?*

39. *He saith to them: Come and see. They came, and saw where he abode, and they staid with him that day: now it was about the tenth hour.*

39. *Dicit eis: Venite, et videte. Venerunt et viderunt ubi maneret, et apud eum manserunt die illo: hora autem erat quasi decima.*

40. *And Andrew the brother of Simon Peter was one of the two who had heard of John, and followed him.*

40. *Erat autem Andreas frater Simonis Petri unus ex duobis, qui audierant a Joanne, et secuti fuerant eum.*

41. *He findeth first his brother Simon, and saith to him: We have found the Messias, which is, being interpreted, the Christ.*

Text.	Commentary.
41. *Invenit hic primum fratrem suum Simonem, et dicit ei: Invenimus Messiam. (Quod est interpretatum Christus.)*	"*We have found,*" Him who was so long expected and ardently desired, and we are anxious that you should have your longing desires of finding Him now fully gratified. We have found Him, the term of whose advent, according to the ancient Prophecies, is fully expired—the desired of the everlasting hills, whom the Patriarchs and Prophets, with sighs and with groans, called on the clouds of heaven to rain down and on the earth to open and deliver up from her bowels. "*The Messiah, which is interpreted, Christ.*" (See Matthew i. 1, Commentary on.) Most likely, Andrew communicated to him, the knowledge of what our Lord imparted the night before.
42. *And he brought him to Jesus. And Jesus looking upon him, said: Thou art Simon the son of Jona: thou shalt be called Cephas, which is interpreted, Peter.* 42. *Et adduxit eum ad Jesum. Intuitus autem eum Jesus, dixit: Tu es Simon filius Jona: tu vocaberis Cephas, quod interpretatur Petrus.*	42. "*And Jesus looking on him*" with the eyes of His soul, penetrating into him by that divine vision, which has before it the future as well as the present, "*He said,*" after closely scanning him, "*Thou art Simon the son of Jona,*" showing His knowledge of everything present, however hidden, and His prescience in regard to the future, by saying, "*thou shalt be called Cephas,*" etc. Our Lord does not change his original name of "*Simon,*" He only adds that of "*Peter,*" in token of the future, exalted dignity of Primacy, which He meant to confer on him. Whether our Lord actually bestowed this name on him at present, is warmly disputed. St. Augustine maintains that the name, "*Peter,*" was given him at this moment, although spoken in a future form. "*Shalt be called,*" just as in the case of Abraham, who received this name of honour on the spot, although spoken of, in the future. "*Vocaberis Abraham*" (Genesis xvii. 5). St. Cyril holds it was only promised, and given afterwards (Mark iii. 16). For the meaning of "*Cephas,*" and the nature of the authority signified and actually conveyed in the term (see Matthew xvi., Commentary on).
43. *On the following day he would go forth into Galilee, and he findeth Philip. And Jesus saith to him: Follow me.* 43. *In crastinum voluit exire in Galilæam, et invenit Philippum. Et dicit ei Jesus : Sequere me.*	43. The Evangelist here records another vocation almost at the same time. "*The following day,*" immediately after that on which he said, "*tu vocaberis Cephas*"; but not the day immediately following that, on which the disciples followed Him (v. 40). For, most likely, these remained with our Lord till the following morning; and then, after sunrise, Andrew brought Peter to Him on the day following that, on which it is said, they followed Him (v. 40). "*He would go forth,*" from Judea, where He was, "*into Galilee.*" This was not by mere chance. But, with the predetermined divine counsel of meeting Philip and calling him. "*He found Philip,*" either on His journey, or, in Galilee. "*Follow Me,*" or, become My disciple. To this exterior call, was added the still more powerful influence of interior grace, drawing him towards his Lord. Philip at once obeyed the voice of God. It was the same voice that raised Lazarus from the

Commentary.

tomb, and performed so many miraculous wonders, in the cure of those affected with various bodily evils and diseases.

44. "*Bethsaida,*" a town on the border of the Lake of Galilee. Our Lord refers in terms of reproach to this town as well as to Corozain, on account of their infidelity and abuse of grace (Matthew xi. 21). Likely, the Evangelist refers to it here, as the native place of Andrew and Peter, to show that our Lord honoured it notwithstanding its unworthiness, by selecting from its poor inhabitants, three glorious Apostles, as trophies of His supernatural grace ; and to reproach the Jews who spurned Him, by showing, that He called His Apostles from the refuse of the earth, the despised fishermen of Galilee.

45. Philip having followed our Lord into Galilee, sought diligently for his friend Nathanael, who was a native of Cana of Galilee (xxi. 2), with a view of making him a sharer in the heavenly treasure, which he himself had found. He brought him to Jesus.

Who this Nathanael was, of whom we have mention only here, and c. xxi. 2, we cannot know for certain. By some, among them, Patrizzi, he is said to be Bartholomew the Apostle. We are told by St. Chrysostom (Hom. 19), and St. Cyril (Lib. 2), that Nathanael was profoundly versed in the SS. Scriptures ; and hence, accommodating himself to Nathanael's character for sacred erudition, Philip said, " *We have found Jesus the son of Joseph of Nazareth, of whom Moses wrote,*" etc., Him of whom Moses wrote in the Law and the Prophets, the long expected of the Jewish nation—who is no other, than Jesus the son of Joseph, from Nazareth. He was reputed to be the son of Joseph of the Royal House of David. Our Lord was a Galilean, being educated and brought up at Nazareth. "*Of Nazareth,*" is to be joined with the word "*Jesus,*" not with *Joseph,*" as is clear from the Greek. The words of this verse are precisely the same as those briefly addressed by Andrew to Peter (*v.* 41), " *We have found the Messiah.*"

46. "*Can any good come out of Nazareth ?* " Nathanael, versed in the SS. Scriptures, knew that Christ was to come from Bethlehem (Micheas v.), and the Scribes, in their reply to Herod, said the same (Matthew ii. 5)., The Jews, in reply to Nicodemus (John vii. 52), said that no Prophet could come out of Nazareth. Hence, Nathanael, in admiration, asks, can any thing extraordinary, can so great a blessing come from this obscure, mean village, in the despised Province of Galilee ? Still, Nathanael does not deny it. He only seems to wonder at it. It might be true. For, although Micheas pointed to Bethlehem as his birthplace ; still, other Prophecies said he would come from Nazareth

Text.

44. *Now Philip was of Bethsaida, the city of Andrew and Peter.*

44. *Erat autem Philippus a Bethsaida civitate Andreæ et Petri.*

45. *Philip findeth Nathanael, and saith to him: We have found him of whom Moses in the law, and the prophets did write, Jesus the son of Joseph of Nazareth.*

45. *Invenit Philippus Nathanael, et dicit ei: Quem scripsit Moyses in lege, et Prophetæ invenimus Jesum filium Joseph a Nazareth.*

46. *And Nathanael said to him : Can any thing of good come from Nazareth? Philip saith to him : Come and see.*

46. *Et dixit ei Nathanael : A Nazareth potest aliquid boni esse? Dicit ei Philippus : Veni, es vide.*

Text.

47. *Jesus saw Nathanael coming to him, and he saith of him; Behold an Israelite indeed, in whom there is no guile.*

47. *Vidit Jesus Nathanael venientem ad se, et dicit de eo ; Ecce vere Israelita, in quo dolus non est.*

48. *Nathanael saith to him: Whence knowest thou me? Jesus answered and said to him: Before that Philip called thee, when thou wast under the fig-tree, I saw thee.*

48. *Dicit ei Nathanael : Unde me nosti? Respondit Jesus, et dixit ei ; Priusquam se Philippus vocaret, cum esses sub ficu, vidi te.*

49. *Nathanael answered him, and said: Rabbi, thou art the Son of God, thou art the king of Israel.*

49. *Respondit ei Nathanael, et ait; Rabbi, tu es Filius Dei tu es Rex Israel.*

Commentary.

(Matthew ii. 23). Hence, the prudence of Nathanael, who, answering in hesitation, does not deny it, but only expresses surprise at such a great blessing coming from Nazareth, since the prevalent opinion among the people was, that He was to come from the seed of David and the town of Bethlehem (c. vii. 42). "*Come and see.*" Philip had no doubt that a brief conversation with our Lord would at once convince Nathanael that He was the promised Messiah.

47. Seeing Nathanael coming to Him on the invitation of Philip, our Lord shows in his hearing, that He was the searcher of hearts, intimately acquainted with the inmost thoughts and dispositions of men, so that Nathanael might see who He was. "*An Israelite indeed,*" a true follower and imitator of Israel, who is praised for His guileless simplicity (Genesis xxv. 2), "*in whom there is no guile,*" no deceit, dissimulation, or duplicity. He saw that Nathanael came not from any captious or deceitful design, or with the view of arguing against Him from the SS. Scriptures, in which he was well versed ; but, with all simplicity of heart, unlike those who, born of Israel according to the flesh, are still devoid of His spirit (Rom. ix. 6); unlike those, who came to question John in the name of the Sanhedrim (*v.* 19, etc.).

48. "*Whence knowest thou Me?*" Nathanael wishes to know how could our Lord know his character and interior dispositions, as they were not acquainted with one another. In order to show him that He was not speaking rashly, in disclosing His inmost thoughts, our Lord manifests to him two other things which he supposed to be most occult, viz., that he was under the fig-tree, hidden he supposed from human eye, probably engaged in prayer, or some pious thoughts, humanly speaking, known to himself alone ; and again, that he was called by Philip, after going forth from under the fig-tree.

"*I saw thee.*" I was present on both occasions. He does not say, *I knew thee.* But in virtue of my Divine Immensity, I was present and saw thee.

49. Owing to the supernatural knowledge displayed by our Lord, in knowing things absent as if they were present, the secret thoughts of the heart, as if they were public, Nathanael, aided by Divine grace, at once acknowledges the truth of what Philip stated, and proclaims our Lord, the true Son of God and King of Israel. "*Rabbi, Thou art the Son of God, Thou art the King of Israel.*"

Nathanael declares three things, which had been predicted of our Lord in the SS. Scriptures. 1st, he declares Him a doctor and teacher, "*Rabbi*.' This was prophesied regarding Him by

Commentary.

Joel (ii. 23), who calls Him "*a teacher of justice.*" 2nd, "*the Son of God,*" declared long before by the Psalmist, "*filius meus es tu.*" 3rdly, King of Israel, as predicted by Zacharias (ix. 9).

It is disputed whether Nathanael believed or proclaimed our Lord's Divinity, in calling Him "*the Son of God.*" Cardinal Franzelin maintains that he proclaimed His Divinity in the words just quoted, and His Messiahship in the words, "*King of Israel.*" Others maintain the contrary, inasmuch, as the mystery of the Trinity was not yet commonly revealed, to the just of old, save, perhaps, in a certain way, to some of the Prophets. Hence, according to them, Nathanael termed our Lord the "*Son of God,*" in the sense commonly understood by the Jews, as implying a filiation above all others, angels and saints. But, they did not believe in His Divinity or regard Him as consubstantial with the Father (see Toletus). Our Lord reserved for Himself to promulgate commonly the mystery of the Trinity. "*Pater, manifestavi nomen tuum hominibus*" (John xvii. 6).

Although the revealing of the secrets of his heart would hardly, *per se*, warrant Nathanael in proclaiming our Lord as the Eternal Son of God—do we not find Elizeus declaring the secrets of his servant Giezi (4 Kings v. 26), and of the King of Syria (vi. 9, 10, 12, 32)? Still, Nathanael might have done so. For, he knew the fulness of time had arrived. He probably heard from Philip, that the Baptist had proclaimed our Lord as the Messiah. To this add, the general opinion regarding Him, and the disclosure of his own secrets. All these considerations, with the help of Divine grace, most likely, impressed him with the conviction expressed in the words taken in their natural sense, "*Thou art the Son of God.*"

A. Lapide thinks, Nathanael and Philip believed Christ to be the Son of God, but only in a confused and indistinct way; not precisely understanding whether He was the Son of God by an eternal generation, consubstantial with the Father, or merely by adoption.

50. "*Thou believest*" Me to be "*the Son of God,*" in whatever sense understood by thee, and "*the King of Israel.*" Our Lord, while commending Nathanael's confession, tacitly insinuates that this confession, however imperfect, will be increased by still greater motives.

"*Thou shalt see greater things than these.*" Greater wonders than the revelation of occult and secret things, which will heighten thy opinion of Me, so as to believe and confess greater things regarding Me, viz., that I am the natural, consubstantial Son of God, and not only "*the King of Israel,*" but the King also and Sovereign Ruler of the universe, angels and men.

Text.

50. *Jesus answered, and said to him: Because I said unto thee, I saw thee under the fig-tree, thou believest, greater things than these shalt thou see.*

50. *Respondit Jesus et dixit ei: Quia dixi tibi: Vidi te sub ficu, credis: majus his videbis.*

Text.

51. And he saith to him: Amen, amen I say to you, you shall see the heaven opened, and the Angels of God ascending and descending upon the Son of man.

51. Et dicit ei: Amen, amen dico vobis, videbitis cælum apertum, es Angelos Dei ascendentes, et descendentes supra Filium hominis.

Commentary.

51. "*Amen, amen,*" point to the solemnity of the declaration about to follow, viz., that Nathanael and those present on this occasion, would see the heavens opened and "*the angels ascending and descending*" to minister to our Redeemer, who would thus be shown to be "*the Son of God*" and Lord of Angels. Our Redeemer calls Himself "*the Son of Man,*" out of humility, and His apparent condition of lowliness at the time in His assumed human nature. As our Lord was spoken of throughout the chapter in His Divine nature, He now refers to the other nature He assumed, so that He was true God and true man.

When did this vision take place? Some say, at His Passion and Resurrection—His Baptism was now past—others, at His Ascension; others, understand it of the ministration of Angels in the Church to be founded by Him, of which the stone, whereon Jacob lay, was a mere figure; others, of the Day of Judgment. A. Lapide holds, it had reference to some particular vision calculated to increase the faith of His hearers. Some say, this particular and wonderful manifestation, like many other acts of our Lord, was left unrecorded by the Evangelist. The words, "*the heaven opened,*" would seem to refer to some special wonderful manifestation calculated to beget or increase faith in the spectators, relative to our Lord's Divinity.

CHAPTER II.

1 And the third day there was a marriage in Cana of Galilee: and the mother of Jesus was there.
2 And Jesus also was invited, and his disciples, to the marriage.
3 And the wine failing, the mother of Jesus saith to him: They have no wine.
4 And Jesus saith to her: Woman, what is it to me and to thee? my hour is not yet come.
5 His mother saith to the waiters: Whatsoever he shall say to you, do ye.
6 Now there were set there six water-pots of stone, according to the manner of the purifying of the Jews, containing two or three measures apiece.
7 Jesus saith to them: Fill the water-pots with water. And they filled them up to the brim.
8 And Jesus saith to them: Draw out now, and carry to the chief steward of the feast. And they carried it.
9 And when the chief steward had tasted the water made wine, and knew not whence it was, but the waiters knew who had drawn the water; the chief steward calleth the bridegroom,
10 And saith to him: Every man at first setteth forth good wine, and when men have well drank, then that which is worse. But thou hast kept the good wine until now.
11 This beginning of miracles did Jesus in Cana of Galilee: and manifested his glory, and his disciples believed in him.
12 After this he went down to Capharnaum, he and his mother, and his brethren, and his disciples: and they remained there not many days.
13 And the pasch of the Jews was at hand, and Jesus went up to Jerusalem:
14 And he found in the temple them that sold oxen and sheep and doves, and the changers of money sitting.
15 And when he had made as it were a scourge of little cords, he drove them all out of the temple, the sheep also and the oxen, and the money of the changers he poured out, and the tables he overthrew.
16 And to them that sold doves he said: Take these things hence, and make not the house of my Father a house of traffic.
17 And his disciples remembered that it was written: The zeal of thy house hath eaten me up.
18 The Jews therefore answered, and said to him: What sign dost thou shew unto us, seeing thou dost these things?
19 Jesus answered and said to them: Destroy this temple, and in three days I will raise it up.
20 The Jews then said: Six and forty years was this temple in building, and wilt thou raise it up in three days?
21 But he spoke of the temple of his body.
22 When therefore he was risen again from the dead, his disciples remembered that he had said this, and they believed the scripture, and the word that Jesus had said.

23 *Now when he was at Jerusalem at the pasch, upon the festival day, many believed in his name, seeing his signs which he did.*

24 *But Jesus did not trust himself unto them, for that he knew all men,*

25 *And because he needed not that any should give testimony of man: for he knew what was in man.*

CAPUT II.

1 *Et die tertia nuptiæ factæ sunt in Cana Galilææ: et erat mater Jesu ibi.*

2 *Vocatus est autem et Jesus, et discipuli ejus ad nuptias.*

3 *Et deficiente vino, dicit mater Jesu ad eum: Vinum non habent.*

4 *Et dicit ei Jesus: Quid mihi, et tibi est mulier? nondum venit hora mea.*

5 *Dicit mater ejus ministris: Quodcumque dixerit vobis, facite.*

6 *Erant autem ibi lapideæ hydriæ sex positæ secundum purificationem Judæorum, capientes singulæ metretas binas vel ternas.*

7 *Dicit eis Jesus: Implete hydrias aqua. Et impleverunt eas usque ad summum.*

8 *Et dicit eis Jesus: Haurite nunc, et ferte architriclino. Et tulerunt.*

9 *Ut autem gustavit architriclinus aquam vinum factam, et non sciebat unde esset, ministri autem sciebant, qui hauserant aquam: vocat sponsum architriclinus.*

10 *Et dicit ei: Omnis homo primum bonum vinum ponit: et cum inebriati fuerint, tunc id, quod deterius est: Tu autem servasti bonum vinum usque adhuc.*

11 *Hoc fecit initium signorum Jesus in Cana Galilææ: et manifestavit gloriam suam, et crediderunt in eum discipuli ejus.*

12 *Post hoc descendit Capharnaum ipse, et mater ejus, et fratres ejus, et discipuli ejus: et ibi manserunt non multis diebus.*

13 *Et prope erat Pascha Judæorum, et ascendit Jesus Jerosolymam:*

14 *Et invenit in templo vendentes boves, et oves, et columbas, et numularios sedentes.*

15 *Et cum fecisset quasi flagellum de funiculis, omnes eiecit de templo, oves quoque, et boves, et numulariorum effudit æs, et mensas subvertit.*

16 *Et his, qui columbas vendebant, dixit: Auferte ista hinc, et nolite facere domum patris mei, domum negotiationis.*

17 *Recordati sunt vero discipuli ejus quia scriptum est: Zelus domus tuæ comedit me.*

18 *Responderunt ergo Judæi, et dixerunt ei: Quod signum ostendis nobis quia hæc facis?*

19 *Respondit Jesus, et dixit eis: Solvite templum hoc, et in tribus diebus excitabo illud.*

20 *Dixerunt ergo Judæi: Quadraginta et sex annis ædificatum est templum hoc, et tu in tribus diebus excitabis illud?*

21 *Ille autem dicebat de templo corporis sui.*

22 *Cum ergo resurrexisset a mortuis, recordati sunt discipuli ejus, quia hoc dicebat, et crediderunt scripturæ, et sermoni, quem dixit Jesus.*

23 *Cum autem esset Jerosolymis in pascha in die festo, multi crediderunt in nomine ejus, videntes signa ejus, quæ faciebat.*

24 *Ipse autem Jesus non credebat semetipsum eis, eo quod ipse nosset omnes.*

25 *Et quia opus ei non erat ut quis testimonium perhiberet de homine: ipse enim sciebat quid esset in homine.*

ANALYSIS.

In this chapter is recorded the marriage feast in Cana of Galilee, at which our Lord, His Blessed Mother and disciples were present (1, 2). The miracle of the conversion of the water into wine, with all its circumstances (3–11). Our Lord's brief visit to Capharnaum (12). The wonderful display of His Majesty in driving the profane traffickers out of the Temple of Jerusalem, whither He ascended to celebrate the Pasch (13–16). Its effect on His disciples (17). His reply to the Jews, who called for some sign, as a proof of His authority (18–21). The happy result of His miracles, in gaining over many to the Faith (22–25).

Commentary.

1. After having explained the mystery of the Incarnation and recorded several testimonies, among them, that of the Baptist, regarding the Divinity and mission of our Lord, as the long expected Messiah, the Evangelist now proceeds to record the first public miracle wrought by Him, after having gathered round Him some few followers.

"*The third day*" is commonly computed from that on which our Lord set out for Galilee, the same on which He called Philip (i. 42), this being the last point of time definitely described by the Evangelist.

"*Marriage*," marriage feast.

"*Cana of Galilee.*" *Lower* Galilee in the tribe of Zabulon, to distinguish it from Cana near Cidon in the Tribe of Aser (Jos. xix. 28) in Upper Galilee, commonly known as Galilee of the Gentiles. The "Cana" mentioned was quite near Nazareth, about six miles distant from it.

"*The Mother of Jesus was there.*" Very likely, she came beforehand, more as a friend, who took particular interest in managing and making arrangements for the feast, than as an invited guest. It is not said, that she was "*invited*," as is said of others. She, likely, came of herself as a friend of the family (*v.* 5). The Evangelist, very likely, makes special mention of her, on account of her part in the subsequent miracle. Who the bride and bridegroom were, cannot be known for certain. It is generally thought, they were relations of the Blessed Virgin. From the absence of all allusion to him, it is conjectured that Joseph, by this time, was dead.

2. "*And His disciples.*" Probably, the four referred to in the preceding chapter, were among them with the Evangelist himself, who minutely describes the whole scene. These followed our Lord for some time, and afterwards returned to their boats and the ordinary occupation of fishermen. Being called again by our Lord they clung to Him. (Matthew iv.)

Our Lord assisted at the marriage, 1st, as a matter of social civility; 2ndly, to bless and sanctify, by His presence, the holy

Text.

1. *And the third day there was a marriage in Cana of Galilee: and the mother of Jesus was there.*

1. *Et die tertia nuptiæ factæ sunt in Cana Galilææ: et erat mater Jesu ibi.*

2. *And Jesus also was invited, and his disciples, to the marriage.*

2. *Vocatus est autem Jesus, et discipuli ejus ad nuptias.*

Text.

3. *And the wine failing, the mother of Jesus saith to him: They have no wine.*

3. *Et deficiente vino, dicit mater Jesu ad eum: Vinum non habent.*

4. *And Jesus saith to her: Woman, what is it to me and to thee? my hour is not yet come.*

4. *Et dicit ei Jesus: Quid mihi, et tibi est mulier? nondum venit hora mea.*

Commentary.

state of matrimony, of which He was the founder, and to obviate the *objections* raised against it at future times by Heretics (1 Tim. iv. 3). Marriage has been always regarded in the Catholic Church as "*a great Sacrament in Christ,*" a *holy state.* Still, however, as a *state*, inferior to *virginity.* (1 Cor. vii.)

3. "*The wine failing,*" or beginning to fall short. The pious and tender solicitude of the Virgin Mother and her merciful consideration for the feelings of the hosts are here displayed. Likely, as a friend of the family, taking special interest in the management of things, she was among the first to be apprised, by the waiters, of the apprehended failure of the wine. She did not wait till the wine was exhausted, and the hosts put to the blush; but relying on the power of Her Son, in whose Divinity and omnipotence she so firmly believed, she at once, unasked, spontaneously anticipates any embarrassment on the part of the entertainers, by gently hinting the state of things to her Divine Son, from whom, as appears from the context, she confidently expected miraculous relief (*v.* 5).

"*They have no wine*" remaining. The wine is about being exhausted. In these words, she mildly hints and tacitly requests the exercise of His sovereign power, to consult for the feelings of the hosts. Similar was the modest proceeding on the part of the sisters of Lazarus, who, without directly preferring a request for the resuscitation of their brother, simply say, "Lord, *behold he whom Thou lovest is sick.*" (John xi. 3).

"*Quid mihi et tibi?*" Whatever meaning may be attached to these words—and they have taxed the learning and ingenuity of the ablest commentators, ancient and modern—we must reject every interpretation that would imply, that they convey a censure, of any kind, on our Blessed Lady, or that our Lord, in any way, reprimanded her. In truth, the feelings of every Catholic would at once recoil from such a supposition. It is the doctrine of the Catholic Church (Council of Trent, SS. vi., Can. xxiii.) that "*the B. Virgin, by a special privilege of God, had avoided all, even venial, sins, during her whole life.*" The great light and Doctor of the Church, St. Augustine, (Lib. *de natura et gratia* c. xxxvi.) says, "*When we speak of sin, I wish to have no question whatever, of the B. Virgin.*" It would not be reverential to say, that our Lord would administer a reproof to that mother whom He loved so tenderly, without some fault on her part. There was no fault committed here to call for a reprimand of any sort. The whole action of the Virgin was dictated by charity and a merciful consideration for the hosts, suggested by the necessity of the case. She merely informed her Divine Son, in the most modest way, at a seasonable time, of how matters stood. No doubt, a request is implied—but in a spirit of conformity to God's holy will—that He would seasonably interpose

Commentary.

by an exercise of Divine power. If the object of this implied request were censurable, surely, our Lord would not immediately accede to it, as He had done. The same is to be said of all *its circumstances*, time, place, etc., for the same reason.

Moreover, from the instructions given by her to the waiters (*v*. 5), it is clear the Virgin Mother did not regard her Son's words, whatever be their meaning, which, at this remote period, it is difficult to determine, as conveying reproof or reprimand of any kind.

The manner of uttering them, likely, most tender, the tone of voice, would remove all appearance of acerbity.

The word, "*woman*," (γυναι) is frequently used as a term of respect, signifying *Mistress, Lady*, as appears from its use, in this sense, by Pagan authors. (Xenophon, Cyroped, vii. 3, 4; Homer, Odyss. 221, 555, etc.) Even the most respectable Protestant commentators are in accord with us, on this point. Our Lord himself, who loved his beloved Mother with such filial tenderness, addresses the term to her, on the most affecting occasion, when hanging on the cross, on the point of breathing His last, on taking His final farewell, He says, "WOMAN, *behold thy Son*" (John xix. 26).

The phrase, τι μοι και σοι—"*Quid mihi et tibi*," literally translated, would be, "*what to me and to thee?*" leaving the verb, "*is*," out altogether. Hence, the words are not faithfully rendered, either in the Douay or Authorized Version. It might have been better to translate the words literally from the Greek, without adding or taking away from them; and then, leave the meaning to be determined, from either the context or any other available source of interpretation. The phrase is sometimes used in the Old Testament as well as in the New. The instances being so well known, it is unnecessary to quote them here at any length. In no one instance, can it be shown that they convey censure or reproof of any kind. The context clearly shows, as has been already stated, that here, they could not possibly imply censure or reproof

"*My hour is not*," etc. The Word, "*hour*," though generally referring to our Lord's Passion, when He speaks of "*My hour*," is not necessarily to be restricted to that meaning. It signifies in general, a time suitable for accomplishing any event. Circumstances are to determine what that suitable time may be, as, for instance, in (c. vii. 6), "*My time*," (the same as, "*My hour, is not yet come*") it refers to His going up to attend the Festival at Jerusalem. Here, it most probably means, the time marked out, in the eternal decrees of his Father's Providence, for publicly working miracles, and thereby manifesting His Divinity to the world. That time, so far as God's general decree was concerned, had not yet come. But, simultaneously and concurrently with this general decree, was another Eternal decree, ordering that in view of the merits

Commentary.

of his Immaculate Mother, our Lord, breaking through the ordinary arrangement of His Providence, would perform this miracle, at the request of His Blessed Mother, without which request, preordained from eternity, He would not have performed the miracle so soon. Both decrees are perfectly consistent and compatible.

The precise meaning of the phrase, owing to the many and conflicting interpretations, given regarding it, can hardly be determined with certainty. But, at the same time, it may be said, that the determination of its precise meaning, however important, must be *secondary* to the grave consideration of vindicating our Lord's filial devotion to His Blessed Mother, and her most powerful Intercessory influence with her Divine Son. The words, "*My hour is not come*," would seem to suggest that, however charitable her views, however praiseworthy her motives, the working of the miracle, was attended with some difficulty, arising from the general arrangements of God's Providence; however, according to the decree of God, it could not be refused, because she requested it. The most probable meaning of the words would then seem to be, " My Lady, the miracle, regarding which " thou givest me a suggestive hint, is a work which cannot ema- " nate from My human nature, received from thee, which alone, " therefore is "*common to you and to Me*," " *quid mihi et tibi*." ' It is a work peculiar to my Divine nature. There is some " difficulty in the way, arising from the decrees of My Father's " Providence as to the time, "*the hour*," for My public mani- " festation to the world, *is not yet come*." But, thy powerful " intercession cannot be frustrated ; thou askest it, let it, there- " fore, be done." Accordingly, fully understanding the views of her Divine Son, she gave instructions to the waiters (*v.* 5).

What more calculated to inspire all her children with the greatest confidence in the wonderful intercessory power of the *Blessed Virgin* ?

Patrizzi observes here : " From the narrative given in this place, we are taught, that God, out of respect for the prayers of this Virgin, has decreed that certain things would be done otherwise, than He would have decreed, had the Virgin not interposed her prayers." (See John xix. 26. Commentary.)

Considering the profundity of SS. Scripture, and the manifold lessons it conveys in several passages, it may be held, that these words in themselves, most respectful and devoid of all reproof, were meant by our Lord, to convey to all future generations a declaration of His Divinity, in virtue of which alone He performed miracles. For this Divinity or Divine nature, he was not indebted to His Blessed Mother. "*Quid mihi et tibi, mulier.*"

The words may also be meant to convey to parents, at all times, a lesson, as to how they should act in regard to their children,

ST. JOHN, CHAP. II.

Commentary.

when duty to God and a regard for their own perfection would demand a sacrifice, such as is involved in embracing a religious life, and giving up all to follow Christ.

Similar is the meaning of the words of our Lord to His parents, when on being found, after an anxious and diligent search, in the Temple, He said: "*Did you not know, that I must be about My Father's business?*" (Luke ii. 49.)

5. From the action of the Virgin, as recorded in this verse, it is clear, she did not regard the words referred to, as in any way reproachful, or her implied request, as untimely. In verse 1, it is not said, she was an *invited* guest, like the others. From this, as well as from her mode of acting, as mentioned here, it is inferred, she was present, as a friend of the hosts, charitably undertaking to superintend the management of the Feast. From her instructions to the waiters, it is clear, she knew her Divine Son would perform the miracle in compliance with her request; that although "*His hour*," looking to God's general decree, in reference to our Lord's manifestation to the world, and apart from her interposition, was "*not come*," in the first instance; still, so far as the will of God, in relation to her interposition, was concerned, it was come, in the second instance. Hence, she wished, by issuing timely instructions to the waiters, that they should be ready at a call to remove every obstacle, and have everything ready for the performance of the miracle.

Whence the Blessed Virgin derived the knowledge, or rather foreknowledge of what was to occur, it is not easy to conjecture; whether it was from revelation or supernatural knowledge, contained in the fulness and abundance of heavenly gifts conferred on her; or from some private intimation which her Divine Son might have given her, cannot be fully ascertained. One thing is certain that she knew all about the coming miracle; and also, that she could not have regarded the words addressed to her by her Son, as reproachful. It was also wisely arranged to hold communication beforehand with the waiters only, to prevent any suspicion of collusion between our Lord and the hosts.

6. The Evangelist now commences to describe the miracle with all its circumstances.

"*Six water pots of stone*," destined for holding water and not wine; and hence, is removed the suspicion that some wine could have remained in these vessels, which might impart to water mixed with it the flavour of wine without having any new wine super-added, or, change effected. They were "*set*" or fixed there; this, together with their being of large and capacious size, removed all ground for suspecting, that they were carried there, full of wine for the purpose of deception.

Text.

5. *His mother saith to the waiters: Whatsoever he shall say to you, do ye.*

5. *Dicit mater ejus ministris: quodcumque dixerit vobis, facite.*

6. *Now there were set there six water pots of stone, according to the manner of the purifying of the Jews, containing two or three measures a piece.*

6. *Erant autem ibi lapideæ hydriæ sex positæ secundum purificationem Judæorum, capientes singulæ metretas binas vel ternas.*

Text	Commentary

"*After the manner of the purification of the Jews.*" They were placed there, that the Jews might perform the usual ablutions practised by them at their feasts, washing their hands before and after meals (Matthew xv. 2). Washing vessels and furniture (Luke xi. 39), was quite common with them. This is more minutely described by Mark (vii. 1–5). The purifications referred to here, were not those prescribed for legal uncleanness in the Law; but rather ablutions in connexion with meals, as handed down from the traditions of the ancients. The legal uncleanness contracted from contact with a corpse, or with a leper, etc., were not removed by purifications through water. It remained till evening.

"*Containing two or three measures each.*" Some contained two measures; some, three. It is difficult to determine the precise quantity, contained in each measure. Likely, it is the same as the Hebrew measure, *Bath*, used for liquids, and generally supposed to be equal to seven and a half gallons. The quantity of wine must, therefore, have been very large, which showed the splendour, of the miracle and the munificence of our Lord. *Bath* and *Epha* were measures of the same capacity; the former, for *liquids*; the latter, for *solids*.

7. *Jesus saith to them: Fill the waterpots with water. And they filled them up to the brim.*

7. *Dicit eis Jesus: Implete hydrias aqua. Et impleverunt eas usque ad summum.*

7.—"*Jesus saith to them,*" the servants—"*Fill the water pots with water.*" So that no room would be left for pouring in wine to mix with the water. Likely, the banquet being by this time nearly over, the pots were emptied of water owing to the frequent purifications during the banquet; and now He tells the servants "*to fill them up,*" which they did, "*to the brim,*" so that there could be no possibility of a mixture or addition of any other ingredient. Moreover, the servants, indifferent disinterested witnesses, are employed, so that it could not be said that either our Lord Himself or His disciples brought the wine to give the colour of a miracle to the whole occurrence.

"*Water pots,*" never employed for holding wine, but only for holding water for ablution purposes; which served to remove all suspicion of any fraud or deception.

8. *And Jesus saith to them: Draw out now, and carry to the chief steward of the feast. And they carried it.*

8. *Et dicit eis Jesus: Haurite nunc, et ferte architriclino. Et tulerunt.*

8. "*Draw out now,*" immediately after the pots were filled with water. This shows that the miracle was wrought on the spot, without any delay; and it, therefore, demonstrates the Divine power. And in order to guard against any suspicion of deception, the servants are ordered to carry it, not to the host or bridegroom; but "*to the chief steward of the feast,*" the man who presided at the head of the table; who having charge of the entertainment, gave instruction to the servants in attendance, and from his office was bound to practise sobriety. He was, therefore, the best judge of the quality of the wine, after tasting it.

Commentary

9. *"And knew not whence it was."* This circumstance gives great weight to his spontaneous evidence. It shows, that the judgment borne by him to the reality and superior excellence of the wine produced, was free from bias or prejudice. His was, therefore, a most important testimony, in regard to the reality of the miracle wrought, without any form of words, or any external action of our Blessed Lord, who effected the change *immediately*, in virtue of the same Omnipotent Power, by which He evoked all things out of nothing, " *Quia ipse dixit et facta sunt; ipse mandavit et creata sunt*" (Psa. cxlviii.).

" *He calls the bridegroom.*" " *The chief steward of the feast*" was seated or reclined at the upper end or top of the table to see what was going on, and give instructions to the attendants. The bridegroom was, probably, going about and attending to his guests. Hence, " *the chief steward*" of the feast calls to him.

10. He charges him with want of tact and practical knowledge, in departing from the practice usually observed in supplying wine at feasts. The *usual practice* was to serve up the best wine at the beginning; and then, after the guests had drunk freely, and their palates had become, to some extent, blunted—this is the meaning of, " *have drunk well*" " *inebriati sunt*"—they, serve up an inferior kind of wine. From this, it by no means follows, that there was any intemperance at this feast. They are the words, not of our Lord, but the chief steward of the feast, stating what *usually* occurs, without any reference to the present feast. Neither do they express any toleration, much less approbation of intemperance. They simply refer to a fact or common occurrence.

11. " *This beginning of miracles*," etc. This was the first of *public* miracles wrought by our Lord, and wrought in Cana of Galilee. There seems to be no good grounds for interpreting the words to mean, that this was the first of the miracles wrought by our Lord in Cana of Galilee, as if He afterwards performed other miracles there. The Greek construction, however, would bear this meaning. There is no reason, why the Evangelist should refer to His miracles at Cana any more than to His miracles at Capharnaum or Jerusalem. I, said " *public* miracles," as there is nothing to prevent us from thinking, that He might have *privately* manifested His Divine power to His parents in their home at Nazareth. Of this, however, there is no evidence. The result of this His first *public* miracle was, as He intended, twofold. 1st, To " *manifest His glory*," to show His Divine attributes of omnipotence and goodness. The end of all His miracles was " *the glory of God, that the Son of Man may be glorified*" (x. 4). This was the effect, so far as He was concerned, which His miracles were calculated to produce. If men did not correspond, this was the result of

Text

9. And when the chief steward had tasted the water made wine, and knew not whence it was, but the waiters knew who had drawn the water; the chief steward calleth the bridegroom.

9. *Ut autem gustavit architriclinus aquam vinum factam, et non sciebat unde esset, ministri autem sciebant, qui hauserant aquam: vocat sponsum architriclinus.*

10. And saith to him: Every man at first setteth forth good wine, and when men have well drank, then that which is worse. But thou has kept the good wine until now.

10. *Et dicit ei: Omnis homo primum bonum vinum ponit: et cum inebriati fuerint, tunc id, quod deterius est: Tu autem servasti bonum vinum usque adhuc.*

11. This beginning of miracles did Jesus in Cana of Galilee: and manifested his glory, and his disciples believed in him.

11. *Hoc fecit initium signorum Jesus in Cana Galilææ: et manifestavit gloriam suam, et crediderunt in eum discipuli ejus.*

Text.	Commentary.
	their own perversity." 2ndly, To increase the faith of His disciples so that they not only believe Him to be the promised Messiah, relying on the testimony of John and their own conversation with him; but now, on witnessing an exercise of Divine Power, that He was also the Eternal Son of God. Faith may be more or less intense. "*Lord increase our faith*" (Luke xvii. 5). The very fact of their being His *disciples* shows that they had already believed in Him. Now, their faith is *increased* or *strengthened* on witnessing this miracle, which is the meaning of the words, "*believed in Him.*" The faith of His Divine Mother, who was "*full of grace,*" needed no increase.
12. *After this he went down to Capharnaum, he and his mother, and his brethren, and his disciples: and they remained there not many days.* 12. *Post hoc descendit Capharnaum ipse, et mater ejus, et fratres ejus, et discipuli ejus: et ibi manserunt non multis diebus.*	12. Probably, He proceeded at once from Cana to Nazareth, His native home. For, we have no account of His brethren being at the marriage feast. So, He met them at Nazareth; and thence went down with them to Capharnaum, which was situated in a lower place, on the brink of the Lake of Galilee. He remained there only for a short time. This is, therefore, different from His visit there, when after returning from Judea, He made it His permanent place of abode, the centre of His missionary excursions to the surrounding districts (Matthew iv. 13). "*Capharnaum.*" See Matthew iv. 13 (Commentary). "*His brethren.*" See Matthew xiii. 55, 56 (Commentary). "*Remained there not many days.*" We have no record of any miracles being performed on this occasion, as we have, when He afterwards fixed His abode there; nor of His preaching, though likely, He employed His time in privately teaching and attracting disciples to Himself. Leaving Nazareth, where He knew He would not be received with proper respect, and His teaching might be disregarded and undervalued, He selects Capharnaum, as the theatre of His preaching and miracles (Matthew iv. 13).
13. *And the pasch of the Jews was at hand, and Jesus went up to Jerusalem:* 13. *Et prope erat Pascha Judæorum, et ascendit Jesus Jerosolymam:*	13. "*And the Pasch of the Jews,*" etc. "*And*" signifies, *because, for,* as assigning a reason why our Lord tarried not for any time on this occasion, at Capharnaum. He says, "*of the Jews,*" because when St. John wrote, the Christians kept *their* Pasch also. The Pasch was the most solemn of the three great Jewish Festivals, viz., Pasch, Pentecost, Tabernacles, on which the Lord commanded every male among the Jews, from every quarter, to adore and sacrifice in Jerusalem (Exodus xxiii.; Deut. xvi.). They were allowed to offer sacrifice nowhere else. "*Went up to Jerusalem.*" Jerusalem was on a higher elevation than Capharnaum.
14. *And he found in the temple them that sold oxen and sheep and doves, and*	14. This ejection of the profane traffickers from the Temple, recorded by St. John only, took place at the opening of our Lord's mission. The other, which took place three years after, recorded

Commentary.

by St. Matthew xxi. 12 (see Commentary), and the two other Evangelists (Mark xi. 11; Luke xix. 45) occurred at the close of His mission; and as the lesson administered here was forgotten and the offenders more culpable, in the second instance, on account of their greater resistance to grace, than in the former recorded here; hence, the language of reproach addressed to them is stronger and more severe. Here, He only charges them with turning the house of His Father *into a mart of traffic;* in St. Matthew, He charges them with converting it into "*a den of robbers.*" See Commentary. (Matthew xxi. 12, etc.)

"*The house of my Father.*" As Son of God, He here claims His strict right, to defend from profanation, the house of His Heavenly Father.

15. "*Having made, as it were, a scourge,*" etc. This is not mentioned by the other Evangelists, on the occasion of His second visit, before His Passion. The scourge was evidently intended for the cattle only, but not for the people; since, after casting out the cattle, etc., He says, "*take hence these things,*" etc., which supposes the people to have remained. "*Take these things hence,*" refers to the doves which could not be driven out. Their possessors were ordered to carry them away. It may seem surprising that these profane traffickers should at once yield such obedience to the commands of our Lord, whom they could hardly regard as vested with any authority. (See in explanation St. Jerome's words. Matthew xxi. 13, Commentary.)

Speaking on this subject, St. Jerome observes, "For my part, "I regard what occurred here, as the most marvellous of all the "miraculous signs of our Lord's power. A man, who was looked "upon with scorn and was treated as the last of men, so as to be "crucified, has the power to banish with a simple whip of cords so "great a multitude, upset their tables and do other things, which "an armed force could hardly accomplish; and this, in the presence "of the Pharisees and Doctors of the Law, transported with rage "against Him, as well as of those whose traffic He ruined. The "eyes of the Saviour must have emitted some sparks of fire and "heavenly rays, and the splendour of Divine Majesty on His "countenance must have completely overwhelmed them, *igneum* "*enim quiddam ac sidereum radiebat in oculis ejus; et Divinitatis* "*Majestas radiebat in facie.*"

17. "*His disciples remembered,*" etc. Our Lord's disciples, who heard the SS. Scriptures, and especially the Psalms, read in the Synagogues, on the Sabbath days, were sufficiently versed in sacred knowledge—Nathanael was so in an especial way—so as to remember the words spoken in the person of David, which they were aware were predicted of Christ, whom they knew to be the

Text.

the changers of money sitting.

14. *Et invenit in templo vendentes boves, et oves, et columbas, et numularios sedentes.*

15. *And when he had made as it were a scourge of little cords, he drove them all out of the temple, the sheep also and the oxen, and the money of the chargers he poured out, and the tables he overthrew.*

15. *Et cum fecisset quasi flagellum de funiculis, omnes eiecit de templo, oves quoque, et boves, et numulariorum effudites, et mensas subvertit.*

16. *And to them that sold doves, he said: Take these things hence and make not the house of my Father a house of traffic.*

16. *Et his, qui columbas vendebant, dixit: Auferte ista hinc, et nolite facere domum patris mei, domum negotiationis.*

17. *And his disciples remembered that it was written: The zeal of thy house hath eaten me up.*

17. *Recordati sunt vero discipuli ejus quia*

Text.

scriptum est: Zelus domus tuæ comedit me.

Commentary.

Messiah promised in the Law and the Prophets. These words, as applicable to Christ, came before their minds on seeing the extraordinary zeal which our Lord so courageously displayed in vindicating the honour of His Father's house on this occasion.

"*The zeal of Thy house,*" etc. The burning anxiety and intense solicitude for the honour of Thy Temple, the dwelling place of Thy glory, the "*house*" wherein Thou dwellest, the indignation I have conceived against its profaners, "*hath eaten me up,*" is the chief, absorbing, burning thought of My mind, the great object of My solicitude. Our Lord commences and closes His sacred mission with a remarkable display of power, in vindicating the honour of His Father's house; thus leaving a memorable lesson of instruction to stimulate the zeal of all who have charge of our Churches in which the glorious but veiled Majesty of God is substantially and personally present. Woe to those who are indifferent in regard to God's glory and interests in this matter. "*If any man violate the temple of God, him will the Lord destroy*" (1 Cor. iii. 17).

18. *The Jews therefore answered and said to him: What sign dost thou shew unto us, seeing thou dost these things?*

18. *Responderunt ergo Judæi, et dixerunt ei: Quod signum ostendis nobis quia hæc facis?*

18. "*The Jews, therefore, answered,*" etc. "*Therefore.*" On seeing the wonderful zeal displayed by our Lord and its results in driving the profane traffickers out of the Temple, "*answered.*" This word frequently means, to begin to speak (Matthew xi. 25).

"*What sign dost Thou shew unto us,*" etc.? The Jews, blinded by avarice, and seeing their temporal emoluments interfered with, regarded our Lord's action in a different light from that in which the Apostles, remembering the words of David, regarded it. They ask for some miracle or supernatural sign, to prove His authority for doing "*these things.*" Similar are the words (Matthew xxi. 23). "*By what authority dost Thou these things?*" The whole occurrence, in connexion with the expulsion from the Temple—all concerned tamely submitting; while the authorities of the Temple were probably looking on—was, in itself, the greatest sign that He could exhibit, and was amply sufficient to convince them of His Divine authority, without asking any other, if their hearts were not hardened and their eyes blinded by passion and prejudice.

19. *Jesus answered and said to them: Destroy this temple, and in three days I will raise it up.*

19. *Respondit Jesus, et dixit eis: Solvite templum hoc, et in tribus diebus excitabo illud.*

19. Our Lord well knew, that if He were to work a new miracle in proof of His Divine mission to convince men, whom this last exhibition of power, with all its circumstances, did not move; they would not, owing to their malignity, believe Him. He now refers, under the metaphor of a body representing a temple—St. Paul often addresses the body of a Christian as the temple of the Holy Ghost—to an overwhelming proof of His power, as well as the most convincing proof, He could give of His Divinity. He speaks of the resuscitation of Himself, by His own power, from the dead; and this, after minutely describing beforehand all its circumstances. No doubt, the Prophets sometimes raised others

Commentary

from the dead. But, this they did, by the Divine Power granted to them. Whereas, our Lord raised *Himself* by *His own innate* power, which God only could do. This is the great proof of our Lord's Divinity constantly adduced, and deservedly so, by St. Paul thoughout his Epistles.

Our Lord gives this sign, however, only in an enigmatical, obscure way, a thing not unusual with Him, when dealing with obstinate, carping unbelievers, "*that seeing, they may not see*," etc. (Luke viii. 10.)

The Temple in which they were, suggested the idea of His own body, which is often represented by a Temple. For, as God resides in His Temple, our Lord dwelt personally in the plenitude of the Divinity, within His own body.

"*Destroy this temple,*" is not a precept; but, a mere prediction of what they would do. It is, what is called, a *permissive imperative*, like "*quod facis, fac citius.*" Some suppose, that in uttering the words, "*this temple,*" He pointed to His own body.

"*And in three days I will raise it up.*" This was the sign our Lord gave the unbelieving Jews on more than one occasion; "*the sign of the Prophet, Jonas.*" (Matthew xii. 40; John viii. 28, etc.)

They "*destroyed*" His life, by separating His soul in death from His body, His Divinity being always inseparably united to each.

20. The Jews understood our Lord, who spoke enigmatically, as treating of the material Temple. It may be, they did so on purpose, with a view of cavilling, and ridiculing His razing the Temple and building it up in three days; and hence, they laugh at His claims to authority. They quote His words on this occasion, or rather pervert them, as the ground of a charge against Him at His trial (Matthew xxvi. 61; xxvii. 40).

The Temple spoken of here is commonly understood of the second or Zorobabelic Temple, built after the return of the Jews from the Babylonish captivity. The first Temple built by Solomon in eight years (3 Kings vi. 38), was utterly demolished by the Chaldeans. There is, therefore, no question of Solomon's Temple here; but, of the second Temple, which it took forty-six years to rebuild, from the time they began to rebuild it, in the second year of Cyrus, to the ninth year of Darius Hystaspes, when it was finished. The work was frequently given over, during that period, owing to several obstacles, so that forty-six years were not spent in building it. But, from the commencement to the close of the building, a period of forty-six years elapsed. In the time of Herod, this second Temple was in a condition bordering on dilapidation. Hence, Herod undertook the work of repairing it on a magnificent scale. The work of rebuilding, which Herod commenced in the eighteenth year of his reign, sixteen years before the birth of Christ, was still going on, at this time—viz., the thirtieth year of our Lord.

Text

20. *The Jews then said: Six and forty years was this temple in building, and wilt thou raise it up in three days?*

20. *Dixerunt ergo Judæi: Quadraginta et sex annis ædificatum est templum hoc, et tu in tribus diebus excitabis illud?*

Text.	Commentary.
	Hence, a period of forty-six years elapsed from the time Herod first began to rebuild or repair it, up to the present time. It was called the second Temple still; because it was still, the Zorobabelic Temple repaired by Herod. We are not bound to vindicate the accuracy of this statement. They are the words, not of our Lord; but, of the Jews, uttered by them, perhaps, inaccurately, as on another occasion, they implied that our Lord was bordering on forty years. "*Quadraginta annos nondum habeset Abraham vidisti.*"
	"*Wilt Thou raise it up,*" etc.? This is asked scornfully, as if a poor, despised man could accomplish in three days, what it took potentates, with all their wealth and influence, over forty years to accomplish. Hence, they fancied that this assertion of His, proved, He had no authority for what He was after doing in the Temple.
21. *But he spoke of the temple of his body.*	21. The Evangelist mentions this to guard us against the mistake the Jews fell into regarding the material Temple, and to show that the accusation made by the Jews at His Passion (Matthew xxvi.), "*I can destroy the temple of God,*" was a calumny. He did not say, "*the temple of God,*" but only, "*this temple,*" probably indicating at the time, by some gesture, what temple He referred to.
21. *Ille autem dicebat de templo corporis sui.*	
22. *When therefore he was risen again from the dead, his disciples remembered, that he had said this, and they believed the scripture and the word that Jesus hath said.*	22. The disciples did not then, fully understand the words of our Lord. But, after His Resurrection, they remembered what He said on this occasion when He predicted His death and Resurrection, and they believed all that He said to be true.
22. *Cum ergo resurrexisset a mortuis, recordati sunt discipuli ejus, quia hoc dicebat et crediderunt scripturæ, et sermoni, quem dixit Jesus.*	"*They believed,*" not only our Lords words, regarding His death and Resurrection; but also, "*the Scripture,*" not the Scriptures in general which they always believed to be true; but, they believed that the portion of the Scripture of the Old Testament, which predicted our Lord's death and Resurrection, was fully verified and accomplished in Christ.
23. *Now when he was at Jerusalem at the pasch, upon the festival day, many believed in his name, seeing his signs which he did.*	23. "*At the Pasch, on the Festival day.*" During the continuation of the festival, which lasted for eight days (John vi.). The Evangelist does not record the miracles wrought by our Lord, on this occasion. But, whatever they were, they had a very salutary effect. "*Many*"—in consequence of these signs—"*believed in His name,*" that is, believed Him to be the Christ, the promised Messiah. Our Lord wrought many miracles not recorded by the Evangelists. (See also iv. 45; vi. 2.)
23. *Cum autem esset Jerosolymis in pascha in die festo, multi crediderunt in nomine ejus, videntes, signa ejus, quæ faciebat.*	
24. *But Jesus did not trust himself unto them, for that he knew all men.*	24. He did not confide or place too much trust in them. He acted with prudent caution, withdrawing and keeping aloof from them, as the appointed hour of His death had not yet come. He, possibly, foresaw that some of those, who now believed in Him,

Commentary.

would again give up the faith, and persecute Him at the instigation of the Jewish leaders, whom He knew to be incensed against Him, though still concealing their hatred and rancour.

"*He knew all men*," their inconstancy and fickleness.

25. "*He needed not that any man should give testimony*," etc. Unlike most men placed in authority, who must derive information from others, He needed not this; "*for He knew what was in man.*" He saw not only the exterior, but, the very secrets, the inmost recesses, of the human heart; nay, even man's future line of free action. As God, He knew the secrets of man's hearts, the future, as well as the present. Hence, He knew of Himself, how far man was to *be trusted*. This is a strong testimony in favour of His Omniscient Divinity. For God alone can search the heart. (Jeremiah xvii. 10; 3 Kings viii. 39; 1 Par. xxvii. 9; Job xlii. 2; Psa. vii. 10, etc.)

Text.

24. *Ipse autem Jesus non credebat semetipsum eis, eo quod ipse nosset omnes.*

25. *And because he needed not that any should give testimony of man: for he knew what was in man.*

25. *Et quia opus ei non erat ut quis testimonium perhiberet de homine: ipse enim sciebat quid esset in homine.*

CHAPTER III.

1 *And there was a man of the Pharisees, named Nicodemus, a ruler of the Jews.*

2 *This man came to Jesus by night, and said to him: Rabbi, we know that thou art come a teacher from God: for no man can do these signs which thou dost, unless God be with him.*

3 *Jesus answered, and said to him: Amen, amen I say to thee, unless a man be born again, he cannot see the kingdom of God.*

4 *Nicodemus saith to him: How can a man be born when he is old? can he enter a second time into his mother's womb, and be born again?*

5 *Jesus answered: Amen, amen I say to thee, unless a man be born again of water and the Holy Ghost, he cannot enter into the kingdom of God.*

6 *That which is born of the flesh, is flesh: and that which is born of the Spirit, is spirit.*

7 *Wonder not, that I said to thee, you must be born again.*

8 *The Spirit breatheth where he will; and thou hearest his voice, but thou knowest not whence he cometh and whither he goeth: so is every one that is born of the Spirit.*

9 *Nicodemus answered, and said to him: How can these things be done?*

10 *Jesus answered, and said to him: Art thou a master in Israel, and knowest not these things?*

11 *Amen, amen I say to thee, that we speak what we know, and we testify what we have seen, and you receive not our testimony.*

12 *If I have spoken to you earthly things, and you believe not: how will you believe if I shall speak to you heavenly things?*

13 *And no man hath ascended into heaven, but he that descended from heaven, the son of man who is in heaven.*

14 *And as Moses lifted up the serpent in the desert, so must the son of man be lifted up:*

15 *That whosoever believeth in him, may not perish, but may have life everlasting.*

16 *For God so loved the world, as to give his only begotten Son; that whosoever believeth in him, may not perish, but may have life everlasting.*

17 *For God sent not his Son into the world, to judge the world, but that the world may be saved by him.*

18 *He that believeth in him is not judged. But he that doth not believe, is already judged: because he believeth not in the name of the only begotten Son of God.*

19 *And this is the judgment: because the light is come into the world, and men loved darkness rather than the light: for their works were evil.*

20 *For every one that doth evil hateth the light, and cometh not to the light, that his works may not be reproved.*

21 *But he that doth truth, cometh to the light, that his works may be made manifest, because they are done in God.*

22 *After these things Jesus and his disciples came into the land of Judea; and there he abode with them, and baptized.*

23 And John also was baptizing in Ænnon near Salim; because there was much water there, and they came, and were baptized.

24 For John was not yet cast into prison.

25 And there arose a question between some of John's disciples and the Jews concerning purification:

26 And they came to John, and said to him: Rabbi, he that was with thee beyond the Jordan, to whom thou gavest testimony, behold he baptizeth, and all men come to him.

27 John answered and said: A man cannot receive anything, unless it be given him from heaven.

28 You yourselves do bear me witness, that I said, I am not Christ, but that I am sent before him.

29 He that hath the bride, is the bridegroom: but the friend of the bridegroom, who standeth and heareth him, rejoiceth with joy because of the bridegroom's voice. This my joy therefore is fulfilled.

30 He must increase but I must decrease.

31 He that cometh from above, is above all. He that is of the earth, of the earth he is, and of the earth he speaketh. He that cometh from heaven, is above all.

32 And what he hath seen, and heard, that he testifieth: and no man receiveth his testimony.

33 He that hath received his testimony, hath set to his seal that God is true.

34 For he whom God hath sent, speaketh the words of God: for God doth not give the spirit by measure.

35 The Father loveth the Son: and he hath given all things into his hand.

36 He that believeth in the Son, hath life everlasting: but he that believeth not the Son, shall not see life, but the wrath of God abideth on him.

CAPUT III.

1 Erat autem homo ex Pharisæis, Nicodemus nomine, princeps Judæorum.

2 Hic venit ad Jesum nocte, et dixit ei: Rabbi, scimus quia a Deo venisti magister, nemo enim potest hæc signa facere, quæ tu facis, nisi fuerit Deus cum eo.

3 Respondit Jesus, et dixit ei: Amen, amen dico tibi, nisi quis renatus fuerit denuo, non potest videre regnum Dei.

4 Dicit ad eum Nicodemus: Quomodo potest homo nasci, cum sit senex? numquid potest in ventrem matris suæ iterato introire, et renasci?

5 Respondit Jesus: Amen, amen dico tibi, nisi quis renatus fuerit ex aqua, et Spiritu sancto, non potest introire in regnum Dei.

6 Quod natum est ex carne, caro est: et quod natum est ex spiritu, spiritus est.

7 Non mireris quia dixi tibi: oportet vos nasci denuo.

8 Spiritus ubi vult spirat: et vocem ejus audis, sed nescis unde veniat, aut quo vadat: sic est omnis, qui natus est ex spiritu.

9 Respondit Nicodemus, et dixit ei: Quomodo possunt hæc fieri?

10 Respondit Jesus, et dixit ei: Tu es magister in Israel, et hæc ignoras?

11 Amen, amen dico tibi, quia quod scimus loquimur, et quod vidimus testamur, et testimonium nostrum non accipitis.

D

12 *Si terrena dixi vobis, et non creditis : quomodo, si dixero vobis cælestia, credetis ?*

13 *Et nemo ascendit in cælum, nisi qui descendit de cælo, Filius hominis, qui est in cælo.*

14 *Et sicut Moyses exaltavit serpentem in deserto : ita exaltari oportet Filium hominis :*

15 *Ut omnis, qui credit in ipsum, non pereat, sed habeat vitam æternam.*

16 *Sic enim Deus dilexit mundum, ut Filium suum unigenitum daret : ut omnis, qui credit in eum, non pereat, sed habeat vitam æternam.*

17 *Non enim misit Deus filium suum in mundum, ut judicet mundum, sed ut salvetur mundus per ipsum.*

18 *Qui credit in eum, non judicatur : qui autem non credit, jam judicatus est : quia non credit in nomine unigeniti Filii Dei.*

19 *Hoc est autem judicium : quia lux venit in mundum, et dilexerunt homines magis tenebras, quam lucem : erant enim eorum mala opera.*

20 *Omnis enim, qui male agit, odit lucem, et non venit ad lucem, ut non arguantur opera ejus :*

21 *Qui autem facit veritatem, venit ad lucem, ut manifestentur opera ejus, quia in Deo sunt facta.*

22 *Post hæc venit Jesus, et discipuli ejus in terram Judæam : et illic demorabatur cum eis, et baptizabat.*

23 *Erat autem et Joannes baptizans in Ænnon, juxta Salim : quia aquæ multæ erant illic, et veniebant, et baptizabantur.*

24 *Nondum enim missus fuerat Joannes in carcerem.*

25 *Facta est autem quæstio ex discipulis Joannis cum Judæis de Purificatione.*

26 *Et venerunt ad Joannem, et dixerunt ei : Rabbi, qui erat tecum trans Jordanem : cui tu testimonium perhibuisti, ecce hic baptizat, et omnes veniunt ad eum.*

27 *Respondit Joannes, et dixit : Non potest homo accipere quidquam, nisi fuerit ei datum de cælo.*

28 *Ipsi vos mihi testimonium perhibetis, quod dixerim : Non sum ego Christus : sed quia missus sum ante illum.*

29 *Qui habet sponsam, sponsus est : amicus autem sponsi, qui stat, et audit eum, gaudio gaudet propter vocem sponsi. Hoc ergo gaudium meum impletum est.*

30 *Illum oportet crescere, me autem minui.*

31 *Qui desursum venit, super omnes est. Qui est de terra, de terra est, et de terra loquitur. Qui de cælo venit, super omnes est.*

32 *Et quod vidit, et audivit, hoc testatur : et testimonium ejus nemo accipit.*

33 *Qui accepit ejus testimonium, signavit quia Deus verax est.*

34 *Quem enim misit Deus, verba Dei loquitur : non enim ad mensuram dat Deus spiritum.*

35 *Pater diligit Filium : et omnia dedit in manu ejus.*

36 *Qui credit in Filium, habet vitam æternam : qui autem incredulus est Filio, non videbit vitam, sed ira Dei manet super eum.*

ANALYSIS.

In this chapter, the Evangelist records our Lord's discourse with Nicodemus, in which he instructs him in the doctrine of spiritual regeneration—the absolute necessity, by the decree of God, to be born again spiritually, in order to enter the Kingdom of Heaven. He replies to Nicodemus's doubts by adducing several illustrations (1–13).

He next records our Lord's teaching on the subject of faith, its necessity, and the heavy judgment in store for such as wilfully closing their eyes against Divine truth, refuse to believe (14–21).

He next records our Lord's ministry of baptizing simultaneously with John (22–24).

We have next an account of the jealousy which the disciples of John entertained in regard to our Lord. John's mild reproof, and his humble testimony in favour of our Lord's Divinity, whom he proclaimed, as infinitely exalted above himself (25–36).

Commentary.

1. "*And there was,*" etc. Among those who believed in our Lord, on seeing the miracles He performed at the Paschal Festival (c. ii. 23), was a certain man named Nicodemus, of whom the Evangelist makes special mention, both on account of his religious profession—he belonged to the sect of the "*Pharisees*"—as well as his high repute among the Jews, and his elevated rank. He was "*a ruler of the Jews.*" He was a member of the Sanhedrim, or Supreme Council (c. vii. 45–50).

2. "*This man came to Jesus by night.*" Some say he came by night, because, our Lord, owing to His labours by day, was accessible only by night for private instruction. The more probable opinion, however, is that he did so from shame. He felt ashamed, that one so exalted in rank and distinguished for learning, should publicly place himself at the feet of the humble Jesus, to receive instruction; and also, like many of the Rulers, who would not publicly confess Him from fear of the Jews (John xii. 19–39), from a fear of incurring the displeasure and anger of his own sect, whom he knew to be the deadly enemies of our Lord. His faith in our Lord and his love were, evidently, very imperfect. He believed Him to be "*a teacher come from God,*" or possibly, the Messiah. But, it is clear he did not believe Him to be the Son of God. The slave of human respect with his love of our Lord, he wished to unite the love of the world: and achieve what was impossible, viz., the serving of two masters, God and the world. He, then, came by night, from human respect and fear of his colleagues.

"*Rabbi*"—*my master.* A title of honour and eminence among the Jews.

"*We know,*" both myself and several others, that Thou art sent by God, as a teacher, to instruct men in the true principles of religion. In proof of this, thou dost exhibit God's own credentials.

"*For no man can do these things,*" etc. While Nicodemus does

Text.

1. *And there was a man of the Pharisees, named Nicodemus, a ruler of the Jews.*

1. *Erat autem homo ex Pharisæis, Nicodemus nomine, princeps Judæorum.*

2. *This man came to Jesus by night, and said to him: Rabbi, we know that thou art come a teacher from God: for no man can do these signs which thou dost, unless God be with him.*

2. *Hic venit ad Jesum nocte, et dixit ei: Rabbi, scimus quia a Deo venisti magister, nemo enim potest hæc signa facere, quæ tu facis, nisi fuerit Deus cum eo.*

Text.

3. *Jesus answered and said to him: Amen, amen I say to thee, unless a man be born again, he cannot see the kingdom of God.*

3. *Respondit Jesus, et dixit ei: Amen, amen dico tibi, nisi quis renatus fuerit denuo, non potest videre regnum Dei.*

Commentary.

not seem to have believed in our Lord, as the Son of God—had he believed it, he would have said so—he believes Him, however, to be a true teacher. He regards the works performed by Him, as true miracles, beyond the power of natural or diabolical agency, both from their number, variety, and mode of operation. He may have regarded Him as the Messiah also.

"*Unless God be with Him,*" unless he be aided by Divine power. Our Redeemer's miracles, such as raising the dead, giving instantaneous sight to the blind, hearing to the deaf, etc., were of such a nature, as to be the result of the Divine Power only. Their avowed *end* and object was, to prove Jesus to be the Son of God; and as God could not, consistently with His own veracity, set the seal of miracles on what was false; hence, they proved Our Lord's Divinity. Moreover, these miracles were predicted, as special marks of the Messiah (Isaias xxxv. 2–6). None among the Prophets performed miracles like those of our Divine Redeemer. Nicodemus, as Doctor of the Jews, could easily have known, that these were predicted of the Messiah (Isaias xxxv. 2–6), and that the Messiah was God and Son of God. (Isaias ix. 6, etc.) Hence, Nicodemus's faith and love, though laudable, were still imperfect.

3. "*Jesus answered him,*" etc. It may be, that the words of our Lord here, are but an answer to some question put by Nicodemus, as to what was necessary for entering the Kingdom of God; or, our Lord seeing what was in his mind, may have answered him, by anticipation. Far from reproaching him for his weakness and timidity in coming at night, our Lord mercifully pities his weakness.

"*Unless a man,*" no matter what his rank, learning, age, country or respectability—no exception made in the Divine decree regarding the mode of entering God's Kingdom. Neither Nicodemus nor anyone else could claim exemption.

"*Be born again.*" The Greek word, ανωθεν, could be also rendered, *from above*. But, "*again,*" is the more probable rendering, and in this sense, it was understood by Nicodemus. This spiritual regeneration, afterwards explained by our Lord, was the indispensable means decreed by God, for every child born of Adam and sinning in him, to enter the Kingdom of Heaven, viz., God's Church here and His eternal Kingdom of Glory hereafter. Whoever was born of Adam, should be re-born or spiritually *regenerated*, in order to be cleaned from the stain of original sin.

"*Cannot see,*" that is, cannot enter into "*the Kingdom of God,*" as above explained. Nicodemus's object being, to know how he was to obtain the Kingdom of God; hence, our Lord opens His instructions with this point.

Commentary.

4. Nicodemus, whose ideas on spiritual things were imperfect, like the sensual man who "*cannot perceive the things of the Spirit of God,*" understands our Lord's words literally, of carnal regeneration; and asks, how can it be possible for one grown old like himself and sincerely anxious for his salvation, to be born again of a mother now possibly resting in her grave? Our Lord spoke obscurely, in order to humble the pride of the Pharisee, by showing him his ignorance, and wishes to raise his mind thus humbled, from carnal to spiritual conceptions.

5. Our Lord seeing that Nicodemus came to Him with good dispositions, and a sincere desire of learning what was necessary for salvation, far from being offended at the question rather bluntly put, mercifully condescends to enlighten him, by explaining in clear terms, that He spoke, not of *carnal* generation, as Nicodemus fancied; but, of *spiritual* regeneration through "*water and the Holy Ghost,*" repeating the same truth in clearer terms.

"*Holy Ghost.*" In the Greek "*Holy*" is omitted. It is, however, read by some ancient Fathers, Cyril, Chrysostom, etc. It is admitted on all hands to mean, the "*Holy Spirit.*"

This is certain from the words of the Baptist (Matthew iii. 11), and the form of Baptism given by our Lord Himself—"*Unless a man be born again of water*"—the *instrumental* cause, the matter employed in this process of spiritual regeneration, signifying the spiritual cleansing of the soul by sanctifying grace, which it at the same time produces.

"*And the Holy Ghost*"—the *efficient* cause, which imparts this spiritual efficacy to the rite through water, of cleansing and purifying the soul.

"*He cannot enter,*" etc. The word "*enter*" clearly conveys the same idea as "*see*" in preceding verse.

Almost all the Catholic Commentators agree in interpreting this verse of the Sacrament of Baptism. The Council of Trent SS. vii. c. 2, *de Baptismo*, defines it, as *de fide*, that true and natural water is necessary for baptism, and condemns such as would distort the words of this verse, "*unless a man be born again,*" etc., to any methaphorical meaning.

The word, "*born again,*" or *regenerated*, signifies a new existence, in which we are fit to become Sons of God, by a twofold process or effect. 1st, by the remission of our sins, through the instrumentality of *water* after due penance (Acts ii. 28), when the old man of sin for ever destroyed, is buried in the waters of baptism (Rom. vi. 4–6). 2ndly, by the infusion of sanctifying grace, which is effected by one and the same process, "*et accipietis donum Spiritus Sancti,*" of which our Lord's Resurrection was a type. This is effected by "*the Holy Ghost.*" The rite or sacrament instituted by our Lord was proclaimed as essential for

Text.

4. *Nicodemus saith to him: How can a man be born when he is old? can he enter a second time into his mother's womb, and be born again?*

4. *Dicit ad eum Nicodemus: Quomodo potest homo nasci, cum sit senex? numquid potest in ventrem matris suæ iterato introire, et renasci?*

5. *Jesus answered: Amen, amen I say to thee, unless a man be born again of water and the Holy Ghost, he cannot enter into the kingdom of God.*

5. *Respondit Jesus: Amen, amen dico tibi, nisi quis renatus fuerit ex aqua, et Spiritu sancto non potest introire in regnum Dei.*

Text.

6. *That which is born of the flesh, is flesh: and that which is born of the Spirit, is spirit.*

6. *Quod natum est ex carne, caro est: et quod natum est ex spiritu, spiritus est.*

7. *Wonder not, that I said to thee, you must be born again.*

7. *Non mireris quia dixi tibi: oportet vos nasci denuo.*

8. *The Spirit breatheth where he will; and thou hearest his voice, but thou knowest not whence he cometh and whither he goeth: so is every one that is born of the Spirit.*

Commentary.

salvation (Mark xvi. 16); here, too, it is said, no one without it, can enter the Kingdom of God. This Baptism was to be in water. (See Acts viii. 36; also the words of the Eunuch to Philip), and of St. Peter to the family of Cornelius (Acts x. 47). It is clear from the complaints of the disciples of John, that our Lord Himself baptized in water (John iii. 22–26).

Our Lord's Baptism was in the Holy Ghost. For (Acts ii. 38), the receiving of the Holy Ghost is attributed to Baptism. Hence, called the "*laver of regeneration and renovation of the Holy Ghost*" (Titus iii. 5).

Commentators remark, that, as in *carnal generation*, a twofold principle is necessary; so, is it also in spiritual regeneration. Water and the Holy Ghost, both are needed. As in our Lord's own Incarnation, the Holy Ghost was the principal agent; so also does it happen in the spiritual regeneration of all the Sons of God, in the Sacrament of Baptism.

Whether Baptism was instituted here, to be of obligation only after the promulgation of the New Law at Pentecost, or whether it was only promised here and afterwards instituted, as in the case of the Holy Eucharist, is disputed.

6. "*That which is born of the flesh,*" etc. This second birth will not necessitate, what is impossible, as you suppose. It shall be a *spiritual* birth, whereby man will receive a new spiritual existence, superadded to his natural, human existence. In this new birth, he will not be born of man. For, so, he would receive a new human natural existence, because, the new being will be assimilated to the principle of generation. Hence, what is born of man, by natural human process of generation, is man. But what is "*born of the Spirit is spirit,*" or receives not a new natural, but a new spiritual existence.

7. Possibly, our Lord saw, either as searcher of hearts, or from Nicodemus's manner, that from a feeling of incredulity, he was astonished at what he heard. Hence, He tells him not to be surprised, that in order to enter the Kingdom of Heaven, which flesh and blood can never possess, a man must receive a new spiritual existence, superadded to his natural being—a thing quite possible, not requiring a second human birth.

8. The leading interpretations of the verse are reduced to two, founded chiefly on the meaning attached to the word "*spirit.*" Some understand it to mean "*the wind,*" as if our Lord meant to illustrate His teachings by a sensible matter, the operations and effects of the *wind*, which blows as "*it wills,*" according to its natural tendency; and one knows not whence it comes or where it spends itself. But, its voice or sound is heard, either in the

Commentary.

hurricane or the gentle breeze rustling through the trees; and then, applying the comparison, our Lord adds: "*so is every one that is born of the Spirit*," as if to say, the operation of the Divine Spirit, in the work of spiritual regeneration is invisible and imperceptible by the senses. You cannot know how it commences or how it terminates. But you only hear it in its effects, in its external operations. No wonder, then, if you cannot understand it. This is the interpretation of SS. Cyril, Chrysostom, etc. The comparison instituted by our Lord between the operations of this power denoted by "*spirit*," whatever it means, and the Holy Ghost favors this interpretation, "*sic est omnis qui natus est de spiritu.*" The words of our Lord in v. 12, are in favor of it, "*If I have spoken to you earthly things,*" etc. The allusion to the wind here would be the only *earthly thing* referred to by our Lord in His conversation with Nicodemus. All the other illustrations are of a purely spiritual and heavenly character. Against it, the chief difficulties are, that it can hardly be said we know not, whence the *wind* goes or whither it cometh. Again, it is hard to attribute personal operations to it, "*as it wills,*" not to speak of the confusion, the use of the same word "*spirit*", (το πνευμα) in different meanings, in the same sentence, would be apt to engender in the mind of Nicodemus, to whom our Lord was explaining the process and effects of spiritual regeneration.

Others—SS. Augustine, Ambrose, Gregory, etc., understand the words, "*the spirit breathes,*" etc., of the Holy Ghost, who breathes and infuses the impulses of faith, penance and grace just as He pleases, "*singulis dividens, prout vult*" (1 Cor. xii. 4-11). The voice of this Holy Spirit is heard in the wonderful effects and conversions brought about by His invisible grace and secret inspirations, in the preaching of His ministers, in the utterances of the Prophets, in the total change effected in the heroes of the Old and New Testaments, Samson, Gideon, Paul, etc., who were transformed into new men, through the operations and impulses of the Holy Ghost, of which Nicodemus, so learned, could not be ignorant.

These Expositors say, that, in the words, "*so is every one that is born of the Spirit,*" there is no application of a comparison; that the words are merely illustrative of the preceding operations of the Holy Ghost in general, as if He said: such, too, is His action or operation, in the case of every one spiritually born of Him in Baptism.

Maldonatus holds a peculiar view of his own, not shared in by any other Commentator of note. He understands "*spirit*" of the human soul, whose entrance into the body or existence in it, or exit from same, no one can understand, although its power is proved from external operations and effects; and, then, the con-

Text.

8. *Spiritus ubi vult spirat: et vocem ejus audis, sed nescis unde veniat, aut quo vadat: sic est omnis, qui natus est ex spiritu.*

Text.	Commentary.
	nexion would be: as you cannot understand, or account for, the operations and effects of corporal existence; so, it is not a matter of surprise, if you cannot understand what relates to the spiritual nativity in the Holy Ghost.
9. *Nicodemus answered, and said to him: How can these things be done?* 9. *Respondit Nicodemus, et dixit ei: Quomodo possunt hæc fieri?*	9. Nicodemus, after being instructed by our Lord, no longer thinks of carnal regeneration; still, not clearly perceiving the meaning of our Redeemer's words relative to spiritual regeneration, unable to understand how a man can become a spirit or spiritual being, asks for further information. "*How?*" a favourite exclamation with infidels and unbelievers in all ages, though, indeed, hardly applicable to Nicodemus here, in its full perverse sense.
10. *Jesus answered, and said to him: Art thou a master in Israel, and knowest not these things?* 10. *Respondit Jesus, et dixit ei: Tu es magister in Israel, et hæc ignoras?*	10. Our Lord reproaches him for his ignorance, on a subject in which he ought to be well versed, considering his position and repute for learning. "*A master in Israel.*" The Greek article prefixed (ὁ διδασκαλος), shows, that the word denotes a distinguished doctor among the the Jews. "*And knowest not these things?*" ignorant of what one learned in the Law ought to know, and able to comprehend when explained. For, the Prophets, with whom He was, or should be, conversant, had predicted spiritual regeneration through water (Ezechiel xxxvi. 24; Zacharias xiii. 1). Hence, while perplexed regarding the mystery or mode of operation, he should unhesitatingly believe it, as regards the *fact*.
11. *Amen, amen I say to thee, that we speak what we know, and we testify what we have seen, and you receive not our testimony.* 11. *Amen, amen dico tibi, quia quod scimus loquimur, et quod vidimus testamur, et testimonium nostrum non accipitis.*	11. Our Lord had, in the preceding, gently alluded to Nicodemus's ignorance without any asperity, however, on account of his good dispositions. In the same spirit of gentleness, He now points to his incredulity. Nicodemus himself had borne testimony to our Lord's veracity and Divine mission. Our Lord, now, in order to attach greater weight to His statements, declares in the most solemn way, as the words, "*Amen, amen,*" indicate, that He only stated, what was most certain and most true, as He stated only what He "*had seen.*" He thus conveys to Nicodemus, that He ought to believe firmly on His testimony, what was stated without further reasoning or questioning, although the *mode* of its existence might be incomprehensible. He uses the plural, "*we know,*" etc., either for greater solemnity sake; or, because the Father and the Holy Ghost testified along with Him; so that the legal number of witnesses were forthcoming. As *God*, our Lord had the knowledge of all things, of Himself, and by His Divine Omniscience. As *man*, through the Beatific Vision and infused science. "*And you*"—referring to Nicodemus and the bulk of the incredulous Jews—"*receive not our testimony.*"

Commentary.

12. "*Earthly things*," are understood by some of the comparison regarding the *wind*, to which the word, "*spirit*," according to them, refers; "*and heavenly things*," of the spiritual regeneration through water.

Others, by "*earthly things*," understand the spiritual regeneration of man termed, *earthly*; because, it regards an earthly being, man; and by "*heavenly things*," the more sublime mysteries relating to the eternal generation of the Son of God—a *heavenly* and Divine Person—to the Trinity, God's attributes, etc. Our Lord here reproaches Nicodemus and the unbelieving Jews, who heard His discourses, with their slowness of belief; and He insinuates, that they should believe what He proposed, without further questioning, if they meant to deserve the communication of more exalted truths of faith, and not to be deprived of the precious gift of faith altogether.

13. "*And no man hath ascended into heaven*," etc. "*And*," meaning, *and yet*, as if to say, you are slow in believing Me, *and yet*, you can learn these abstruse heavenly truths from no one else. For, no one else ever "*ascended into heaven*," not even the Prophets, in whom you believe, which is the same as, *ever was in heaven*, to learn and contemplate and fully comprehend these things, but Myself, who am always there, the only-begotten Son, "*who is in the bosom of the Father*" (1-18), who came down from heaven to assume human nature and appear visibly in human flesh. Our Lord here very significantly conveys to Nicodemus, that He was God, being always in heaven, "*who is in heaven*," and man at the same time, by *descending* from heaven; thus becoming "*the Son of man*," in virtue of human nature assumed by Him on earth, still retaining the nature and Personality of the Divine Word. "*He descended from heaven*" without leaving it; since in His Divine nature he fills heaven and earth, nay, all space, by His glorious, Divine Immensity.

The words, then, mean, that our Lord alone could fully enlighten Nicodemus, on heavenly subjects. For, no one could securely do so, except one who mounted up to heaven and was in heaven, and no one else was in heaven, so as fully to become acquainted with heavenly things and come down to earth to teach mankind these heavenly mysteries, save "*the Son of man*," our Lord Himself, who is always in heaven, in virtue of His Divinity, and never leaving it, came down by assuming nature, to teach mankind.

Our Lord is said to be "*in heaven*" as "*Son of man*," by, what is theologically termed, *the communication of Idioms*, which means; that, as our Lord had two natures and one Person, to which Person the actions of both natures are attributed (*actiones sunt suppositorum*), we can predicate of one nature of Christ what peculiarly belongs to the other, on account of His unity of Person.

Text.

12. *If I have spoken to you earthly things, and you believe not; how will you believe if I shall speak to you heavenly things?*

12. *Si terrena dixi vobis, et non creditis? quomodo, si dixero vobis cælestia, credetis:*

13. *And no man hath ascended into heaven, but he that descended from heaven, the son of man who is in heaven.*

13. *Et nemo ascendit in cælum, nisi qui descendit de cælo, Filius hominis, qui est in cælo.*

Text.	Commentary.
	The words, "*ascending*" and "*descending*," in reference to our Lord, are used by way of accommodation; and, strictly speaking, do not apply to Him at all; but are used in reference to all other men. "*Descended*," and "*is in heaven*," express our Lord's twofold nature and unity of Person.
14. *And as Moses lifted up the serpent in the desert, so must the son of man be lifted up.*	14. "*And as Moses lifted up the serpent in the desert.*" The desert refers to the desolate district south of Mount Horeb, near Edom. In the preceding verse, our Lord instructs Nicodemus regarding *His Divinity*. Here, He speaks of His *humanity*.
14. *Et sicut Moyses exaltavit serpentem in deserto: ita exaltari oportet Filium hominis:*	Allusion is made to Numbers (xxi. 9, etc.), where it is recorded that Moses, by the command of God, raised up, on an elevated pole, to be visible to all, a brazen serpent, so that such as would look upon it, would be cured of the effects of the bite of the poisonous serpent; and such as would refuse doing so, would be left to perish.
	"*So the Son of man must be lifted up.*" By the Divine decree, our Lord must be raised aloft on the cross and put to death. This is the meaning of the words, "*lifted up*," in several passages of this Gospel (viii. 28; xii. 32–34). Those who will look upon Him by faith, will be saved from the effects of the bite of the infernal serpent, from sin and its consequences, temporal and everlasting. But, as in the case of those bitten by the fiery serpent, such as either refused or neglected looking on the brazen serpent were sure to die of the effects of this bite; so, those who refuse or neglect to look up to our Lord hanging on the cross, and believe in Him, will, surely, be lost for ever.
15. *That whosoever believeth in him, may not perish, but may have life everlasting.*	15. "*That whosoever believeth in Him,*" etc., looks up to Him suspended on the cross, by faith in His Divinity and humanity "*may not perish,*" etc. This faith, in order to secure, "*life everlasting,*" must be animated by charity and good works; since, our Lord declares elsewhere, that, in order to gain eternal life, we must keep the Commandments. The proposition, "faith saves us," like every other affirmative proposition, has its attribute taken, as logicians term it, *particularly*, implying, that other essential conditions are present or attended to.
15. *Ut omnis, qui credit in ipsum, non pereat, sed habeat vitam æternam.*	
15. *For God so loved the world, as to give his only begotten Son; that whosoever believeth in him, may not perish, but may have life everlasting.*	16. In this verse our Lord, as if answering an objection which might present itself to Nicodemus, viz., why should the Son of God be suspended on an ignominious gibbet, assigns the true, efficient cause, viz., the boundless love of God for man. Every word is expressive and suggestive. "*So,*" to such a boundless extent, with such mighty effort and vehemence, "*did God,*" not a king or emperor, but, *God*, this Infinite Being—Infinite in all perfections—"*love*" freely and gratuitously, without any claim on Him, "*the world*," all mankind, His enemy by sin (Rom. v. 6–9),
16. *Sic enim Deus dilexit mundum, ut Filium suum unigenitum daret: ut omnis, qui credit in*	

Commentary.

"*as to give,*" deliver over to torture and punishment, not for His own, but for their outrages and sins, "*His only begotten* (His natural) Son." What a mystery of godliness. *God* becoming *man*. The *Highest* and the *lowest* united. The Great Creator showing His love for a wretched, sinful worm of the earth, by submitting to excruciating, ignominious tortures. "*Laudetur in eternum Summa Dei Majestas. Venite, adoremus et procidamus ante Deum.*"

The *cause* of the Incarnation and death of the Son of God was the boundless and incomprehensible love of God for the world.

The *end* was, not to exercise justice in condemning, but mercy in saving.

The *fruit*, was the saving of man from perishing eternally, and bestowing on him life eternal through faith, accompanied by the observance of God's commandments.

17. This is explanatory of the last verse in regard to God's object in sending His Son, which was to bestow on them "*everlasting life.*" For, although looking to God's justice, the world would deserve condemnation for its sins; still, it was not to display His justice, in judging and condemning the world that God sent His Son in the first instance, but to exercise His mercy, which is over all His works, "*that the world may be saved by Him,*" by rescuing them from everlasting death, and bestowing on them, everlasting life. Hence, God wills, by a sincere antecedent will, the salvation of all mankind. Such of them as are lost, are lost through their own fault. No doubt, at His second coming on the day of judgment, the Son of God will display His justice, rewarding and punishing men, according to their deserts, judging every man, according to his works.

18. In this verse is proved by a kind of implied dilemma, that God did not send His Son "*to judge the world.*" For, either a man believes in Him, or refuses to do so. If he believes; then, he is not judged; but is rescued and saved by the mercy of God and the superabundant merits of our Saviour, from the general condemnation, in which all men would be involved, and receives abundance of grace.

If he believes not; then, no further sentence is needed. He remains in the state of damnation, in which all men are involved, as "*children of wrath.*" He is condemned by the original decree of God and his own determined obstinacy of will to persevere in his unbelief, "*because he believeth not in the name of the only begotten Son of God,*" thus rejecting the only means instituted by God, to save and rescue him from damnation.

St. Augustine (Tract 12), illustrates this by the example of a physician who comes to cure all the infirm. Such as refuse his ministrations, die; not on account of the physician, as if he came

Text.

cum, non pereat, sed habeat vitam æternam.

17. *For God sent not his Son into the world, to judge the world, but that the world may be saved by him.*

17. *Non enim misit Deus Filium suum in mundum, ut judicet mundum, sed ut salvetur mundus per ipsum.*

18. *He that believeth in him, is not judged. But he that doth not believe, is already judged: because he believeth not in the name of the only begotten Son of God.*

18. *Qui credit in eum, non judicatur: qui autem non credit, jam judicatus est: quia non credit in nomine unigeniti Filii Dei.*

Text.	Commentary.
	to cause their death; but, on account of the infirmities already contracted by them, which they refuse to have cured by the physician.
19. And this is the judgment: because the light is come into the world, and men loved darkness rather than the light: for their works were evil. 19. *Hoc est autem judicium: quia lux venit in mundum, et dilexerunt homines magis tenebras, quam lucem: erant enim eorum mala opera.*	19. "*This is the judgment.*" The *cause* of judgment or condemnation, "*because the light*," which is our Lord Himself, who enlightens every man, whether naturally or supernaturally, "*is come into the world*" to dissipate, by the diffusion of true doctrine, the darkness of infidelity and sin. "*He was the light of the world*" (viii. 12), "*and men*," wallowing in the mire of corruption, culpably, "*loved the darkness*" of infidelity, in which they were enveloped, "*rather than the light*," which, by a little inquiry, they might easily ascertain to be the true light. They then acted perversely. For, had they embraced the light and true teaching of Christ, they would be compelled to abandon their present evil courses, which they were determined on pursuing. "*Their works are evil.*" They shun the light, lest they should be convicted by the light, which the teaching of Christ would shed upon them. Moral perversity is, ordinarily, the cause, why men persevere in rejecting the teachings of truth. The words of the verse may also mean: the judgment of condemnation which they pass on themselves consists in this; that, having a full opportunity of walking in the light, performing the works of light, they prefer remaining in darkness, "*for, their deeds,*" in which they glory and mean to persevere, "*are evil.*"
20. For every one that doth evil hateth the light, and cometh not to the light, that his works may not be reproved. 20. *Omnis enim, qui male agit, odit lucem, et non venit ad lucem, ut non arguantur opera ejus:*	20. "*For every one that doth evil,*" and perversely means to persevere in its commission, "*hateth the light, and cometh not,*" etc., because the effect of the light would be, to expose his wicked works, which he would fain conceal. They would show him to be deserving of reprehension, "*that his works be not reproved,*" not to speak of their generating remorse of conscience (Eph. v. 11–13).
21. But he that doth truth, cometh to the light, that his works may be made manifest, because they are done in God. 21. *Qui autem facit veritatem, venit ad lucem, ut manifestentur opera ejus, quia in Deo sunt facta.*	21. "*Doth truth.*" There is question of practical truth, of actions or works done in accordance with the law of rectitude and justice—"*doth,*" sincerely intends and purposes to do good works, to do what is right and true. Such a man, unlike him who means to persevere in his perversity, far from flying and shunning the light, "*cometh to the light, that his works may be made manifest,*" that his *future works,* which he means to perform in the new course of life which the light will point out to him, may "*be done in God,*" done in accordance with the will and commands of God. The words may also have reference to his *past* works, done in grace, before embracing the light of faith. Pagans may do good works, aided by grace, before embracing the faith. The proposition, "*Faith is the first grace,*" was condemned by Pius VI.

Commentary.

in the Bull, AUCTOREM FIDEI, as put forward in the Schismatical Council of Pistoia, under its Bishop, Scipio Ricci.

22. "*Came into the land of Judea.*" The Evangelist records this circumstance, as an introduction to the following incident relative to the jealousy of John's disciples and the testimony borne to our Lord by John.

23. "*Near Salem,*" to distinguish it from another Ennon, near Damascus (Ezechiel xlvii. 17). Likely, John selected this place preferably to Bethania, or Bethabara, where our Lord baptized, in order to traverse the entire country, baptizing and preaching, and thus be enabled to witness to our Lord, through every part of the country. Some infer from this, that *immersion* was the form of Baptism employed by John. But this does not clearly follow, as John would select a place well supplied with water to accommodate the multitudes flocking to his Baptism, in whatever form administered.

24. From reading the other Evangelists, one would be apt to suppose (Matthew iv. 12, etc.) that John was cast into prison immediately after baptizing our Lord. Hence, the Evangelist here states that our Lord had entered on His ministry soon before John's imprisonment; that some interval occurred, during which the Baptist continued to baptize and bear testimony to our Lord. St. John alone, of the four Evangelists, records what our Lord did after His Baptism, and before the Baptist was cast into prison.

25. "*And there arose a question,*" etc. The Greek for, "*and*," is (ουν), *therefore,* as if he meant to say, that from the circumstance of our Lord and John baptizing at the same time, there arose, in consequence, a discussion, to which the simultaneous administration of both Baptisms gave rise between "*some of John's disciples,*" and some "*Jews,*" who, without being numbered among our Lord's disciples and constant followers, probably came to His Baptism in preference to John's. It may refer to certain leading men among the Jews, members of the Sanhedrim. "*Concerning purification,*" or the relative merits and excellence of the Baptism of John and the Baptism of our Lord, which has the effect of purifying and cleansing the body as well as the soul; hence, termed "*purification.*" The complaint made, out of jealousy and envy, by John's disciples, as in next verse, favours this interpretation. In many Greek MSS. the reading for "*Jews*" is, a *certain Jew,* who, no doubt, belonged to the class already referred to.

Text.

22. *After these things Jesus and his disciples came into the land of Judea; and there he abode with them, and baptized.*

22. *Post hæc venit Jesus, et discipuli ejus in terram Judæam: et illic demorabatur cum eis, et baptizabat.*

23. *And John also was baptizing in Ennon near Salim; because there was much water there, and they came, and were baptized.*

23. *Erat autem et Joannes baptizans in Ænnon, juxta Salim: quia aquæ multæ erant illic, et veniebant, et baptizabantur.*

24. *For John was not yet cast into prison.*

24. *Nondum enim missus fuerat Joannes in carcerem.*

25. *And there arose a question between some of John's disciples and the Jews concerning purification:*

25. *Facta est autem quæstio ex discipulis Joannis cum Judæis de Purificatione.*

Text.

26. *And they came to John, and said to him: Rabbi, he that was with thee beyond the Jordan, to whom thou gavest testimony, behold he baptizeth, and all men came to him.*

26. *Et venerunt ad Joannem, et dixerunt ei: Rabbi, qui erat tecum trans Jordanem: cui tu testimonium perhibuisti, ecce hic baptizat, et omnes veniunt ad eum.*

27. *John answered, and said: A man cannot receive any thing, unless it be given him from heaven.*

27. *Respondit Joannes, et dixit: Non potest homo accipere quidquam, nisi fuerit ei datum de cælo.*

28. *You yourselves do bear me witness, that I said, I am not Christ; but that I am sent before him.*

28. *Ipsi vos mihi testimonium perhibetis, quod dixerim: Non sum ego Christus: sed quia missus sum ante illum.*

Commentary.

26. "*And they*"—the disciples of John probably worsted in the discussion—"*came to John,*" out of feelings of envy—a state of mental infirmity to which the saints of old were not wholly strangers—(see history of Joseph's brethren, Genesis xxxvii., etc.), and also from a feeling of undue jealousy for the honour and celebrity of their master, relate the affair to John, in the hope, that he might suggest new grounds for a successful discussion, and possibly, retract the exalted testimony he gave of Jesus, whom they regarded not as the Messiah, but as the rival of their master. "*And said to him: Rabbi, He that was with thee beyond the Jordan.*" They would not mention any particular good quality or epithet applied to Him—"*Lamb of God,*" etc.—"*and to whom thou gavest testimony,*" for which He should manifest due feelings of gratitude, as it exalted Him so much in public estimation. Far from that, He seeks to lower you, by Himself assuming your office of baptizing, thus attracting vast multitudes, whom He withdraws from thee and attracts to His own Baptism. This causes you to be deserted. "*And all men come to Him,*" that is, great numbers. For many still had recourse to the Baptism of John. He should, therefore, be restrained.

27. Far from encouraging, the Baptist vigorously represses their feelings of jealousy, saying that neither he nor any other man should claim any prerogatives or dignity or elevated position, save in as far as it was granted him by God; and, therefore, he should not contend with Him whom God had sent as His Eternal Son, whose precursor and minister only he was.

Others, with St. Chrysostom, explain the words thus: If Christ claims pre-eminence and superiority, and attracts, as is meet, all men to Him, He is only carrying out the will of Heaven, and displaying the gifts and powers bestowed on Him by Heaven. He should not, therefore, be impeded or obstructed. The former interpretation, which understands it of the Baptist himself, is more in accordance with the following verse.

28. Out of their own mouth, he convicts them. I call yourselves to witness, that on a former occasion, I declared I was not the Christ.

This "*was not given me from Heaven*" (*v.* 27). "*But that I am sent before him,*" as His minister and precursor, to prepare His ways. Why should I now contradict my former truthful testimony, and exceeding the measures given me from Heaven, claim to be what I am not? Why should you tempt me to contend with Him for superiority or equality, who is infinitely my superior? Before whom, my Creator and my God, I, a mere creature, the work of His hands, should humble myself to the very dust; to whom, therefore, you and I should transfer all our homage and services.

Commentary.

29. By a familiar illustration, the Baptist conveys to them, that far from being chagrined at seeing all men come to Him (Christ) he is rather rejoiced at it, just as the friend of the bridegroom, the bridesman, who is in attendance at the nuptials, is delighted at seeing all the honours transferred to the party to be principally honoured, viz., the bridegroom; is rejoiced at hearing his voice, his conversation with the spouse and the language of affection interchanged between them, without himself aspiring to any share in the affection bestowed. The application of the example, though not given, is, however, quite obvious. Our Lord is the *bridegroom*; the Church or assembly of the Faithful, the *bride*; John, the bridesman or *friend* of our Lord, standing humbly to attend; as His friend, rejoices on hearing His voice on occasion of His Baptism, and when in prison hearing of His miracles and preaching, he sent his disciples to witness His miracles in order that they would become His followers. Hence, far from feeling jealous, he was rejoiced, while acting a subordinate part, as His precursor appointed to prepare His ways, at seeing the people in crowds attach themselves to Him.

"*This my joy, therefore, is fulfilled,*" filled up and perfected, on seeing the end and object of my baptizing and preaching fully realized, when He is now acknowledged and followed by the people. John calls himself as our Lord's *friend*, as he really was; the term "*friend*," being better suited to the occasion. For, the comparison was one of joy; and John, as our Lord's *friend*, would rejoice, with peculiar great joy, on hearing Him converse with the *bride*, His Church and His people.

30. By the decree of God's Providence in regard to our Lord and the Baptist, our Lord "*must increase,*" not in Himself, not in merit or virtue; but, in the estimation of the people, by the external manifestation of His power, "*and I must decrease,*" in public estimation. I must pass out of public observation and give up the exercise of my ministry, its end being now accomplished in the public manifestation and reception of Christ. He is the SUN; I, the *morning star*, to announce His near rising. The more He mounts in His course through the heavens, the more must my feeble light be dimmed. I was regarded as the Messiah. He, as a Prophet. He must now be regarded as the true Messiah, the Eternal Son of God, as He really is. I, as His servant and precursor.

31. "*He that cometh from above,*" from the bosom of the Eternal Father, having a Divine origin, as the only begotten Son of God, "*is above all.*" Therefore, above me, above all angels and men. Hence, it is fit He should increase, and be devoutly reverenced and received by all.

Text.

29. *He that hath the bride is the bridegroom: but the friend of the bridegroom who standeth and heareth him, rejoiceth with joy because of the bridegroom's voice. This my joy therefore is fulfilled.*

29. *Qui habet sponsam, sponsus est: amicus autem sponsi, qui stat, et audit eum, gaudio gaudet propter vocem sponsi. Hoc ergo gaudium meum impletum est.*

30. *He must increase, but I must decrease.*

30. *Illum oportet crescere, me autem minui.*

31. *He that cometh from above, is above all. He that is of the earth he is, and of the earth he speaketh. He that*

Text.	Commentary.

cometh from heaven, is above all.

31. *Qui desursum venit, super omnes est. Qui est de terra, de terra loquitur. Qui de cælo venit, super omnes est.*

"*He that is of the earth, of the earth he is,*" etc. In this, the Baptist shows the superiority of our Lord's person and doctrine beyond himself and his doctrine. The Baptist and all other men are formed from the slime of the earth, mere earthly beings; and their teaching, earthly, derived from human knowledge and human principles. This is true of man, considered in himself, abstracting from revelation and the knowledge derived from God. If he speaks Divine things, it is owing to the illumination communicated from above. "*He that cometh from Heaven,*" essentially participating in the Divine nature, is heavenly, and above all.

32. *And what he hath seen, and heard, that he testifieth: and no man receiveth his testimony.*

32. *Et quod vidit et audivit, hoc testatur: et testimonium ejus nemo accipit.*

32. "*And what He hath seen,*" etc., a form of expression accommodated to our conceptions, the senses of seeing and hearing being the means, through which men acquire knowledge. The words mean, in relation to our Lord, what He knows by Divine Omniscience and intuition, that He testifies to us on earth in His assumed nature, wherein He converses with us.

"*And no one,*" but very few—In next verse, it is stated there were some exceptions—"*receiveth His testimony.*" In this the Baptist reproaches his own envious disciples. They tell the Baptist, that all men come to Christ. He says, but very few, comparatively, embrace His heavenly doctrines, not excepting John's own disciples.

33. *He that hath received his testimony, hath set to his seal that God is true.*

33. *Qui accepit ejus testimonium, signavit quia Deus verax est.*

33. "*Receiveth His testimony,*" by giving the assent of faith to what He says, "*hath set to His seal,*" etc. By the very fact of believing the words of our Lord, such a person, like a man who puts his seal to a document, to a bond or deed, in testimony of his conviction regarding the truth of its contents, has shown his conviction, by his firm belief openly professed, "*that God*"—who has spoken—"*is true,*" the primary and infallible truth, who speaks through the mouth of His Son. Such a man honours God's veracity.

34. *For he whom God hath sent, speaketh the word of God: for God doth not give the spirit by measure.*

34. *Quem enim misit Deus, verba Dei loquitur: non enim ad mensuram dat Deus spiritum.*

34. He sets his seal to the truth of God; because, He whom God sent into the world to teach mankind, speaks not from Himself, but the words of the Father who sent Him. He, therefore, who believes the Son, believes the Father, whose words the Son utters.

"*For God doth not give His Spirit by measure,*" to His Son. This proves that the Son speaks the words of God; because, as He has the Spirit without measure, He, therefore, always acts and speaks under the influence of the Spirit, and so speaks the words of God; unlike the men who receiving it in measure, sometimes speak from themselves.

If there be question of our Lord, *as God*, then, by communicating the Divine substance in His *first* birth from eternity, the Father communicated His Spirit and the gifts of His Spirit in an

Commentary.

infinite degree. If there be question of Him, as *man*, at His *second* birth; then, the Spirit was given abundantly, most copiously. The whole plenitude of the Divinity dwelt in Him corporally (Coll. ii. 9), as *man*. In Him, as *man*, were concealed all the treasures of wisdom and knowledge (Coll. ii. 3), and God poured forth on Him the whole plenitude of the gifts of His Spirit without stint or measure. So that none of them was wanting to Him in all perfection. He unceasingly possessed them all at once, to the greatest extent of which human nature is capable, unlike men, who possess them partially and successively, one, having one gift; another, another. To give a thing "*by measure*," implies, sparingly, as is done by those who give a thing by measuring or weighing it. *Without measure*, conveys, abundantly, copiously.

35. Here is assigned a reason why the Spirit is not given by measure, because the love of the Father for His Son was *infinite*, without measure; and hence, He handed over to His control and without measure, "*into His hand*," as man, "*all things*" in heaven and on earth, visible and invisible, to distribute them at will. But He has especially granted to Him, as *man*, to bestow all the gifts of the Spirit necessary for the salvation of the human race. The words of this and the following verses are almost identical with the words of our Lord (*v.* 16). "*God so loved the world . . . may have life everlasting.*"

36. As the Father hath handed over all things for dispensation and distribution into the hands of His Son, whoever, therefore, wishes to have eternal life, which God alone can give, must receive it from the hands of His Son. This can be only through faith, our only way for approaching Him—faith accompanied with good works.

"*Hath life everlasting*," in an inchoate state, at present, through justification, which gives a claim to it, and is an earnest of it; and in its full enjoyment and possession hereafter, provided he persevere in grace and in the performance of good works.

"*Believeth not . . . shall not see life.*" The future is used to denote the privation of all present and future hope. He shall be excluded not only from the possession or enjoyment of eternal life; but, he shall not even taste it or get a glimpse of it.

"*But the wrath of God*," the vengeance of God in inflicting punishment, "*abideth in him*," shall abide in him for all eternity in hell's torments. Similar are the words (*v.* 18), "*Qui non credit, jam judicatus est.*" They were in a state of sin and damnation before our Lord came, "*natura, filii iræ*" (Eph. ii. 3), and by refusing to adopt the means decreed by God to rescue them from this state of damnation, viz., faith, "*that worketh by charity*" (Gal. v. 6), they continue under it, and the wrath of God and judgment of damnation always abides with them.

Text.

35. *The Father loveth the Son: and he hath given all things into his hand.*

35. *Pater diligit Filium: et omnia dedit in manu ejus.*

36. *He that believeth in the Son, hath life everlasting: but he that believeth not the Son, shall not see life, but the wrath of God abideth on him.*

36. *Qui credit in Filium, habet vitam æternam: qui autem incredulus est Filio, non videbit vitam, sed ira Dei manet super eum.*

> **Commentary.**
>
> The Baptist discloses all these mysteries of God to his disciples—the Trinity, Incarnation, necessity of faith, etc.—in order that they should become detached from himself, and attached to Christ, to whose Divinity he bore such unequivocal testimony, whose faith they must embrace—the end of John's preaching and baptism—if they wish to secure eternal life; otherwise they shall be the victims of God's everlasting wrath.

CHAPTER IV.

1 *When Jesus therefore understood that the Pharisees had heard that Jesus maketh more disciples, and baptizeth more than John,*

2 *(Though Jesus himself did not baptize, but his disciples,)*

3 *He left Judea, and went again into Galilee.*

4 *And he was of necessity to pass through Samaria.*

5 *He cometh therefore to a city of Samaria which is called Sichar; near the land which Jacob gave to his son Joseph.*

6 *Now Jacob's well was there. Jesus therefore being wearied with his journey, sat thus on the well. It was about the sixth hour.*

7 *There cometh a woman of Samaria to draw water. Jesus saith to her: Give me to drink.*

8 *For his disciples were gone into the city to buy meats.*

9 *Then that Samaritan woman saith to him: How dost thou, being a Jew, ask of me to drink, who am a Samaritan woman? For, the Jews do not communicate with the Samaritans.*

10 *Jesus answered, and said to her: If thou didst know the gift of God, and who he is that saith to thee, Give me to drink; thou perhaps wouldst have asked of him, and he would have given thee living water.*

11 *The woman saith to him: Sir, thou hast nothing wherein to draw, and the well is deep: from whence then hast thou living water?*

12 *Art thou greater than our father Jacob, who gave us the well, and drank thereof himself, and his children, and his cattle?*

13 *Jesus answered, and said to her: Whosoever drinketh of this water, shall thirst again: but he that shall drink of the water that I will give him, shall not thirst for ever;*

14 *But the water that I will give him shall become in him a fountain of water springing up into life everlasting.*

15 *The woman saith to him: Sir, give me this water, that I may not thirst, nor come hither to draw.*

16 *Jesus saith to her: Go, call thy husband, and come hither.*

17 *The woman answered, and said: I have no husband. Jesus said to her: Thou hast said well, I have no husband:*

18 *For thou hast had five husbands: and he whom thou now hast, is not thy husband. This thou hast said truly.*

19 *The woman saith to him: Sir, I perceive that thou art a prophet.*

20 *Our fathers adored on this mountain, and you say, that at Jerusalem is the place where men must adore.*

21 Jesus saith to her: Woman, believe me, that the hour cometh, when you shall neither on this mountain, nor in Jerusalem adore the Father.

22 You adore that which you know not: we adore that which we know; for salvation is of the Jews.

23 But the hour cometh, and now is, when the true adorer shall adore the Father in spirit and in truth. For the Father also seeketh such to adore him.

24 God is a spirit, and they that adore him, must adore him in spirit and in truth.

25 The woman saith to him: I know that the Messias cometh (who is called Christ) therefore when he is come, he will tell us all things.

26 Jesus saith to her: I am he who am speaking with thee.

27 And immediately his disciples came: and they wondered that he talked with the woman. Yet no man said: What seekest thou, or why talkest thou with her?

28 The woman therefore left her water-pot, and went her way into the city, and saith to the men there:

29 Come, and see a man who has told me all things whatsoever I have done. Is not he the Christ?

30 They went therefore out of the city, and came unto him.

31 In the meantime the disciples prayed him, saying: Rabbi, eat.

32 But he said to them: I have meat to eat which you know not.

33 The disciples therefore said one to another: Hath any man brought him to eat?

34 Jesus said to them: My meat is to do the will of him that sent me, that I may perfect his work.

35 Do not you say, there are yet four months, and then the harvest cometh? Behold I say to you, lift up your eyes, and see the countries, for they are white already to harvest.

36 And he that reapeth receiveth wages, and gathereth fruit unto life everlasting: that both he that soweth and he that reapeth, may rejoice together.

37 For in this is the saying true: that it is one man that soweth, and it is another that reapeth.

38 I have sent you to reap that in which you did not labour: others have laboured, and you have entered into their labours.

39 Now of that city many of the Samaritans believed in him, for the word of the woman giving testimony: He told me all things whatsoever I have done.

40 So when the Samaritans were come to him, they desired him that he would tarry there. And he abode there two days.

41 And many more believed in him because of his own word.

42 And they said to the woman: We now believe, not for thy saying: for we ourselves have heard him, and know that this is indeed the Saviour of the world.

43 Now after two days he departed thence; and went into Galilee.

44 For Jesus himself gave testimony that a prophet hath no honour in his own country.

45 And when he was come into Galilee, the Galileans received him, having seen all the things he had done at Jerusalem on the festival day; for they also went to the festival day.

46 He came again therefore into Cana of Galilee, where he made the water wine. And there was a certain ruler whose son was sick at Capharnaum.

47 He having heard that Jesus was come from Judea into Galilee, went to him, and prayed him to come down and heal his son: for he was at the point of death.

48 Jesus therefore said to him: Unless you see signs and wonders, you believe not.

49 The ruler saith to him: Lord, come down before that my son die.

50 *Jesus saith to him: Go thy way, thy son liveth. The man believed the word which Jesus said to him, and went his way.*

51 *And he was going down, his servants met him: and they brought word, saying, that his son lived.*

52 *He asked therefore of them the hour, wherein he grew better. And they said to him: Yesterday at the seventh hour the fever left him.*

53 *The father therefore knew that it was at that same hour, that Jesus said to him, Thy son liveth; and himself believed and his whole house.*

54 *This is again the second miracle that Jesus did, when he was come out of Judea into Galilee.*

CAPUT IV.

1 *Ut ergo cognovit Jesus quia audierunt Pharisæi quod Jesus plures discipulos facit et baptizat, quam Joannes,*

2 *(Quamquam Jesus non baptizaret, sed discipuli ejus)*

3 *Reliquit Judæam, et abiit iterum in Galilæam.*

4 *Oportebat autem eum transire per Samariam.*

5 *Venit ergo in civitatem Samariæ, quæ dicitur Sichar: juxta prædium, quod dedit Jacob Joseph filio suo.*

6 *Erat autem ibi fons Jacob. Jesus ergo fatigatus ex itinere, sedebat sic supra fontem. Hora erat quasi sexta.*

7 *Venit mulier de Samaria haurire aquam. Dicit ei Jesus: Da mihi bibere.*

8 *(Discipuli enim ejus abierunt in civitatem ut cibos emerent.)*

9 *Dicit ergo ei mulier illa Samaritana: Quomodo tu Judæus cum sis, bibere a me poscis, quæ sum mulier Samaritana? non enim coutuntur Judæi Samaritanis.*

10 *Respondit Jesus, et dixit ei: Si scires donum dei, et quis est, qui dicit tibi: Da mihi bibere: tu forsitan petisses ab eo, et dedisset tibi aquam vivam.*

11 *Dicit ei mulier: Domine, neque in quo haurias habes, et puteus altus est: unde ergo habes aquam vivam?*

12 *Numquid tu major es patre nostro Jacob, qui dedit nobis puteum, et ipse ex eo bibit, et filii ejus, et pecora ejus?*

13 *Respondit Jesus, et dixit ei: Omnis, qui bibit ex aqua hac, sitiet iterum: qui autem biberit ex aqua, quam ego dabo ei, non sitiet in æternum:*

14 *Sed aqua, quam ego dabo ei, fiet en eo fons aquæ salientis in vitam æternam.*

15 *Dicit ad eum mulier: Domine, da mihi hanc aquam, ut non sitiam, neque veniam huc haurire.*

16 *Dicit ei Jesus: Vade, voca virum tuum, et veni huc.*

17 *Respondit mulier, et dixit: Non habeo virum. Dicit ei Jesus: Bene dixisti, quia non habeo virum:*

18 *Quinque enim viros habuisti, et nunc, quem habes, non est tuus vir: hoc vere dixisti.*

19 *Dicit ei mulier: Domine, video quia Propheta es tu.*

20 *Patres nostri in monte hoc adoraverunt, et vos dicitis, quia Jerosolymis est locus, ubi adorare oportet.*

21 *Dicit ei Jesus: Mulier crede mihi, quia venit hora, quando neque in monte hoc, neque in Jerosolymis adorabitis Patrem.*

22 *Vos adoratis quod nescitis: nos adoramus quod scimus, quia salus ex Judæis est.*

23 *Sed venit hora, et nunc est, quando veri adoratores adorabunt Patrem in spiritu et veritate. Nam et Pater tales quærit, qui adorent eum.*

24 *Spiritus est Deus: et eos, qui adorant eum, in spiritu et veritate oportet adorare.*

25 *Dicit ei mulier: Scio quia Messias venit, (qui dicitur Christus) cum ergo venerit ille, nobis annuntiabit omnia.*

26 *Dicit ei Jesus: Ego sum, qui loquor tecum.*

27 *Et continuo venerunt discipuli ejus: et mirabantur quia cum muliere loquebatur. Nemo tamen dixit: Quid quæris, aut quid loqueris cum ea?*

28 *Reliquit ergo hydriam suam mulier, et abiit in civitatem, et dicit illis hominibus:*

29 *Venite, et videte hominem, qui dixit mihi omnia quæcumque feci: numquid ipse est Christus?*

30 *Exierunt ergo de civitate, et veniebant ad eum.*

31 *Interea rogabant eum discipuli, dicentes: Rabbi, manduca.*

32 *Ille autem dicit eis: Ego cibum habeo manducare, quem vos nescitis.*

33 *Dicebant ergo discipuli ad invicem: Numquid aliquis attulit ei manducare?*

34 *Dicit eis Jesus: Meus cibus est ut faciam voluntatem ejus, qui misit me, ut perficiam opus ejus.*

35 *Nonne vos dicitis, quod adhuc quatuor menses sunt, et messis venit? Ecce dico vobis: Levate oculos vestros, et videre regiones, quia albæ sunt jam ad messem.*

36 *Et qui metit, mercedem accipit, et congregat fructum in vitam æternam: ut, et qui seminat, simul gaudeat, et qui metit.*

37 *In hoc enim est verbum verum: quia alius est qui seminat, et alius est qui metit.*

38 *Ego misi vos metere quod vos non laborastis: alii laboraverunt, et vos in labores eorum introistis.*

39 *Ex civitate autem illa multi crediderunt in eum Samaritanorum, propter verbum mulieris testimonium perhibentis: Quia dixit mihi omnia quæcumque feci.*

40 *Cum venissent ergo ad illum Samaritani, rogaverunt eum ut ibi maneret. Et mansit ibi duos dies.*

41 *Et multo plures crediderunt in eum propter sermonem ejus.*

42 *Et mulieri dicebant: Quia jam non propter tuam loquelam credimus: ipsi enim audivimus, et scimus, quia hic est vere Salvator mundi.*

43 *Post duos autem dies exiit inde: et abiit in Galilæam.*

44 *Ipse enim Jesus testimonium perhibuit quia Propheta in sua patria honorem non habet.*

45 *Cum ergo venisset in Galilæam, exceperunt eum Galilæi, cum omnia vidissent quæ fecerat Jerosolymis in die festo: et ipsi enim venerant ad diem festum.*

46 *Venit ergo iterum in Cana Galilææ, ubi fecit aquam vinum. Et erat quidam regulus, cujus filius infirmabatur Capharnaum.*

47 *Hic cum audisset quia Jesus adveniret a Judæa in Galilæam, abiit ad eum, et rogabat eum ut descenderet, et sanaret filium ejus: incipiebat enim mori.*

48 *Dixit ergo Jesus ad eum: Nisi signa, et prodigia videritis, non creditis.*

49 *Dicit ad eum regulus: Domine, descende prius quam moriatur filius meus.*

50 *Dicit ei Jesus: Vade, filius tuus vivit. Credidit homo sermoni, quem dixit ei Jesus, et ibat.*

51 *Jam autem eo descendente, servi occurrerunt ei, et nunciaverunt dicentes, quia filius ejus viveret.*

52 *Interrogabat ergo horam ab eis, in qua melius habuerit. Et dixerunt ei: Quia heri hora septima reliquit eum febris.*

53 *Cognovit ergo pater, quia illa hora erat, in qua dixit ei Jesus: Filius tuus vivit: et credidit ipse, et domus ejus tota.*

54 *Hoc iterum secundum signum fecit Jesus, cum venisset a Judæa in Galilæam.*

ANALYSIS.

In this chapter is recorded our Lord's journey to Galilee through Samaria (1–3.) His long and interesting colloquy with the Samaritan woman, which ended in the conversion of this sinful woman (3–28). His conversation with His disciples, whose approach interrupted His discourse with her (28–38). The conversion of a great number of the Samaritans (39–43).

Our Lord cures the Ruler's son, who was sick unto death, at Capharnaum (46–54).

Text.	Commentary.
1. *When Jesus therefore understood that the Pharisees had heard that Jesus maketh more disciples, and baptizeth more than John,* 1. *Ut ergo cognovit Jesus quia audierunt Pharisæi quod Jesus plures discipulos facit, et baptizat, quam Joannes,* 2. *(Though Jesus himself did not baptize, but his disciples.)* 2. *(Quamquam Jesus non baptizaret, sed discipuli ejus.)* 3. *He left Judea, and went again into Galilee.* 3. *Reliquit Judæam et abiit iterum in Galilæam.*	1–3. Our Lord had known, in virtue of His Divine Omniscience, "*that the Pharisees,*"—probably members of the Sanhedrim, composed chiefly of Pharisees, who, out of jealousy, on seeing John's popularity, and their own influence lessened among the people, had delivered John up to Herod—(Matthew xvii. 12), had heard that He had more disciples and baptized more than John had heretofore baptized. At this time, John was in prison. Our Lord Himself did not commonly baptize, He did so through His disciples, who baptized with His sanction and authority, thus showing His superiority over John, whose Baptism was performed by Himself only. If our Lord Himself had baptized some few, as is generally stated, this would not be opposed to the statement made here. He did not usually baptize the multitudes indiscriminately, which statement will admit of His baptizing a few. "*He (therefore) left Judea, and went again into Galilee.*" This was a second time. His first return to Galilee is mentioned (c. i. 43). Our Lord retired not from fear ; but, as the time marked out for His Passion had not yet arrived, He avoided the Pharisees, who, as He knew, would, out of jealousy and hatred, endeavour to compass His death before the appointed time, by denouncing Him to the authorities, with whom, as appears from John's case, they had vast influence (Matthew xvii. 12). John was, at this time, cast into prison. This was partly owing to the machinations and envy of the Pharisees, who were offended at his bold denunciations, his great influence and popularity, to the consequent lessening of their own influence with the people ; and partly, to the offence given to Herod, in being reproached with his incestuous connexion with his brother's wife.
4. *And he was of necessity to pass through Samaria.* 4. *Oportebat autem eum transire per Samariam.*	4. His direct route was through Samaria—a district which lay between Judea and Galilee inhabited by the tribe of Ephraim and half tribe of Manasse (see Matthew x. 4, Commentary on). The Evangelist mentions this circumstance, to introduce us naturally to the following interesting colloquy with the Samaritan woman.
5. *He cometh therefore to a city of Samaria which is called*	5. "*Sichar,*" formerly called *Sichem,* one of the oldest cities of Palestine (Genesis xii. 6). But, the Evangelist adopts the name

Commentary

by which it was commonly called in his time. It was in the tribe of Ephraim (Jos. xxi. 21). This city of Sichem is celebrated on account of the many remarkable events recorded of it in the Old Testament. (Jos. xxiv. etc.). It was destroyed by Abimelech (Judges ix. 45) and afterwards rebuilt by Jeroboam, who dwelt there (3 Kings xii. 25). It was waste in the time of St. Jerome, and a city built close by, called Neapolis in the Roman age; now, *Naplous*, situated "*near the land which Jacob gave to his son Joseph.*" On his return from Mesopotamia, Jacob purchased a piece of land from the children of Hemor for a hundred lambs (Genesis xxxiii. 19). This piece of land Jacob gave, at his death, in addition to his other inheritance, to his son Joseph (Genesis xlviii. 22). Here the bones of Joseph were buried (Josue xxiv. 32).

6. "*Jacob's well*," which he dug and secured while living there for his own use (*v.* 12).

"*Was there*," either within the ground or near it, a little distance from "*Sichar*" or *Sichem*.

"*Wearied with his journey*," which he performed on foot. "*Sat thus on the well.*"

"*Thus*," is understood by some to mean, sat in the position of one fatigued, without any seat, but carelessly, as might best secure refreshing rest. By others, it is understood to mean, "*therefore.*" Being wearied, He, *therefore*, sat down to rest and refresh His wearied limbs. It is a common acceptation of the word, "*so.*" We say of a man, he travelled far, and *so* (therefore) sat down to rest.

"*On the well*," by the side of it; or, on the covering of the well, which was sunk deep in the ground.

"*About the sixth hour.*" Midday, when the heat is greatest. It was the hour of taking food and rest in Judea. Hence, the disciples went to procure food (*v.* 8). This was another reason for His sitting down, and it introduces us actually to the subsequent narrative.

7. "*There cometh*," from the town of Sichem close by, "*a woman of Samaria*," a native of the district of Samaria, "*to draw water*," and carry it home for domestic use.

8. In this is assigned a reason for His asking the Samaritan woman to give him to drink. The disciples who were in the habit of ministering to Him were away, and our Lord had providentially so arranged it, in order to be able to converse more fully with this wretched woman, when alone.

Text

Sichar; near the land which Jacob gave to his son Joseph.

5. Venit ergo in civitatem Samariæ, quæ dicitur Sichar: juxta prædium, quod dedit Jacob Joseph filio suo.

6. Now Jacob's well was there. Jesus therefore being wearied with his journey, sat thus on the well. It was about the sixth hour.

6. Erat autem ibi fons Jacob. Jesus ergo fatigatus ex itinere, sedebat sic supra fontem. Hora erat quasi sexta.

7. There cometh a woman of Samaria to draw water. Jesus saith to her: Give me to drink.

7. Venit mulier de Samaria haurire aquam. Dicit ei Jesus: Da mihi bibere

8. For his desciples were gone into the city to buy meats.

8. (Discipuli enim ejus abierant in civitatem ut cibos emerent.)

Text.

9. *Then that Samaritan woman saith to him: How dost thou, being a Jew, ask of me to drink, who am a Samaritan woman? For the Jews do not communicate with the Samaritans.*

9. *Dicit ergo ei mulier illa Samaritana: Quomodo tu Judæus cum sis, bibere a me poscis, quæ sum mulier Samaritana? non enim coutuntur Judæi Samaritanis.*

10. *Jesus answered, and said to her: If thou didst know the gift of God, and who he is that saith to thee, Give me to drink; thou perhaps wouldst have asked of him, and he would have given thee living water.*

10. *Respondit Jesus, et dixit ei: Si scires donum Dei, et quis est, qui dicit tibi: Da mihi bibere: tu forsitan petisses ab eo, et dedisset tibi aquam vivam?*

Commentary.

9. From His dress and accent, the woman knew Him to be a Jew; and hence, she reproachfully asks, how could He, a Jew, ask any request of a Samaritan. A deadly hatred existed between the Jews and Samaritans; and hence, the woman takes an opportunity of reproaching our Lord, with the deep hatred His nation bore her people.

"*For the Jews do not communicate*," etc. The Jews refused all social and familiar intercourse with the Samaritans. She throws the whole blame on the Jews. She does not say, the Samaritans refuse all intercourse with the Jews, throwing the whole blame of this national hate on the Jews. The Jews held the Samaritans in special aversion, for several reasons. First, on account of their mixed origin, being partly descended from the Assyrians, who cruelly oppressed the Jews; again, on account of their possessing the inheritance of the Jews, the lands formerly held by the Israelites; again, on account of their mixing up false and idolatrous rites with the Jewish worship; again, on account of their encouraging and giving refuge to every scandalous and refractory Jew, who passed over to them. It was not considered a departure from the social exclusion the Jews determined on, in relation to the Samaritans, to relieve individual distress, to buy or sell food. Hence, the Samaritan woman drew too fast a line in reproaching our Lord for asking of her to drink.

10. "*The gift of God,*" most likely, means our Lord Himself (iii. 16), in whom were eminently contained all we want: who was sent to be the Saviour of all mankind. This gift was common to her with all others. It may also refer to what was peculiarly granted herself, the special favour bestowed on her of having this opportunity of conversing with Him, whom God sent into this world. This latter meaning seems expressed in the words, "*and who He is that saith to thee,*" etc., the Eternal Son of God, who would cheerfully, if asked, instead of refusing, as she did, have granted all her requests.

"*Thou perhaps wouldst have asked,*" etc. "*Perhaps*" (αν), is generally understood to mean, *surely*, though rendered in the Vulgate, *forsitan*, "*perhaps,*" to express free will on the part of the woman to petition Him, to receive or reject God's gift. "*Living water.*" She refused Him water from the well. He, on the other hand, would have given her "*living water,*" the Holy Ghost, to dwell in her with His gifts, to slake her thirst and purify her soul of the stains with which it was covered, as natural water has the effect of removing stains from the body, and this water would not be stagnant or become putrid, or corrupted; but, like the running water, would ever vivify her, and "*spring up into life everlasting*" (v. 14).

Commentary.

Allusion to "*living water*," is not unusual in the Old Testament. (Zacharias xiv. 8; Jeremias ii. 13, etc.)

11. The words of our Lord in the preceding verse impressed the woman with a sense of respect. Hence, although before scornfully addressing Him as a Jew, the enemy of her people; now, altering her tone, she says, "*Sir*," etc. She understood our Lord to speak of elementary natural water, which was better than that in the well, and as she saw no other *water* save that of the well, which He had no means of reaching, she cannot understand where He could get the water He promises to give, if asked for.

12. *Our father Jacob.*" The Samaritans claimed descent from the Patriarchs, and they occupied the portion of the Land of Promise assigned to Ephraim, who was reckoned among his sons by Jacob (Genesis xlviii. 15). The Samaritans were descended from the Gentiles and Jews united (2 Paralip. xxxv. 18). For, on the abduction of the ten tribes into Assyria, there were left behind many Jews, who formed one people with the Babylonian colony, who were sent to inhabit the country. Whenever the kingdom of *Juda* was prosperous, the Samaritans, as representing Ephraim and Manasses, claimed descent from the Patriarchs; when otherwise, the Samaritans disowned them (Josephus, Lib. Antiq. 9).

Jacob and his family used the water of this well, a proof of its superior quality—"*and his cattle*," a proof of its abundance.

The woman's mind is undergoing a gradual change. She changes her tone, and asks, without denying it, if He could claim to be greater than Jacob, to be endowed with greater power and sagacity, so as to dig a well and find out better water than that which Jacob procured at such trouble; and from the fact of his drinking of it himself, was considered the best to be found in the locality. From the superior quality of the water, she would seem to infer the superiority of the party giving it. Hence, taking advantage of her ideas, our Lord, in order to prepare her for faith in Himself, as the Messiah, points, in the next verse, to the superior excellence of the living water He speaks of.

13. Our Lord leaves her to infer the superiority of the person from the superior excellence of the water He gives.

The water from the well which you refused Me, can only slake one's thirst for a time, only to return again. But, the living water I will give, slakes all thirst in future and for ever, unless through their own fault men reject it.

"*Shall not thirst for ever.*" Whether we regard bodily thirst, or the thirst of the soul, these words have reference to the world to come, when the bodies of the just, who have drunk plentifully of the gifts and grace of the Holy Ghost, shall rise glorious, not

Text.

11. *The woman saith to him: Sir, thou hast nothing wherein to draw, and the well is deep; from whence then hast thou living water?*

11. *Dicit ei mulier: Domine, neque in quo haurias habes, et puteus altus est: unde ergo habes aquam vivam?*

12. *Art thou greater than our father Jacob, who gave us the well, and drank thereof himself, and his children, and his cattle?*

12. *Numquid tu major es patre nostro Jacob, qui dedit nobis puteum, et ipse ex eo bibit, et filii ejus, et pecora ejus?*

13. *Jesus answered, and said to her: Whosoever drinketh of this water, shall thirst again: but he that shall drink of the water that I will give him, shall not thirst for ever;*

13. *Respondit Jesus, et dixit ei: Omnis, qui bibet ex aqua hac, sitiet iterum: qui*

| **Text.** | **Commentary.** |

autem biberit ex aqua, quam ego dabo ei, non sitiet in æternum:

subject any longer to animal wants, miseries or passions of any sort, and their souls shall be fully satiated. "*Satiabor cum apparuerit gloria tua*"—"*Non esurient neque sitient amplius.*"—"*Inebriabuntur ab ubertate domus tuæ.*"—"*Quoniam ipsi saturabuntur.*"

14. *But the water that I will give him, shall become in him a fountain of water springing up into life everlasting.*

14. *Sed aqua, quam ego dabo ei, fiet in eo fons aquæ salientis in vitam æternam.*

14. "*But the water which I shall give him*"—and shall not be drawn from without—"*shall become in him a fountain of water springing up into life everlasting.*" The Holy Spirit whom Christ shall give with all His graces and gifts, shall cause these waters of grace so to bubble up and gush forth from the fountain, like springs of elementary water, which mount up sometimes as high as their source, that they will cause them to mount up to heaven to their heavenly source, and resuscitate their mortal bodies by the power of the Holy Ghost who dwells in them, so as to become sharers in a glorious immortality in heaven.

That water in the minds of men will bound up to God and eternal life, because, it makes men possessors of life eternal.

15. *The woman saith to him: Sir, give me this water, that I may not thirst, nor come hither to draw.*

15. *Dicit ad eum mulier: Domine, da mihi hunc aquam, ut non sitiam: neque veniam huc haurire.*

15. Although the carnal mind of the woman did not fully comprehend our Lord's allusion to the spiritual waters of grace; still, she was undergoing a gradual change, so as to become divested of the aversion shown our Lord in the first instance. She respectfully addresses Him, "*Sir*" or "*Lord,*" and seemed inclined to believe, He would give her this superior water, and to regard Him, therefore, as superior to Jacob, and to have the remote dispositions for embracing the faith. She did not ask for eternal life, but only for the water which would spare her the drudgery of coming again so far for refreshing water. Our Lord told her if she asked for it, He would give it. She who before refused Him for water from the well, now asks for the living water spoken of by Him. Some Commentators think it likely the woman understood our Lord to have spoken of the spiritual waters of grace at His disposal; but that she disbelieved Him, and feigning belief, derisively asked Him to give what she fancied He could not do. At all events, our Lord, in order to bring conviction to her mind regarding His sacred character and mission, calls her attention to a remarkable feature in her life, and shows His hidden knowledge of the sinful life she was pursuing.

16. *Jesus saith to her: Go, call thy husband and come hither.*

16. *Dicit ei Jesus: Vade, voca virum tuum, et veni huc.*

16. "*Call thy husband,*" etc. Likely, in speaking thus, our Lord had mercifully in view to introduce gradually the subject of her sinful life, to elicit from her a confession of the same, and by thus stimulating her to a course of penance, to prepare her for the due reception of His heavenly gift, sanctifying grace. He, at the same time, wished to show her, that He was endowed with a supernatural knowledge, so that she might know who He was, and be thus

Commentary

inspired with due reverence for Him and confidence in His teaching.

17. Anxious to receive the promised living water without any delay, which would result from her doing what our Lord commanded; she, at once answers evasively, not confessing; still not denying her guilt. "*I have no husband,*" not looking upon the man, with whom she lived in sin, as her lawful husband. Our Lord fully expressed what she had not clearly confessed, and discloses the real state of the case "*Thou hast said well, I have no husband.*"

18. "*Five husbands,*" very likely, lawful husbands—though Maldonatus and others think otherwise. For, our Lord draws a comparison between the five husbands she had had, and the present one. The former "*she had,*" because, legitimate; the present she has *not*. He is not her husband, because unwedded to him. In this, our Lord lets her know the hidden knowledge He had of her past life, and from this, she sees in Him at once something supernatural. She bears well the reprehension and tacit correction conveyed in our Lord's words, mildly intimating His knowledge of her sinful condition. Hence, she at once, conceiving a high opinion of His exalted station, exclaims:

19. "*Sir, I perceive Thou art a Prophet,*" as if to say—You disclose a knowledge of my sins hidden from You. I admit You state facts. From this knowledge of my wicked life, "*I see Thou art a Prophet,*" by disclosing, although a stranger, a knowledge of things that could not naturally be known to Thee; hence, communicated from above. She admits her guilt by acknowledging that He discloses facts not known by natural means. It was the part of Prophets not only to predict future events, but to make known secret things at present occurring (4 Kings v. 26).

20. She now proposed to Him whom she regarded as a "*Prophet,*" but whom she had not yet believed to be the Messias, (25) to decide a question much controverted among the two peoples regarding the place, where, by Divine ordinance, sacrifices should be offered to God. This is the meaning of the word, "*adore,*" here. Only *one place* was allowed for this purpose. In earlier times, the altar of the Tabernacle (Leviticus xvii. 1–7); in latter times, since the building of the Temple, the Temple of Jerusalem (Deut. xii. 13, 14). There was never any question, as to the lawfulness of privately adoring and worshipping God in any place. This our Lord Himself did and this St. Paul prescribes (1 Timothy ii. 8). The question regarded solely the *offering of Sacrifice*, to which reference is made (Deut. xii) and the *one* place, which God had chosen for that purpose. The Jews contended that

Text

17. *The woman answered and said: I have no husband. Jesus said to her: Thou hast said well, I have no husband.*

17. *Respondit mulier, et dixit: Non habeo virum. Dicit ei Jesus: Bene dixisti, quia non habeo virum:*

18. *For thou hast had five husbands: and he whom thou now hast, is not thy husband. This thou hast said truly.*

18. *Quinque enim viros habuisti, et nunc quem habes, non est tuus vir: hoc vere dixisti.*

19. *The woman saith to him: Sir, I perceive that thou art a prophet.*

19. *Dicit ei mulier: Domine, video quia Propheta es tu.*

20. *Our fathers adored on this mountain, and you say, that at Jerusalem is the place where men must adore.*

20. *Patres nostri in monte hoc adoraverunt, et vos dicitis, quia Jerosolymis est locus, ubi adorare oportet.*

| Text. | Commentary. |

this place was Jerusalem, where Solomon, by divine sanction, built the Temple and offered sacrifices pleasing to God. (2 Par. ii. 6) Our Lord (*v.* 22) approves of this.

"*Our fathers*," are understood by some to refer to the fathers, common to Jews and Samaritans, viz., the Patriarchs, Jacob and his sons (Genesis xxxiii. 20). Others say, she refers to the fathers of the Samaritans.

"*Adored*," offered up sacrifices "*on this mountain*," within sight, viz., Garazim, overhanging Sichem. The Samaritans, at least, were persuaded of this. The woman states the case in a way to favour her own people, as if she said: they were only following the example of their fathers, in sacrificing on Mount Garazim. But the Jews, she insinuates, said on their own authority—without proving it, "*You say, that at Jerusalem*," etc. The Temple of Garazim was built, out of a schismatical spirit of revenge, by one of the Persian Governors, to gratify the spleen of Manasses, the High Priest, who was deprived of his place in the Temple, for having married, contrary to law, the daughter of Sanaballeth, Persian Governor of Samaria, whom he refused to send away. Upon this, Manasses had recourse to his father-in-law Sanaballeth, who built a Temple on Mount Garazim, to rival that of Jerusalem, constituting Manasses, High Priest. The latter was afterwards joined by other reprobates, and established a rival schismatical form of worship. This rendered the breach between the Jews and Samaritans irreparable, and was among the chief causes, why the Jews had such aversion for the Samaritans.

As has been already remarked, in only one place which the Lord had chosen, was it allowable to offer sacrifices. This, in the first instance, was the altar of the Tabernacle (Levit. xvii.). And as the Temple of Jerusalem succeeded the Tabernacle, the Jews contended, therefore, that Jeruselem was the place, while the Samaritans contended for Mount Garazim. The dispute being referred to Ptolemy Philometer, King of Egypt, he decided in favour of the Jews (Josephus 13, Antiq. c 6). Our Lord conveys, very significantly, in the following verses, that the solution of the question was, at present, but of little consequence, owing to the changes to take place, in the near future, in their religious relations, consequent on the coming of the Messias.

21. *Jesus saith to her: Woman, believe me, that the hour cometh, when you shall neither on this mountain, or in Jerusalem adore the Father.*

21. "*Woman, believe Me*," invests the following words with great weight. As she regarded Him as a Prophet, then, let her place more trust in Him, more reliance on the truth of what He was about to announce, than in the supposed acts of her fathers referred to.

21. *Dicit ei Jesus: Mulier crede mihi,*

"*The hour cometh*," is just at hand, when the pure worship of the true God is no longer to be confined to the narrow precincts of Judea, as the Jews imagined, or of Samaria, as the Samaritans

Commentary.

fancied, but was to extend to the entire earth; hence, the present controversy is of no consequence.

"*Adore the Father*," implying that they were to be *children* of God. The word, "*Father*," refers to the fundamental mystery of the Trinity, obscurely, however, so as to let the light of faith gradually dawn on the mind of this still unbelieving and sinful woman.

22. Lest it might be inferred from the abolition of both forms of worship, that they were both on terms of equality, our Lord approves of the Jewish worship preferably to that of the Samaritans. "*You*," Samaritans, "*adore what you know not*." The words might, perhaps, be more easily understood by inversion. "*You know not, what you adore*," because, although the Samaritans believed in the God of Israel as the true God; still, they mixed up with His worship several idolatrous rites, at least in the beginning (4 Kings xvii. 33), and even in the time of our Lord, although the grosser form was removed by Manasses and the Priests who served with him, in the schismatical worship at Garazim; some leaven of idolatry could still be found. Having lost the true faith, and being in ignorance, they were adoring what they had no accurate conception of. They had no solid foundation for their worship or religion, no certain form sanctioned by God, no priests nor pastors legitimately sent.

"*We*," Jews—with whom our Lord, who was born of the Jews, identifies Himself—"*adore that which we know*," without any admixture of error. The Jews knew the true God, believed in Him, and retained His true worship. They knew what they worshipped; because, they worshipped in a place prescribed by God and pointed out by the Prophets. As a people, they retained the true faith, whatever might be the wanderings of individuals at certain times. Hence, our Lord, in reply to her question, decides in favor of the Jewish claims, and conveys, at the same time, that the controversy was but of little practical consequence at present, owing to the abolition of both forms of worship, in the near future; the Samaritan, as bad and idolatrous; the Jewish, as imperfect, its shadows soon to be replaced by the reality.

He assigns a reason why the Jews should know the proper mode and place of true worship, "*because salvation*," promised to the world, the Saviour of the world is admittedly to come "*from the Jews*" (Genesis xlix. 10). The promises of salvation through the Messias and fully accomplished by Him, were made to the Jews, and through them, to the rest of mankind. It would be preposterous to suppose, that the Saviour of mankind would spring from a race ignorant of the true God and of His true worship; or, that He would allow the true faith and consequent true worship to pass away from His own race and nation, although in some matters,

Text.

quia venit hora quando neque in monte hoc, neque in Jerosolymis adorabitis Patrem.

22. *You adore that which you know not: we adore that which we know; for salvation is of the Jews.*

22. *Vos adoratis quod nescitis: nos adoramus quod scimus quia salus ex Judæis est.*

Text.	Commentary.
	there might be a departure from it, for which He often reproved them.
23. *But the hour cometh, and now is, when the true adorers shall adore the Father in spirit and in truth. For the Father also seeketh such to adore him.* 23. *Sed venit hora, et nunc est, quando veri adoratores adorabunt Patrem in spiritu et veritate. Nam et Pater tales quærit, qui adorent eum.*	23. After interposing the statement contained in v. 22, which might be regarded as parenthetical, our Lord now resumes and perfects His teaching referred to in v. 21. By *"adoration,"* she meant sacrifice. Our Lord also uses the word in the same sense. *"The true,"* genuine, heartfelt, sincere *"adorers," "in spirit and in truth."* Their adoration, their sacrifices (for, it is of sacrifices, the woman and our Lord speak) however corporeal in their external form, will chiefly proceed from an interior *"spirit,"* unlike the Jewish oblations, which were all external. They will not be associated with any gross false ideas regarding the true God, like the sacrifices of the Samaritans. Both forms of worship, Jewish and Samaritan, are soon to be abolished, and succeeded by a true form of worship of which spiritual, interior feelings of reverence towards God, and correct notions of Him, shall be the chief characteristics. It is adorers of this description that God always seeks and always cherishes. Such adorers alone can please Him. *"Spirit,"* is opposed to the Jewish; *"truth,"* to the Samaritan form of worship.
24. *God is a spirit, and they that adore him must adore him in spirit and in truth.* 24. *Spiritus est Deus: et eos, qui adorant eum, in spiritu et veritate oportet adorare.*	24. As *"God is a Spirit,"* and also a true Spirit, *"they that adore Him,"* must offer Him worship suited to His nature and true attributes. It must proceed from spiritual feelings, *"in spirit,"* dictated by a clear knowledge of His true and adorable perfections, *"and in truth."* As both forms of worship, Jewish and Samaritan, were soon to be abolished, the new form alone pleasing to God, shall be distinguished chiefly by interior feelings of religion, so much wanting in the purely exterior Jewish worship, and by truthful external profession in regard to the attributes, and adorable perfections of God, so much wanting in the false worship, the outcome of false ideas regarding God, practised by the Samaritans. Some say, *"spirit"* and *"truth"* mean the same. For, he who adores *"in spirit,"* by acts proceeding from grace and faith, thereby adores *"in truth,"* or, in a manner becoming a true adorer. Then as *"God is a Spirit,"* the sacrifices offered to Him must be chiefly spiritual. This cannot exclude external worship, accommodated to the nature of man, who is composed of a body as well as of a soul; and it is through the medium of actions performed by the body, this spiritual worship must be presented. Hence, temples and external rites cannot be excluded, otherwise, our Lord would contradict Himself when purifying not abolishing the temple, and in exercising external worship (Luke xxiv. 50; xxii. 41).

Commentary.

The Apostles, too, would have disobeyed our Lord's instructions (Acts ix. 40; xvi. 25; Eph. iii. 14).

The only sacrifice referred to, as excluded here, is that of the Jews, consisting almost in mere external and corporeal oblations. Our Sacrifice of the Mass, although containing something external and corporeal, is still "*in spirit and truth,*" appertaining to the supernatural order of faith, grace and glory. The same holds in regard to the sacraments. Our Lord reproves those who, addicted to external rites of worship, undervalue and neglect the interior spirit. The just of old were true adorers; because, in presenting Jewish sacrifices, they did so, not regarding them as pleasing in themselves; but, as figures of Him who was to come, "*the Lamb slain from the beginning of the world.*"

The word, "*adoration,*" is here taken in a general sense also, so as to include all acts of religious worship, interior acts proceeding from faith and grace, prayer, of every description. Hence, as God is a Spirit; a Spirit, however, who is omnipresent, filling all space with His glorious and adorable immensity, He can be adored in every place: and such worship is pleasing to Him (1 Tim. ii. 8).

25. "*I know that the Messias cometh,*" etc. The Samaritans admitted the Pentateuch, in which was contained the promise of the coming of Christ (Deut. xviii. 18). Hence, our Lord says (v. 46), "*if you believe Moses, you would also believe Me.*" However, they could not learn His near approach from Deuteronomy. Hence, it is likely the woman was made aware of His *near* approach from the rumours prevalent amongst her neighbours, the Jews, regarding the fulfilment of the time marked out for His coming; and also from the testimony of the Baptist, which must have reached even to the Samaritans. Probably, not pleased with our Lord's decision in favour of the Jews, and unable fully to understand His words, she, waiving all further discussion, remits the whole case to the Messiah now at hand, whose decision all were prepared to abide by, "*who is called the Christ.*" These are likely the words of the Evangelist himself, as the woman could hardly be expected to know the meaning of the word "*Messias,*" which signifies, *Christ*, or *anointed*.

"*When He comes, He will tell us all things.*" This shows she herself expected to see the day of His coming.

26. Having gradually prepared her mind to accept the great truth; seeing her docile dispositions, He now at once tells this sinful woman, who He was—a thing He refused telling the haughty Jews, who so often asked Him in order to persecute Him. He thus exhorts her to embrace the faith, at the same time, pouring His grace into her soul. Wonderful condescension of our

Text.

25. *The woman saith to him: I know that the Messias cometh (who is called Christ) therefore when he is come, he will tell us all things.*

25. *Dicit ei mulier: Scio quia Messias venit, (qui dicitur Christus,) cum ergo venerit ille, nobis annunciabit omnia.*

26. *Jesus saith to her: I am he, who am speaking with thee*

26. *Dicit ei Jesus: Ego sum, qui loquor tecum.*

Text.	Commentary.
	Lord. "*Qui in altis habitat, ac humilia respicit in cœlo et in terra.*" (Psalm cxii.)
27. *And immediately his disciples came; and they wondered that he talked with the woman. Yet no man said: What seekest thou, or why talkest thou with her?*	27. "*And immediately*," after this declaration, and revelation of his Divinity—when He had said all that was needed, and no sooner, "*the disciples came*," after having purchased food at Sichem. "*And they wondered that He talked with the woman*," which is understood by some in praise of His condescension to engage in conversation with so poor and humble a person—others, more probably, interpret the words to mean, they wondered, at seeing Him, with whom it was unusual to speak to any woman apart, save His immediate relatives, engaged in conversation with a strange, unknown woman, alone in such a place. Our Lord always set an example of modesty and circumspection to His followers, by His holy reserve, in regard to females. This He intended for our instruction. "*Yet no one said, what seekest thou?*" etc. Their profound reverence for their Master prevented them from asking any questions regarding His interview with the woman, knowing He was engaged in some useful and instructive conversation.
27. *Et continuo venerunt discipuli ejus: et mirabantur quia cum muliere loquebatur. Nemo tamen dixit: Quid quæris, aut quid loqueris cum ea?*	
28. *The woman therefore left her water-pot, and went her way into the city, and saith to the men there:*	28. "*Therefore*," on hearing the wonderful announcement, which she believed from one who had already disclosed secret sins, "*the woman*," inflamed with ardour of faith—"*left her waterpot*," wherewith she came to carry water home from the well. Indifferent about her temporal and domestic wants, she went in haste into the city, to announce to her people and fellow-citizens, the wonderful tidings communicated to her, in order that they might come out, to see our Lord before leaving, and thus become sharers with her in the heavenly treasures of grace.
28. *Reliquit ergo hydriam suam mulier, et abiit in civitatem, et dicit illis hominibus:*	
29. *Come, and see a man who has told me all things whatsoever I have done. Is not he the Christ.*	29. "*All things whatsoever I did.*" It may be, our Lord spoke more than is recorded here, or she may have inferred from His disclosing the leading features of her life, that He knew all. She thus prepares them to receive the faith. "*Is He not the Christ?*" Although she had no doubt herself, she, still, speaks the language of hesitation, and puts the matter in an interrogative, rather than affirmative form; lest, by betraying too much anxiety, she would create doubt or prejudice in their minds. She excites their curiosity, and invites them to come, see, and judge for themselves in which she displayed consummate prudence.
29. *Venite, et videte hominem, qui dixit mihi omnia quæcumque feci: numquid ipse est Christus?*	
30. *They went therefore out of the city, and came unto him.*	
30. *Exierunt ergo de civitate, et veniebant ad eum.*	

ST. JOHN, CHAP. IV.

Commentary.

31. In the meantime, whilst the woman is in the city speaking to her fellow-citizens, the Apostles press Him to partake of the food they procured in the city.

32. Our Lord, in rather obscure language, which He afterwards clears up (v. 34), replies to the invitation of His disciples to eat. He referred to the spiritual hunger, he had for the conversion of the Samaritan.

33. The disciples misunderstand Him, as if He spoke of material food.

34. Our Lord explains. His food was to do His Father's will, and accomplish the work of God, which, although in general, referring to the salvation of mankind, in this instance, regarded the conversion of the Samaritans.

35. Our Lord, in response to the invitation of His disciples, asking Him to partake of the material food they procured in the city, said, His principal food was the doing of the will of His Father who sent Him. Now, the will of His Father in sending Him was, that He should engage in the work of salvation, and gather in a harvest of souls; and that harvest was just ripe and fit for the sickle, as might be seen from the crowds of Samaritans coming out to see Him. If men, generally, were so solicitous about bodily food, that from the time the seed is committed to the earth, they are looking forward from a long period, and preparing to gather it in when it is sufficiently ripe: how much more solicitous should they be, in regard to the spiritual harvest of souls, which they themselves could see is now ripe and fit for the sickle.

"*Do you not say?*" etc., which means; are not men generally in the habit of saying? These words are to be taken in their literal sense, as conveying, that a period of four months intervened between the time they were spoken and the coming harvest; and as the fruits were ripe in Palestine in the month of May, between the Pasch and Pentecost, it is inferred that our Lord spoke these words about the end of January. "*And then the harvest cometh,*" which being then ripe, is at once to be cut down.

Text.

31. *In the mean time the disciples prayed him, saying: Rabbi, eat.*
31. *Interea rogabant eum discipuli, dicentes: Rabbi, manduca.*

32. *But he said to to them: I have meat to eat which you know not.*
32. *Ille autem dicit eis: Ego cibum habeo manducare, quem vos nescitis.*

33. *The disciples therefore said one to another: Hath any man brought him to eat?*
33. *Dicebant ergo discipuli ad invicem: Numquid aliquis attulit ei manducare?*

34. *Jesus saith to them: My meat is to do the will of him that sent me, that I may perfect his work.*
34. *Dicit eis Jesus: Meus cibus est ut faciam voluntatem ejus, qui misit me, ut perficiam opus ejus.*

35. *Do not you say, there are yet four months, and then the harvest cometh? Behold I say to you, lift up your eyes, and see the countries, for they are white already to harvest.*
35. *Nonne vos dicitis, quod adhuc quatuor menses sunt, et messis venit? Ecce dico vobis: Levate oculos vestros, et videte regiones, quia albae sunt jam ad messem.*

Text.	Commentary.
	"*Lift up your eyes,*" the eyes of the body to see the crowds coming out from Sichem, and the eyes of the soul as well, to contemplate a sinful world, whereof Sichem, which was sending forward its people with such promptitude, was a type, prepared to receive the Gospel, and be gathered into the granary of God's Church. Prepare, therefore, to attend to it at once, the ripe harvest calls for the sickle.
36. *And he that reapeth, receiveth wages, and gathereth fruit unto life everlasting: that both he that soweth, and he that reapeth, may rejoice together.*	36. He stimulates His fellow labourers in the spiritual harvest, to labour zealously in this spiritual work of salvation, not on account of the temporal, but of the everlasting abiding reward they have to treasure up for themselves in the life to come; unlike the reapers of the material harvest, who labour for their masters, and treasure up fruits soon to be consumed.
36. *Et qui metit, mercedem accipit, et congregat fructum in vitam æternam: ut, et qui seminat, simul gaudeat, et qui metit.*	So that the sower and the reaper may again rejoice together. That is to say, the consequence will be, that the joy on seeing the abundant spiritual fruit of the seed they had sown, in other words, at seeing numberless souls saved through their labours, will not be confined to the reaper, as generally happens in regard to the material harvest; but will also extend to the sower, who laboured hard in his day. Both will rejoice together; as having laboured for God and as co-operators with God, from whom alone the increase can come, in beholding the abiding and abundant fruits of their toil. This fruit, unlike the material harvest, will abide for ever, so that all may enjoy it in the eternal life to come.
37. *For in this is the saying true: that it is one man that soweth, and it is another that reapeth.*	37. For in the case of the spiritual harvest, which I now point out to you as ripe for the sickle, is verified and fulfilled, the trite adagial saying—"*It is one man that soweth, it is another that reapeth,*" both, in this case, enjoying the fruit and reward. The saying is verified in reference to the difference of persons engaged in sowing and reaping; but, not in reference to the fruit and reward. For, in the spiritual harvest, both sower and reaper receive the reward.
37. *In hoc enim est verbum verum: quia alius est qui seminat, et alius est qui metit.*	
38. *I have sent you to reap that in which you did not labour: others have laboured, and you have entered into their labours.*	38. Our Lord illustrates this adage in His dealing with the Apostles, and accommodates it to their case, in this way: "*I sent you to reap*" in Judea, to labour for the lost sheep of the house of Israel, "*wherein you did not labour.*" Likely, our Lord here immediately refers to the mission among the Jews, which was to be succeeded by a more general, nay, a universal, mission hereafter, "*to all nations.*"
38. *Ego misi vos metere quod vos non laborastis: alii laboraverunt, et vos in labores eorum introistis.*	"*Others have laboured,*" viz., Moses, the Patriarchs and Prophets, toiled hard in instructing and enlightening a stiff-necked people, to prepare them for Jesus and His law, at great personal risks and sacrifice; so did the Baptist, not to speak of

Commentary.

His own labours and privations, and fructifying graces, so abundantly tendered.

"*And you have entered into their labours,*" by perfecting their teaching, and bringing men to heaven, the abiding fruit of eternal life, to be enjoyed in common by all. Of this the spiritual toilers of old could not be partakers, until they would enjoy it in common with us (Heb xi. 40).

He thus encourages them to labour hard in the work of saving souls. The harvest is to be plentiful; the reward, not far distant By His death, He is soon to fling open the gates of heaven, so long closed against the human race.

39. "*Believed in Him,*" as the Christ, or Messiah, on account of the testimony of the woman whom, all things considered, viz., the absence of motive to deceive, the confession of her own guilty and sinful life, etc., they prudently regarded as truthful, and a safe medium of conveying Divine revelation. To this was added, the powerful influence of God's grace. Not unlikely, she told them of His declaration, that He was the Messiah or Christ. They believed on account of the assertion of the woman, before they came out of the city to see Him.

40. His brief stay was, no doubt, very interesting to them. Possibly, He may have baptized them through His disciples. If He tarried longer among them, the Jews would calumniate Him, as preaching to the Samaritans and not to the Jews, to whom He was promised.

41. His own preaching drew a greater number of believers, than had already embraced the faith, owing to the testimony of the woman.

42. "*Now we believe,*" refers to the portion of the Samaritans who had already believed in the testimony of the woman; but, not to those who believed, only after seeing and hearing our Lord.

"*Not for thy saying*" only. Their faith was strengthened and corroborated by the teaching of our Lord. "*The Saviour of the world,*" not of the Jews only, or any other section of men; but, of the entire human race sunk in sin, and in need of a Redeemer. This one article of faith comprised everything else.

Text.

39. *Now of that city many of the Samaritans believed in him, for the word of the woman giving testimony: He told me all things whatsoever I have done.*

39. *Ex civitate autem illa multi crediderunt in eum, Samaritanorum, propter verbum mulieris testimonium perhibentis: Quia dixit mihi omnia quaecumque feci.*

40. *So when the Samaritans were come to him, they desired him that he would tarry there. And he abode there two days.*

40. *Cum venissent ergo ad illum Samaritani, rogaverunt eum ut ibi maneret. Et mansit ibi duos dies.*

41. *And many more believed in him because of his own word.*

41. *Et multo plures crediderunt in eum propter sermonem ejus.*

42. *And they said to the woman: We now believe, not for thy saying: for we ourselves have heard him, and know that this is indeed the Saviour of the world.*

42. *Et mulieri dicebant: Quia jam non propter tuam loquelam credimus: ipsi enim audivimus, et scimus quia hic est vere Salvator mundi.*

Text.	Commentary.
43. *Now after two days he departed thence ; and went into Galilee.* 43. *Post duos autem dies exiit inde: et abiit in Galilæam.*	43. He prosecuted His intended journey through the Province of Samaria into Galilee (*v.* 3), which was interrupted by His short stay in Samaria.
44. *For Jesus himself gave testimony that a prophet hath no honour in his own country :* 44. *Ipse enim Jesus testimonium perhibuit quia Propheta in sua patria honorem non habet.*	44. The force of "*for*," is seen by supplying the narrative omitted here, and recorded by the other Evangelists, viz., that our Lord passed by Nazareth, His native place, and came to Capharnaum. (Matthew. iv. 13). "*A Prophet,*" etc. (See Matthew xiii. 57.) Some connect it with the preceding, giving "*for*," the meaning of *although*, as if He said : "*Although*, Jesus Himself gave testimony by word and act, "*that a Prophet had no honour*," etc., He may still anticipate some good results from His visit, owing to the miracles they saw Him perform, during the Festival, in Jerusalem. How these are warranted in giving "*for*," the meaning of *although*, cannot well be seen. It seems somewhat arbitrary. Others, among them, Patrizzi, say, "*His own country*," was Judea ; and hence, He left it for Galilee. The former interpretation is warranted by the history given in St. Matthew (ix.), and we learn from St. Matthew xiii., Luke iv., that our Lord uttered the words, "*a Prophet*," etc., in reference to Nazareth.
45. *And when he was come into Galilee, the Galileans received him, having seen all the things he had done at Jerusalem on the festival day : for they also went to the festival day.* 45. *Cum ergo venisset in Galilæam, exceperunt eum Galilæi, cum omnia vidissent quæ fecerat Jerosolymis in die festo: et ipsi enim venerant ad diem festum.*	45. The Galileans received Him with great honour, as they witnessed His miracles, on the Festival day at Jerusalem. In this the simple and confiding faith of the Samaritans is tacitly commended, who believed, without seeing any miracles. Whether the Galileans *believed* in Him, is not stated here. They received Him, however, with honour. But the Jews, although witnessing His miracles, neither received Him with honour nor believed in Him. Who these Galileans were, the Evangelist does not mention.
46. *He came again therefore into Cana of Galilee, where he made the water wine. And there was a certain ruler whose son was sick at Capharnaum.* 46. *Venit ergo iterum in Cana Galilæa, ubi fecit aquam vinum. Et erat quidam regulus, cujus filius infirmabatur Capharnaum.*	46. "*He came again therefore.*" "*Therefore,*" because He passed by His native place, Nazareth ; He came again to the place nearest it, as more convenient for remaining ; and, moreover, He was there among His friends and relatives. Allusion is made to the miracle performed there, to distinguish it from another Cana, which was far off. "*A certain ruler whose son was sick,*" etc. Several conjectures are hazarded, as to who he was. They are, however, only conjectures. Some say, he was of the Royal family, a connexion of Herod Antipas, or, one of the officers of his Court, whether related to him or not. At all events, he must have been a man of

Commentary

high station and wealth, having a retinue of servants (*v.* 51). Most likely, he was a Jew, as the reproaches commonly addressed to the Jews, "*unless you see,*" etc. (*v.* 48) would seem to indicate. Our Lord addresses reproaches to the Jews, for their stubborn unbelief, more frequently than to the Gentiles.

47. The fame of our Lord's miracle wrought at Cana, and of those performed by Him at Jerusalem during the festival days, rendered Him celebrated all over the country. This ruler, who resided ordinarily at Capharnaum, which was not far from Cana, on hearing of His arrival, besought Him "*to come down*"—the site of Capharnaum was lower than Cana—"*and heal his son.*" If this man had any faith at all, it must have been very imperfect and weak, indeed. How different from the Centurion, on another occasion, "*on the point of death,*" probably despaired of by the physicians, he was so far gone that healing art could be but of little use to him.

48. Our Lord's preaching ought to be sufficient to beget faith in him. He also had the testimony of the Baptist, which should be sufficient, especially as the Jews regarded him as sent by God; nay, even some regarded him as the Messiah. Our Lord Himself worked several miracles; and, still, the Galileans were slow in believing; and the Jews utterly rejected and despised Him. On this account it is, that He reproaches the ruler, and the Jews, to whom He refers in addressing Him—hence, using the plural—that unles they *see*—it won't do to *hear* of—a constant succession of signs and wonders, they cannot bring themselves to believe. Our Lord speaks of them not believing, which one would think to be foreign to the object the ruler had in view—viz., the cure of his son; He does so, because, all His miracles, all His works of beneficence, such as curing the bodies of the infirm, had for object a greater work of mercy still; viz., to cure their souls and remove the still greater evil of spiritual blindness, nay, spiritual death, from which He meant to resuscitate them by His all-powerful grace.

49. The ruler althogether engrossed with the concern for his dying son, again urges his request to our Lord to go down and save his son from death. His faith, if he had any, must be very weak; he had no idea, that our Lord's power would restore his son, absent as well as present, and he would seem also to think, that if his son once breathed his last, our Lord could not raise him up from the dead.

50. Our Lord, seeing that His just reproaches had no effect on the ruler, now attaches him to Himself, and induces him to embrace the faith by acts of kindness. He tells him, "*Go,*" and be of good

Text

47. *He having heard that Jesus was come from Judea into Galilee, went to him, and prayed him to come down and heal his son: for he was at the point of death.*

47. *Hic cum audisset quia Jesus adveniret a Judea in Galilæam, abiit ad eum, et rogabat eum ut descenderet, et sanaret filium ejus: incipiebat enim mori.*

48. *Jesus therefore said to him Unless you see signs and wonders you believe not.*

48. *Dixit ergo Jesus ad eum: Nisi signa et prodigia videritis, non creditis.*

49. *The ruler saith to him: Lord, come down before that my son die.*

49. *Dicit ad eum regulus: Domine, descende prius quam moriatur filius meus.*

50. *Jesus saith to him: Go thy way, thy son liveth. The man believed the word which*

Text.	Commentary.
Jesus said to him, and went his way.	cheer, that at that very moment, his son was perfectly restored to health; thus, curing him without being present.
50. *Dicit ei Jesus: Vade, filius tuus vivit. Credidit homo sermoni, quem dixit ei Jesus, et ibat.*	"*The man believed the word which Jesus said to him.*" It is not said he believed in our Lord, but only, knowing our Lord to be a holy, truthful man, he believed that He announced what was true. But he did not seem to believe that our Lord had Himself, by His omnipotent power, effected the cure. This he afterwards discovered after minutely questioning his servants. The result was, that he fully believed (as in verse 53) in our Lord and His Divine mission. The belief referred to in this verse is merely belief in the specific assurance of our Lord, not in His Divinity.
51. *And as he was going down, his servants met him: and they brought word, saying, that his son lived.* 51. *Jam autem eo descendente, servi occurrerunt ei, et nunciaverunt dicentes quia filius ejus viveret.* 52. *He asked therefore of them the hour, wherein he grew better. And they said to him, Yesterday at the seventh hour the fever left him.* 52. *Interrogabat ergo horam ab eis, in qua melius habuerit Et dixerunt ei: Quia heri hora septima reliquit eum febris.*	51, 52. His servants hastened to meet their master in order to convey the joyous tidings, and save our Lord the trouble of going down. The ruler, remembering that our Lord has informed him of his son's recovery, was anxious to know from his servants the precise time at which this took place. "*Yesterday at the seventh hour.*" This corresponds with one o'clock after midday, as the Jews had, by this time, adopted the Roman division of time. Their days commenced at sunrise; their night, at sunset; and were divided into twelve equal parts, which varied in length, according to the season of the year. In summer, the hours were longer in day time; shorter, in winter.
53. *The father therefore knew that it was at the same hour, that Jesus said to him, Thy son liveth; and himself believed and his whole house.* 53. *Cognovit ergo pater, quia illa hora erat, in qua dixit ei Jesus: Filius tuus vivit: et credidit ipse, et domus ejus tota.*	53. Finding the time of his son's recovery to correspond exactly with the time fixed by our Lord, the ruler at once recognised our Lord's power and Divinity in the miraculous cure of his son, though absent; and aided by Divine grace, he, with his entire household, embraced the faith and believed in our Lord's Divinity. It is but of trifling importance, to ascertain the hour at which his servants met the ruler on his way home.
54. *This is again the second miracle that Jesus did, when he was come out of Judea into Galilee.* 54. *Hoc iterum secundum signum fecit Jesus, cum venisset a Judæa in Galilæam.*	54. This miracle Jesus performed, it being His second, on His return again from Judea to Galilee. He performed several miracles in *Judea* (c. ii. 26). But, this was His second in Galilee, the conversion of water being his first (c. ii. 1–6). The Greek reading is confused. The above is the meaning. "*Again,*" is to be joined with, "*when He was come out again,*" on His second return from Judea to Galilee.

CHAPTER V.

1 *After these things was a festival day of the Jews, and Jesus went up to Jerusalem.*
2 *Now there is at Jerusalem a pond, called Probatica, which in Hebrew is named Bethsaida, having five porches.*
3 *In these lay a great multitude of sick, of blind, of lame, of withered, waiting for the moving of the water.*
4 *And an Angel of the lord descended at certain times into the pond; and the water was moved. And he that went down first into the pond after the motion of the water, was made whole of whatsoever infirmity he lay under.*
5 *And there was a certain man there that had been eight and thirty years under his infirmity.*
6 *Him when Jesus had seen lying, and knew that he had been now a long time, he saith to him: Wilt thou be made whole?*
7 *The infirm man answered him: Sir, I have no man, when the water is troubled, to put me into the pond. For whilst I am coming, another goeth down before me.*
8 *Jesus saith to him: Arise, take up thy bed, and walk.*
9 *And immediately the man was made whole: and he took up his bed and walked. And it was the sabbath that day.*
10 *The Jews therefore said to him that was healed: It is the sabbath, it is not lawful for thee to take up thy bed.*
11 *He answered them: He that made me whole, he said to me: Take up thy bed, and walk.*
12 *They asked him therefore: Who is that man who said to thee: Take up thy bed, and walk?*
13 *But he who was healed, knew not who it was. For Jesus went aside from the multitude standing in the place.*
14 *Afterwards Jesus findeth him in the temple, and saith to him: Behold thou art made whole: sin no more, lest some worse thing happen to thee.*
15 *The man went his way, and told the Jews that it was Jesus made him whole.*
16 *Therefore did the Jews persecute Jesus, because he did these things on the sabbath.*
17 *But Jesus answered them: My father worketh until now; and I work.*
18 *Hereupon therefore the Jews sought the more to kill him, because he did not only break the sabbath, but also said God was his Father, making himself equal to God. Then Jesus answered, and said to them:*
19 *Amen, amen, I say unto you: the Son cannot do anything of himself, but what he seeth the Father doing: for what things soever he doth, these the Son also doth in like manner.*
20 *For the Father loveth the Son, and sheweth him all things which himself doth: and greater works than these will he shew him, that you may wonder.*
21 *For as the Father raiseth up the dead, and giveth life: so the Son also giveth life to whom he will.*
22 *For neither doth the Father judge any man: but hath given all judgment to the Son.*

23 *That all men may honour the Son, as they honour the Father. He who honoureth not the Son, honoureth not the Father who hath sent him.*

24 *Amen, amen, I say unto you that he who heareth my word, and believeth him that sent me, hath life everlasting; and cometh not into judgment, but is passed from death to life.*

25 *Amen, amen, I say unto you, that the hour cometh, and now is, when the dead shall hear the voice of the Son of God, and they that hear shall live.*

26 *For as the Father hath life in himself; so he hath given to the Son also to have life in himself:*

27 *And he hath given him power to do judgment, because he is the son of man.*

28 *Wonder not at this, for the hour cometh wherein all that are in the graves shall hear the voice of the Son of God.*

29 *And they that have done good things, shall come forth unto the resurrection of life: but they that have done evil, unto the resurrection of judgment.*

30 *I cannot of myself do anything. As I hear, so I judge: and my judgment is just, because I seek not my own will, but the will of him that sent me.*

31 *If I bear witness of myself, my witness is not true.*

32 *There is another that beareth witness of me: and I know that the witness which he witnesseth of me is true.*

33 *You sent to John: and he gave testimony to the truth.*

34 *But I receive not testimony from man: but I say these things that you may be saved.*

35 *He was a burning and a shining light. And you were willing for a time to rejoice in his light.*

36 *But I have a greater testimony than that of John. For the works which the Father hath given me to perfect: the works themselves, which I do, give testimony of me, that the Father hath sent me.*

37 *And the Father himself, who hath sent me, hath given testimony of me: neither have you heard his voice at any time, nor seen his shape.*

38 *And you have not his word abiding in you: for whom he hath sent, him you believe not.*

39 *Search the scriptures, for you think in them to have life everlasting: and the same are they that give testimony of me:*

40 *And you will not come to me that you may have life.*

41 *I receive not glory from men.*

42 *But I know you, that you have not the love of God in you.*

43 *I am come in the name of my Father, and you receive me not: if another shall come in his own name, him you will receive.*

44 *How can you believe, who receive glory one from another: and the glory which is from God alone, you do not seek?*

45 *Think not that I will accuse you to the Father. There is one that accuseth you, Moses, in whom you trust.*

46 *For if you did believe Moses, you would perhaps believe me also. For he wrote of me.*

47 *But if you do not believe his writings: how will you believe my words?*

CAPUT V.

1 *Post hæc erat dies festus Judæorum, et ascendit Jesus Jerosolymam.*

2 *Est autem Jerosolymis Probatica piscina, quæ cognominatur Hebraice Bethsaida, quinque porticus habens.*

3 *In his jacebat multitudo magna languentium, cæcorum, claudorum, aridorum expectantium aquæ motum.*

4 *Angelus autem Domini descendebat secundum tempus in piscinam: et movebatur aqua. Et qui prior descendisset in piscinam post motionem aquæ, sanus fiebat a quacumque detinebatur infirmitate.*

5 *Erat autem quidam homo ibi triginta et octo annos habens in infirmitate sua.*

6 *Hunc cum vidisset Jesus jacentem, et cognovisset quia jam multum tempus haberet, dicit ei: Vis sanus fieri?*

7 *Respondit ei languidus: Domine, hominem non habeo, ut cum turbata fuerit aqua, mittat me in piscinam: dum venio enim ego, alius ante me descendit.*

8 *Dicit ei Jesus: Surge, tolle grabatum tuum, et ambula.*

9 *Et statim sanus factus est homo ille: et sustulit grabatum suum, et ambulabat. Erat autem sabbatum in die illo.*

10 *Dicebant ergo Judæi illi, qui sanatus fuerat: Sabbatum est, non licet tibi tollere grabatum tuum.*

11 *Respondit eis: Qui me sanum fecit, ille mihi dixit: Tolle grabatum tuum, et ambula.*

12 *Interrogaverunt ergo eum: Quis est ille homo, qui dixit tibi, Tolle grabatum tuum, et ambula.*

13 *Is autem, qui sanus fuerat effectus, nesciebat quis esset. Jesus enim declinavit a turba constituta in loco.*

14 *Postea invenit eum Jesus in templo, et dixit illi: Ecce sanus factus es: jam noli peccare, ne deterius tibi aliquid contingat.*

15 *Abiit ille homo, et nuntiavit Judæis quia Jesus esset, qui fecit eum sanum.*

16 *Propterea persequebantur Judæi Jesum, quia hæc faciebat in sabbato.*

17 *Jesus autem respondit eis: Pater meus usque modo operatur, et ego operor.*

18 *Propterea ergo magis quærebant eum Judæi interficere: quia non solum solvebat sabbatum, sed et patrem suum dicebat Deum, æqualem se faciens Deo. Respondit itaque Jesus, et dixit eis:*

19 *Amen, amen dico vobis: non potest Filius a se facere quidquam, nisi quod viderit Patrem facientem: quæcumque enim ille fecerit, hæc et Filius similiter facit.*

20 *Pater enim diligit Filium, et omnia demonstrat ei, quæ ipse facit: et majora his demonstrabit ei opera, ut vos miremini.*

21 *Sicut enim Pater suscitat mortuos, et vivificat: sic et Filius, quos vult, vivificat.*

22 *Neque enim Pater judicat quemquam: sed omne judicium dedit Filio,*

23 *Ut omnes honorificent Filium, sicut honorificant Patrem: qui non honorificat Filium, non honorificat Patrem, qui misit illum.*

24 *Amen, amen dico vobis, quia qui verbum meum audit, et credit ei, qui misit me, habet vitam æternam, et in judicium non venit, sed transiit a morte in vitam.*

25 *Amen, amen dico vobis, quia venit hora, et nunc est, quando mortui audient vocem Filii Dei: et qui audierint, vivent.*

26 *Sicut enim Pater habet vitam in semetipso: sic dedit et Filio habere vitam in semetipso:*

27 *Et potestatem dedit ei judicium facere, quia Filius hominis est.*

28 *Nolite mirari hoc, quia venit hora, in qua omnes, qui in monumentis sunt, audient vocem Filii Dei:*

29 *Et procedent qui bona fecerunt, in resurrectionem vitæ: qui vero mala egerunt, in resurrectionem judicii.*

30 *Non possum ego a meipso facere quidquam. Sicut audio, judico: et judicium meum justum est: quia non quæro voluntatem meam, sed voluntatem ejus, qui misit me.*

31 *Si ego testimonium perhibeo de meipso, testimonium meum non est verum.*

32 *Alius est, qui testimonium perhibet de me: et scio quia verum est testimonium, quod perhibet de me.*

33 *Vos misistis ad Joannem: et testimonium perhibuit veritati.*

34 *Ego autem non ab homine testimonium accipio: sed hæc dico ut vos salvi sitis.*

35 *Ille erat lucerna ardens, et lucens. Vos autem voluistis ad horam exultare in luce ejus.*

36 *Ego autem habeo testimonium majus Joanne. Opera enim, quæ dedit mihi Pater ut perficiam ea: ipsa opera, quæ ego facio, testimonium perhibent de me, quia Pater misit me:*

37 *Et qui misit me Pater, ipse testimonium perhibuit de me: neque vocem ejus umquam audistis, neque speciem ejus vidistis.*

38 *Et verbum ejus non habetis in vobis manens: quia quem misit ille, huic vos non creditis.*

39 *Scrutamini Scripturas, quia vos putatis in ipsis vitam æternam habere: et illæ sunt, quæ testimonium perhibent de me:*

40 *Et non vultis venire ad me ut vitam habeatis.*

41 *Claritatem ab hominibus non accipio.*

42 *Sed cognovi vos, quia dilectionem Dei non habetis in vobis.*

43 *Ego veni in nomine Patris mei, et non accipitis me: si alius venerit in nomine suo, illum accipietis.*

44 *Quomodo vos potestis credere, qui gloriam ab invicem accipitis: et gloriam quæ a solo Deo est, non quæritis?*

45 *Nolite putare quia ego accusaturus sim vos apud Patrem: est qui accusat vos Moyses, in quo vos speratis.*

46 *Si enim crederetis Moysi, crederetis forsitan et mihi: de me enim ille scripsit.*

47 *Si autem illius litteris non creditis: quomodo verbis meis credetis?*

ANALYSIS.

In this chapter we have an account of a miracle wrought by our Divine Redeemer at Jerusalem in the cure of an infirm man, who had been suffering under his infirmity for eight and thirty years, after having waited in vain for the miraculous cures witnessed from time to time, at the pond of Probatica (1–9).

The attempts on the part of the Jews, as was their wont, to arraign our Lord for a violation of the Sabbath, and their persecution of Him (10–16). Our Lord justifies His mode of acting, by declaring His Divinity, His identity of nature, and operation with His Father, who conferred on Him all power, especially the power to judge the world, and by His all-powerful voice to raise the dead from their graves, and pass upon them, an immutable judgment, entailing everlasting misery or happiness (16–30).

He refers to several witnesses of His Divinity, the Baptist, His own works—the testimony of His Father Himself, and, finally, the testimony of Scripture, of which they boasted so much (30–39).

He charges them with vain glory and pride, the great obstacles to their embracing the faith (40–44).
He charges them with paying no attention to the writings of Moses, who bore testimony of Him (44–47).

Commentary.

1. *"After these things,"* etc. The Evangelist here passes over several occurrences that took place in connexion with our Lord in Galilee; His many miracles, the vocation of the Apostles, the sermon on the Mount, etc., recorded by St. Matthew (iv.–xii.).

"A festival." It is a subject of controversy among Commentators, what festival is here referred to. Some understand it of the Feast of *Purim* or *Lots*, instituted by Mardochai (Book of Esther ix. 17); others, of the Feast of Tabernacles; others, with St. Chrysostom, Cyril, etc., of the Feast of Pentecost; others, with St. Ireneus, etc., whose opinion seems the more probable, of the Pasch, the Great Festival, *by excellence*. This corresponds best with the time referred to in iv. 25, where our Lord speaks of the harvest being four months off. Now, the harvest occurred between the Pasch and Pentecost. Hence, the Pasch was the next great festival. It is generally held by the learned, that our Lord attended four Paschs after his baptism, during the three years and a half of His public mission. The first (ii. 13); the second, here; the third (iv. 6); and the last (xix. 14). If the festival referred to here were not the Pasch, he would have attended only *three* Paschs. To these reasons may be added, that the article is prefixed in the Greek ἡ ἑορτη, to indicate that there was question of *the* feast, the greatest of the three, which were annually celebrated at Jerusalem. But even were the article omitted, it would not militate against this opinion, as it is omitted in several places, where the Pasch is referred to (xix. 14; Matthew xxvii. 15; Mark xv. 6; Luke xxiii. 17).

Our Lord went up to Jerusalem on the occasion of each recurring festival, to show that far from being the enemy of the Law, He was most observant of all its ordinances. He also had in view, to work miracles and deliver His heavenly doctrines, when the people assembled in great crowds at the several festivals.

2. *"A pond called Probatica."* There is reference here to a pool of water, called *"Probatica,"* because it was close to the gate through which the sheep destined for sacrifice passed. According to St. Jerome (*de locis Hebraicis*), the sheep were washed in this pool in preparation for sacrifice. In the ordinary Greek, the reading is, επι τη προβατικη, near the sheep, gate, πυλη, is understood. That προβατικη, refers to a *gate*, may be seen from Nehemias or 2 Esdras (iii. 1), where there is reference to this flock-gate built by the Priests. *"A pond"*—κολυμβηθρα. It was of sufficient dimensions to form a swimming ground.

Text.

1. *After these things was a festival day of the Jews, and Jesus went up to Jerusalem.*

1. *Post hæc erat festus Judæorum, et ascendit Jesus Jerosolymam.*

2. *Now there is at Jerusalem a pond, called Probatica, which in Hebrew is named Bethsaida, having five porches.*

2. *Est autem Jerosolymis Probatica piscina, quæ cognominatur Hebraice Bethsaida, quinque porticus habens.*

Text.	Commentary.

"*Which in Hebrew is named Bethsaida.*" The common reading is *Bethesda*.

"*Having five porches,*" fronting the pool, and roofed, as a protection against the sun and rain.

3. In these lay a great multitude of sick, of blind, of lame, of withered, waiting for the moving of the water.

3. "*Waiting for the movement,*" etc. The reason is assigned in the next verse, because the time of such movement was uncertain.

3. In his jacebat multitudo magna languentium, excorum, claudorum, aridorum expectantium aquae motum.

4. And an Angel of the Lord descended at certain times into the pond; and the water was moved. And he that went down first into the pond after the motion of the water, was made whole of whatsoever infirmity he lay under.

4. Angelus autem Domini descendebat secundum tempus in piscinam: et movebatur aqua. Et qui prior descendisset in piscinam post motionem aquae, sanus fiebat a quacumque detinebatur infirmitate.

4. The authenticity of this verse, owing to its having been omitted in several versions and MSS., has been called in question by the Anabaptists. They, moreover, chiefly rely on this circumstance, that no mention has been made of it by Josephus. But, the preponderance of evidence from versions and the Fathers is in favour of its authenticity. The context requires it: otherwise, the answer of the man (*v.* 7), would be unintelligible. As for Josephus, he was the enemy of Christianity, and would not speak of this pool, as it would seem to corroborate the miracle wrought by our Redeemer. The same author passes over several other matters (*v. g.*), the coming of the Magi, the infanticide, etc. Surely, the positive description by St. John ought to carry with it greater weight than the omission on the part of Josephus.

"*The Angel of the Lord.*" "*Lord*" is not in the Greek. The sense, however, is the same, as, doubtless, there is question of an Angel sent by God. In the Greek we have, "*For, an Angel descended,*" etc., giving a reason for the foregoing "*at certain times,*" at some unknown time. How often in the year cannot be ascertained, as we have no information respecting the pool anywhere else save here.

"*And the water was troubled.*" The more probable reading is in the active form, και εταρασσε το υδωρ, *and he troubled the water.*

"*And he who went down first,*" etc. Besides this statement of the Evangelist, the fact of invalids of every description (*v.* 3), remaining in the porches would seem to show, that the healing power of the water was not confined to any one sort of disease; that it had an universal efficacy, extending to diseases of every description, which would show the miraculous and supernatural character of the cure, which is corroborated by the circumstance that on every occasion, the cure was confined to the *first* who entered, after the movement of the waters, and that, *immediately* and *invariably*.

Even if these waters had a natural curative efficacy, this would not militate against the truth of the Gospel narrative, as the Angel

ST. JOHN, CHAP. V.

Commentary.

might invisibly use such natural curative power to impart to it, on occasions, supernatural efficacy also.

The Evangelist refers to this pool, etc., by way of preparing us for the subsequent history of the miracle wrought by our Blessed Redeemer.

5. "*Under his infirmity*," generally supposed to be paralysis. It is not stated, how long He lay in the porch.

8. Our Lord's words here were not only expressive; but, practical and effective of what He wished.

9. The intervening verses need no explanation.

10. The chief men of influence who met Him carrying His bed, said to Him, "*It is not lawful for thee to take thy bed.*" (Jeremias xvii. 21: "Take heed to your souls, and carry no burdens on the Sabbath day," etc.) (See Matthew xii. 6, 7.)

Text.

5. *And there was a certain man there that had been eight and thirty years under his infirmity.*

5. *Erat autem quidam homo ibi triginta et octo annos habens in infirmitate sua.*

6. *Him when Jesus had seen lying, and knew that he had been now a long time, he saith to him: Wilt thou be made whole?*

6. *Hunc cum vidisset Jesus jacentem, et cognovisset quia jam multum tempus haberet, dicit ei: Vis sanus fieri?*

7. *The infirm man answered him: Sir, I have no man, when the water is troubled, to put me into the pond. For whilst I am coming, another goeth down before me.*

7. *Respondit ei languidus: Domine, hominem non habeo, ut cum turbata fuerit aqua, mittat me in piscinam: dum venio enim ego, alius ante me descendit.*

8. *Jesus saith to him: Arise, take up thy bed, and walk.*

8. *Dicit ei Jesus: Surge, tolle grabatum tuum, et ambula.*

9. *And immediately the man was made whole: and he took up his bed, and walked: And it was the sabbath that day.*

9. *Et statim sanus factus est homo ille: et sustulit grabatum suum, et ambulabat. Erat autem sabbatum in die illo.*

10. *The Jews therefore said to him that was healed: It is the sabbath, it is not lawful for thee to take up thy bed.*

10. *Dicebant ergo Judæi illi, qui sanatus fuerat: Sabbatum est, non licet tibi tollere grabatum tuum.*

11. *He answered them: He that made me whole, he said to me: Take up thy bed, and walk.*

11. *Respondit eis: Qui me sanum fecit, ille mihi dixit: Tolle grabatum tuum, et ambula.*

12. *They asked him therefore: Who is that man who said to thee: Take up thy bed, and walk?*

12. *Interrogaverunt ergo eum: Quis est ille homo, qui dixit tibi: Tolle grabatum tuum, et ambula.*

13. *But he who was healed, knew not who it was. For Jesus went aside from the multitude standing in the place.*

13. *Is autem, qui sanus fuerat effectus, nesciebat quis esset. Jesus enim declinavit a turba constituta in loco.*

Text.	Commentary.
14. *Afterwards Jesus findeth him in the temple, and saith to him: Behold thou art made whole: sin no more, lest some worse thing happen to thee.* 14. *Postea invenit eum Jesus in templo, et dixit illi: Ecce sanus factus es: jam noli peccare, ne deterius tibi aliquid contingat.*	14. "*Sin no more*," etc. From this it would appear his infirmity was the punishment of sin. Our Lord also in this showed His Omniscience. He knew the cause from which the man's infirmity had sprung. Hence, in some cases, diseases are the punishment of sin. In other cases, God sends diseases to test His servants, to try their patience; thus to increase their merit and save them from sin, by chastening them in this life, as an antidote against sin.
15. *The man went his way, and told the Jews that it was Jesus who had made him whole.* 15. *Abiit ille homo, et nunciavit Judæis quia Jesus esset, qui fecit eum sanum.*	15. As it is incredible that this man would mean, in giving this information, to betray his benefactor, who cured him of his inveterate disease of soul and body, one being the effect of the other, Commentators, in general, hold that he did this out of a feeling of gratitude, to make known and proclaim the glory of his benefactor, and possibly, with a view of making known to others labouring under bodily distempers, to what source they might profitably have recourse, for the recovery of bodily health. St. Chrysostom observes, that in informing the Jews, the man made no mention of the charge preferred against our Lord by the Jews, of His having told him to take up his bed on the Sabbath day. He only mentions the act of beneficence; or the cure effected. "*It was Jesus who made him whole.*"
16. *Therefore did the Jews persecute Jesus, because he did these things on the sabbath.* 16. *Propterea persequebantur Judæi Jesum, quia hæc faciebat in sabbato.*	16. "*Therefore did the Jews*," especially the Scribes and Pharisees, "*persecute Jesus.*" Some Greek copies have, "*and sought to kill Him.*" They make this apparent violation of the letter of the Law, a pretext; the real cause being envy, on account of the glory our Lord received, and His denunciation of their crimes and hypocrisy, which affected them the more, as they affected such sanctity of life.
17. *But Jesus answered them: My Father worketh until now; and I work.* 17. *Jesus autem respondit eis: Pater meus usque modo operatur, et ego operor.*	17. The Evangelist enumerates, without expressing it, that the Jews came to our Lord, after being informed by the sick man, that it was He who worked the cure, and charged Him with a violation of the Sabbath. Hence, in reply, He defends His conduct. On other occasions, He defends His action, in like cases, on human grounds, and adduces reasons from human examples, among the rest that of David (Matthew xii. 3, 4). Here, He defends His action on higher grounds, viz., on the ground of His Divinity, of His equality and identity in nature with the Eternal Father. He says, "My *Father,*" not OUR Father, since the paternity of which He speaks no one else had in common with Him. *They* are the *adopted* sons, *He,* the *natural* Son of God. "*Worketh until now.*" As if He said: you charge Me with violating the Sabbath, which was instituted in commemoration and celebration of God's

Commentary

rest on the seventh day, after having, on the six preceding days, perfected the works of creation. Now, My Father did not rest on the seventh day, save as regards the creation of new species. But, He always continues to work, "*and works until now,*" even on the Sabbath, in preserving, holding together, conserving creation, in governing the world, in moving the heavens, in nourishing and feeding every creature—a work by no means servile, but truly benevolent. Were He to withdraw His protecting hand, all creation would crumble. Hence, His work did not cease, on the seventh day. On His conserving Power, every creature depends.

"*And I work.*" "*And,*" in like manner; I, who am His eternal, consubstantial Son, work jointly with Him. As well, then, might you accuse the Eternal Father of violating the Sabbath, as accuse Me. As the Father is exempt from the Sabbatical law; so, am I, His Eternal Son.

18. "*Hereupon, therefore, the Jews sought the more to kill Him.*" The Jews were anxious to put our Lord to death, on the pretext of having violated the Sabbath. But now they were stimulated the more to kill Him; "*but also said God was His Father,*" making Himself not only God's ADOPTED Son, like the saints and just; but, His *natural* Son, "*My Father.*"

"*Making Himself equal to God,*" as His natural, consubstantial Son, who works not only after His example, but conjointly with Him. "*And I work,*" "*and*" meaning, I work conjointly with Him. Hence, according to them, He was guilty of the shocking crime of blasphemy, which the Law punished with death (Leviticus xxiv. 16).

19. Far from repudiating the conclusion arrived at by the Jews, viz., that He made Himself equal with God, He rather confirms it.

The words, "*Amen, amen,*" show the solemn importance of the statement to which they are prefixed.

"*The Son cannot do any thing of Himself, but what He sees the Father doing.*" In this our Lord proves that in curing on the Sabbath day—a work of mercy—He did not violate the Sabbath any more than the Father, who still works, violated it: nor can the Son do anything contrary to what the Father does. From this follows unity and identity of operation in the Father and the Son. Both work together. What one does, the other does. The Son does nothing of Himself; because, owing to unity of operation, the Son does nothing without the Father, nor does the Father act without the Son. Hence, the words imply no imbecility in the Son, any more than in the Father; because, both operate conjointly and inseparably.

Our Lord speaks of His Divine nature. For, as man, even as

Text

18. *Hereupon therefore the Jews sought the more to kill him, because he did not only break the sabbath, but also said God was his Father, making himself equal to God.*

18. *Propterea ergo magis quærebant eum Judæi interficere: quia non solum solvebat sabbatum, sed et patrem suum dicebat Deum, æqualem se faciens Deo.*

19. *Then Jesus answered, and said to them: Amen, amen. I say unto you: the Son cannot do anything of himself, but what he seeth the Father doing: for what things soever he doth, these the Son also doth in like manner.*

19. *Respondit itaque Jesus, et dixit eis: Amen, amen dico vobis: non potest Filius a se facere quidquam, nisi quod viderit Pat em facientem: quæcumque enim ille fecerit, hæc et Filius similiter facit.*

Text.	Commentary.
	man God, He does some things which the Father doth not (*v. g.*), pray, walk on the waters, etc. The words, "*sees the Father doing*," imply no dependence or imperfection. They only indicate the relation of Divine origin in the eternal generation of the Son from the Father, as His eternally begotten Word. "*Videndo enim natus est et nascendo videt.*"— "*Videre est accipere Divinam Cognitionem.*"—St. Augustine. "*For whatever things He doth,*" etc. The Jews preferred a twofold charge against Him, viz.: the violation of the Sabbath, and making Himself equal to God. The former charge He refutes in the preceding words; far from denying the latter, He proves it by declaring in the most general, unexceptionable terms, that every thing done by the Father is done by the Son "*in like manner.*"
20. *For the Father loveth the Son, and sheweth him all things which himself doth: and greater works than these will he shew him, that you may wonder.* 20. *Pater enim diligit Filium, et omnia demonstrat ei, quæ ipse facit: majora his demonstrabit ei opera, ut vos miremini.*	20. "*For the Father loveth the Son, and sheweth Him all things,*" etc., and communicates to Him all knowledge of doing what He does. In this verse, is assigned a reason why the Son does all the Father doth. It arises from the identity of nature in both. In begetting His son by an eternal generation, the Father singularly loves Him, and communicates to Him, with the fulness of the Divine nature, a knowledge of all He does and conceives in the Divine mind. The word, "*sees,*" in reference to the Son (*v.* 19), and "*shows,*" in reference to the Father, are correlative terms, indicating the communication of the Divine nature from the Father to the Son, and the eternal generation of the Son, in which He receives all things. To "*show,*" on the part of the Father, refers to the generation of the Son, "*to see,*" on the part of the Son, denotes his generation from the Father.—St. Augustine. "*And greater works than these will He show Him, that you may wonder.*" This showing on the part of the Father, was communicated from eternity, in the eternal generation of the Son. The power then given Him was displayed in past times, and lately exhibited in the cure of the paralytic; and it shall be exhibited in future, in works and effects still more brilliant than the cure of the paralytic, such as raising the dead and the exercise of judiciary power over all men. These will be calculated to excite your wonder and astonishment, though they may fail in their intended effect of generating in you the divine virtue of faith. "*Will show Him,*" is used in the future, in accommodation to human ideas, there being question of a future event; but as regards God, with whom every thing is present, it is not *future*. As regards Him, it is eternal, though the result be future in regard to man.
21. *For as the Father raiseth up the dead, and giveth life:*	21. This is one of the greater works, He will show and communicate to His Son, viz., the power of *raising up* the dead and

ST. JOHN, CHAP. V.

Commentary.

restoring them to life. "*As the Father raiseth,*" etc. The present tense, "*raiseth,*" denotes perpetuity.

"*So, the Son giveth life,*" etc. This indicates equality of Divine power. Unlike the Prophets of old, He raises them by His own innate power. To God is it peculiarly attributed, that He alone can restore life to the dead (1 Kings ii). "*Dominus mortificat et vivificat.*" "*Ego, Dominus occidam et ego vivere faciam.*" He adds, "*to whom He wills,*" to show full liberty and independence of power, equal, with the Father, without subjection to Him. The Father always wills to vivify those whom the Son wills to restore to life, there being but *one will* in the Godhead. The Son raised Lazarus to life, and also the only son of the widow of Naim, etc. He will resuscitate all men in the day of judgment, and He will restore to spiritual life sinners who are spiritually dead. He exercises, just as He wills, His spiritual power in their regard.

22. "*For neither doth the Father judge any one,*" etc. This is interpreted by some as expressing another instance of greater works, and in proof of *v*. 20. Although the Father and the Holy Ghost judge equally with the Son, since they cannot abdicate their power; they do not, however, judge visibly. Hence, the Father from eternity communicated to His Son the power of judging all mankind, to be exercised by Him alone visibly. This, too, proves the Divine nature of the Son; since, to God alone does it belong to judge the world in equity. The Father, who ceases not to be judge, will not display the majesty of judge visibly. This He leaves to the Son to be exercised, in time, in the visible nature He was to assume.

Many Commentators of note understand resurrection, or resuscitation to life referred to, of the spiritual life of grace. It is likely, however, that, in this entire passage, as far as *v*. 30, our Lord speaks *principally*, in a literal sense, of the resurrection of the body, as an instance of the greater works referred to, and incidentally, in a mystical or *spiritual sense*, of the spiritual life of grace, which although a no less stupendous exercise of power, is still less perceptible—to encourage us to gain that life, which is a necessary means of securing the glorious life, in the resurrection. For, resurrection to punishment can hardly be called life.

23. "*That all may honour the Son, as they honour the Father.*" In conferring this supreme judiciary power on His Son, which was communicated from eternity, to be exercised by Him visibly, as man God, after His Incarnation, the Father had in view that all men would honour the Son with the same Divine worship which was due to the Father. The Jews, who here refused to honour the Son of God, or acknowledge Him as such, will, on the day of judgment, on seeing the majesty of the man God, the Sovereign Judge,

Text.

so the Son also giveth life to whom he will.

21. *Sicut enim Pater suscitat mortuos, et vivificat : sic et Filius, quos vult, vivificat,*

22. *For neither doth the Father judge any man : but hath given all judgment to the Son.*

22. *Neque enim Pater judicat quemquam : sed omne judicium dedit Filio,*

23. *That all men may honour the Son, as they honour the Father. He who honoureth not the Son, honoureth not the Father who hath sent him.*

23. *Ut omnes honorificent Filium sicut*

Text.

honorificant Patrem: qui non honorificat Filium, non honorificat Patrem, qui misit illum.

Commentary.

be reluctantly forced to honour Him. "*As they honour,*" etc. "*As,*" denotes equality; since it has reference to subjects, who have the same common or Divine nature.

"*He who honoureth not the Son,*" etc. The dishonour shown the Son is also shown the Father, the nature and majesty of both being the same, and their claims to Divine honour being, therefore, equal.

"*Who sent Him,*" not as His servant or inferior; but, as His equal, to be honoured, as such, by men. If he who dishonours the legate, dishonours Him whose legate He is, how much more is this the case when both, as here, are equal. In this, He would seem to censure the Jews, who pretended that they meant to honour God the Father, while withholding due honour from His Son, who, as consubstantial with the Father, is entitled to the same undivided supreme worship and honour due to God alone.

24. *Amen, amen, I say unto you that he who heareth my word, and believeth him that sent me, hath life everlasting; and cometh not into judgment, but is passed from death to life.*

24. *Amen, amen dico vobis, quia qui verbum meum audit, et credit ei, qui misit me, habet vitam æternam, et in judicium non venit, sed transiit a morte in vitam.*

24. "*Amen, amen.*" This repetition of the word shows the great importance of the statement about to be made, "*that he who heareth,*" with a docile heart, in other words, *obeys* "*My word,*" My commandments, both in regard to subjects of faith and morals, "*and believeth Him that sent Me,*" in which is contained belief in our Lord Himself. For, the Father sent His Son to teach the world. Their word is the same, and in this, is also implied the Mystery of the Trinity. For, the Holy Ghost proceeds from the Father and the Son. He who believes in this fundamental truth, and all other truths revealed by God, "*hath life everlasting,*" in an inchoate state here, through grace; and he has a right to eternal life, should he finally persevere in grace and faith.

"*And cometh not,*" will not come—the present is used for the future—"*into judgment,*" shall not be condemned.

"*But is passed from death to life.*" "*Is passed,*" has already, by anticipation, before the time of judgment, passed from the death of the soul, and consequent liability to eternal death induced by sin, to spiritual life by grace, which is the prelude to life everlasting.

"*Is passed,*" may also have a future signification—will surely pass—as if He had already done so—from the death of the body, to the eternal life enjoyed by the saints in heaven.

25. *Amen, amen, I say unto you: that the hour cometh, and now is when the dead shall hear the voice of the Son of God, and they that hear, shall live.*

25. *Amen, amen dico vobis, quia venit hora, et nunc est, quando mortui*

25. Our Lord here refers to the exercise of His Divine power, in the resuscitation which He was soon to accomplish in three particular cases, viz., the son of the widow of Naim, the daughter of the ruler of the Synagogue, and Lazarus. "*The hour cometh, and now is,*" near at hand, before our Lord Himself departed out of life. Others, understand it of the general resurrection, which they say is to occur in "*the last hour,*" or during the religious dispensation, which "*now is.*" For, the period of the Christian religion is

Commentary.

termed in Sacred Scripture, "*the last hour.*" But the words (*v.* 28,) referring to *all* who are in their graves, militates against this opinion; and the Lord refers to this latter event, as a subject of greater wonder. Some understand this of the power exercised in the spiritual resuscitation to a life of grace; because, He says restrictively, "*they who shall hear shall live.*" It may be, He refers to this too. The restrictive clause, "*those who shall hear, shall live,*" may, in the literal sense, also be interpreted, those who shall hear, or, to whom the power of His voice shall be addressed, shall be resuscitated and shall live.

26. "*For, as the Father hath life in Himself,*" being essentially life, the source of all life, which He communicates at will, preserves at will, in all creatures, or takes away at will.

"*So He hath given to the Son also,*" in His eternal generation, "*to have life in* HIMSELF," to be Himself essential life, the source of all life, in every thing that exists, in every thing made by Him. Those therefore, who hear His voice and are called by Him, with a command to arise, will come forth to life.

27. As *God*, He had, from his eternal generation from the Father, essential life, with the power of imparting it to others. As *God man*, appearing visibly in the flesh, in which He vouchsafed to redeem mankind, He received from His Father, who Himself judges no one (*v.* 22), the power which, as *God*, He had from eternity to judge mankind, to be exercised in time.

"*Because He is the Son of man.*" It is on account of His having assumed human nature, that He is constituted judge of mankind; so that those who here below despised Him, may see their judge visibly in majesty. The wicked cannot see Him, in the form of God. The vision of God is withheld from them. Hence, they who maltreated Him (Apoc. i. 7) shall see Him, in the form of man, coming in great power and majesty (Matthew xxvi. 64).

28. "*Wonder not at this,*" viz., at My saying that the Father hath given Me the power of raising the dead at will, and of judging mankind. "*For, the hour cometh,*" is just at hand—(this shall occur at the close of the Gospel dispensation)—when this twofold power shall be exercised by Me. "*All who are in their graves,*" all the dead, whether their ashes are consigned to their graves, or scattered any where else, "*shall hear the voice of the Son of God,*" viz., the Archangel's trumpet, to which the power of rousing the dead shall be imparted by our Lord; hence, called "*The voice of an Archangel.*" (1 Thess. iv. 15, etc.) It is also called "*the trumpet of God,*" "*the last trumpet*" (1 Cor. xv. 52), "*trumpet and a great voice*" (Matthew xxiv. 30).

Text.

audient vocem Filii Dei: et qui audierint, vivent.

26. For as the Father hath life in himself: so he hath given to the Son also to have life in himself:

26. Sicut enim Pater habet vitam in semetipso: sic dedit et Filio habere vitam in semetipso:

27. And he hath given him power to do judgment, because he is the son of man.

27. Et potestatem dedit ei judicium facere, quia Filius hominis est.

28. Wonder not at this, for the hour cometh, wherein all that are in the graves shall hear the voice of the Son of God.

28. Nolite mirari hoc, quia venit hora, in qua omnes, qui in monumentis sunt, audient vocem Filii Dei:

Text.	Commentary.
29. *And they that have done good things, shall come forth unto the resurrection of life; but they that have done evil, unto the resurrection of judgment.*	29. "*Shall come forth*"—from their graves—"*unto the resurrection of life,*" to enter on a life of eternal happiness. "*Resurrection of judgment,*" viz., condemnation to hell's eternal torments, which is contrasted with the "*life*" of the just. That, which is but an eternal dying life, can hardly be called "*life*" on the part of the reprobate. "*They that have done good.*" It is by our *works*, we shall be rewarded or condemned. Hence, faith alone without good works, cannot save us. Oh! how the reprobate would wish for their annihilation? how they must curse the day they were born, "*melius illi, si natus non fuisset.*" What a dread subject for reflection is the last judgment, with all its horrors, which are so vividly depicted for us beforehand by a merciful Saviour, in order to save us from the eternal anguish of the damned.
29. *Et procedent qui bona fecerunt, in resurrectionem vitæ: qui vero mala egerunt, in resurrectionem judicii.*	
30. *I cannot of myself do any thing. As I hear, so I judge; and my judgment is just, because I seek not my own will, but the will of him that sent me.*	30. Having said that He had all power of judging, "*because He is the Son of man,*" He now shows that all His judgments are righteous and just, whether, as *Son of God*, or *Son of man*. For, as God, He can do nothing of Himself alone (v. 19). Every thing He does, as *God*, is done by the Father also. Every thing He does, as *man*, is in accordance with what God wishes. He judges as He "*hears*" his Father judging. This, in reference to his Divinity, regards eternal generation. In reference to His humanity, He judges "*as*" inspired by the Father. "*Hearing*" is the same as "*seeing*" (v. 19). "*My judgment is just,*" as God's judgment must ever be. "*Because I seek not my own will.*" My will, as God, is identical with that of the Father, and My *human* will is ever conformable to the Divine will; hence, when judging, as man God, I judge in accordance with the Divine will, and, therefore, justly.
30. *Non possum ego a meipso facere quidquam. Sicut audio, judico: et judicium meum justum est; quia non quæro voluntatem meam, sed voluntatem ejus, qui misit me.*	
31. *If I bear witness of myself, my witness is not true.*	31. "*My testimony is not true.*" If I am alone in bearing witness regarding myself as the Eternal Son of God, as having received judiciary power to judge the world, etc., my testimony, from a human point of view, or according to the rules of human evidence (since no one would be admitted without other evidence as witness in his own cause), "*is not true,*" worthy of acceptance; nor, from a human point of view, legitimate or beyond suspicion. However, granting this in general for a moment, without admitting it, in My particular case, it does not hold.
31. *Si ego testimonium perhibeo de meipso, testimonium meum non est verum.*	
32. *There is another that beareth witness of me: and I know that the witness which he witnesseth of me is true.*	32. I can appeal to other witnesses both on earth and in Heaven. On earth, to Moses and the Prophets; in heaven, to my Father, who is "*another that beareth testimony of Me.*" This he did at my baptism, declaring Me to be His well-beloved Son.
32. *Alius est, qui testimonium perhibet de me: et scio quia*	"*And I know,*" from the infinite knowledge and science imparted to me from eternity, that the testimony rendered by

Commentary.

Him "*is true,*" undoubted and beyond suspicion. Some Expositors understand, "*another,*" of the Baptist (next verse).

33. Our Lord adduces different testimonies in His own favour. He commences with John the Baptist, although He had still stronger evidence in reserve (verse 36).

"*You sent to John*" (c. i. vv. 19, etc.), whom you regarded as deserving of the highest veneration, as a witness deserving of all credit.

"*And he bore testimony to the truth,*" both in regard to himself, as a "*mere voice,*" etc., and Me, as "*the Lamb of God,*" also: "*This is the Son of God*" (i. 34); thus proclaiming Me to be the promised Messiah.

34. When I appeal to the testimony of John, I do not mean that I require testimony from any man living. I have not done so on my own account, who am the Eternal Son of God, who received glory from my Father, before the world began; by whom John and the Prophets were taught; and from whom they derive all their holiness. It is solely on your account, I adduce his testimony, "*that you may be saved,*" by receiving his testimony regarding Me, "*saved,*" by believing in Me.

35. Lest it might be imagined, that in the foregoing He undervalued John, he adds, "*He* (John) *was a burning and shining light,*" "*a light,*" or rather *lamp*, enlightened by the true light, Christ. He was not himself the true light; but he borrowed all his brightness and lustre from the source of all light, Christ. He was "*burning*" with charity, zeal and sanctity of life. "*Shining*" with the light of true faith and doctrine. A Prophet who, after a long silence on the part of other Prophets, closed the old Dispensation and ushered in the new, holding, as it were, a middle place between both.

"*You rejoiced in his light.*" Showed singular pleasure and exultation in seeing and hearing him, but it was only "*for a time,*" until he began fearlessly to upbraid you with your vices, to summon you, to do penance, denouncing you, as a "*brood of vipers,*" calling on you to "*fly from the wrath to come,*" to point Me out, in My humility, as your long-expected Messiah. Then it was the "*Pharisees and lawyers despised the counsels of God against themselves, not being baptized by him*" (Luke vii. 30), and charged him with *having a devil*" (vii. 33). In the words, "*for a time,*" He taxes the inconstancy and perversity of the chief men among the Jews.

36. "*I have a greater testimony than that of John.*" "*Greater,*" less liable to cavil or exception, less liable to be ascribed to human friendship or earthly consideration, than the testimony of John, which you rejected, after he had boldly spoken the truth.

Text.

verum est testimonium quod perhibet de me.

33. You sent to John: and he gave testimony to the truth.

33. Vos misistis ad Joannem: et testimonium perhibuit veritati.

34. But I receive not testimony from man: but I say these things that you may be saved.

34. Ego autem non ab homine testimonium accipio: sed hæc dico ut vos salvi sitis.

35. He was a burning and a shining light. And you were willing for a time to rejoice in his light.

35. Ille erat lucerna ardens, et lucens. Vos autem voluistis ad horam exultare in luce ejus.

36. But I have a greater testimony than that of John. For the works which the Father hath given me to

Text	Commentary
perfect: the works themselves which I do, give testimony of me, that the Father hath sent me.	"*The works which the Father hath given Me to perfect.*" The miracles of every description, performed without number, at every time and at every place; performed, also in proof of my Divine Sonship, performed also by my own Divine power, foretold of me by the Prophets, the revelation of the most hidden thoughts of the human heart, the prediction of future events,—all these are the works, which I received the essential power of performing from My Father, in My eternal generation, and the limited faculty of performing, conferred on My human nature, at My Incarnation.
36. *Ego autem habeo testimonium majus Joanne. Opera enim, quæ dedit mihi Pater ut perficiam ea: ipsa opera, quæ ego facio, testimonium perhibent de me, quia Pater misit me:*	"*The works themselves*" (I say) "*which I do, give testimony that My Father hath sent Me.*" For, they were performed in proof of His having done this, and they sealed this truth with the Divine seal, which cannot be counterfeited or falsified, God's own veracity being pledged to it (see c. x. 37, 38).
37. *And the Father himself who hath sent me, hath given testimony of me; neither have you heard his voice at any time, nor seen his shape.*	37. And not only has My Father borne testimony to me through the medium of works; but, He has borne testimony immediately Himself, when at my baptism, He loudly and openly declared Me to be His well-beloved Son. Besides this direct testimony of the Father; others say, there is also reference made to the testimony rendered by the Father in former times, through the Scriptures, Moses and the Prophets, as in next verse.
37. *Et qui misit me Pater, ipse testimonium perhibuit de me: neque vocem ejus unquam audistis, neque speciem; ejus vidistis.*	"*Nor have you heard His voice,*" etc. The connection of this with the preceding is not easily seen. It seems to be allusive to the occurrences that took place on the occasion of the people receiving the Law in Sinai (Exod. xx. 19–21; Deut. iv. 12 v. 22–27; xviii. 15). The people, terrified at all the dreadful appearances there exhibited, earnestly prayed that God would discontinue these frightful and terrifying phenomena, and appoint a mediator, Moses, who would communicate to them his commands (Exodus xx. 19; Deut. v. 27). "*Let me* (the people) *not hear any more the voice of the Lord my God neither let me see any more this exceeding great fire, lest I die*" (Deut. xviii. 16). The Lord yielding to their earnest prayer, of which He approved, "*they have spoken all things well*" (v. 17), withheld the terrifying sound of His voice, and withdrew His appearance, manifested in the burning fire, thunders and lightning. He entered into a solemn covenant with them, that He would send them a Prophet, whose voice they should hear; at the same time, threatening His Divine vengeance against such as would disregard His voice (Deut. xviii. 19). The Lord had observed His part of the covenant, while they did not keep theirs.
38. *And you have not his word abiding in you: for whom he hath sent, him you believe not.*	38. "*His word,*" or command, about hearing the Prophet, "*you have not abiding in you.*" They refused to obey. "*For whom He hath sent, you believe not.*" Far from believing, they rather despised and scornfully rejected Himself, the Prophet referred to, "*whom God hath sent.*"

Commentary.

The words of preceding verse, "*you have not heard his voice*," etc., are clearly allusive to the passage, "*we will not hear His voice nor see His shape.*" What you formerly prayed for through fear, from your Father, He granted you. You have not heard the terrible voice of God, nor seen His frightful shape; His word, however, or covenant by which you bound yourselves, you have not kept, viz., to hear the Prophet of your own nation, whom He was to send you. What you have engaged to do, you have not done, viz., to believe in Me, the Prophet whom He promised to send. Hence, "*His word*," does not abide in you.

39. "*Search the Scriptures.*" Both in the Greek and Latin versions, these words are of doubtful construction. They may be understood, either in the Indicative or Imperative mood. Some, with St. Cyril, understand them Indicatively. "*You search the Scriptures; for, in them you think to have life everlasting.*" You think, that by observing what is prescribed or commanded in them, as well in regard to faith as to morals, you have in them the means of salvation. This could not be, unless you found Christ in them. "*They bear testimony of me.*" This construction derives great probability from the entire context, in which all the words are in the Indicative; also from the words, "*For in them you think*," etc., a reason, why they read them; also from the words, "*and you will not come to Me*," etc. (*v.* 40), as if He said, although you are in the habit of searching the Scriptures, and find in them undoubted evidence in favour of Me; still, owing to your obstinate and perverse wills, you will not come to me. Others, with St. Chrysostom, understand these words, Imperatively, as conveying an exhortation to them to "*search the Scriptures*" of the Old Testament; and that thus, they will find in them new evidence. By this appeal to Scripture, He adduces a new argument in His own favour.

"*And the same are they*," etc. "*And*," signifies, *for*. They bear testimony of our Lord in every part, both in the Law and in the Prophets. For, "*the end of the Law is Christ*" (Rom. x. 4). "*To Him all the Pophets bear testimony*" (Acts x. 43).

In what sense soever understood, whether indicatively or imperatively, this passage furnishes no ground for argument in favour of the indiscriminate reading of Scripture by all classes of people; nor do they convey any precept to that effect.

Taken *indicatively*, as they are understood by several Protestant Commentators, it is evident they convey no precept to read the Scripture. They only convey a reproach, to the Jews, who derived such little profit from the reading of the Sacred Scriptures.

If read in the *imperative* mood, they have reference to the Scribes and Pharisees, those learned in the Law, whom alone our

Text.

38. *Et verbum ejus non habetis in vobis manens: quia quem misit ille, huic vos non creditis.*

39. *Search the scriptures, for you think in them to have life everlasting; and the same are they that give testimony of me.*

39. *Scrutamini Scripturas, quia vos putatis in ipsis vitam æternam habere: et illæ sunt, quæ testimonium perhibent de me:*

Commentary.

Lord here addresses. Any precept they might possibly be construed to convey, is addressed, not to the followers of our Lord, but to the Jews, and not to the Jews generally; not to the multitude; but, to the Scribes and Pharisees, as is clear from the attempt of this latter class to persecute our Lord (*v.* 16), and from their receiving glory from one another. (*v.* 44). Now, this is true only of the Priests, the Scribes, etc.; but, not of the people, who always glorified God, on witnessing the wonderful works of our Lord. Far from denying that the Priests, the pastors and teachers of the people, are bound to read and search the Scriptures, as is mentioned here, we rather affirm it, as "*the lips of the Priest should keep knowledge, and the Law they should require at his mouth*" (Malachias ii. 7).

As regards the great body of the Jewish people, it was not from their own private reading of the Scriptures, they were, ordinarily, to derive a knowledge of the Law; but, from the teachers legitimately constituted, viz., the Priests, Scribes, Levites, appointed for this purpose (Matthew xxiii. 2, 3). On this account, the Levites and Priests dwelt among the several tribes. (Josue xxi.) In case of doubt, they should have recourse to the proper authority. (Deuter. xvii. 8, etc.) It was necessary that the Priests should teach the Law to the people. It was impossible for the people, generally, to read the Scripture. For, in the interval between the captivity and our Lord's time, the Jews of Palestine, who spoke the Syro-Chaldaic, had no version in that language. Moreover, it was impossible to multiply a sufficient number of copies. We know that, even in the kingdom of Judea, the pious King Josephat sent teachers among the people, carrying with them, for that purpose, "*the Book of the Law of the Lord*" (2 Paralip. xvii. 7–9). Hence, the copies were not in indiscriminate use among the people.

The Catholic Church does not interdict the reading of the Sacred Scripture, in the *original* languages. It is not forbidden to the Priests, in any language, nor to the people generally, save with some salutary restrictions, which experience and common sense would dictate, as necessary against the profane and injurious use of the Bible. The people are allowed to read them in the vulgar tongue, if they do so with proper dispositions, the chief among which is, a due feeling of respect and subordination in regard to the teaching of the Church, and to the interpretation of the Holy Fathers.

Without meaning to disparage the reading of the SS. Scripture by the laity, when done in accordance with the wise prescriptions of the Church and the proper dispositions, it may not be undeserving of remark, as showing the evil of reading the SS. Scripture without the proper dispositions, that among even the Jews, it was the rulers who read them, that rejected our Lord; whereas, it was

Commentary

the people who were charged with being ignorant of the Law, that received Him. "*Hath any of the rulers believed in Him, or of the Pharisees? But this mutitude that knoweth not the Law are accursed*" (John vii. 48, 49).

The discipline of the Church in interdicting the indiscriminate reading of the SS. Scriptures in the vulgar tongue can be easily justified :—

1. From the declaration of St. Peter regarding the difficulties of certain passages of Scripture, which "*the unstable and unlearned*" even in his day, "*wrested and distorted to their own destruction*" (2 Peter iii. 16).

2. From the practice of the Apostles, in withholding certain doctrines, from that description of men, who were incapable of comprehending them, for whom such doctrines, however true and indisputable, were utterly unsuited, nay, noxious. Just as strong food would injure those, who were only fit to receive the milk of babes.

3. From a consideration of the different subjects contained in the Bible, relating to history, obscure doctrinal teachings, morals, passages apparently contradictory, literal and figurative language, legislation, precepts, some of passing; others, of permanent obligation; some, dispensable; others, unchangeable, admitting of no dispensation, under any circumstances. Do not all these subjects require a master mind, to elucidate and explain their meaning and import? Into what confusion would not the indiscriminate consideration of these various subjects throw the mind of an untutored peasant; or of a doubting, unstable Christian, be he ever so learned? Common sense itself justifies the wise economy of the Church, on this all-important subject.

4. From sad experience of the disastrous results of this indiscriminate reading, as testified by the history and the shocking conduct of modern heretics; all, directly traceable to this abuse of the SS. Scriptures, to this "*giving holy things to dogs, this casting of pearls before swine.*"

40. "*And you will not come to Me*," notwithstanding that the Scriptures of the Old Testament—the only books of Scripture then extant—by clearly attesting my Divine mission, sent you to Me, as the only source of eternal life. "*For, I am the way, the truth and the life.*" Still, owing to your perversity and malice, you refuse to embrace the only means of salvation pointed out to you, in your own inspired Scriptures, of which you boast, and in which you glory so much.

41. Having adduced several testimonies in His own favour, He now upbraids the Jews with their stubborn incredulity. If you charge Me with proclaiming Myself as the Son of God, the

Text

40. And you will not come to me that you may have life.

40. Et non vultis venire ad me ut vitam habeatis.

41. I receive not glory from men.

41. Claritatem ab hominibus non accipio.

| Text. | Commentary. |

divinely sent teacher, in order that I might reap glory from man, and exalt Myself unduly, you are guilty of injustice. You do Me a wrong.

"*I receive not glory from man.*" I undervalue it. In thus proclaiming My own Divine mission, I have only in view your salvation, which can be secured only through faith in Me.

42. *But I know you, that you have not the love of God in you.*

42. *Sed cognovi vos, quia dilectionem Dei non habetis in vobis.*

42. "*But I know,*" etc. In virtue of that Divine insight into the secrets of hearts, "*I know that you have not the love of God in you,*" that you are full of pride and ambition, which are the cause of your rejecting the clear testimonies adduced in My favour, and of your refusal to believe in Me.

Some make verse 41 parenthetical, as if He said, think not that I reproach you thus, because, I receive glory from men. Then, in verse 42, He upbraids them with incredulity, which proceeded not from the obscurity of Scripture, bearing testimony of Him; but, from their want of the love of God, owing to which they cannot comprehend the things of God.

43. *I am come in the name of my Father, and you receive me not: if another shall come in his own name, him you will receive.*

43. *Ego veni in nomine Patris mei, et non accipitis me: si alius venerit in nomine suo, illum accipietis.*

43. In proof of your not having the love of God in your hearts, "*I am come in the name of My Father,*" performing all My works by His authority and for His glory, proving My Divine mission beyond all doubt, by My works, and by fulfilling all the Prophecies that regarded Me.

"*And you receive Me not,*" as sent by My Father, having the same Divine nature, and doing all My works in union with Him. Such is your perversity, that, "*if another shall come in his own name,*" self sent, on his own authority, "*him you will receive.*" Our Lord here tacitly predicts the coming of false prophets, who were soon to make their appearance before the final destruction of Jerusalem. (Matt. xxiv.) Among them was *Barchochebas,* or *Son of the Star,* who arose in the days of Adrian. Likely, Antichrist, who is to precede the final end of all things, is also included.

44. *How can you believe, who receive glory one from another: and the glory which is from God alone, you do not seek?*

44. *Quomodo vos potestis credere, qui gloriam ab invicem accipitis: et gloriam quæ a solo Deo est, non quæritis?*

44. "*How can you believe,*" etc. They placed an insuperable obstacle to their embracing the faith, on account of their hypocrisy and vain glory, with which our Lord taxes them here, as He did elsewhere. He gently makes a retort on them, in regard to His supposed love of human applause. The Pharisees were hypocrites, who performed all their actions to please men and gain human applause. This was their damning fault. (Matt. xxiii.) They preferred to be honoured by men, rather than that they themselves would honour God.

"*And the glory which is from God,*" etc., the true glory which God bestows on the humble, who perform good actions to please Him, they undervalue and despise.

Pride is one of the chief obstacles to embracing the faith, as well

Commentary.

in the case of individuals, as of entire nations. It is simply folly to expect that a nation, that has lost the faith will ever return, till first they are humbled by God, and made to feel their own misery and dependence on Him. Pride, and an insatiable desire to indulge in sensuality are leading obstacles to the conversion of a country as well as of individuals. While addicted to these two kindred vices—one being inflicted in punishment of the other—we can never hope for the conversion of a people or of individuals.

45. The Pharisees would have justified themselves for rejecting our Lord, on the ground, that they did so out of love of God and zeal for His honour. Our Lord convicts them of the contrary feelings, in the foregoing. He convicts them, viz., of having been influenced by ambition, personal jealousy, and vain glory. He now deprives them of another plea of justification, viz., that they rejected Him, on account of their adhering to the teachings of Moses (John ix. 28). He says, that He Himself need not be the first to accuse them, that Moses, in whom they believed and so much confided, as their advocate; in turn, accuses, and would be the first to accuse them before the Father, of disbelief in his teachings and of the injury done him by such disbelief. The accusation by Moses simply means, that their sin of incredulity against the testimony of Moses, will render them deserving of condemnation before God.

46. "*For, if you did believe Moses, you would perhaps believe in Me.*" The Greek word for "*perhaps*" (αν) is generally rendered, *surely*. Its meaning of "*perhaps*," would indicate the liberty of action on the part of the believer, under the influence of Divine grace; but, certainty, as regards the effect or event. "*For he wrote of Me.*" Moses proclaimed our Lord as the Messiah, whom they should, if they believed in Moses' words, receive as such. Special reference is made to Deut. xviii. 18, "*I will raise them up a Prophet out of the midst of their brethren,*" etc.; also, to the prophecy of Jacob (Genesis xlix.) and the several passages in the Pentateuch, referring to our Lord. The end, the scope of the Law and the Prophets, was Christ.

47. "*If you believe not his writings,*" in My favour, which you receive as authoritative. If you believe not Him whom you place far above Me, "*how will you believe My words?*" not, My *writings*. Our Lord had not written anything, save the few words (John viii. 6). Our Lord, here has recourse to an *argumentum ad hominem*, in which He makes a comparison between Himself and Moses, between *words* and *writing*. The Jews could easily have seen, that our Lord was referred to by Moses, had they approached this solemn subject, with the proper dispositions; or, had they not been blinded by jealousy and pride. Hence, their gross, affected ignorance was grievously culpable.

Text.

45. *Think not that I will accuse you to the Father. There is one that accuseth you, Moses, in whom you trust.*

45. *Nolite putare quia ego accusaturus sim vos apud Patrem: est qui accusat vos Moyses, in quo vos speratis.*

46. *For if you did believe Moses, you would perhaps believe me also. For he wrote of me.*

46. *Si enim crederetis Moysi, crederetis forsitan et mihi: de me enim ille scripsit.*

47. *But if you do not believe his writings: how will you believe my words?*

47. *Si autem illius litteris non creditis: quomodo verbis meis credetis?*

CHAPTER VI.

1 *After these things, Jesus went over the sea of Galilee, which is that of Tiberias:*

2 *And a great multitude followed him, because they saw the miracles which he did on them that were diseased.*

3 *Jesus therefore went up into a mountain, and there he sat with his disciples.*

4 *Now the pasch, the festival day of the Jews, was near at hand.*

5 *When Jesus therefore had lifted up his eyes, and seen that a very great multitude cometh to him, he said to Philip: Whence shall we buy bread that these may eat?*

6 *And this he said to try him: for he himself knew what he would do.*

7 *Philip answered him: Two hundred penny-worth of bread is not sufficient for them, that every one may take a little.*

8 *One of his disciples, Andrew, the brother of Simon Peter, saith to him:*

9 *There is a boy here that hath five barley loaves, and two fishes: but what are these among so many?*

10 *Then Jesus said: Make the men sit down. Now there was much grass in the place. The men therefore sat down, in number about five thousand.*

11 *And Jesus took the loaves: and when he had given thanks, he distributed to them that were sat down. In like manner also of the fishes as much as they would.*

12 *And when they were filled, he said to his disciples: Gather up the fragments that remain, lest they be lost.*

13 *They gathered up therefore, and filled twelve baskets with the fragments of the five barley loaves, which remained over and above to them that had eaten.*

14 *Now those men, when they had seen what a miracle Jesus had done, said: This is of a truth the prophet that is to come into the world.*

15 *Jesus therefore when he knew that they would come to take him by force and make him king, fled again into the mountain himself alone.*

16 *And when evening was come, his disciples went down to the sea.*

17 *And when they had gone up into a ship, they went over the sea to Capharnaum: and it was now dark, and Jesus was not come unto them.*

18 *And the sea arose, by reason of a great wind that blew.*

19 *When they had rowed therefore about five and twenty or thirty furlongs, they see Jesus walking upon the sea, and drawing nigh to the ship, and they were afraid.*

20 *But he saith to them: It is I: be not afraid.*

21 *They were willing therefore to take him into the ship, and presently the ship was at the land, to which they were going.*

22 *The next day, the multitude that stood on the other side of the sea, saw that there was no other ship there but one, and that Jesus had not entered into the ship with his disciples, but that his disciples were gone away alone.*

23 *But other ships came in from Tiberias, nigh unto the place where they had eaten the bread, the Lord giving thanks.*

24 *When therefore the multitude saw that Jesus was not there, nor his disciples, they took shipping, and came to Capharnaum seeking for Jesus.*

25 And when they had found him on the other side of the sea, they said to him: Rabbi, when camest thou hither?

26 Jesus answered them and said: Amen, amen, I say to you, you seek me, not because you have seen miracles, but because you did eat of the loaves, and were filled.

27 Labour not for the meat which perisheth, but for that which endureth unto life everlasting, which the son of man will give you. For him hath God, the Father, sealed.

28 They said therefore unto him: What shall we do that we may work the works of God?

29 Jesus answered, and said to them: This is the work of God, that you believe in him whom he hath sent.

30 They said therefore to him: What sign therefore dost thou shew that we may see, and may believe thee? what dost thou work?

31 Our fathers did eat manna in the desert as it is written, He gave them bread from heaven to eat.

32 Then Jesus said to them: Amen, amen, I say to you: Moses gave you not bread from heaven, but my Father giveth you the true bread from heaven.

33 For the bread of God is that which cometh down from heaven, and giveth life to the world.

34 They said therefore unto him: Lord, give us always this bread.

35 And Jesus said to them: I am the bread of life, he that cometh to me shall not hunger; and he that believeth in me, shall never thirst.

36 But I said unto you, that you also have seen me, and you believe not.

37 All that the Father giveth me shall come to me; and him that cometh to me, I will not cast out.

38 Because I came down from heaven, not to do my own will, but the will of him that sent me.

39 Now this is the will of the Father who sent me; that of all that he hath given me, I should lose nothing, but should raise it up again in the last day.

40 And this is the will of my Father that sent me; that every one who seeth the Son, and believeth in him, may have life everlasting, and I will raise him up in the last day.

41 The Jews therefore murmured at him, because he had said, I am the living bread which came down from heaven.

42 And they said: Is not this Jesus the son of Joseph, whose father and mother we know? How then saith he, I came down from heaven?

43 Jesus therefore answered and said to them: Murmur not among yourselves.

44 No man can come to me, except the Father, who hath sent me, draw him, and I will raise him up in the last day.

45 It is written in the prophets: And they shall all be taught of God. Every one that hath heard of the Father, and hath learned, cometh to me.

46 Not that any man hath seen the Father, but he who is of God, he hath seen the Father.

47 Amen, amen, I say unto you: He that believeth in me hath everlasting life.

48 I am the bread of life.

49 Your fathers did eat manna in the desert, and are dead.

50 This is the bread which cometh down from heaven: that if any man eat of it, he may not die.

51 *I am the living bread, which came down from heaven.*

52 *If any man eat of this bread, he shall live for ever: and the bread that I will give, is my flesh for the life of the world.*

53 *The Jews therefore strove among themselves, saying: How can this man give us his flesh to eat?*

54 *Then Jesus said to them: Amen, amen, I say unto you: Except you eat the flesh of the son of man, and drink his blood, you shall not have life in you.*

55 *He that eateth my flesh, and drinketh my blood, hath everlasting life: and I will raise him up in the last day.*

56 *For my flesh is meat indeed: and my blood is drink indeed:*

57 *He that eateth my flesh, and drinketh my blood, abideth in me, and I in him.*

58 *As the living Father hath sent me, and I live by the Father: so he that eateth me, the same also shall live by me.*

59 *This is the bread that came down from heaven. Not as your fathers did eat manna, and are dead. He that eateth this bread shall live for ever.*

60 *These things he said teaching in the synagogue, in Capharnaum.*

61 *Many therefore of his disciples hearing it, said: This saying is hard, and who can hear it?*

62 *But Jesus knowing in himself, that his disciples murmured at this, said to them: Doth this scandalize you?*

63 *If then you shall see the son of man ascend up where he was before?*

64 *It is the spirit that quickeneth: the flesh profiteth nothing. The words that I have spoken to you, are spirit and life:*

65 *But there are some of you that believe not. For Jesus knew from the beginning who they were that did not believe, and who he was that would betray him.*

66 *And he said: Therefore did I say to you, that no man can come to me, unless it be given him by my Father.*

67 *After this many of his disciples went back; and walked no more with him.*

68 *Then Jesus said to the twelve: Will you also go away?*

69 *And Simon Peter answered him: Lord, to whom shall we go? thou hast the words of eternal life.*

70 *And we have believed and have known that thou art the Christ the Son of God.*

71 *Jesus answered them: Have not I chosen you twelve; and one of you is a devil?*

72 *Now he meant Judas Iscariot, the son of Simon: for this same was about to betray him, whereas he was one of the twelve.*

CAPUT VI.

1 *Post hæc abiit Jesus trans mare Galilææ, quod est Tiberiadis:*

2 *Et sequebatur eum multitudo magna, quia videbant signa, quæ faciebat super his, qui infirmabantur.*

3 *Subiit ergo in montem Jesus: et ibi sedebat cum discipulis suis.*

4 *Erat autem proximum Pascha, dies festus Judæorum.*

5 *Cum sublevasset ergo oculos Jesus, et vidisset quia multitudo maxima venit ad eum, dixit ad Philippum: Unde ememus panes, ut manducent hi?*

6 *Hoc autem dicebat tentans eum: ipse enim sciebat quid esset facturus.*

ST. JOHN, CHAP. VI.

7 *Respondit ei Philippus: Ducentorum denariorum panes non sufficiunt eis, ut unusquisque modicum quid accipiat.*

8 *Dicit ei unus ex discipulis ejus, Andreas frater Simonis Petri:*

9 *Est puer unus hic, qui habet quinque panes hordeaceos, et duos pisces: sed hæc quid sunt inter tantos?*

10 *Dixit ergo Jesus: Facite homines discumbere. Erat autem fœnum multum in loco. Discubuerunt ergo viri, numero quasi quinque millia.*

11 *Accepit ergo Jesus panes: et cum gratias egisset, distribuit discumbentibus: similiter et ex piscibus quantum volebant.*

12 *Ut autem impleti sunt, dixit discipulis suis: Colligite quæ superaverunt fragmenta, ne pereant.*

13 *Collegerunt ergo, et impleverunt duodecim cophinos fragmentorum ex quinque panibus hordeaceis, quæ superfuerunt his, qui manducaverant.*

14 *Illi ergo homines cum vidissent quod Jesus fecerat signum, dicebant: Quia hic est vere propheta, qui venturus est in mundum.*

15 *Jesus ergo cum cognovisset, quia venturi essent ut raperent eum, et facerent eum regem, fugit iterum in montem ipse solus:*

16 *Ut autem sero factum est, descenderunt discipuli ejus ad mare.*

17 *Et cum ascendissent navim, venerunt trans mare in Capharnaum: et tenebræ jam factæ erant: et non venerat ad eos Jesus.*

18 *Mare autem, vento magno flante, exurgebat.*

19 *Cum remigassent ergo quasi stadia vigintiquinque aut triginta, vident Jesum ambulantem supra mare, et proximum navi fieri, et timuerunt.*

20 *Ille autem dicit eis: Ego sum, nolite timere.*

21 *Voluerunt ergo accipere eum in navim: et statim navis fuit ad terram, in quam ibant.*

22 *Altera die, turba, quæ stabat trans mare, vidit quia navicula alia non erat ibi nisi una, et quia non introisset cum discipulis suis Jesus in navim, sed soli discipuli ejus abiissent.*

23 *Aliæ vero supervenerunt naves à Tiberiade juxta locum ubi manducaverant panem, gratias agente Domino.*

24 *Cum ergo vidisset turba quia Jesus non esset ibi, neque discipuli ejus, ascenderunt in naviculas, et venerunt Capharnaum quærentes Jesum.*

25 *Et cum invenissent eum trans mare, dixerunt ei: Rabbi, quando huc venisti?*

26 *Respondit eis Jesus, et dixit: Amen, amen dico vobis: quæritis me, non quia vidistis signa, sed quia manducastis ex panibus, et saturati estis.*

27 *Operamini non cibum, qui perit, sed qui permanet in vitam æternam, quem Filius hominis dabit vobis: Hunc enim Pater signavit Deus.*

28 *Dixerunt ergo ad eum: Quid faciemus ut operemur opera Dei?*

29 *Respondit Jesus, et dixit eis: Hoc est opus Dei, ut credatis in eum, quem misit ille.*

30 *Dixerunt ergo ei: Quod ergo tu facis signum ut videamus, et credamus tibi? quid operaris?*

31 *Patres nostri manducaverunt manna in deserto, sicut scriptum est: Panem de cælo dedit eis manducare.*

32 *Dixit ergo eis Jesus: Amen, amen dico vobis: Non Moyses dedit vobis panem de cælo, sed Pater meus dat vobis panem de cælo verum.*

33 *Panis enim Dei est, qui de cælo descendit, et dat vitam mundo.*
34 *Dixerunt ergo ad eum: Domine, semper da nobis panem hunc.*
35 *Dixit autem eis Jesus: Ego sum panis vitæ: qui venit ad me, non esuriet, et qui credit in me, non sitiet umquam.*
36 *Sed dixi vobis, quia et vidistis me, et non creditis.*
37 *Omne, quod dat mihi Pater, ad me veniet: et eum, qui venit ad me, non ejiciam foras:*
38 *Quia descendi de cælo, non ut faciam voluntatem meam, sed voluntatem ejus, qui misit me.*
39 *Hæc est autem voluntas ejus, qui misit me, Patris: ut omne, quod dedit mihi, non perdam ex eo, sed resuscitem illum in novissimo die.*
40 *Hæc est autem voluntas patris mei, qui misit me: ut omnis, qui videt filium, et credit in eum, habeat vitam æternam, et ego resuscitabo eum in novissimo die.*
41 *Murmurabant ergo Judæi de illo, quia dixisset: Ego sum panis vivus, qui de cælo descendi,*
42 *Et Dicebant: Nonne hic est Jesus, filius Joseph, cujus nos novimus patrem, et matrem? Quomodo ergo dicit hic: Quia de cælo descendi?*
43 *Respondit ergo Jesus, et dixit eis: Nolite murmurare in invicem?*
44 *Nemo potest venire ad me, nisi Pater, qui misit me, traxerit eum: et ego resuscitabo eum in novissimo die.*
45 *Est scriptum in Prophetis: Et erunt omnes docibiles Dei. Omnis, qui audivit a Patre, et didicit, venit ad me.*
46 *Non quia Patrem vidit quisquam, nisi is, qui est a Deo, hic vidit Patrem.*
47 *Amen, amen dico vobis: Qui credit in me, habeat vitam æternam.*
48 *Ego sum panis vitæ.*
49 *Patres vestri manducaverunt manna in deserto, et mortui sunt.*
50 *Hic est panis de cælo descendens: ut si quis ex ipso manducaverit, non moriatur.*
51 *Ego sum panis vivus, qui de cælo descendi.*
52 *Si quis manducaverit ex hoc pane, vivet in æternum: et panis, quem ego dabo, caro mea est pro mundi vita.*
53 *Litigabant ergo Judæi ad invicem, dicentes: Quomodo potest hic nobis carnem suam dare ad manducandum?*
54 *Dixit ergo eis Jesus: Amen, amen, dico vobis: Nisi manducaveritis carnem Filii hominis, et biberitis ejus sanguinem, non habebitis vitam in vobis.*
55 *Qui manducat meam carnem, et bibit meum sanguinem, habet vitam æternam: et ego resuscitabo eum in novissimo die.*
56 *Caro enim mea, vere est cibus: et sanguis meus, vere est potus.*
57 *Qui manducat meam carnem, et bibit meum sanguinem, in me manet, et ego in illo.*
58 *Sicut misit me vivens Pater, et ego vivo propter Patrem: et qui manducat me, et ipse vivet propter me.*
59 *Hic est panis, qui de cælo descendit. Non sicut manducaverunt patres vestri manna, et mortui sunt. Qui manducat hunc panem, vivet in æternum.*
60 *Hæc dixit in synagoga docens, in Capharnaum.*
61 *Multi ergo audientes ex discipulis ejus, dixerunt: Durus est hic sermo, et quis potest cum audire?*
62 *Sciens autem Jesus apud semetipsum quia murmurarent de hoc discipuli ejus, dixit iis: Hoc vos scandalizat?*

ST. JOHN, CHAP. VI.

63 *Si ergo videritis Filium hominis ascendentem ubi erat prius?*

64 *Spiritus est, qui vivificat: caro non prodest quidquam: verba, quæ ego locutus sum vobis, spiritus et vita sunt.*

65 *Sed sunt quidam ex vobis, qui non credunt. Sciebat enim ab initio Jesus qui essent non credentes, et quis traditurus esset eum.*

66 *Et dicebat: Propterea dixi vobis, quia nemo potest venire ad me, nisi fuerit ei datum a Patre meo.*

67 *Ex hoc multi discipulorum ejus abierunt retro: et jam non cum illo ambulabant.*

68 *Dixit ergo Jesus ad duodecim: Numquid et vos vultis abire?*

69 *Respondit ergo ei Simon Petrus: Domine, ad quem ibimus? verba vitæ æternæ habes.*

70 *Et nos credidimus, et cognovimus quia tu es Christus Filius Dei.*

71 *Respondit ei Jesus: Nonne ego vos duodecim elegi: et ex vobis unus diabolus est?*

72 *Dicebat autem Judam Simonis Iscariotem: hic enim erat traditurus eum, cum esset unus ex duodecim.*

ANALYSIS.

In this chapter we have an account of a miracle wrought by our Lord in the multiplication of five barley loaves and two fishes, so as to satisfy the wants of about five thousand persons. The admiration expressed by the crowd, who were witnesses of this miracle (1–15).

The miracle wrought on the sea, when immediately after having entered the boat in which the disciples laboured hard against the storm, our Lord had the boat suddenly brought to shore (17–22).

The anxious search of the multitude for Him, whom they at last succeeded in finding (24, 25).

Our Lord's discourse, in which after having referred indistinctly and rather obscurely, to the Eucharistic bread He meant to give them (*v.* 27), He fully explains the most effectual means of securing this bread, viz., faith in Himself, upon which, after several interruptions, He fully dilates as far as *v.* 51.

At *v.* 51, He commences to deliver distinctly, His consoling doctrine regarding His real presence, and the necessity of partaking of His body and blood in the Holy Eucharist. This He inculcates by a threat of exclusion from eternal life, in case of disobedience, and repeated promises of eternal life, to those who obey. At the same time, He refers to the superior excellence of this promised gift (54–60).

After repeatedly corroborating the ideas which the Jews had conceived from His own words, regarding the real manducation of His body, which proves they were right; He next, in reply to their rebellious murmurings, corrects their erroneous carnal ideas regarding the *mode* of receiving Him.

He points out the source of their murmurings, viz., want of faith in His Divine mission, which they had not humility to pray for, to His Heavenly Father, the source of all blessings (65, 66).

The Evangelist next describes our Lord's stern resolve, to allow His disciples and apostles leave Him, sooner than withdraw or modify or correct a word of what He delivered, regarding His real presence in the Eucharist (67, 68). He next records the confession of Peter, on behalf of the twelve, in our Lord's Divinity—our Lord's reference to the treason of Judas (71, 72).

Text.

1. *After these things Jesus went over the sea of Galilee, which is that of Tiberias:*

1. *Post hæc abiit Jesus trans mare Galilææ, quod est Tiberiadis:*

Commentary.

"*After these things,*" etc. The occurrences referred to in the preceding chapter, took place about the Pasch or Pentecost of the second year of our Lord's public ministry. The events the Evangelist is now about recording in this chapter, occurred about the Pasch of the following year. So, that, nearly an interval of a year elapsed between the occurrences recorded in this and the preceding chapter. St. John here passes over the election of the twelve Apostles, the Sermon on the Mount, etc., recorded fully by St. Matthew.

Although the miraculous multiplication of bread was recorded by the other Evangelists; still, St. John repeats it here with some additional circumstances as an appropriate introduction to the discourse, He was about to deliver regarding the heavenly food—His own adorable body—which He promised to give them, and gave them, by a permanent rite, at the Last Supper. The other Evangelists (Matthew xiv. 13 ; Mark vi. 32 ; Luke ix. 10, etc., record what is narrated here by St. John up to *v*. 14). It is not known precisely when our Lord left Judea, where the events recorded in the preceding chapter took place.

"*The Sea of Galilee.*" According to Hebrew usage, any large expanse of water is designated a "*sea.*" Hence, the large lake in question is called, "*the Sea of Galilee,*" as it was in the province of that name, and "*of Tiberias,*" situated on its borders. The town was so called, after Tiberius Cæsar, by Herod the Tetrarch, who built it in honour of that Emperor (Josephus, Lib. 18, Antiq. c. 3).

"*Went over.*" (See Matthew xiv. 13, Commentary on.) Some Commentators maintain, He did not cross the lake from one side to the other, from east to west; but, only crossed several creeks on the same side, the people thus following Him on foot, being even before Him at the several points of destination, owing to the difficulties in sailing. It may be also, that He Himself wished to cross these creeks slowly, so that the people could meet Him.

2. *And a great multitude; followed him, because they saw the miracles which he did on them that were diseased.*

2. "*And a great multitude followed Him,*" etc. He went by boat; they, on foot. (See Mark vi. 32 ; Mathew xiv. 13.)

2. *Et sequebatur eum multitudo magna, quia videbant signa, quæ faciebat super his, qui infirmabantur.*

3. *Jesus therefore went up into a mountain, and there he sat with his disciples.*

3, 4. "*The Pasch, the Festival day of the Jews,*" their greatest and chief festival. The Pasch is mentioned on account of those, who were not well versed in Jewish history or in Jewish religious rites.

3. *Subiit ergo in montem Jesus: et ibi sedebat cum discipulis suis.*

4. *Now the pasch, the festival day of the Jews, was near at hand.*

4. *Erat autem proximum Pascha dies festus Judæorum.*

Commentary.

5-16. (See Matthew xiv. 15-22.)

Text.

5. *When Jesus therefore had lifted up his eyes, and seen that a very great multitude cometh to him, he said to Philip: Whence shall we buy bread that these may eat?*

5. *Cum sublevasset ergo oculos Jesus, et vidisset quia multitudo maxima venit ad eum, dixit ad Philippum: Unde ememus panes, ut manducent hi?*

6. *And this he said to try him: for he himself knew what he would do.*

6. *Hoc autem dicebat tentans eum: ipse enim sciebat quid esset facturus.*

7. *Philip answered him: Two hundred penny-worth of bread is not sufficient for them, that every one may take a little.*

7. *Respondit ei Philippus: Ducentorum denariorum panes non sufficiunt eis, ut unusquisque modicum quid accipiat.*

8. *One of his disciples Andrew, the brother of Simon Peter, saith to him:*

8. *Dicit ei unus ex discipulis ejus, Andreas frater Simonis Petri:*

9. *There is a boy here that hath five barley loaves, and two fishes; but what are these among so many?*

9. *Est puer unus hic qui habet quinque panes hordeaceos, et duos pisces: sed hæc quid sunt inter tantos?*

10. *Then Jesus said: Make the men sit down. Now there was much grass in the place. The men therefore sat down, in number about five thousand.*

10. *Dixit ergo Jesus: Facite homines discumbere. Erat autem fœnum multum in loco. Discubuerunt ergo viri, numero quasi quinque millia.*

11. *And Jesus took the loaves: and when he had given thanks, he distributed to them that were set down. In like manner also of the fishes as much as they would.*

11. *Accepit ergo Jesus panes: et cum gratias egisset, distribuit discumbentibus: similiter et ex piscibus quantum volebant.*

12. *And when they were filled, he said to his disciples: Gather up the fragments that remain, lest they be lost.*

12. *Ut autem impleti sunt, dixit discipulis suis: Colligite quæ superaverunt fragmenta, ne pereant.*

13. *They gathered up therefore, and filled twelve baskets with the fragments of the five barley loaves, which remained over and above to them that had eaten.*

13. *Collegerunt ergo, et impleverunt dudodecim cophinos fragmentorum ex quinque panibus hordeaceis, quæ superfuerunt his, qui manducaverunt.*

14. *Now those men, when they had seen what a miracle Jesus had done said: This is of a truth the prophet that is to come into the world.*

14. *Illi ergo homines cum vidissent quod Jesus fecerat signum, dicebant: Quia hic est vere propheta, qui venturus est in mundum.*

15. *Jesus therefore when he knew that they would come to take him by force and make him king, fled again into the mountain himself alone.*

15. *Jesus ergo cum cognovisset, quia venturi essent ut raperent eum, et facerent eum regem, fugit iterum in montem ipse solus.*

16. *And when evening was come, his disciples went down to the sea.*

16. *Ut autem sero factum est, descenderunt discipuli ejus ad mare.*

---

17. "*They went over the sea to Capharnaum,*" that is, they directed their course to Capharnaum. They intended going there and making for it. In St. Mark (vi. 45) it is said, they were ordered by Him, while dismissing the crowds, to make for Bethsaida, which is near Capharnaum. Possibly, the tempest drove them past Bethsaida; and they, then, made for Capharnaum.

17. *And when they had gone up into a ship, they went over the sea to Capharnaum: and it was now dark, and Jesus was not come unto them.*

17. *Et cum ascendissent navim, venerunt trans mare in Capharnaum: et tenebræ jam factæ erant: et non venerat ad eos Jesus.*

Text.	Commentary.
18. *And the sea arose, by reason of a g eat wind that blew.*	18–22. See Matthew xiv. 24–33 (Commentary on.)

18. *Mare autem, vento magno flante, exurgebat.*

19. *When they had rowed therefore about five and twenty or thirty furlongs, they see Jesus walking upon the sea, and drawing nigh to the ship, and they were afraid.*

19. *Cum remigassent ergo quasi stadia viginti quinque aut triginta, vident Jesum ambulantem, supra mare, et proximum navi fieri, et timuerunt.*

20. *But he saith to them: It is I: be not afraid.*

20. *Ille autem dicit eis: Ego sum, nolite timere.*

21. *They were willing therefore to take him into the ship: and presently the ship was at the land, to which they were going.*

21 *Voluerunt ergo accipere eum in navim: et statim navis fuit ad terram, in quam ibant.*

22. *The next day, the multitude that stood on the other side of the sea, saw that there was no other ship there but one, and that Jesus had not entered into the ship with his disciples, but that his disciples were gone away alone.*	22. "*The next day,*" viz., the day after our Lord miraculously multiplied the bread, with which He fed 5,000. "*The multitude that stood on the other side of the sea,*" the side opposite Capharnaum, where our Redeemer and His disciples had been, after crossing the lake, on which He calmed the storm. "*Saw that there was no other ship there but one, and that Jesus had not entered into the ship*" (the one ship referred to) "*with His disciples, but that His disciples were gone away alone.*" The Greek for "*saw*" (ἰδὼν) is, "*having seen.*" Hence, the sentence is imperfect or suspensive, and the following or some such words must be added to perfect the sense, "*sought Jesus,*" unless we connect it with *v.* 24, where it would be repeated thus: "*when therefore* (I say) *they saw,*" etc.

22. *Altera die, turba, quæ stabat trans mare, vidit quia navicula alia non erat ibi nisi una, et quia non introisset cum discipulis suis Jesus in navim, sed soli discipuli ejus abiissent.*

23. *But the other ships came in from Tiberias, nigh unto the place where they had eaten the bread, the Lord giving thanks.*	23. "*Other ships came*" the following day—"*from Tiberias*"—the rumour of the miracle having spread, people came in crowds to hear and see our Lord—"*nigh unto the place where they had eaten the bread,*" etc.

23. *Aliæ vero supervenerunt naves a Tiberiade juxta locum ubi manducaverant panem, gratias agentes Domino.*

24. *When therefore the multitude saw that Jesus was not there, nor his disciples, they took shipping, and came to Capharnaum seeking for Jesus.*	24. Seeing, then, that our Lord, whom they sought, was not there, as they fancied He would have been, since they saw His disciples cross the lake towards Capharnaum without Him, the previous evening, in the only boat that was there, they had no idea of His walking on the waters, and meeting on the way the boat, which carried the disciples—disappointed in their search for Him on their side of the lake, where they expected to find Him, "*they took shipping,*" entering the boats that had come from Tiberias. In these they crossed the lake, and "*came to Capharnaum, seeking for Jesus,*" expecting to find Him at His usual place of abode.

24. *Cum ergo vidisset turba quia Jesus non esset ibi, neque discipuli ejus, ascenderunt in naviculas, et venerunt Capharnaum quærentes Jesum.*

25. *And when they had found him on the other side of the sea, they said to him:*	25. Having succeeded in their search, and finding Him at last, surprised at how He could have crossed the lake, and come there, they ask Him, "*Rabbi,*" etc.

Commentary.

"*Rabbi, when camest Thou hither?*" The question was rather rude and frivolous. The term, however, "*Rabbi*" shows it was blended with some feeling of respect. Our Lord does not reply, as He did not choose, out of feelings of modesty, to say *how* He came, viz., by walking on the waters. Indeed, the question *how* was implied in asking "*when.*" Declining to answer their frivolous questions, our Lord speaks to them in terms of reprehension, as He well knew their minds. He also wished to repress their excessive demonstration of feeling displayed the preceding day, in wishing to make Him king. He also shows, He cared not much for their praise, and was not affected by their bland address, when calling Him "*Rabbi.*" He answers, however, in a way that interested them most, by instructing them to seek for the food of the soul, rather than that of the body, which they were expecting to be perpetuated among them ; and on account of which they thus sought and crowded round Him.

26. "*Amen, amen,*" shows the solemn importance of what He was about uttering. "*Not because you have seen miracles,*" which should have the effect of producing feelings of faith, penance, and the other evangelical virtues, that would conduct you to life everlasting, about which you seem so indifferent ; you seek Me, not to procure the food of the soul, but of the body. You seek Me for your own sakes, not for Mine—St. Augustine—"*but because you did eat of the loaves,*" etc. You were actuated by carnal motives, by a desire to have the multiplication of bread continued amongst you, whereby to relieve your corporal necessities.

Our Lord, while mildly rebuking them and showing them He had the Divine faculty of scanning their inward motives, and of knowing the thoughts of their hearts, takes occasion, from allusion to corporal bread, to speak of that spiritual food of their souls, conferring everlasting life, which the Son of Man had in store for them.

27. "*Labour not for the food which perisheth,*" etc. Our Lord takes occasion, from the discourse regarding corporal bread, and the desire which the people had for it, to speak of a more exalted description of food—His own adorable Body—just as He raised the mind of the Samaritan woman, to desire and ask for the spiritual waters of faith and grace, by speaking of the material water, of which He asked her to give Him to drink.

When our Lord tells us to labour not for perishable food, He, by no means, prohibits our working for corporal nourishment ; since, all are bound by the Law of God, to toil and labour for their bodily sustenance (2 Thess. iii. 10). He uses the word, in an exclusive sense, "*labour not for,*" etc., *alone*, and He wishes to convey, that we should labour *chiefly* for the food of which He means

Text.

Rabbi, when camest thou hither?

25. *Et cum invenissent eum trans mare, dixerunt ei : Rabbi, quando huc venisti?*

26. *Jesus answered them, and said: Amen, amen, I say to you, you seek me not because you have seen miracles, but because you did eat of the loaves, and were filled.*

26. *Respondit eis Jesus, et dixit: Amen, amen dico vobis : quæritis me non quia vidistis signa, sed quia manducastis ex panibus, et saturati estis.*

27. *Labour not for the meat which perisheth, but for that which endureth unto life everlasting, which the son of man will give you. For him hath God, the Father, sealed.*

27. *Operamini non cibum qui perit sed qui permanet in vitam æternam, quem Filius hominis dabit vobis. Hunc enim Pater signavit Deus.*

Commentary.

to speak. "*the meat which perisheth*," viz., corporal food, that perishes with the body which it is meant to support.

"*But for that which endureth*"—in itself imperishable—"*unto life everlasting*," which, unlike corporal food, that only upholds the life of the body, supports, "*unto everlasting life*," which it confers and to which it leads us.

"*Which the Son of Man will give you.*" He speaks of it, as a *future* gift, not as yet bestowed on the world ; it is also peculiarly the gift of our Lord, as *Son of Man*. This would seem to indicate what that gift is.

"*For Him hath God the Father sealed.*" First, when in eternally begetting Him, He communicated to His Eternal Son, His own Divine nature, and impressed upon Him the substantial, living, eternal image of His substance. "*The figure of His substance*" (Heb. i. 3), thus communicating His omnipotence and the power of giving the promised gift or heavenly food, showing Him to be the Eternal Son of God as well as the Son of Man. Secondly, in His Incarnation, when the Son of God united human nature, under His own Divine person. Thus, the Son of Man, at the same time, became the Son of God. Thirdly, He testified by words, "*Thou art my beloved Son*," etc., and by miracles, that our Lord was the Son of God.

It is disputed to what "*meat*" or food there is reference made here. There is almost a universal consensus among Catholic Commentators, that towards the close of this chapter, commencing with *v.* 48, our Lord refers to the Blessed Eucharist, which He promises here to give, and did graciously give and institute, a year after this, at the Last Supper. Only a few Catholic Commentators deny this. There is, however, a great diversity of opinion, whether the Blessed Sacrament is referred to, in this verse. Although it is quite certain and undeniable, that, in the latter part of the chapter, our Lord promises to give His body and blood in the adorable Eucharist, and did so at the Last Supper ; still, we are not bound to believe, as a matter of faith, that He refers to the Blessed Eucharist in this chapter, at all. But it is a point of faith, which no one is free to question or reject, that there is reference to the Blessed Eucharist and the real Presence in the words of Institution, "*This is My Body*," etc. (Council of Trent, SS. xiii., de Euch. c. i.)

A great number of distinguished interpreters say, that while our Lord is preparing the people, in the preceding part of the chapter, and in this portion of it, as far as *v.* 48, for the sublime doctrine which He means to deliver there regarding His real Presence, He does not refer to it here. Others maintain, that the "*meat*" or food referred to in this *v.* 27, is His body and blood in the adorable Eucharist. This latter seems by far the most probable opinion. For 1. Our Lord here clearly distinguishes between the "*meat*," or food, and the works which were to be performed, as the *means* for

Commentary.

securing this food. Now, the chief of these works is faith in Him (v. 29). Hence, the food being the *end* or *object*, cannot be confounded with the works, which are the *means* for obtaining it; and hence, the opinion of a large section of distinguished Commentators and Theologians, who say that the food refers to faith, doctrine, etc., is hardly tenable. 2. Our Lord says, He "*will give*" it, at a future time; but He had already bestowed faith, doctrine, etc. 3. He distinguishes between the bread which He Himself *will* give them in the *future*, and that which the *Father gives* (v. 32), at *present*. The Father *gives* us His Incarnate Son; He, as *Son of Man, will give* His body and blood. To Him it peculiarly belongs to bestow this gift. If our Lord turns aside from continuing this subject, regarding His body and blood, to treat, in a subsequent part of the chapter, of faith, as a necessary disposition for securing and worthily receiving this heavenly bread, it was, owing to their untimely questions and interruptions, to resume the subject afterwards.

28. "*The works of God.*" Works pleasing to God, and required by Him for obtaining this heavenly food. This question was suggested by the preceding words of our Lord, v. 27, "*Operamini cibum,*" "*labour, work for the meat*" or food. They then ask what *works*, does God, who "*sealed His Son,*" the bestower of this gift, require of us, in order to secure this food?

29. Our Lord marks out one special work, which they must do by the aid of God, who by His all powerful grace, Himself produces this work in them, they at the same time co-operating with His grace and concurring in the work, viz., "*to believe in Him whom He hath sent.*" He specially selects faith, as, in the first place, indispensable, because, on it must be founded all the works necessary for securing this food. Though speaking to them of Himself, as if He said, "that you believe in Me;" still our Lord, out of modesty, employs the third person, "*Him . . . sent,*" instead of *Me*, referring all to His Father.

From His saying, that faith is the chief work, or *means*, necessary for securing this food, it would seem to follow, that the food itself is not faith, that faith is distinguished from the food, as *means* from the *end*, this food being no other than His own adorable body and blood, which is given as the reward of faith; and therefore, distinct from it.

30. In consequence of His requiring faith in Himself as the Son of God, they, thererefore, said to Him, what sign doest Thou show to convince us of this? Signs were hitherto wrought, such as the multiplication of bread, which has just taken place, but no sign of a nature to convince us of this.

Text.

28. They said therefore unto him: What shall we do that we may work the works of God?

28. *Dixerunt ergo ad eum : Quid faciemus ut operemur opera Dei?*

29. Jesus answered and said to them: This is the work of God, that you believe in him whom he hath sent.

29. *Respondit Jesus, et dixit eis: Hoc est opus Dei, ut credatis in eum quem misit ille.*

30. They said therefore to him: What sign therefore dost thou show that we may see, and may believe thee? what dost thou work?

Text.

30. *Dixerunt ergo ei: Quod ergo tu facis signum ut videamus et credamus tibi? quid operaris.*

31. *Our fathers did eat manna in the desert as it is written, He gave them bread from heaven to eat.*

31. *Patres nostri manducaverunt manna in deserto, sicut scriptum est: Panem de cælo dedit eis manducare.*

32. *Then Jesus said to them: Amen, amen, I say to you, Moses gave you not bread from heaven, but my Father giveth you the true bread from heaven.*

32. *Dixit ergo eis Jesus: Amen, amen dico vobis: Non Moyses dedit vobis panem de cælo, sed Pater meus dat vobis panem de cælo verum.*

33. *For the bread of God is that which cometh down from heaven and giveth life to the world.*

33. *Panis enim Dei est, qui de cælo descendit, et dat vitam mundo.*

34. *They said therefore unto him: Lord, give us always this bread.*

34. *Dixerunt ergo ad eum: Domine, semper da nobis panem hunc.*

Commentary.

"*What dost Thou work?*" as if to say, the works hitherto performed, the signs hitherto given are insufficient, to supply due motives of credibility for begetting in us such faith as you require.

31. This miracle just wrought, is not to be compared with the sign given us by Moses, who fed our fathers with manna for forty years in the desert, "*as it is written, He gave them bread,*" etc. As if they said, Moses, to whom they evidently allude, as appears from our Lord's answer, gave an incomparably greater sign, by feeding our fathers in the desert, not once, but for forty years, not with earthly bread, but "*with bread from heaven,*" and still, he did not ask our fathers or us to believe in him. If the men referred to here be the same spoken of (*v.* 14), they must have changed their minds. Likely, they are different parties altogether.

32. In reply to their assertion, that Moses gave them bread from heaven, our Lord, prefixing His declaration with "*Amen, amen,*" declares in the most emphatic way, that "*Moses did not give them bread from heaven,*" in the strict sense of the word. It was called "*bread from heaven,*" because, generated in the air, it came down from the clouds. Hence, said in a general, but inaccurate, way, to be "*from heaven,*" just as we term the birds of the air that fly aloft towards heaven and descend on the earth, *volucres cæli*, and it is said of the Lord "*intonuit de cælo Dominus*" (Psa. xvii. 14). "*But My Father,*" with whom He is identified, for He Himself gives this gift, which as Son of Man, He promised (*v.* 27). His Father He contrasts with Moses, "*gives you the true bread from heaven,*" where He dwells, as in His own habitation, "*true bread,*" really come down from heaven, of which the bread given by Moses, rained down from the clouds, was a mere type and figure. This bread is the reality, no other than Himself, who came down from heaven, to nourish us, with His own adorable Body and Blood.

33. "*For the bread of God,*" really divine and heavenly in its *origin*, "*is that which cometh down from heaven,*" cometh of itself, by its own power. (The manna was sent or rained down), and is really divine in its *effects*. For, "*it gives life* (eternal) *to the world,*" including the entire human race, rescued at a great price from hell and the power of the devil, unlike the manna, which was confined to the Jewish people, to one particular nation.

34. No longer concerned about signs, or proofs of His Divinity, they are enticed by a desire to receive from Him "*this bread*" not *once*, but "*always,*" perpetually, which He extolled so much, beyond the manna of Moses. Their faith—if they had any, which is implied in the word, "*Lord,*" and in their conceiving that He would give the bread which the Father gives—was still very

Commentary.

imperfect. For, like the Samaritan woman, who made a similar request (iv. 15), they do not regard it as spiritual bread, but only corporal, more excellent than the manna, which they would wish to have always at hand, to remove bodily hunger.

35. "*I am the bread of life,*" etc. In reply to their anxious desire to receive this life-giving bread, our Lord says, that He Himself, inasmuch as He means to give His own Body and Blood in the Eucharist, which He was surely to institute, is that life-giving bread, which came down from heaven, and which the Father gives (*vv.* 32, 33).

"*He that cometh to Me.*" Clearly, He means by faith, as in next clause, "*he that believeth,*" etc.—"*shall not hunger,*" etc. From *v.* 27, it seems quite clear that our Lord in speaking of Himself, is speaking, though not quite so explicitly, as He does hereafter, of His real sacramental presence, of His Body and Blood in the Eucharist. In *v.* 29 He speaks of faith as a *means,* for procuring this food. He says the same, in this verse. He speaks of faith, as the chief *means* of deriving profit from partaking of this heavenly life-giving bread. Our Lord does not explicitly up to this, state, how He is to communicate Himself to us as food. He merely refers to His own *Sacred Person,* as the bread of life. But, He states this more explicitly hereafter. In verses 52–54 He says: it is received by *eating His flesh and drinking His blood.*

36. "*But I have said unto you,*" etc. You seek for some greater miracles, than those I have already performed, thereby implying, that, if wrought, you would believe in Me. But, I have already told you (*v.* 26), and, perhaps, elsewhere, and I now repeat it, that "*you have seen Me,*" in other words, you have *known Me,* or *should have known Me.* For, you have sufficient reasons to know who I am ; and, still, "*You do not believe in Me,*" and, hence, it is to this obstinate refusal to believe in Me, notwithstanding the abundant motives of credibility furnished to you, in My many miracles, and other testimonies regarding Me, you may attribute your being deprived of this heavenly food.

37. Every description of men, without distinction of rank, sex, or degree, be they Jew, Gentile, Greek, or Barbarian, "*whom the Father,*" who had already given Me the nations for inheritance, "*giveth Me,*" and predestinated, according to the purpose and counsel of His will (Ephes. i. 11), for eternal life, "*will come to Me,*" by faith and by co-operation with grace, as My Father's decree, who wishes all men to be saved, cannot be voided or frustrated. If they come not, it will be owing to their own stubborn incredulity and perverse will.

"*And him that cometh to me,*" aided by Divine grace, and

Text.

35. And *Jesus* said to them: *I am the bread of life, he that cometh to me, shall not hunger ; and he that believeth in me, shall never thirst.*

35. Dixit autem eis *Jesus*: *Ego sum panis vitæ : qui venit ad me, non esuriet : et qui credit in me, non sitiet umquam.*

36. *But I said unto you, that you also have seen me, and you believe not.*

36. Sed dixi vobis quia et vidistis me, et non creditis.

37. *All that the Father giveth me, shall come to me : and him that cometh to me, I will not cast out.*

37. Omne, quod dat mihi Pater, ad me veniet : et eum, qui venit ad me, non ejiciam foras :

| Text. | Commentary. |

embraces My faith, "*I will not cast out,*" nor cast his lot among the reprobate, who are to be cast out from the society of the saints in My Church, or from a share in My spiritual and eternal blessings, but I shall place him securely within the saving enclosure of My fold, in order, in the end, to attain eternal life.

Our Lord implies in this verse, that the rejection of some is traceable to a higher cause, viz., their abandonment of God, whose graces they spurn and neglect.

38. *Because I came down from heaven, not to do my own will, but the will of him that sent me.*

38. *Quia descendi de cælo, non ut faciam voluntatem meam, sed voluntatem ejus, qui misit me.*

38. In thus aggregating to My Church, and not rejecting those whom My Father gives Me, I am only carrying out My object in assuming human nature, coming down from the throne of My Father in heaven, which was, not to do My own human will, as far as it might conflict with My Father's heavenly will—with which, however, it was ever in accord—but, to carry out the adorable will of Him who sent Me.

39. *Now this is the will of the Father who sent me; that of all that he hath given me, I should lose nothing, but should raise it up again in the last day.*

39. *Hæc est autem voluntas ejus, qui misit me, Patris: ut omne, quod dedit mihi, non perdam ex eo, sed resuscitem illud in novissimo die.*

39. "*Now, this is the will,*" etc. The adorable will of His Father is, that of all whom He has given the Son, and whom He predestined for faith and grace here, and for glory hereafter, from every age, sex, condition, country, whether Jew or Gentile, He would lose none. Hence, instead of "*casting him out,*" He would receive such into the enclosure of His Church and fold here, and bestow on them eternal happiness, both as to soul and body, by "*raising them up again in the last day.*"

40. *And this is the will of my Father that sent me; that every one who seeth the Son, and believeth in him, may have life everlasting, and I will raise him up on the last day.*

40. *Hæc est autem voluntas Patris mei, qui misit me: ut omnis qui videt Filium, et credit in eum, habeat vitam æternam, et ego resuscitabo eum in novissimo die.*

40. He more fully explains who they are that His Father gives Him, viz., they who, having a knowledge of the Son, and having known Him and seen His miracles, furnished with sufficient motives of credibility, perseveringly believe in Him, with a faith enlivened by good works. Faith and obedience to God's precepts are essential conditions for securing God's promises of life eternal. It is in their thus believing and obeying, the Father hands them over to His Son, to guard them safely, and by raising them up at the last day, to bestow on them a glorious immortality.

Our Lord makes no allusion to the resuscitation of the wicked; because, He is here speaking of the eternal rewards of the just, and the resurrection of the wicked will be rather a curse than a blessing.

41. *The Jews therefore murmured at him because he had said, I am the living bread, which came down from heaven.*

41, 42, 43. "*The Jews, therefore,*" the Doctors of the Synagogue, "*murmured against Him,*" for claiming a Divine origin, by saying, "*I am the living bread that came down from heaven.*" They looked upon His coming down from heaven as utterly incompatible with His earthly parentage and origin, so well known

ST. JOHN, CHAP. VI.

Commentary.

to them, Capharnaum being in the neighbourhood of Nazareth, where He was educated. It was His saying, that He "*came down from heaven,*" that chiefly elicited their murmurs.

42. *And they said: Is not this Jesus the son of Joseph, whose father and mother we know? How then saith he, I came down from heaven?*

42. *Et dicebant: Nonne hic est Jesus filius Joseph, cujus nos novimus patrem, et matrem? Quomodo ergo dicit hic: Quia de cælo descendi.*

43. *Jesus therefore answered and said to them: Murmur not among yourselves.*

43. *Respondit ergo Jesus, et dixit eis: Nolite murmurare in invicem.*

44. "*No one can come to Me . . . draws Him.*" In these words, our Lord mildly conveys to the murmurers, the cause of their obstinate unbelief and resistance to His teaching. For, as faith is the gift of God, no one can come to Christ but by faith, "*unless His* (Heavenly) *Father,*" by the sweet and powerful influence of His grace, which interferes not with man's free will, "*draw him*"—draws him by pleasure, not by compulsion, draws him by sweet moral persuasion, draws him by his preventing and co-operating graces, while freely co-operating with the powerful and attractive inspirations of heaven.

No doubt, there may be violence implied on the part of the subject himself, who, attracted by God's grace, offers violence to his passions, inveterate habits, and, by great exertions, practises virtues, the opposite of the vices of which he was so long the slave. Hence, it is said, "*the Kingdom of Heaven suffereth violence,*" etc. (Matthew xi. 12).

This grace they do not humbly pray for. Hence, it is their own fault, if this heavenly light and spiritual attraction are withheld from them. Our Lord insinuates in these words, that their murmuring and incredulity were the result of their not receiving or asking for grace from His Father. Also, that faith cannot be in man's own power, that it must come from God. He also wishes, to terrify them by insinuating that they were destitute of God's grace and heavenly aid.

"*And I shall raise him up,*" etc. In this, He shows that their murmuring, caused by His saying, He came down from heaven, was quite unmeaning. For, He hath the power of raising up, on the last day, all those to whom the Father gives the gift of faith in Him. Surely, such power argues heavenly descent.

In these words, He also wishes to point out the fruit, as the result of this drawing on the part of His Father, and of the faith received therefrom, viz., that He will bestow on such as believe in Him and shall obey Him, life everlasting, provided they persevere in grace and obedience to God's commandments to the hour of death.

Text.

41. *Murmurabant ergo Judæi de illo, quia dixisset: Ego sum panis vivus qui de cælo descendi.*

44. *No man can come to me, except the Father, who hath sent me, draw him, and I will raise him up in the last day.*

44. *Nemo potest venire od me, nisi Pater, qui misit me, traxerit eum et ego resuscitabo eum in novissimo die.*

Text.

45. *It is written in the prophets:* And they shall all be taught of God. *Every one that hath heard of the Father, and hath learned, cometh to me.*

45. *Est scriptum in Prophetis: Et erunt omnes docibiles Dei. Omnis, qui audivit a Patre, et didicit, venit ad me.*

46. *Not that any man hath seen the Father, but he who is of God, he hath seen the Father.*

46. *Non quia Patrem vidit quisquam nisi is, qui est a Deo, hic vidit Patrem.*

47. *Amen, amen I say unto you: He that believeth in me, hath everlasting life.*

47. *Amen, amen dico vobis: Qui credit in me, habet vitam æternam.*

Commentary.

45. "*It is written in the Prophets.*" He confirms by a prophetic quotation so much prized by the Jews, that no one can have faith unless the Father draw him—"*in the Prophets,*" may mean, the writings of the several Prophets; or, in that portion of the sacred volume termed "*The Prophets.*" All the children of God and of the Church shall be taught of God in the New Law, taught by the interior inspirations of Divine grace, to understand fully and obey the teachings of SS. Scripture, and of those who are appointed to instruct mankind.

That this furnishes no argument against the external ministry of teaching in the Church. (See Hebrews viii. 11, Commentary on.)

"*Every one who has heard,*" etc. Accommodating the prophetic quotation to His purpose, our Lord says, that "*every one who hath heard of the Father,*" whose intellects are enlightened and wills influenced by His grace.

"*And hath learned,*" under this illumination of intellect and impulse of will, to obey.

"*He cometh to Me,*" by faith. The words, "*learn* and *hear,*" denote the same thing, in substance. To "*hear of God,*" is to apprehend the mysteries of faith through revelation and the influence of enlightening grace. "*To learn,*" is, under the influence of Divine grace, to give assent to the truths proposed. Both denote, coming to Christ through faith, and they indicate how men "*are taught of God.*"

46. "*Not that any one hath seen the Father.*" It is not to be inferred from the words, "*all taught of God,*" that God can be seen visibly instructing men, and bringing to faith and salvation such as place no obstacle to the operation of grace. His teaching is interior, invisible. His Eternal Son alone, eternally begotten of Him, identical with Him in His Divine nature and substance, "*He* (alone) *hath seen the Father.*" Of course, He speaks of Himself, the eternally begotten Son of God, who is in the bosom of His Father (John i. 18), the splendour of His glory (Heb. i. 3). "*He hath seen the Father,*" knows His nature, His attributes, designs, and, as equal with the Father, possesses a knowledge superior to what any mere "*man*" possesses.

47. He now resumes the subject of the necessity of faith in Him as a means of obtaining the bread of life, from which he was diverted, in repressing their murmuring, and reproaching them for their incredulity.

"*Amen, amen.*" The repetition of the words shows the solemnity of the utterance He is about making.

"*Hath life everlasting.*" Has it, to be given on the last day; or, has it in certain hope, and faith, accompanied by good works, with perseverance, which are a sure pledge of it.

Commentary.

48-51. In regard to the preceding portion of this chapter, it is admitted on all hands, as beyond all dispute, that from its commencement to *v.* 27, there is only question of material bread, which our Lord miraculously multiplied. At verse 27, it is asserted, by many, as most probable, though not admitted by all Commentators, that our Lord commences to treat, in a general and rather obscure way, alternately of His Body and Blood to be given in the Eucharist, and of faith, as the means and the most necessary disposition for securing and partaking of it worthily. It is almost universally maintained by Catholic Commentators, with some very few exceptions, that, at verse 48, He commences to treat explicitly of His Body and Blood, and explains in the clearest terms, in what manner this promised heavenly nourishment of His own adorable Body and Blood is to be received, viz.: that it is to be partaken by way <u>of *eating* and *drinking*</u>.

Some few Catholic Commentators, among them, Jansenius Gandavensis, hold, that our Lord is not treating of the Eucharist at all, in this chapter. Maldonatus, while referring to these interpreters in terms of praise, regards their opinion, on this point, as temerarious, and all but erroneous.

Text.

48. *I am the bread of life.*

48. *Ego sum panis vitæ.*

49. *Your fathers did eat manna in the desert, and are dead.*

49. *Patres vestri manducaverunt manna in deserto, et mortui sunt.*

50. *This is the bread which cometh down from heaven: that if any man eat of it, he may not die.*

50. *Hic est panis de cœlo descendens: ut si quis ex ipso manducaverit, non moriatur.*

OBJECTION.

"*Your fathers did eat . . . and are dead . . . that if any man eat of it, he may not die.*" A grave objection suggests itself here, which militates no less against the interpretation, which understands the whole chapter to refer to faith, than against our interpretation, which refers it to the Eucharist. It is this: if there be question *of the death of the body.* Why, all, who have faith, or who partake of our Lord's body, yield to the universal decree, "*it is appointed for men once to die*" (Heb. ix. 27), as well, as did the Jews of old, who partook of the manna. Hence, so far as the death of the *body* is concerned, there seems to be no difference. If there be question of the *death of the soul,* many of those who have faith, or who partake of the Blessed Eucharist, fall off from grace (1 Cor. xi. 30), die in their sins, and are lost. Would it not be hard to say, that those who partook of the manna in the desert, were eternally lost? What of Moses, Aaron, Josue, etc.?

The only Commentator I find treating of this objection is Maldonatus. The substance of his reply is this: the comparison instituted by our Lord is between the manna and the promised food, and their relative excellence shown from their *effects.* The superior excellence claimed for the bread, which our Lord promises over the manna, judging from *effects,* consists in this. The manna, which was only given for a *time,* while the Jews were sojourning in the desert ("*did eat manna in the desert,*") and ceased when they reached the Land of Promise (Josue v. 12), had no *intrinsic* efficacy in itself, to rescue from corporal death those who partook of it "*Your fathers . . . and are dead,*" without the hope of being ever recalled to a glorious, immortal life. So far as the *intrinsic* virtue of the manna is concerned, it had no power, *of itself,* to save men from death or recall them to a glorious immortality after their short sleep in the grave; whereas, this food which I will give, accomplishes what is to be infinitely more prized; it possesses the *intrinsic* efficacy *of itself,* not only to bestow everlasting glorious life on *the soul*, and rescue it from eternal death ; but, also to bestow a glorious *immortality on the body*. In other words, this bread can, of its own *intrinsic* excellence and efficacy, bestow what is *greater*, viz., eternal life on the *soul*, it will bestow what is less also, by restoring the life of *the body*. For, although we all return to the dust from which we were formed, this is but a passing state of sleep (1 Thess. iv. 12), as our bodies are to be resuscitated, by the power of the lifegiving body of Christ, "*et ego resuscitabo eum in novissimo die.*" Hence, unlike the manna, which could not of *itself*, either ward off death or confer immortal life "*and are dead ;*" this bread of *itself* virtually preserves from *temporal* death, by restoring us to life, and confers a glorious immortality on the soul. This is Maldonatus's answer to the objection just made. The body of Christ is, *of itself, of its own efficacy*, the seed of a glorious immortality for our bodies, so necessary in the present order of Divine Providence to complete the full happiness of the soul. If men, after receiving the body of Christ, desert the Church or die in mortal sin, this is owing to their own perversity, which destroys the effect which the worthy participation of our Lord's body would produce in bestowing eternal happiness on the soul, and as its necessary complement, a glorious immortality on the body; thus rendering happy the entire man, soul and body.

If those who partook of the manna in the desert are destined for a glorious immortality, as, no doubt, some of them are, this was not owing to the manna, which of *itself*, unlike the bread our Lord promised, had no such efficacy; but owing rather to their faith and good works, in view of the retrospective merits of Christ. The manna was given only to support bodily life, and had no power to resuscitate after death those who had partaken of it.

Text.

51. *I am the living bread, which came down from heaven.*

51. *Ego sum panis vivus, qui de cælo descendi.*

52. *If any man eat of this bread, he shall live for ever: and the bread that I will give, is my flesh for the life of the world.*

52. *Si quis manducaverit ex hoc pane, vivet in æternum : et panis, quem ego dabo, caro mea est pro mundi vita.*

Commentary.

51. "*I am the living bread,*" *living* in Myself— unlike the manna, which was an inanimate substance—*and life-giving* to others.

"*Which came down from heaven,*" really from God's heaven, where He reigns in glory. The manna was only distilled from the clouds.

52. "*If any man eat of this bread,*" with the proper dispositions, and persevere in grace, "*he shall live for ever,*" enjoy eternal happiness, both as to soul and body, as already explained. This bread has the efficacy of raising the body, in a glorious state, from the tomb, to enjoy eternal happiness in union with the soul, so necessary to complete the happiness of the entire man.

"*And the bread that I will give*"—to be eaten—"*is My flesh,*" to which is added in the Greek ("*which I shall give*"—to be immolated on the cross) "*for the life of the world.*" Here, our Lord explicitly states in *what form*, or *how*, this life-giving bread, which He eulogizes so much, whose wonderful effects He extols so much in the foregoing, is to be received. *What* it is, viz., His own real flesh—the same which He was to " *give* "—which He was to sacrifice on the cross—"*for the life of the world,*" for the redemption of mankind, for whom He meant to pay a full ransom, by the blood

Commentary.

of the cross. Similar are the words of Institution, "*Hoc est Corpus meum, quod pro vobis datur.*" The words in the future, "*which I will give,*" cannot refer to faith, which He had given them already. The just of the Old Law had it. Faith belongs to all times. It was from the beginning. (Heb. xi.)

53. "*How can this man,*" etc. This fresh outburst on the part of the Jews, after our Lord had already satisfied them (30—47), and repressed their murmurings on the subject of faith, or of believing in Him, renders it clear that they here understood Him to speak literally of the real manducation of His flesh. Hence, their rebellious murmurings and incredulity.

"*How,*" is the favourite exclamation with all heretics, who measure the power of God by their own capacity to understand. The words are also as expressive of scorn as of rebellious incredulity. "*How can* THIS MAN," so mean, so lowly, of no earthly consideration? etc.

54. Far from correcting their impression, which resulted from their having understood His words in their plain and literal signification, our Lord rather confirms it, by repeating the same in still stronger terms, with a solemn, repeated asseveration, almost equivalent to an oath, menacing them also with eternal death, in case of refusal to obey an ordinance founded on the literal meaning of His words, to which they so strongly object as impossible, in their minds, utterly absurd. If their impression were erroneous, founded on the plain and literal meaning of His words, could our Lord, knowing their minds, confirm their error? They were, therefore, right substantially in understanding His words, in the literal sense, however mistaken they might be as to the mode in which His words, regarding real manducation, could be carried out. Our Lord does not directly answer their question, "*how?*" But, He insists on the fact or mandate.

The objections raised here against the practice of the Church in giving Communion to the *laity* under one kind only, are sufficiently refuted in Treatises of Theology, where, at the same time, the Catholic discipline is sufficiently vindicated.

The Council of Trent on this subject (SS. xxi., c. 1), says, "*From the words, however differently understood, it can by no means be fairly inferred, that Communion under both kinds, is commanded by our Lord.* For, He who said, 'EXCEPT YOU EAT . . . AND drink,' etc., also said, 'IF ANY MAN EAT OF THIS BREAD, HE SHALL LIVE FOR EVER' (*v.* 52); also, 'THE BREAD THAT I WILL GIVE YOU, IS MY FLESH,' etc. (*v.* 52). 'HE THAT EATETH THIS BREAD, SHALL LIVE FOR EVER'" (*v.* 59). (See also St. Paul, 1 Cor. xi. 27, Commentary on.)

The conjunction "*and,*" may be understood disjunctively, as it

Text.

53. *The Jews therefore strove among themselves, saying: How can this man give us his flesh to eat?*

53. *Litigabant ergo Judæi ad invicem, dicentes: Quomodo potest hic nobis carnem suam dare ad manducandum?*

54. *Then Jesus said to them: Amen, amen I say unto you: Except you eat the flesh of the son of man, and drink his blood, you shall not have life in you.*

54. *Dixit ergo eis Jesus: Amen, amen dico vobis: Nisi manducaveritis carnem Filii hominis, et biberitis ejus sanguinem non habebitis vitam in vobis.*

Text.	Commentary.
	often is, according to Scriptural usage. (Exod. xxi. 23 ; xxii. 10 ; Acts iii. 6, etc.)

The Greek for "*except*" is (ἐὰν μὴ), *if you do not*. The meaning then would be, if you do not eat the flesh of the Son of Man, and if you do not drink His blood, that is, if you do neither one nor the other.

The usage of the Church, at one period, giving Communion under both kinds ; at another, allowing it, for wise reasons, only under one, is the best proof, that, while we are obliged by Divine precept to receive "really, truly and substantially," the Body and Blood of our Lord, the *mode* of receiving it is not obligatory ; since, under one species or the other, we receive our Lord's body, which is contained in either species, His flesh and blood being necessarily inseparable, in a living body, such as our Lord's is, after His Resurrection. We have the body of our Lord under the species of bread, and His blood under the species of wine, *vi verborum*; but, we have the body under the species of wine also, and the blood under the species of bread, and the soul under both, *vi concomitantiæ* (Council of Trent SS. xiii., c. 3). What is of obligation is, that we receive the Body and Blood of Christ, which is done by receiving either species, the Body and Blood being contained in each. Our Lord, four different times, promises eternal life to eating alone, in this chapter.

On *Priests* alone, is it obligatory to receive, under both species, when sacrificing, in order perfectly to represent our Lord's sacrifice on the cross, of which the Mass is a continuation. On the cross, His flesh and blood were separated in death. If the particle, "*and*," is to be understood as a conjunction, then, it would be used in that sense, in order to show us, that we should keep in mind His sacred Passion, of which the Eucharist is a permanent memorial.

55. *He that eateth my flesh, and drinketh my blood, hath everlasting life : and I will raise him up in the last day.*

55. *Qui manducat meam carnem, et bibit meum sanguinem habet vitam æternam : et ego resuscitabo eum in novissimo die.*

55. What our Lord had, in the preceding verse, commanded, under a threat of forfeiture of eternal life, in case of refusal to obey, He now solemnly repeats, with a promise of eternal life in case of compliance, "*eateth My flesh*," etc., of course, with worthy dispositions, "*hath everlasting life*," has a right to it, unless he forfeits it through his own fault.

56. *For my flesh is meat indeed; and my blood is drink indeed.*

56. *Caro enim mea, vere est cibus: et sanguis meus, vere est potus.*

56. "*Indeed*," in reality. It is true food and true drink, since no other food or drink can give everlasting life to the soul or to the body. This the promised food effects.

"*I shall raise him up*," etc. The innate virtue and efficacy of our Lord's body worthily received, will communicate a glorious immortality to the soul. The body, after a short time in the grave, will be raised up, so that it might be virtually said not to

Commentary.

have died at all. Hence, St. Paul calls it a sleep, "*de dormientibus,*" etc. (1 Thess. iv. 12.) The Apostle speaks so, in view of the coming general Resurrection, as appear from that passage.

57. He shows again, how the man "*who eats His flesh,*" etc., hath everlasting life; because, he is united with Christ, Himself life eternal and the source of it in others, as the food is with the man who receives it, so that after the dwelling of our Lord's *humanity* in us is dissolved, his *Divinity* remains, and we are, in some measure, made partakers of the Divine nature. St. Cyril illustrates this, by the example of liquefied wax mixed with wax similarly liquefied, which becomes one mixed mass or body. Hence, when the soul is thus united with Christ, it receives supernatural life.

58. "*Living Father*"—the fountain and source of all life—"*sent Me*" to assume human nature, and in My Incarnation, communicated life, which, on account of this union in My Incarnation, I, in turn, impart to others, "*and I live by the Father.*" The Greek for "*by*" (διὰ) would, perhaps, be better rendered, not, *propter* Patrem, "*by the Father,*" but, *per,* "*through the Father,*" in consequence of the essential life, communicated in My eternal generation.

"*The same shall live by (or through) Me.*" As the Father, with whom I was identified in My eternal generation—He thus being one with Me—communicated essentially life to Me : so the man, who receiving me as food, thus, becoming identified with Me, in a certain sense—on account of the union established by receiving Me as food—though not so closely united as I with the Father, receives through Me, immortal life, which will be fully conferred on the last day.

The words, "*as the living Father hath sent Me,*" would seem to be prefixed to the comparison He means to institute in a limited sense—for, no union can equal that of the Father and his Eternal Son—for the purpose of showing, how it is our Lord was in a position to bestow life on creatures, who received His flesh as food. This resulted from His mission to earth by His Eternal Father.

59. This would seem to be a summary and concluding repetition of His doctrine, in the preceding parts of this chapter (*vv.* 32–41– 49, 50–52–55). In these verses, the contents of this verse have been already fully explained.

59. *Hic est panis, qui de cælo descendit. Non sicut manducaverunt patres vestri manna, et mortui sunt. Qui manducat hunc panem, vivet in æternum.*

60. This is mentioned by the Evangelist to show, that no one could question the fact, that this discourse was delivered by our Lord. These words were not spoken in an obscure corner. The

Text.

57. *He that eateth my flesh and drinketh my blood, abideth in me, and I in him.*

57. *Qui manducat meam carnem, et bibit meum sanguinem in me manet, et ego in illo.*

58. *As the living Father sent me, and I live by the Father so he that eateth me, the same also shall live by me.*

58. *Sicut misit me vivens Pater, et ego vivo propter Patrem: et qui manducat me, et ipse vivet propter me.*

59. *This is the bread that came down from heaven. Not as your fathers did eat manna, and are dead. He that eateth this bread, shall live for ever.*

60. *These things he said teaching in the synagogue, in Capharnaum.*

I

Text.

60. *Hæc dixit in synagoga docens, in Capharnaum.*

61. *Many therefore of his disciples hearing it, said: This saying is hard, and who can hear it?*

61. *Multi ergo audientes ex discipulis ejus, dixerunt: Durus est hic sermo, et quis potest eum audire?*

62. *But Jesus knowing in himself that his disciples murmured at this, said to them: Doth this scandalize you?*

62. *Sciens autem Jesus apud semetipsum quia murmurarent de hoc discipuli ejus, dixit eis: Hoc vos scandalizat?*

63. *If then you shall see the son of man ascend up where he was before?*

63. *Si ergo videritis filium hominis ascendentem ubi erat prius?*

Commentary.

place was public, in some respects, sacred, "*the Synagogue*," devoted to prayer and the exposition of the Word of God; resorted to by all classes, Scribes, Priests, and people. The city of "*Capharnaum*" was, on account of its position, a mart of traffic, and a place of public resort. Our Lord also delivered these words in an official capacity, "*teaching*" the doctrines of eternal life.

61. "*Many* (even) *of His disciples*,"—no doubt; a still greater number of His enemies—"*hearing it*," the doctrines recorded in the preceding part of the chapter and summed up in *v.* 59. There is reference to the seventy-two disciples, and not to all of them. "*Many.*" Nor are the twelve Apostles included, as appears from *v* 68 "*This saying*," viz., relating to His having come down from heaven, but principally and chiefly to the necessity of eating His flesh, "*is hard*," incredible, difficult to be conceived and digested in the mind, like hard indigestible food, received into the stomach.

"*And who can bear it?*" The precept imposed is, as they fancy simply intolerable, utterly revolting. While they were right in their literal apprehension of our Lord's words, respecting the real manducation of His flesh, which our Lord Himself confirms; they erred, as to the *mode*. There was nothing unnatural, nothing revolting in the real manducation of His body, which He imparted under the *species* or appearance of bread and wine.

62. Likely, the murmuring, unbelieving portion of His disciples durst not express themselves openly. They did so privately. Our Lord, knowing the thoughts of their hearts and the secret expressions of their unbelief and their murmurings, "*said, doth this scandalize you?*" After all My miracles amongst you in such numbers and variety, to prove My Divine mission from the Father, and My undoubted veracity, are My words just spoken, a stumbling block to you? and are you disposed to desert Me?

"*If then you shall see the Son of Man*," etc. The words, *What shall you say*, are understood, in order to complete the sentence. These words are understood by some, as a reply to their murmuring about His having come down from heaven, as if He said: your difficulties on this head will vanish, when at My Ascension you shall see Me, or, if unworthy of witnessing it yourselves, you shall hear from My disciples, who shall soon see Me, in virtue of My own power and majesty, in My assumed human nature, as Son of Man, mount up to heaven, "*where I was before*," in my Divine nature; whence I descended, without leaving it, in assuming human nature for your redemption. Then, you will be able to know, that having been in heaven, I came down from heaven; that I am not only veracious in My words and promises, but, a true Prophet, God, the Eternal

Commentary.

Son of God, to whom all things are possible; that there is nothing impossible for Me in what I said, and that I can, therefore, give My own flesh to eat, and raise the dead to life, as I promised.

Others, with Maldonatus, interpret the words to mean, if you are scandalized at My saying, that I will give you My flesh, etc., now while I am with you on earth, and regard this as impossible and utterly incredible, how much greater cause of scandal, how much greater difficulty will you have, in believing this, when the flesh which I promised to give you is mounted up to heaven? It was not unusual with our Lord to rebuke such unreasoning unbelievers by proposing to their belief truths involving greater difficulty, which they should, however, believe. (John i. 50.; iii. 12).

64. "*It is the spirit that vivifies*," etc. These words mean, it is My Divine Spirit, or My Divinity, which is inseparably united with My flesh, that gives it a life-giving property, which it imparts to those who partake of Me. But My flesh of itself, the human element, regarded apart from this Spirit, and not united with it, "*profiteth nothing.*"

"*The words I have spoken to you*," on the subject of My Body and Blood, are to be understood in a spiritual sense—opposed to the gross, carnal meaning attached to them by the Jews, who understood them of partaking of His body, as ordinary flesh, but not as opposed to the literal reality. The *spiritual* sense of words is one thing; the *metaphorical* or *figurative*, another. Our Lord could never have meant His words on the subject of the manducation of His body, etc., to be understood *figuratively*, as excluding the *reality*. He only wished them to be understood in a *spiritual* sense, by no means excluding reality, and quite different from the carnal conceptions of the Capharnaites, who fancied that our Lord's flesh was to be eaten, like flesh purchased in the shambles.

"*The words I have spoken to you*," etc. The words which have caused you so much scandal regarding My flesh, etc., are not to be understood in a gross, carnal sense, such as you entertain; but, *spiritually*, as referring to My Divine Spirit, animating My body, which you really and substantially receive. Understood in a spiritual sense, as referring to My real flesh and blood animated by My Divinity, My words will be to you a source of spiritual life.

Others understand, the word, "*spirit*," of the spiritual understanding of His words, by man's intellect, aided and enlightened by grace, and practised in the principles of faith.

"*Flesh*," the material, carnal understanding of them without the aid of grace or faith, such as caused scandal in the minds of the Jews. Understood in the former sense, the words are the source of life; in the latter sense, they are of no avail whatever.

Similar is the idea conveyed by St. Paul, when he speaks of the sensual, compared with the spiritual man (1 Cor. ii.), relative to the

Text.

64. *It is the spirit that quickeneth the flesh profiteth nothing. The words that I have spoken to you, are spirit and life.*

64. *Spiritus est, qui vivificat: caro non prodest quidquam, verba, quæ ego locutus sum vobis, spiritus et vita sunt.*

Text.	Commentary.

understanding of what appertains to the Spirit of God (see Commentary on). The words which I have spoken, are to be understood in the spiritual sense referred to; and thus understood, they are the source of life.

Which ever of the above interpretations we adopt, we can clearly see, the utter absurdity of those outside the Church, when they interpret the words *figuratively*, as excluding the real presence of His flesh, and the real manducation of the same; since their interpretation of these words in a figurative sense, as if our Lord meant by them to correct the ideas of the Capharnaites, and exclude His real manducation, is utterly gratuitous and unfounded. Our Lord commanded men to eat His flesh, under pain of eternal death. He could not, therefore, say of that flesh, "*it profits nothing.*" The words of our Lord in this verse, could not be regarded as corrective of the impressions of the Capharnaites; since He had already repeated the words which gave offence, with a solemn asseveration equivalent to an oath, and repeats the same several times. It would be late at this period, after having before impressed them so strongly, to come out with a correction, especially as He had been after positively corroborating their ideas. Moreover, neither apostles nor disciples understood these words, as corrective of the preceding.

65. *But there are some of you that believe not. For Jesus knew from the beginning who they were that did not believe, and who he was that would betray him.*

65. *Sed sunt quidquam ex vobis, qui non credunt. Sciebat enim ab initio Jesus qui essent non credentes, et quis traditurus esset eum.*

65. Our Lord here points out the cause of their rebellious murmurings. It arose from their incredulity; their want of faith in His Divine mission, notwithstanding the many and splendid miracles He had wrought. "*Some of them,*" for want of humility of heart, "*did not believe.*" Hence, their murmurings, and incapacity, to understand Him fully, as to the *mode* of receiving His flesh. ("*For, Jesus knew from the beginning,*" etc.) These words, to the end of the verse, are to be read parenthetically, "*from the beginning,*" in virtue of His Divine Omniscience, He knew from the very time He selected them, who among them would be alienated and incredulous, and who among them was to turn traitor; and still He selected and called them, so that He did so with a full knowledge of what was to happen. The Evangelist explains here beforehand the contents of (*vv.* 71 and 72). "*Beginning,*" would be true of eternity and of the time of His Incarnation. Judas was among the incredulous murmurers; and it is here insinuated, that in consequence of our Lord's discourse in this chapter, he became alienated; and this led finally to his act of shocking treason.

66. *And he said: Therefore did I say to you, that no man can come to me, unless it be given him by my Father.*

66. "*Therefore did I say to you,*" at least substantially (in verse 44). Some of them do not believe, owing to their not having been blessed with the gift of faith, which must come from grace and not from man's free will only. It must come from "*My Father,*" who would give it to all who would place no

Commentary

obstacle. Hence, they may ascribe their want of faith to their own stubborn resistance to grace, and to their pride, which will not stoop to ask this grace fervently and humbly from God.

67. "*After this*," after having heard our Lord repeatedly corroborating their impressions regarding the real manducation of His flesh, "*many of His disciples*," whose faith, no doubt, was infirm, and who were disappointed in their hopes of receiving bread from the hands of our Lord, miraculously multiplied for their bodily sustenance, and were manifestly disgusted with His promising them His own flesh instead, "*went back*," left His society, "*and walked no more with Him*," ceased to be any longer His disciples.

The Evangelist does not refer to the twelve (verse 70), who remained with Him, not excepting Judas, who had an eye to His betrayal; nor to the seventy-two disciples, who were not yet selected. They were chosen, after our Lord left for Galilee.

From this and the following verse it is clear, these men understood our Lord's words literally of His real flesh and blood; otherwise, they could have no difficulty or cause for offence; since being already His disciples, they must have believed in Him. Would our Lord have allowed them to depart with the certain risk of losing their souls, which He came down from heaven to save, without explaining Himself and correcting their false conceptions, if they were mistaken in their interpretation of His words? Would He not have corrected their false ideas and explained His words? They must, therefore, have been right; and our Lord must have spoken of the real manducation of His flesh.

The plain and necessary inference from this and next verse is, that our Lord's words were properly understood, in a literal sense; and that this could not, therefore, be corrected. No doubt, our Lord would have done this, if He could, rather than allow His disciples and apostles to desert Him.

68. This shows how correctly our Lord was understood, as to the literal meaning of His words, since rather than offer a word of explanation or correction, He was prepared to allow even His chosen twelve to depart, for whom He shows here singular regard and affection. Seeing the others depart, He said. "*Will you also go away?*" As it is free for the others to depart or stay, and they could remain and be attracted by the grace of My Father, if they were humbly to pray for it, and not obstruct its operation by their stubborn and rebellious wills; so, it is free for you also, to go or stay.

69. "*Simon Peter*," from his innate fervour, which he displayed on other occasions also, speaking in the name of his companions, whose opinions, he felt he was giving expression to, answered:

Text

66. *Et dicebat. Propterea dixi vobis quia nemo potest venire ad me, nisi fuerit ei datum a Patre meo.*

67. *After this many of his disciples went back; and walked no more with him.*
67. *Ex hoc multi discipulorum ejus abierunt retro: et jam non cum illo ambulabant.*

68. *Then Jesus said to the twelve: Will you also go away?*

68. *Dixit ergo Jesus ad duodecim: numquid et vos vultis abire?*

69. *And Simon Peter answered him: Lord, to whom shall we go? thou hast the words of eternal life.*

Text.	Commentary.

69. *Respondit ergo ei Simon Petrus: Domine, ad quem ibimus? verba vitæ æternæ habes.*

"*To whom shall we go?*" Where else can we go? From what other teacher are we to seek for guidance and truth?

"*Thou hast the words of eternal life,*" for such as believe and obey your doctrine; you alone can confer eternal life. From you alone, not from Jewish Doctors or heathen philosophers, can we hope for true doctrine which leads to eternal life. Others may regard it as harsh, repulsive; not so with us. We regard it as sweet and attractive; since it alone leads to everlasting happiness.

You alone can, by your words, which are infallibly true, point out to us the way to eternal life, and surely confer it.

70. *And we have believed and have known that thou art the Christ the Son of God.*

70. *Et nos credidimus, et cognovimus quia tu es Christus filius Dei.*

70. "*And we have believed*"—and believe still—"*and have known*"—and still know—from undoubted sources of evidence, from the testimony of the Baptist, from your own miracles, from your heavenly doctrines, sanctity of life, etc.—Hence, ours is not a blind, unreasoning faith—"*that Thou art the Christ,*" the long expected Messiah, "*the Son of God,*" the natural, eternally begotten, co-equal Son of God, whose words, be they ever so incomprehensible, we believe to be most true, whose promises are sure to be fulfilled. Hence, we embrace with all our hearts, Thy doctrine regarding Thy real flesh, which Thou wilt give us to eat, unto life eternal, and a pledge and principle of a glorious immortality.

71. *Jesus answered them: Have not I chosen you twelve; and one of you is a devil?*

71. *Respondit eis Jesus: Nonne ego vos duodecim elegi: et ex vobis unus diabolus est.*

71. "*Have I not chosen you twelve,*" specially selected you, out of all My followers, to be the future pillars of My Church. "*And one of you is a devil?*" Our Lord here refers to the treason of Judas—1st, in order to correct the assertion of Peter, that the twelve, without exception, believed in Him. 2ndly, He also refers to it, in order to save them from being scandalized when it would happen, by showing them He knew it beforehand, and by preparing them for it. 3rdly, to put them on their guard against presumption and over confidence in themselves; and thus, to inspire them with humility and diffidence in themselves, and stimulate them to secure, by fear and trembling, the great gift of final perseverance.

"*A devil,*" Far from contenting Himself with disbelieving My words; even at this moment, he is harbouring thoughts of betraying Me, and of co-operating with the devil, in handing Me over to death. For meaning of word, "*devil,*" see Matt. iv. 1; Mark i. 23 (Commentary on).

72. *Now he meant Judas Iscariot, the son of Simon: for this same was about to betray him, whereas he was one of the twelve.*

72. He alluded to Judas Iscariot, the son of Simon (see Matthew x. 3).

"*Whereas he was one of the twelve,*" shows the magnitude of his guilt and black ingratitude.

72. *Dicebat autem Judam Simonis Iscariotem: hic enim erat traditurus eum, cum esset unus ex duodecim.*

PROOF OF THE REAL PRESENCE OF OUR LORD IN THE BLESSED EUCHARIST.

It is but right we should acknowledge our indebtedness for a portion of the following proof to Cardinal Wiseman's admirable Lecture "ON THE REAL PRESENCE OF THE BODY AND BLOOD OF OUR LORD IN THE BLESSED EUCHARIST."

The proof may be thus briefly stated—In order to establish the doctrine of the Catholic Church regarding the real Presence of our Lord in the Blessed Eucharist, from His words in this chapter, commencing with verse 51, it is merely necessary, to show that His words are to be taken in their plain, obvious, literal signification. Understood thus, they prove, that our Redeemer promised to give, under the form of food, His real flesh—the flesh which He gave for the life of the world. They prove, that men are bound by a Divine precept, to partake from time to time of the same flesh, in the form of food, under pain of eternal death.

This Divine precept shows it must continue, as a permanent rite in the Church. Our religious adversaries themselves admit, that taken literally, our Redeemer's words prove the Catholic doctrine. Hence, regardless of the common consent of the Holy Fathers, of the universal voice of antiquity, and the Decrees of Councils, they leave no means untried, to wrest them to a figurative and forced signification.

Taken literally, then, our Redeemer's words prove our doctrine. Must they be understood literally? Can they admit of any other interpretation? That they can be understood only in a literal sense, will appear clear; if it be borne in mind, in the first place, that they were understood in this sense only, by those whom our Redeemer addressed; and, secondly, that these could not be mistaken in understanding them literally, without involving our Redeemer in a breach of duty, and rendering Him guilty of positively confirming error.

First, the Capharnaites, whom our Redeemer addressed, understood His words in the literal sense of real manducation of His flesh. For, when He required of them in the preceding part of His address, to believe in Him, as having come down from heaven (*vv.* 40, 41); after murmuring and exclaiming, how can He, the Son of Joseph, whose father and mother we know, say, He came down from heaven? On His assigning satisfactory *reasons* or motives for this belief, they acquiesce, and all further murmuring ceases. But, no sooner does He make use of the expression, "*the bread that I will give is my flesh*" (*v.* 52), than they openly and rebelliously cry out, "*How can this man give us his flesh to eat?*" which proves, that they understood Him to speak of a different subject altogether.

Not only do the Capharnaites murmur and understand Him to speak literally; but, even His own disciples exclaim, "*it is a hard saying,*" etc. Now, if these were questions merely of faith in Him, what difficulty could faith in Him present to those who, by the very fact of being His disciples, were already supposed to believe in Him? They, therefore, understood Him to speak literally.

But why dwell on a point which our religious opponents themselves admit, when, in the language of scorn and derision, they taunt Catholics, on account of taking our Lord's words literally, with being gross, carnal Capharnaites.

Those, therefore, whom our Lord addressed at Capharnaum understood Him to speak literally. The next question is, were they right or were they wrong: if they were right, so must we. That the Capharnaites were right in taking the words of our Lord literally, is proved by a reference to our Lord's invariable practice when delivering His sacred doctrine. It was a rule which He invariably observed, that whenever His hearers understood His words *literally*, when He meant to have them understood *figuratively*, He, in every instance, corrected the error by telling His hearers, that His words should be understood *figuratively*. On the other hand, whenever His hearers understood His words literally, and were right in doing so, but took offence at His doctrine founded on the literal signification of His words, our Redeemer repeated the obnoxious form of words, regardless of the offence of His hearers. It will suffice to adduce a few examples, out of the many the Gospel furnishes of our Lord's rule of action, in both instances. First, when His words were understood literally, whereas He had intended them to be understood figuratively. We have the case of Nicodemus (John iii.) who understood our Lord's words regarding a second birth, literally, our Lord corrects him at once, and shows He is to be understood figuratively; of a spiritual birth of water and the Holy Ghost. Again, in this same Gospel (iv. 32), His disciples erroneously understood Him to speak literally of corporal food, He explains His words as referring to spiritual food, viz., doing the work of His Father. Again (xi. 11), speaking of Lazarus, who was already dead, He says, "*Lazarus our friend sleepeth.*" They understood Him literally. He at once explains, "*Lazarus is dead.*" Again (Matthew xvi. 6), He takes care to correct their erroneous ideas regarding the leaven of the Pharisees, and says, He meant their *false doctrine*. Numerous other examples could be adduced in illustration of the same. Were we to search the four Gospels, no single instance could be adduced to the contrary; we would find, that in every single instance, our Lord took care to correct His hearers whenever they misunderstood Him, by taking His words in a literal sense, when He meant to be understood figuratively.

Let us now examine our Saviour's practice, whenever His hearers correctly understood His words in a literal sense; then, no matter what murmurs took place, what objections were raised, what offence was given, He always repeats His words, in a literal sense, and insists on being believed. Of this we have an example in the 9th chapter of St. Matthew, where our Lord insists on having words, regarding His power to remit sins, understood literally, and works a miracle to prove it. Again, in the 8th chapter of 1st John, He repeats His words, which in their literal sense caused the Jews great offence, as to His having seen Abraham, "*before Abraham was, I am.*" They understood Him correctly; He, then, insists on the literal truth of His words, saying, "*before Abraham was, I am*" (viii. 58). Again, in this chapter, He speaks of having come down from heaven. The Jews understood Him correctly in the literal sense; and although they murmured and were offended, He still repeats the obnoxious phrase; and, three times successively, declares that He really came down from heaven. The few examples cited will suffice, out of many. It can be said, without fear of contradiction, that if we read the whole history of our Redeemer's life, from the first chapter of St. Matthew, to the last of St. John, we will find, that whenever our Lord treated a doctrinal subject, and meant His words figuratively, while His hearers erroneously understood them literally, He sets them right by explaining His words. On the other hand, whenever His words were correctly understood, no matter what objections were raised or offences given, He invariably repeats the obnoxious expressions. Therefore, as our Redeemer, in the passage under consideration, six different times, regardless of the offence of His hearers, repeated the obnoxious words, that "they should eat His flesh and drink His blood," we have a right to assume, that He was understood correctly, and His words, therefore, to be taken literally; unless it be proved (and that was never attempted) that in this solitary instance, He departed from His invariable practice.

In the next place, even were we to suppose, that our Redeemer departed from His usual practice in such cases; still, it is clear, His hearers were right in taking His words literally; because, if they were in error, our Redeemer would be bound to correct and set them right. For, every man who assumes the function of teacher, is bound, in virtue of his office, to remove and correct any false conceptions, arising from the plain and obvious signification of His words, and the obligation becomes greater in proportion to the importance of the subject and the disastrous consequences likely to result from any error regarding it.

Now, our Lord filled the office of teacher on this occasion, "*teaching in the Synagogue of Capharnaum*" (*v.* 60). The doctrine was exceedingly important, embracing one of the leading truths of Christianity, regarding which, an error would involve no less disastrous consequences than eternal death. The error of the Capharnaites, had it existed, would flow from the plain and obvious signification of His own words. Hence, as public teacher, He would be strictly bound to correct it. Since, therefore, instead of doing so, He positively confirmed their impressions regarding the real manducation of His flesh, it is clear, that these impressions were substantially correct. This is suggestive of a still stronger argument, viz., that our Redeemer not only omitted correcting, but positively confirmed, the impressions of the Capharnaites. Now, it would be nothing short of blasphemy to assert, that our Redeemer could, for an instant, confirm error. Hence, the impressions of the Capharnaites were quite correct. It should be borne in mind, that the confirmation of the impressions of the Capharnaites by our Lord was not confined to mere simple assertion. He employs the most solemn asseveration, equivalent to an oath. They say, "*how can this man give us His flesh to eat?*" He replies, "*Amen, Amen, I say to you, except you eat,*" etc., words which are supposed by many to be the terms of oath employed by the Almighty in confirming repeatedly His promise to the human race. Now, if there be such a thing as perjury, He surely, would be guilty of it, who would confirm by oath, in a figurative sense, words which He knew to be understood literally, by His hearers. Hence, as our Redeemer confirms by oath, or by, at least, what is equivalent to it, the words repeatedly addressed to the Capharnaites, He must do so, according to their acceptation of them, which we have shown to be in the literal sense. They were, therefore, right in understanding his words literally.

This reasoning is further confirmed by our Redeemer's treatment of His own disciples, many of whom, from that day forward, owing to the offence, they conceived at the literal meaning of His works, desert His society altogether, "*went back and walked no more with Him*" (*v.* 67). Now, I ask, if they were in error, could it, for a moment, be supposed that our Redeemer would permit them, at the risk of their eternal salvation, to desert Him altogether, whom He had specially enrolled in His service, to whom He was in the habit of expounding these truths, which lay beyond the reach of the multitude generally, while He might by a single word remove the error, by simply telling them, they mistook His meaning, that He proposed nothing new, that He was developing these points of faith, which they had already believed! And yet, far from doing so, our Redeemer suffers them to depart, without offering a single word in explanation; nay, He positively confirms their impression, by recurring to the great miracle of His Ascension, after which He says, they would have even greater difficulty in believing His doctrine (v. 63). If, then, He treated merely of faith, His Ascension, far from rendering it more difficult, would, on the contrary, render it more easy; it is, only taken literally, His words would be more difficult of accomplishment after His Ascension, than before it; and, therefore, by recurring to it, our Redeemer would confirm the impression of His disciples, regarding the literal acceptation of His words, which, consequently, could not be erroneous.

His conduct towards His Apostles, is a further confirmation of the arguments already adduced. For, not only does He suffer His *disciples* to depart without offering a single word in explanation; but, addressing His twelve *Apostles*, He asks them will they also go away? (v. 68) Can it be supposed, that He would permit His twelve *Apostles*, the twelve pillars, upon which was about to be reared the spiritual edifice of His Church, to depart without offering a single word in explanation, if they were in error; particularly when that error would flow from the plain and obvious meaning of His words, delivered by Himself in capacity of teacher? Yet, He plainly insinuates, that, He would rather suffer even them to depart, than correct their impression. The line of action adopted by our Redeemer can, therefore, be accounted for on no other supposition, than that they were right in taking His words literally, which impression He did not correct, because, He could not correct it, unless, He wished to correct right, and say it was wrong.

ILLUSTRATION.

To elucidate the course of reasoning now put forward, I will avail myself of a familiar illustration; Suppose, a Protestant missionary, placed in circumstances precisely similar to those, in which our Redeemer addressed the multitude at Capharnaum. Suppose him in some distant wilds, delivering a series of catechetical lectures on the truth of Christianity, to a body of men, who had not yet embraced that religion. Suppose him to have succeeded in forming a few converts, who, relinquishing their secular employments, accompany him everywhere on his missionary excursions among the people. Among other points of instruction, he, for a particular occasion, selects the article of faith in the death of Christ (for, observe, that is the point of faith, upon which, in the minds of our religious opponents, our Redeemer treats in the 6th chap. of St. John); and by way of preparation for this great and important truth, he descants fully, upon the necessity of faith in his divinity, in consequence of His having performed greater wonders than did Moses, or any other of the sacred personages, who were the leading characters in every preceding dispensation. And having fully satisfied them as to the Divinity of the Redeemer, and having repressed the murmurings which they, at first, indulged in, and having exhibited this faith in His Divinity under the figure of *bread* and *food*—terms, with which they are supposed to be acquainted—he at once proposes to them the article of faith in His death, in terms the most extraordinary ever uttered by man, calling that faith, "*eating His flesh*, and *drinking His blood*." They are shocked; they murmur; they exclaim, "*how can He give us His flesh to eat?*" etc. They take the words of this Protestant Missionary literally; he knows this full well, whereas he wishes, they should be understood figuratively, he is fully aware of the errors his hearers labour under; he knows full well, it was caused, by his own words, never employed before in the sense, in which he wishes to have them now understood. I ask, then, what line of conduct, would reason, would religion, would a common regard for truth dictate to that man? Would not the plainest dictates of common sense call upon him to set His hearers right, at once, by telling them they misunderstood him? That he never meant, by any chance, to inculcate the necessity of eating the flesh of the Redeemer; that, such would be, in his mind, an error of the grossest description; that he merely intended to treat of faith in the death of the Redeemer. But, suppose that, instead of doing this, with a perfect knowledge of their error, he re-asserts, with a solemn asseveration, the obnoxious phrase, in the very words in which their errors were expressed, and in a manner, the best calculated to confirm and impress them with the idea of real manducation of the flesh of Christ, he *repeats* it six different times, without offering a single word in explanation to remove the error caused by his own words; he suffers them, the early fruit of his labours, with many of his converts, to give up his instructions, and desert him altogether. If we appeal to the commonest dictates of reason, would not such a person be regarded as perverting the religious commission, with which he may have the good faith, to imagine himself invested? Would he not be accountable for the salvation of those who thus desert him, supposing it possible for them to be saved by his ministry? Would he not be sacrificing all the dictates of reason and religion; and be chargeable with the most malicious falsehood, nothing short of formal perjury? Such would be the character our Divine Redeemer would necessarily assume in the interpretation of our religious opponents. There is but one way of accounting for His line of action, in reference to the multitude and His Apostles. It is, by supposing, according to the Catholic interpretation, that they were right. In this supposition, he could not correct them, unless he wished to correct right, and tell them it was wrong. The words of our Redeemer are, therefore, to be taken literally. Taken literally, they prove our doctrine.

OBJECTION TO PROOF.

There is one difficulty against the arguments now put forward, which I shall briefly explain, not so much on account of the importance of the objection itself, as because, appearing to flow from the words of our Redeemer, it has obtained a considerable degree of popularity. It is founded on the words, "*It is the Spirit that vivifies, the flesh profiteth nothing. The words I have spoken to you are spirit and life*" (v. 64). Here our religious opponents allege, all our reasoning is overturned, these words are corrective of the impression of the Capharnaites. He says, "*It is the Spirit, that vivifies,*" that is, the spiritual or figurative interpretation of the words, as opposed to the literal. "*The flesh,*" that is, the literal interpretation, "*profiteth nothing.*" In answer to this objection, it is to be said, in the first place, granting for a moment the meaning our adversaries give to the words, just quoted, to be the true one; still, it leaves the most conclusive part of the arguments wholly untouched. The only part, of our argument, it would answer, even allowing it to remain in full force, would be, that founded on the omission on the part of our Redeemer to correct the Capharnaites, which He would be bound to do, if they were in error. But, it by no means touches the strongest point of argument, urged from the very beginning, viz., that if the Capharnaites were in error, our Redeemer would not only have *omitted* correcting them, when He should, but He would have *positively confirmed* their error. And do not our religious opponents, by the very objection, suppose the Capharnaites to be in error up to the time our Redeemer had spoken these words; since, by supposing these words corrective, they also suppose the previous impression erroneous? And it has been proved, that, if erroneous, our Redeemer would have positively confirmed that error. In the next place, are these words in reality intended to be corrective of the impression of the Capharnaites? I deny it altogether. The assertion is absolutely unfounded. 1st. I ask if these words were intended as a correction of the false impression of His hearers, would our Redeemer be justified in putting it off so long? Would He not be bound to do so at the very first murmuring of the Capharnaites? In other words, would He be justified, in the first instance, in confirming an erroneous impression in the strongest possible manner, in the most clear and impressive language, and then, in the end, come forward and say it was all wrong?

2ndly. If, these words were sincerely intended by our Redeemer as a correction, would they not be put forward in terms clear enough to remove the erroneous impression caused by His former expressions? Nay, would not our Redeemer be bound to do so much? For, a man, who uses clear language in impressing a pernicious error, is bound, in justice, to use equally clear language in removing it. Would not His words, consequently, have the effect of retaining those, whom the former erroneous impression had estranged from Him? Now, the very reverse is the fact. The men thus estranged, no longer "*walk with Him*," they, therefore, never understood the words of our Redeemer, as corrective of their former impression; and hence, our Redeemer did not intend them as such.

Let us now analyse the words themselves, and see whether they can bear the interpretation put upon them by our adversaries. They say, the word "*flesh*," refers to the literal interpretation of His words; "*spirit*," to the spiritual meaning of them. Now, this can, by no means, be the meaning of the words It is quite gratuitous. And would it be too much to expect, after the long course of reasoning we have gone through, to prove our interpretation to be correct, that they would give something beyond mere assertion, for their view of the text? If, there were a dispute about the meaning of a certain passage in law, and the advocate of one opinion proved his interpretation of the passage, by a dozen or so of satisfactory arguments, would not his opponent be bound to adduce something stronger than mere assertion in support of his? Now, we have adduced our arguments, to prove our interpretation of the 6th chapter of St. John to be correct; and until our adversaries adduce stronger arguments in favour of their interpretation, we have a strict right to insist on their being wrong. I said, until they bring *stronger* arguments, etc. The reason is evident, because, the *onus* of proof rests upon them. Suppose a man to have acquired possession of an estate, held by his fathers for 1,500 years by a title hitherto unquestioned, and that after the lapse of that long period, his right were called in question by a rebellious domestic, who for the purpose of gratifying personal enmity, wishes to deprive him of his sacred inheritance, would not the whole onus of proof devolve upon the claimant? Would he not be bound to prove his claims, even to evidence? Now, when our adversaries sprang into existence, we were the legitimate inheritors of the sacred deposit of faith transmitted to the Church, by her Divine founder. We possessed the dogma of the Eucharist, as proved from the very passage. The onus, therefore, of proof devolves upon our adversaries; of whom we have a right in justice to demand, that, they should prove, even by arguments stronger than we have adduced, in favour of our interpretation, that the words, "*unless you eat the flesh of the Son of Man and drink His blood,*" mean, unless you believe in the death of Christ; and that, in the passage, "*it is the Spirit that vivifies, the flesh profiteth nothing,*" the word "*spirit,*" means, spiritual interpretation, and "*flesh,*" literal meaning, even by arguments stronger, etc. But what is the real state of the case? Why, not a single argument have they yet adduced to show this to be the meaning of the *words*, not a parallel text of Sacred Scripture, for this simple reason that they could not. For, though in many passages of Scripture, the word "*letter,*" as opposed to "*spirit,*" means the literal meaning of words, I challenge them to adduce a single text in which the word "*flesh*" has that meaning. I may be asked then, what meaning do I give it? Why, I give it the same definite and fixed meaning it has in every passage of Sacred Scripture in which the two words stand opposed to each other; and in every such passage, the word "*flesh,*" means the carnal intellect, and natural reason of man unenlightened by Divine grace, and unpractised in the principles of faith; and "*spirit,*" means the same intellect of man practised in the principles of faith, and supernaturally enlightened by Divine grace. Such is the sense in which these words are applied by St. Paul, in every part of his Epistles, and particularly in his Epistle to the Romans, when he tells us, "*the prudence of flesh is death, the prudence of the spirit is life.* The very same idea, as expressed by them, is conveyed by the Apostle to the Corinthians (c. ii.), when he speaks of the spiritual and the sensual man, the one enlightened by grace, and practised and exercised in the things of faith; the other, unenlightened by gace, and unpractised in the principles of faith. You might as well speak to a peasant of the revolution of the heavenly bodies, and the other truths of Philosophy, as speak to such a man about the doctrines of faith; they are folly to him, and he cannot understand them. This is the only objection which is attempted to be urged, with any degree of plausibility, against the arguments I have adduced. Our Redeemer promised to give us His body, really and substantially, under the appearance of food, and His promise is a sufficient guarantee for its accomplishment. This promise He redeemed at the Last Supper, when He instituted the Blessed Eucharist, on the eve of his Sacred Passion.

CHAPTER VII.

1 *After these things Jesus walked in Galilee ; for he would not walk in Judea, because the Jews sought to kill him.*

2 *Now the Jews' feast of tabernacles was at hand.*

3 *And his brethren said to him : Pass from hence, and go into Judea : that thy disciples also may see thy works which thou dost.*

4 *For there is no man that doth any thing in secret, and he himself seeketh to be known openly. If thou do these things, manifest thyself to the world,*

5 *For neither did his brethren believe in him.*

6 *Then Jesus said to them : My time is not yet come ; but your time is always ready.*

7 *The world cannot hate you ; but me it hateth : because I give testimony of it, that the works thereof are evil.*

8 *Go you up to this festival day, but I go not up to this festival day : because my time is not accomplished.*

9 *When he had said these things, he himself staid in Galilee.*

10 *But after his brethren were gone up, then he also went up to the feast, not openly, but as it were in secret.*

11 *The Jews therefore sought him on the festival day, and said : Where is he ?*

12 *And there was much murmuring among the multitude concerning him. For some said : He is a good man. And others said : No, but he seduceth the people.*

13 *Yet no man spoke openly of him, for fear of the Jews.*

14 *Now about the midst of the feast, Jesus went up into the temple, and taught.*

15 *And the Jews wondered, saying : How doth this man know letters, having never learned ?*

16 *Jesus answered them and said : My doctrine is not mine, but his that sent me.*

17 *If any man will do the will of him : he shall know of the doctrine, whether it be of God, or whether I speak of myself.*

18 *He that speaketh of himself, seeketh his own glory: but he that seeketh the glory of him that sent him, he is true, and there is no injustice in him.*

19 *Did not Moses give you the law, and yet none of you keepeth the law ?*

20 *Why seek you to kill me ? The multitude answered, and said : Thou hast a devil ; who seeketh to kill thee ?*

21 *Jesus answered and said to them : One work I have done ; and you all wonder :*

22 *Therefore Moses gave you circumcision, (not because it is of Moses, but of the fathers ;) and on the sabbath-day you circumcise a man.*

23 *If a man receive circumcision on the sabbath-day, that the law of Moses may not be broken ; are you angry at me because I have healed the whole man on the sabbath-day ?*

24 *Judge not according to the appearance, but judge just judgment.*

25 *Some therefore of Jerusalem said : Is not this he whom they seek to kill ?*

26 *And behold he speaketh openly, and they say nothing to him. Have the rulers known for a truth that this is the Christ ?*

27 *But we know this man whence he is: but when the Christ cometh, no man knoweth whence he is.*

28 *Jesus therefore cried out in the temple, teaching and saying: You both know me, and you know whence I am: and I am not come of myself; but he that sent me is true, whom you know not.*

29 *I know him, because I am from him, and he hath sent me.*

30 *They sought therefore to apprehend him: and no man laid hands on him, because his hour was not yet come.*

31 *But of the people many believed in him, and said: When the Christ cometh, shall he do more miracles than these which this man doth?*

32 *The Pharisees heard the people murmuring these things concerning him: and the rulers and Pharisees sent ministers to apprehend him.*

33 *Jesus therefore said to them: Yet a little while I am with you: and then I go to him that sent me.*

34 *You shall seek me, and shall not find me: and where I am, thither you cannot come.*

35 *The Jews therefore said among themselves: Whither will he go, that we shall not find him? will he go unto the dispersed among the gentiles, and teach the gentiles?*

36 *What is this saying that he hath said: You shall seek me, and shall not find me; and where I am, you cannot come?*

37 *And on the last and great day of the festivity, Jesus stood and cried, saying: If any man thirst, let him come to me, and drink.*

38 *He that believeth in me, as the scripture saith,* Out of his belly shall flow rivers of living water.

39 *Now this he said of the spirit which they should receive who believed in him: for as yet the spirit was not given, because Jesus was not yet glorified.*

40 *Of that multitude therefore, when they had heard these words of his, some said: This is the prophet indeed.*

41 *Others said: This is the Christ. But some said: Doth the Christ come out of Galilee?*

42 *Doth not the scripture say: That Christ cometh out of the seed of David, and from Bethlehem the town where David was?*

43 *So there arose a dissension among the people because of him.*

44 *And some of them would have apprehended him: but no man laid hands upon him.*

45 *The ministers therefore came to the chief priests and the Pharisees. And they said to them: Why have you not brought him?*

46 *The ministers answered: Never did man speak like this man.*

47 *The Pharisees therefore answered them: Are you also seduced?*

48 *Hath any one of the rulers believed in him, or of the Pharisees?*

49 *But this multitude that knoweth not the law, are accursed.*

50 *Nicodemus said to them, he that came to him by night, who was one of them:*

51 *Doth our law judge any man, unless it first hear him, and know what he doth?*

52 *They answered, and said to him: Art thou also a Galilean? Search the scriptures, and see that out of Galilee a prophet riseth not.*

53 *And every man returned to his own house.*

CAPUT VII.

1 *Post hæc autem ambulabat Jesus in Galilæam, non enim volebat in Judæam ambulare: quia quærebant eum Judæi interficere.*

2 *Erat autem in proximo dies festus Judæorum, Scenopegia.*

3 *Dixerunt autem ad eum fratres ejus: Transi hinc, et vade in Judæam, ut et discipuli tui videant opera tua, quæ facis.*

4 *Nemo quippe in occulto quid facit, et quærit ipse in palam esse: si hæc facis, manifesta teipsum mundo.*

5 *Neque enim fratres ejus credebant in eum.*

6 *Dicit ergo eis Jesus: Tempus meum nondum advenit: tempus autem vestrum semper est paratum.*

7 *Non potest mundus odisse vos: me autem odit: quia ego testimonium perhibeo de illo quod opera ejus mala sunt.*

8 *Vos ascendite ad diem festum hunc, ego autem non ascendo ad diem festum istum: quia meum tempus nondum impletum est.*

9 *Hæc cum dixisset, ipse mansit in Galilæa.*

10 *Ut autem ascenderunt fratres ejus, tunc et ipse ascendit ad diem festum non manifeste, sed quasi in occulto.*

11 *Judæi ergo quærebant eum in die festo, et dicebant: Ubi est ille?*

12 *Et murmur multum erat in turba de eo. Quidam enim dicebant: Quia bonus est. Alii autem dicebant: Non, sed seducit turbas.*

13 *Nemo tamen palam loquebatur de illo propter metum Judæorum.*

14 *Jam autem die festo mediante, ascendit Jesus in templum, et docebat.*

15 *Et mirabantur Judæi, dicentes: Quomodo hic litteras scit, cum non didicerit?*

16 *Respondit eis Jesus, et dixit: Mea doctrina non est mea, sed ejus, qui misit me.*

17 *Si quis voluerit voluntatem ejus facere, cognoscet de doctrina, utrum ex Deo sit, an ego a me ipso loquar.*

18 *Qui a semetipso loquitur, gloriam propriam quærit: qui autem quærit gloriam ejus, qui misit eum, hic verax est, et injustitia in illo non est.*

19 *Nonne Moyses dedit vobis legem: et nemo ex vobis facit legem?*

20 *Quid me quæritis interficere? Respondit turba, et dixit: Dæmonium habes: quis te quærit interficere?*

21 *Respondit Jesus, et dixit eis: Unum opus feci, et omnes miramini.*

22 *Propterea Moyses dedit vobis circumcisionem: (non quia ex Moyse est, sed ex patribus) et in sabbato circumciditis hominem.*

23 *Si circumcisionem accipit homo in sabbato, ut non solvatur lex Moysi: mihi indignamini quia totum hominem sanum feci in sabbato?*

24 *Nolite judicare secundum faciem, sed justum judicium judicate.*

25 *Dicebant ergo quidam ex Jerosolymis: Nonne hic est, quem quærunt interficere?*

26 *Et ecce palam loquitur, et nihil ei dicunt. Numquid vere cognoverunt principes quia hic est Christus?*

27 *Sed hunc scimus unde sit: Christus autem cum venerit, nemo scit unde sit.*

28 *Clamabat ergo Jesus in templo docens, et dicens: Et me scitis, et unde sim scitis: et a me ipso non veni, sed est verus, qui misit me, quem vos nescitis.*

29 *Ego scio eum: quia ab ipso sum, et ipse me misit.*

30 *Quærebant ergo eum apprehendere: et nemo misit in illum manus, quia nondum venerat hora ejus.*

31 *De turba autem multi crediderunt in eum, et dicebant: Christus cum venerit, numquid plura signa faciet quam quæ hic facit?*

32 *Audierunt Pharisæi turbam murmurantem de illo hæc: et miserunt Principes, et Pharisæi ministros ut apprehenderent eum.*

33 *Dixit ergo eis Jesus: Adhuc modicum tempus vobiscum sum: et vado ad eum, qui me misit.*

34 *Quæretis me, et non invenietis: et ubi ego sum, vos non potestis venire.*

35 *Dixerunt ergo Judæi ad semetipsos: Quo hic iturus est, quia non inveniemus eum? numquid in dispersionem Gentium iturus est, et docturus Gentes?*

36 *Quis est hic sermo, quem dixit. Quæretis me, et non invenietis: et ubi sum ego, vos non potestis venire?*

37 *In novissimo autem die magno festivitatis stabat Jesus, et clamabat, dicens: Si quis sitit, veniat ad me, et bibat.*

38 *Qui credit in me, sicut dicit Scriptura, flumina de ventre ejus fluent aquæ vivæ.*

39 *Hoc autem dixit de Spiritu, quem accepturi erant credentes in eum: nondum enim erat Spiritus datus, quia Jesus nondum erat glorificatus.*

40 *Ex illa ergo turba cum audissent hos sermones ejus, dicebant: Hic est vere propheta.*

41 *Alii dicebant: Hic est Christus. Quidam autem dicebant: Numquid a Galilæa venit Christus?*

42 *Nonne Scriptura dicit: Quia ex semine David, et de Bethlehem castello, ubi erat David, venit Christus?*

43 *Dissensio itaque facta est in turba propter eum.*

44 *Quidam autem ex ipsis volebant apprehendere eum: sed nemo misit super eum manus.*

45 *Venerunt ergo ministri ad Pontifices et Pharisæos. Et dixerunt eis illi: Quare non adduxistis illum?*

46 *Responderunt ministri: Numquam sic locutus est homo, sicut hic homo.*

47 *Responderunt ergo eis Pharisæi: Numquid et vos seducti estis?*

48 *Numquid ex principibus aliquis credidit in eum, aut ex Pharisæis?*

49 *Sed turba hæc, quæ non novit legem, maledicti sunt.*

50 *Dixit Nicodemus ad eos, ille, qui venit ad eum nocte, qui unus erat ex ipsis:*

51 *Numquid lex nostra judicat hominem, nisi prius audierit ab ipso, et cognoverit quid faciat?*

52 *Responderunt, et dixerunt ei: Numquid et tu Galilæus es? Scrutare Scripturas, et vide quia a Galilæa propheta non surgit.*

53 *Et reversi sunt unusquisque in domum suam.*

ANALYSIS.

In this chapter, we have an account of our Lord's conversation with His brethren, who from selfish motives, urge Him, on occasion of the Feast of Tabernacles, to go up to Jerusalem and perform His miraculous wonders, in the face of the world (1–9).

His ascent privately to Jerusalem to join in the celebration of the Festival (10).

The search for Him, and the discourses regarding Him among the people (11–13).

His teaching in the Temple, and the admiration of the crowd, at the learning He displayed, as He had not learned letters (14, 15).

Our Lord's justification of Himself and of His doctrine (16–18).
The reproachful language of the Jews on His having charged them with a design to put Him to death (18–21).
His retort on them as having themselves violated the Sabbath, with the violation of which they unjustly charged Him (21–25).
His declaration as to His heavenly origin, and the rejection of the Jews (28–36).
His invitation to all to come and partake of His abundant graces (37–39).
The result of His discourse. The division caused among the multitude (40–42).
The testimony of those sent to arrest Him (44) and the bitter reproaches addressed to Him, in consequence, by the Pharisees who employed them (44–48).
The fearless defence of our Lord by Nicodemus, and the reproaches he was subjected to, in consequence (50–52.)

Text.

1. *After these things Jesus walked in Galilee; for he would not walk in Judea, because the Jews sought to kill him.*

1. *Post hæc autem ambulabat Jesus in Galilæam, non enim volebat in Judæam ambulare; quia quærebant eum Judæi interficere.*

2. *Now the Jews' feast of tabernacles was at hand.*

2. *Erat autem in proximo dies festus Judæorum, Scenopegia.*

3. *And his brethren said to him: Pass from hence, and go into Judea: that thy disciples also may see thy works which thou dost.*

3. *Dixerunt autem ad eum fratres ejus; transi hinc, et vade in Judæam, ut et discipuli tui videant opera tua, quæ facis.*

Commentary.

2. "*Now, the Jewish feast of Tabernacles,*" etc. This feast was instituted in memory of the Divine protection extended to the Jewish people, when living in tents, during their forty years' sojourn in the desert. It commenced on the 15th day of the seventh month, *Tishri* (September), and lasted seven consecutive days, to which the eighth day was added, a day of special solemnity. It was a most joyous festival. During these eight days, the Israelites were obliged to dwell in tents, hurriedly constructed of wood, branches of trees, skins, etc. They carried in their hands, each day, branches of palm-trees, olives, citrons, myrtles and willows. It was the third of the great festivals of the Jews, the others being the Pasch and Pentecost.

3. "*Brethren,*" His blood relations on His mother's side; or, on St. Joseph's side, who was His reputed father. Not all His relatives spoke, as is stated here. Some of them believed in Him; others, of whom there is question (*v.* 5), did not. These latter were not of His disciples strictly so called. For, these believed in Him.

"*Pass from hence,*" depart from this obscure district, where Thou art hidden, and Thy great works generally unknown, "*and go into Judea,*" show Thyself in Jerusalem, the chief centre of public resort; whence Thy fame is sure to go out, and Thy works made known (Acts ii. 5). These were anxious for His glory, in order that as His relatives, they themselves, might profit thereby.

"*That Thy disciples,*" those desirous of learning Thy doctrine, whom Thy teaching and wonderful works performed heretofore at Jerusalem (c. ii. 23) rendered favourable to Thee, "*may see Thy works,*" may be confirmed in their good opinion, by witnessing the splendour of Thy works. These men would subject the works of our Lord to the test of learned inquiries. They had not yet believed in Him.

Commentary.

4. "*For there is no man that doth any thing,*" etc. Men who perform works calculated to gain them celebrity, as you do, with a view of profiting mankind, whose anointed Saviour you wish to have yourself regarded, don't seek darkness and obscurity; nor do they resort to obscure and unknown places, as is done by you here in Galilee.

"*And He Himself seeketh to be known openly.*" The Greek for "*openly,*" εν παρρησια, means, "*full liberty of speech.*" Such a man wishes to be publicly celebrated and freely spoken of.

"*If,*" which means, *since, whereas,* "*Thou dost these thing*s," since Thou performest wonderful works, calculated to render Thee celebrated. "*Manifest Thyself to the world,*" perform the same works in Jerusalem, the capital of Judea, wherein are found men from every nation under heaven (Acts ii. 5); that thus, Thy fame may spread throughout the entire earth. These clearly had in view their own selfish profit and advancement.

5. These men, even after witnessing His wonderful works, seeing His poverty and humility, did not believe Him to be the Messiah. Had they believed in Him, they would not presume to counsel Him. They would have Him acknowledged as such in Jerusalem, and in order to secure this, they wish Him to perform His miraculous wonders there, so that the priests and scribes would acknowledge Him as the Messiah; and they themselves would derive glory, honour, and emolument therefrom.

6. "*My time,*" for going up to this festival and manifesting Myself to the world, according to the decree of my Eternal Father, "*is not yet come.*" I shall not go up publicly with you, but I mean to go up privately, in order to avoid the fury of the Jews.

"*Your time is always ready.*" You need not apprehend any bad treatment at their hands; you gave them no provocation, no cause of enmity whatever.

7. "*Cannot hate you.*" You offer no resistance to the Scribes and Pharisees. Far from it, you obey them, and in all things carry out their wishes; "*Me it hateth.*" These wicked men entertain a deadly hatred for Me, as the stern reprover of their wicked conduct, "*because I give testimony,*" etc., thus verifying the words of the wise man, "*Let us lie in wait for the just man, because he is contrary to our doings, and upbraideth us with transgressions of the law,*" etc. (Wisdom ii. 12.)

8. "*I do not go up to this festival,*" *publicly,* in your company, and in the way you would expect, as I wish to avoid exciting the hatred of the Jews, already incensed against Me.

"*I do not go up,*" may mean, "*I do not YET go up.*" The Greek

Text.

4. *For there is no man that doth any thing in secret, and he himself seeketh to be known openly. If thou do these things, manifest thyself to the world.*

4. *Nemo quippe in occulto quid facit, et quærit ipse in palam esse: si hæc facis, manifesta teipsum mundo.*

5. *For neither did his brethren believe in him.*

5. *Neque enim fratres ejus credebant in eum.*

6. *Then Jesus said to them: My time is not yet come; but your time is always ready.*

6. *Dicit ergo eis Jesus; Tempus meum nondum advenit: tempus autem vestrum semper est paratum.*

7. *The world cannot hate you; but me it hateth: because I give testimony of it, that the works thereof are evil.*

7. *Non potest mundus odisse vos: me autem odit: quia ego testimonium perhibeo de illo quod opera ejus mala sunt.*

8. *Go you up to this festival day, but I go not up to this festival day; because my time is not accomplished.*

Text.

8. *Vos ascendite ad diem festum hunc, ego autem non ascendo ad diem festum istum: quia meum tempus nondum impletum est.*

9. *When he had said these things, he himself staid in Galilee.*

9. *Hæc cum dixisset, ipse mansit in Galilæa.*

10. *But after his brethren were gone up, then he also went up to the feast, not openly, but as it were in secret.*

10. *Ut autem ascenderunt fratres ejus, tunc et ipse ascendit ad diem festum non manifeste, sed quasi in occulto.*

11. *The Jews therefore sought him on the festival day, and said, Where is he?*

11. *Judæi ergo quærebant eum in die festo, et dicebant: Ubi est ille?*

12. *And there was much murmuring among the multitude concerning him. For some said: He is a good man. And others said: No, but he seduceth the people.*

12. *Et murmur multum erat in turba de eo. Quidam enim dicebant: Quia bonus est. Alii autem dicebant: Non, sed seducit turbas.*

13. *Yet no man spoke openly of him, for fear of the Jews.*

13. *Nemo tamen palam loquebatur de illo propter metum Judæorum.*

Commentary.

for "*not*," οὔπω, is rendered, *not yet*, in this very passage. He did go up, however; but, it was only after the fulfilment of the time, and in the manner marked out in the decrees of His Eternal Father. Whether He went up, the first day, at the beginning of the feast, or only later on, is disputed; most likely, He attended from the very beginning, as is insinuated (*v.* 14). His ascent was *private*; His going to the Temple on the fourth day, *public*.

9, 10. "*Not openly*" acompanied by a great retinue of followers; nor straightway through Samaria; but, through Pærea, after crossing the Jordan near Jericho.

"*But as it were in secret*," accompanied by only a few trusty friends, without any display; to avoid openly encountering the hostility of the Jewish rulers, who sought to compass His death. His ascent was not altogether "*in secret*," but, "*as it were, in secret*." On the fourth day, He publicly appeared in the Temple.

"*The Jews*," or rather the chief men among them, "*sought Him, on the festival day*," in order to meet Him and put Him to death. The day marked out for the worship of God is devoted by them to the works of the devil. Would to God, this was not true in regard to Christian festivals also. On these, God is, sometimes, more outraged than on any other days.

"*Where is He?*" A scornful question—what is become of this impostor? Why does He seek lurking, hiding places? It may be, that some, too, who were friendly to our Lord, asked the question.

12. "*Much murmuring*," great discussion carried on privately among the crowd, as to His character, some saying "*He is a good man*." A true teacher, and Prophet. This was the opinion expressed by those who witnessed His miracles and heard His preaching in Galilee. Others, on the contrary, viz., the Scribes and Pharisees and their followers, charged Him with seducing the people, to make Himself head of a new faction, and create sedition and rebellion.

13. "*Yet no one spoke openly of Him*." The Greek for, *openly*, is the same as in *v.* 4, εν παρρησια. No one of those who were for or against Him spoke openly of Him, owing to a prohibition on the part of the Jewish rulers, that there would be no reference whatsoever to His name, "*for fear of the Jews*," or chief rulers, who had issued the prohibition referred to.

Commentary.

14. "*About the middle of the feast,*" which lasted eight days. Hence, the fourth day is here referred to. "*Jesus went into the Temple and taught.*" Our Lord's ascent to Jerusalem was *private*; His ascent to the Temple, *public*. The festival was celebrated both within the city and outside it, by the people dwelling in temporary tents. Most likely, our Lord was celebrating it from the very first day of the solemnity, having followed His relations, on their departure for Jerusalem; but, only secretly, to give us an example of prudence in dealing with rabid enemies. But, on the fourth day, He courageously and fearlessly braved the fury of His enemies, by publicly presenting Himself in the Temple and preaching there; to give us an example of fortitude, when the call of duty and God's glory requires it; and to inspire us with confidence, to be rescued in due time. By comparing this with *v.* 10, it would appear, that our Lord was present and privately celebrating the festival from the first day; and this well accords with our idea of Him who came to "*fulfil all justice.*" No evil could accrue to Him from being privately present.

15. The teaching of our Lord must have been wonderful, since it had the effect of making His rabid enemies, who sought to put Him to death, regard with admiration and astonishment, the knowledge He displayed without having learned *letters*. The learning in repute among the Jews, was the knowledge of the Sacred Scriptures and their profound mysteries. In this sense, is the Word taken (2 Tim. iii. 15). "*Having never learned,*" in their schools. They knew His position in life, His education; hence, their admiration of the profound knowledge displayed by Him. This should have been an inducement to them, to see and receive Him as a divinely sent teacher. But, owing to their hatred of Him, they contented themselves with stolid and sterile admiration. They, moreover, were attributing it to diabolical influence and agency.

16. "*My doctrine is not Mine, but His that sent Me.*" In His school, I learned all I know. Our Redeemer, knowing well what they were privately and secretely discussing among themselves, said, you cannot understand where I learned what I am delivering to you. It is not from any diabolical source it came, as many of you would be inclined to suppose. The doctrine I deliver is not from Myself: Although, it be My doctrine, inasmuch as I possess it and give utterance to it; still, in another respect, it is *not mine.* It did not originate with Myself; but, it was communicated to Me, as God, by My Father at My eternal generation; and viewed in this way, My doctrine, as well as the nature and essence communicated to Me, is *identical* with that of My Father; or, if there be question of My knowledge, as *man,* it was knowledge of all things infused into My human nature, at My Incarnation, conformably

Text.

14. *Now about the midst of the feast, Jesus went up into the temple, and taught.*

14. *Jam autem die festo mediante, ascendit Jesus in templum et docebat.*

15. *And the Jews wondered, saying: How doth this man know letters, having never learned?*

15. *Et mirabantur Judæi, dicentes: Quomodo hic litteras scit, cum non didicerit?*

16. *Jesus answered them and said: My doctrine is not mine, but his that sent me.*

16. *Respondit eis Jesus, et dixit: Mea doctrina non est mea, sed ejus, qui misit me.*

| Text. | Commentary. |

to the words of the Prophet Isaias (xi. 2), "*And the Spirit of the Lord shall rest upon Him; the Spirit of wisdom and understanding . . . the Spirit of knowledge,*" etc. Although His doctrine *as God*, was *His own;* still, He wishes to attribute it to the Father, to show them that it came from God; and His doctrine, as *man*, what He taught, as *man*, was identical with that of the Father; since what He knew and taught, as *man*, was what His Father wished Him to teach.

17. *If any man will do the will of him: he shall know of the doctrine whether it be of God or whether I speak of myself.*

17. *Si quis voluerit voluntatem jus facere, cognoscet de doctrina, utrum ex Deo sit, an ego a me ipso loquar.*

17. Our Lord here assigns a criterion for knowing, whether His doctrine was divine or human; and tacitly reproaches the Jews with opposing God's will, owing to the hatred and hostility they bore Himself. Their wicked dispositions were the cause of their wilful blindness, in regard to the source from which He derived His teaching, and the obstacles to their seeing things in a true light. If they desired to do the will of God, by a conformity of life to the Divine precepts, they would know, aided by the interior light of grace, which God would not refuse them; whether His doctrine was from God or from Himself, a mere human invention, opposed to that of God. It is only the spiritual man, whose will is conformable to God's will, that shall have his intellect enlightened to see the things that are of the Spirit of God.

18. *He that speaketh of himself, seeketh his own glory: but he that seeketh the glory of him that sent him, he is true, and there is no injustice in him.*

18. *Qui a semetipso loquitur gloriam propriam quærit: qui autem quærit gloriam ejus, qui misit eum, hic verax est, et injustitia in illo non est.*

18. "*He that speaketh of himself,*" etc. Our Lord having, in the preceding verse, pointed to a criterion for knowing that His doctrine was from God, and the reason why the Jews did not know it; now, assigns another criterion for ascertaining His doctrine to be from God, thus: "*He that speaketh from himself,*" or delivers doctrine of His own, as opposed to that of God, *seeketh his own glory,*" wishes to gain a crowd of disciples who would extol him, become his followers, and proclaim him as their chief, thus seeking his own glory. This is seen from the lives of all Heresiarchs. "*But he that seeketh*"—not his own glory, but—"*the glory of Him that sent Him, He is true.*" Our Lord does not say, "*he that speaketh from God, seeketh the glory of God,*" as would seem necessary, in order that the latter clause of the sentence, should be directly contrary to the preceding. But, "*He is true,*" veracious; thus refuting the charge made against Himself, of seducing the people by false teaching, whereas He taught the truth of God, who is infinitely veracious. "*And there is no injustice in Him,*" He is not guilty of unjustly robbing God of His glory; He thus refutes the charge of His having violated the law of the Sabbath. Our Lord charges the Pharisees, by implication, with seeking "*their own glory;*" therefore, *not* true, *mendacious*, preferring the false traditions of men to the Divine Law. *Unjust*, as transgressors of the Divine Law, while arrogating to themselves unjustly the glory of God.

Commentary.

19. Having proved that He was truthful in His teaching, and just in His works, our Lord now charges the Jews with injustice and transgression of the law. They violated the law of Moses, whom they pretended to value so much. They sought to kill Him (v. 16-18), who was just and innocent, and this was strictly prohibited, in the law of Moses (Exodus xxiii. 7). They unjustly charged Him with violating the law of Moses for curing a man on the Sabbath day. (c. v.) But He clearly proves that they were the real prevaricators, by violating it, in a most important point. For, He well knew the murderous designs of the Scribes and Pharisees in reference to Himself. The words, "*and none of you keepeth the law*," may also refer to their violation of the law of the Sabbath, in circumcising infants on the Sabbath, for the alleged imputed violation for which they wished to kill Him (v. 16-18).

20. "*The multitude.*" Of the multitude, some were in favour of Him; others opposed to Him. None of them, however, had any idea of killing Him. But the Pharisees and rulers, of whose machinations the people were ignorant, had such designs; and it is to them our Lord addressed the preceding words. "*Thou hast a devil.*" It is at the suggestion of the devil thou utterest this calumny against us; or, the words may mean—Thou art *crazy*, or *mad*.

21. Passing over in silence the reproaches levelled at Himself personally, by the crowd, our Lord shows that the accusation brought against Him, for having violated the law of Moses was unfounded and unjust. The cure of the paralytic (v. 5-16) occurred several months before this; still, the Jewish rulers bore it in mind, as well as their charge of blasphemy against Him, for claiming God for His Father; and this they make a pretext for wishing to compass His death.

"*One work I have done*," in curing the paralytic.

"*And you all wonder.*" You are in a state of tumultuous, angry excitement; filled with indignation, from which springs your murderous machination against My life.

22. "*Therefore,*" in order to remove all just ground for such indignation on your part, I shall give you an example, or illustration, which you must reverently attend to, while from it, you will see how unfounded your indignation is, arising from my cure of the paralytic on the Sabbath day. (c. v.) The example I adduce is from the Mosaic dispensation regarding circumcision. "*Moses gave you circumcision,*" or, rather, renewed the ordinance relative to it in his law; not that it was originally of Mosaic institution, like the Sabbath law; it was handed down from the "*Fathers,*" the Patriarchs, Abraham, Isaac, Jacob, etc., and pre-

Text.

19. *Did not Moses give you the law, and yet none of you keepeth the law?*

19. *Nonne Moyses dedit vobis legem: et nemo ex vobis facit legem?*

20. *Why seek you to kill me? The multitude answered, and said, Thou hast a devil; who seeketh to kill thee?*

20. *Quid me quæritis interficere? Respondit turba, et dixit: Dæmonium habes: quis te quærit interficere?*

21. *Jesus answered and said to them: One work I have done; and you all wonder.*

21. *Respondit Jesus et dixit eis: Unum opus feci, et omnes miramini.*

22. *Therefore Moses gave you circumcision, (not because it is of Moses, but of the fathers,) and on the sabbath-day you circumcise a man.*

22. *Propterea Moyses dedit vobis circumcisionem: (non quia ex Moyse est, sed ex patribus) et in sabbato circumciditis hominem.*

Commentary.

scribed by God to be binding on their posterity (Genesis xvii. 10, etc.; xxi. 4). This rite was interrupted, during their forty years' sojourn, in the desert. Moses renewed it, in his laws (Leviticus xii. 3).

According to the original command of God given to the Patriarchs, the new-born infant should be circumcised on the eighth day after its birth. Whenever, then, the birth occurred on the Sabbath, the infant should be circumcised on that day week, the eighth day, which fell on the Sabbath, the precept regarding circumcision being of greater importance, and of more binding force, was attended to; the precept regarding the Sabbath, as of less importance, unheeded. Circumcision was of patriarchal origin, originally enjoined by God on Abraham, and being of earlier origin and of greater importance, it superseded, in particular cases, the Sabbatical observance.

"*And on the Sabbath day you circumcise a man.*" We find a new-born infant called, *a man,* elsewhere (John xvi. 21).

There is a great diversity of opinion among Commentators regarding the connection and force of "*therefore.*" Some, with Beelen, etc., connect it with what went before, thus: "And you all wonder, therefore," *on this account,* δια τοῦτο, on account of the work He did. This would render the interpretation comparatively easy, and the connection very smooth. It is, however, more probably connected with what follows. It points to an example or illustration, showing, that our Lord did not violate the Sabbath, in curing, by the mere word of power, the palsied man; since the Jews themselves did not interpret the Sabbatical law so strictly, as not to admit of exception, in conflict with a higher law, like the law of circumcision. These enclose the words ("*not because it is of Moses,*" etc.) in a parenthesis, as found in the Vulgate reading, as if it were incidentally used to meet an objection which might possibly be raised against the saying, that Moses was the institutor or original promulgator of circumcision, which our Lord here Himself seems to assert. "*Moses gave you circumcision,*" etc., and that the parenthetical observation had no force in the argument.

Others, laying great stress on the observation enclosed within the parenthesis, say, that "*therefore*" has direct and immediate reference to these words. It is *because* ("*therefore*") circumcision, which Moses inserted or re-promulgated among his laws, was strictly of patriarchal origin, you circumcise on the Sabbath day; thereby showing that Sabbatical observance, with the violation of which you unjustly charge Me, admits of exception, in case of conflict with a higher or more binding law. So, that "*therefore*" has immediate reference to the words, "*but of the Fathers,*" and it is, because of the conflict with a higher law, they overlooking the law relating to the observance of the Sabbath, circumcise a man on the Sabbath day; or, thus: "*Therefore,*" or on this account, did

Commentary.

Moses give you circumcision, because it was originally handed down from the Patriarchs, and as coming from the Patriarchs, you circumcise on the Sabbath day, as they did, it being older and of greater binding force than the Sabbatical law, originally promulgated by Moses. Why, then, censure Me for doing the same?

23. This, then, is our Lord's crushing refutation of their charge —"*If a man . . . that the law of Moses may not be broken,*" meaning, without violating the law of Moses, although involving servile work in inflicting pain, staunching blood, applying soothing remedies, etc., etc. The words, "*that the law of Moses,*" etc., may also mean, you circumcise on the Sabbath, in order that the law of Moses, commanding that circumcision be administered on the eighth day (Leviticus xii. 3) be not broken. It was a law of Moses, as well as a patriarchal law. For, He re-promulgated it, and made it His own. "*Moses gave you circumcision.*" The law of circumcision involved servile work; our Lord's act of curing involved none; it was a mere word. His was a work of mercy, exceeding in importance Sabbatical observance; circumcision, only conferred a partial benefit; our Lord's case reached the entire man, soul and body. Hence, the natural and Divine precept of mercy, of relieving our brother in distress, should outweigh the law of Moses, relative to the observance of the Sabbath.

24. Let your judgments, then, be not merely according to appearances, or founded on any personal prejudices in regard to Me, or feelings of personal respect, which seems to be the chief motive that influences you in this case, when you judge according to your views of the law of Moses, and your veneration for him, despising Me and My actions.

"*But, judge just judgment.*" Judge the case according to its *intrinsic merits* and deserts, without any regard to persons. Far, from doing so, you are guilty of exception of persons. You accuse Me of violating the Sabbatical ordinance, in restoring health of soul and body to a sick man, by a mere word, while you yourselves perform the work of circumcising on the Sabbath day, with all its accompaniments.

25. "*Some of Jerusalem.*" The Greek has, "*of the Jerusalemites.*" The sense is the same. Some of the inhabitants of Jerusalem, who knew well the wicked designs of the Rulers regarding our Lord. Hence, the Evangelist refers to them as distinguished from the strangers then flocking to Jerusalem, who knew nothing of the wicked machinations of the Rulers. These latter, probably, were friendly to our Lord, having seen His miracles and having heard His doctrine.

"*Is not this He whom they wish to kill.*" They knew well

Text.

23. *If a man receive circumcision on the sabbath-day, that the law of Moses may not be broken; are you angry at me because I have healed the whole man on the sabbath day?*

23. *Si circumcisionem accipit homo in sabbato, ut non solvatur lex Moysi: mihi indignamini quia totum hominem sanum feci in sabbato?*

24. *Judge not according to the appearance, but judge just judgment.*

24. *Nolite judicare secundum faciem, sed justum judicium judicate.*

25. *Some therefore of Jerusalem said: Is not this he whom they seek to kill?*

25. *Dicebant ergo quidam ex Jerosolymis: Nonne hic est, quem quærunt interficere?*

Text.	Commentary.
	the wicked designs of the Rulers, the Scribes, Priests and Pharisees.
26. *And behold he speaketh openly, and they say nothing to him. Have the rulers known for a truth that this is the Christ?*	26. "*Behold, He speaketh openly, and they say nothing to Him.*" They express their astonishment that the Rulers, whose hatred of our Lord they well knew, were now silent, while He was speaking freely and openly regarding them.
26. *Et ecce palam loquitur, et nihil ei dicunt. Numquid vere cognoverunt principes quia hic est Christus?*	"*Have the Rulers known for a truth that this is the Christ?*" These men, seeking some cause for an event so unaccountable, a change so great in the attitude of the Rulers in His regard, concluded, that they must now be convinced that He is truly the Christ, whom they hitherto charged with falsely affecting to be such. It must be, therefore, because they now find Him to be really the Christ. The Rulers have laid aside every feeling of animosity, which arose from zeal for the interests of the true Christ. In this, however, the crowd were deceived. It was not from any feeling of zeal for the interests of the true Christ the Pharisees, etc., were influenced, but by a feeling of pride, jealousy and envy.
27. *But we know this man whence he is; but when the Christ cometh, no man knoweth whence he is.*	27. "*But,*" this is most unlikely; this cannot be; for, "*we know this man whence He is*" (see v. 42). "*But, when the Christ cometh, no one knows whence He is.*" From this it would seem there was some absurd notion afloat among the ignorant portion of the Jews regarding our Lord's parentage, etc. The learned knew well He was to be born in Bethlehem, of the family of David (v. 42). But the ignorant portion came to an erroneous conclusion, probably misunderstanding the words of the Prophet Isaias (xliii.), "*Generationem ejus quis enarrabit?*" "*Egressus ejus ab initio, a diebus æternitatis*" (Micheas ix.), and other such texts, which have reference to His *Divine* nature.
27. *Sed hunc scimus unde sit: Christus autem cum venerit, nemo scit unde sit.*	
28. *Jesus therefore cried out in the temple teaching and saying: You both know me, and you know whence I am: and I am not come of myself; but he that sent me is true, whom you know not.*	28, 29. "Jesus, therefore, knowing their thoughts and conversation, "*cried out in the Temple,*" raised His voice, to render more impressive what He was saying, "*teaching and saying,*" as the only thing you want in Me, in order to acknowledge Me as your Messiah is, not to know me. He then shows they did not know Him. They should, therefore, acknowledge Him.
28. *Clamabat ergo Jesus in templo docens, et dicens: Et me scitis, et unde sim scitis: et a me ipso non veni, sed est verus, qui misit me, quem vos nescitis.*	"*You both know Me and know who I am.*" That is, you assert that you know who I am and My parentage, as you think you know My parents; but, in this you are mistaken. For, "*I have not come of Myself.*" In this our Lord clearly insinuates, that He was the Son of God, sent by Him, in fulfilment of the promises made to their fathers. "*But He that sent Me is true,*" infinitely veracious in His words and acts, and in the testimony He bore to Me as His Son, and as I teach His doctrine, what I teach must, therefore, be true. "*Whom you know not.*" You know not that

Commentary.

He is My Father, who, by word and miraculous wonders, bore testimony to Me as His Son, and not Joseph, whom you fancy to be My real father.

"*But I know Him, because I am from Him,*" His Eternal Son, begotten of Him from eternity, "*and He hath sent Me*" into this world, to assume human nature for your redemption. In these latter words, our Lord refers to His *Divine* and *human* natures. His *Divine*, in the words, "*I am from Him,*" His human, "*and He hath sent Me.*"

Others interpret the words, "*you both know Me,*" etc., as if taken up by Him, and repeated after them in irony, so as to convey, that they were mistaken as to His person and parentage, and, then, He states His true origin and parentage, "*and I am not come of Myself,*" etc. On their own showing, therefore, they should acknowledge Him as their Messiah. Since they would seem to admit that He had all the other qualities to be desired in the Messiah, the only thing wanted was, that they should not know Him, and this too He now shows to be verified regarding Him.

By others, the words, "*you both know Me,*" etc., are read interrogatively, "Do you, indeed, *know Me?*" etc. Conveying, that they did not; and then He proceeds to show who He was and whence He was.

Some Latin Codices have at the end of *v.* 28, as in viii. 55, "*But I know Him, and if I should say I know Him not, I shall be a liar, like you.*" Editions and versions generally omit them here.

30. "*Therefore,*" in consequence of His saying that He came from God the Father, whom *they knew not,* they, blinded from malice and obduracy, instead of being convinced, were more embittered against Him, and would put Him to death, because the people preferred Him to themselves, and regarded Him as the Messias. But, His power restrained them, because the hour marked out in the eternal decrees, for His suffering death, had not yet arrived—"*his hour,*" the time which, of His own free will, in obedience to the decrees of His Eternal Father, He had fixed for suffering the death of the cross.

31. "*Of the people,*" probably, refers to those who had come to the festival, together with some of the better disposed of the inhabitants of Jerusalem. "*Many believed in Him,*" owing to the miracles He performed, which are fully recorded by the other Evangelists. Perhaps, our Lord worked wonders on this occasion also, which St. John passes over here in silence. For, all His miracles were not recorded (xxi. 25).

"*When the Christ cometh,*" that is, if Christ were yet to come,

Text.

29. *I know him, because I am from him, and he hath sent me.*

29. *Ego scio eum: quia ab ipso sum, et ipse me misit.*

30. *They sought therefore to apprehend him: and no man laid hands on him, because his hour was not yet come.*

30. *Quærebant ergo eum apprehendere: et nemo misit in illum manus, quia nondum venerat hora ejus.*

31. *But of the people many believed in him, and said: When the Christ cometh, shall he do more miracles than these which this man doth?*

31. *De turba autem multi crediderunt in eum, et dicebant:*

Text.

Christus cum venerit, numquid plura signa faciet quam quæ hic facit?

Commentary.

supposing Him not to have come already, could He perform greater miracles than this man performs? Surely not. Why not, then, accept Him for the Christ, since He gives us the most undoubted proof that He is the Christ. The Jews were impressed with the belief that the Messias would work many miracles. This opinion derived probability from passages of SS. Scriptures regarding Him, "*then the eyes of the blind shall be opened,*" etc. (Isaias xxxv. 5, 6, etc.)

32. *The Pharisees heard the people murmuring these things concerning him: and the rulers and Pharisees sent ministers to apprehend him.*

32. The Rulers, maddened with envy, on seeing the people acknowledge our Lord as the true Messiah, could no longer dissemble their rage, and throwing off all restraint, sent to have Him apprehended.

32. *Audierunt Pharisæi turbam murmurantem de illo hæc: et miserunt Principes, et Pharisæi ministros ut apprehenderent eum.*

33. *Jesus therefore saith to them: Yet a little while I am with you: and then I go to him that sent me.*

33. *Dixit ergo eis Jesus adhuc modicum tempus vobiscum sum: et vado ad eum, qui me misit.*

33. "*To them,*" the ministers sent to apprehend Him, who would carry back to the Rulers what they would hear Him say.

"*Yet a little while*"—but a very brief period of time, six months from this—"*I am with you.*" I remain on earth, "*and then I go to Him that sent Me.*" Then I shall voluntarily submit to death, and return; but, until that time comes, of which I am fully aware, all your efforts to destroy Me shall be unavailing. I shall, till then, set at nought every attempt against me.

34. *You shall seek me, and shall not find me: and where I am, thither you cannot come.*

34. *Quæretis me, et non invenietis: et ubi ego sum, vos non potestis venire.*

34. "*You shall seek Me,*" etc. Some interpret these words as indicating or promising some good, viz., that after His death, on witnessing the miracles and preaching of His Apostles, they, touched with compunction, shall be converted, and shall desire to see and hear Him whom they now despise; but they will not be able, as He shall then have ascended into heaven. The words bear this construction (xiii. 33), when addressed by our Lord to His apostles. Others understand these words as threatening evil, as if He said: After My death, you will endeavour to abolish My name and every memory of Me. You wish to apprehend Me, and again put Me to death, and utterly wipe out My name and teaching. But, you shall strive in vain. I shall be out of your reach, at the right hand of My Father, and you will never reach that seat of everlasting bliss, in punishment of your obstinacy and unrepented guilt.

Others interpret it: You shall seek and earnestly desire the *Messiah* or *Me*, who am the Messiah, as your deliverer—the deliverer of your people and nation, when in dire straits, to which your city and nation shall be reduced, by the strong hand of the Romans. But, you shall be disappointed. You shall not be able to find Him; you shall not be able to reach where He shall be.

Commentary.

Some reject this interpretation, as, in reality, the Jews in their distress did not seek the Messiah.

Others, with Maldonatus, say the words simply mean, that, although you should seek Me—which they by no means, did—still, you would not find Me, because, where I am, you could not come. It is a phrase signifying, that our Lord was taken away from the earth, so as not to be found among the living. Similar is the phrase (Psa. ix. 16; xxxvi. 10; Isaias xli. 12; Ozee ii. 7).

35. "*The dispersed among the Gentiles,*" is understood by some, of the Jews scattered through every country under heaven. It most likely, signifies the Gentiles themselves dispersed throughout the globe, as the words, "*and teach the Gentiles,*" would denote. In the fulness of their pride, they supposed it to be a matter utterly impossible that He would go to these. Because, it was a thing hitherto unheard of, that a Prophet of God, would go to instruct the impure, idolatrous Gentiles, with whom no Jew could hold intercourse. In this, the Jews unconsciously and unwillingly predicted what afterwards happened, when our Lord, through His Apostles and representatives, after the Jews had spurned their teaching, went and transferred their ministry to the Gentile world; the curse of rejection and reprobation having fallen on the Jews.

For "*Gentiles,*" it is *the Greeks*, in the Greek Version. "The dispersed among *the Greeks*, and teach the *Greeks.*"

The Jews divided the world into Jews and Greeks. Under the latter, best known as the dominant race, since the conquests of Alexander the Great, were included all the other less prominent and least known nations and peoples of the earth.

37. "*And on the last and great day of the festival,*" which is generally understood of the eighth day, when the people assembled in greater crowds, on the eve of their departure.

This eighth day which was, in course of time, added to the seven preceding ones, that originally constituted the Festival, was celebrated with the greatest solemnity (Leviticus xxiii. 36). On this closing day, our Lord availing Himself of the greater assemblage of people, wished to impress on them, the most solid and practical truths.

"*Jesus stood,*" in some elevated position, where He could be best heard; and regardless of the threats and machinations of His enemies, "*cried*" out, fearlessly, and courageously, in order to show that He feared no one while performing the work of His Father, in gaining souls and diffusing the light of His Heavenly truths. Similar should be the spirit in times of danger and opposition, with which all true preachers of the Gospel should be animated. "*Ne formides a facie eorum,*" etc. (Jeremiah i. 17; Ezechiel iii. 9.)

"*If any man thirst,*" feels a vehement desire for eternal happiness, his own salvation. There is hardly any sensation equal to

Text.

35. *The Jews therefore said among themselves: Whither will he go, that we shall not find him? will he go unto the dispersed among the gentiles, and teach the gentiles?*

35. *Dixerunt ergo Judæi ad semetipsos: Quo hic iturus est, quia non inveniemus eum? numquid in dispersionem Gentium iturus est, et docturus Gentes?*

36. *What is this saying that he hath said: You shall seek me, and shall not find me; and where I am, you cannot come?*

36. *Quis est hic sermo, quem dixit: quæretis me, et non invenietis: et ubi sum ego, vos non potestis venire?*

37. *And on the last and great day of the festivity, Jesus stood and cried, saying: If any man thirst, let him come to me, and drink.*

37. *In novissimo autem die magno festivitatis stabat Jesus, et clamabat, dicens: Si quis sitit, veniat ad me, et bibat.*

Text	Commentary
	that of thirst or an anxious craving to slake a desire for drink. "*Quemadmodum desiderat cervus,*" etc. (Psa. xli. 2.) "*Let him come to Me,*" by faith; to Me, who am the inexhaustible fountain of living waters. "*And drink,*" slake his thirst, by drinking to satiety of the abundant graces which I still ungrudgingly dispense, in order to satiate and spiritually inebriate him. It is only those, however, that "*thirst,*" really anxious and desirous for it, that are invited. This is allusive to the words of Isaias (lv. 1), "*Omnes sitientes, venite ad aquas.*"
38. *He that believeth in me, as the scripture saith,* Out of his belly shall flow rivers of living water.	38. "*He that believeth in Me.*" It is by believing we come to Him. Our Lord speaks of faith animated by charity, accompanied by good works, and the observance of God's commandments. For, "*the devils also believe and tremble*" (James ii. 19).
38. *Qui credit in me, sicut dicit Scriptura, flumina de ventre ejus fluent aquæ vitæ.*	"*As the Scripture saith,*" in several passages, referring to the following words, in substance and in sense, if not exactly in so many words. (Joel ii. 28), "*I shall pour out My Spirit on all flesh,*" etc. (Isaias xli. 18; xliv. 3; lv. 1; Ezechiel xxxvi. 25; Eccles. xxiv. 40, etc.)
	"*Out of his belly shall flow rivers of living water.*" His soul, which is the receptacle of spiritual food, as the belly, of corporal aliment, will be filled with the copious abundance of the graces of the Holy Ghost, so that nothing will be wanting to him. "*Living water,*" which shall display itself in external operations, in the practice of all virtues, whereby men shall advance more and more in perfection, and slake their own thirst after justice. They will not confine to themselves the overflowing waters of grace. They shall communicate their happiness to others, whom they shall aid in obtaining life eternal. That "*the living waters,*" refer to the abundant graces of the Holy Ghost, is clear from the words, "*He said of the Spirit*" (v. 39). Our Redeemer, who here quotes no one particular passage of Scripture, explains, in order to prevent misconception, the meaning of the words, "*living water,*" as referring to the Spirit, which was to be given abundantly, hereafter.
39. *Now this he said of the spirit which they should receive who believed in him: for as yet the spirit was not given, because Jesus was not yet glorified.*	39. "*Now, this He said of the Spirit,*" etc. The Evangelist assigns a reason why our Lord speaks in the future, not in the present or past, regarding "*the rivers of living water,*" that *shall* flow; because by them, He meant the abundant gifts of the Spirit which they were to receive. For, although the Holy Ghost with His gifts was given in past times, to the saints and just of old; still, they were not given in such copious and gushing abundance, as on Pentecost Sunday, when the Holy Ghost visibly descended on the Apostles and filled them with the heavenly fire and divine virtue which they displayed on the spot.
39. *Hoc autem dixit de Spiritu, quem accepturi erant credentes in eum: nondum enim erat Spiritus datus, quia Jesus nondum erat glorificatus.*	

"*For as yet the Spirit was not given,*" in the full abundance

Commentary

afterwards displayed, "*because Jesus was not glorified,*" in His Resurrection, and especially in his Ascension. Our Lord referred to the necessity of His going to the Father, in order to send down the Paraclete (John xvi. 7). The glorification of our Lord, the Divine Head of the Church, should, as a matter of congruity, precede the glorification of the members.

By not giving the Holy Ghost in all fulness, till our Lord was in heaven, He wished to show, that the Holy Ghost proceeded from Him as well as from the Father. He also wished to show the Jews, that He was in heaven whom they crucified. Hence, the words of St. Peter (Acts ii. 33).

40. "*The Prophet, indeed.*" The definite article, "*the*," only denotes that He was a distinguished Prophet, not the Messias, the "*Prophet of their own nation,*" etc. (Deut. xviii. 15.) For another class said (v. 41), "*He is the Christ,*" or Messias. The text from Deuteronomy, above referred to, was meant by the Holy Ghost to designate the Messias. But, the Jews erroneously fancied the Prophet thus spoken of to be different from Christ (see John i. 21). It may refer to "*the Prophet,*" who, as was supposed by the Jews, would precede or accompany the Messiah (John i. 21).

41, 42. Some of them may have thought that, as our Lord was brought up at Nazareth in Galilee, He was born there, and of parents, who were not Jews. Others, very likely, knew His parentage and birthplace, but affected to be ignorant of it, and would have Him looked upon as a Galilean, who could not be the Christ; as He was to be born in Bethlehem, of the seed of David.

42. *Doth the scripture say: That Christ cometh of the seed of David, and from Bethlehem the town where David was.*

43. Owing to their difference of opinion regarding Him, there was a division amongst them.

44. Others, had such inveterate hostility towards Him, that they would have arrested Him as an impostor, an abettor of rebellion and revolution, a blasphemer, who affected to be the Son of God, etc.

"*But no one laid hands on Him.*" Our Lord by His innate power restrained them from offering Him violence.

It may be, that those referred to in this verse, who would fain apprehend Him, are the same ministers who received orders to that effect (v. 32). The following (v. 45), renders this view very probable.

Text

40. Of that multitude therefore, when they had heard these words of his, some said: *This is the prophet indeed*

40. *Ex illa ergo turba cum audissent hos sermones ejus, dicebant: Hic est vere propheta.*

41. Others said: *This is the Christ.* But some said: *Doth the Christ come out of Galilee?*
41. *Alii dicebant: hic est Christus. Quidam autem dicebant: Numquid a Galilæa venit Christus?*

42. *Nonne Scriptura dicit; Quia ex semine David, et de Bethlehem castello, ubi erat David, venit Christus?*

43. So there arose a dissension among the people because of him.
43. *Dissensio itaque facta est in turba propter eum.*

44. And some of them would have apprehended him: but no man laid hands upon him.
44. *Quidam autem ex ipsis volebant apprehendere eum, sed nemo misit super eum manus.*

| **Text.** | **Commentary.** |

45. *The ministers came to the chief priests and the Pharisees. And they said to them: Why have you not brought him?*

45. *Venerunt ergo ministri ad Pontifices, et Pharisæos. Et dixerunt eis illi: Quare non adduxistis illum?*

45, 46. The ministers commissioned by the Rulers to arrest Him, when on the first day, or some other day, He appeared in the Temple, did not do so, on that day. They then returned on the eighth day, "*the great day of the festivity*" (v. 37), when He appeared a second time during the Feast in the Temple (vv. 14–37), in order to carry out their commission, and being captivated by His eloquence, came back to their employers to whom, they were naturally so beholden, whose followers they were, and whose principles they had imbibed, and bore the most convincing testimony in His favour. Instead of their arresting and capturing Him, they were led captive by the divine force of His eloquence. "*Never did man speak like this man.*" This was the most convincing evidence in favour of our Lord's teaching and the power of His Divine eloquence.

46. *The ministers answered: Never did man speak like this man.*

46. *Responderunt ministri: Numquam sic locutus est homo sicut hic homo.*

Whether the ministers sent to arrest our Lord (v. 32), came on more than one day to the Temple for that purpose, and deferred arresting Him, or whether they came only on the eighth or last day, is uncertain.

47. *The Pharisees therefore answered them: Are you also seduced?*

47. *Responderunt ergo eis Pharisæi: Numquid et vos seducti estis?*

47. The Pharisees, these implacable enemies of our Lord, confirmed in iniquity, and rendered obdurate by sin, far from yielding to the impressions of grace, only derided and jeered at the testimony of their own servants. "*Are you also,*" as well as the ignorant crowd, you who have shared so largely in our confidence, and learned from us the principles of the law of Moses, "*are you too seduced*" by this impostor, so as to be inclined to receive Him for the Messiah.

48. *Hath any one of the rulers believed in him, or of the Pharisees?*

48. *Numquid ex principibus aliquis credidit in eum, aut ex Pharisæis?*

48. They wished to remove the favourable impressions made by our Lord on their servants, by alleging that if He were a Prophet or the Messiah, "*the Rulers,*" members of the Sanhedrim, who regulated and controlled their religious rites and doctrines, and were themselves versed in the law, and "*the Pharisees,*" noted for their sanctity, filling offices of authority, would not fail to receive Him and believe in Him. But, the contrary was the fact—those men well versed in the law rejected Him. They did so, however, from envy, blind ambition and jealousy, seeing their own power and influence with the people on the wane. In their case were verified the words of our Lord (Matthew xi. 25), "*Abscondisti hæc a sapientibus et revelasti ea parvulis.*" The weapons they employ are scorn and contempt, instead of argument.

49. *But this multitude that knoweth not the law, are accursed.*

49. *Sed turba hæc, quæ non novit legem, maledicti sunt.*

49. "*This multitude*"—they speak of them in terms of scorn—"*who knoweth not the law,*" and, therefore, neglect to observe it, or believe the truths it announces; "*are accursed,*" that is, liable to the penalties threatened by God on the transgressors of the law. "*Cursed is he who abideth not in the words of this law*" (Deut.

Commentary

xxvii. 26). The words may mean, deserving of contempt, of no consideration whatever.

50. Nicodemus (c. iii.), this sincere, but hitherto timid follower of our Lord, "*he that came to Him by night, who was one of them,*" a member of the Sanhedrim or Supreme Council, now displays apostolic courage in defence of our Lord, and in reproaching His enemies with acting unjustly towards Him, and in violation of, at least, the spirit of the law in condemning Him unheard, and in pronouncing His followers as liable to a curse. Although it might be difficult to point out the text of the law, prohibiting what is here referred to; still, it is quite certain, that the whole *spirit* of the law of Moses, as seen in several places (Lev. xix. 15–18), was, that justice should be done to the accused party, by a fair trial. The same was the practice of the Jews, as evidenced in the case of Susanna (Daniel). The same is dictated by the law of nature, or the law of justice itself, God's own original law, with which the law of Moses is always in accord. It was strictly adhered to by moral Pagans and by the Romans in particular (Acts xxv. 16.)

What an example is held out here by Nicodemus to those placed in authority to defend the rights of God and religion, when unjustly assailed.

52. Far from listening to reason, they assail Nichodemus with cutting, scornful reproaches, calling him in terms of contempt, "*a Galilean,*" a follower of this impostor from Galilee. Art thou an abettor of this despised Galilean? "*Galilean*" was a term of reproach at this time. Julian, the apostate, mortally transfixed with the arrow or javelin of a Persian, cries out in defiant scorn, "*Vicisti Galilæa.*" They knew well Nicodemus was not from Galilee. But, they class him, a member of the Sanhedrim, with these despised Galileans. Ridicule is at all times a favourite weapon with infidels, for want of argument, in assailing the truths and practices of religion. In the Greek for "*Galilean,*" is read "*from Galilee.*"

"*Search the Scriptures.*" "*Scriptures*" is wanting in the Greek, in which the sentence runs thus:—"*Search and see that out of Galilee a Prophet riseth not.*" In the Greek, "*ariseth*" is in the past tense, "*hath arisen.*" A foolish argument, indeed. For, even if true, which is disputed by many, that hitherto no Prophet came out of Galilee, it would not follow, that a Prophet might not come out of it, hereafter. If urged, the argument would prove that the *first* Prophet, who came out of a country, was no Prophet. Some one must come forth, *first.* It would prove that *Elias the Thesbite* was no Prophet; for, he first came out of Thesbis. Besides, the fact is questioned by many. Some say, Debora, the Prophetess,

Text

50. *Nicodemus said to them, he that came to him by night, who was one of them:*

50. *Dixit Nicodemus ad eos, ille qui venit ad eum nocte, qui unus erat ex ipsis:*

51. *Doth our law judge any man, unless it first hear him, and know what he doth?*

51. *Numquid lex nostra judicat hominem, nisi prius audierit ab ipso, et cognoverit quid faciat?*

52. *They answered and said to him: Art thou also a Galilean? Search the scriptures, and see that out of Galilee a prophet riseth not.*

52. *Responderunt, et dixerunt ei: Numquid et tu Galilæus es? Scrutare Scripturas, et vide quia a Galilæa propheta non surgit.*

L

Text.	**Commentary.**
	was a Galilean, of the tribe of Zabulon and Nepthali. So was Anna the Prophetess, of the tribe of Aser (Luke ii. 36).
	The argument of the Pharisees is beside the point; since, Nicodemus said nothing of our Lord being a Prophet. He only spoke of the injustice of condemning Him unheard and unconvicted.
53. *And every man returned to his own house.* 53. *Et reversi sunt unusquisque in domum suam.*	53. The remarks of Nicodemus had some effect for the present. For, the assembly broke up in confusion, without giving them an opportunity, this time, of carrying out their murderous designs, against our Blessed Lord. God's Providence had so arranged it, as His hour was not yet come.

CHAPTER VIII.

1 *And Jesus went unto Mount Olivet.*

2 *And early in the morning he came again into the temple, and all the people came to him, and sitting down he taught them.*

3 *And the scribes and Pharisees bring unto him a woman taken in adultery; and they set her in the midst.*

4 *And said to him: Master, this woman was even now taken in adultery.*

5 *Now Moses in the law commanded us to stone such a one. But what sayest thou?*

6 *And this they said tempting him, that they might accuse him. But Jesus bowing himself down, wrote with his finger on the ground.*

7 *When therefore they continued asking him, he lifted up himself and said to them: He that is without sin among you, let him first cast a stone at her.*

8 *And again stooping down, he wrote on the ground.*

9 *But they hearing this went out one by one, beginning at the eldest. And Jesus alone remained, and the woman standing in the midst.*

10 *Then Jesus lifting up himself, said to her: Woman, where are they that accused thee? Hath no man condemned thee?*

11 *Who said: No man, Lord. And Jesus said: Neither will I condemn thee. Go, and now sin no more.*

12 *Again therefore Jesus spoke to them, saying: I am the light of the world: he that followeth me, walketh not in darkness, but shall have the light of life.*

13 *The Pharisees therefore said to him: Thou givest testimony of thyself: thy testimony is not true.*

14 *Jesus answered, and said to them: Although I give testimony of myself, my testimony is true: for I know whence I came, and whither I go: but you know not whence I come, or whither I go.*

15 *You judge according to the flesh: I judge not any man.*

16 *And if I do judge, my judgment is true: because I am not alone, but I and the Father that sent me.*

17 *And in your law it is written, that the testimony of two men is true.*

18 *I am one that give testimony of myself: and the Father that sent me, giveth testimony of me.*

19 *They said therefore to him: Where is thy Father? Jesus answered: Neither me do you know, nor my Father: if you did know me, perhaps you would know my Father also.*

20 *These words Jesus spoke in the treasury, teaching in the temple: and no man laid hands on him, because his hour was not yet come.*

21 *Again therefore Jesus said to them: I go, and you shall seek me, and you shall die in your sin. Whither I go, you cannot come.*

22 *The Jews therefore said: Will he kill himself, because he said: Whither I go, you cannot come?*

23 *And he said to them: You are from beneath, I am from above. You are of this world, I am not of this world.*

24 *Therefore I said to you, that you shall die in your sins. For if you believe not that I am he, you shall die in your sin.*

25 *They said therefore to him: Who art thou? Jesus said to them: The beginning, who also speak unto you.*

26 *Many things I have to speak and to judge of you. But he that sent me is true: and the things I have heard of him, these same I speak in the world.*

27 *And they understood not that he called God his father.*

28 *Jesus therefore said to them: When you shall have lifted up the son of man, then shall you know that I am he, and that I do nothing of myself, but as the Father taught me, these things I speak:*

29 *And he that sent me is with me, and he hath not left me alone: for I do always the things that please him.*

30 *When he spoke these things, many believed in him.*

31 *Then Jesus said to those Jews who believed him: If you continue in my word, you shall be my disciples indeed.*

32 *And you shall know the truth, and the truth shall make you free.*

33 *They answered him: We are the seed of Abraham, and we have never been slaves to any man: how sayest thou: You shall be free?*

34 *Jesus answered them: Amen, amen, I say unto you: that whosoever committeth sin, is the servant of sin.*

35 *Now the servant abideth not in the house for ever: but the son abideth for ever.*

36 *If therefore the son shall make you free, you shall be free indeed.*

37 *I know that you are the children of Abraham: but you seek to kill me, because my word hath no place in you.*

38 *I speak that which I have seen with my Father: and you do the things that you have seen with your father.*

39 *They answered, and said to him: Abraham is our father. Jesus saith to them: If you be the children of Abraham, do the works of Abraham.*

40 *But now you seek to kill me, a man who have spoken the truth to you, which I have heard of God. This Abraham did not.*

41 *You do the works of your father. They said therefore to him: We are not born of fornication: we have one Father even God.*

42 *Jesus therefore said to them: If God were your father, you would indeed love me. For from God I proceeded, and came: for I came not of myself, but he sent me:*

43 *Why do you not know my speech? Because you cannot hear my word.*

44 *You are of your father the devil, and the desires of your father you will do. He was a murderer from the beginning, and he stood not in the truth; because truth is not in him. When he speaketh a lie, he speaketh of his own, for he is a liar, and the father thereof.*

45 *But if I say the truth, you believe me not.*

46 *Which of you shall convince me of sin? If I say the truth to you, why do you not believe me?*

47 *He that is of God, heareth the words of God. Therefore you hear them not, because you are not of God.*

48 *The Jews therefore answered, and said to him: Do not we say well that thou art a Samaritan, and hast a devil?*

49 *Jesus answered: I have not a devil: but I honour my Father, and you have dishonoured me.*

50 *But I seek not my own glory: there is one that seeketh and judgeth.*

51 *Amen, amen, I say to you: if any man keep my word, he shall not see death for ever.*

52 *The Jews therefore said: Now we know that thou hast a devil. Abraham is dead, and the prophets; and thou sayest: If any man keep my word, he shall not taste death for ever.*

53 *Art thou greater than our father Abraham, who is dead? and the prophets are dead. Whom dost thou make thyself?*

54 *Jesus answered: If I glorify myself, my glory is nothing. It is my Father that glorifieth me, of whom you say that he is your God.*

55 *And you have not known him, but I know him. And if I shall say that I know him not, I shall be like to you, a liar. But I do know him, and do keep his word.*

56 *Abraham your father rejoiced that he might see my day: he saw it, and was glad.*

57 *The Jews therefore said to him: Thou art not yet fifty years old, and hast thou seen Abraham?*

58 *Jesus said to them: Amen, amen, I say to you, before Abraham was made I am.*

59 *They took up stones therefore to cast at him But Jesus hid himself, and went out of the temple.*

CAPUT VIII.

1 *Jesus autem perrexit in montem Oliveti:*

2 *Et diluculo iterum venit in templum, et omnis populus venit ad eum, et sedens docebat eos.*

3 *Adducunt autem Scribæ, et Pharisæi mulierem in adulterio deprehensam: et statuerunt eam in medio,*

4 *Et dixerunt ei: Magister, hæc mulier modo deprehensa est in adulterio.*

5 *In lege autem Moyses mandavit nobis hujusmodi lapidare. Tu ergo quid dicis?*

6 *Hoc autem dicebant tentantes eum, ut possent accusare eum. Jesus autem inclinans se deorsum, digito scribebat in terra.*

7 *Cum ergo perseverarent interrogantes eum, erexit se, et dixit eis: Qui sine peccato est vestrum, primus in illam lapidem mittat.*

8 *Et iterum se inclinans, scribebat in terra.*

9 *Audientes autem unus post unum exibant, incipientes a senioribus : et remansit solus Jesus, et mulier in medio stans.*

10 *Erigens autem se Jesus, dixit ei : Mulier, ubi sunt, qui te accusabant ? nemo te condemnavit ?*

11 *Quæ dixit : Nemo, Domine. Dixit autem Jesus : Nec ego te condemnabo : Vade, et jam amplius noli peccare.*

12 *Iterum ergo locutus est eis Jesus, dicens : Ego sum lux mundi : qui sequitur me, non ambulat in tenebris, sed habebit lumen vitæ.*

13 *Dixerunt ergo ei Pharisæi : Tu de te ipso testimonium perhibes : testimonium tuum non est verum.*

14 *Respondit Jesus, et dixit eis : Et si ego testimonium perhibeo de meipso, verum est testimonium meum : quia scio unde veni, et quo vado : vos autem nescitis unde venio, aut quo vado.*

15 *Vos secundum carnem judicatis : ego non judico quemquam :*

16 *Et si judico ego, judicium meum verum est, quia solus non sum : sed ego, et qui misit me Pater.*

17 *Et in lege vestra scriptum est, quia duorum hominum testimonium verum est.*

18 *Ego sum, qui testimonium perhibeo de meipso : et testimonium perhibet de me, qui misit me, Pater.*

19 *Dicebant ergo ei : Ubi est Pater tuus ? Respondit Jesus : Neque me scitis, neque Patrem meum : si me sciretis, forsitan et Patrem meum sciretis.*

20 *Hæc verba locutus est Jesus in gazophylacio, docens in templo : et nemo apprehendit eum, quia necdum venerat hora ejus.*

21 *Dixit ergo iterum eis Jesus : Ego vado, et quæretis me, et in peccato vestro moriemini. Quo ego vado, vos non potestis venire.*

22 *Dicebant ergo Judæi : Numquid interficiet semetipsum, quia dixit : Quo ego vado, vos non potestis venire ?*

23 *Et dicebat eis : Vos de deorsum estis, ego de supernis sum. Vos de mundo hoc estis, ego non sum de hoc mundo :*

24 *Dixi ergo vobis quia moriemini in peccatis vestris : si enim non credideritis quia ego sum, moriemini in peccato vestro.*

25 *Dicebant ergo ei : Tu quis es ? Dixit eis Jesus : Principium, qui et loquor vobis.*

26 *Multa habeo de vobis loqui, et judicare. Sed qui misit me, verax est : et ego quæ audivi ab eo, hæc loquor in mundo.*

27 *Et non cognoverunt quia Patrem ejus dicebat Deum.*

28 *Dixit ergo eis Jesus : Cum exaltaveritis Filium hominis, tunc cognoscetis quia ego sum, et a meipso facio nihil, sed sicut docuit me Pater, hæc loquor :*

29 *Et qui me misit, mecum est, et non reliquit me solum : quia ego quæ placita sunt ei, facio semper.*

30 *Hæc illo loquente, multi crediderunt in eum.*

31 *Dicebat ergo Jesus ad eos, qui crediderunt ei, Judæos : Si vos manseritis in sermone meo, vere discipuli mei eritis :*

32 *Et cognoscetis veritatem, et veritas liberabit vos.*

33 *Responderunt ei : Semen Abrahæ sumus, et nemini servivimus umquam : quomodo tu dicis : Liberi eritis ?*

34 *Respondit eis Jesus: Amen, amen dico vobis: quia omnis, qui facit peccatum, servus est peccati.*
35 *Servus autem non manet in domo in æternum: filius autem manet in æternum.*
36 *Si ergo vos filius liberaverit, vere liberi eritis.*
37 *Scio quia filii Abrahæ estis: sed quæritis me interficere, quia sermo meus non capit in vobis.*
38 *Ego quod vidi apud Patrem meum, loquor: et vos quæ vidistis apud patrem vestrum, facitis.*
39 *Responderunt, et dixerunt ei: Pater noster Abraham est. Dicit eis Jesus: Si filii Abrahæ estis, opera Abrahæ facite.*
40 *Nunc autem quæritis me interficere, hominem, qui veritatem vobis locutus sum, quam audivi a Deo: hoc Abraham non fecit.*
41 *Vos facitis opera patris vestri. Dixerunt itaque ei: Nos ex fornicatione non sumus nati: unum patrem habemus Deum.*
42 *Dixit ergo eis Jesus: Si Deus pater vester esset: diligeretis utique me. Ego enim ex Deo processi, et veni: neque enim a meipso veni, sed ille me misit.*
43 *Quare loquelam meam non cognoscitis? Quia non potestis audire sermonem meum.*
44 *Vos ex patre diabolo estis: et desideria patris vestri vultis facere. Ille homicida erat ab initio, et in veritate non stetit: quia non est veritas in eo: cum loquitur mendacium, ex propriis loquitur, quia mendax est, et pater ejus.*
45 *Ego autem si veritatem dico, non creditis mihi.*
46 *Quis ex vobis arguet me de peccato? Si veritatem dico vobis, quare non creditis mihi?*
47 *Qui ex Deo est, verba Dei audit. Propterea vos non auditis, quia ex Deo non estis.*
48 *Responderunt ergo Judæi, et dixerunt ei: Nonne bene dicimus nos quia Samaritanus es tu, et dæmonium habes?*
49 *Respondit Jesus: Ego dæmonium non habeo: sed honorifico Patrem meum, et vos inhonorastis me.*
50 *Ego autem non quæro gloriam meam: est qui quærat, et judicet.*
51 *Amen, amen dico vobis: si quis sermonem meum servaverit, mortem non videbit in æternum.*
52 *Dixerunt ergo Judæi: Nunc cognovimus quia dæmonium habes. Abraham mortuus est, et Prophetæ: et tu dicis: Si quis sermonem meum servaverit: non gustabit mortem in æternum.*
53 *Numquid tu major es patre nostro Abraham, qui mortuus est? et Prophetæ mortui sunt. Quem te ipsum facis?*
54 *Respondit Jesus: Si ego glorifico meipsum, gloria mea nihil est: est Pater meus, qui glorificat me, quem vos dicitis quia Deus vester est,*
55 *Et non cognovistis eum: ego autem novi eum: Et si dixero quia non scio eum, ero similis vobis, mendax. Sed scio eum, et sermonem ejus servo.*
56 *Abraham pater vester exultavit ut videret diem meum, vidit, et gavisus est.*
57 *Dixerunt ergo Judæi ad eum: Quinquaginta annos nondum habes, et Abraham vidisti?*
58 *Dixit eis Jesus: Amen, amen dico vobis, antequam Abraham fieret, ego sum.*
59 *Tulerunt ergo lapides, ut jacerent in eum: Jesus autem abscondit se, et exivit de templo.*

ST. JOHN, CHAP. VIII.

ANALYSIS.

The last verse (53) of preceding chapter, "*and they returned each one to his own home,*" is clearly in contrast with v. 1 of this c. viii., from which, in the division of chapters, it ought not to have been separated. They went to their own homes to enjoy themselves and concert measures against our Lord, But, He went out to Mount Olivet to spend the night, as was His wont, in prayer. The portion from verse 53 of preceding chapter to verse 11 of this inclusive, is wanting in several MSS., and ancient copies of the Gospel. Hence, the authenticity of the passage is questioned by many. It is classed with the portions of SS. Scripture commonly termed, *Deutero-Canonical*. Several arguments, extrinsic and intrinsic, are adduced in favour of, and against its authenticity. The preponderance, however, is in favour of it. But, whatever may be said of the arguments on both sides, no Catholic can question it, after the solemn declaration of the Council of Trent (SS. iv.), "*Decreto de Canonicis Scripturis,*" in which all are commanded, under pain of Anathema, "*to receive as sacred and canonical the entire books themselves*" (which are there recounted), "*with all their parts, as they are wont to be read in the Catholic Church, and are found in the old Latin Vulgate.*"

This chapter commences with an account of the woman caught in the act of adultery, and our Lord's merciful treatment of her, while He baffles the insidious designs of her accusers (1–11).

Our Lord's declaration of the truth of His doctrine, and of His heavenly mission, which, according to the rules of evidence sanctioned in their Law, they should admit (11–19). These things He spoke in the most frequented part of the Temple, fearlessly and openly (20).

He resumes His discourse, threatening them with eternal reprobation, in case they persisted in their unbelief regarding His Divinity, after all the testimonies borne in His favour (21–31).

He next declares that they were not genuine sons of Abraham, in whom they so much gloried, as they did not imitate His works; but, rather children of the devil, of whose wicked works they were imitators, in rejecting Him and harbouring murderous designs regarding Him (31–51).

He next declares His superiority over Abraham, as Abraham "WAS MADE"—created; whereas He *always was* (52–58).

Our Lord, in virtue of His Divine power, hides Himself from them and leaves the Temple (59).

Commentary.	Text.
1. "*Went unto Mount Olivet,*" which was distant, a Sabbath day's journey, from Jerusalem to the east. Between it and the city ran the little brook or rivulet, Cedron. Close by it was the Garden of Gethsemane. The house of Martha and Mary was near. Our Lord frequently spent the night in Mount Olivet, communing with His Heavenly Father in prayer. On this account, it was that the traitor, who well knew His habits and places of resort, directed or conducted there the armed band sent to apprehend Him, thinking it to be the place, where He was most likely to be found.	1. And Jesus went unto mount Olivet. 1. *Jesus autem perrexit in montem Oliveti:*
2. "*Early in the morning*" He came *again*—according to custom—"*into the Temple.*"	2. And early in the morning he came again into the temple, and all the people came to him, and sitting down he taught them.

2. *Et diluculo iterum venit in templum, et omnis populus venit ad eum, et sedens docebat eos.*

Text.

3. And the Scribes and Pharisees bring unto him a woman taken in adultery; and they set her in the midst.
3. Adducunt autem Scribæ, et Pharisæi mulierem in adulterio deprehensam: et statuerunt eam in medio.
4. And said to him: Master, 'this woman was even now taken in adultery.
4. Et dixerunt ei: Magister, hæc mulier modo deprehensa est in adulterio.

5. Now Moses in the law commanded us to stone such a one. But what sayest thou?
5. In lege autem Moyses mandavit nobis huiusmodi lapidare. Tu ergo quid dicis?

6. And this they said tempting him, that they might accuse him. But Jesus, bowing himself down, wrote with his finger on the ground.

6. Hoc autem dicebant tentantes eum, ut possent accusare eum. Jesus autem inclinans se deorsum, digito scribebat in terra.

Commentary.

3, 4. "*The Scribes*"—who gloried in the knowledge—"*and the Pharisees*," in their strict and religious observance of the law, now come to test His knowledge and religious sentiments in regard to the law, of which His decision in the following case, which they submit to Him, would be regarded as a true test, "*taken in adultery*." From the Greek reading of following verse (4), "*this woman was taken in adultery*" (μοιχευομενη), it is clear she was caught in the actual commission of crime.

"*Master.*" They wish to conciliate Him and gain His good will, by affecting respect for His opinions, as teacher. "*What sayest Thou?*" as teacher.

5. The law of Moses commanded, that in case a virgin espoused to a man was found guilty of crime with another, both should be stoned (Deut. xxii. 24). In regard to adulterers also, death was enacted. No mention, however, was made of the kind of death (Levit. xx. 10; Deut. xxii. 22). The Jews, however, following tradition, and guided by the interpretation of the ancients, extended the specific punishment of stoning to adultery, as being a still more grievous crime. That it was the kind of death actually inflicted on adulterers, is clear from Ezechiel xvi. 40. Likely, it was the kind of death in reserve for Susanna, as the elders underwent it, at the hands of the multitude. This would point to stoning, as their mode of action conjointly (Daniel xiii. 62).

6. "*Tempting Him.*" Their object was, according to several Commentators, to involve Him in a dilemma, so that whatever answer He gave, they would have an opportunity of accusing Him, either with the civil authorities or the people. If He decided, she should be stoned; then, they would charge Him with excessive severity and want of that spirit of mercy, so often hitherto commended and practised by Him. Moreover, He would be acting as judge; and thus amenable to the civil authorities. If He said, she should *not* be stoned; then, He would be the enemy of the law of Moses, a charge so often before made against Him. He would be thus amenable to the Mosaic or religious authorities. Others say, "*tempting,*" had solely for object, to elicit from Him an opinion or decision at variance with, or in modification of, the sentence of the law, which the Jews quote for Him. This, they hoped would bring Him into disrepute as an enemy of the law.

This seems to be their object in quoting the law. It is not easy to see, how our Lord could be charged with want of clemency in agreeing in the sentence of the law of Moses. Hence, there seems to be no ground for the dilemma above referred to.

Commentary.

"*Wrote with His finger on the ground.*" What did He write? It is idle to conjecture, since He Himself has not vouchsafed to tell us. Why did He write? The reason generally assigned is, that He wished to convey, that He would decline giving any answer to a question so captious and so dishonestly intended. Hence, He delineated some character on the pavement of the Temple.

7. Perceiving, probably, from His stooping down and delineating some characters on the pavement or the dust, with which it might have been covered, that He meant to decline having anything to say to them, they persevered in asking for an explicit answer to their captious, insidious questions, thus interrupting Him. "*He lifted up Himself and said to them, he that is without sin among you, let him first cast,*" etc. "*Without sin,*" may refer to sin in general, or to the sin with which this adulterous woman was charged. For, there is abundant evidence, as testified by Josephus, regarding the low state of morality at the time, even among those who affected sanctity and religious observance of the moral law.

"*Let him first cast a stone at her.*" The law prescribed (Deut. xvii. 7), that the accuser or witness should be the first to cast a stone at the guilty party; doubtless, with a view to make men more cautious in bringing forward accusations, from a sense of their responsibility, in being executioners. The throwing of the first stone was a signal to the bystanders for a general attack on the culprit.

Our Lord does not say the adulterous woman was to be set free, or, that she was undeserving of the punishment provided by the law against such transgressions; and hence, does not interfere with the just sentence of the law. He implies that she deserved death; and thus baffled the insidious attempts of His enemies. At the same time, He mercifully stays the execution, which the Roman Governor alone could warrant, although the Sanhedrim might pass sentence, by remitting each to the tribunal of conscience, which convicted them of the crime, for which they would fain execute vengeance on their fellow-creature. Our Lord does not here mean, that no judge could pass sentence on a convicted criminal, if the judge himself were in sin. He merely remits His enemies to the tribunal of conscience. They ask Him to give judicial sentence; this He declines doing. It belonged to the public authority to do so. He conveys to us that, in a private capacity, it would be congruous, that a man who, in private, sits in judgment on another and condemns him, would himself be free from the crime for which he judges others. There is no reference whatever here to *public authority*, but only to the execution of a sentence by *private* authority. "*First cast a stone.*" Our Lord

Text.

7. *When therefore they continued asking him, he lifted up himself and said to them: He that is without sin among you, let him first cast a stone at her.*

7. *Cum ergo perseverarent interrogantes eum, erexit se, et dixit eis: Qui sine peccato est vestrum, primus in illam lapidem mittat.*

Text.	Commentary.

knowing their guilty consciences, knew well they would not dare submit to the test.

8. *And again stooping down, he wrote on the ground.*

8. *Et iterum se inclinans, scribebat in terra.*

8. He then resumes the operation of writing on the ground, in which they had interrupted Him by their importunity. He probably intended by this to give them, in the exercise of clemency, an opportunity of quietly retiring without being put to excessive confusion or shame.

9. *But they hearing this went out one by one, beginning at the eldest. And Jesus alone remained, and the woman standing in the midst.*

9. *Audientes autem unus post unum exibant, incipientes a senioribus: et remansit solus Jesus, et mulier in medio stans.*

9. "*When they heard this*—(the Greek adds, "*being convicted by their own conscience*") *they went out one by one, beginning at the eldest*"—(to which the Greek adds, "*unto the last*").

The "*eldest*" may mean those who, advanced in life, were most hardened in iniquity, like the old judges who falsely accused Susanna (Daniel xiii.); or, the word may refer not to age; but to dignity. The whole sentence means, that all the accusers meanly sneaked away, without exception, either as regards age or dignity.

"*Jesus alone remained,*" etc. "*Alone,*" regards the accusers, but not the multitude, who remained, as appears from verse 12.

10. *Then Jesus lifting up himself, said to her: Woman, where are they that accused thee? Hath no man condemned thee?*

10. *Erigens autem se Jesus, dixit ei: Mulier, ubi sunt, qui te accusabant? nemo te condemnavit?*

10, 11. Our Lord mercifully inspiring her with true sorrow for her sin, pardons her guilt, without passing any judicial sentence on her. "*Neither will I condemn thee*"—to legal punishment. He implies her moral guilt, which was manifest. "*Sin no more.*" At the same time, He shows, in these words, His abhorrence of sin.

11. *Who said: No man, Lord. And Jesus said: Neither will I condemn thee. Go, and now sin no more.*

11. *Quæ dixit: Nemo, Domine. Dixit autem Jesus: Nec ego te condemnabo: Vade, et jam amplius noli peccare.*

12. *Again therefore Jesus spoke to them, saying: I am the light of the world; he that followeth me, walketh not in darkness, but shall have the light of life.*

12. *Iterum ergo locutus est eis Jesus, dicens: Ego sum lux mundi: qui sequitur me, non ambulat in tenebris, sed habebit lumen vitæ.*

12. "*Again, therefore, Jesus spoke to them.*" After being interrupted in His course of teaching (*v.* 2) by this unhappy incident regarding the adulterous woman, our Lord now resumes His discourse to the people.

"*I am the light of the world,*" not only considered in My *Divine* nature, as eternal wisdom and truth, but in My *human* nature, of which it was predicted, "*populus . . . vidit lucem magnam.*" (Isaias ix.) He is the light of the world, enlightening minds, by His teaching and example. "*Of the world,*" not merely of one nation, but all the nations of the earth.

"*He that followeth Me.*" When pointing out the true path, by My teaching and example. "*Walketh not in darkness,*" of error, which the light of My teaching dissipates; or, of sin, which My conversation and life condemns.

Commentary.

"*But shall have the light of life.*" When at the close of His mortal pilgrimage, He shall reach His eternal home (Ps. xxxv., "*et in lumine tuo, videbimus lumen*")—others understand it of the light of faith, which is opposed to walking "*in darkness,*" and faith is said to be "*the light of life,*" inasmuch as it leads and gives the knowledge of the way that leads to life, and even in this world, united to charity, it gives life to the soul.

13. "*The Pharisees.*" Some of them, who remained in the crowd, when the others had retired in confusion, after they were baffled by His answer in the case of the adulterous woman.

"*Is not true,*" that is, not worthy of credit, receivable in evidence. The testimony of two witnesses was required to be produced in evidence.

14. "*My testimony is true,*" deserving of being received in evidence. "*For I know whence I came,*" etc. It is an obscure way of saying, "BECAUSE I AM GOD, THE ETERNAL SON OF GOD, THE INFALLIBLE TRUTH." Our Lord uses this obscure way of conveying the sacred truth, in accommodation to the weakness of His hearers. "*I know, whence I came,*" descending from the bosom of My Eternal Father, God of God, light of light, to assume human nature and redeem mankind. Thus, He conveys to them the fundamental truth regarding His Divinity and humanity, His Divine nature and Incarnation. "*And whither I go.*" After My work on earth is accomplished, I ascend to the Father, to be seated next Him, at His right hand of majesty in glory. As the Son of God, My own assertion is sufficient. As well might one question the existence of the sun in the midst of noon-day splendour. Had He plainly conveyed to them this truth, "I am the Son of God," and, therefore, entitled to undoubting belief, they would have recoiled from Him, as a blasphemer. He, however, conveyed the same truth in an obscure way, and proved it by undoubted arguments and reasons, independently of His personal testimony, which reasons and arguments superadded to His own personal testimony, were in a moral point, equivalent to an additional witness.

"*But you know not, whence I come or whither I go.*" It is because you know Me not, nor wish to know Me, though you have had already evident proofs of it in many ways, that you disbelieve or affect to disbelieve My words.

15. Your judgment regarding Me is according to your carnal notions, and the external appearances you behold; or, you judge of Me, merely from the appearance of the flesh in which I am clothed. You judge of Me, the man God, and of My words, as you would of any other human being, or mere man.

Text.

13. *The Pharisees therefore said to him: Thou givest testimony of thyself: thy testimony is not true.*

13. *Dixerunt ergo ei Pharisæi: Tu de te ipso testimonium perhibes: testimonium tuum non est verum.*

14. *Jesus answered and said to them: Although I give testimony of myself, my testimony is true: for I know whence I came, and whither I go: but you know not whence I come, or whither I go.*

14. *Respondit Jesus, et dixit eis: Et si ego testimonium perhibeo de meipso, verum est testimonium meum: quia scio unde veni, et quo vado: vos autem nescitis unde venio, aut quo vado.*

15. *You judge according to the flesh: I judge not any man.*

15. *Vos secundum carnem judicatis: ego non judico quemquam.*

Text.	Commentary.
	"*I*"—considered as mere man—"*judge not any man.*" I am not alone in judging any man, which means, in bearing testimony regarding any man. My testimony, which forms the chief part in determining any judicial process, is not Mine only. I am joined in it by another. The word "*judge*," as appears from the entire context, refers to bearing witness, which is the chief thing in determining any judgment, as it is by evidence, the judge is guided in his decision.
16. *And if I do judge, my judgment is true: because I am not alone, but I and the Father that sent me.* 16. *Et si judico ego, judicium meum verum est quia solus non sum: sed ego, et qui misit me, Pater.*	16. And if I were to judge and bear testimony, "*My judgment*" or testimony "*is true*" and admissible according to the strictest rules of evidence; "*because I am not alone.*" I am not a single or solitary witness. My Father also testifies along with Me.
17. *And in your law it is written, that the testimony of two men is true.* 17. *Et in lege vestra scriptum est, quia duorum hominum testimonium verum est.*	17. He refers them to their own, the Mosaic, law, "*Your law.*" "*Your,*" in the observance of which you glory so much, as if no one else observed it so well. He merely quotes the substance of the law, which applies to His case regarding *two witnesses.* (The words of the law, Deut. xvii. 6; xix. 15, are, "*In the mouth of two or three witnesses every word shall stand.*") In the words of this verse, our Lord conveys, that two human witnesses will decide any case, and their testimony be accepted, as legal evidence—("*is true*")—though in several instances the testimony of two has been proved to be false; for example, in the case of Susanna, and others. If this be so, of how much greater force ought the testimony of God the Father, and the Son, be regarded, to whose united evidence, reference is made in the following verse? The word "*true,*" means accepted as legal evidence.
18. *I am one that give testimony of myself: and the Father that sent me, giveth testimony of me.* 18. *Ego sum, qui testimonium perhibeo de me ipso: et testimonium perhibet de me, qui misit me, Pater.*	18. No doubt, in the sense of the law, there are required two witnesses, distinct from the party in whose favour testimony is borne. We are, however, to bear in mind, that our Lord had two natures, and one person. As *God*, or, in His *Divine nature*, He could, and did bear testimony, through the works peculiar to the Divinity and other undoubted evidence, to the fact or fundamental truth, that under His visible *human* nature was concealed the Divine nature and person of the Son of God. Of Himself as *man*, with a distinct nature, He Himself, as God in His Divine nature, bore testimony; and adduced besides His testimony, reasons and additional arguments in proof of it.
19. *They said therefore to him: Where is thy Father? Jesus*	19. "*Where is your Father?*" Who is this Father, of whom you boast so often? Where is He? Show Him to us, as bearing

ST. JOHN, CHAP. VIII.

Commentary.

testimony to you. They feign a desire of knowing the truth, and wish to elicit from Him an explicit declaration, that He was the Son of God, which they knew well He meant; and thus, have a pretext for carrying out what they intended, viz., to stone Him, as a blasphemer (v. 18; x. 31).

Our Lord does not directly and clearly answer, My Father is in heaven. They wished to elicit this, in order to catch Him in His words. He, however, answers these hypocrites indirectly. "*Neither Me do you know*," etc., bywhich He meant to convey, that they were mistaken, in regarding Him as mere man, having Joseph for His father. They knew not the truth as to His Incarnation, His assuming human flesh, being at the same time, the Son of God; neither did they know God to be His Father, paternity and filiation being relative designations. He performed several miracles, to prove this, which they blindly and obstinately ignored.

"*If you did know Me, perhaps,*" etc. "*Perhaps,*" Greek (άν) means, *surely*. If they knew Him to be God, a truth, He often proved to them, they would know that His Father was God, to be sought for not on earth; but, in heaven. The Eternal and Divine Sonship of our Lord connotes the relation of paternity in the Eternal Father.

20. "*In the treasury*"—the entire portico surrounding the chest or ark, in which the moneys and valuable property of the Temple were deposited and preserved. As this was a very public part of the Temple, the Evangelist wishes to convey, that our Lord spoke not in private or in any obscure corner, but rather in the most public place, and with the greatest freedom of speech. This seems to be the point He had in view in alluding to the place where our Lord spoke—still, they did not apprehend Him. His divine power restrained them, as the time, He had Himself fixed for freely and voluntarily undergoing death, had not yet arrived.

21. "*Again, therefore, Jesus spoke,*" etc. "*Therefore,*" as they durst not seize on Him; and as they were persevering in their feelings of hatred and malice. "*Jesus again,*" as He had spoken already, repeats the words addressed to the servants sent to apprehend Him (vii. 33, 34). "*I go,*" returning, after My death, to the bosom of My Father. "*And you shall seek Me,*" which is understood by some to mean: in your blind hatred and malice, you shall desire to crucify Me again. But, your efforts shall be in vain, as I shall be beyond your reach, sitting in glory at the right hand of My Father (vii. 33).

"*And you shall die in your sin.*" You shall persevere and die in your sinful state of infidelity and refusal to believe in Me.

Text.

answered: Neither me do you know nor my Father: if you did know me, perhaps you would know my Father also.

19. *Dicebant ergo ei: Ubi est Pater tuus? Respondit Jesus: Neque me scitis, neque Patrem meum: si me sciretis, forsitan et Patrem meum sciretis.*

20. *These words Jesus spoke in the treasury, teaching in the temple: and no man laid hands on him, because his hour was not yet come.*

20. *Hæc verba locutus est Jesus in gazophylacio, docens in templo: et nemo apprehendit eum, quia necdum venerat hora ejus.*

21. *Again therefore Jesus said to them: I go, and you shall seek me, and you shall die in your sin. Whither I go you cannot come.*

21. *Dixit ergo iterum eis Jesus: Ego vado, et quæretis me, et in peccato vestro moriemini. Quo ego vado, vos non potestis venire.*

Text.	Commentary.
	"*Whither I go, you cannot come.*" While I shall ascend up to heaven, you shall descend into hell, in punishment of your malice and sin. In vain, then, shall you seek Me on earth, when I shall be seated in majesty at the right hand of My Heavenly Father.
22. *The Jews therefore said: Will he kill himself, because he said: Whither I go, you cannot come?* 22. *Dicebant ergo Judæi; Numquid interficiet semetipsum, quia dixit: Quo ego vado, vos non potestis venire?*	22. The servants of the Pharisees, on receiving a similar answer, took a more benignant view of His expressed intentions, not being blinded, like their employers, with hatred and malice. They said; "*Will He go into the dispersed,*" etc. (vii. 34). But the Pharisees, who harboured murderous designs against Him, thinking He could not escape their hands, go where He might, by any other means than self destruction, ask, "*will He*"—to escape our hands—"*kill Himself?*"
23. *And he said to them: You are from beneath, I am from above. You are of this world, I am not of this world.* 23. *Et dicebat eis; Vos de deorsum estis, ego de supernis sum. Vos de mundo hoc estis, ego non sum de hoc mundo?*	23. "*You are from beneath,*" "*of the earth, earthly,*" only thinking of earthly things, measuring everything by your earthly conceptions. "*I am from above.*" You are altogether bent on things of earth, persevering in your sins, and shall be punished eternally in the lower regions. You cannot, therefore, come to Me, who am dwelling in heaven. Or, the words may be assigned by our Lord, as a cause why they understood perversely, of His intending to put Himself to death, what He meant regarding His return to heaven. They thus thought perversely; because, they were earthly and carnal in their ideas and conceptions. "*You are of this world,*" a further explanation, or rather a confirmatory repetition of the above. Being "*of this world,*" they were blinded by the passions and corrupt leading maxims of this wicked world, in their judgments regarding our Lord. The phrase, "*of the world,*" implies blindness of intellect; low, earthly, grovelling ideas and corruption of heart, the latter being in great measure the cause of the former.
24. *Therefore I said to you, that you shall die in your sins. For if you believe not that I am he, you shall die in your sin.* 24. *Dixi ergo vobis quia moriemini in peccatis vestris: si enim non credideritis quia ego sum, moriemini in peccato vestro.*	24. It is on account of low, earthly ideas regarding Me, you cannot believe in Me as your long expected Messiah, as the Saviour sent to redeem the world, the Eternal Son of God, begotten of the Father before all ages. "*I am He,*" the eternal uncreated, self-existent, only begotten Son of the Father before all ages, the great essential source of light and life in creatures.
25. *They said therefore to him: Who art thou? Jesus said to them: The beginning*	25. Forgetful of all our Lord's miraculous wonders, which would prove His Divinity, or, at least, affecting to forget them, they insolently and scornfully ask, "*Who art Thou?*" "*Who,*" being

Commentary

emphatic. You say, "*I am He.*" You threaten us with everlasting misery, with a bad death, unless we believe that "*Thou art He.*" "*Who art Thou?*" What are we to believe regarding you?

Our Lord knowing they wished to entrap Him, answers, not directly or explicitly, "*The beginning, who also speak unto you.*" This passage presents great difficulties, chiefly owing to the Greek reading, which has "*the beginning*" not in the nominative as the Vulgate has it, but in the accusative case (την αρχην). Some Expositors, following the Vulgate reading, which they regard as giving the sense of the words, expound them thus : I am the beginning, the principle of all things with the Father and the Holy Ghost, "*who also speak unto you.*" Although viewed according to My *Divine* nature, to you invisible, I am "*the beginning*" of all things; still, viewed according to My *human* nature, assumed by Me for your sakes, under the personality of the Divine Word, I now "*speak to you,*" and reveal to you heavenly truths, hitherto concealed from the children of men. Briefly ; according to My Divinity, "*the beginning*" of all things, being one and the same with My Father ; but, according to My *Humanity,* which I also possess with My Divine nature, I speak to you, teaching you what you are to believe concerning Me. These Expositors regard ὅτι or, ὅ τι, not as an adverb, but as a pronoun, agreeing not with *principium,* "*beginning,*" but with "*ego,*" "I, the beginning, who speak to you."

The Greek reading, however, will hardly admit of this construction. Hence, St. Augustine retaining the accusative, την αρχην, interprets it thus : You ask Me who I am, that you may believe in Me. I say, *believe Me* to be the beginning, etc. Hence, St. Augustine adds or prefixes the word *credite, believe,* this being understood as the object of their question.

Others understand the Greek word for "*beginning*" in an adverbial sense, prefixing, κατα, to it, κατα την αρχην, meaning, *omnino, altogether, by all means,* as if He said ; I am by all means what I have been saying and proclaiming all along to you, the Eternal Son of God, the light of the world, the bread of life, etc.

Others understand it to mean, *from the beginning.* I am what I have been saying to you, *from the beginning,* and still say to you, viz., the Word, by whom all things were made, born of the Father before all ages ; the source of life and light to all creatures. Hence, the Evangelist supposes that our Lord here refers to His eternal generation, when he adds (*v.* 27), "*they understood not that He called God His Father.*" The Vulgate giving the sense of the Greek words, renders it, "*the beginning,*" the source and fountain of existence to all creatures.

Some Catholic Expositors follow the Greek reading, and render it, "*as from the beginning,*" *I also speak to you*" (Kenrick). I

Text

who also speak unto you.

25. *Dicebant ergo ei : Tu quis es? Dixit eis Jesus : Principium qui et loquor vobis.*

Text.

26. *Many things I have to speak and to judge of you. But he that sent me is true: and the things I have heard of him, these same I speak in the world.*

26. *Multa habeo de vobis loqui, et judicare sed qui me misit, verax est: et ego quæ audivi ab eo, hæc loquor in mundo.*

27. *And they understood not that he called God his Father.*

27. *Et non cognoverunt quia Patrem ejus dicebat Deum.*

28. *Jesus therefore said to them: When you shall have lifted up the son of man, then shall you know that I am he, and that I do nothing of myself, but as the Father hath taught me, these things I speak;*

28 *Dixit ergo eis Jesus: Cum exaltaveritis Filium hominis, tunc cognoscetis quia ego sum, et a meipso facio nihil, sed sicut docuit me Pater, hæc loquor:*

Commentary.

am what I affirmed from the beginning, and still affirm, etc. (as above).

26. I have many things whereon to expostulate with you and condemn you. "*But he that sent Me is true.*" But, passing over these, I will content Myself with saying, that the Father "*who sent Me,*" whose doctrine I preach, is infinitely veracious. Hence, My doctrines, which you deride, are true, and should be believed. Since "*the things I have heard, I speak,*" etc. I proclaim to the world those things only which I have heard from Him.

27. "*... called God His Father.*" In the Greek the word "*God*" is wanting ... "*that He spoke to them of the Father.*" The sense, however, is more clearly expressed in our Vulgate. Our Lord, in verses 25, 26, referred to His Father in heaven, of whom He was eternally begotten before all ages. This, however, He uttered obscurely, lest, by saying in clear terms, He was the Eternal Son of God, they would charge Him with blasphemy, and stone Him. Hence, they did not clearly understand Him, nor had they any clear grounds of proceeding against Him as a blasphemer, God having providentially so arranged it, as the hour marked out for the death of His Son, had not yet arrived.

28. "*Therefore,*" as you do not now clearly understand, you shall understand it, "*when you shall have lifted up,*" etc., that is, raised Him and suspended Him on the cross, as explained by Himself (xii. 33). Commentators carefully note, regarding the word, "*lifted up,*" "*exaltaveritis,*" that the humiliation and scandal of the cross was the source of our Lord's greatest exaltation (Phil. ii. 8, 9).

"*Then you shall know that I am He.*" The result following from Christ's death, owing to the great miracles which took place on occasion of it—the verification of His predictions regarding it—His Resurrection which soon followed it, was, that many of the Jews proclaimed Him to be the Son of God, and regarded Him in quite a different light from that in which His unbelieving hearers viewed Him. They looked upon Him, not as a mere man, but as God.

"*I am He,*" the Messiah promised to you; the Eternal Son of God, whom I proclaimed Myself to be.

"*And that I do nothing of Myself,*" having the same Divine will and operation with My Father, with whom I act simultaneously and in perfect concert and harmony.

"*But as the Father,*" with whom I have the same knowledge, "*taught Me,*" being thus, Omniscient in My eternal generation, born of Him, God of God, light of light.

ST. JOHN, CHAP. VIII.

Commentary.

29. To prevent any erroneous inference, that might be deduced from the foregoing, He conveys that the Father, by sending Him, did not desert or relinquish Him either as to His Divinity or Humanity. In His *Divinity*, He is identical, and, therefore, always with the Father. In His *Humanity*, the Father so guided, directed, and led Him, that all His works were pleasing to God, ever in accordance with His Holy will, exalted, meritorious in the highest degree; nay, Divine.

30. Many of the simple, unsophisticated crowd, captivated by His words, the grace of God, at the same time interiorly enlightening and aiding them, believed in Him; but, very few, if any, from among the carping, envious Pharisees.

31. Addressing those who believed, our Lord, in order to strengthen their faith, says to them: if you persevere in the faith and doctrine you have received, and in obedience to My words, you will merit the name of being, in reality, My disciples, and after trials and persecutions during life, you will receive the eternal inheritance reserved by Me for My faithful followers. "*He that shall persevere to the end, shall be saved.*"

32. "*And you shall know the truth.*" By persevering in My doctrine, you shall know by experience and practice, and shall taste how true are all things you believe of Me, and how salutary is My doctrine and teaching. This knowledge of faith and truth will free and emancipate you from the servitude of sin and the tyranny of your passions (*v.* 34). It will inspire you with true sentiments of penance, contrition and charity, and will cause you to see God, not from fear of punishment peculiar to slaves, but from love and affection.

33. "*They answered Him.*" "*They*," are understood of the unbelieving Jews (*v.* 27), not of those that believed. Both were among His hearers, and a speaker addressing an assembly, may direct his words to one portion, in particular.

"*And we have never been slaves,*" etc. This, in reference to their fathers, would be untrue, who were slaves to the Egyptians, Babylonians, etc. "*Egypto manum dedimus et Assyriis,*" etc. "*Servi dominati sunt nobis*" (Jeremiah, iv. 6-8). It is, therefore, most likely, the Jews spoke not of past times, but of the generation then alive; and, although subject to the Romans, they were not slaves. They enjoyed, in a great measure, their own institutions and laws. Our Lord, as appears from next verse, refers to a different kind of bondage, the bondage of sin. He addresses to them a twofold reproach: ignorance and servitude. Overlooking the former

Text.

29. *And he that sent me is with me, and he hath not left me alone: for I do always the things that please him.*

29. *Et qui me misit, mecum est, et non reliquit me solum: quia ego quæ placita sunt ei, facio semper.*

30. *When he spoke these things, many believed in him.*

30. *Hæc illo loquente, multi crediderunt in eum.*

31. *Then Jesus said to those Jews who believed in him: If you continue in my word, you shall be my disciples indeed.*

31. *Dicebat ergo Jesus ad eos, qui crediderunt ei, Judæos: Si vos manseritis in sermone meo, vere discipuli mei eritis:*

32. *And you shall know the truth, and the truth shall make you free.*

32. *Et cognoscetis veritatem, et veritas liberabit vos.*

33. *They answered him: We are the seed of Abraham, and we have never been slaves to any man: how sayest thou: You shall be free?*

33. *Responderunt ei: Semen Abrahæ sumus, et nemini servivimus unquam: quomodo tu dicis: Liberi eritis?*

M

Text.	Commentary.
	charge, the Jews expressed indignation, and murmured against the latter.
34. *Jesus answered them: Amen, amen I say unto you, that whosoever committeth sin, is the servant of sin.* 34. *Respondit eis Jesus: Amen, amen dico vobis: quia omnis, qui facit peccatum, servus est peccati.*	34. "*Amen, amen.*" The Hebrews expressed a superlative by repeating a word, as if He said, *most truly*. Our Lord tells them, He speaks not of civil bondage; but, of the bondage of sin. He speaks in very general terms and in the third person, while specially intending it for them, to avoid offence. What He really meant was: you are slaves to sin; and this is the servitude from which I rescue you and all others, involved in it. I alone can do it. "*Whosoever*," without exception, be he slave, in a civil sense, or a freeman; be he born of Abraham, or of Gentile parents, "*committeth sin, is the servant of sin*," bound over by its corrupt passions and concupiscences.
35. *Now the servant abideth not in the house for ever: but the son abideth for ever.* 35. *Servus autem non manet in domo in æternum: filius autem manet in æternum.*	35. From the condition of his existence, the slave has no fixed right to remain always in the house of his master. He is liable to be cast out at a moment's notice, and sold to some other master. It is different with the son, who has a right to his father's fortune and inheritance. The implied conclusion from this generally admitted truth, in its application is, that the Jews, being the slaves of sin, had no fixed right to remain in the house, that is, the Church of God. They were liable to be cast out, and if they persevered in their unbelief, would be cast out of the Church, God's inheritance, which would be transferred to others. This may contain a latent allusion to the exclusion, or reprobation of the Jews, and the call of the Gentiles.
36. *If therefore the son shall make you free, you shall be free indeed.* 36. *Si ergo vos filius liberaverit, vere liberi eritis.*	36. "*If, therefore, the Son shall make you free.*" If, I who am the Son of God, eternal truth, the heir in My Father's house, make you free, and I alone can do it, "*you shall be free indeed.*" As the heir emancipates his slaves, so you will receive from Me, a liberty far exceeding civil liberty, a true liberty, from the tyranny of sin and the bondage of your passions.
37. *I know that you are the children of Abraham; but you seek to kill me, because my word hath no place in you.* 37. *Scio quia filii Abrahæ estis: sed quæritis me interficere, quia sermo meus non capit in vobis.*	37. 'I know you are descendants of Abraham according to the flesh. But, you are degenerate sons, neither imitating his virtues nor walking in his footsteps; since you seek to kill Me, the true son of Abraham, your descent from Abraham will only condemn you the more. On the day of Judgment, Abraham will disown you, "*because My word hath no place in you.*" On account of the servitude of sin, in which you are involved, your hearts are too corrupt, too full of pride, envy and other passions, to obey My words; your intellects are too obscured, and darkened to comprehend them properly.

ST. JOHN, CHAP. VIII.

Commentary.

38. "*I speak and teach what I have seen with My Father.*" "*You*"—in turn—"*do the things which you have seen with your father,*" implying that Abraham was not their father. They had another father, the Devil, whose works they performed, whose wishes they execute, when they wish to kill Him. Their father "*was a murderer from the beginning*" (v. 44).

39. The Jews understanding our Lord to assign to them tacitly a father different from Abraham, now repeat that Abraham, and no one else, was their father. In him, there is no bad example given us to imitate.
Our Lord tells them, if they were the true, genuine sons of Abraham, the children, not merely according to the flesh, but the children of benediction, who were to be heirs of his promises, they should imitate his example, and do his good works.

40. "*This Abraham did not do.*" He never injured any one. He never sought to compass the death of a teacher of truth. Hence, while compassing My death, you are not doing the work of Abraham; you are proving yourselves to be degenerate, undutiful children.

40. *Nunc autem quæritis me interficere, hominem, qui veritatem vobis locutus sum, quam audivi a Deo: hoc Abraham non fecit.*

41. Our Lord repeats his assertion that the Jews were not the true children of Abraham, that they had a different father, whose works they did, whose example they followed. He forbears mentioning, who that father is. He mentions it in v. 44. From the work they did, it might be easily seen who their father was, whose works they imitated.
"*We are not born of fornication.*" They understood our Lord, in denying their descent from Abraham, to speak not of carnal, but of spiritual, generation. Now, idolatry was regarded as spiritual fornication by the Jews. Hence, here they meant to say, that they were not idolators, the worshippers of false gods, like the Gentiles. They worshipped the true God, whom they regarded as their Spiritual Father, God Himself, on account of His special predilection for the Jewish people, his special Providence in their regard, and the special blessings bestowed on them preferably to all other nations. He calls them His *first-born*, *His Son*, *Ex Egypto vocavi filium meum.*" (Exod. iv)

42. "*If God were your Father,*" if you were His adopted children, "*you would love Me,*" who am His eternal, only begotten Son,

Text.

38. *I speak that which I have seen with my Father: and you do the things that you have seen with your father.*
38. *Ego quod vidi apud Patrem meum, loquor: et vos quæ vidistis apud patrem vestrum, facitis.*

39. *They answered, and said to him: Abraham is our father. Jesus saith to them: If you be the children of Abraham, do the works of Abraham.*
39. *Responderunt, et dixerunt ei: Pater noster Abraham est. Dicit eis Jesus: Si filii Abrahæ estis, opera Abrahæ facite.*

40. *But now you seek to kill me, a man who have spoken the truth to you, which I have heard of God. This Abraham did not.*

41. *You do the works of your father. They said therefore to him: We are not born of fornication: we have one Father even God.*
41. *Vos facitis opera patris vestri. Dixerunt itaque ei: Nos ex fornicatione non sumus nati: unum patrem habemus Deum.*

42. *Jesus therefore said to them: If God were your father,*

Text.	Commentary.
you would indeed love me. For from God I proceeded, and came; for I come not of myself, but he sent me;	It is but meet, that the adopted children should love the natural, genuine offspring of the same father, rather than hate him, as you hate me. "*For, I proceeded from God, and came.*" I, who had been begotten of the Father before all ages, proceeded from Him, and came into the world in my Incarnation. The words, most likely, refer to the Incarnation of our Lord, and His coming amongst us in human flesh. They suppose also his eternal generation. "*For I came not of Myself.*" I am not self-sent, like false teachers, reproached by the Prophet. "*I did not send Prophets, yet they ran,*" etc. (Jer. xxiii. 21) "*But He sent Me.*"
42. *Dixit ergo eis Jesus: Si Deus pater vester esset: diligeretis utique me. Ego enim ex Deo processi, et veni: neque enim a meipso veni, sed ille me misit.*	
43. *Why do you not know my speech? Because you cannot hear my word.*	43. If you are the adopted sons of God, having God for your Father, as you boast, "*why then not know My speech?*" who am the natural Son of God? Why not recognise My speech, as suited to and indicative of my eternal Sonship? Domestics easily recognise the language and peculiar manner of speaking of their master. The reason is, "*because you cannot*"—you will not—"*hear My word.*" You are so blinded by passion and hatred of Me, that you are unwilling to attend to My words, and to the proofs I have so abundantly given of My Divinity.
43. *Quare loquelam meam non cognoscitis? Quia non potestis audire sermonem meum.*	
44. *You are of your father the devil, and the desires of your father you will do. He was a murderer from the beginning, and he stood not in the truth; because truth is not in him. When he speaketh a lie, he speaketh of his own, for he is a liar, and the father thereof.*	44. Our Lord now plainly expresses, what He merely insinuated (*v.* 41), viz.: that the devil was their father. By imitation of his conduct, by their crimes of murder and lying, they are his children, and in this way he was their father, just as, on the other hand, believers are, by imitation of his faith, the children of Abraham. "*And the desires of your father,*" etc. In this is assigned the cause why they are children of the devil; because, they mean to carry out his wicked desires, suggestions and instincts. They were only carrying out his desires in putting our Lord to death. Our Lord specifies two special traits in the Evil One, wherein they were his imitators. "*He was a murderer from the beginning*" of man's creation. For, in order to be a murderer, he must have some one to murder. By persuading our first parents to disobey God, he murdered the entire human race spiritually, and was the cause of the temporal death of their bodies. By the envy of the devil, death entered into the world. (Wisdom ii.) So, they now, from envy, wish to put our Lord to death (37–40). Like Satan, they were murderers. Like him, who was a liar, and the father of lies, they turned away from the truth (13, 32, 37, 40, 43), "*and he stood not in the truth.*" Created in justice and sanctity, he persevered not, however, in this state. By his rebellion against God, he lost all his primeval integrity and sanctity. The word "*truth,*" includes also veracity, truthfulness in language, as seems from the following words—"*When he speaketh a lie,*" etc. So that both senses are conveyed. Before his fall, his nature was such, that had he spoken at all—of which there is no evidence, before he deceit-
44. *Vos ex patre diabolo estis: et desideria patris vestri vultis facere. Ille homicida erat ab initio, et in veritate non stetit: quia non est veritas in eo: cum loquitur mendacium, ex propriis loquitur, quia mendax est, et pater ejus.*	

Commentary.

fully addressed Eve (*eritis sicut Dii*)—he would have uttered the truth. It may mean, he did not embrace the truth addressed by God to Adam, "*Morte morieris*"; on the contrary he falsely said, "*Non morieris*." (Jan. Gandav.)

"*Because truth is not in him.*" "*Because*," denotes effect. It is clear, he did not persevere in truth, because he is now altogether "*a liar*," "*and the father of lies.*" Hence, the Angels were created in grace, as Theologians infer from this passage.

"*When he speaketh a lie, he speaketh of his own.*" He speaks from his own perverse will and nature, corrupted by his fall; he need not be taught lying by anyone else. It is innate in his corrupt, fallen nature.

"*For he is a liar*," delights in telling what is false, with the intention of deceiving.

"*And the Father thereof*," that is, of lying he was the first author, when, by telling a lie, he persuaded Eve to commit sin.

45. "*But if I speak the truth.*" "*If*," means, *because* (οτι). He had already convicted them of having imitated the murderous designs of their father; he now shows they are imitators, and as such, children of the devil, in their lying spirit and aversion to truth. It is, because our Lord speaks the truth they refuse to believe Him; whereas, His speaking the truth should be a reason for their believing Him. Hence, He shows them to be lovers of lies, and, in this leading trait, children of the devil, the father of lies.

46. "*Which of you*," etc, as if he said, I can confidently challenge any of you to come forward, and by bringing any solid proofs against Me, to convict Me of sin, whether in regard to morals or faith; any violation of the law of God, in point of morals, or of any error in point of faith or doctrine, however unsparing in your vain, unproven accusations. In neither point, can you do so. There is no reason, therefore, why you should turn a deaf ear to My teaching, and refuse to believe Me.

"*If I say the truth*," as you must admit from the several proofs exhibited before your eyes, "*why do you not believe Me?*" They should first convict Him of sin or error. Failing such proof, they should believe Him.

47. He assigns the cause of their not believing or obeying His words, viz., because "*they are not of God.*" They are not children of God, sharers in His Spirit; but rather, children of the devil, filled with His spirit, so opposed to the Spirit of God. For, all the children of God willingly hear and obey His words. They, on the contrary, despise His teachings, disobey His precepts, indulge in vice, which proves they are not the sons of God, but sons of a different father, viz., the devil.

Text.

45. *But if I say the truth, you believe me not.*

45. *Ego autem si veritatem dico, non creditis mihi.*

46. *Which of you shall convince me of sin? If I say the truth to you, why do you not believe me?*

46. *Quis ex vobis arguet me de peccato? Si veritatem dico vobis quare non creditis mihi?*

47. *He that is of God, heareth the words of God. Therefore you hear them not, because you are not of God.*

47. *Qui ex Deo es', verba Dei audit. Propterea vos non audititis, quia ex Deo non estis.*

Text.

Commentary.

St. Gregory infers from this passage, that it is a sign of predestination, to hear the Word of God, and obey His holy inspirations. "*Beati qui audiunt,*" etc. (Luke x.) "*Oves meæ vocem meam audiunt.*" (John x.) But, a sign of reprobation to refuse, "*because I called, and you refused,*" etc. (Proverbs i.)

43. *The Jews therefore answered, and said to him: Do not we say well that thou art a Samaritan, and hast a devil?*

48. *Responderunt ergo Judæi, et dixerunt ei: Nonne bene dicimus quia Samaritanus es tu, et dæmonium habes?*

"*Do we not say?*" etc. Are we not justified in what we are in the habit of calling you? "*Say,*" habitually. Hence, it appears, although not recorded, that they used to address to Him these opprobrious epithets. Driven to madness by the truthful charges of our Lord, accusing them of murder and of love for lying, in which respect they were children of the devil, the Pharisees, in their impotent rage, address the most abusive language to our Blessed Lord. They retort by saying, that while He charges them with not being children of Abraham, He was Himself "*a Samaritan.*" While He charges them with being "*children of the devil,*" they say, He Himself has a devil, who inspires Him and works miracles through Him. "*Samaritan*" was a term of insult and reproach among the Jews, the Samaritans being Schismatics separated from God's people. They had partly turned to the worship of the false gods of the Assyrians (4 Kings xviii.); nor did they duly value the law of Moses. Moreover, they had but very little esteem or respect for the Jews, who gloried in being the true descendants of Abraham.

"*And hast a devil,*"—a delirious madman, madly uttering foolish things, while asserting that his own doctrine was from God; theirs, from the devil, whose children he reproachfully calls them.

It may be, they also meant, that as the devil (Lucifer), impiously sought to be regarded as God, and would fain arrogate to himself God's glory; so did our Lord imitate Lucifer, by claiming to be considered the Son of God. This latter meaning is borne out by our Lord's words, "*I seek not My own glory*" (v. 50).

49. *Jesus answered: I have not a devil: but I honour my Father, and you have dishonoured me.*

49. *Respondit Jesus: Ego dæmonium non habeo: sed honorifico Patrem meum, et vos inhonorastis me.*

49. Our Lord passes over as a purely personal insult, the first charge. Every one knew He was a Jew, and not a Samaritan. It might be He did not deny it, looking to the etymology of the word, "*Samaritan*" which means, "*Guardian.*" Our Lord was guardian of the entire human race, "*Nisi Dominus custodierit civitatem,*" etc. "*Custos, quid de nocte.*" This is the mystical meaning given the words by St. Gregory (Hom. 18), "*Duo ei allata fuerunt; unum negavit, alterum, tacendo consensit.*" But when doctrine or teaching is assailed, He vigorously repels and repudiates the charge, in defence of His Father's glory. "*I have no devil.*" Far from dishonouring, "*I honour My Father*" in all things, by My good works. To Him, I refer all I do, giving Him the glory of every good work I perform.

"*But, you dishonour Me.*" By reviling Me and wishing to com-

Commentary.

pass My death. You thus dishonour My Father, by dishonouring Me, His only and well-beloved Son, whom He has sent into the world, and to whom He has given, to be exhibited, His Divine credentials.

50. "*But I seek not,*" etc., so far as I am personally concerned, I regard not, from a human point of view, or, as man, any dishonour or insults you may offer Me. I am concerned only about the glory of My Father, not my own.

"*There is one,*" God the Father, "*that seeketh,*" to promote My glory, "*and judgeth,*" will avenge all dishonour and insults offered to Me.

The Father wishes that all men should honour His Son as Himself, and He will severely punish such as act otherwise. Elsewhere, our Lord says, "*the Father judges no one*" (v. 22), but there, He speaks of *general* public judgment *Here*, there is question of *private* and every day judgment, exercised on those who insult the Son, just as was done, when through the Romans, Titus and Vespasian, He utterly destroyed the Jewish race, and had them scattered abroad, as vagabonds, over the face of the earth.

51. Unmoved by the gross insulting reproach of the Jews, our Lord, far from seeking revenge, assures them in the most solemn manner, "*Amen, amen,*" He has only their salvation in view "*If any man keep My word,*" observes My precepts, believes My doctrine, although he may pass through the gates of temporal death, as is insinuated, by saying, they shall escape eternal death, "*he shall not see death for ever,*" shall be saved from everlasting death. Our Lord may be said to speak of the death of the body also, for the death of the body being but of the shortest duration, may be termed not death, but sleep. For, our Lord shall one day raise up the believer from the grave to live for ever in glory. Similar is our Lord's promise (vi. 52, 53, 59), regarding His sacred flesh, thus putting His word and His flesh, to some extent, on a level, both being the nourishment of man's soul.

52. "*Now we know,*" etc. The Jews becoming now still more insulting, while our Lord shows the greatest meekness and forbearance, exclaim, "*now we know,*" we are more and more convinced, that Thou art possessed of a devil, who inspires Thee with such blasphemous arrogance.

They understood our Lord to speak of the temporal death of the body, and exultingly exclaim, "*Abraham and the Prophets*" observed God's law ; and still, this did not save them from death.

Text.

50. *But I seek not my own glory, there is one that seeketh and judgeth.*

50. *Ego autem non quaero gloriam meam : est qui quaerat, et judicet.*

51. *Amen, amen I say to you : if any man keep my word, he shall not see death for ever.*

51. *Amen, amen dico vobis: si quis sermonem meum servaverit, mortem non videbit in aeternum.*

52. *The Jews therefore said: Now we know thou hast a devil. Abraham is dead, and the prophets and thou sayest: If any man keep my word, he shall not taste death for ever.*

52. Dixerunt ergo Judaei: Nunc cognovimus quia daemonium habes. Abraham mortuus est, et Prophetae: et tu dicis : Si quis sermonem meum servaverit: non gustabit mortem in aeternum.

Text.

53. *Art thou greater than our father Abraham, who is dead? and the prophets are dead. Whom dost thou make thyself?*

53. *Numquid tu major es patre nostro Abraham, qui mortuus est, et Prophetæ mortui sunt. Quem te ipsum facis?*

54. *Jesus answered: If I glorify myself, my glory is nothing. It is my Father that glorifieth me, of whom you say that he is your God.*

54. *Respondit Jesus: Si ego glorifico meipsum, gloria mea nihil est: est Pater meus, qui glorificat me, quem vos dicitis quia Deus vester est,*

55. *And you have not known him, but I know him. And if I shall say that I know him not, I shall be like to you, a liar. But I do know him, and do keep his word.*

55. *Et non cognovistis eum: ego autem novi eum: Ei si dixero quia non scio eum, ero similis vobis, mendax sed scio eum, et sermonem ejus servo.*

Commentary.

53. "*Art Thou greater than Abraham,*" the father of the faithful, the father of the Synagogue, the friend of God "*or the Prophets,*" who never swerved from the observance of God's law; and, still, never obtained what is here promised. Art Thou greater than God Himself, whose Word could not save Abraham from death, whereas Thou boastest that Thy word can do more?

"*Whom makest thou Thyself?*" when indulging in this blasphemous boasting.

54. In reply to their question, "*whom makest Thou Thyself?*" He answers, "*If I glorify Myself, My glory is nothing,*" if in thus speaking of Myself, I have only in view My own glory, as you suppose; My glory is of little value or weight amongst men. He speaks from common estimation, and the general opinion among men regarding self praise. Similar is His saying (v. 31), "*If I bear testimony of Myself,*" etc. Hence, it is said in the Book of Proverbs, "*Let another praise thee, and not thy own mouth*" (Proverbs xxvii. 2). It may be also a reason for the words (v. 50), "*I seek not,*" etc., because, if I did, it would be worthless. *But there is one who glorifies Me,* viz., "*My Father,*" by the oracles of the Prophets, by the wonders wrought through Me, by testimonies from heaven, proving that all I say is true. And if you ask who is My Father? I reply, it is He "*of whom you say that He is your God,*" implying that He was not in reality their God, as they boasted. For, if He were truly their God, they would have honoured Him. In this our Lord conveys, that He was Himself the natural Son of God. For, He calls the God of the Jews, His own Father.

55. And while worshiping Him, "*you have not known Him,*" to be what is true regarding Him, *one* in *Nature* and *three* in *Person*; or, you have not known Him, as My Father, glorifying Me by signs and miraculous wonders. Had they known the Father, they would have known our Lord and believed in Him, as the Eternal Son of the Father, as He says, on the other hand, had you known Me, you would have surely known My Father (xiv. 7). They did not know Him, since they did not acknowledge His words nor the works wrought through His Son. Nor did they observe His precepts. It is implied that their minds were so blinded by indulgence in passion, that they could not come to a true knowledge of God. Hence, He adds, "*but I know Him, and keep His word,*" thus showing, in what sense they did not know Him. Similar are the words (John ii. 3, 4). I know the Father, His power and majesty; therefore, as man, I reverence Him and keep His Commandments, which you violate, because you know not His majesty and attributes. He also wishes to convey, that He speaks not unknown things, but what He received from the Father.

Commentary.

Hence, the Jews should abide by His testimony, since, through Him alone could they know the Father. "*I know Him*," as My Father, "*and if I shall say that I know Him not, I shall be like you, a liar.*"

56. In reply to their question, "*Art Thou greater than our father Abraham?*" (v. 53), He says that Abraham, in whom they gloried, acknowledged His superiority. "*He rejoiced*" that is; in ecstacy of spirit, he earnestly desired, longed and yearned to "*see His day.*" There is a diversity of opinion, as to what day, reference is made here, whether the day of our Lord's eternal generation, born of the Father before the day star (Psa. cix), *before all* ages ; or, His day in the flesh, when, in time, He assumed human flesh. It most likely refers to the entire course of our Redeemer's life on earth, from His Incarnation in the womb of the Virgin, to His Ascension. Abraham (of whose seed He was to be born), the Father of the faithful, the friend of God, having been gifted with faith, in the coming of Him, in whom all the nations of the earth were to be blessed, the entire human race redeemed from the slavery of Satan and sin, longed for the day of His coming ; so did all the Prophets. From their prison in Limbo, with sighs and with tears, they sent up their loud cries, praying for the coming of this deliverer. They called on the dews of heaven, to rain Him down, and on the earth to open and deliver Him up from her bowels. "*Rorate cœli desuper,*" etc. (Isaias xlv. 8.) "*Utinam disrumperes cælos et descenderes*" (Isaias lxiv. 1).

"*He saw it and was glad.*" Most likely, this refers to the knowledge, which, we can hardly doubt, was communicated to Abraham in Limbo, by the angels of God, not to speak of the Baptist, holy Simeon, etc.

"*He saw it,*" as all the Prophets longed to see it, in its reality and accomplishment.

"*And was glad,*" overjoyed at the happy tidings, at the knowledge that his desires were accomplished, the sighs and groans of the Patriarchs and Prophets in the prison of Limbo were now fully heard. Our Lord Himself preached in Limbo ; but, at a period subsequent to this.

Besides showing in this, His superiority over Abraham, our Lord reproaches the Jews, who pretended to be imitators of Abraham, with spurning Him now present amongst them, for whose advent Abraham had so earnestly yearned, as his blessed seed, in whom all the nations of the earth were to be blessed.

57. "*Fifty years old.*" Our Lord, according to the common opinion throughout the entire Church, had only reached his *thirty-third* or thirty-fourth year. But, the Jews fix on a period exceeding that ; a period or age which they were sure He had not reached,

Text.

56. *Abraham your father rejoiced that he might see my day he saw it, and was glad.*

56. *Abraham pater vester exultavit ut videret diem meum, vidit, et gavisus est.*

57. *The Jews therefore said to him Thou art not yet fifty years old, and hast thou seen Abraham?*

Text.

57. *Dixerunt ergo Judæi ad eum: Quinquaginta annos nondum habes, et Abraham vidisti?*

58. *Jesus said to them: Amen, amen I say to you, before Abraham was made, I am.*

58 *Dixit eis Jesus: Amen, amen dico vobis antequam Abraham fieret, ego sum.*

59. *They took up stones therefore to cast at him. But Jesus hid himself, and went out of the temple.*

59. *Tulerunt ergo lapides, ut jacerent in eum: Jesus autem abscondit se, et exivit de templo.*

Commentary.

and which they were safe in mentioning without fear of a contradictory reply, or of being charged by Him with falsehood. Some say, that although only thirty-three years, our Lord, owing to His mortified, laborious life, seemed to be near fifty.

"*And hast Thou seen Abraham?*" The proper phrase should be, "*and Abraham saw Thee,*" since it was of Abraham having seen His day, our Lord spoke. But, with the Jews, to have seen Abraham and be seen by Abraham, amounted to the same, signifying to have lived with Abraham, to have been in the world at the same time with Abraham.

58. "*Before Abraham was made,*"—created—"*I am,*" existing from eternity, existing before Abraham or any other created being existed. When they came into existence, "I AM." I was before them, existing from eternity. Similar are the words, "I AM, WHO AM," self-existent, uncreated, from Myself, existing by the force of My Divine nature and essence. "I AM," in the *present* tense, denotes continued, unchanged existence, without respect to time, in His case, before all ages, from eternity. The force of "*was made,*" applied to Abraham, and "I AM," applied to our Blessed Lord, is very expressive and significant. The Jews fancied our Lord could not see nor be seen by Abraham, owing to the long interval of time that was between them, fancying our Lord to be mere man. But He here asserts His Divine nature and consequent eternal existence.

59. "*They, therefore, took up stones to cast at Him,*" as a blasphemer, who preferred Himself to Abraham and compared Himself to the Eternal God. The punishment of blasphemers in the law was stoning (Leviticus xxiv. 16).

"*Hid Himself,*" by an effort of Divine power, rendered Himself invisible, so as to escape the murderous effect of their fury; He thus passed unseen in their midst from the Temple.

CHAPTER IX.

1 And Jesus passing by, saw a man who was blind from his birth;

2 And his disciples asked him: Rabbi, who had sinned, this man, or his parents, that he should be born blind?

3 Jesus answered: Neither hath this man sinned, nor his parents; but that the works of God should be made manifest in him.

4 I must work the works of him that sent me, whilst it is day: the night cometh when no man can work.

5 As long as I am in the world, I am the light of the world.

6 When he had said these things, he spat on the ground, and made clay of the spittle, and spread the clay upon his eyes,

7 And said to him: Go, wash in the pool of Siloe, which is interpreted, Sent. He went therefore, and washed, and he came seeing.

8 The neighbours therefore, and they who had seen him before that he was a beggar, said: Is not this he that sat, and begged? Some said: This is he.

9 But others said: No, but he is like him. But he said: I am he.

10 They said therefore to him: How were thy eyes opened?

11 He answered: That man that is called Jesus, made clay, and anointed my eyes, and said to me: Go to the pool of Siloe, and wash. And I went, I washed, and I see.

12 And they said to him: Where is he? He saith: I know not.

13 They bring him that had been blind to the Pharisees.

14 Now it was the sabbath when Jesus made the clay and opened his eyes.

15 Again therefore the Pharisees asked him how he had received his sight. But he said to them: He put clay upon my eyes, and I washed, and I see.

16 Some therefore of the Pharisees said: This man is not of God, who keepeth not the sabbath. But others said: How can a man that is a sinner do such miracles? And there was a division among them.

17 They say therefore to the blind man again: What sayest thou of him that hath opened thy eyes? And he said: He is a prophet.

18 The Jews then did not believe concerning him, that he had been blind and had received his sight, until they called the parents of him that had received his sight,

19 And asked them, saying: Is this your son, who you say was born blind? How then doth he now see?

20 His parents answered them, and said: We know that this is our son, and that he was born blind;

21 But how he now seeth, we know not: or who hath opened his eyes, we know not: ask himself; he is of age, let him speak for himself.

22 These things his parents said, because they feared the Jews: for the Jews had already agreed among themselves, that if any man should confess him to be Christ, he should be put out of the synagogue.

23 Therefore did his parents say; He is of age, ask him.

24 They therefore called the man again that had been blind, and said to him: Give glory to God. We know that this man is a sinner.

25 He said therefore to them: If he be a sinner, I know not: one thing I know, that whereas I was blind, now I see.

26 They said then to him: What did he to thee? How did he open thy eyes?

27 He answered them: I have told you already, and you have heard: why would you hear it again? will you also become his disciples?

28 They reviled him therefore, and said: Be thou his disciple; but we are the disciples of Moses.

29 We know that God spoke to Moses: but as to this man, we know not from whence he is.

30 The man answered, and said to them: Why herein is a wonderful thing that you know not from whence he is, and he hath opened my eyes.

31 Now we know that God doth not hear sinners: but if a man be a server of God, and doth his will, him he heareth.

32 From the beginning of the world it hath not been heard, that any man hath opened the eyes of one born blind.

33 Unless this man were of God, he could not do anything.

34 They answered, and said to him: Thou wast wholly born in sins, and dost thou teach us? And they cast him out.

35 Jesus heard that they had cast him out: and when he had found him, he said to him: Dost thou believe in the Son of God?

36 He answered, and said: Who is he, Lord, that I may believe in him?

37 And Jesus said to him: Thou hast both seen him; and it is he that talketh with thee.

38 And he said: I believe, Lord. And falling down he adored him.

39 And Jesus said: For judgment I am come into this world; that they who see not, may see: and they who see, may become blind.

40 And some of the Pharisees, who were with him, heard; and they said unto him: Are we also blind?

41 Jesus said to them: If you were blind, you should not have sin: but now you say: We see. Your sin remaineth.

CAPUT IX.

1 *Et præteriens Jesus vidit hominem cæcum a nativitate:*

2 *Et interrogaverunt eum discipuli ejus: Rabbi, quis peccavit, hic, aut parentes ejus, ut cæcus nasceretur?*

3 *Respondit Jesus: Neque hic peccavit, neque parentes ejus: sed ut manifestentur opera Dei in illo.*

4 *Me oportet operari opera ejus, qui misit me, donec dies est: venit nox, quando nemo potest operari.*

5 *Quamdiu sum in mundo, lux sum mundi.*

6 *Hæc cum dixisset, expuit in terram, et fecit lutum ex sputo, et linivit lutum super oculos ejus,*

7 *Et dixit ei: Vade, lava in natatoria Siloe (quod interpretatur Missus.) Abiit ergo, et lavit, et venit videns.*

ST. JOHN, CHAP. IX.

8 *Itaque vicini, et qui viderant eum prius, quia mendicus erat, dicebant: Nonne hic est, qui sedebat, et mendicabat? Alii dicebant: Quia hic est.*

9 *Alii autem: Nequaquam, sed similis est ei. Ille vero dicebat: Quia ego sum.*

10 *Dicebant ergo ei: Quomodo aperti sunt tibi oculi?*

11 *Respondit: Ille homo, qui dicitur Jesus, lutum fecit: et unxit oculos meos, et dixit mihi: Vade ad natatoria Siloe, et lava. Et abii, et lavi, et video.*

12 *Et dixerunt ei: Ubi est ille? Ait: Nescio.*

13 *Adducunt eum ad Pharisæos, qui cæcus fuerat.*

14 *Erat autem sabbatum quando lutum fecit Jesus, et aperuit oculos ejus.*

15 *Iterum ergo interrogabant eum Pharisæi quomodo vidisset. Ille autem dixit eis: Lutum mihi posuit super oculos, et lavi, et video.*

16 *Dicebant ergo ex Pharisæis quidam; Non est hic homo a Deo, qui sabbatum non custodit. Alii autem dicebant: Quomodo potest homo peccator hæc signa facere? Et schisma erat inter eos.*

17 *Dicunt ergo cæco iterum: Tu quid dicis de illo, qui aperuit oculos tuos? Ille autem dixit: Quia propheta est.*

18 *Non crediderunt ergo Judæi de illo, quia cæcus fuisset, et vidisset, donec vocaverunt parentes ejus, qui viderat:.*

19 *Et interrogaverunt eos, dicentes: Hic est filius vester, quem vos dicitis quia cæcus natus est? Quomodo ergo nunc videt?*

20 *Responderunt eis parentes ejus, et dixerunt: Scimus quia hic est Filius noster, et quia cæcus natus est:*

21 *Quomodo autem nunc videat, nescimus: aut quis aperuit oculos, nos nescimus: ipsum interrogate: ætatem habet, ipse de se loquatur.*

22 *Hæc dixerunt parentes ejus, quoniam timebant Judæos: jam enim conspiraverant Judæi, ut si quis eum confiteretur esse Christum, extra synagogam fieret.*

23 *Propterea parentes ejus dixerunt: Quia ætatem habet, ipsum interrogate.*

24 *Vocaverunt ergo rursum hominem, qui fuerat cæcus, et dixerunt ei: Da gloriam Deo; nos scimus quia hic homo peccator est.*

25 *Dixit ergo eis ille: Si peccator est, nescio: unum scio, quia cæcus cum essem, modo video.*

26 *Dixerunt ergo illi: Quid fecit tibi: quomodo aperuit tibi oculos?*

27 *Respondit eis: Dixi vobis jam, et audistis; quid iterum vultis audire? numquid et vos vultis discipuli ejus fieri?*

28 *Maledixerunt ergo ei, et dixerunt: Tu discipulus illius sis: nos autem Moysi discipuli sumus.*

29 *Nos scimus quia Moysi locutus est Deus: hunc autem nescimus unde sit.*

30 *Respondit ille homo, et dixit eis: In hoc enim mirabile est, quia vos nescitis unde sit, et aperuit meos oculos:.*

31 *Scimus autem quia peccatores Deus non audit: sed si quis Dei cultor est, et voluntatem ejus facit, hunc exaudit.*

32 *A sæculo non est auditum quia quis aperuit oculos cæci nati.*

33 *Nisi esset hic a Deo, non poterat facere quidquam.*

34 *Responderunt, et dixerunt ei: In peccatis natus es totus, et tu doces nos? Et ejecerunt eum foras.*

35 *Audivit Jesus quia ejecerunt eum foras: et cum invenisset eum, dixit ei: Tu credis in Filium Dei?*

36 *Respondit ille, et dixit: Quis est, Domine, ut credam in eum?*
37 *Et dixit ei Jesus: Et vidisti eum, et qui loquitur tecum, ipse est.*
38 *At ille ait: Credo Domine. Et procidens adoravit eum.*
39 *Et dixit Jesus: In judicium ego in hunc mundum veni: ut qui non vident videant, et qui vident, cæci fiant.*
40 *Et audierunt quidam ex Pharisæis, qui cum ipso erant, et dixerunt ei: Numquid et nos cæci sumus?*
41 *Dixit eis Jesus: Si cæci essetis, non haberetis peccatum: nunc vero dicitis: Quia videmus. Peccatum vestrum manet.*

ANALYSIS.

This chapter commences with an account of the miraculous cure, performed by our Lord in restoring sight to a man who was born blind. The questions proposed by the disciples, as to the cause of his blindness. Our Redeemer's reply. At the same time, He declares Himself to be the light of the world (1–5). The manner in which the cure was effected (6–13). The bitter animadversion of the Pharisees, as usual, denouncing the violation of the Sabbath. The discussion among them, as to our Lord's character. The appeal to the man who was cured, as to his opinion respecting our Lord. The appeal to the man's parents, as to his identity (15–24). Their vile abuse of the man for showing an inclination to respect and speak in terms of praise of our Lord (24–29). His courageous reply, and his expulsion from the place of meeting, in consequence (30–34). The gift of faith or spiritual enlightenment, bestowed on him by our Lord (34–39). Our Lord's denunciation of the Pharisees for their perversity and resistance to God's heavenly light, thereby entailing on themselves the more grievous sin (39–41).

Text.

1. And Jesus passing by, saw a man who was blind from his birth;

1. *Et præteriens Jesus vidit hominem cæcum a nativitate:*

2. And his disciples asked him: Rabbi, who hath sinned, this man, or his parents, that he should be born blind?

2. *Et interrogaverunt cum discipuli ejus: Rabbi, quis*

Commentary.

1. "*And Jesus passing by,*" etc. The common opinion is, that the occurrences here referred to took place in connexion with the foregoing, immediately after our Lord left the Temple. This is, however, questioned by others, who hold that some interval elapsed. These say, it may refer to some other time, when the Pharisees sought an occasion for assailing our Redeemer, on which account, the Evangelist now records it, and they ground their opinion, chiefly on our Lord's disappearance, coupled with the fact, that His disciples were present. There is nothing, however, to prevent one from holding, that His disciples may have met Him outside, as, most likely, on His disappearing, they, too, left the Temple.

"*A man blind from his birth,*" which rendered his case the more difficult, and the miracle wrought more remarkable.

2. "*Who hath sinned,*" etc. This question probably took its rise from the prevailing popular opinion, that diseases and corporal ailments were the punishment of sin. This may be true; but, not always, as may be seen from the case of Job, as well as of Tobias, etc. Great calamities, sudden deaths, by no means argue any particular commission of sin (Luke xiii. 1–4). Others hold, that the question was suggested by our Lord's admonition to

Commentary.

the man sick of the palsy. "*Go, sin no more, lest anything worse*," etc. (v. 14).

The question as regards the man himself committing sin, so as to induce the curse of blindness, is quite unmeaning, as if he could commit *actual* sin, before he was born. It is intelligible, so far as it may concern his parents, since God often punishes children, on account of the sins of their fathers. "*A jealous God visiting the iniquity of the Fathers upon the children unto the third and fourth generation*" (Exodus xx. 5).

St. Chrysostom and Theophylact say the disciples speak thus, not by way of interrogation, as if they suspected that either child or parents were in fault, but by way of doubting, as much as to say; neither of them could give rise to it.

3. "*Neither this man sinned*," etc. The question requires the words to be added, "*that he should be born blind.*" Our Lord does not deny that this man or his parents had been guilty of sin, besides original sin—(the source of all our misfortunes)—in which we were all born. What He denies is that this blindness was the result or effect of any particular sin of theirs, on account of which it was inflicted.

"*That the works of God,*" etc. It happened, in order that an occasion would be afforded, for having the works of God's power and goodness manifested in his miraculous cure by our Lord; and that thus, it would be proved that our Lord was sent by God, and men would be stimulated to believe in Him and follow Him.

4. "*I must*"—considering My Father's decree—"*work the works of Him that sent Me,*" which My Father, commissioned Me, as His legate to perform, so as to bring men to the faith and to eternal salvation, "*whilst it is day,*" during the course of My mortal life and during my corporal presence among men. "*The night cometh*"—the time of My death and of My absence from among men, is fast drawing to a close. "*When no man can work.*" I can no more work among men, after My departure out of this world, than any one else can. After death, men can perform no work, neither can I. "Neither work, nor reason, nor wisdom in hell (Ecclesiastes ix. 10). Our Lord wishes to convey that after death, He cannot work by His own visible personal operation, as He did in life. He can neither suffer, nor die, nor teach men, nor perform miracles for man's salvation; though, indeed, after death, He works through His holy Spirit, and by means of Apostolic men.

5. "*As long,*" etc. Therefore, must I work while it is day. I must not hide my light under a bushel. I must not be idle. I must enlighten the world. Not that He ceased to enlighten the

Text.

peccavit, hic, aut parentes ejus, ut cæcus nasceretur?

3. *Jesus answered: Neither hath this man sinned, nor his parents; but that the works of God should be made manifest in him.*

3. *Respondit Jesus: neque hic peccavit, neque parentes ejus: sed ut manifestentur opera Dei in illo.*

4. *I must work the works of him that sent me, whilst it is day: the night cometh when no man can work.*

4. *Me oportet operari opera ejus, qui misit me. donec dies est: venit nox, quando nemo potest operari.*

5. *As long as I am in the world, I am the light of the world.*

Text.

5. *Quamdiu sum in mundo, lux sum mundi.*

6. *When he had said these things, he spat on the ground, and made clay of the spittle, and spread the clay upon his eyes.*

6. *Hæc cum dixisset, expuit in terram, et fecit lutum ex sputo, et linivit lutum super oculos ejus.*

Commentary.

world after His departure. For, even now, it is He, "*that enlightens every man that cometh into the world.*" But, He would not enlighten it, as He did during His life time, by personally working miracles, and instructing men in person.

These words are also allusive to the miracle of restoring sight to the blind man, and enlightening him, which our Lord is about to effect.

6. "*When He had said,*" etc., as if to show practically, in a partial way, that He was the light of the world, destined to enlighten those who sat in darkness, whether spiritually or corporally, He, at once, proceeds to effect the cure of the blind man. He might have accomplished this by His sole word of command, but He employs the instrumentality of His creatures, in a way, that conveys some mystery, and contains some recondite, hidden meaning. "*He spat on the ground, and made clay of the spittle, and spread it on the eyes*" of the blind man.

Various conjectures are hazarded, as to why He did this. Some say, He wished to show, that as He originally formed man out of the slime of the earth; so, He employed the same material for the repairing of human nature, that He used in its formation. He makes use, in restoring sight, of the very thing, which if applied to the eyes of a sound man, would render him perfectly blind, to convey that the restoration of his sight would appear from the contrary and inadequate means employed, attributable, not to human natural agency, but solely as the effect of Divine power. Sometimes, in the Old Testament, did the Prophets employ such means and instrumentality. For instance, see Miracles of Eliseus (4 Kings xx. 21; vi. 5, 6), thereby showing that the wonderful results are the effects of God's power, owing to the inadequacy of the human means employed.

Similar is the economy of God's Providence in carrying out His greatest work, the work of man's redemption (see 1 Cor. i., Commentary on).

Our Lord mixed with the clay, spittle, the foam of His own mouth, to show how salutary was every thing emanating from Him.

Those, who impiously jeer at the use of ceremonies, and material elements in connexion with spiritual effects, which they symbolize, have a clear refutation in this action, and several similar actions on the part of our Divine Redeemer for similar effects (Mark vii. 33; viii. 23).

To try his obedience, our Lord, who might have cured the blind man on the spot, tells him, "*Go and wash in the pool of Siloe.*" He might have also in view, to have the miracle, which He wrought on the Sabbath, more generally known, when the people saw this man passing a long way through the midst of the city, towards the

Commentary.

pool, with the clay on his eyes, thus taking away from the unbelievers all excuse for rejecting Him. The Prophet Elizeus acted similarly with Naaman, the Syrian (2 Kings v. 10).

7. "*Wash in the pool of Siloe.*" Siloe or Siloam, had its origin in a fountain at the foot of Mount Sion, which, as we are told by St. Jerome (in Isaias viii.), sent forth its waters, not continuously, but, only intermittently, at certain seasons and certain days, discharging them with great noise through subterranean passages and the fissures of the hardest rocks, till they formed the pool now spoken of, called the pool of Siloam.

St. Epiphanius (in vita Prophetarum c. 7) tells us, the waters gushed from the rock at the prayer of Isaias. The waters having passed through the cavities of the rocks with great noise, formed the pool here referred to, in the western side of the valley of Josaphat, outside, but quite close to Jerusalem; and from the pool, the waters glided gently (Isaias viii.) into the little brook of Cedron, of which mention is made in the history of our Lord's Passion (John xviii. 1). Allusion is made to the pool of Siloam in Nehemias (ii. 15).

"*Which is interpreted*, SENT," being derived from the Hebrew *Shalach, to send*. It is not without some latent cause, the Evangelist gives the meaning and interpretation of "*Siloe*" to signify "*sent*." It was a type of our Lord who was sent from the bosom of His Father to save and enlighten mankind, and of His mysteries and ordinances; especially of the rite of Baptism, instituted by Him to cleanse and wash us from our spiritual defects, and enlighten us spiritually by the light of Divine grace, of which St. Augustine tells us the waters of Siloe were a type.

"*He went therefore*," asking no questions, raising no doubts as to our Lord's meaning, believing in His miraculous curative powers. "*Washed*," as he was ordered, in reward of which "*He came, seeing*," his sight being perfectly restored.

8. "*The neighbours*," etc. This blind man was well known, and the remarks of his neighbours served to place the reality of His miraculous cure in the clearest light.

9, 10, 11. "*The man called Jesus*," etc. This he did not say out of disrespect; but merely to show that he was yet a stranger to Him. He heard of Him, he knew Him only by report.

Text.

7. And said to him: Go, wash in the pool of Siloe, which is interpreted, Sent. He went therefore, and washed, and he came seeing.

7. Et dixit ei: Vade, lava in natatoria Siloe (quod interpretatur Missus) Abiit ergo, et lavit, et venit videns.

8. The neighbours therefore, and they who had seen him before that he was a beggar, said: Is not this he that sat, and begged? Some said: This is he.

8. Itaque vicini, et qui viderant eum prius quia mendicus erat, dicebant: Nonne hic est, qui sedebat, et mendicabat? Alii dicebant: Quia hic est.

9. But others said: No, but he is like him. But he said: I am he:

9. Alii autem? Nequaquam, sed similis est ei. Ille vero dicebat: Quia ego sum

Text.	Commentary.

10. They said therefore to him: How were thy eyes opened?

10. Dicebat ergo ei: Quomodo aperti sunt tibi oculi?

11. He answered: That man that is called Jesus, made clay and anointed my eyes, and said to me: Go to the pool of Siloe, and wash: And I went, I washed, and I see.

11. Respondit: Ille homo, qui dicitur Jesus, lutum fecit: et unxit oculos meos, et dixit mihi: Vade ad natatoria Siloe, et lava. Et abii, et lavi, et video.

12. And they said to him: Where is he? He saith: I know not.

12. Et dixerunt ei: Ubi est ille? Ait: Nescio.

13. They bring him that had been blind, to the Pharisees.

13. Adducunt eum ad Pharisæos, qui cæcus fuerat.

12, 13, 14. As this miracle and the entire operation occurred on the Sabbath, the people doubt as to whether it could come from God. Hence, they bring the blind man before the Pharisees—members of the Sanhedrim—as judges in such cases. God's Providence so arranged it, that the Pharisees themselves could not deny the fact of the miracle. "*Cæcus confitebatur et cor impiorum frangebatur.*" (St. Augustine.)

Our Lord, in order to refute the false notions of the Pharisees regarding Sabbatical observances, frequently fixed on the Sabbath, as the time for performing miracles.

14. Now it was the sabbath when Jesus made the clay, and opened his eyes.

14. Erat autem sabbatum quando lutum fecit Jesus, et aperuit oculos ejus.

15. Again therefore the Pharisees asked him how he had received his sight. But he said to them: He put clay upon my eyes, and I washed, and I see.

15. Iterum ergo interrogabant eum Pharisæi quomodo vidisset. Ille autem dixit eis: Lutum mihi posuit super oculos, et lavi, et video.

16. Some therefore of the Pharisees said: This man is not of God, who keepeth not the sabbath. But others said: How can a man that is a sinner do such miracles? And there was a division among them.

16. Dicebant ergo ex Pharisæis quidam: Non est hic homo a Deo, qui sabbatum non custodit. Alii autem dicebant: Quomodo potest homo peccator hæc signa facere? Et schisma erat inter eos.

17. They say therefore to the blind man again: What sayest thou of him that hath opened thy eyes? And he said: He is a prophet:

17. Dicunt ergo cæco iterum: Tu quid dicis de illo, qui aperuit oculos tuos? Ille autem dixit: Quia propheta est.

15, 16. They had their own ideas about keeping the Sabbath, to which they wished all others to conform. The reality of the miracle they could not deny. Indeed, the reality of all our Lord's miracles were undeniable. The *facts* were patent. So undeniable were they, that even in the Synagogue, they secured followers for our Lord, timid followers, however, on account of the violent persecution from the Jews.

"*A sinner*," an impostor or deceiver. Could God possibly grant the power of such miracles, performed in such a way, in proof of His own sanctity and Divine mission, to an impostor? Unable to deny the reality of our Lord's miracles, His enemies, then, as also happened at all future periods, ascribed them to other than Divine agency.

"*There was a division*," etc. A schism. They were divided into two separate parties.

17. The disputants refer to the blind man himself, each party being anxious to strengthen their views by the judgment of the man who was cured. Some Expositors say, the question was put by those who were favourable to our Lord; others say, by the opposite party. However, it seems likely, as above, that both parties proposed it. The enemies of our Lord likely intended to cast the blind man out of the Synagogue, if he favoured our Lord.

"*He is a Prophet*," a holy man, sent and commissioned by God.

Commentary.

18. Seeing their views were not strengthened by the opinion of the blind man, to whom they appealed; the enemies of our Lord unable to deny the miraculous fact, now question the man's identity, and have recourse to his parents to know if he were their son; thus, hoping in case of any difference of testimony, to discredit the miracle.

19, 20, 21. The Pharisees propose *three* questions. The man's parents answer *two* of them. For prudential reasons, they decline answering the *third*, viz., *how* he was cured, as they did not wish to run the risk of excommunication. He is no longer an infant; he is of age to answer for himself and give testimony. The age for giving testimony among the Jews was the age of *thirteen*.

22. "*Put out of the Synagogue*," was a kind of excommunication among the Jews entailing the heaviest religious and social penalties. The excommunicated were deprived of all *religious* intercourse; excluded from religious worship and sacrifice. They were deprived of all *social* intercourse also, even with their nearest and dearest friends. The very necessaries of life could not be sold to them.

23, 24 "*Give glory to God.*" This was a form of adjuration or obtestation; or of administering an oath in use among the Jews (Josue vii. 19; 1 Kings vi. 5; Jeremiah xii. 16). They did not mean, give glory to *God for thy cure*. This they scornfully denied. Tell the truth, as in the presence of God, for the glory of God, whose sovereign veracity is thus honoured, as essentially loving the truth. Admit that there is an imposition in this case, that thou hast told us a lie, and endeavoured to impose on us; and thus thou wilt give glory to God, who hates and condemns all imposture, as He is the essential and eternal truth. To induce Him to make this acknowledgment, they say, "*we*"—who are the proper authority to decide such matters—"*know*," we declare "*this man*," this violator of the Sabbath, far from being a

Text.

18. *The Jews then did not believe concerning him, that he had been blind and had received his sight, until they called the parents of him that had received his sight,*

18. *Non crediderunt ergo Judæi de illo, quia cæcus fuisset et vidisset, donec vocaverunt parentes ejus qui viderat:*

19. *And asked them, saying: Is this your son, who you say was born blind? How then doth he now see?*

19. *Et interrogaverunt eos. dicentes: Hic est filius vester, quem vos dicitis quia cæcus natus est? Quomodo ergo nunc videt?*

20. *His parents answered them, and said: We know that this is our son, and that he was born blind;*

20. *Responderunt eis parentes ejus, et dixerunt: Scimus quia hic est filius noster, et quia cæcus natus est:*

21. *But how he now seeth, we know not: or who hath opened his eyes we know not: ask himself; he is of age, let him speak for himself.*

21. *Quomodo autem nunc videat, nescimus: aut quis ejus aperuit oculos, nos nescimus: ipsum interrogate: ætatem habet, ipse de se loquatur.*

22. *These things his parents said, because they feared the Jews: For the Jews had already agreed among themselves, that if any man should confess him to be Christ, he should be put out of the synagogue.*

22. *Hæc dixerunt parentes ejus, quoniam timebant Judæos: jam enim conspiraverant Judæi, ut si quis eum confiteretur esse Christum, extra synagogam fieret.*

23. *Therefore did his parents say: he is of age, ask him.*

23. *Propterea parentes ejus dixerunt: Quia ætatem habet, ipsum interrogate.*

24. *They therefore called the man again that had been blind, and said to him: Give glory to God. We know that this man is a sinner.*

24. *Vocaverunt ergo rursum hominem, qui fuerat cæcus, et dixerunt ei: Da*

Text.

gloriam Deo, nos scimus quia hic homo peccator est.

25. *He said therefore to them: If he be a sinner, I know not: one thing I know, that whereas I was blind, now I see.*
25. *Dixit ergo eis ille: Si peccator est, nescio: unum scio, quia caecus cum essem, modo video.*

26. *They said then to him: What did he to thee? How did he open thy eyes.*
26. *Dixerunt ergo illi: Quid fecit tibi? quomodo aperuit tibi oculos?*

27. *He answered them: I have told you already, and you have heard: why would you hear it again? will you also become his disciples?*
27. *Respondit eis: Dixi vobis jam, et audistis: quid iterum vultis audire? numquid et vos vultis discipuli ejus fieri?*

28. *They reviled him therefore, and said: Be thou his disciple; but we are the disciples of Moses.*
28. *Maledixerunt ergo ei, et dixerunt: Tu discipulus illius sis: nos autem Moysi discipuli sumus.*

29. *We know that God spoke to Moses: but as to this man, we know not whence he is.*
29. *Nos scimus quia Moysi locutus est Deus: hunc autem nescimus unde sit.*

30. *The man answered, and said to them: Why, herein is a wonderful thing that you know not from whence he is, and*

Commentary.

"Prophet" commissioned by God, to be "*a sinner,*" a blasphemous seducer.

25. "*I know not.*" I have no opinion to offer. Facts speak for themselves. "*One thing I know, that whereas I was blind, now I see,*" owing to His having opened my eyes.

26. They want to confound Him by their questions, and to elicit from Him some contradiction, in order to injure the credibility of the miraculous cure.

27. Justly indignant at their conduct and factious persistency, he loses patience on clearly seeing the wicked passions that prompted this unmeaning cavilling, and asks, "*will you also,*" as well as His other followers, become His disciples? What other object can you have in thus sifting my case, unless after discovering the truth, to become, like others among them, myself included, "*His disciples?*" This stinging, reproachful irony was calculated to annoy them. He saw well their determined malice, and their incurable hatred of our Lord.

28. "*They reviled Him,*" heaping imprecations on Him, especially by saying, what they considered the most insulting and ignominious charge. You are His disciple, "*or, be you His disciple,*" the follower of an impostor—a fate which your seeming attachment to Him merits for you. Or, "*You* ARE *His disciple.*" You show yourself so degraded, as to be a fit follower of such a blasphemous *impostor.*

As for us, "*we are disciples of Moses.*" We follow his law regarding Sabbatical and other observances, unlike the man, who impiously prides himself in trampling on them.

29. "*We know that God spoke to Moses.*" Therefore, in following his law, we obey God's law. "*As for this man*"—they speak contemptuously—"*we know not from whence He is.*" Whatever His country or descent may be, we know not whether He derives His commission or doctrine from God or from the devil. Of this we are totally ignorant.

30. "*Herein is a wonderful thing.*" It is a matter to be greatly wondered at, viz., "*that you,*" who are the teachers of the people, you, who boast of being so learned in the law—"*know not whence He is,*" cannot see, whence He derives His mission and

Commentary.

authority. "*And—yet—He hath opened my eyes.*" Whence could He derive His mission, but from God, who, in proof of His Divine mission, has performed such stupendous miracles, among the rest, opening my eyes, who was born blind—a miracle that you cannot, in any way, question?

31. "*Now we know*," as a matter commonly and generally believed. In this, the blind man gives expression to the opinion commonly entertained. Hence, he says, "*we know.*"

"*That God doth not hear sinners.*" This, taken in a general or universal sense, is not true; for, God does hear sinners and lends an ear to their petitions when they approach Him with proper dispositions of penance and sorrow. But, the words have here a restricted meaning, from the context, which has reference to the working of miracles, and then the words mean: God does not hear sinners, who persevere in a sinful course, so as to give them the power of working miracles, in proof of their Divine mission and personal sanctity, as in the case of miracles wrought by our Divine Lord. God never gives the seal of His power in the operation of miracles, to prove men to be holy who are not so, or to be sent by Him, who were not sent, but ran of themselves.

These are the words of the blind man. We are not bound to defend their accuracy. All the Scriptures are committed to is, that he uttered the words, which is no doubt true.

"*But if a man be a server of God,*" a true sincere worshipper, announcing true, sound doctrine, and in addition, "*doth His will,*" observes His commandments, "*him He heareth,*" whenever He calls upon him, when necessary, for power to work wonders. Then, God grants Him this power. In this, it is implied, that whenever men work miracles, they do so, not by their own innate power, but by the power of God.

32. "*From the beginning of the world.*" In the whole history of miracles wrought from the beginning of the world, whether by Moses or the Prophets, or any one else, there is no instance of restoring sight to a man born blind in so extraordinary a way, by rubbing and wiping off clay. Hence the superiority of this man, whom you spurn and reject, over Moses or the Prophets who have gone before us.

33. The conclusion is, that this, being so rare and stupendous a miracle, could only come from the power of God, especially as it had for object, like all the other miracles of our Redeemer, to prove His sanctity and mission from God. "*Unless this man were from God, He could not do any thing,*" like the miracle just wrought by Him.

Text.

he hath opened my eyes.

30. *Respondit ille homo, et dixit eis: In hoc enim mirabile est, quia vos nescitis unde sit, et aperuit meos oculos:*

31. *Now we know that God doth not hear sinners: but if a man be a server of God, and doth his will, him he heareth.*

31. *Scimus autem quia peccatores Deus non audit: sed si quis Dei cultor est, et voluntatem ejus facit, hunc exaudit.*

32. *From the beginning of the world it hath not been heard, that any man hath opened the eyes of one born blind.*

32. *A sæculo non est auditum quia quis aperuit oculos cæci nati.*

33. *Unless this man were of God, he could not do any thing.*

33. *Nisi esset hic a Deo, non poterat facere quidquam.*

Text.

34. *They answered, and said to him: Thou wast wholly born in sins, and dost thou teach us! And they cast him out.*

34. *Responderunt, et dixerunt ei: In peccatis natus es totus, et tu doces nos? Et ejecerunt eum foras.*

35. *Jesus heard that they had cast him out and when he had found him, he said to him: Dost thou believe in the Son of God?*

35. *Audivit Jesus quia ejecerunt eum foras et cum invenisset eum, dixit ei: Tu credis in Filium Dei?*

Commentary.

34. Finding they could neither shake the confidence nor impugn the veracity, nor answer the arguments of this man, now laying aside their affected mildness, assumed in order to elicit inconvenient replies, they show themselves in their true colours, and indulge in abuse of the grossest kind.

"*Thou*"—a wretched ignorant mendicant—"*wast born wholly in sins*," defiled with sin, soul and body, from your birth to this day; and in punishment of these sins hast been cursed with blindness from your very birth. Likely, these men entertained the notions regarding the infliction of bodily maladies in punishment of sin, expressed by our Lord's disciples (*v.* 2).

"*And dost thou teach us?*" "*Thou*" and "*us*" are emphatic. "*Teach us*," so famed for sanctity of life, and a profound knowledge of the law.

"*And they cast him out,*" from the place of meeting, whatever it was. Some say, the Synagogue, thus excommunicating Him. This latter opinion is hardly likely, as the man did not yet explicitly declare that our Lord was the Messiah.

35. Our Lord arranged to find out this man, so dishonoured for his intrepid defence of his heavenly deliverer and the avowal of his miraculous cure. In order to compensate him for this injury, He now bestows on him the priceless spiritual enlightenment of faith, for which the restoration of his bodily sight had gradually disposed him.

He asked him, "*Dost thou believe in the Son of God?*" Our Lord asked him this, when there was question of his spiritual enlightenment, or the gift of faith about to be bestowed on him, to secure his co-operation; while in regard to corporal enlightenment, no co-operation was needed, according to the teaching of St. Augustine. "*Qui fecit te sine te, non justificat te sine te; fecit nescientem, justificat volentem.*" (Sermo, 15, de verbis Apostoli.)

He uses the words, "*Dost thou believe in the Son of God?*" rather than, "*Dost thou believe in Me?*" as He gradually wished to reveal Himself to him, and cause him no sudden surprise, by declaring Himself at once the Son of God. Likely, the man cured, did not know it was our Lord cured him, since he was sent to the Pool of Siloe to be healed, and had not seen our Lord up to this. He believed our Lord to be a Prophet, and proclaimed Him as such. He did not, however, as yet fully believe, though, no doubt, well disposed, to do so, in His Divinity. It may be, the man knew from His voice, that it was our Lord cured him; but, in any case, he did not believe in His Divinity. He knew in case he recognised Him as his benefactor, that He would not deceive him; and hence, he cried out.

Commentary.

36. "*Who is He, Lord?*" etc. The word, "*Lord,*" is a term of respect, and might be rendered, "*Sir.*" From his heart, he was ready to believe, but he did not precisely know who the person was, in whom he was to believe. Hence, the question.

37. Our Lord then manifests Himself to him. "*Thou hast seen Him,*" reminding him of the blessing of sight conferred on him, "*and it is He that talketh with thee.*"

38. By words—"*I believe, Lord*"—by acts, "*and falling down, he adored Him,*" the man who was blind proclaimed his faith in our Lord's Divinity, whom hitherto he regarded, on account of the great miracle, in the light of a holy man sent by God; but, in that light only.

39. "*And Jesus said*"—as is clear from verse 40—to the Pharisees. "*For judgment,*" in order to exercise a judgment of discernment, to separate the humble believers from the haughty unbelievers—or, "*judgment*" may mean, to execute the high and mysterious decree of God, giving the faith to the blind unbelieving Gentiles, who, like this blind man, are disposed humbly to embrace the faith; and rejecting the haughty Jews, wise and enlightened in their own opinion.

"*That*"—so that, as a consequence. For, their own perversity was the *cause* of the rejection of the Jews and of the haughty.

"*They who see not,*" who are in ignorance and error of the true faith and spiritually blind, but disposed to lay aside their errors and embrace the truth.

"*May see,*" and be enlightened.

"*And they who see,*" who fancy they are rich in faith and gifts of sanctity, may, in punishment of their pride and haughty resistance to grace, "*see not,*" become obdurate and impenitent. Like the Pagan philosophers referred to by St. Paul (Rom. i.), "*Dicentes se esse sapientes, stulti facti sunt.*" Our Lord did not come for the purpose of blinding the Jews; but He *permitted* them to continue blind, as a punishment of their resistance to grace.

40. "*Some of the Pharisees who were with Him,*" tracking His footsteps, wherever He went, in order to catch Him in His words, "*heard,*" and understanding that they were pointedly alluded to as spiritually blind, "*said*"—in an arrogant and malignant spirit— "*Are we also blind?*" "*We also,*" as well as the man whom You pretend to have enlightened. "*Are we,*" the rulers and teachers

Text.

36. He answered, and said: Who is he, Lord, that I may believe in him?

36. Respondit ille, et dixit: Quis est, Domine, ut credam in eum?

37. And Jesus said to him: Thou hast both seen him; and it is he that talketh with thee.

37. Et dixit ei Jesus: Et vidisti eum, et qui loquitur tecum, ipse est.

38. And he said: I believe, Lord, and falling down he adored him.

38. At ille ait: Credo Domine. Et procidens adoravit eum.

39. And Jesus said: For judgment I am come into this world; that they who see not, may see; and they who see, may become blind.

39. Et dixit Jesus In judicium ego in hunc mundum veni: ut qui non vident videant, et qui vident cæci fiant.

40. And some of the Pharisees, who were with him, heard; and they said unto him: Are we also blind?

40. Et audierunt quidam ex Pharisæis,

Text.	Commentary.
qui cum ipso erant, et dixerunt ei: Numquid et nos cæci sumus?	of the people, pronounced by you to be *struck* with spiritual blindness?
41. *Jesus said to them; If you were blind, you should not have sin, but now you say: We see. Your sin remaineth.* 41. *Dixit eis Jesus: Si cæci essetis, non haberetis peccatum: nunc vero dicitis: Quia videmus, Peccatum vestrum manet.*	41. "*If you were blind,*" in your own estimation and judgment—it is opposed to "*but now you say we see*"—and humbly acknowledged yourselves blind and ignorant and foolish in the affairs of your salvation, "*You should not have sin.*" You would cease to be overwhelmed with the weight of sin in which you are; because, you would humbly have had recourse to Me for your spiritual cure, owing to the consciousness of your miseries. "*But now you say we see.*" Now, you, arrogantly regard yourselves as having light and sanctity, you scorn any exhortation to have recourse to Me—the true Son of justice—"*the true light, that enlightens every man that cometh into this world.*" Hence, "*your sin remaineth.*" You continue, on account of your self-esteem, pride and arrogance, in your infidelity and sinful state. It may also mean, "*If you were blind,*" and had not the knowledge of SS. Scriptures proclaiming Me to be the Son of God, and of the many miracles wrought by Me, which should convince you that I am come from God; then, indeed, you might have some excuse. I would have treated you leniently and have attracted you to Myself by My grace. Your sin would be comparatively trifling. But, now, you sin in the face of the light, and "*your sin remains*" unremitted, and, so you persevere in your infidelity.

CHAPTER X.

1 *Amen, amen, I say to you: he that entereth not by the door into the sheepfold, but climbeth up another way, that same is a thief and a robber.*

2 *But he that entereth in by the door, is the shepherd of the sheep.*

3 *To him the porter openeth; and the sheep hear his voice: and he calleth his own sheep by name, and leadeth them out.*

4 *And when he hath let out his own sheep, he goeth before them: and the sheep follow him, because they know his voice.*

5 *But a stranger they follow not, but fly from him, because they know not the voice of strangers.*

6 *This proverb Jesus spoke to them. But they understood not what he spoke to them.*

7 *Jesus therefore said to them again: Amen, amen, I say to you, I am the door of the sheep.*

8 *All others as many as have come, are thieves and robbers: and the sheep heard them not.*

9 *I am the door. By me, if any man enter in, he shall be saved: and he shall go in, and go out, and shall find pastures.*

10 *The thief cometh not, but to steal and to kill and to destroy. I am come that they may have life, and may have it more abundantly.*

11 *I am the good shepherd. The good shepherd giveth his life for his sheep.*

12 *But the hireling and he that is not the shepherd, whose own the sheep are not, seeth the wolf coming and leaveth the sheep, and flieth: and the wolf catcheth, and scattereth the sheep:*

13 *And the hireling flieth, because he is a hireling; and he hath no care for the sheep.*

14 *I am the good shepherd; and I know mine, and mine know me.*

15 *As the Father knoweth me, and I know the Father: and I lay down my life for my sheep.*

16 *And other sheep I have, that are not of this fold: them also I must bring, and they shall hear my voice, and there shall be one fold and one shepherd.*

17 *Therefore doth the Father love me: because I lay down my life, that I may take it again.*

18 *No man taketh it away from me: but I lay it down of myself, and I have power to lay it down: and I have power to take it up again. This commandment have I received of my Father.*

19 *A dissension rose again among the Jews for these words.*

20 *And many of them said: He hath a devil, and is mad: why hear you him?*

21 *Others said: These are not the words of one that hath a devil: Can a devil open the eyes of the blind?*

22 *And it was the feast of the dedication at Jerusalem: and it was winter.*

23 *And Jesus walked in the temple in Solomon's porch.*

24 *The Jews therefore came round about him, and said to him: How long dost thou hold our souls in suspense? if thou be the Christ tell us plainly.*

25 *Jesus answered them: I speak to you, and you believe not: the works that I do in the name of my Father, they give testimony of me.*

26 *But you do not believe: because you are not of my sheep.*

27 *My sheep hear my voice: and I know them, and they follow me.*

28 *And I give them life everlasting; and they shall not perish for ever, and no man shall pluck them out of my hand.*

29 *That which my Father hath given me, is greater than all: and no one can snatch them out of the hand of my Father.*

30 *I and the Father are one.*

31 *The Jews then took up stones to stone him.*

32 *Jesus answered them: Many good works I have shewed you from my Father; for which of those works do you stone me?*

33 *The Jews answered him: For a good work we stone thee not, but for blasphemy; and because that thou being a man, makest thyself God?*

34 *Jesus answered them: Is it not written in your law:* I said you are gods?

35 *If he called them gods, to whom the word of God was spoken, and the scripture cannot be broken;*

36 *Do you say of him, whom the Father hath sanctified and sent into the world: Thou blasphemest, because I said, I am the son of God.*

37 *If I do not the works of my Father, believe me not.*

38 *But if I do, though you will not believe me, believe the works: that you may know and believe that the Father is in me, and I in the Father.*

39 *They sought therefore to take him: and he escaped out of their hands.*

40 *And he went again beyond the Jordan into that place where John was baptizing first; and there he abode.*

41 *And many resorted to him, and they said: John indeed did no sign.*

42 *But all things whatsoever John said of this man were true. And many believed in him.*

CAPUT X.

1 *Amen, amen dico vobis: qui non intrat per ostium in ovile ovium, sed ascendit aliunde: ille fur est, et latro.*

2 *Qui autem intrat per ostium, pastor est ovium.*

3 *Huic ostiarius aperit, et oves vocem ejus audiunt, et proprias oves vocat nominatim, et educit eas.*

4 *Et cum proprias oves emiserit, ante eas vadit: et oves illum sequuntur, quia sciunt vocem ejus.*

5 *Alienum autem non sequuntur, sed fugiunt ab eo: quia non noverunt vocem alienorum.*

6 *Hoc proverbium dixit eis Jesus. Illi autem non cognoverunt quid loqueretur eis.*

7 *Dixit ergo eis iterum Jesus: Amen, amen dico vobis, quia ego sum ostium ovium.*

8 *Omnes, quotquot venerunt, fures sunt, et latrones, et non audierunt eos oves.*

9 *Ego sum ostium. Per me si quis introierit, salvabitur: et ingredietur, et egredietur et pascua inveniet.*

10 *Fur non venit nisi ut furetur, et mactet, et perdat. Ego veni ut vitam habeant, et abundantius habeant.*

11 *Ego sum pastor bonus. Bonus pastor animam suam dat pro ovibus suis.*

12 Mercenarius autem, et qui non est pastor, cujus non sunt oves propriæ, videt lupum venientem, et dimittit oves, et fugit : et lupus rapit, et dispergit oves :

13 Mercenarius autem fugit, quia mercenarius est, et non pertinet ad eum de ovibus.

14 Ego sum pastor bonus ; et cognosco meas, et cognoscunt me meæ.

15 Sicut novit me Pater, et ego agnosco Patrem : et animam meam pono pro ovibus meis.

16 Et alias oves habeo, quæ non sunt ex hoc ovili et alias oportet me adducere, et vocem meam audient, et fiet unum ovile, et unus pastor.

17 Propterea me diligit Pater : quia ego pono animam, meam, ut iterum sumam eam.

18 Nemo tollit eam a me : sed ego pono eam a meipso, et potestatem habeo ponendi eam : et potestatem habeo iterum sumendi eam : Hoc mandatum accepi a Patre meo.

19 Dissensio iterum facta est inter Judæos propter sermones hos.

20 Dicebant autem multi ex ipsis : Dæmonium habet, et insanit : quid cum auditis ?

21 Alii dicebant : Hæc verba non sunt dæmonium habentis : Numquid dæmonium potest cæcorum oculos aperire ?

22 Facta sunt autem Encænia in Jerosolymis : et hiems erat.

23 Et ambulabat Jesus in templo, in porticu Salomonis.

24 Circumdederunt ergo eum Judæi, et dicebant ei : Quousque animam nostram tollis ? si tu es Christus, dic nobis palam.

25 Respondit eis Jesus : Loquor vobis, et non creditis. Opera, quæ ego facio in nomine Patris mei, hæc testimonium perhibent de me ?

26 Sed vos non creditis, quia non estis ex ovibus meis.

27 Oves meæ vocem meam audiunt : et ego cognosco eas, et sequuntur me :

28 Et ego vitam æternam do eis : et non peribunt in æternum, et non rapiet eas quisquam de manu mea.

29 Pater meus quod dedit mihi, majus omnibus est : et nemo potest rapere de manu Patris mei.

30 Ego, et Pater unum sumus.

31 Sustulerunt ergo lapides Judæi, ut lapidarent eum.

32 Respondit eis Jesus : Multa bona opera ostendi vobis ex Patre meo, propter quod eorum opus me lapidatis ?

33 Responderunt ei Judæi : De bono opere non lapidamus te, sed de blasphemia, et quia tu homo cum sis, facis teipsum Deum.

34 Respondit eis Jesus : Nonne scriptum est in lege vestra : quia Ego dixi, dii estis ?

35 Si illos dixit deos, ad quos sermo Dei factus est, et non potest solvi scriptura :

36 Quem Pater sanctificavit, et misit in mundum, vos dicitis : Quia blasphemas ; quia dixi, Filius Dei sum ?

37 Si non facio opera Patris mei, nolite credere mihi.

38 Si autem facio : et si mihi non vultis credere, operibus credite, ut cognoscatis, et credatis quia Pater in me est, et ego in Patre.

39 Quærebant ergo eum apprehendere : et exivit de manibus eorum.

40 Et abiit iterum trans Jordanem in eum locum, ubi erat Joannes baptizans primum : et mansit illic :

41 Et multi venerunt ad eum, et dicebant : Quia Joannes quidem signum fecit nullum.

42 Omnia autem quæcumque dixit Joannes de hoc, vera erant. Et multi crediderunt in eum.

ANALYSIS.

In this chapter, our Lord treats of the Parable of the good Shepherd (1–6). His hearers understood not its object or tendency (7). He then explains the parable, and applying it to Himself, He states that He is Himself the good Shepherd. He points out the characteristics or qualities of a good Shepherd, and contrasts him with selfish hirelings, who desert their flocks at the first approach of danger (7–15).

He conveys that He is Himself prepared, at His Father's command, to give His life freely for His flock (15–19).

He reproaches the Jews with refusing to believe in Him, notwithstanding the evidence of works proving His Divinity (19–25).

He asserts His identity with His Father (30). The Jews understanding Him correctly to claim equality with God, threaten to stone Him as a blasphemer. Our Lord confirms this impression, as it was correct on the part of the Jews, by several arguments, and repeats His claim to be regarded as the Eternal Son of God, consubstantial with the Father (31–38).

By an exercise of His Almighty power, He escapes from them and crosses the Jordan into Pærea, where He remained for some time (39–42).

Text.

1. *Amen, amen, I say to you: he that entereth not by the door into the sheepfold, but climbeth up another way, the same is a thief and a robber.*

1. *Amen, amen dico vobis: qui non intrat per ostium in ovile ovium, sed ascendit aliunde; ille fur est, et latro.*

Commentary.

1. "*Amen, amen.*" The repetition of the word, "*Amen*," when prefixed by our Lord to any assertion, conveys the most solemn asseveration.

"*I say unto you, he that entereth,*" etc. This parable of the sheepfold, etc., was uttered by our Lord, in connexion with the preceding, including the cure of the blind man, as appears from v. 19.

Some, however, hold that some interval elapsed between what is recorded here and the preceding. But, the words "*Amen, amen,*" with which the present account commences, would show, that He is not entering on a new subject, as these words are not employed for the commencement of a discourse, and the whole discourse looks like a continuation of what goes before.

Some Expositors, therefore, maintain, that this tenth chapter should begin at v. 19 of c. ix. "*For judgment am I come unto the world.*" The division of chapters was made, not by the Evangelist; but, by Cardinal Hugo de Sancto Caso, about the middle of the 13th century.

The casting out of the man, cured by our Lord, from their place of meeting, possibly, the Synagogue of the Jews (c. ix. v. 34), with the view of showing that our Lord was a false teacher—He and all His followers having been cast out from the Jewish Church, apostates from the Jewish religion, placed outside the Synagogue or true assembly of God's people—gave occasion to this parable of the sheepfold.

In it, our Lord wishes to convey, the opposite of what they thought, viz., that far from being a false Prophet, in consequence of His exclusion from the Synagogue, He was, on the contrary, on the way into the sheepfold—the authority of the Synagogue being

ST. JOHN, CHAP. X.

Commentary.

now abolished—and as the Scribes and Pharisees refused to enter into His sheepfold, they were rejected and reprobated by God. The parable continues up to v. 11, and there our Lord Himself makes the application.

"*He that entereth not by the door*," that is, the passage open for all who have no sinister design in entering "*into the sheepfold*," "*climbeth up another way*," whether through a window or any breach in the wall of the enclosure, "*the same is a thief*," whose only object is to steal away the sheep privately and unobserved, "*and a robber*," whose object is to carry them off forcibly, "*to kill and destroy them*." The sheepfold was open above; it was made of hurdles and wicker work. He enters not by the door, who enters not by Christ, the door of the Church, and possessing no legitimate delegation from God, assumes an office to which he is not called by God, like Aaron. Our Lord alludes to such men as Theodas and Judas of Galilee (Acts v. 36, 37), who claimed to be regarded as the Messias. He also refers to the Pharisees, who were opposing Him and turning away the people from Him. In a word, He refers to all who undertook, unsent, to guide the people, like those referred to by Jeremias, c. xxiii. 21: "*I did not send Prophets, yet, they ran; I have not spoken to them, yet, they prophesied.*"

2. "*He that entereth by the door is the shepherd*," etc. His entering by the door is a proof that He is the owner, who has a right to go in and go out, on His legitimate business, in caring and looking after the flock.

Christ, who is the door, enters through Himself into the sheepfold. It is by His authority, all others legitimately enter into it. Moreover, as our Lord has two natures, Christ, as *man*, enters through Himself, *as God*; although, in the literal sense, the door and the Pastor are different. In the application, they are the same thing, "*Intrat per Christum, tanquam ostium, qui in illum credit; et qui illum in regimine fidelium imitatur*."—(St. Augustine.)

3. "*The porter*," designates the man appointed to guard the entrance, to admit all having a claim, and exclude intruders. This true Pastor knows all His sheep, and has a different name for each. The sheep "*hear*," that is, recognise "*His voice*," His peculiar tone or whistle, leaving their pasture to follow Him; so do the faithful, recognising the voice of Christ, receive His doctrines and obey His precepts.

"*He calleth His own sheep by name*," taking special care of each, and attending to their individual wants. So does Christ by Himself, and also through the pastors of His Church, specially attend to the spiritual wants and necessities of each member of His flock.

Text.

2. *But he that entereth in by the door, is the shepherd of the sheep.*

2. *Qui autem intrat per ostium, pastor est ovium.*

3. *To him the porter openeth; and the sheep hear his voice: and he calleth his own heep by name, and leadeth them out.*

3. *Huic ostiarius aperit, et oves vocem ejus audiunt, et proprias oves vocat nominatim, et educit eas.*

Text.

4. *And when he hath let out his own sheep, he goeth before them; and the sheep follow him, because they know his voice.*
4. *Et cum proprias oves emiserit, ante eas vadit: et oves illum sequuntur, quia sciunt vocem ejus.*

5. *But a stranger they follow not, but fly from him, because they know not the voice of strangers.*
5. *Alienum autem non sequuntur, sed fugiunt ab eo: quia non noverunt vocem alienorum.*

6. *This proverb Jesus spoke to them. But they understood not what he spoke to them.*
6. *Hoc proverbium dixit eis Jesus. Illi autem non cognoverunt quid loqueretur eis.*

Commentary.

"*The porter*," means the Holy Ghost, who opens the door into the Church to Christ, giving Him authority, by the wonderful works wrought through Him, as also by the descent on Him at Baptism. The same Holy Ghost, it is, that places other pastors over the Church. " *Quos posuit Spiritus Sanctus, Episcopos, regere Ecclesiam Dei.*" (Acts xx)

4. "*The sheep follow Him.*" The contrary usage prevails in the *West;* the shepherd follows the sheep and drives them before him. In the EAST, the shepherd precedes them. Here, it is meant to point out the care which the pastors of the Church should show in protecting their flocks from the inroads of wolves, and guarding them against all dangers. There is allusion also to their holding out before them the light and guidance of a good example.

5. The sheep "*know not,*" the peculiar tone of "*voice,*" nor the whistling "*of strangers.*" The true faithful shun those, who deliver doctrines or precepts different from what had been pointed out to them by the voice of their true pastors, whom they recognise as inculcating doctrines and precepts that emanate from God.

6. "*The proverb.*" It may be called a "*parable,*" which is longer than a "*proverb.*" By a "*proverb,*" is meant a trite, short, pithy sentence, expressing some well-known truth, or some common fact, ascertained from experience. The three other Evangelists call such, "*parables.*" St. John, "*proverbs.*" The Greek word for "*parable*" only occurs in the three first Evangelists. St. John, in every instance, terms such illustrations not παραβολαι (*parables*); but, παροιμιαι (*proverbs*). The Hebrew for both is the same, *Marshah.* Hence, the Septuagint translators of the Book of Solomon, translate the word, at one time, *parable;* at another, *proverb*. Both words are often interchanged and used as convertible terms. The proverb is but a condensed parable; the essence and substance of a parable.

"*They understood not what He spoke.*" They understood well the familiar allusions literally contained in the parable, as these were drawn from common life, regarding sheep, shepherds and sheepfolds, well known to them. But, the scope and tendency of the parable, or what it was meant to illustrate, they understood not, and this our Lord, very probably, intended, so as to avoid rousing their anger too soon against Him, as " *His hour had not yet come.*" The foregoing is the parable in its literal sense, containing, like almost all parables, several ornamental parts not meant to illustrate the principal subject for elucidation; and although our Lord applies its most prominent parts in the following verses 7–10; there are, still, several parts, the mystical or spiritual meaning of

Commentary

which is left to be explained by others. On these points, Commentators hold different opinions. Our Redeemer only explains the sense or principal part of the parable; viz., that He Himself is the door; and that no one can be saved except through Him. He Himself explains v. 7, states who or what is meant by "*the door*."

7. In the most solemn way, "*Amen, amen,*" He assures them, that He Himself is "*the door of the sheep,*" that it is only by faith in Him, as the Eternal, consubstantial Son of God, sent into the world to save sinners, man can be justified. "*No other name under Heaven whereby man can be saved*" (Acts iv. 12). He employs the similitude of the pastor to convey that all others are mercenaries, seeking themselves, and not their flocks, like Him whom alone, therefore, they should follow.

8. "*All* OTHERS, *as many as have come,*" of themselves, unsent by Me, not in connexion with Me or subordinate to Me, affecting to be duly commissioned.

"*Are thieves and robbers.*" The Prophets of old, who were sent, and entered the fold through Christ's future merits, are not, therefore, referred to.

He also, very probably, refers to those who came, claiming to be *the* Pastor—the Messias or Christ so long expected—such as Theodas, Simon Magus, etc. This interpretation derives probability from our Lord, calling Himself "*the Pastor*" (ὅ ποιμην) (v. 14). In this sense only, could it be said, that, "*the others*" were "*thieves,*" etc., since the true Prophet did not claim to be *the* Pastor or Messias. Hence, He speaks of those (the false Prophets) who pretended to be sent by God, as the Messias. He would seem to note specially the Pharisees, etc., who, seeing the mark of the Messiah in Christ, rejected Him, and taking upon themselves to govern the people, burst into the fold in His own time. The word, "*are*," gives this interpretation great probability.

"*And the sheep heard them not.*" The pious and humble portion of the Jewish nation, "*did not hear them,*" or embrace their teachings. If they followed them, they would cease to belong to Christ's sheepfold.

9. "*He shall be saved,*" by entering through Me and by faith in Me, it being understood that he shall persevere in performing everything necessary, good works, etc.

"*And he shall go in, and go out,*" not go out from the Church; but, to find pastures without any fear, under my guidance, as Shepherd. Or, it may mean: shall, freely, and with all confidence and a sense of security, discharge the duties assigned to him.

"*And shall find pastures,*" the pastures and spiritual nourishment of true, sound doctrine. It is disputed among Commentators

Text

7. *Jesus therefore said to them again, Amen, amen, I say to you, I am the door of the sheep.*

7. *Dixit ergo eis iterum Jesus: Amen, amen dico vobis quia ego sum ostium ovium.*

8. *All others as many as have come, are thieves and robbers: and the sheep heard them not.*

8. *Omnes, quotquot venerunt, fures sunt et latrones et non audierunt eos oves.*

9. *I am the door. By me if any man enter in, he shall be saved: and he shall go in, and go out, and shall find pastures.*

9. *Ego sum ostium. Per me si quis introierit, salvabitur: et ingredietur, et egredietur, et pascua inveniet.*

Text.	Commentary.
	whether this refers to the *sheep* or to the *Pastors*. It is in favour of the former, that it is the *sheep, that are saved*, the *Pastor*, that *saves*.
10. *The thief cometh not, but for to steal and to kill and to destroy. I am come that they may have life, and may have it more abundantly.* 10. *Fur non venit nisi ut furetur, et mactet, et perdat. Ego veni ut vitam habeant, et abundantius habeant.*	10. "*The thief*," who does not enter by the door, but privately steals in, the Heretic, the Schismatic, the Scribe and Pharisee, the false Christ, "*come not, but to steal*," the flock from Christ and the Church; to carry them off to the synagogue of Satan, and thus "*kill*" their souls—"*and destroy them*," in the everlasting torments which await them. This they, doubtless, do for the selfish purposes of securing pelf and self aggrandizement. My object in coming is, not only that they may have life, bare existence; but also, that they have what is required to make that life supereminently happy, viz., "*have it more abundantly*," or superabundantly, that is, have an abundance of heavenly gifts and graces, which stimulate men to perform acts of heroic merit; and, as a reward, an abundance of glory hereafter, in the kingdom of everlasting bliss, and at the final resurrection.
11. *I am the good shepherd. The good shepherd giveth his life for his sheep.* 11. *Ego sum pastor bonus. Bonus pastor animam suam dat pro ovibus suis.*	11. "*I am the good shepherd.*" "*I*," unlike the mercenary Scribes and Pharisees, unlike the thieves who come like wolves, "*am the good shepherd.*" That good shepherd, promised by God in the law, revealed to Moses, foretold by the Prophets, destined to redeem and govern the people of God—and even in a literal view, it often happens that the shepherd exposes his life, like David (2 Kings xvii.). "*The good shepherd giveth his life for his sheep.*" This, in its application, whatever may be said of the literal parable, is quite true, in reference to our Lord, who did so, and the pastors of His Church, who sacrifice their temporal life, as happens every day, in times of pestilence or persecution, for the spiritual life of their flocks.
12. *But the hireling and he that is not the shepherd, whose own the sheep are not, seeth the wolf coming and leaveth the sheep, and flieth: and the wolf catcheth, and scattereth the sheep:* 12. *Mercenarius autem, et qui non est pastor, cujus non sunt oves propriæ, videt lupum venientem et dimittit oves, et fugit: et lupus rapit, et dispergit oves:*	12. Our Lord not only contrasts Himself, as above, with the thief, but also with another wicked class of pastors—the hirelings. "*The hireling*," the man who cares the flock for temporal gain and hire. In this verse is shown the character of the good shepherd, in contrast with the conduct of the hireling. "*Seeth the wolf coming.*" By "*the wolf*," is meant, whatever causes danger to himself and the flock; it may be, it refers to bad men, soldiers, etc. ; but, "*the wolf*" is put for all, as being the more common enemy of the flock. "*He leaves the sheep*" to their fate, and takes safety himself in flight. The consequence is, that, so far as he is concerned, the wolf devours and scattereth the sheep.

Commentary

13. "*The hireling ... because he is a hireling.*" All the concern he feels is, for his wages. He feels no special interest in the welfare of his flock. In this, our Lord notes and censures the mercenary Scribes and Pharisees.

When, and in what circumstances, it may be permissible and lawful for a pastor to flee, in times of persecution, (see Matthew x. 23, Commentary on)..

14. Our Lord here shows that He possesses—and applies to Himself—the qualities appertaining to a good shepherd, viz., that "*He knows His sheep,*" as in v. 3, "*He calleth them by name,* and *they hear His voice.*" Our Lord's "knowledge" here is a knowledge, accompanied by practical benevolence, a knowledge of love and beneficence. "*And His sheep know Him.*" "*And,*" expresses the effect of this knowledge on His part; it is, that they in turn, know Him, they believe in Him; they hope in Him; they love Him. His love for them reciprocally begets love from them towards Him.

15. "*As the Father knoweth Me,*" etc.. This is to be connected with the foregoing, as if He said: My love for My sheep and their love for Me, is like to—though infinitely inferior to and beneath—the infinite and boundless love and knowledge My Father has for Me, and I, for Him. This boundless love is the source and origin of the mutual love between My sheep and Me; because, the Divine and increated love is the source and origin of all created love. My Father wishes Me, His natural and Increated Son, to love His adopted children, who, in turn, faithfully repay My love. The knowledge and love are of the *same kind;* one, however, being infinite, the other, finite. There is a *similarity;* not an *equality* of love and knowledge in both cases.

"*And I lay down My life for My sheep.*" This is another quality already predicated of the Good Shepherd. These words are immediately connected with the words (*v.* 14), "*I know Mine.*" The intermediate words—"*As the Father,*" etc., being an expression of the quality of His knowledge and love for His sheep. "*And I lay down My life.*" I am prepared to lay down My life, and mean to do it shortly, "*for My sheep.*" This is a proof of His practical benevolent knowledge and love.

16. "*And other sheep I have,*" etc. He refers to the Gentile world, whom He meant to call into His Church, bestowing on them the priceless gift of faith (Isaias xlix.), "*Ecce dedi te in lucem gentium,*" etc. "*Other,*" than the Jewish people, whom He was sent to preach to first, and gather into His fold.

He uses the present, "*I have,*" and calls them His "*sheep*" by anticipation, as He foresaw their call, at no distant period, into the

Text

13. And the hireling *flieth, because he is a hireling; and he hath no care for the sheep.*

13. *Mercenarius autem fugit, quia mercenarius est, et non pertinet ad eum de ovibus.*

14. *I am the good shepherd; and I know mine, and mine know me.*

14. *Ego sum pastor bonus: et cognosco meas, et cognoscunt me mea.*

15. *As the Father knoweth me, and I know the Father: and I lay down my life for my sheep.*

15. *Sicut novit me Pater, et ego agnosco Patrem: et animam meam pono pro ovibus meis.*

16. *And other sheep I have, that are not of this fold; them also I must bring, and they shall hear my voice, and there shall be one fold and one shepherd.*

Text.

16. *Et alias oves habeo, quæ non sunt ex hoc ovili: et alias oportet me adducere, et vocem meam audient, et fiet unum ovile, et unus pastor.*

17. *Therefore doth the Father love me: because I lay down my life, that I may take it again.*

17. *Propterea me diligit Pater; quia ego pono animam meam, ut iterum sumam eam.*

18. *No man taketh it away from me: but I lay it down of myself, and I have power to lay it down; and I have power to take it up again. This commandment have I received of my Father.*

18. *Nemo tollit eam a me; sed ego pono eam a meipso, et potestatem habeo ponendi eam: et potestatem habeo iterum sumendi eam. Hoc mandatum accepi a Patre meo.*

Commentary.

sheepfold of His Church, and their faithful correspondence with His grace, "*and they shall hear My voice.*"

"*That are not of this fold.*" Scattered abroad, like sheep without a fold, wherein safely to congregate.

"*Them also I must bring,*" into the fold, bestowing on them the light of faith, as I am constituted by My Father, the "*light to enlighten the Gentiles.*" This verse seems to be parenthetically introduced, and verse 15 to be immediately connected with verse 17.

"*And they*"—the two peoples, Jews and Gentiles—"*shall be one fold.*" All the sheep shall form one fold founded by Me, who am to be the "*one*" only chief "*shepherd.*" All other shepherds are dependent on and subordinate to Me (Gal. iii. 28; Ezechiel xxxiv. 13–16).

17. "*Therefore doth the Father love Me,*" because out of love for Him, and in obedience to His command, "*I lay down My life for Him,*" of My own free will and accord; however, this I do, "*that I may take it again.*" "*That,*" is the same as, *so that,* expressive of a result or consequence. "*I lay down My life,*" in obedience to My Father's command, for My flock, by paying the due ransom for the sins of My people, but in such a way, "*that I may take it up again,*" and perfect this act of ransom, by being gloriously resuscitated to bring about their justification. The cruel and ignominious death of the cross is sweet to Me; because, pleasing to My Father, who in reward for obedience and humiliation, has bestowed on Me glory and exaltation (Philip. ii. 8–11).

18. "*No man taketh it away from Me,*" forcibly, against My will. "*But I lay it down of Myself,*" of My own free will and accord. The violence of the Jews would be of no avail against Him. The instruments of torture employed could not affect Him. He could, if He pleased, by the power of His Divinity, render His body, like the bodies of the glorified saints, impassible and proof against any impression. The power He had of crying out with a loud voice, on the point of expiring, could be exerted in saving Him from dying. Hence, the Centurion, on witnessing Him in dying, utter a loud voice, as well as witnessing the other phenomena, also, exclaimed, "*Indeed, this was the Son of God*" (Matthew xxvii. 54).

"*I have power to lay it down,*" by a free and voluntary death—"*and power to take it up again,*" by a glorious Resurrection. He shows He was God and man. As *man*, He died; as *God*, He raised Himself up.

"*This commandment have I received,*" etc. Our Lord's death, while it was His own free act, was undergone by Him, in fulfilment of the command of His Father.

Commentary.

19. "*A dissension rose again,*" as on several former occasions, for instance (c. ix. 16), "*for these words.*" This may denote the words of the parable, which they understood not; or, His words, regarding His power of life and death.

20. "*He hath a devil,*" proudly imitating Lucifer in his claims and arrogant assumption. He is driven on by the demon who possesses Him. "*He is mad.*" "*Why hear ye Him?*" Why listen to a madman of His sort?

21. Others defend Him. They declare that the curing of a blind man and restoring his sight cannot be the work of the devil, but of God. Hence, this man who effected so great a cure (opening the eyes of a blind man), cannot in His speech be under the influence of any diabolical agency.

22. "*Dedication,*" literally, of the renewing or renovation. It, most likely, refers to the renewing and dedication of the Temple by Judas Machabeus, after it had been profaned and partly destroyed by Antiochus Epiphanes. (1 Machabees iv. 52–59; 4 Machabeus x. 5–8). After purifying the Temple, Judas Machabeus decreed that this festival should be celebrated for eight days, in each succeeding year, which was done with great demonstrations of joy. It occurred in the month of *Casleu,* or, about the middle of our December.

23. "*Walked.*" As it was cold, wintry weather, He walked about publicly; prepared to give instruction, if required.

"*In Solomon's porch.*" This was covered, adjoining the Temple to the East. It was called so, either because it was originally built by Solomon.—It was left undestroyed by the Chaldeans and preserved amidst the ruins of the Temple,—or, because it was built anew on the site of the porch built by Solomon on the eastern side of the hill (Josephus de Bello, c. v.).

24. "*The Jews came round Him, and said to Him, how long dost thou hold our souls in suspense?*" These men, very likely, pressed Him for an answer, out of feelings of malice, in order to elicit a plain answer from Him; and then either accuse Him to the Romans, as affecting sovereign power; or, stone Him for blasphemy. Hence, their insidious question.

"*If Thou be the Christ, tell us plainly.*" "*The Christ,*" the promised, expected, *Messias.* If we even admit that our Lord

Text.

19. *A dissension rose again among the Jews for these words.*

19. *Dissensio iterum facta est inter Judæos propter sermones hos.*

20. *And many of them said: He hath a devil, and is mad. why hear you him?*

20. *Dicebant autem multi ex ipsis: Dæmonium habet, et insanit: quid eum auditis?*

21. *Others said: These are not the words of one that hath a devil. Can a devil open the eyes of the blind?*

21. *Alii dicebant: Hæc verba non sunt dæmonium habentis: numquid dæmonium potest cæcorum oculos aperire?*

22. *And it was the feast of the dedication at Jerusalem; and it was winter.*

22. *Facta sunt autem Encænia in Jerosolymis: et hiems erat.*

23. *And Jesus walked in the temple in Solomon's porch.*

23. *Et ambulabat Jesus in templo, in porticu Salomonis.*

24. *The Jews therefore came round about him, and said to him: How long dost thou hold our souls in suspense? If thou be the Christ, tell us plainly.*

24. *Circumdederunt ergo eum Judæi, et dicebant ei: Quousque animam nostram*

Text	Commentary
tollis? si tu es Christus, dic nobis palam.	had not declared this directly, He did so equivalently, on several occasions, and by stupendous miracles, proved it.
25. *Jesus answered them: I speak to you, and you believe not: the works that I do in the name of my Father, they give testimony of me.* 25. *Respondit eis Jesus: Loquor vobis. et non creditis. Opera, quæ ego facio in nomine Patris mei, hæc testimonium perhibent de me:*	25. Our Lord answers them, that He had already told them, at least equivalently (viii. 12–18–24) that He was the Christ, and they did not believe Him. They cast discredit on His testimony, as the testimony of one speaking in his own favour (viii. 13). He therefore, now refrains from answering them in words, knowing their malicious motives ; He refers them to His stupendous works done in the name and by the authority of His Father. These works wrought in proof of His Divine mission are the strongest testimony He can give.
26. *But you do not believe: because you are not of my sheep.* 26. *Sed vos non creditis, quia non estis ex ovibus meis.*	26. Taxing their obstinate malice, He accounts for their not believing in Him, although, besides His own assurance, they had such testimony of works. The reason was, that they were not of His flock, either at present, or at any future time.
27. *My sheep hear my voice, and I know them, and they follow me.* 27. *Oves meæ vocem meam audiunt: et ego cognosco eas, et sequuntur me:*	27. He shows they are not of His sheep ; because, destitute of the distinguishing qualities of such, the chief quality being to hear and obey His words, a thing they refuse to do. Hence, they are not of His sheep. Of them He shall, one day, say, instead of knowing them, "*I know you not*" (Matthew vii. 23).
28. *And I give them life everlasting; and they shall not perish for ever, and no man shall pluck them out of my hand.* 28. *Et ego vitam æternam do eis: et non peribunt in æternum, et non rapiet eas quisquam de manu mea.*	28. In order to stimulate them to become "*His sheep,*" His obedient followers, He points out the blessings in store for His followers. "*I give them life everlasting,*" so far as I am concerned, unless they wish to desert Me of their own free will, and refuse to co-operate with My grace. "*I give them life everlasting.*" I have in store for them hereafter life everlasting, of which My grace here is a sure earnest, "*and no man shall pluck them out of My hand.*" No power in existence, men or devils, can forcibly take them away from Me.
29. *That which my Father hath given me, is greater than all: and no man can snatch them out of the hand of my Father.* 29. *Pater meus quod dedit mihi, majus omnibus est: et nemo potest rapere de manu Patris mei.*	29. "*That which My Father hath given Me,*" viz., My Divine nature in My eternal generation, "*is greater than all,*" than any thing or power in existence, it being the Divinity itself. "*And no one can snatch them out of the hand of My Father.*" Therefore, nor out of Mine, our power being the same. The Greek reading is different. "*My Father who gave to Me,*" viz., My sheep—"*is greater than all, and no one can snatch them out the hand of My Father.*" Therefore, nor out of Mine, as our power is the same (*v.* 30). This reading is sustained by the external authority of Versions and MSS., and renders the reasoning clear and less involved. According to the Vulgate reading, the words of verse, 30, would be only a repetition, in clearer terms, of verse 29. However, the Vulgate reading makes good sense, and from a doc-

Commentary.

trinal point of view, conveys the same adorable truth regarding our Lord's *Divinity* and *Humanity*.

Verses 29, 30, express the *identity* of the Father and of the Son and the *Omnipotent power of both*.

30. The meaning is: no one can snatch them out of the hand of My Father, nor, therefore, out of Mine, since, "*the Father and I are one*," possessing the same Omnipotent power, the same identical Divine nature, the same Divine will. The reasoning here requires, that our Lord should speak of unity of *power* and *nature*. "*One*," denotes unity of nature. "*Are*," distinction of persons (St. Augustine, Oratio de Hæres). In answering, He declares more than they asked, viz., that He was not only the Messias, such as they fancied in their minds, but even God.

31, 32. This clearly shows, they understood our Lord to speak of Himself as God, consubstantial, equal in power, with God. Hence, their intention of stoning Him, stoning being the punishment marked out for blasphemers (Leviticus xxiv. 14–16).

Our Lord does not remove nor correct this impression; but rather confirms it here, as it was correct, by an argument derived from His stupendous works proceeding from the Father. "*Many good works I have shewed you from My Father*," from whom I derive My power of performing the works of the Divinity, along with my Divine nature. These works prove Him to be the Son of God, and this He means to say here. Hence, He here again confirms the impression of the Jews by re-affirming His consubstantiality with the Father, as demonstrated by His works.

33. "*For a good work*"—if ever you performed such—"*we stone Thee not, but for blasphemy*, in making Thyself God." It is, then, clear, they understood our Lord's meaning.

34. If our Lord had not meant to assert His identity in nature with the Father, He could easily have silenced them by saying, they misunderstood Him; that He did not mean what they understood Him to say. Far from it, He confirms their views, by an *argumentum a minore ad majus*, an *argumentum*, also, as it is called, *ad hominem*, showing their inconsistency in charging Him with blasphemy in the application of the term, "*God*," to Himself.

"*Written in your law.*" The whole of the Sacred Scriptures in use among the Jews, as in xv. 25. Sometimes the law denotes the Pentateuch (Luke xxiv. 44).

Text.

30. *I and the Father are one.*

30. *Ego, et Pater unum sumus.*

31. *The Jews then took up stones to stone him.*

31. *Sustulerunt ergo lapides Judæi, ut lapidarent eum.*

32. *Jesus answered them: Many good works I have shewed you from my Father: for which of those works do you stone me?*

32. *Respondit eis Jesus, Multa bona opera ostendi vobis ex Patre meo, propter quod eorum opus me lapidatis?*

33. *The Jews answered him: For a good work we stone thee not, but for blasphemy, and because that thou being a man makest thyself God.*

33. *Responderunt ei Judæi: De bono opere non lapidamus te, sed de blasphemia: et quia tu homo cum sis, facis teipsum Deum.*

34. *Jesus answered them: Is it not written in your law: I said, you are gods?*

34. *Respondit eis Jesus: Nonne scriptum est in lege vestra: quia Ego dixi, dii estis?*

Text

35. *If he called them gods, to whom the word of God was spoken, and the scripture cannot be broken;*
35. *Si illos dixit deos, ad quos sermo Dei factus est, et non potest solvi scriptura:*

36. *Do you say of him, whom the Father hath sanctified and sent into the world; Thou blasphemest, because I said, I am the Son of God?*
36. *Quem Pater sanctificavit, et misit in mundum, vos dicitis: Quia blasphemas: quia dixi Filius Dei sum?*

37. *If I do not the works of my Father, believe me not.*
37. *Si non facio opera Patris mei, nolite credere mihi.*

Commentary.

"*I said, you are gods.*" These words are taken from Psalm (lxxxi. 6), addressed to judges, whom God invests with His own legitimate power, and makes to share in His name, as His vicars and representatives. They are called "*gods*," in administering justice.

35. "*If He called them gods, to whom the Word of God was spoken,*" addressing them as gods, "*and the Scripture,*" which records this, "*cannot be broken,*" be declared nugatory, or to have recorded an undue appellation, emanating from the mouth of God; in other words, cannot be charged with attributing improper language to God. They, therefore, are properly termed, *gods*.

36. "*Whom the Father sanctified,*" bestowing on Him, as *God*, His essential sanctity with the Divine nature in His Eternal generation; and sanctifying Him, as *man*, in the Hypostatic union; so as, to fit Him for His mission in the world, "*and sent into the world*" as His Son, which the relation of *Father* clearly implies—a relation of the closest character—"*sent*" Him, to exercise an office far more exalted than that of judges, justly termed "*gods.*" Is it not very wrong of you, therefore, to say, "*Thou blasphemest, because I said, I am the Son of God?*"

It is clear, "*the Father and I are one*" (*v.* 30), and "*I am the Son of God*" (*v.* 36), are the same thing; since, it is verse 30, our Lord refers to, in this verse. Both, therefore, express His identity of nature with the Father.

Our Lord here uses an *argumentum a minore ad majus*. If men can legitimately be termed *gods* in the exercise of judicial power, simply because God called them such, with how much more reason can He call Himself, without blasphemy, "*the Son of God,*" whom God, the Father, implying the relation of Son, sent, as His Son, into the world. He thus, fully refutes their charge, prescinding from the more exalted sense in which He calls Himself the Son of God, which is not expressed in this verse. But, in verses 30–36, is clearly expressed His meaning. In these verses He, in the most explicit terms, calls Himself "*the Son of God,*" consubstantial, and equal in all things, as well in power, as in all other Divine attributes. "*Sanctified,*" may signify, destined, set apart for the office of Saviour, and "*sent into the world*" for that purpose. In this sense, the word is used (Jer. i. 5), *Antequam exires de vulva*, SANCTIFICAVI *te*," destined you to be a Prophet, "*et Prophetam in gentibus,*" etc.

37. Our Lord once more confirms their conviction, that He meant to call Himself the Son of God, by referring to the works which proved that He possessed the same power and Divine nature with the Father, "*the works of My Father,*" works

Commentary.

peculiar to My Father. Hence, as the works are common to both, they must both be the same in nature, power, and operation.

38. If you do not believe Me on my own assertions, believe Me on account of My works, which can proceed from no other than My Father. These prove the truth of My words and assertions. "*That you may know and believe.*" That you may know My works to be Divine, and knowing them to be such, you may "*believe that the Father is in Me*," performing His Divine works, by His Divine nature, "*and I in Him*," by My Divine nature, by the same Deity and Omnipotence. This refers to *circuminsession*. The works of our Lord prove His declaration, that "He is the Son of God," to be true.

Verse, 30, declares the *consubstantiality* of our Lord with His Father. Verse, 36, His Divine *filiation*. Verse, 37, His *circuminsession*. It is clear from verse 39, that the Jews understood Him in these two last verses to refer to His Divinity. Hence, their efforts to apprehend and punish Him, as a blasphemer.

39. "*They sought to take Him*," on account of His again repeating His equality with God. "*He escaped*," etc., rendering Himself invisible by His omnipotent power.

40. In order to appease the rage of His enemies, He crossed the Jordan into Perea, "*into that place where John was baptizing first*." This was Bethany or Bethabara (i. 28). Here it is, our Lord was baptized, and testimony borne to Him, by John, of which, the place and surroundings would remind the crowds that followed Him.

"*And abode there*," until, towards the approach of the Pasch and His Passion, He went into Judea and raised Lazarus from the dead.

41. "*Many resorted to Him.*" They were reminded of what formerly occurred there by the place itself. Likely, these occurrences were fresh in their memory. Hence, they said, "*John indeed did no sign*," and we believed in Him, even fancied Him to be the promised Messiah; with how much greater reason ought we have believed in this man, who has performed so many miracles, in proof of His assertion, that He is the Son of God.

42. Again, we have further proof of this in the testimony of John regarding Him. "*And all things whatsoever John said of Him were true*," and confirmed by events. Hence, influenced by these motives of credibility, we should have received Him, as the true Messiah and Son of God. "*And many believed in Him.*"

Text.

38. *But if I do, though you will not believe me, believe the works: that you may know and believe that the Father is in me, and I in the Father.*

38. *Si autem facio: et si mihi non vultis credere, operibus credite, ut cognoscatis, et credatis quia Pater in me est, et ego in Patre.*

39. *They sought therefore to take him; and he escaped out of their hands.*

39. *Quærebant ergo eum apprehendere: et exivit de manibus eorum.*

40. *And he went again beyond the Jordan into that place where John was baptizing first; and there he abode.*

40. *Et abiit iterum trans Jordanem in eum locum, ubi erat Joannes baptizans primum: et mansit illic:*

41. *And many resorted to him, and they said; John indeed did no sign.*

41. *Et multi venerunt ad eum, et dicebant: Quia Joannes quidem signum fecit nullum.*

42. *But all things whatsoever John said of this man were true. And many believed in him.*

42. *Omnia autem quæcumque dixit Joannes de hoc, vera erant. Et multi crediderunt in eum.*

CHAPTER XI.

1 *Now there was a certain man sick named Lazarus, of Bethania, of the town of Mary and of Martha her sister.*

2 *(And Mary was she that anointed the Lord with ointment and wiped his feet with her hair: whose brother Lazarus was sick).*

3 *His sisters therefore sent to him, saying: Lord, behold, he whom thou lovest is sick.*

4 *And Jesus hearing it, said to them: This sickness is not unto death, but for the glory of God: that the Son of God may be glorified by it.*

5 *Now Jesus loved Martha, and her sister Mary, and Lazarus.*

6 *When he had heard therefore that he was sick, he still remained in the same place two days:*

7 *Then after that he said to his disciples: Let us go into Judea again.*

8 *The disciples say to him: Rabbi, the Jews but now sought to stone thee: and goest thou thither again?*

9 *Jesus answered: Are there not twelve hours of the day? If a man walk in the day, he stumbleth not, because he seeth the light of this world:*

10 *But if he walk in the night he stumbleth, because the light is not in him.*

11 *These things he said; and after that he said to them: Lazarus our friend sleepeth; but I go that I may awake him out of sleep.*

12 *His disciples therefore said: Lord, if he sleep, he shall do well.*

13 *But Jesus spoke of his death; and they thought that he spoke of the repose of sleep.*

14 *Then therefore Jesus said to them plainly: Lazarus is dead;*

15 *And I am glad for your sakes, that I was not there, that you may believe: but let us go to him.*

16 *Thomas therefore, who is called Didymus, said to his fellow-disciples: Let us also go, that we may die with him.*

17 *Jesus therefore came and found that he had been four days already in the grave.*

18 *(Now Bethania was near Jerusalem, about fifteen furlongs off.)*

19 *And many of the Jews were come to Martha and Mary, to comfort them concerning their brother.*

20 *Martha therefore, as soon as she heard that Jesus was come, went to meet him; but Mary sat at home.*

21 *Martha therefore said to Jesus: Lord, if thou hadst been here, my brother had not died.*

22 *But now also I know that whatsoever thou wilt ask of God, God will give it thee.*

23 *Jesus saith to her: Thy brother shall rise again.*

24 *Martha saith to him: I know that he shall rise again in the resurrection at the last day.*

25 *Jesus said to her: I am the resurrection and the life: he that believeth in me although he be dead, shall live ·*

26 *And every one that liveth, and believeth in me, shall not die for ever. Believest thou this?*

27 *She saith to him: Yea, Lord, I have believed that thou art Christ the Son of the living God, who art come into this world.*

28 *And when she had said these things, she went, and called her sister Mary secretly, saying: The master is come and calleth for thee.*

29 *She, as soon as she heard this, riseth quickly and cometh to him.*

30 *For Jesus was not yet come into the town: but he was still in that place where Martha had met him.*

31 *The Jews therefore, who were with her in the house and comforted her, when they saw Mary that she rose up speedily and went out, followed her, saying: She goeth to the grave, to weep there.*

32 *When Mary therefore was come where Jesus was, seeing him she fell down at his feet, and saith to him: Lord, if thou hadst been here, my brother had not died.*

33 *Jesus therefore, when he saw her weeping, and the Jews that were come with her, weeping, groaned in the spirit, and troubled himself,*

34 *And said: Where have you laid him? They say to him: Lord, come and see.*

35 *And Jesus wept.*

36 *The Jews therefore said: Behold how he loved him.*

37 *But some of them said: Could not he that opened the eyes of the man born blind, have caused that this man should not die?*

38 *Jesus therefore again groaning in himself, cometh to the sepulchre: now it was a cave; and a stone was laid over it.*

39 *Jesus saith: Take away the stone. Martha, the sister of him that was dead, saith to him: Lord, by this time he stinketh, for he is now of four days.*

40 *Jesus saith to her: Did not I say to thee, that if thou believe, thou shalt see the glory of God?*

41 *They took therefore the stone away: and Jesus lifting up his eyes said: Father, I give thee thanks that thou hast heard me.*

42 *And I knew that thou hearest me always, but because of the people who stand about have I said it; that they may believe that thou hast sent me.*

43 *When he had said these things, he cried with a loud voice: Lazarus, come forth.*

44 *And presently he that had been dead came forth, bound feet and hands with winding-bands, and his face was bound about with a napkin. Jesus said to them: Loose him and let him go.*

45 *Many therefore of the Jews who were come to Mary and Martha, and had seen the things that Jesus did, believed in him.*

46 *But some of them went to the Pharisees, and told them the things that Jesus had done.*

47 *The chief priests therefore and the Pharisees gathered a council, and said: What do we, for this man doth many miracles?*

48 *If we let him alone so, all will believe in him, and the Romans will come, and take away our place and nation.*

49 *But one of them named Caiphas, being the high-priest that year, said to them: You know nothing.*

50 *Neither do you consider that it is expedient for you that one man should die for the people, and that the whole nation perish not.*

51 *And this he spoke not of himself: but being the High-Priest of that year, he prophesied that Jesus should die for the nation.*

52 *And not only for the nation, but to gather together in one the children of God, that were dispersed.*

53 *From that day therefore they devised to put him to death.*

54 *Wherefore Jesus walked no more openly among the Jews, but he went into a country near the desert, unto a city that is called Ephrem, and there he abode with his disciples.*

55 *And the pasch of the Jews was at hand: and many from the country went up to Jerusalem before the pasch, to purify themselves.*

56 *They sought therefore for Jesus; and they discoursed one with another, standing in the temple: What think you, that he is not come to the festival day? And the chief priests and the Pharisees had given a commandment, that if any man knew where he was, he should tell, that they might apprehend him.*

CAPUT XI.

1 *Erat autem quidam languens Lazarus a Bethania, de castello Mariæ, et Marthæ sororis ejus.*

2 *(Maria autem erat, quæ unxit Dominum unguento, et extersit pedes ejus capillis suis: cujus frater Lazarus infirmabatur.)*

3 *Miserunt ergo sorores ejus ad eum dicentes: Domine, ecce quem amas infirmatur.*

4 *Audiens autem Jesus dixit eis: Infirmitas hæc non est ad mortem, sed pro gloria Dei, ut glorificetur Filius Dei per eam.*

5 *Diligebat autem Jesus Martham, et sororem ejus Mariam, et Lazarum.*

6 *Ut ergo audivit quia infirmabatur, tunc quidem mansit in eodem loco duobus diebus.*

7 *Deinde post hæc dixit discipulis suis: Eamus in Judæam iterum.*

8 *Dicunt ei discipuli: Rabbi, nunc quærebant te Judæi lapidare: et iterum vadis illuc?*

9 *Respondit Jesus: Nonne duodecim sunt horæ diei? Si quis ambulaverit in die, non offendit, quia lucem hujus mundi videt:*

10 *Si autem ambulaverit in nocte, offendit, quia lux non est in eo.*

11 *Hæc ait, et post hæc dixit eis: Lazarus amicus noster dormit: sed vado ut a somno excitem eum.*

12 *Dixerunt ergo discipuli ejus: Domine, si dormit, salvus erit.*

13 *Dixerat autem Jesus de morte ejus: illi autem putaverunt quia de dormitione somni diceret.*

14 *Tunc ergo Jesus dixit eis manifeste: Lazarus mortuus est:*

15 *Et gaudeo propter vos, ut credatis, quoniam non eram ibi. Sed eamus ad eum.*

16 *Dixit ergo Thomas, qui dicitur Didymus, ad condiscipulos: Eamus et nos, ut moriamur cum eo.*

17 *Venit itaque Jesus: et invenit eum quatuor dies jam in monumento habentem.*

18 *(Erat autem Bethania juxta Jerosolymam quasi stadiis quindecim.)*

19 *Multi autem ex Judæis venerant ad Martham, et Mariam, ut consolarentur eas de fratre suo.*

20 *Martha ergo ut audivit quia Jesus venit, occurrit illi : Maria autem domi sedebat.*

21 *Dixit ergo Martha ad Jesum : Domine, si fuisses hic, frater meus non fuisset mortuus :*

22 *Sed et nunc scio quia quæcumque poposceris a Deo, dabit tibi Deus.*

23 *Dicit illi Jesus : Resurget frater tuus.*

24 *Dicit ei Martha : Scio quia resurget in resurrectione in novissimo die.*

25 *Dixit ei Jesus : Ego sum resurrectio et vita : qui credit in me, etiam si mortuus fuerit, vivet :*

26 *Et omnis, qui vivit, et credit in me, non morietur in æternum. Credis hoc ?*

27 *Ait illi : Utique Domine, ego credidi, quia tu es Christus filius Dei vivi, qui in hunc mundum venisti.*

28 *Et cum hæc dixisset, abiit, et vocavit Mariam sororem suam silentio, dicens : Magister adest, et vocat te.*

29 *Illa ut audivit, surgit cito, et venit ad eum.*

30 *Nondum enim venerat Jesus in castellum : sed erat adhuc in illo loco, ubi occurrerat ei Martha.*

31 *Judæi ergo, qui erant cum ea in domo, et consolabantur eam, cum vidissent Mariam quia cito surrexit, et exiit, secuti sunt eam dicentes : Quia vadit ad monumentum, ut ploret ibi.*

32 *Maria ergo, cum venisset ubi erat Jesus, videns eum, cecidit ad pedes ejus, et dicit ei : Domine, si fuisses hic, non esset mortuus frater meus.*

33 *Jesus ergo, ut vidit eam plorantem, et Judæos, qui venerant cum ea, plorantes, infremuit spiritu, et turbavit seipsum,*

34 *Et Dixit : Ubi posuistis eum ? Dicunt ei : Domine, veni, et vide.*

35 *Et lacrymatus est Jesus.*

36 *Dixerunt ergo Judæi : Ecce quomodo amabat eum.*

37 *Quidam autem ex ipsis dixerunt : Non poterat hic, qui aperuit oculos cæci nati facere ut hic non moreretur ?*

38 *Jesus ergo rursum fremens in semetipso, venit ad monumentum. Erat autem spelunca : et lapis superpositus erat ei.*

39 *Ait Jesus : Tollite lapidem. Dicit ei Martha soror ejus, qui mortuus fuerat : Domine, jam fœtet, quatriduanus est enim.*

40 *Dicit ei Jesus : Nonne dixi tibi quoniam si credideris, videbis gloriam Dei ?*

41 *Tulerunt ergo lapidem : Jesus autem elevatis sursum oculis, dixit : Pater gratias ago tibi quoniam audisti me.*

42 *Ego autem sciebam quia semper me audis, sed propter populum, qui circumstat, dixi : ut credant quia tu me misisti.*

43 *Hæc cum dixisset, voce magna clamavit : Lazare, veni foras.*

44 *Et statim prodiit qui fuerat mortuus, ligatus pedes, et manus institis, et facies illius sudario erat ligata. Dixit eis Jesus : Solvite eum, et sinite abire.*

45 *Multi ergo ex Judæis, qui venerant ad Mariam, et Martham, et viderant quæ fecit Jesus, crediderunt in eum.*

46 *Quidam autem ex ipsis abierunt ad Pharisæos, et dixerunt eis quæ fecit Jesus.*

47 *Collegerunt ergo Pontifices et Pharisæi concilium, et dicebant : Quid facimus, quia hic homo multa signa facit ?*

48 *Si dimittimus eum sic, omnes credent in eum : et venient Romani, et tollent nostrum locum, et gentem.*

49 *Unus autem ex ipsis Caiphas nomine, cum esset Pontifex anni illius, dixit eis:
Vos nescitis quidquam,*

50 *Nec cogitatis quia expedit vobis ut unus moriatur homo pro populo, et non tota
gens pereat.*

51 *Hoc autem a semetipso non dixit: sed cum esset Pontifex anni illius, prophetavit,
quod Jesus moriturus erat pro gente,*

52 *Et non tantum pro gente, sed ut filios Dei, qui erant dispersi, congregaret in
unum,*

53 *Ab illo ergo die cogitaverunt ut interficerent eum.*

54 *Jesus ergo jam non in palam ambulabat apud Judæos, sed abiit in regionem juxta
desertum, in civitatem, quæ dicitur Ephrem, et ibi morabatur cum discipulis suis.*

55 *Proximum autem erat Pascha Judæorum: et ascenderunt multi Jerosolymam de
regione ante Pascha, ut sanctificarent seipsos.*

56 *Quærebant ergo Jesum: et colloquebantur ad invicem, in templo stantes: Quid
putatis, quia non venit ad diem festum? Dederant autem Pontifices, et Pharisæi
mandatum, ut si quis cognoverit ubi sit, indicet, ut apprehendant eum.*

ANALYSIS.

In this chapter, we have an account of the message despatched by the sisters of
Lazarus to inform our Lord of the sickness of their brother—our Lord's observations
thereon (1–11).

His journey into Judea, in order to resuscitate Lazarus from the sleep of death,
though dissuaded from going by His disciples (11–16).

His consoling words addressed to Martha, who at once proceeded to meet Him
at the grave, on hearing of His arrival. His exposition of the doctrine of the
General Resurrection (17–28). The meeting of Mary with our Lord, after she had
been secretly informed by her sister of His arrival (29–34). The miraculous
resuscitation of Lazarus, and the circumstances connected with it (34–45). The
jealous, envious feelings which the account of this miracle created in the Jewish
Rulers, who, in accordance with the counsel given them by Caiphas, the High Priest,
conspire to put Him to death (46–58).

Text.

1. *Now there was a certain man sick named Lazarus, of Bethania, of the town of Mary and of Martha her sister.*

1. *Erat autem quidam languens Lazarus a Bethania, de castello Mariæ, et Marthæ sororis ejus.*

Commentary.

1. It is supposed generally that an interval of about three
months elapsed between this and the occurrences recorded in the last
chapter, at the Feast of the Renovation. These took place about
the middle of December—and those mentioned in this chapter,
took place about the middle of March, at the near approach of the
Pasch, when our Lord was put to death.

"*Now there was a certain man sick named Lazarus,*" etc. He
was supposed to be in good circumstances, quite different from
the Lazarus mentioned in connexion with the rich glutton. (Luke
xvi.) "*Of Bethania, of the town of Mary and Martha, her
sister.*" These latter words are put in apposition to the former,
meaning, "*Bethania,*" that is to say, the town or village in which
Martha and Mary lived, just as Bethsaida is called, "*the town of
Peter and Andrew*" (i. 41), not that they were owners of it, but
only lived there. This Bethania was about two miles from
Jerusalem, to the east of Mount Olivet. The Evangelist narrates

Commentary.

every thing in detail, connected with the great miracle, which He is about to describe.

2. The more probable opinion, though warmly disputed (see *Corlui, in hunc locum*) is, that Mary Magdalen (Luke viii. 2 ; Matthew xxviii. 5, 6, and 7), the Mary referred to here, the sister of Lazarus, as also in Luke x. 38; John xii. 3–8, and the sinful woman, Luke vii. 36–50, are one and the same person (see Matthew xxvi. 7, Commentary on).

3. The sisters of Lazarus respectfully hint, or rather modestly request, that our Lord would cure their sick brother. This expresses their great faith in our Lord, their confidence and love. Their *faith*, shown in their belief that our Lord, though absent, could cure him. Their *hope*, in the expectation that, on receiving the message, He would restore him. Their *charity*—"*behold whom Thou lovest*," etc., which implied reciprocal great love on their part. They say, "*whom Thou lovest*," etc., not Lazarus; not our brother, to excite our Lord's tender compassion and pity, the more effectually, to move Him to cure their brother.

4. "*Said to them*," viz., the sisters, through the messenger, "*not unto death*," will not terminate in death, but has for object, the glory of God ; or, is not meant to end in the death which, as you apprehend, will close his mortal life; since, he was to be soon again resuscitated.

"*But for the glory of God.*" To promote and manifest God's glory ; when men seeing the miracle, would believe in our Lord, as Son of God, and thus glorify the Father and the Son. This is explained in the following words, "*that the Son of God may be glorified by it.*" The glory of the Father and of the Son is the same. The death and resuscitation of Lazarus was meant for a signal display of the glory of God, by proving the Divine mission of His Son.

5. He loved them with an *eternal* love, as God ; with a *human* love, as good, virtuous people, and also on account of their singular love, devotion and liberality, in hospitably entertaining Himself and His disciples, on several occasions.

6. He did not wish to go to Bethania till Lazarus would be some time dead, and no cavilling questions raised about the reality of his death, and the subsequent miracle of his resuscitation. It is likely, that Lazarus died soon after the messengers left our Lord, on their return home. The circumstance of our Lord's

Text.

2. (*And Mary was she that anointed the Lord with ointment and wiped his feet with her hair, whose brother Lazarus was sick.*)

2. (*Maria autem erat, quæ unxit Dominum unguento, et extersit pedes ejus capillis suis: cujus frater Lazarus infirmabatur.*)

3. *His sisters therefore sent to him saying : Lord, behold, he whom thou lovest is sick.*

3. *Miserunt ergo sorores ejus ad eum dicentes : Domine, ecce quem amas infirmatur.*

4. *And Jesus hearing it, said to them : This sickness is not unto death, but for the glory of God : that the Son of God may be glorified by it.*

4. *Audiens autem Jesus dixit eis : Infirmitas hæc non est ad mortem, sed pro gloria Dei, ut glorificetur Filius Dei per eam.*

5. *Now Jesus loved Martha, and her sister Mary, and Lazarus.*

5. *Diligebat autem Jesus Martham, et sororem ejus Mariam, et Lazarum.*

6. *When he had heard therefore that he was sick he still remained in the same place two days :*

Text.	Commentary.
6. *Ut ergo audivit quia infirmabatur, tunc quidem mansit in eodem loco duobus diebus.*	remaining two days at Bethabara, thirty miles from Bethania, where this disconsolate family lived, whom He knew to be plunged in the deepest sorrow, would seem to indicate, that He meant to compensate for this apparent indifference in remaining so long away, by raising him, as He did, from the grave.
7. *Then after that he said to his disciples: Let us go into Judea again.* 7. *Deinde post hæc dixit discipulis suis: Eamus in Judæam iterum.*	7. "*Then after that.*" After the lapse of two days, from the departure of the messengers. Up to that, He said nothing of His intended journey, or of the death of Lazarus. "*Let us go into Judea*"—the portion occupied by the Tribes of Juda and Benjamin—"*again.*" They had left it not long before when the Jews meant to stone Him (x. 31–39). He knew the disciples had no wish to return to Judea, from a sense of danger. He now prepares them for it by this announcement of His intention.
8. *The disciples say to him: Rabbi, the Jews but now sought to stone thee; and goest thou thither again?* 8. *Dicunt ei discipuli: Rabbi, nunc quærebant te Judæi lapidare, et iterum vadis illuc?*	8. His disciples, who were ignorant of His design to die, wish to dissuade Him from encountering certain death. They knew not His designs of Redemption, which was now on the eve of accomplishment.
9. *Jesus answered: Are there not twelve hours of the day? If a man walk in the day, he stumbleth not, because he seeth the light of the world:* 9. *Respondit Jesus: Nonne duodecim sunt horæ diei? Si quis ambulaverit in die, non offendit, quia lucem hujus mundi videt:* 10. *But if he walk in the night he stumbleth, because the light is not in him.* 10. *Si autem ambulaverit in nocte, offendit, quia lux non est in eo.*	9, 10. Since the return from the Babylonish captivity, the Jews divided their days from sunrise to sunset into twelve parts, which were longer or shorter, according to the season of the year. This was the division in use among the Romans, to whom the Jews were now subject. Our Lord means to employ an allegory wherein the twelve hours of the *day* denote the period of human life; the *night*, death. He, therefore, means to convey, that as a man walking in day-time, is sure to avoid all obstacles, against which he might impinge, and thus stumble, because he has the light of the day to guide him; so, as there is a certain time marked out for Him in the decrees of His heavenly Father to continue in life, they need not fear any danger till "*His hour is come,*" and the time has expired. Now that time will expire then only, when He shall voluntarily hand Himself over to His cruel executioners. Hence, they need be under no apprehension in accompanying Him now into Judea.
11. *These things he said; and after that he said to them: Lazarus our friend sleepeth: but I go that I may awake him out of sleep.* 11. *Hæc ait, et post hæc dixit eis: Lazarus amicus noster dormit: sed vado ut a somno excitem eum.*	11. After having strengthened them against indulging in fear, He announces the death of Lazarus. "*Sleepeth.*" Death is but a kind of sleep. The SS. Scriptures often term it such, in view of the future general Resurrection. "*Awake him.*" He thus modestly refers to the exercise of His Almighty power, soon to be displayed in the resuscitation of Lazarus.

Commentary.

12, 13. If he only sleeps, he is sure of recovery. Let us allow him to sleep. It would seem that by the observation, "*he shall do well*," they meant to dissuade our Lord from undertaking an unnecessary journey.

13. But Jesus spoke of his death; and they thought that he spoke of the repose of sleep.
13. *Dixerat autem Jesus de morte ejus: illi autem putaverunt quia de dormitione somni diceret.*

14. The messenger only spoke of Lazarus's illness. Our Lord showed His Divine insight into secret, hidden events, by saying, "*plainly*," literally, without any figure, "*Lazarus is dead*."

15. "*I am glad . . . not there*," because, if there at the time of Lazarus's death, He would have been moved by the tears and entreaties of his sisters to ward off death, or to raise him up at once. Neither course would so strongly contribute to the faith of His Apostles, as did what took place in his resuscitation, after he was in the grave for some time. "*That you may believe*," that is, be more and more confirmed in your faith.

16. "*Thomas, called Didymus.*" The word, "*Thomas*," translated into Greek, means, "*Didymus*," or *twin*, just as *Cephas*, in Greek, means, *Petros* or *rock*.
"*Let us go and die*," etc. He did not seem to understand our Saviour's words (verses 9 and 10). Hence, fancying our Lord meant to go to death, he intrepidly encourages his fellow Apostles to share in his fate.

17. "*Four days already in the grave.*" Commentators explain it thus: most likely, Lazarus died on the day the messenger was despatched to our Lord, and was buried the following day. Our Lord set out from Bethabara the *third* day after Lazarus's death, and the *second* of his burial. The distance was rather long; and our Lord, on the *third* day of Lazarus's burial, travelled leisurely, delivering instructions as He went along. Most likely, He remained for the night at some midway place. The following or *fourth* day He arrived near Bethany about mid-day. It would not be congruous, that the miracle, with all its circumstances, should occur at any other time save the day-time.

18. Bethany was about two miles distant from Jerusalem.

18. (*Erat autem Bethania juxta Jerosolymam quasi stadiis quindecim.*)

Text.

12. *His disciples therefore said: Lord, if he sleep, he shall do well.*
12. *Dixerunt ergo discipuli ejus: Domine, si dormit, salvus erit.*

14. *Then therefore Jesus said to them plainly: Lazarus is dead;*
14. *Tunc ergo Jesus: dixit eis manifeste: Lazarus mortuus est,*

15. *And I am glad for your sakes, that I was not there, that you may believe; but let us go to him.*
15. *Et gaudeo propter vos, ut credatis, quoniam non eram ibi. sed eamus ad eum.*

16. *Thomas therefore, who is called Didymus, said to his fellow-disciples: Let us also go, that we may die with him.*
16. *Dixit ergo Thomas qui dicitur Didymus, ad condiscipulos: Eamus et nos, ut moriamur cum eo.*

17. *Jesus therefore came and found that he had been four days already in the grave.*
17. *Venit itaque Jesus: et invenit eum quatuor dies jam in monumento habentem.*

18. (*Now Bethania was near Jerusalem about fifteen furlongs off.*)

Text.

19. *And many of the Jews were come to Martha and Mary, to comfort them concerning their brother.*

19. *Multi autem ex Judeis venerant ad Martham, et Mariam, ut consolarentur eas de fratre suo*

20. *Martha therefore, as soon as she heard that Jesus was come, went to meet him ; but Mary sat at home.*

20. *Martha ergo ut audivit quia Jesus venit, occurrit illi : Maria autem domi sedebat.*

21. *Martha therefore said to Jesus: Lord, if thou hadst been here, my brother had not died.*

21. *Dixit ergo Martha ad Jesum : Domine, si fuisses hic, frater meus non fuisset mortuus :*

22. *But now also I know that whatsoever thou wilt ask of God, God will give it thee.*

22. *Sed et nunc scio quia quæcumque poposceris a Deo, dabit tibi Deus.*

23. *Jesus saith to her: Thy brother shall rise again.*

23. *Dicit illi Jesus: Resurget frater tuus.*

Commentary.

19. The family of Lazarus likely occupied a respectable position, and had many friends in the neighbouring city ; probably, men of eminence and learning. They came out to condole with the sisters of the deceased. The testimony of these, some of them, no doubt, hostile to our Lord, would have great weight in regard to the stupendous miracle of which they were witnesses.

20. It is clear our Lord did not, at this time, reach the house of Martha ; but only came to the place of the sepulchre, which was outside the town or village, according to the custom of the Jews. "*Martha,*" to whom, as mistress of the house (Luke x. 38), the tidings of our Lord's arrival was communicated, on hearing of His approach went out at once—without waiting to intimate it to her sister—to meet our Lord, sure to receive greater and more practical consolation than she could expect from any of the sympathizing Jews.

"*But Mary sat at home,*" receiving the expression of condolence from those who came to sympathize with them. Likely, too, she had not at once heard of our Lord's arrival (*v.* 28), and Martha, in her hurry, did not tell her at the time. Moreover, had she left, all the Jews in the house would have followed ; and confusion at their meeting our Lord, to whom some of them were hostile, might ensue.

21, 22. Martha's faith in our Lord's power was somewhat imperfect, since He could as easily operate when absent, as when present. And although she believed Him to be "*the Christ, the Son of the living God*" (*v.* 27) ; still, it is likely she did not clearly apprehend His identity of nature and power with the Father; since, she regards His power as dependent on the Father, who would surely grant all His petitions. She does not say, *if Thou wilt, Thou canst raise my brother*. It may be, she tacitly expects He would, in virtue of His acceptance with His Father, raise her brother again, relying on the message received from Him (*v.* 4). He had already cured men on the point of death. Hence, she says, if present, He would have cured her brother. It is hardly likely, that she hoped, He would perform the stupendous miracle of raising the dead to life. The words of this verse, clearly denote that she expected our Lord would obtain any thing from God necessary to console them in their affliction. Possibly, even to the extent of raising up her brother, though, it does not seem clear that she expected this (*vv.* 24–39).

23, 24. "*Thy brother shall rise again.*" Our Lord, while referring to the near resurrection of Lazarus, uses ambiguous language, which would apply to the General Resurrection, as Martha understood it, possibly in order to prepare her for the miracle He was

Commentary.

about to perform, and to elicit from her the act of faith she expressed in reply to His question, arising out of this subject (*v.* 27). Martha heard our Lord often treating of the General Resurrection of all men; and now she hears Him in language harmonizing with His former teaching, proclaim the same doctrine, but, in her words, would seem to be implied, the latent or suppressed complaint, viz.: what particular consolation does this bring us now in our excessive grief? What particular or special favour is now conferred on us?

25. Our Lord then said to her, "*I am the Resurrection*," etc. I am the *cause*, the *power* by which all men are raised from the dead, raising up and giving life to whom I will—"*the life*," the source of life eternal to all the good who deserve it. For, as regards the life to which the reprobate are restored, this is but a living death, a perpetuation of everlasting torture. Better for them, they were never born ("*Melius illi fuisset si natus non esset iste homo*"—Matthew xxvi. 24), never raised to life. By saying, He is "*the Resurrection and the life*," our Lord wishes to convey, that every one who is resuscitated, is raised by Him and Him alone; that every one, who lives, lives by Him alone. Hence, it would be just as easy for Him now to raise up Lazarus, as it will be to raise up all men, at the General Resurrection.

"*He that believeth in Me*," etc. In this, He points out the means of securing a happy Resurrection and everlasting glory. This means is faith. He that hath faith in Him, with the other dispositions, during life, "*although now dead*—in the body"—"*shall live*," shall be raised to a life of everlasting glory, both in regard to soul and body.

26. "*And every one that liveth*," etc.—now living in the body —"*and believeth in Me*," although his body may soon return to earth, still, "*he shall not die for ever.*" The bodies and souls of men, like him who believes, shall, after a time, be restored to a life of glorious immortality. Our Lord wishes to convey a proof, not only of His Omnipotent Power in restoring to life all who die; but, a still greater manifestation of His Power and boundless beneficence as well, in bestowing on them everlasting happiness. Hence, as Martha's brother, though now dead, believed, and had faith in our Lord, she should not be disturbed at what has taken place, she should expect for him a glorious immortality; nay, perhaps, a near resurrection.

"*Believest thou this?*" That is to say, My assertion regarding Myself, as the source of Resurrection and life?

27. Martha, not fully understanding what our Lord wished her to believe and profess, makes an act of faith which fully contained all she was asked. She professes to have believed Him to be the

Text.

24. *Martha saith to him: I know that he shall rise again in the resurrection at the last day.*

24. *Dicit ei Martha: Scio quia resurget in resurrectione in novissimo die.*

25. *Jesus said to her; I am the resurrection and the life; he that believeth in me although he be dead, shall live.*

25. *Dixit ei Jesus: Ego sum resurrectio et vita: qui credit in me, etiam si mortuus fuerit vivet.*

26. *And every one that liveth, and believeth in me, shall not die for ever. Believest thou this?*

26. *Et omnis, qui vivit, et credit in me, non morietur in aeternum. Credis hoc?*

27. *She saith to him: Yea, Lord, I have believed that thou art Christ the Son of the*

P

Text.	Commentary.
living God, who art come into this world.	natural, genuine Son of God, God Himself; and that, therefore, every thing He taught was true, and that He was, therefore, as He asserted, "*the Resurrection and the life.*"
27. Ait illi: Utique Domine, ego credidi, quia tu es Christus filius Dei vivi, qui in hunc mundum venisti?	"*I have believed,*" heretofore, and my faith still continues the same, "*that Thou art the Christ,*" the promised Messiah, nay, more, "*the Son of the living God,*" the true, genuine, natural Son of God, "*who art come,*" or as the Greek has it, "*who was to come,*" long before predicted and expected, "*into this world,*" to enlighten and save the entire human race, Jew and Gentile alike.

Some Commentators, think that Martha did not believe as St. Peter did (Matthew xvi.), though the form of words is similar. While expressing her belief in Him as the Son of God, she did not distinguish whether He was the natural or adopted Son of God. (St. Chrysostom, etc.) They in proof of this refer to Martha's words (*v.* 22).

| 28. *And when she had said these things, she went, and called her sister Mary secretly, saying: The master is come and calleth for thee.* | 28. "*She went,*" evidently at our Lord's instance. "*The Master is come, and calleth thee.*" But for brevity sake, it is omitted here by the Evangelist, that our Lord suggested this to Martha, "*secretly,*" to escape being noticed by the Jews, who were with her. |

28. *Et cum hæc dixisset abiit, et vocavit Mariam sororem suam silentio, dicens: Magister adest, et vocat te.*

| 29. *She, as soon as she heard this, riseth quickly and cometh to him.* 29. *Illa ut audivit, surgit cito et venit ad eum.* | 29, 30. Our Lord remained outside the village near the tomb, which, according to Jewish custom, was outside the town or village. He did not wish to go to the house of Mary, in the first instance, as He should return again to perform the miracle at the grave. |

30. *For Jesus was not yet come into the town: but he was still in that place where Martha had met him.*
30. *Nondum enim venerat Jesus in castellum: sed erat adhuc in illo loco, ubi occurrerat ei Martha.*

| 31. *The Jews therefore, who were with her in the house and comforted her, when they saw Mary that she rose up speedily and went out, followed her, saying: She goeth to the grave, to weep there.* | 31. "*When they saw that she rose up speedily,*" as Martha had whispered into her ear the tidings of our Lord's arrival, "*followed her.*" It was thus providentially arranged, that they should witness the miracle. |

31. *Judæi ergo, qui erant cum ea in domo, et consolabantur eam, cum vidissent Mariam quia cito surrexit, et exiit, secuti sunt eam dicentes; Quia vadit ad monumentum, ut ploret ibi.*

| 32. *When Mary therefore was come where Jesus was, seeing him, she fell down at his feet, and saith to him: Lord, if thou hadst been here, my brother had not died.* | 32. "*Fell down at His feet,*" in testimony of her great reverence and gratitude for His having rescued her from her passions and sins. This she did, regardless of the presence of the Jews, who entertained hostile feelings against our Lord. |

32. *Maria ergo, cum venisset ubi erat Jesus, videns eum, cecidit ad pedes ejus, et dicit ei: Domine, si fuisses hic, non esset mortuus frater meus.*

Commentary.

33. "*Groaned in spirit and troubled Himself.*" There is a great diversity of opinion regarding the meaning of these words, owing to the peculiar signification of the Greek *word* (ενεβριμησατο), which generally means, *to be indignant*. However, this word, rigorously speaking, denotes the *commotion* or excitement of any of the violent passions, anger, sorrow, etc. Looking to the context, the circumstances of the people weeping around Him, it, most likely, denotes the commotion of tenderness and sympathetic sorrow caused by our Lord's seeing the tears and affliction of those present, and especially of His dear friends, who were plunged in sorrow; and by His own free will, which always kept in check all His passions, He excited Himself to feelings of tenderness and humanity, which manifested themselves afterwards in tears. Some who understand, "*groaned in spirit*," to mean *indignation*, say, He was indignant at the hypocritical expression of sorrow on the part of the Jews, mingling with the sincere lamentation of Mary. He always showed His horror of hypocrisy.

34. "*Where have you laid him?*" He spoke thus, as if He were acting in a human way. For, He knew it Himself. He wishes to excite their attention to the great miracle about to be performed.

"*Lord, come and see.*" They went before Him to point out the precise spot.

35. "*Jesus wept,*" in sympathy with His friends, to show His true humanity and sympathetic feelings of tenderness. He conformed to the admonition, "*lugere cum lugentibus*" (Rom. xii. 15). As He meant to display His Divinity in the miracle He was about performing; so, He here manifests His humanity in sentiments of tenderness and compassion, proving He had not a hard, unfeeling heart.

Only on *three* occasions have we any record of our Lord's weeping. 1. Here. 2. When weeping over Jerusalem (Luke xix. 41). 3. On the cross (Heb. v., "*Cum clamore magno et lacrymis*"). No doubt, in each case, there were strong mystical reasons. Most likely, He wept over the dreadful evil of sin, the havoc it wrought, and over the ingratitude of man.

36. Some of the Jews, who were well affected towards our Lord, said, "*Behold*," etc. Tears, in a grown man, are a great sign of sorrow. These Jews admired our Lord's fast friendship and humanity.

37. But others, who were unfriendly and unfavourably disposed, attributed it to weakness. If He had the power of warding off death from this man, and did not do it, why now weep over what

Text.

33. *Jesus therefore, when he saw her weeping, and the Jews that were come with her, weeping, groaned in the spirit, and troubled himself.*

33. *Jesus ergo, ut vidit eam plorantem, et Judæos, qui venerant cum ea, plorantes infremuit spiritu, et turbavit seipsum.*

34. *And said: Where have you laid him? They say to him: Lord, come and see.*

34. *Et dixit: Ubi posuistis eum? Dicunt ei: Domine, veni, et vide.*

35. *And Jesus wept.*

35. *Et lacrymatus est Jesus.*

36. *The Jews therefore said: Behold how he loved him.*

36. *Dixerunt ergo Judæi: Ecce quomodo amabat eum.*

37. *But some of them said: Could not he, that opened the eyes of the man born*

Text.

blind, have caused that this man should not die?

37. *Quidam autem ex ipsis dixerunt: Non poterat, hic, qui aperuit oculos cæci nati, facere ut hic non moreretur?*

38. *Jesus therefore again groaning in himself, cometh to the sepulchre: Now it was a cave; and a stone was laid over it.*

38. *Jesus ergo rursum fremens in semetipso, venit ad monumentum, erat autem spelunca: et lapis superpositus erat ei.*

39. *Jesus saith: Take away the stone. Martha the sister of him that was dead, saith to him: Lord, by this time he stinketh, for he is now of four days.*

39. *Ait Jesus: Tollite lapidem. Dicit ei Martha soror ejus, qui mortuus fuerat: Domine, jam fœtet, quatriduanus est enim.*

40. *Jesus saith to her; Did not I say to thee, that if thou believe, thou shalt see the glory of God?*

40. *Dicit ei Jesus: Nonne dixi tibi quoniam si credideris, videbis gloriam Dei.*

41. *They took therefore the stone away: and Jesus lifting up his eyes said: Father, I give thee thanks that thou hast heard me.*

41. *Tulerunt ergo lapidem: Jesus autem elevatis sursum oculis, dixit: Pater gratias ago tibi quoniam audisti me.*

Commentary.

He could have prevented? They sneeringly ask, "*Could not He that opened the eyes,*" a more difficult thing, do what was easier, viz., cure this infirm man and ward off death? All admit the death of Lazarus. All admit the cure of the blind man. Yet still they refer to it, out of malice, in a sneering, sarcastic manner.

38. "*Groaning in Himself.*" The near approach to the grave excited His sensibility and compassionate tenderness.

"*It was a cave,*" sunk into the earth, "*a stone laid over it,*" unlike the grave of our Lord, which was over ground, and "*a stone rolled to the mouth of the sepulchre.*"

39. "*Take away the stone.*" He might, if He pleased, have removed it by the sole act of His will, and have raised up Lazarus without removing it. But, He preferred calling on them to remove it, to leave no possibility of doubt regarding the identity and death of Lazarus. Martha imagined our Lord only wished to see the remains. It would seem she did not anticipate or expect that He could raise him up in this state of decomposition. Hence, the reproach addressed by our Lord to her in the following verse. All these circumstances detailed by the Evangelist take away all grounds for suspecting imposture.

40. "*Did I not say to thee?*" It is disputed at what time He said this. Some say, through the messenger (*v.* 4). "*His sickness is not unto death, but for the glory of God, that the Son of God,*" etc. Others refer it to verse 25. "*Thou shalt see the glory of God,*" which shall be manifested in the great miracle of the resuscitation of Lazarus. This shall promote My glory, by showing the power I possess, and the proof it gives of My Divine mission. He confirms the faith of Martha, which would seem, at this critical point, to be somewhat *wavering* (*v.* 41).

41. The removal of the stone left no doubt of the identity and death of Lazarus, his remains approaching a state of decomposition.

"*Lifting up His eyes,*" to heaven, to His Eternal Father, thus showing whence the power of performing the great miracle emanated—and referring all to Him, said: "*Father, I give Thee thanks, that Thou hast heard Me,*" in regard to the resuscitation of Lazarus. It may be, too, that whilst He groaned in spirit, He prayed to His Father—the Evangelist makes no special mention of any expressed prayer—or, He may have simply wished it in His heart, and His Father attended to this desire, "*desiderium animæ ejus tribuisti ei*" (Psa. ix. 1). Our Lord teaches us how to com-

Commentary

mence our petitions to God. It is, by thanking Him for past favours, so as to render Him propitious and bountiful in granting those we now ask.

42. It was not on My own account, I thanked Thee, for hearing Me. This is not new to Me. For, "*I knew that Thou always hearest Me;*" "*but, because of the people who stand about have I said it,*" that is, have I said the words. "*I give Thee thanks*"—uttering them aloud—"*that they may believe that Thou hast sent Me,*" on beholding the miracle, I am now about to perform by Thy Divine power, in proof of My mission from Thee to earth.

43. "*With a loud voice,*" to render those present more attentive, and to demonstrate His own great power and authority, whereby this miracle was accomplished; and some add, to show that He summoned the soul of Lazarus from afar, from Limbo, where it reposed in the bosom of Abraham; or, it may be, that he spoke in a loud voice, as to a dead man, just as we speak in a loud voice to the deaf. Theophylact observes, that this loud voice of our Redeemer was a symbol of the loud trumpet of the Archangel, which is to sound at the General Resurrection.

"*Lazarus, come forth.*" He mentions him by name, lest it might be supposed that any of the others who might have been laid in the tomb, answered the Divine call and command. "*Lazarus,*" the person of Lazarus, soul and body, "*come forth,*" from the tomb. This implied his resurrection, the union of soul and body, effected by our Lord's power. For, He invokes no other power to assist Him. He does it all by His own sole command and authority. "*Come forth,*" and show yourself, resuscitated by My power, to all here present.

44. "*And presently,*" without any delay, the power of our Lord producing an instantaneous effect.

"*He that was dead,*" Lazarus, who in person, was summoned by the voice of God, burst forth at once from the embrace of death.

"*Bound hand and feet with winding bands,*" according to the custom of the Jews, in burying their dead. "*And his face was bound about with a napkin,*" quite common among the Jews in preparing their dead for burial.

"*Loose him and let him go.*" Instead of freeing him at once Himself, our Lord calls on them to perform these offices, to leave no room for doubt as to his identity, death and resuscitation.

Text

42. *And I knew that thou hearest me always, but because of the people who stand about have I said it; that they may believe that thou has sent me.*

42. *Ego autem sciebam quia semper me audis, sed propter populum, qui circumstat, dixi: ut credant quia tu me misisti.*

43. *When he had said these things, he cried with a loud voice: Lazarus come forth.*

43. *Hæc cum dixisset, voce magna clamavit: Lazare veni foras,*

44. *And presently he that had been dead came forth, bound feet and hands with winding-bands, and his face was bound about with a napkin. Jesus said to them: Loose him and let him go.*

44. *Et statim prodiit qui fuerat mortuus, ligatus pedes, et manus institis, et facies illius sudario erat ligata. Dixit eis Jesus: Solvite eum, et sinite abire.*

Text.

45. *Many therefore of the Jews who were come to Mary and Martha, and had seen the things that Jesus did, believed in him.*

45. *Multi ergo ex Judæis, qui venerant ad Mariam, et Martham, et viderant quæ fecit Jesus, crediderunt in eum;*

46. *But some of them went to the Pharisees, and told them the things that Jesus had done.*

46. *Quidam autem ex ipsis abierunt ad Pharisæos, et dixerunt eis quæ fecit Jesus.*

47. *The chief priests therefore and the Pharisees gathered a council, and said; What do we, for this man doth many miracles?*

47. *Collegerunt ergo Pontifices et Pharisæi concilium, et dicebant: Quid facimus, quia hic homo multa signa facit?*

48. *If we let him alone so, all will believe in him and the Romans will come, and take away our place and nation.*

48. *Si dimittimus eum sic, omnes credent in eum et venient Romani, et tollent nostrum locum, et gentem.*

Commentary.

45. "*Believed in Him.*" On seeing the proof they just saw of His Divinity. They were aided by Divine grace.

46. Others, blindly closing their eyes against the light, became still more obstinate; and, going maliciously, reported the whole occurrence to the Pharisees, with a view of injuring our Lord, by exciting still greater feelings of envy. These are contrasted with such as believed (*v.* 45). They are supposed to be the men referred to in *v.* 37, as speaking sneeringly and scornfully of the miracle performed on the blind man. Hence, the opinion of those who credit them with good motives, in reporting the matter to the Pharisees, is exceedingly improbable.

47. "*The Chief Priests, therefore, and the Pharisees gathered a Council.*" The right to assemble a Council of the Sanhedrim or 72, was vested exclusively in the High Priest. But, the Pharisees are said to convene it; because, it was at their instigation, to whom the matter was reported (*v.* 46), the High Priest convened it. "*The Chief Priests,*" were Caiphas and Annas. For explanation of this, as only one High Priest could officiate or minister, and the office of High Priest was for life; see Luke (c. iii. 2, Commentary on).

"*What do we?*"—an expression of self-reproach—in thus indolently folding our arms, and permitting "*this man*"—they would not deign to mention His name—Who "*doth many miracles,*" to seduce our people, and withdraw them from the allegiance they owe their legitimate spiritual rulers?

They cannot deny the miracles of our Lord. "*He doth many miracles?*"—the evidences of which were placed beyond all possibility of being successfully gainsayed.

48. "*If we let Him alone so,*" allow Him to go on working miracles, "*all will believe in Him.*" The entire population will regard Him as the promised Messiah, who, according to their prevailing false and erroneous notions, was destined to free Israel from the yoke of the Gentiles. Seditions will be the consequence of such notions on the part of our people, who will raise Him up as king, in opposition to the ruling civil powers. To quell such commotions, and popular risings, "*the Romans,*" who now rule us, and can tolerate no one to be king except one of their own appointment, will regard us as rebelling against Cæsar, in favour of our Messiah, and they "*will come and take away,*" destroy "*our place,*" our holy place, our temple, "*and nation,*" lay

Commentary.

waste our entire nation, possibly transferring us elsewhere, as did the Babylonians of old. They hypocritically put forward the public safety and the necessity of securing the interest of their nation, as their pretext for opposing and doing away with our Lord; while, in reality, envy and jealousy were the chief motives that influenced them.

49. Most probably, as is implied in the words, "*you know nothing*," there was a diversity of opinion among the members of the Sanhedrim, as to the wisdom or justice of either preventing our Lord from working miracles or compassing His death. Likely, some, as Nicodemus and other such, were in favour of our Lord. Hence, Caiphas, "*the High Priest of that year*," addressing them in his official capacity. (It is this the Evangelist seems to convey; for, he speaks of him afterwards, as imbued with a prophetic spirit.)

"*Said to them*," superciliously charging them with ignorance and inconsiderateness, and with being bereft of all power of reasoning, "*you know nothing.*" In your private capacity, you understand nothing about the case under discussion.

50. "*Neither do you consider*" what I, who am High Priest, in my official capacity, specially enlightened by God, now solemnly decree and promulgate, "*that it is expedient*," profitable, advantageous, "*for you*"—The Greek has "*for us*," for you and for me, for us all,—that "*one man should die for the people*," irrrespective of whether he is guilty or innocent, whether he deserves death or not, —"*and that the whole nation perish not*"—rather than that the entire nation should perish. As if He said, in other words, it is a lesser evil to put one man to death, although innocent, than that the entire nation should perish. Therefore, we should embrace the alternative of doing away with this man.

The words of Caiphas has a two-fold meaning, one, his declaration that Jesus should be put to death; the other, contained under it, emanating from the Holy Gost. The former, Caiphas, understood and meant; the latter, he did not.

51. "*This he spoke not of himself,*" so far as the wicked mind of Caiphas was concerned, in impiously and unjustly recommending the murder of an innocent man—and although he did not mention His name, he clearly referred to our Lord—Caiphas spoke from himself, and meant what he said. But so far as his utterance contained a hidden truth, he was ignorant of the hidden and mysterious meaning of the words he uttered. Under his words was contained a great and important truth. The Holy Ghost arranged his words, so wonderfully, and their form of utterance, that without knowing it, He predicted what was true, viz., that

Text.

49. *But one of them named Caiphas, being the high-priest of that year, said to them; You know nothing.*

49. *Unus autem ex ipsis Caiphas nomine, cum esset Pontifex anni illius, dixit eis: vos nescitis quidquam.*

50. *Neither do you consider that it is expedient for you that one man should die for the people, and that the whole nation perish not.*

50. *Nec cogitatis quia expedit vobis ut unus moriatur homo pro populo, et non tota gens pereat.*

51. *And this he spoke not of himself: but being the high-priest of that year, he prophesied that Jesus should die for the nation.*

51. *Hoc autem a semetipso non dixit: sed cum esset Pontifex anni illius, prophetavit, quod Jesus moriturus erat pro gente.*

Text.	Commentary.

it was expedient, nay, useful and necessary, that Jesus should die, and be offered up as a victim of propitiation, to make atonement for the sins of the entire nation, and save them from eternal ruin. "*He prophesied.*" God made use of him, as he before made use of other wicked men, to prophesy or predict a future event, which would certainly come to pass (*v.g.*), Nabuchodonosor, Pharaoh, Balaam, etc. This would not constitute him a Prophet, nor is he said to be inspired. But, to show the respect due to the office of High Priest, which he filled, God singled him out, on account of his office, though personally wicked and impious, as the instrument of uttering a most important truth, which was surely to take place, viz., that, in the designs of God, Jesus was to die for the salvation of the entire Jewish *nation*.

52. *And not only for the nation, but to gather together in one the children of God that were dispersed.*

52. *Et non tantum pro gente, sed ut filios Dei, qui erant dispersi congregaret in unum.*

52. "*And not only for the nation*," but for the entire human race; so that He would "*gather together in one the children of God*," those whom He had determined to call to His Church out of the entire Gentile world, dispersed over the face of the globe. This observation is incidentally made by the Evangelist himself lest the prophecy might be regarded, as restricted to the Jewish nation. Our Lord had resolved to cement into one, the hitherto separated Jewish and Gentile peoples, so that there would be one fold and one pastor, under the guidance of His visible vicar, on whom He conferred the plenitude of power to rule His Church. Similar is the idea expressed (Ephes. ii.), "*Ipse enim est pax nostra qui fecit utraque unum,*" etc.

By "*the children of God,*" among the Gentiles, are meant, not those who were then actually children of God, but those who, at a future day, were certainly to be called by the predestinating decree of God, to the Church, and made partakers, in the beneficent designs of Providence, of eternal salvation.

53. *From that day therefore they devised to put him to death.*

53. *Ab illo ergo die cogitaverunt ut interficerent eum.*

53. "*From that day, therefore,*" after the High Priest had decreed, that our Lord should die, "*they devised,*" they took counsel together, as to the means they should employ, in some legal form or other, for putting Him to death, in accordance with the decree of the High Priest, without exciting a tumult among the people (Matthew xxvi. 5).

Knowing their designs, our Lord no more appeared in public, in their towns and cities, for fear of precipitating events, as His "hour had not yet come."

54. *Wherefore Jesus walked no more openly among the Jews, but he went into a country near the desert, unto a city that is called Ephrem, and there he abode with his disciples.*

54. "*Near the desert . . . a city called Ephrem.*" The Greek has *Ephraim.* What this desert, or this city was, is uncertain. By the "*desert,*" some understand "*the desert*" of Judea, which extended to the confines of Jericho.

By "*Ephrem,* or, *Ephraim,*" some, among them St. Jerome and Eusebius, understand the city of Hebron, in the tribe of Juda,

Commentary.

which was according to Eusebius, eight miles north of Jerusalem; according to St. Jerome, it was 20.

Others understand by it, a small town in the Tribe of Ephraim, about five miles west of Jericho.

55. "*The Pasch of the Jews*," which had ceased, when St. John wrote this. The Christians celebrated the *Christian Pasch*. This was the fourth and last Pasch in the public life of Christ, which He celebrated a few days after, with His disciples. "*Was at hand.*" Our Lord was spending a few days at Ephraim, preparing with alacrity to be offered up, as the true Paschal Lamb, for the sins of mankind.

"*And many from the country*," such as needed to be purified from the several districts of the country. "*To purify themselves*," by prayers and sacrifices for sin, according to the precepts of the law, from all legal defilements, if contracted (c. xviii. 28), in order worthily to celebrate the coming Festival of the Pasch. It is not said, *all* came, as probably *all* needed it not.

56. "*What think you, that He is not come to the Festival day.*" The Greek could be rendered, "*What seems to you—will He not come to the Festival ?*" It is disputed, who they were that thus spoke, whether the friends or enemies of our Lord. Most likely, the latter, as appears from the following words:—"*The Chief Priests and the Pharisees had given a commandment,*" etc. On this account, it was, these people were on the look out to find our Lord and have Him handed over to the Chief Priests and Pharisees to be put to death. To show their folly, our Lord, a few days after, approached Jerusalem in the most public, demonstrative way, accompanied by a rejoicing multitude. They could not lay hands on Him up to this, as it would be against His will. But when "*His hour had come,*" He, then, willingly handed Himself over to them for execution.

Text.

54. *Jesus ergo jam non in palam ambulabat apud Judæos, sed abiit in regionem juxta desertum, in civitatem, quæ dicitur Ephrem, et ibi morabatur cum discipulis suis.*

55. *And the pasch of the Jews was at hand: and many from the country went up to Jerusalem before the pasch, to purify themselves.*

55. *Proximum autem erat Pascha Judæorum: et ascenderunt multi Jerosolymam de regione ante Pascha, ut sanctificarent se ipsos.*

56. *They sought therefore for Jesus; and they discoursed one with another, standing in the temple: What think you, that he is not come to the festival day? And the chief priests and the Pharisees had given a commandment, that if any man knew where he was, he should tell, that they might apprehend him.*

56. *Quærebant ergo Jesum: et colloquebantur ad invicem, in templo stantes: Quid putatis, quia non venit ad diem festum? Dederant autem Pontifices, et Pharisæi mandatum, ut si quis cognoverit ubi sit, indicet, ut apprehendant eum.*

CHAPTER XII.

1 *Now six days before the Pasch, Jesus came to Bethania, where Lazarus had been dead, whom Jesus raised to life.*

2 *And they made him a supper there: and Martha served, but Lazarus was one of them that were at table with him.*

3 *Mary, therefore, took a pound of ointment of right spikenard, of great value, and anointed the feet of Jesus, and wiped his feet with her hair: and the house was filled with the odour of the ointment.*

4 *Then one of his disciples, Judas Iscariot, he that was about to betray him, said:*

5 *Why was not this ointment sold for three hundred pence, and given to the poor?*

6 *Now he said this, not because he cared for the poor, but because he was a thief, and having the purse, carried what was put therein.*

7 *But Jesus said: Let her alone, that she may keep it against the day of my burial.*

8 *For the poor you have always with you: but me you have not always.*

9 *A great multitude, therefore, of the Jews knew that he was there: and they came, not for Jesus's sake only, but that they might see Lazarus, whom he had raised from the dead.*

10 *But the chief priests thought to kill Lazarus also:*

11 *Because many of the Jews, by reason of him, went away, and believed in Jesus.*

12 *And on the next day a great multitude, that was come to the festival day, when they had heard that Jesus was coming to Jerusalem:*

13 *Took branches of palm-trees, and went forth to meet him, and cried: Hosannah, blessed is he that cometh in the name of the Lord, the king of Israel!*

14 *And Jesus found a young ass, and sat upon it; as it is written:*

15 *Fear not, daughter of Sion: behold, thy king cometh, sitting on the colt of an ass.*

16 *These things his disciples did not know at the first: but when Jesus was glorified, then they remembered that these things were written of him: and that they had done these things to him.*

17 *The multitude, therefore, gave testimony, which was with him, when he called Lazarus out of the grave, and raised him from the dead.*

18 *For which reason also the people came to meet him: because they heard that he had done this miracle.*

19 *The Pharisees, therefore, said among themselves: Do you see that we prevail nothing? Behold, the whole world is gone after him.*

20 *Now there were certain Gentiles among them, that came up to adore on the festival day.*

21 *These, therefore, came to Philip, who was of Bethsaida of Galilee, and desired him, saying: Sir, we would willingly see Jesus.*

22 *Philip cometh, and telleth Andrew: Again Andrew and Philip told Jesus.*

23 *But Jesus answered them, saying: The hour is come that the Son of man should be glorified.*

24 *Amen, amen, I say to you, unless the grain of wheat fall into the ground and die,*

25 *Itself remaineth alone. But if it die, it bringeth forth much fruit. He that loveth his life, shall lose it: and he that hateth his life in this world, keepeth it unto life everlasting.*

26 *If any man minister to me, let him follow me: and where I am, there also shall my minister be. If any man minister to me, him will my Father honour.*

27 *Now is my soul troubled. And what shall I say? Father, save me from this hour. But for this cause I came unto this hour.*

28 *Father, glorify thy name. A voice, therefore, came from heaven: I have both glorified it, and I will glorify it again.*

29 *The multitude, therefore, that stood and heard, said that it thundered. Others said: An angel spoke to him.*

30 *Jesus answered, and said: This voice came not for me, but for your sake.*

31 *Now is the judgment of the world: now shall the prince of this world be cast out.*

32 *And I, if I be lifted up from the earth, will draw all things to myself.*

33 *(Now this he said, signifying what death he should die.)*

34 *The multitude answered him: We have heard out of the law, that Christ abideth for ever: and how sayest thou: The Son of man must be lifted up? Who is this Son of man?*

35 *Jesus, therefore, said to them: Yet a little while, the light is among you. Walk whilst you have the light, that the darkness overtake you not: and he that walketh in darkness, knoweth not whither he goeth.*

36 *Whilst you have the light, believe in the light, that you may be the children of light. These things Jesus spoke, and he went away, and hid himself from them.*

37 *And whereas he had done so many miracles before them, they believed not in him:*

38 *That the saying of Isaias, the prophet, might be fulfilled, which he said: Lord, who hath believed our hearing? And to whom hath the arm of the Lord been revealed?*

39 *Therefore they could not believe, for Isaias said again:*

40 *He hath blinded their eyes, and hardened their heart: that they should not see with their eyes, nor understand with their heart, and be converted, and I should heal them.*

41 *These things said Isaias, when he saw his glory, and spoke of him.*

42 *However, many of the chief men also believed in him: but because of the Pharisees, they did not confess it, that they might not be cast out of the synagogue.*

43 *For they loved the glory of men, more than the glory of God.*

44 *But Jesus cried out, and said: He that believeth in me, doth not believe in me, but in him that sent me.*

45 *And he that seeth me, seeth him that sent me.*

46 *I, the light, am come into the world; that whosoever believeth in me, may not remain in darkness.*

47 *And if any man hear my words, and keep them not, I do not judge him: for I came not to judge the world, but to save the world.*

48 *He that despiseth me, and receiveth not my words, hath one that judgeth him. The word that I have spoken, the same shall judge him in the last day.*

49 *For I have not spoken of myself, but the Father who sent me, he gave me command what I should say, and what I should speak.*

50 *And I know that his command is life everlasting. The things, therefore, that i speak, even as the Father said unto me, so do I speak.*

CAPUT XII.

1 *Jesus ergo ante sex dies Paschæ venit Bethaniam, ubi Lazarus fuerat mortuus, quem suscitavit Jesus.*

2 *Fecerunt autem ei cœnam ibi: et Martha ministrabat: Lazarus vero unus erat ex discumbentibus cum eo.*

3 *Maria ergo accepit libram unguenti nardi pistici, pretiosi, et unxit pedes Jesu, et extersit pedes ejus capillis suis: et domus impleta est ex odore unguenti.*

4 *Dixit ergo unus ex discipulis ejus, Judas Iscariotes, qui erat eum traditurus:*

5 *Quare hoc unguentum non væniit trecentis denariis, et datum est egenis?*

6 *Dixit autem hoc, non quia de egenis pertinebat ad eum, sed quia fur erat, et loculos habens, ea, quæ mittebantur, portabat.*

7 *Dixit ergo Jesus: Sinite illam ut in diem sepulturæ meæ servet illud.*

8 *Pauperes enim semper habetis vobiscum: me autem non semper habetis.*

9 *Cognovit ergo turba multa ex Judæis quia illic est: et venerunt, non propter Jesum tantum, sed ut Lazarum viderent, quem suscitavit a mortuis.*

10 *Cogitaverunt autem principes sacerdotum, ut et Lazarum interficerent:*

11 *Quia multi propter illum abibant ex Judæis, et credebant in Jesum.*

12 *In crastinum autem turba multa, quæ venerat ad diem festum, cum audissent quia venit Jesus Jerosolymam:*

13 *Acceperunt ramos palmarum, et processerunt obviam ei, et clamabant: Hosanna, benedictus, qui venit in nomine Domini, Rex Israel.*

14 *Et invenit Jesus asellum, et sedit super eum, sicut scriptum est:*

15 *Noli timere filia Sion: ecce rex tuus venit sedens super pullum asinæ.*

16 *Hæc non cognoverunt discipuli ejus primum: sed quando glorificatus est Jesus, tunc recordati sunt quia hæc erant scripta de eo: et hæc fecerunt ei.*

17 *Testimonium ergo perhibebat turba, quæ erat cum eo quando Lazarum vocavit de monumento, et suscitavit eum a mortuis.*

18 *Propterea et obviam venit ei turba: quia audierunt eum fecisse hoc signum.*

19 *Pharisæi ergo dixerunt ad semetipsos: Videtis quia nihil proficimus? ecce mundus totus post eum abiit.*

20 *Erant autem quidam Gentiles ex his, qui ascenderant ut adorarent in die festo.*

21 *Hi ergo accesserunt ad Philippum, qui erat a Bethsaida Galilææ, et rogabant eum, dicentes: Domine, volumus Jesum videre.*

22 *Venit Philippus, et dicit Andreæ: Andreas rursum et Philippus, dixerunt Jesu.*

23 *Jesus autem respondit eis, dicens: Venit hora, ut clarificetur Filius hominis.*

24 *Amen, amen dico vobis, nisi granum frumenti cadens in terram, mortuum fuerit:*

25 *Ipsum solum manet. Si autem mortuum fuerit, multum fructum affert. Qui amat animam suam, perdet eam : et qui odit animam suam in hoc mundo, in vitam æternam custodit eam.*

26 *Si quis mihi ministrat, me sequatur: et ubi sum ego, illic et minister meus erit. Si quis mihi ministraverit, honorificabit eum Pater meus.*

27 *Nunc anima mea turbata est. Et quid dicam ? Pater, salvifica me ex hac hora. Sed propterea veni in horam hanc.*

28 *Pater, clarifica nomen tuum. Venit ergo vox de cælo : Et clarificavi, et iterum clarificabo.*

29 *Turba ergo, quæ stabat, et audierat, dicebat tonitruum esse factum. Alii dicebant : Angelus ei locutus est.*

30 *Respondit Jesus, et dixit : Non propter me hæc vox venit, sed propter vos.*

31 *Nunc judicium est mundi : nunc princeps hujus mundi ejicietur foras.*

32 *Et ego si exaltatus fuero a terra, omnia traham ad meipsum.*

33 *(Hoc autem dicebat, significans qua morte esset moriturus.)*

34 *Respondit ei turba : Nos audivimus ex lege, quia Christus manet in æternum : et quomodo tu dicis, Oportet exaltari Filium hominis ? Quis est iste Filius hominis ?*

35 *Dixit ergo eis Jesus : Adhuc modicum lumen in vobis est. Ambulate dum lucem habetis, ut non vos tenebræ comprehendant : et qui ambulat in tenebris, nescit quo vadat.*

36 *Dum lucem habetis, credite in lucem, ut filii lucis sitis. Hæc locutus est Jesus et abiit, et abscondit se ab eis.*

37 *Cum autem tanta signa fecisset coram eis, non credebant in eum :*

38 *Ut sermo Isaiæ prophetæ impleretur, quem dixit : Domine, quis credidit auditui nostro ? et brachium Domini, cui revelatum est?*

39 *Propterea non poterant credere, quia iterum dixit Isaias :*

40 *Excæcavit oculos eorum, et induravit cor eorum : ut non videant oculis, et non intelligant corde, et convertantur, et sanem eos.*

41 *Hæc dixit Isaias, quando vidit gloriam ejus, et locutus est de eo.*

42 *Verumtamen et ex principibus multi crediderunt in eum : sed propter Pharisæos non confitebantur, ut e synagoga non ejicerentur.*

43 *Dilexerunt enim gloriam hominum magis, quam gloriam Dei.*

44 *Jesus autem clamavit, et dixit : Qui credit in me, non credit in me, sed in eum, qui misit me.*

45 *Et qui videt me, videt eum, qui misit me.*

46 *Ego lux in mundum veni : ut omnis, qui credit in me, in tenebris non maneat.*

47 *Et si quis audierit verba mea, et non custodierit : ego non judico eum. Non enim veni ut judicem mundum, sed ut salvificem mundum.*

48 *Qui spernit me, et non accipit verba mea : habet qui judicet eum. Sermo, quem locutus sum, ille judicabit eum in novissimo die.*

49 *Quia ego ex meipso non sum locutus, sed qui misit me Pater, ipse mihi mandatum dedit quid dicam, et quid loquar.*

50 *Et scio quia mandatum ejus vita æterna est. Quæ ergo ego loquor, sicut dixit mihi Pater, sic loquor.*

ANALYSIS.

In this chapter, we have an account of the banquet at Bethany, where our Lord had arrived a few days before the Pasch. The anointing of His feet by Magdalen. The murmuring of Judas, prompted by avarice. Our Lord's defence of Magdalen (1–9).

We have a short account of His triumphal entry into Jerusalem on Palm Sunday, and the applause of the crowd, who extol Him on account of His miracles (10–18).

The fury of the Pharisees on seeing the multitude follow Him (19).

The mediation of Philip, on behalf of some Gentiles, who wished to be introduced to our Lord (20–22).

Our Lord's allusion to His death, as necessary for His exaltation and glorification (22–26). His appeal to His Father in His distress of mind, and the loud testimony rendered in answer to His appeal (27, 28).

The results of His death, the nature of which He alludes to (29–37).

The incredulity of the Jews predicted by Isaias (37–41).

The rewards of such as believe in Him, and the punishment of the disobedient (42–48). The source from which He derives His authority, to speak and preach (49, 50).

Text.

1. *Jesus therefore six days before the pasch came to Bethania, where Lazarus had been dead, whom Jesus raised to life.*

1. *Jesus ergo ante sex dies Paschæ venit Bethaniam, ubi Lazarus fuerat mortuus, quem suscitavit Jesus.*

Commentary.

1. "*Jesus, therefore, six days before the Pasch.*" "*Therefore,*" because the Pasch was near (xi. 55), Jesus wished to go Jerusalem; or, "*therefore,*" on account of the commandment above referred to (xi. 56), not wishing to come into the power of His enemies before the time appointed had come, He left Ephrem, or Ephraim, where He had been sojourning a few days. "*Six days before the Pasch,*" at which He was Himself to be sanctified, as the true Paschal Lamb, for the redemption of mankind. Instead of going straightway to Jerusalem, He came to Bethany, where lived Lazarus, who had been resuscitated from the grave. Here, our Lord had many friends, and the recollection of His recent miracle would induce the people to conduct Him in triumph to Jerusalem, on the following Sunday, the *third* day, after His arrival at Bethany. "*Whom Jesus raised to life.*" The Greek has not, "*Jesus,*" but only, "*whom He raised from the dead.*" "*Where Lazarus had been dead.*" The Greek has, "*Where was Lazarus, who had been dead?*"

2. *And they made him a supper there: and Martha served, but Lazarus was one of them that were at table with him.*

2. St. Matthew (xxvi. 6), tells us, this banquet was given in the house of Simon the leper.

1–3–8. (See Matthew xxvi. 6–13, Commentary on.)

2. *Fecerunt autem ei cœnam ibi: et Martha ministrabat, Lazarus vero unus erat ex discumbentibus cum eo.*

3. *Mary, therefore, took a pound of ointment of right spikenard, of great price, and anointed the feet of Jesus and wiped his feet with her hair, and the house was filled with the odour of the ointment.*

3. "*Anointed the feet of Jesus and wiped,*" etc. There is a transposition or inversion of order in this. She first wiped His feet with her hair, removing the dust that adhered to them; and then, as Matthew and Mark tell us, anointed His head, which was usually done. Had she wiped His feet after anointing them, she would be only oiling her own hair; and St. John adds, that, in addition to washing His head, she did what was quite unusual,

Commentary.

viz., anointed His feet, in proof of her excessive love, and in gratitude for the remission of her sins, which she obtained at His sacred feet. She did not wipe His feet *after* anointing them, for the reason already assigned. *After* anointing His head and feet, she left the oil, without wiping it off, as above explained, to produce the intended effect of anointing in such cases.

4, 5. "*Judas Iscariot.*" The Greek has, "*Judas of Simon or, the son of Simon.*" The other Evangelists say, that the other disciples joined in the murmuring. They did so, from feelings of charity; Judas, from avarice, as in next verse.

6. He was entrusted with carrying the common purse, in which were deposited the means contributed as a sort of sustentation fund for the support of our Redeemer and His disciples. Abusing the confidence reposed in him, he used to purloin or carry away stealthily, for his own private use, some of its contents. He felt indignant, that the price of this ointment was not thrown with the rest into the common fund, so that he might thus be enabled to set some of it aside for his own use. While affecting great concern for the poor, the gratification of avarice was his real motive. For the poor he felt no concern whatever. How many hypocritical followers of Judas are to be found, at all times, men who talk loudly in favour of the poor, and never contribute a farthing for their relief?

Matthew and Mark, after giving the history of this banquet, refer to the impious compact entered into by Judas with the Chief Priests, as if he wished to compensate himself for the loss of the price of the ointment, by the amount of the reward secured for his base betrayal of his Master.

7, 8. (See Matthew xxvi. 7–12, Commentary on.)

9. "*A great multitude,*" etc. They came out from Jerusalem, not merely out of respect for our Lord, but also, out of a feeling of curiosity to see Lazarus, the fame of whose resuscitation from the grave reached far and near. They wished to see both, Lazarus resuscitated, and Jesus who had raised him.

Text.

3. *Maria ergo accepit libram unguenti nardi pistici, pretiosi, et unxit pedes Jesu, et extersit pedes ejus capillis suis: et domus impleta est ex odore unguenti.*

4. Then one of his disciples, Judas Iscariot, he that was about to betray him, said:

4. *Dixit ergo unus ex discipulis ejus, Judas Iscariotes, qui erat eum traditurus:*

5. Why was not this ointment sold for three hundred pence, and given to the poor?
5. *Quare hoc unguentum non væniit trecentis denariis, et datum est egenis?*

6. Now he said this not because he cared for the poor; but because he was a thief, and having the purse, carried the things that were put therein.

6. *Dixit autem hoc, non quia de egenis pertinebat ad eum, sed quia fur erat, et loculos habens, ea, quæ mittebantur, portabat.*

7. Jesus therefore said: Let her alone, that she may keep it against the day of my burial.

7. *Dixit ergo Jesus: Sinite illam ut in diem sepulturæ meæ servet illud.*
8. *For the poor you have always with you; but me you have not always.*
8. *Pauperes enim semper habetis vobiscum: me autem non semper habetis.*

9. A great multitude therefore of the Jews knew that he was there: and they came not for Jesus' sake only, but that they might see Lazarus whom he had raised from the dead.

9. *Cognovit ergo turba multa ex Judæis quia illic est: et venerunt, non propter Jesum tantum, sed ut Lazarum viderent, quem suscitavit a mortuis.*

Text.

10. *But the chief priests thought to kill Lazarus also.*

10. *Cogitaverunt autem principes sacerdotum ut et Lazarum interficerent:*

Commentary.

10. "*The Chief Priests thought*"—conspired together—"*to kill Lazarus also*," as well as our Lord, for the reason assigned in following verse. They were influenced purely by malice and envy, as Lazarus harmed none of them. It may be that the Chief Priests, most of them Sadducees, had another reason. Lazarus now brought back to life, would be a standing, living refutation of their doctrine, that there was no Resurrection (Acts xxiii. 18). This does not imply a formal meeting of the Sanhedrim, as in (xi. 47). The Pharisees are not mentioned here, though, no doubt, they had a hand in the business. They dreaded the influence which Lazarus, now walking abroad in full life, might have on the crowds, assembled from every quarter for the Pasch.

St. Augustine (Tract 50), jeeringly derides them, and exposes their blind malice and folly, as if our Lord, who raised up the *dead* Lazarus, could not raise up the *murdered* Lazarus as well. "*O stulta cogitatio ac cæca sævitia ! Dominus, Christus, qui suscitare potuit* MORTUUM, *non posset* OCCISUM.*"*

11. *Because many of the Jews by reason of him went away, and believed in Jesus.*

11. *Quia multi propter illum abibant ex Judæis, et credebant in Jesum.*

11. "*Went away*," not out of the Synagogue, but withdrew all connexion with the murderous faction of the High Priests and Pharisees, and adhered to Jesus.

12. *And on the next day a great multitude, that was come to the festival day, when they had heard that Jesus was coming to Jerusalem,*

12. *In crastinum autem turba multa, quæ venerat ad diem festum, cum audissent quia venit Jesus Jerosolymam.*

13. *Took branches of palm trees, and went forth to meet him and cried: Hosanna, blessed is he that cometh in the name of the Lord, the king of Israel.*

12–16. "*The next day*," that is, the day after the Sabbath, on which our Lord was entertained at a banquet in the house of Simon the leper, the same as the second day of the Sabbath, or our Palm Sunday. "*A great multitude.*" A great number, including strangers and foreigners also, "*that was come to the Festival day,*" who came from every quarter to Jerusalem, a few days before hand, to prepare for the due celebration of the Pasch. "*Having heard that Jesus,*" the fame of whose teaching and miracles, especially the last, viz., the raising up of Lazarus, was spread abroad every where, "*was coming to Jerusalem.*" Our Lord selected the day after the Sabbath, our Sunday, for His triumphal entry into Jerusalem, preparatory to His death, or immolation, as the true Paschal Lamb, destined to "*take away the sins of the world.*" (See all this explained, Matthew xxi. 1–9.)

13. *Acceperunt ramos palmarum, et processerunt obviam ei, et clamabant: Hosanna, benedictus qui venit in nomine Domini, Rex Israel.*

14. *And Jesus found a young ass, and sat upon it, as it is written:*

14. *Et invenit Jesus asellum, et sedit super eum, sicut scriptum est:*

15. Fear not, daughter of Sion, behold, thy king cometh sitting on an ass's colt.

15. *Noli timere filia Sion: ecce rex tuus venit sedens super pullum asinæ.*

ST. JOHN, CHAP. XII.

Commentary.

16. The disciples did not understand that these things were foretold of our Lord by the Prophet, with all their circumstances. "*But when Jesus was glorified,*" had ascended into heaven, and sent down His holy Spirit to enlighten them and teach them all truth, "*they, then, remembered,*" etc.

16. *Hæc non cognoverunt discipuli ejus primum: sed quando glorificatus est Jesus, tunc recordati sunt quia hæc erant scripta de eo: et hæc fecerunt ei.*

17. Those who were eye-witnesses of the raising up of Lazarus, bore witness to the fact; and circulated it, as indisputable, throughout Jerusalem.

17. *Testimonium ergo perhibebat turba, quæ erat cum eo quando Lazarum vocavit de monumento, et suscitavit eum a mortuis.*

18. On account of which stupendous miracle, the people, on the occasion of His entry into Jerusalem, came out in crowds to meet one who had the power of working such marvels.

18. *Propterea et obviam venit ei turba: quia audierunt eum fecisse hoc signum.*

19. "*The Pharisees*"—the enemies of our Lord—maddened with rage on seeing the triumphal entry of our Lord, accompanied by such crowds, young and old, Jews and Gentiles (*v.* 20), "*said among themselves,*" conferring with one another, "*Do you see that we prevail nothing?*" as if to say: we have foolishly put off carrying out our resolve, of putting Him to death, according to the counsel of Caiphas. The result of our procrastination and supineness is, that He is getting strength every day, His followers increasing "*The whole world*"—an hyperbolical form of expression—meaning great multitudes, "*are gone after Him.*" We must, therefore, carry out at once, our resolve, to put Him to death.

20. "*Certain Gentiles.*" In Greek, "*certain Hellenists, or Greeks.*" The Greek language was the most extensively used among the Gentiles. Hence, the word "*Greeks,*" was commonly used by the Jews to designate all the Pagan nations; as most of the Pagans, whom they knew, spoke the Greek language. The Apostle (St. Paul), commonly uses the word, when speaking of the Gentile or Pagan world, as contra-distinguished from the Jews. (Rom. i. 16; xi. 9), etc. The Evangelist appropriately introduces this, when describing the rage and envy of the Pharisees, to signify, that both Jews and Gentiles were to join in receiving and believing in our Lord.

Who these Gentiles were, cannot be easily determined. Some say, they were Jews who spoke the Greek language, and dwelt

Text.

16. *These things his disciples did not know at the first: but when Jesus was glorified, they remembered that these things were written of him, and that they had done these things to him.*

17. *The multitude therefore gave testimony, which was with him when he called Lazarus out of the grave, and raised him from the dead.*

18. *For which reason also the people came to meet him: because they heard that he had done this miracle.*

19. *The Pharisees therefore said among themselves: Do you see that we prevail nothing? behold, the whole world is gone after him.*

19. *Pharisæi ergo dixerunt ad semetipsos: Videtis quia nihil, proficimus? ecce mundus totus post eum abiit.*

20. *Now there were certain gentiles, among them who came up to adore on the festival day.*

20. *Erant autem quidam Gentiles ex his, qui ascenderant ut adorarent in die festo.*

Q

Text.

Commentary.

in some of the Greek cities of Asia Minor, Greece, Egypt, where they had their Synagogues. Others say, they were *Proselytes*, from among the Gentiles. Others, Gentiles and idolaters, who came to bring offerings to the God of Israel and worship Him. These holding, that there was one God, and seeing Him adored, with such majesty, by the Jews in the glorious Temple of Jerusalem, came to join in his worship, and present their gifts. The Temple was greatly venerated by Pagan Monarchs, who bestowed on it the richest gifts. Cyrus (1 Esdras; Darius Hystaspes, c. 6), and other Kings of Asia. (2 Machabees iii.) The neighbouring Pagans frequently attended the great feasts of the Jews. Hence, the outer Court of the Temple was called, the *Court of the Gentiles*.

21. *These therefore came to Philip, who was of Bethsaida of Galilee, and desired him, saying: Sir, we would see Jesus.*

21. *Hi ergo accesserunt ad Philippum, qui erat a Bethsaida Galilææ, et rogabant eum dicentes: Domine, volumus Jesum videre.*

21. They came to Philip, either because he was the first of our Lord's disciples they met; or, because they knew him before. Some say, the mention of his native place, "*Bethsaida of Galilee*," would show that these dwelt in the neighbourhood of Galilee; and hence, knew Philip, who was a Galilean. This is not likely; as among the disciples, there were other Galileans also.

Besides, knowing that the Jews would not wish to hold converse with Gentiles, the Gentiles in question had the deepest feelings of reverence for our Lord, and would not presume to approach Him in person. Hence, they employ Philip as an intermediary. "*We wish to see*," that is, converse with "*Jesus*," For, as regards "*seeing*," all could see Him, as He was preaching. It means, therefore, to *converse* with Him.

22. *Philip cometh and telleth Andrew. Again Andrew and Philip told Jesus.*

22. *Venit Philippus, et dicit Andreæ: Andreas rursum, et Philippus dixerunt Jesu.*

22. Philip declined the task of introducing them, and had recourse to Andrew, his countryman, for the purpose. Andrew, it seems, enjoyed greater influence with our Lord, being His oldest disciple. It was he introduced Peter, his brother (i. 40). Likely, Philip's hesitation may have resulted from our Lord's command, "*in viam Gentium, ne abieritis.*" Before exposing themselves to transgress, in any way, our Lord's wish in this matter, they both lay the matter before our Lord.

23. *But Jesus answered them saying: The hour is come, that the son of man should be glorified.*

23. *Jesus autem respondit eis, dicens: Venit hora, ut clarificetur Filius hominis.*

23 "*Jesus answered them.*" Likely, the Gentiles, too, were near, and within hearing, as we find no other answer made to Philip's appeal, which would seem not to be unacceptable to our Lord. Whether He admitted them to conversation with Him is not stated. He, however, granted them more than was asked (v. 23–28).

"*The hour is come*," the appointed time for His death, which was to be followed by His Resurrection, Ascension, "*is come*," so near at hand, that it may be said to have come, "*that the Son of Man,*" whose name the Pharisees would fain blot out from the minds of mankind and utterly obliterate.

ST. JOHN, CHAP. XII.

Commentary.

"*Should be glorified*," made known to the Gentile world, of whom these are the first fruits; and after His Glorious Resurrection, Ascension, and sending down of the Holy Ghost, joined with the preaching of the Gospel, throughout the world, he would be acknowledged, adored and proclaimed by the entire earth, Jew and Gentile, as the Eternal Son of God. Our Lord frequently employs this epithet, "*the Son of Man*," rather than the "*Son of God*," as denoting His union with human nature, which He so honoured, denoting also His humble lowliness, in which through His humiliation, He was to receive the honours due to the Messiah; glory being exchanged, as its reward, for humiliation. (Philip. ii.)

Some Expositors (among whom Patrizzi), say, the "*hour*," refers to the present day, on which He was so honoured, by the multitude, and on which a glorious testimony was soon to be borne to Him by His Father (v. 28), in the hearing of so many; the day whereon He was approaching Jerusalem, to enter on that course of suffering so often predicted by Him (Matthew xx. 17–19; Mark x. 32; Luke xviii. 31–34), as the prelude to His glory.

Most likely, it refers to the testimony rendered to Him by His Father, in His Resurrection, Ascension, preaching of the Gospel, which would make known to all, the economy of Redemption, founded chiefly on His humiliation and death.

24. As His glorification was the fruit and reward of His humiliation and death (Philip. ii.), which was now at hand, He illustrates the subject by a familiar similitude, and thus removes any grounds of offence or scandal which it might create in their minds. This being an important and solemn utterance, He prefaces it, with "*Amen, amen*," usual with Him in such cases. His death would purchase a vast harvest of worshippers from all nations and peoples and tongues, etc. (Apoc. vii). For this, His death was necessary, just as it was necessary, in order that from a grain of corn, a crop or harvest would proceed, that the grain should first die and be dissolved, after being committed to the bosom of the earth. Unless it dies, it produces no fruit. It remains sterile and alone. But, if it dies, it produces much fruit When, after I die, I am committed to the earth, an uncommon harvest of faithful followers shall rise up, who are, in some limited sense, to partake of My nature, by a communication of My choicest graces, as the harvest is of the same nature with the seed. These shall proclaim My glory throughout the world.

25. He wishes to fortify them against the sufferings and persecutions in store for His followers who are destined to tread the same path that He has trodden. Sufferings and trials and mortification are the only means of securing eternal happiness.

"*He that loveth his life*," with an inordinate, sensual love, at the

Text.

24. *Amen, amen I say to you, unless the grain of wheat falling into the ground, die;*

24. *Amen, amen dico vobis, nisi granum frumenti cadens in terram, mortuum fuerit.*

25. *Itself remaineth alone. But if it die, it bringeth forth much fruit. He that loveth his life shall lose it: and he that hateth his life in this world,*

Text.

keepeth it unto life eternal.

25. *Ipsum solum manet. Si autem mortuum fuerit, multum fructum affert. Qui amat animam suam, perdet eam: qui odit animam suam, in hoc mundo, in vitam æternam custodit eam.*

26. *If any man minister to me let him follow me: and where I am, there also shall my minister be. If any man minister to me, him will my Father honour.*

26. *Si quis mihi ministrat, me sequatur: et ubi sum ego, illic et minister meus erit. Si quis mihi ministraverit, honorificabit eum Pater meus.*

27. *Now is my soul troubled. And what shall I say? Father save me from this hour. But for this cause I came unto this hour.*

27. *Nunc anima mea turbata est. Et quid dicam? Pater, salvifica me ex hac hora. Sed propterea veni in horam hanc.*

Commentary.

expense of the law of God, which he hesitates not to violate in order to save His life, "*shall lose it,*" shall lose his soul in the world to come. It is clear from the following clause, that to this clause, "*he that loveth his life*" should be added (*in this world*) shall lose it in the world to come.

"*And he that hateth,*" etc. (See Matthew x. 39; xvi. 25, Commentary on.) This was a favourite principle or kind of axiom with our Lord. It is the compendium of a Christian life.

26. Our Lord insinuates, that He Himself would lose His life in this world; that the triumphs He was now enjoying would not last; that sufferings and death were near; and, then, He exhorts His followers to follow His example and walk in His footsteps.

"*If any man minister to Me,*" etc., or, would wish to show himself My minister and true disciple, "*let him follow Me,*" imitate Me, in My disregard for temporal life, in order to secure life eternal (Matthew x. 38). By following Me, he shall not lose His life in the world to come. He shall be sharer with Me in everlasting happiness. "*Where I am,*" being now, as to My Divinity, in heaven; and sure to ascend there shortly, in My human nature, "*there also shall My minister be,*" sharing with Me, the ineffable joys of heaven.

This true minister and faithful persevering follower in humiliation, sorrows and death, here, shall be exalted and honoured hereafter by My Father in heaven, before the angels and the blessed, by rendering him a partaker of the glory, which shall be the reward of My humiliation, sufferings and death.

"*I am,*" clearly shows our Lord was then in heaven. This, of course, refers to His *Divine* nature; at a future day, He will ascend there, in His *glorified humanity.*

27. "*Now is My soul troubled,*" etc. The reference to the grain, which dies in the earth, to which He compared Himself, brought before our Lord's mind, the horrors of His approaching death, its tortures and gloomy accompaniments. Thus, in order to show that He Himself endured what He encouraged others to endure after Him; and also, to prove His human nature, and point out what we are to do, when terrified by death, impending evils, viz., to have recourse to God; He voluntarily permits His human nature and inferior faculties to be disturbed; to shrink from the contemplation of His impending Passion, and to endure in some measure beforehand, the agony He endured in the garden. (See Matthew xxvi. 38; Luke xxii. 42–44, Commentary on.)

Likely this "*man of sorrows,*" often during life, voluntarily permitted the inferior faculties of His human nature to be troubled at the foresight and anticipation of His Passion and final suffering on earth.

ST. JOHN, CHAP. XII.

Commentary.

"*And what shall I say?*" Expresses His doubts, fears and perplexity, as if deliberating within Himself, if He could endure this torture; or, if the work of Redemption should be given up, and He should call on God to rescue Him (Luke xxii. 42).

"*Father, save Me from this hour.*" These words, in this Indicative form, contain a petition to save Him (Matthew xxvi. 39), in which He at once checks Himself. Some read them, as the Greek admits, interrogatively, "*Shall I say, Father, save Me?*" Shall I ask of God to rescue Me? Or, shall I submit to these tortures? The former reading is preferable, as it better expresses the parallelism between these words and His prayer in the garden.

"*From this hour,*" from this agony which awaits Me, at the time fixed in the Divine decrees.

"*But, for this cause,*" as if correcting His inferior appetite, which naturally shrank from death, He, at once, absolutely wishes, in His superior faculties, will and intellect, that the desires of His inferior appetite should not be complied with; and that He would go forward to certain death. Similar are His words and feelings (Matthew xxvi.)—"*Non mea, sed tua voluntas fiat.*" "*Transeat a me calix iste.*" Here it is, "*Nunc turbata est anima mea.*" In the garden, He prayed, "*transfer calicem istum.*" Here, "*Pater, Salvifica me ex hac hora.*" In the garden, He subjected His natural desire of life to His Father's will, "*Non sicut ego volo, sed sicut tu.*" Here, "*clarifica nomen tuum.*"

"*But for this cause,*" for the purpose of dying to save mankind, have I reached this hour of agony and suffering.

28. "*Father, glorify Thy name,*" by My death, which is to be cheerfully undergone in obedience to Thy will. By it, Thy name shall be celebrated all over the earth. The words convey the same signification as, "*Nevertheless, not My will; but, Thine be done.*"

"*Then came a voice from heaven: I have both glorified it,*" by My testimony at your Baptism. "*This is My beloved Son,*" etc., by the stupendous miracles wrought through you, by your preaching, doctrines, etc.

"*And I shall glorify it again,*" by Thy death and the wonders that shall take place thereat; by thy subsequent glory and exaltation, in thy Resurrection and Ascension. By our Lord's death and exaltation, the faith and worship of God was propagated among Jews and Gentiles, and His name thus glorified. As an angel from heaven was sent by the Heavenly Father to strengthen our Lord in His agony in the garden; so here too, was a voice sent from above to sustain Him, in His troubles.

29. Very likely this trumpet voice from heaven was distinctly heard by all, uttering an articulate sound. For, "*it was for their sakes it came*" (*v.* 30). Some of them, on account of its loudness,

Text.

28. *Father glorify thy name. A voice therefore came from heaven: I have both glorified it, and will glorify it, again.*

28. *Pater, clarifica nomen tuum. Venit ergo vox de cælo: Et clarificavi, et iterum clarificabo.*

29. *The multitude therefore that stood and heard, said that it thundered. Others*

Text.	Commentary.
said, *An angel spoke to him.* 29. *Turba ergo, quæ stabat, et audierat dicebat tonitruum esse factum. Alii dicebant: Angelus ei locutus est.*	pronounced it to be thunder; and possibly, said so out of envy, not wishing to attend to the testimony it bore. Hence, they would wish to regard it, as a natural phenomenon. Others, better disposed, regarded it as uttered by the trumpet voice of an angel. The Evangelist conveys, that all heard it, as it sounded so loud and clear.
30. *Jesus answered, and said: This voice came not because of me, but for your sakes.* 30. *Respondit Jesus, et dixit: Non propter me hæc vox venit, sed propter vos.*	30. "*Not for Me,*" as if I needed to be assured that My Father hears Me. For, I know that He always hears me (xi. 42). "*But for your sakes,*" that you may learn from it and believe, that I am sent from God the Father, and that the same glory is common to us both.
31. *Now is the judgment of the world: now shall the prince of this world be cast out.* 31. *Nunc judicium est mundi: nunc princeps hujus mundi ejicietur foras.*	31. He points out the mode in which His Father is to glorify Him. "*Now is the judgment of the world.*" "*Now,*" at My approaching death, a judgment of condemnation shall be passed on those obstinate unbelievers, who reject Me, and after so many splendid proofs, refuse to believe in Me; nay, go so far as to put Me unjustly to death. The signal vengeance of God, shall, therefore, be justly visited on them.

"*Now shall the Prince of this world,*" that is, Satan, who exercised unbounded sway over mankind, by holding them captive in the chains of sin, shall now be dislodged, by the powerful grace merited by My death, from the hearts of men, as from a citadel in which he ruled. Others, understand it of a judgment or sentence of *remission* or *absolution*, thus: now shall a sentence of remission be pronounced in favour of men who hitherto were kept bound in the chains of sin. This remission shall be obtained by My death; whereby, I ransom them, pay their debt, and set them free from the tyranny of sin and Satan, who shall himself be dethroned and dislodged from the citadel and stronghold he possessed in the souls of men. Thus shall the name of God be glorified; His Attributes, Mercy, Power, etc., proclaimed throughout the world. The devil is often called in SS. Scripture, "*the Prince of the Power of this air,*" etc., on account of the dominion he exercises over the children of unbelief. His dominion was destroyed by the death of Christ, on whom, though innocent, the punishment of sin was inflicted (Rom. viii. 3; Heb. ii. 14), and although Satan still exercises power over men; still, it is owing to their own fault. So far as the liberation through Christ is concerned, it embraces all, who do not obstinately resist the influences of Divine grace. Now, that the Liberator and Saviour of the human race has appeared, the effusion of grace is *universal*.

Formerly, in regard to the just of old, it was only *partial;* and that, in virtue of the future merits of Christ *now* purchased by the blood of the cross.

Commentary.

32. *"And,"* the same as, *for,* *"if,"* *(whereas),*—*"I be lifted up from the earth,"* raised aloft on the tree of the cross (John iii. 14; viii. 28), which is clearly referred to, next verse. He shows how the devil is to be cast out and stripped of his power, viz., by His death.

"I shall draw all things to Myself." *"All things,"* all men, of every description, from every clime and country, Jews and Gentiles. The neuter form, *"all things,"* *"omnia,"* is a more emphatic way of expressing universal subjection to Christ. *"Shall draw,"* voluntarily, as regards man; *forcibly,* as regards the demon snatching forcibly his prey from His hands. *"Draw,"* expresses the resistance of the devil and the superior power of the grace of Christ, forcibly wresting men from the tyrannical grasp and dominion of Satan.

33. The words of this verse are not the words of our Lord; but, of the Evangelist, and should be enclosed in a parenthesis, and interpreted as such.

34. The crowd, it would seem, understood our Lord as referring to His own death.

"The law," includes the entire SS. Scripture in its widest extent. In several passages of Scripture it was said, His power would be eternal, *"abideth for ever"* (Isaias ix. 6, 7; Psalm cix. 4, lxxi.; 5, lxxxviii. 30–38; Daniel xi. 44; vii. 14). There is question, in these passages, of Christ's glorious kingdom. From the interpretation given by their teachers, whom they followed, the crowd understood these passages to refer to an earthly reign, which, they hoped, would exceed in splendour the days of David and Solomon. They could not reconcile this teaching, founded on SS. Scripture, with His death; and they seemed to pay no heed to other passages of Scripture which referred to His death, as the prelude to the inauguration of His glorious reign (Isaias liii.; Daniel ix. 26; xi. 19).

"And how sayest thou, the Son of Man MUST *be lifted up?"* This question they put, not quoting the words of our Lord literally, but their sense. Their question, *"must be,"* etc., was virtually included in the words, *"if I be lifted up,"* etc. *"The Son of Man"*—the designation constantly applied by our Lord to Himself—and supposed to refer to the Messiah, who was, according to Scripture, to reign for ever—how can He be lifted up and submit to death? From these questions, it seems they regarded the Messiah (Christ) and *the Son of Man* as the same person.

"Who is this Son of Man?" Must He not be different from the Messiah or Christ, whose reign is to be eternal, according to Daniel? At one time, the splendid miracles of our Lord would

Text.

32. *And I, if I be lifted up from the earth will draw all things to myself.*

32. *Et ego si exaltatus fuero a terra, omnia traham ad me ipsum.*

33. *(Now this he said, signifying what death he should die.*

33. *(Hoc autem dicebat, significans qua morte esset moriturus.)*

34. *The multitude answered him: We have heard out of the law, that Christ abideth for ever; and how sayest thou: The son of man must be lifted up? Who is this son of man?*

34. *Respondit ei turba: Nos audivimus ex lege, quia Christus manet in æternum: et quomodo tu dicis, Oportet exaltari Filium hominis? Quis est iste Filius hominis?*

Text.	Commentary.
	prove what He asserted Himself to be, viz., that He was the promised, long-expected Messiah. Now, His teachings, regarding His own death, would seem opposed to the Scripture teachings regarding His never-ending reign. The Jews would now seem to doubt, if our Lord be the promised Messiah. Possibly, this question was put, out of a feeling of contempt and scorn.
35. *Jesus therefore said to them: Yet a little while, the light is among you. Walk whilst you have the light that the darkness overtake you not. And he that walketh in darkness knoweth not whither he goeth.*	35, 36. Our Lord might have referred them to the texts above quoted, regarding the death of the Messiah, which was to precede His exaltation. But, knowing their passions and prepossessions regarding Him and His reign, which, by blinding their intellects, rendered them incapable of understanding the truth regarding the Messiah, He gives them no direct answer. He only answers them, allegorically and indirectly. He gives them a solemn warning and earnest exhortation, not to shut their eyes against
35. *Dixit ergo eis Jesus: Adhuc modicum lumen in vobis est. Ambulate dum lucem habetis ut non vos tenecomprehendant: et qui ambulat in tenebris, nescit quo vadat.*	the lights and graces now so plenteously tendered to them. He, at the same time, indirectly conveys, that they had but a short time to enjoy His presence, and that He would soon be taken away from them. "*Yet a little while,*" for only a short time, "*the light is among you.*" *I*, who am "*the true Son of justice*," "*the true light that enlightens every man that cometh into this world,*" shall be among you in person, teaching, instructing, conversing with
36. *Whilst you have the light, believe in the light, that you may be the children of light. These things Jesus spoke and he went away, and hid himself from them.*	you. Therefore, "*whilst you have the light, walk in the light,*" by believing in Me, by consulting Me, who will solve all your doubts, especially in regard to My death and the eternal exaltation and glory, which is to be consequent on it. I shall shortly leave you; and, then, if you neglect the present opportunity, the darkness of error, the night of infidelity and sin, will be sure to
36. *Dum lucem habetis, credite in lucem ut filii lucis sitis. Hæc locutus est Jesus: et abiit, et abscondit se ab eis:*	overtake and envelop you. "*He that walketh in darkness,*" by neglect of proffered grace, entails on himself blindness of intellect, hardness of heart, or obduracy of will—the assured forerunner of final impenitence. "*Knoweth not whither He goeth.*" Will never reach the desired goal of salvation, and shall blindly be precipitated into the gulf of eternal perdition. "*And hid Himself from them.*" He knew their secret thoughts and murderous designs; and hence, He left them for a short time, "*hid Himself,*" lest they should prematurely carry out their designs before His hour would have arrived. Likely, He went to Bethany. For, during the three last days of His life, He preached in the Temple, and at night retired to Mount Olivet (Luke xxi. 37), and thence, to Bethany (Matthew xxi. 17; Mark xi. 11).
37. *And whereas he had done so many miracles before them, they believed not in him:*	37. "*And whereas He had done many signs,*" performed so many and such stupendous miracles during the course of His public ministry; still, owing to their carnal views, their corrupt passions, their want of appreciation of the heavenly doctrines

Commentary.

preached by our Lord, their false pre-conceived notions, regarding the splendour of the Messiah's reign, not to speak of their fear of the authorities and human respect, the chiefs and the great bulk of the people, "*believed not in Him.*" On this account, it was He exhorted them above (*v.* 36), whilst they had time, "*to believe in the light.*"

38. "*That the saying of Isaias,*" etc. "*That,*" expresses the event, not the *cause.* The consequence was, that the words of Isaias were fulfilled. The prediction took place, *because,* the event predicted was to happen. The prevision followed the *futurition.* Foreseeing what would happen, our Lord inspired Isaias to predict it; so that their incredulity *would* not come on men by surprise, or occasion scandal to any one.

"*Lord, who has believed?*" etc. How few are there to believe the doctrine communicated by our preaching of the Gospel, the preaching of which they hear from ûs. *Hearing,* signifies, the thing heard.

And "*the arm of the Lord,*" the Power of God, working such miracles through Christ, to how few of the Jews has it been disclosed, so as to ensure their believing in it. "*Arm,*" is employed by a common figure of speech, to denote strength and power. "*The arm of the Lord,*" may mean, Christ, who is the Power, the Word, by whom all things are made; by how few is He acknowledged through faith. This had reference, in a special way, to the time of our Redeemer and the Jews of His day.

39. In verse 37, He says, "*they did not believe.*" Here, it is stronger still, "*they could not believe.*"

"*Therefore, they could not believe, because Isaias said,*" etc. "*Therefore,*" "*because.*" These two causal particles express, not a *cause* or *final motive*; but, a *consequence.* The unbelief or inability to believe, on the part of men, did not take place, on account of the prediction of the Prophet, or, in order that the words of Isaias would be fulfilled. But, God inspired the Prophet to foretell their unbelief, on account of the prevision he had, or, because He foresaw, that they, of their own free will, and out of obstinacy, *would not* believe. The events referred to did not take place, on account of the prediction, or, in order to verify the prediction; but, the prediction was made, founded on God's *prescience,* because, the events were surely to take place, freely, in time on the part of man. The prescience of these events was posterior in the Divine mind, to the futurition of events which were freely to take place on the part of man, uninfluenced by such prevision.

"*They could not believe,*" expresses a *consequent,* but not an *antecedent,* inability to believe; Isaias having predicted, that they

Text.

37. *Cum autem tanta signa fecisset coram eis, non credebant in eum.*

38. *That the saying of Isaias the prophet might be fulfilled, which he said:* Lord, who hath believed our hearing? and to whom hath the arm of the Lord been revealed?

38. *Ut sermo Isaiæ prophetæ impleretur, quem dixit: Domine, quis credidit auditui nostro? et brachium Domini cui revelatum est?*

39. *Therefore they could not believe, because Isaias said again:*

39. *Propterea non poterant credere, quia iterum dixit Isaias:*

Text.

40. He hath blinded their eyes, and hardened their heart, that they should not see with their eyes, nor understand with their heart, and be converted, and I should heal them:

40. *Excæcavit oculos eorum, et induravit cor eorum; ut non videant oculis, et non intelligant corde, et convertantur, et sanem eos.*

Commentary.

would not believe, this prediction should infallibly be verified: and it was impossible, therefore, that they would believe, consistently with this prophecy, which was founded on the Divine prevision, that by their own free act and obstinacy of will, they would reject the preaching of Christ. Events do not take place, because God foresaw them; but God foresaw them, because they were to take place in time, by the free and voluntary act of man.

In truth, supposing men voluntarily to blind their eyes and harden their hearts against the inspirations of grace; in this state of mind, their conversion is, at least, morally impossible. The grace of God could, however, change them, and under its influence, they *could* believe; but, in punishment of their perverse resistance, it shall not be given them. God can foresee only what is surely to take place.

40. "*He hath blinded their eyes,*" etc. The past tense is used, though there is reference to a future event, meaning, "*He will blind,*" etc., as in Matthew (xiii. 14, 15), on account of the certainty of its taking place. In the Hebrew of Isaias (vi. 10), the words are in the Imperative form, and are so rendered literally by St. Jerome, "*blind the hearts,*" etc. But, the Septuagint version, which gives the meaning of the passage, is followed here by the Evangelist. When God is said to inflict blindness of intellect and hardness of heart, He does so *negatively*, by withholding the graces, indispensable for men, to avoid sin; and *positively*, in a certain sense, by throwing in their way, obstacles, such as riches, honours, etc.—things good or indifferent, not necessarily inducing to sin, but which, owing to the abuse of them, will as infallibly prove the cause of sin, as if God had given them over to sin. (See Matthew xiii. 13, 14; Rom. i. 24, Commentary on.)

Commenting on the words of this verse, above referred to, "*they could not believe.*" St. Chrysostom and St. Augustine understand the words, of *moral* inability. "*They could not believe, because they would not*" (St. Chrysostom).

"If asked why '*they could not believe?*' I answer, without hesitation, because they *would not;* because God, foreseeing their *evil will*, announced it beforehand by the Prophet" (St. Augustine).

Others understand it, "*they could not believe,*" because, they were blinded, and also obstinate, as Isaias predicted.

The words would, then, denote *moral* inability, or very great necessity; or they are meant conditionally, on their indulging their passions, maliciously and voluntarily blinding themselves. For, though *obcæcuti et obdurati*, they still had free will and sufficient grace.

ST. JOHN, CHAP. XII.

Commentary.

41. "*These things Isaias said, when he saw His glory,*" etc. (Isaias vi. 1–6), saw the Lord seated on a throne surrounded by the Seraphim. It is clear, from the entire passage, it is of our Lord Jesus Christ, St. John here speaks, as the supreme Lord of Glory, who was seen by Isaias. For, in verse 37, it is said, "*they believed not in Him;*" in verse 42, "*they believed in Him.*" The pronoun, "*Him*"; in both these verses, manifestly refers to our Blessed Lord. In this intermediate verse, 41, "*His glory,*" *and spoke of Him,* must also refer to the same person. Now, in these latter words, the Evangelist speaks of Him, whom Isaias "*saw sitting on His throne;*" and Isaias tells us, He was the Jehovah or great God. What greater proof, therefore, can we have of our Lord's Divinity, unless we hold, that the Evangelist misunderstood the Prophet Isaias? We have "HIS GLORY," the glory of the Messiah, spoken of, by the Evangelist in this passage.

Jehovah whom Isaias saw, was the incommunicable name of God, held in the greatest reverence by the Jews. It was hardly ever uttered by them. Briefly; the Evangelist declares, it was the glory of the Messiah that was seen by Isaias. Now, Isaias asserts, that it was Jehovah he saw. Hence, our Lord is the great Jehovah. What clearer proof of our Lord's Divinity?

It is disputed whether Isaias did not, at the same time, see the Trinity represented by the appearance presented to him, as Abraham saw *three*, and adored *one*. Some hold, he did ; and hence the Trisagion, the threefold acclamation, "*Holy, Holy, Holy*" (Isaias vi. 3). Others hold, it was the Second Person he saw.

"*His glory,*" denotes an appearance of splendour and majesty ; some external sign of the Divinity.

"*And spoke of Him,*" viz., the Messiah, as is clear from the entire context.

While the triple acclamation, "*Holy, Holy Holy,*" pointed to the Trinity of Persons ; the unity or nature is expressed in the words, "*I saw the Lord,*" etc. (Isaias vi. 1). The Evangelist shows that the blindness and incredulity of the Jews, furnished a new argument of our Lord's Divinity ; because, it was predicted, that they would not believe in Him, as God ; and here this prediction of Isaias (vi. 10) was verified to the letter. In the same prediction He was spoken of, as God (Isaias vi. 1–3).

42. "*However, many of the chief men,*" etc. Some members of the Sanhedrim, as well as the common people, convinced by His teaching, His sanctity of life and miracles, "*believed in Him,*" as the promised Messiah. This the Evangelist says, to remove any erroneous impression that might be conceived from verse 37, where it is said, "*they believed not in Him.*" The great mass of the people did not. But, some did. We know of Nicodemus, Joseph of Arimathea, etc., as sincere believers.

Text.

41. *These things said Isaias when he saw his glory and spoke of him.*

41. *Hæc dixit Isaias, quando vidit gloriam ejus, et locutus est de eo.*

42. *However many of the chief men also believed in him: but because of the Pharisees they did not confess him, that they might not be cast out of the synagogue.*

42 *Verumtamen et ex principibus multi*

Text.	Commentary.
crediderunt in eum: sed propter Pharisæos non confitebantur, ut e synagoga non ejicerentur.	"*But, because of the Pharisees*"—the declared enemies of our Lord—"*they do not confess Him.*" Their faith was weak, dead, merely speculative, not reduced to practice, not enlivened by charity; lest, through the great influence of the Pharisees, they would be cast out of the Synagogue.
43. *For they loved the glory of men, more than the glory of God.* 43. *Dilexerunt enim gloriam hominum magis, quam gloriam Dei.*	43. "*They loved the glory of men more than the glory of God.*" They preferred the praises and honours derived from pertinaciously adhering to the religion of their fathers, to the glory which God has in store for His faithful confessors, who suffer reproach and persecution for His sake. Great glory would redound to God from their firmness and constancy.
44. *But Jesus cried and said: He that believeth in me, doth not believe in me, but in him that sent me.* 44. *Jesus autem clamavit, et dixit: Qui credit in me, non credit in me, sed in eum, qui misit me.*	44. The Evangelist does not state when the following words were spoken. Some say, they were spoken in connection with His discourse (verse 30–36), before He hid Himself. Others conjecture, that our Lord may have more than once repeated them. It is, however, quite uncertain. Seeing the incredulity of some and the cowardly fears of others, He publicly states the result of receiving or rejecting Him. In a loud voice, "*He cried out,*" He publicly states, in the presence of the Pharisees, in order to dissipate the fears of the timid and inspire them with confidence to avow their belief in Him. "*He that believeth in Me,*" he that believeth in Me not merely as man, as the abject being you suppose Me to be, while I am, at the same time, God; "*doth not believe in me,*" only, "*but in Him,*" God the Father, "*who sent Me.*" In this, He boldly asserts His consubstantiality and identity with God the Father. They should not, therefore, be ashamed to believe in Him; because, by believing in Him, they believe in God. No one should be ashamed of believing in God. The Jews even gloried in believing in God.
45. *And he that seeth me, seeth him that sent me.* 45. *Et qui videt me, videt eum, qui misit me.*	45. "*And He that seeth Me,*" by faith, and perceives the dignity of My Divine nature, concealed under the veil of My humanity. "*Seeth Him that sent Me,*" because we are one, having identically the same Divine nature. He said the same elsewhere. "*I and the Father are one.*" (c. x. 30). These words would have no meaning, unless He and the Father had one and the same Divine nature.
46. *I am come a light into the world; that whosoever believeth in me may not remain in darkness.* 46. *Ego lux in mundum veni: ut*	46. "*A light,*" eternal with My Father, without a beginning, the increated, immense source of light, from which all created light in men and angels, sun, moon, and stars, borrow their lustre, compared with which, they are a mere ray. "*I am come into the world,*" by assuming human nature, to dissipate the darkness of sin and error in which all mankind,

Commentary.

Jew and Gentile, are involved, so "*that whosoever believes in Me,*" etc., be he Jew or Gentile, whosoever embraces the all-saving doctrines which I preach, should "*remain no longer in darkness,*" in the darkness of idolatry, vice or error here, or in eternal darkness, hereafter. This is one of the effects, or rather, the chief effect, of My coming.

47. "*If any man hear My words,*" through the bodily organ of hearing, "*and keep them not.*" The Greek is, "*and believe them not.*" The meaning is the same, keep it not, retain it by faith in his mind, by firmly believing and persevering in that belief, and exhibiting obedience to My precepts and the observance of the moral law.

"*I do not judge Him*" (John iii. 17). Although deserving of condemnation; still, I refrain from judging him, *at present;* because, "*I came*" into the world, *not* to condem or *judge, but to save,* thus insinuating that, at a *future* day, He shall exercise judgment on such, when He shall come in majesty to judge the world. So, let not the refractory and disobedient fancy they shall transgress God's law with impunity. "*Now is the time of mercy; hereafter, of justice*" (St. Augustine).

48. "*He that despiseth Me,*" etc., and shows this, by "*not receiving My words,*" whereby I proclaim Myself the light of the world, and the Saviour of mankind. The latter sentence is an illustration or explanation of the former. Such a man will not be allowed to pass unpunished, without a judge to condemn him. "*Hath one that judgeth him,*" and condemns him, viz., "*the word that I have spoken,*" with the view of imparting to him the true faith and light of grace, which he obstinately rejects, against which he closes his eyes. "*The same shall judge him,*" will rise in judgment against him, and proclaim him deserving of hell, by testifying to his guilt "*on the last day,*" before Him whose words he despises. For, it is our Lord Himself who will judge and condemn men for rejecting His words and teaching.

"*In the last day,*" are found only in this Gospel, and refer to the general judgment, which is to take place at the end of the world.

49. He assigns a reason why His word would judge and condemn such as would not believe, or more accurately, why He, as judge, would condemn them for despising His words, viz., because His words were not merely His own, uttered by His own private authority, or uttered by Him, as mere man; but, by the command of His Father, whom they despise, by despising Him and rejecting His teaching.

"*But, the Father who sent Me, He gave Me commandment what*

Text.

omnis, qui credit in me, in tenebris non maneat.

47. *And if any man hear my words, and keep them not: I do not judge him: for I came not to judge the world, but to save the world.*

47. *Et si quis audierit verba mea, et non custodierit: ego non judico eum, non enim veni ut judicem mundum, sed ut salvificem mundum.*

48. *He that despiseth me, and receiveth not my words, hath one that judgeth him: the word that I have spoken, the same shall judge him in the last day.*

48. *Qui spernit me, et non accipit verba mea : habet qui judicet eum. Sermo, quem locutus sum, ille judicabit eum in novissimo die.*

49. *For I have not spoken of myself, but the Father who sent me, he gave me commandment what I should say, and what I should speak,*

49. *Quia ego ex me ipso non sum locutus, sed qui misit me Pater,*

Text.

ipse mihi mandatum dedit quid dicam, et quid loquar.

50. *And I know that his commandmen' is life everlasting. The things therefore that I speak; even as the Father said unto me, so do I speak.*

50. *Et scio quia mandatum ejus vita æterna est. Quæ ergo ego loquor, sicut dixit mihi Pater, sic loquor.*

Commentary.

I should say," etc. In several occasions, He impresses on them, that God is His Father. "*Say*" and "*speak*" small things, as well as great things, including actions. All His words and actions were regulated by the will and command of His Father.

50. My word will condemn the disobedient; because, it is the commandment of My Father.

"*And I know that His commandment is life everlasting,*" the *cause* of life eternal, the way to it, for such as obey it, "*si vis ad vitam ingredi, serva mandata;*" the *cause* also of judgment and condemnation, not of itself; but, on account of their perversity, for such as disobey it; and therefore, it is, I instruct you benevolently, knowing it will turn to your profit and advantage, if you properly receive it. "*Momentaneum, quod cruciat; æternum, quod delectat; momentaneum quod delectat; æternum, quod cruciat.*" "*Even as the Father said unto Me, so do I speak.*" Our Lord confines Himself to His Father's command. He exceeds it not in speaking. Hence, all He says is worthy of undoubting belief. To reject His words, is to reject the words of God.

CHAPTER XIII.

1 *Before the festival day of the Pasch, Jesus knowing that his hour was come, that he should pass out of this world to the Father: having loved his own who were in the world, he loved them to the end.*

2 *And when supper was done, the devil having now put into the heart of Judas, the son of Simon, the Iscariot, to betray him:*

3 *Knowing that the Father had given him all things into his hands, and that he came from God, and goeth to God.*

4 *He riseth from supper, and layeth aside his garments: and having taken a towel, he girded himself.*

5 *After that, he poureth water into a basin, and began to wash the feet of the disciples, and to wipe them with the towel, wherewith he was girded.*

6 *He cometh, therefore, to Simon Peter. And Peter saith to him: Lord, dost thou wash my feet?*

7 *Jesus answered, and said to him: What I do, thou knowest not now, but thou shalt know hereafter.*

8 *Peter saith to him: Thou shalt never wash my feet. Jesus answered him: If I wash thee not, thou shalt have no part with me.*

9 *Simon Peter saith to him: Lord, not only my feet, but also my hands and my head.*

10 *Jesus saith to him: He that is washed, needeth not but to wash his feet, but is clean wholly. And you are clean, but not all.*

11 *For he knew who he was that would betray him; therefore he said: You are not all clean.*

12 *Then after he had washed their feet, and taken his garments, having sat down again, he said to them: Know you what I have done to you?*

13 *You call me, Master, and Lord: and you say well, for so I am.*

14 *If I then, being Lord and Master, have washed your feet: you also ought to wash one another's feet.*

15 *For I have given you an example, that as I have done to you, so you do also.*

16 *Amen, amen, I say to you: The servant is not greater than his lord: neither is an apostle greater that he that sent him.*

17 *If you know these things, you shall be blessed if you do them.*

18 *I speak not of you all: I know whom I have chosen: but that the Scripture may be fulfilled: He that eateth bread with me, shall lift up his heel against me.*

19 *At present I tell you before it come to pass: that when it shall come to pass, you may believe, that I am.*

20 *Amen, amen, I say to you, he that receiveth whomsoever I send, receiveth me: and he that receiveth me, receiveth him that sent me.*

21 *When Jesus had said these things, he was troubled in spirit: and he protested, and said: Amen, amen, I say to you, that one of you will betray me.*

22 *The disciples, therefore, looked one upon another, doubting of whom he spoke.*

23 *Now there was leaning on Jesus's bosom one of his disciples, whom Jesus loved.*

24 *Simon Peter, therefore, beckoned to him: and said to him: Who is it, of whom he speaketh?*

25 *He, therefore, leaning on the breast of Jesus, saith to him: Lord, who is it?*

26 *Jesus answered: He it is, to whom I shall reach bread dipped. And when he had dipped the bread, he gave it to Judas Iscariot, the son of Simon.*

27 *And after the morsel, satan entered into him. And Jesus said to him: That which thou dost, do quickly.*

28 *Now no man at the table knew for what intent he said this to him.*

29 *For some thought, because Judas had the purse, that Jesus had said to him: Buy those things which we have need of for the festival day: or that he should give something to the poor.*

30 *He then having received the morsel, went out immediately. And it was night.*

31 *When, therefore, he was gone out, Jesus said: Now is the Son of man glorified: and God is glorified in him.*

32 *If God be glorified in him, God will also glorify him in himself: and immediately will he glorify him.*

33 *Little children, yet a little while I am with you. You shall seek me: and as I said to the Jews: Whither I go, you cannot come: so now I say to you.*

34 *I give you a new commandment: That you love one another, as I have loved you, that you also love one another.*

35 *By this shall all men know that you are my disciples, if you have love one for another.*

36 *Simon Peter saith to him: Lord, whither goest thou? Jesus answered: Whither I go, thou canst not follow me now: but thou shalt follow me afterwards.*

37 *Peter saith to him: Why cannot I follow thee now? I will lay down my life for thee.*

38 *Jesus answered him: Wilt thou lay down thy life for me? Amen, amen, I say to thee, the cock shall not crow, till thou deny me thrice.*

CAPUT XIII.

1 *Ante diem festum Paschæ, sciens Jesus quia venit hora ejus ut transeat ex hoc mundo ad Patrem: cum dilexisset suos, qui erant in mundo, in finem dilexit eos.*

2 *Et cœna facta, cum diabolus jam misisset in cor, ut traderet eum Judas Simonis Iscariotæ:*

3 *Sciens quia omnia dedit ei Pater in manus, et quia a Deo exivit, et ad Deum vadit:*

4 *Surgit a cœna, et ponit vestimenta sua: et cum accepisset linteum, præcinxit se.*

5 *Deinde mittit aquam in pelvim, et cœpit lavare pedes discipulorum, et extergere linteo, quo erat præcinctus.*

6 *Venit ergo ad Simonem Petrum. Et dicit ei Petrus: Domine, tu mihi lavas pedes?*

7 *Respondit Jesus, et dixit ei: Quod ego facio, tu nescis modo, scies autem postea.*

8 *Dicit ei Petrus: Non lavabis mihi pedes in æternum. Respondit ei Jesus: Si non lavero te, non habebis partem mecum.*

9 *Dicit ei Simon Petrus: Domine, non tantum pedes meos, sed et manus, et caput.*

10 *Dicit ei Jesus: Qui lotus est, non indiget nisi ut pedes lavet, sed est mundus totus. Et vos mundi estis, sed non omnes.*

11 *Sciebat enim quisnam esset qui traderet eum: propterea dixit: Non estis mundi omnes.*

12 *Postquam ergo lavit pedes eorum, et accepit vestimenta sua: cum recubuisset iterum, dixit eis: Scitis quid fecerim vobis?*

13 *Vos vocatis me Magister, et Domine: et bene dicitis: sum etenim.*

14 *Si ergo ego lavi pedes vestros, Dominus et Magister: et vos debetis alter alterius lavare pedes.*

15 *Exemplum enim dedi vobis, ut quemadmodum ego feci vobis, ita et vos faciatis.*

16 *Amen, amen dico vobis: Non est servus major domino suo: neque Apostolus major est eo, qui misit illum.*

17 *Si hæc scitis, beati eritis si feceritis ea.*

18 *Non de omnibus vobis dico: ego scio quos elegerim: sed ut impleatur Scriptura: Qui manducat mecum panem, levabit contra me calcaneum suum.*

19 *Amodo dico vobis, priusquam fiat: ut cum factum fuerit, credatis, quia ego sum.*

20 *Amen, amen dico vobis: Qui accipit si quem misero, me accipit: qui autem me accipit, accipit eum qui me misit.*

21 *Cum hæc dixisset Jesus, turbatus est spiritu: et protestatus est, et dixit: Amen, amen dico vobis: Quia unus ex vobis tradet me.*

22 *Aspiciebant ergo ad invicem discipuli, hæsitantes de quo diceret.*

23 *Erat ergo recumbens unus ex discipulis ejus in sinu Jesu, quem diligebat Jesus.*

24 *Innuit ergo huic Simon Petrus, et dixit ei: Quis est, de quo dicit?*

25 *Itaque cum recubuisset ille supra pectus Jesu, dicit ei: Domine quis est?*

26 *Respondit Jesus: Ille est, cui ego intinctum panem porrexero. Et cum intinxisset panem, dedit Judæ Simonis Iscariotæ.*

27 *Et post buccellam introivit in eum satanas. Et Dixit ei Jesus: Quod facis, fac citius.*

28 *Hoc autem nemo scivit discumbentium ad quid dixerit ei.*

29 *Quidam enim putabant, quia loculos habebat Judas, quod dixisset ei Jesus Eme ea, quæ opus sunt nobis ad diem festum: aut egenis ut aliquid daret.*

30 *Cum ergo accepisset ille buccellam, exivit continuo. Erat autem nox.*

31 *Cum ergo exisset, dixit Jesus: Nunc clarificatus est filius hominis: et Deus clarificatus est in eo.*

32 *Si Deus clarificatus est in eo, et Deus clarificabit eum in semetipso: et continuo clarificabit eum.*

33 *Filioli, adhuc modicum vobiscum sum. Quæretis me: et sicut dixi Judæis: Quo ego vado, vos non potestis venire: et vobis dico modo.*

34 *Mandatum novum do vobis: Ut diligatis invicem, sicut dilexi vos, ut et vos diligatis invicem.*

35 *In hoc cognoscent omnes quia discipuli mei estis, si dilectionem habueritis ad invicem.*

36 *Dicit ei Simon Petrus: Domine, quo vadis? Respondit Jesus: Quo ego vado, non potes me modo sequi: sequeris autem postea.*

37 *Dicit ei Petrus: Quare non possum te sequi modo? animam meam pro te ponam.*

38 *Respondit ei Jesus: Animam tuam pro me pones? Amen, amen dico tibi: Non cantabit gallus, donec ter me neges.*

R

ANALYSIS.

In this chapter, is recorded the washing of His disciples' feet by our Lord, with all its circumstances, calculated to point out the great humility practised by our Lord (1–8). His threat addressed to Peter, who, out of reverence, first refused to have his feet washed by his heavenly Master. Peter's instant submission (8–12). Our Lord's address to His disciples, inculcating, after His own example, the practice of humility (12–17). His allusion to the treason of Judas, which He expressed in a rather general way (18–21). The trepidation into which the Apostles were thrown in consequence (22). The questioning of our Lord by St. John, at the instance of Peter, to know who the traitor was (23–25). Our Lord gives a sign for having him known, after which the traitor left, to carry out his wicked designs (25–31). He inculcates brotherly love, as a distinctive mark of His followers (32–35). He predicts the denial of Him by Peter (38).

Text.

1. *Before the festival day of the pasch, Jesus knowing that his hour was come that he should pass out of this world to the Father : having loved his own who were in the world, he loved them unto the end.*

1. *Ante diem festum Paschæ sciens Jesus quia venit hora ejus ut transeat ex hoc mundo ad Patrem ; cum dilexisset suos, qui erant in mundo, in finem dilexit eos.*

Commentary.

1. "*Before the festival day of the Pasch.*" This occurred on the evening of the fourth month (Nisan). According to the Jewish computation of festivals, the feast of the following day, commenced on the evening of the preceding, and closed on the evening of the day itself. Hence, the Pasch was celebrated "*between the two evenings*," of Thursday and Friday. The other Evangelists agree in saying (Matthew xxvi. 17 ; Luke xxii. 7 ; Mark xiv. 22), that our Lord celebrated the Pasch on the first day of Azyms. St. John says it occurred on the day before. Both accounts are true. It was on the festival itself, according to the Jewish computation of festivals, which commenced on the previous evening. It was on the day *before*, according to the *civil* computation of time which St. John, who wrote sixty years after this, followed. Hence, he uses the phrase, "*before the festival day of the Pasch.*" He does not say, *before the Pasch,* because the Pasch had commenced, when the occurrence here referred to regarding the supper, etc., took place.

"*Jesus knowing,*" as *God,* from eternity ; as *man,* from His conception ; "*that He should pass*" through the gates of death, now at hand—and His Resurrection and Ascension—"*from this world to the Father.*" There seems to be an allusion to the meaning of the word, "*Pasch,*" which signifies, *a passage.* The words also convey, that our Lord, when the destined hour had come, had voluntarily offered Himself for death, which He foresaw.

"*Having loved His own.*" Apostles and familiar friends and domestics, as is clear from the following history. "*Who were in the world,*" whom He was about to leave behind Him, exposed to the miseries and perils of this world, from which He was about to depart, when returning to a place of rest in His Father's bosom. These He now views with an eye of compassionate tenderness, and with feelings of increased pity and love.

"*Unto the end.*" Some understand, the end of His life. Others, the consummation or perfect exhibition of love, which He manifested by washing their feet—a thing He never did before— also by

Commentary

giving His sacred body and blood in the Eucharist, and by the following discourse, breathing love and affection. Finally, by giving His life for them.

"*Loving to the end,*" according to those, would mean, the most perfect, most intense and demonstrative love.

2. "*And when supper was ended.*" On this occasion the Paschal supper took place, when the Paschal lamb was partaken of in a standing posture. To this Paschal supper, there cannot be reference here, as our Lord clearly partook of the supper referred to here in a reclining posture, for "*He rose from it*" (*v.* 4). There was, besides, a common or ordinary Jewish supper, which took place, immediately after the Paschal supper, in order to satiate the cravings of hunger, for which the Paschal lamb would not suffice, considering the number who should, by law, partake of one lamb. The guests partook of this, as of any other supper, in a reclining posture. It is very likely that it is to this latter supper, reference is made here, at the close of which took place the washing of the Apostles' feet. The washing of the feet occurred *before* the institution of the Blessed Eucharist, our Lord having again resumed His reclining posture (*v.* 12), before He instituted it. The circumstance of the washing of the disciples' feet before the institution of the Blessed Eucharist, denoted or symbolized the purity of heart required at all times, for the proper reception of the adorable sacrament. On the very eve of His ignominious death, rendered bitter by the fact that the treason of one of His own disciples, whom the devil impelled to so horrible a crime, had a great share in bringing it about, He leaves us an undying memorial of His love in instituting the Blessed Eucharist, and an unexampled manifestation of humility, in washing His disciples' feet; the traitor, not excluded, who was an instrument in the hands of the devil.

The Evangelist uses the words, "*the devil having put it into the heart,*" etc., to denote the enormity of the crime, which was more than human; nay, even diabolical, in its nature.

3. "*Knowing that the Father,*" etc. This shows the excess of our Lord's humility, in washing His disciples feet. He did this with a full knowledge that He was Lord of the universe. That although in a state of passing weakness, His Father had already, by an ineffable communication, bestowed on Him, all power, "*had given Him all things*"—without exception—"*into His hands.*" He knew His origin, "*that He came from God,*" by an eternal generation, and came forth from Him, in time, by assuming human flesh in His Incarnation; and that He was about to return to His Father, "*and goeth to God,*" to reap the full fruit of glory, which He so well merited. The predestined "*hour*" having now

Text

2. *And when supper was done, (the devil having now put into the heart of Judas Iscariot the son of Simon, to betray him.)*

2. *Et cœna facta, cum diabolus jam misisset in cor ut traderet eum Judas Simonis Iscariotæ:*

3. *Knowing that the Father had given him all things into his hands, and that he came from God, and goeth to God:*

3. *Sciens quia omnia dedit ei Pater in manus, et quia a Deo exivit, et ad Deum vadit,*

Text.

4. *He riseth from supper and layeth aside his garments, and having taken a towel, girded himself.*

4. *Surgit a cœna, et ponit vestimenta sua: et cum accepisset linteum, præcinxit se.*

5. *After that, he putteth water into a basin, and began to wash the feet of his disciples, and to wipe them with the towel wherewith he was girded.*

5. *Deinde mittit aquam in pelvim, et cœpit lavare pedes discipulorum, et extergere linteo, quo erat præcinctus.*

6. *He cometh therefore to Simon Peter. And Peter saith to him: Lord, dost thou wash my feet?*

6. *Venit ergo ad Simonem Petrum. Et dicit ei Petrus: Domine, tu mihi lavas pedes?*

Commentary.

arrived, He wishes to leave an example of the most exalted virtues—love and humility—to all future generations.

In this, two things are worthy of observation: 1st, Our Lord while about to perform a great act of humility, had before Him a full knowledge of His infinite dignity, which rendered His humility more conspicuous; 2ndly, that He did this, on the eve of His Passion, to show His excessive love for His disciples, and for us all.

4. "*He riseth from supper.*" This refers to the common or ordinary Jewish supper, which succeeded the Paschal supper. Likely, there still lay scattered on the table, some of the food used.

"*And layeth aside His garments.*" "*Garments,*" in the plural, by common scriptural usage, is employed for the singular. It designates one, viz., the outer garment, which our Lord laid aside, to be more expedite, and in order to assume more perfectly the appearance and costume of a slave, who wore one, and only one short garment. A slave was not allowed flowing robes.

"*And having taken a towel, girded Himself.*" The Evangelist records not only the washing of the feet, but, all the circumstances, which clearly demonstrate how perfectly our Lord, in order to show His excessive humility, put on the appearance of a slave, on this occasion.

5. "*Began to wash the feet,*" etc. This is an account, in a general way, of what took place. It is not meant to be conveyed that our Lord washed the feet of any other of the disciples before He washed those of Peter; or, that having washed the feet of the others, He proceeded to wash his. In this verse, is contained only a general statement of what took place. The Evangelist comes to particulars, and describes things in order afterwards; or, the words of the verse may mean, He commenced to make preparation for the coming operation.

6. "*He cometh, therefore, to Simon Peter.*" "*Therefore,*" in order to commence what He intended, He came to Simon Peter, in the first place, as having been constituted head of the Apostolic College.

"*Dost thou?*" etc. Thou, and *my*, are emphatic, expressive of the infinite distance between them in point of dignity. "*Thou,*" the Eternal Son of God, Himself, God. *I*, a contemptible worm, a miserable sinner. Peter speaks thus out of feelings of the profoundest reverence, as the Baptist did at Baptism (Matthew iii. 14).

"*Dost Thou wash,*" prepare or mean to wash? Peter not knowing the full import or mysterious significance of our Redeemer's mode of acting, fancied our Lord meant merely to consult for their bodily comfort.

Commentary.

7. Our Lord conveys to Peter, that He did not well comprehend the import of what He was saying, regarding the washing of his feet; that this action had a deep meaning, a mysterious signification, which Peter would understand hereafter. Our Lord Himself seems to explain it, to a certain extent, in verse 14, where He says, it was meant to convey a lesson of humility. As to other mysterious meanings, it was very likely reserved for him, to know after the Spirit of truth would have come down on them.

8. Peter, whose natural vehemence showed itself on many occasions, is now vehement in his humility and reverence for his Lord, of whom he believed it to be unworthy, as supreme Lord and master, to condescend to wash His disciples' feet. Out of humility and reverence, he refuses to submit to it. Our Lord then, alluding to the mystical signification of this washing of the feet, which probably denoted purity of soul, tells him, if he persists in his refusal, which would amount to obstinate disobedience; then, he would be excluded from all participation in the great Eucharistic banquet, which He was about instituting. "*No part with Me*," most probably, refers to the Blessed Eucharist, in which the devout communicant is made one with our Lord, who becomes his food, and forms a portion of him.

Likely, our Lord's threat does not include utter exclusion from Him, and reprobation from grace and glory; though it seems likely, from following verse 9, that this was the sense in which Peter understood it, as the threat urges him to an opposite extreme, as consenting to more than was asked from him.

9. Peter, at once terrified by the threat of exclusion from our Lord, which he undersood in the strictest sense, consents to more than was required. He would have Him wash his head also and his hands. From which it is clear, the foregoing refusal sprang from love and reverence, rather than from disobedience.

10. Our Lord says, alludes to 'the condition of those coming forth from a bath, who having washed their entire person, now only need to remove from their feet the stains they contracted from walking naked in the dust. This was elicited by Peter's desire to have his hands and head also washed. He wishes to convey to Peter and the disciples present, that they needed no further washing than that of their feet; that they were by His grace, free from grievous sins, and only needed to be cleansed from these sins contracted through human frailty in their passage through life. Of this the cleansing of their feet was symbolical. It may be, He alludes to venial transgressions. Or, if He alludes to mortal sins contracted by men, who had been heretofore in grace, they need to be purified from those before approaching the Holy

Text.

7. *Jesus answered, and said to him: What I do, thou knowest not now, but thou shalt know hereafter.*

7. *Respondit Jesus, et dixit ei: Quod ego facio, tu nescis modo, scies autem postea.*

8. *Peter saith to him: Thou shalt never wash my feet. Jesus answered him: If I wash thee not, thou shalt have no part with me.*

8. *Dicit ei Petrus: Non lavabis mihi pedes in æternum. Respondit ei Jesus: Si non lavero te, non habebis partem mecum.*

9. *Simon Peter saith to him: Lord not only my feet, but also my hands, and my head.*

9. *Dicit ei Simon Petrus: Domine, non tantum pedes meos, sed et manus, et caput.*

10. *Jesus saith to him: He that is washed, needeth not but to wash his feet, but is clean wholly. And you are clean, but not all.*

10. *Dicit ei Jesus. Qui lotus est, non indiget nisi ut pedes lavet, sed est mundus totus. Et vos mundi estis, sed non omnes.*

Text.

Commentary.

Eucharist. In this allusion to bodily cleanliness, is evidently contained an allusion to moral or spiritual purity, as is clear from the application made in the following words, "*and you are clean, but not all*," which is allusive to Judas, as in following verse, "*They were clean*," either by the water of Baptism; or, by faith in Him and obedience to His words (xv. 3).

11. *For he knew who he was that would betray him; therefore he said: you are not all clean.*

11. Out of consideration for the feelings of Judas, of whose treasonable designs He was well aware, He refrained from mentioning his name. He reminds him of his state, with a view to his correction and repentance.

11. *Sciebat enim quisnam esset qui traderet eum: propterea dixit: Non estis mundi omnes.*

12. *Then after he had washed their feet, and taken his garments, being set down again, he said to them: Know you what I have done to you?*

12. "*Being sat down again*," in continuation of the supper, before instituting the Eucharist, "*He said to them*," calling their attention, to the spiritual lesson He meant to convey in the washing of their feet, as appears from His words to St. Peter (v. 7).

12. *Postquam ergo lavit pedes eorum, et accepit vestimenta sua: cum recubuisset iterum dixit eis: Scitis quid fecerim vobis?*

13. *You call me Master, and Lord: and you say well, for so I am.*
13. *Vos vocatis me Magister, et Domine: et bene dicitis: sum etenim.*

13. "*Master and Lord, and you say well; for, I am so.*" Not only as God, but also as Man, was He their Lord and Master, who not only taught them exteriorly; but, by His interior grace, enlightened their intellects and impelled their wills to do good and obey His heavenly precepts.

14. *If then I, being your Lord and Master have washed your feet; you also ought to wash one another's feet.*
14. *Si ergo ego lavi pedes vestros Dominus, et Magister: et vos debetis alter alterius lavare pedes.*

14. If He, their Lord and Superior, condescended to wash their feet, they should, with greater reason, wash each other's feet. This He inculcates literally, when necessity or charity required it, as was sometimes done in the infancy of the Church. Hence, among the commendations of widows is mentioned, "*Si sanctorum pedes lavit*," (1 Tim. v. 10). But what is particularly inculcated here, is, the *thing signified* by this washing of feet, viz., the exercise of charity and humility towards our neighbour.

"*To wash each other's feet*," is to be understood more according to the spirit, than the letter; always in a moral, rather than a literal sense; though, on occasions, the literal sense, or literally washing each other's feet, is enjoined.

15. *For I have given you an example, that as I have done to you, you do also.*
15. *Exemplum enim dedi vobis, ut quemadmodum ego feci vobis, ita et vos faciatis.*

15. Our Lord now teaches, by act, what He before taught by words, when He said, "*Learn of Me, because, I am meek and humble of heart*" (Matthew xi. 29). Similar is His teaching (Matthew xx. 25-28; Luke xx. 26, 27).

Commentary.

16. By a proverbial expression, He inculcates the equity of His precept. He thus perseveres in inculcating humility, and feelings of self-abasement, as He foresaw, that some among them would inordinately aspire to superiority and authority over their fellows.

17. "*If you knew these things,*" viz., that charity and humility are to be practised, as I make no doubt you do, and understand them speculatively.

"*You shall be blessed,*" in hope and peace of soul here, and eternal fruition hereafter, "*if you do them,*" by accomplishing them in deed, and persevering to the end.

18. In saying you shall be happy in the fulfilment of My precepts, I cannot say so of you all. "*I know whom I have chosen,*" to the Apostolic office. I know the hearts and dispositions of all, who are deserving of that office, and who are not; who are to persevere in My love and service, and who are not; who, on the contrary, are to betray Me and sell me to My enemies.

"*I elected twelve, and one is a devil*" (vi. 70).

"*But,* I have still chosen him among my Apostles;" (the sentence is to be filled up by the addition of the above clause), that My passion and death for mankind being brought about by him, whom I loaded with favours; the Scriptures which principally regarded Me, be fulfilled. "*He that eateth bread with Me,*" etc. The Scripture in question regarded originally the trials of David, and the ingratitude shown Him by His trusted, but faithless councillor, Achitophel. (2 Kings xx. 16, etc.) It principally, however, and mystically referred to Christ and His Passion, which was to commence with the treason of His ungrateful Apostle and be brought about by him. Our Lord, foreseeing the treason of His apostate disciple, and knowing his evil disposition, had still chosen him to the Apostleship; thus drawing good out of evil and verifying the Scripture, which contained the decree of God regarding His Passion and its mode of accomplishment. "*Eateth bread with Me,*" indicates great familiarity and friendship. "*Shalt lift his heel against Me,*" is allusive to the kick of vicious animals injuring their master. Others understand the figure to be allusive to wrestlers, who strive to trip up each other; or to men, who in a race, strive to trip their rivals and cause them to fall.

In the Septuagint reading, it is (Psalm xl. 10), "*Magnificavit super me supplantationem,*" "*hath greatly supplanted Me.*"

19. "*At present I tell you,*" etc. I now forewarn you of it, lest you might be scandalized at My admitting a traitor among My

Text.

16. *Amen, amen I say to you: The servant is not greater than his Lord: neither is the apostle greater than he that sent him.*

16. *Amen, amen dico vobis: Non est servus major Domino suo: neque apostolus major est eo, qui misit illum.*

17. *If you know these things, you shall be blessed if you do them.*

17. *Si hæc scitis beati eritis si feceritis ea.*

18. *I speak not of you all: I know whom I have chosen: but that the scripture may be fulfilled, He that eateth bread with me, shall lift up his heel against me.*

18. *Non de omnibus vobis dico: ego scio quos elegerim: sed ut adimpleatur Scriptura: Qui manducat mecum panem, levabit contra me calcaneum suum.*

19. *At present I tell you, before it come to pass that when it*

Text.

shall come to pass, you may believe that I am he.

19. *Amodo dico vobis, priusquam fiat: ut cum factum fuerit, credatis, quia ego sum.*

20. *Amen, amen I say to you, he that receiveth whomsoever I send, receiveth me: and he that receiveth me, receiveth him that sent me.*

20. *Amen, amen dico vobis: Qui accipit si quem misero, me accipit: qui autem me accipit, accipit cum, qui me misit.*

21. *When Jesus had said these things, he was troubled in spirit; and he testified, and said: Amen, amen I say to you, one of you shall betray me.*

21. *Cum hæc dixisset Jesus, turbatus est spiritu: et protestatus est, et dixit: Amen, amen dico vobis: Quia unus ex vobis tradet me.*

Commentary.

friends, as if I did not know it; so that seeing My prescience and My prediction on the subject verified by the event, "*you may believe*" in My Divinity, "*that I am He*," the long expected Messiah, whom I proclaimed Myself to be, viz., the Saviour of mankind.

20. "*Amen, Amen, I say to you.*" The words of this verse are explained in Commentary on Matthew (c. x. 40). Commentators are perplexed as to their connexion in the context with what precedes or follows. This great diversity of opinion shows it to be no easy matter to explain it.

There is a great preponderance of authorities in favour of the opinion, which holds that our Lord has in view in this verse to strengthen and console His followers, in the several trials they would have to endure in the faithful discharge of their duty, by the recollection, that they were His own vicegerents and representatives; and, if they should have to suffer, so had He; and it was by suffering, they would be partakers of His rewards and glory.

Corlui, however (*in hunc locum*), is of opinion, that there is no connexion whatever; that the Evangelist omits words spoken by our Redeemer, between which words omitted by the Evangelist and the words of this verse, there is a connexion; so that the connexion is traceable to some other words spoken by our Redeemer, but omitted here.

21. "*When Jesus said these things, He was troubled in spirit.*" He voluntarily permitted the inferior faculties of His soul to feel sorrow and indignation at the criminal treachery of Judas, which he was soon to carry into effect, as well as his base ingratitude. No doubt, the fore-knowledge of his damnation, which was to follow his act of suicide in hanging himself with a halter, deeply affected the merciful soul of our Divine Lord. (For a full explanation of this passage to *v.* 30, see Matthew xxvi. 21–26, Commentary.)

"*And He testified,*" openly declared what He before had only insinuated (*v.* 19), "*and said,*" adding, solemnly, to His seemingly incredible declaration, "*Amen, amen, I say to you, one of you shall betray Me.*"

When did our Lord say this? Was it *before* the institution of the Blessed Eucharist? Some hold it was. Others, following the order of narrative given by St. Luke (xxii. 21), hold that it was *after* the institution, He uttered these words; and that Matthew and Mark describe this by anticipation. St. Augustine (Lib. 3, *de Consensu Evang.* c. 1), and other Expositors, reconcile the narrative of the Evangelists, by saying, our Lord referred to the treason of Judas both *before* and *after* the institution of the Blessed Eucharist. The order of events was, probably, as follows;

Commentary.

after the Paschal supper was over, and when the common Jewish supper, which succeeded it, had commenced, our Lord rose from table, while they were engaged at the common supper, and washed His disciples' feet, and then reclining, said all that is recorded in this chapter from verse 12 to this verse 21. Then, troubled in spirit, He refers to the traitor, and on each one asking, "*Is it I, Lord?*" and Jesus replying, "*Thou hast said it*" (Matthew xxvi. 25), He instituted the Blessed Eucharist. After which, He again refers to the traitor, as in Luke (xxii. 21). Then, Peter asked John, to know of whom He spoke, and our Lord answers, "*to whom I shall reach bread dipped*" (v. 26). Whereupon, Judas, on receiving the morsel at our Lord's hands, after the devil had entered into Him, withdraws. After that, our Lord delivered the following beautiful discourse to His disciples.

22. The disciples, in their terror and anxious state of perplexity, each asked, "*Is it I, Lord?*" (Matthew xxvi. 22).

23. Our Lord then institutes the Blessed Sacrament, and this is omitted by St. John, as this Adorable Institution is fully recorded by the three other Evangelists. St. John fully details (vi.), the promise of this institution, with all its circumstances. After the institution of the Blessed Eucharist, our Lord again refers to the treason of Judas, and the events occurred, which are recorded in this verse (23), and the subsequent part of this chapter.

"*Leaning on Jesus's bosom.*" This happened owing to the mode of sitting or reclining at table, according to the custom then prevalent in Judea. It does not mean, that he was actually lying on our Saviour's bosom; but, that he sat *next* Him, so that his head naturally fell back on our Saviour's bosom, when he spoke to Him. This was a mark of special favour.

"*One of His disciples whom Jesus loved.*" This refers to St. John himself. He omits expressly mentioning his own name, out of a feeling of modest humility.

24. "*Beckoned to him,*" either by signs, or in a very low tone of voice, so as not to be heard by others. Peter may, possibly, have in view, to prevent the actual betrayal of our Lord, if necessary, by force, as in the case of Malchus, the High Priest's servant.

25. "*He, therefore, leaning on the breast of Jesus.*" From the position John held at table next to our Lord, he had his head quite near the breast of his Divine Master (v. 23). Now, on being

Text.

22. *The disciples therefore looked one upon another, doubting of whom he spoke.*
22. *Aspiciebant ergo ad invicem discipuli, hæsitantes de quo diceret.*

23. *Now there was leaning on Jesus' bosom one of his disciples, whom Jesus loved.*
23. *Erat ergo recumbens unus ex discipulis ejus in sinu Jesu, quem diligebat Jesus.*

24. *Simon Peter therefore beckoned to him, and said to him: Who is it, of whom he speaketh?*
24. *Innuit ergo huic Simon Petrus, et dixit ei: Quis est, de quo dicit?*

25. *He therefore leaning on the breast of Jesus saith to him: Lord, who is it?*

Text.

25. *Itaque cum recubuisset ille supra pectus Jesu, dicit ei: Domine quis est?*

26. *Jesus answered: He it is to whom I shall reach bread dipped. And when he dipped the bread, he gave it to Judas Iscariot, the son of Simon.*

26. *Respondit Jesus: Ille est, cui ego intinctum panem porrexero. Et cum intinxisset panem, dedit Judae Simonis Iscariotae.*

27. *And after the morsel, satan entered into him. And Jesus said to him: That which thou dost, do quickly.*

27. *Et post buccellam, introivit in eum satanas. Et dixit ei Jesus: Quod facis, fac citius.*

28. *Now no man at the table knew to what purpose he said this unto him.*

28. *Hoc autem nemo scivit discumbentium ad quid dixerit ei.*

Commentary.

asked by Peter, he turned towards him, and again leaning on the breast of Jesus, questioned Him, "*Who is it?*" It would appear from verses 28, 29, that all this was said in so low a tone of voice, as not to reach the other Apostles.

26. "*Bread dipped.*" The prevalent custom in the East was to use the hand as the instrument for conveying food to the mouth. It was also customary to have a dish filled with some *sauce*, into which all were wont, in common, to dip pieces of bread before eating it. Hence, when our Lord says, "*he that dippeth his hand with Me in the dish,*" etc. (Matthew xxvi. 23), He only refers to the traitor, in a general way, as forming part of the company, and as one of His intimate friends. Now, He gives a secret, special intimation by saying, "*he, to whom I shall reach bread dipped,*" and suiting the action to the word, handed it to Judas Iscariot. From this, St. John clearly saw Judas was the person referred to. Very likely, Judas, purse-bearer and almoner to our Lord and to the Apostolic College, occupied a place near our Lord, St. John being on the other side of Him, as it would be difficult to reach a morsel except to one immediately near Him. This distinction both as to the place he held, and the handing a morsel dipped, which was also regarded as a privilege and mark of special favour, only helped to aggravate the heinous ingratitude of Judas.

27. "*Satan entered into him.*" Already had Judas yielded to the suggestions and temptations of the devil (*v.* 2). But, now, the fiend takes full possession of him, rendering him utterly reprobate, driving him on recklessly to destruction. Judas now becomes a tool in his hands, to perpetrate the greatest crime, the betrayal of his Divine Master and benefactor. The communication between our Lord and St. John relative to the horrid treason of Judas was conducted in an under-tone, unperceived by others. Now, our Lord, in an audible tone, addresses Judas, "*that which thou dost, do it quickly.*" This is *permissive*, not *mandatory*, as if He said in the language of stern, indignant reproach: I know your wicked designs; I fear not your worst; I am prepared for the consequences of your base treason. "*What you do,*" you are prepared and determined to do, you may as well do at once.

28, 29. Although some at least may have known, that Judas was the traitor referred to; still, they did not understand the words of our Lord to convey that the execution of his treasonable designs was so near at hand. They thought that Judas was only commissioned to procure at once what might be required for the coming week or seven days of the Paschal solemnity, or to distribute alms to the poor.

Commentary.

29. *For some thought, because Judas had the purse, that Jesus had said to him: Buy those things which we have need of for the festival day or that he should give something to the poor.*

29. *Quidam enim putabant, quia loculos habebat Judas, quod dixisset ei Jesus Eme ea, quæ opus sunt nobis ad diem festum : aut egenis ut aliquid daret.*

30. The two preceding verses, 28, 29, would seem to convey, parenthetically an observation of the Evangelist, who returns to the narrative regarding Judas. He, on receiving the morsel, and being informed by our Lord, in reply to his question (Matthew xxvi. 25), that it was to him reference was made, "*went out immediately,*" on seeing that his treasonable design was discovered, and that he was excluded by our Lord from His society for ever. He may have been resolved on losing no time; lest our Redeemer might possibly arrange to escape, as He often did before ; and so, he would lose the stipulated sum of thirty pieces of silver. He may have been also apprehensive that the other Apostles, on discovering his wicked designs, might lay violent hands on him.

"*And it was night.*" A time well suited for carrying out treasonable designs.

From this, to chapter xviii., the Evangelist records the beautiful discourse, which our Lord delivered as a valedictory address to His beloved disciples, on the eve of His departure from them, full of tenderness, and replete with solid instruction as to their line of action in the future circumstances of difficulty and peril which awaited them, when His visible presence would be withdrawn from them.

31. "*When, therefore, he was gone out.*" The Evangelist refers to this circumstance, solely for the purpose of accurately noting the time.

"*Glorified,*" or shortly to be glorified. The past tense is put, to denote what would certainly take place in the future, just at hand. The *Son of Man* was to be *glorified* in His Passion, through which the redemption of man was to be accomplished, and His victory over death, sin and hell brought about.

He was also to be "*glorified*" in the wonderful events that were to occur at His death—the darkness, the earthquake—which proclaimed that God was suffering; also in the events that were to succeed it, His glorious Resurrection and Ascension, the sending down of the Holy Ghost as promised, all which proclaimed Him to be God. Now, this Passion, the source of His glory, was about to commence, owing to the betrayal of His apostate disciple.

"*And God is glorified in Him,*" since, by Him and His Sacred Passion, the leading Attributes of God, His justice, and hatred of sin, His eternal mercy and love for His creatures, are set forth in the clearest light.

Text.

30. *He therefore having received the morsel, went out immediately. And it was night.*

30. *Cum ergo accepisset ille buccellam, exivit continuo. Erat autem nox.*

31. *When he therefore was gone out, Jesus said: Now is the son of man glorified, and God is glorified in him.*

31 *Cum ergo exisset, dixit Jesus: Nunc clarificatus est filius hominis: et Deus clarificatus est in eo.*

Text.	Commentary.

Text.

32. *If God be glorified in him. God also will glorify him in himself, and immediately will he glorify him.*

32. *Si Deus clarificatus est in eo, et Deus clarificabit eum in semetipso: et continuo clarificabit eum.*

33. *Little children, yet a little while I am with you. You shall seek me, and as I said to the Jews. Whither I go, you cannot come: so I say to you now.*

33. *Filioli, adhuc modicum vobiscum sum. Quæretis me: et sicut dixi Judæis: Quo ego vado, vos non potestis venire: et vobis dico modo.*

34. *A new commandment I give unto you: That you love*

Commentary.

32. "*And if God is glorified in Him.*" "*If*," means *since—since* God is glorified in Him . . . "*will also* (in time) *glorify Him*," render this Son of Man and his humanity, glorious, "*in Himself*," by Himself, since the latent Deity, to which his humanity is united, will display itself and show Him to be the Son of God; and that, "*immediately*," in the miraculous and stupendous events accompanying His Passion now at hand, and in the wonderful events, which are to succeed, to be completed by His Assumption, or, rather, Ascension, when He shall enter into the glory of His Father.

33. "*Little children.*" This is the consoling language of endearment and tender affection expressed by Him, now on the point of leaving them.

"*Yet a little while*," etc. He refers to His approaching Passion just at hand, which had virtually commenced with the treason of Judas, who had just left, to put in execution his criminal designs. In these words, He confirms His assertion that He was to be glorified immediately. Some understand, "*yet a little while*," of the interval that was to elapse between this and His Ascension. But, as His intercourse with them between His Resurrection and Ascension was that of an Immortal and Divine Being, rather than of a mortal man, and as He will not be with them then in His usual mortal condition and familiarity as heretofore; hence, His words are generally understood of His approaching Passion.

"*You shall ask Me*," in your difficulties and perplexities, with a view of receiving strength, advice and consolation, "*and as I said to the Jews*," meaning the Jewish people generally, or their chief men in Jerusalem, on two occasions (vii. 34; viii. 21, and on the last occasion, repeating the dreadful prediction of their reprobation, "*you shall die in your sins.*" "*Whither I go, you cannot come.*" The Apostles will be anxious to follow Him to heaven and share in His glory, and rest from their labours. But, they will not be able to attain to it "*now*," as they are destined to spread the Gospel throughout the earth. It is only after great labours, persecution and suffering, to be completed by shedding their blood, they will be allowed to follow Him and share in His rest. Unlike the Jews, who would not find Him, and die in their sins, He consoles His disciples, His "*own children*," with the assurance that, after having passed through the gates of death and an ordeal of suffering, final glory and rest shall be their assured portion (*v.* 36).

Some Expositors connect "*now*," not with, "*I say to you*," but with "*come.*" "*You cannot come now*," implying, as He says, verse 36, "*Thou shalt follow hereafter.*"

34. "*A new Commandment I give unto you, that you love one another.*" In this sentence, after which should be placed a full

Commentary.

stop, is conveyed the *substance* of the precept. In the next sentence, commencing with the words, "*As I have loved you, that you also love one another*," is conveyed the *mode*, or rather, standard of its fulfilment. There is a diversity of opinion, as to how it could be called "*new*," since love for one another was a leading principle of the old law (Leviticus xix. 18). (See also Commentary, Matthew v. 43.) It is generally agreed upon, that our Lord calls it "*new*," as promulgated by Himself; 1st, because He made it the badge or distinguishing mark of his followers; 2ndly, because of the *new* and exalted standard proposed for its observance, "*as I have loved you*," or, because of the persons to whom it was first promulgated, who ignored it *speculatively*, owing to the false glossary of the Pharisees, who inferred from the word, "*love thy neighbour or friend;*" therefore, hate thy enemy; and *practically* ignored it owing to the universal selfishness and corruption prevalent, when the Gospel was first preached.

35. This was the distinctive mark or badge by which Christians were known and distinguished from all others. There were several distinctive marks for distinguishing men of several countries, of different religions, and professions in life; but, the marks of our Lord's true followers, without distinction of country, rank, profession, was the sincere and practical love of one another, a love, such as Christ had for us, who unselfishly made every sacrifice for us, even to the laying down of His life for us. "*Greater love no man hath*," etc. (xv. 13), "*and we ought to lay down our life for our brethren*" (1 John iii. 16). The love of the early Christians for one another was a subject of admiration to Pagans, who frequently exclaimed, "*See, how these Christians love one another!*" and the happy source of many conversions to the Christian faith.

36. St. Peter, absorbed in the thought that his Master was to depart from him, and seemingly listening in a heedless way, to the rest of the discourse, now with characteristic ardour, joined to great love for his Divine Master, asks, "*Lord, whither goest Thou?*" Our Lord, answering not Peter's question regarding the *place;* but, replying to Peter's intention of following Him to danger, even to death, tells how "*he cannot follow Him now.*" He is not yet prepared to die. His faith is not sufficiently strong to enable him to face death, *now*. So his hour is not yet come. His work for the Gospel is still before him; and his death, which will not be unlike that of his Divine Master, will open for him the gates of everlasting bliss. He will follow Him, *hereafter*, at some future day.

37. In the fulness of his love and zeal, and over confident in his own strength, which was partly the cause of his fall, by exposing

Text.

one another: as I have loved you, that you also love one another.

34. *Mandatum novum do vobis: Ut diligatis invicem, sicut dilexi vos, ut et vos diligatis invicem.*

35. *By this shall all men know that you are my disciples, if you have love one for another.*

35. *In hoc cognoscent omnes quia discipuli mei estis, si dilectionem habueritis ad invicem.*

36. *Simon Peter saith to him: Lord, whither goest thou? Jesus answered, Whither I go, thou canst not follow me now, but thou shalt follow hereafter.*

36. *Dicit ei Simon Petrus: Domine, quo vadis? Respondit Jesus: Quo ego vado, non potes me modo sequi: sequeris autem postea.*

37. *Peter saith to him: why cannot I follow thee now? I*

Text.	Commentary.
will lay down my life for thee. 37. *Dicit ei Petrus: Quare non possum te sequi modo? animam meam pro te ponam.*	himself unnecessarily to the proximate occasion of sinning against faith, he professes himself ready and willing to follow his Master to any place, ever so beset with danger: nay, ready to lay down his life for Him.
38. *Jesus answered him: Wilt thou lay down thy life for me? Amen, amen, I say to thee, the cock shall not crow till thou deny me thrice.* 38. *Respondit ei Jesus: Animam tuam pro me pones? Amen, amen dico tibi: Non cantabit gallus, donec ter me neges.*	38. Our Lord tells Peter that far from going to death with Him, he will deny Him, and that before dawn of the following morning (see Matthew xxvi. 34). Likely, our Lord predicted this twice, 1st, in the Supper Hall, as here, and Luke (xxii. 34); 2ndly, on their way to Gethsemane, after leaving the Supper Hall, as in Matthew and Mark (xiv. 30). St. Mark says, "*before the cock crows twice,*" referring to the first and second crowing of the cock. The first crowing of the cock occurred at midnight; and took place after Peter's first denial. The second, at day dawn. This latter took place after Peter's third denial—so that before the second crowing of the cock, Peter denied Him *thrice*, as is here clearly predicted.

CHAPTER XIV.

1 *Let not your heart be troubled. You believe in God, believe also in me.*
2 *In my Father's house there are many mansions. If not, I would have told you: because I go to prepare a place for you:*
3 *And if I shall go, and prepare a place for you: I will come again, and will take you to myself, that where I am, you also may be.*
4 *And whither I go you know, and the way you know.*
5 *Thomas saith to him: Lord, we know not whither thou goest; and how can we know the way?*
6 *Jesus saith to him: I am the way, and the truth, and the life. No man cometh to the Father, but by me.*
7 *If you had known me, you would surely have known my Father also: and from henceforth you shall know him, and you have seen him.*
8 *Philip saith to him: Lord, show us the Father, and it is enough for us.*
9 *Jesus saith to him: Have I been so long a time with you; and you have not known me? Philip, he that seeth me, seeth the Father also. How sayest thou, Show us the Father?*
10 *Do you not believe, that I am in the Father, and the Father in me? The words that I speak to you, I speak not of myself. But the Father who abideth in me, he doth the works.*
11 *Believe you not that I am in the Father, and the Father in me?*
12 *Otherwise believe for the works themselves. Amen, amen, I say to you, he that believeth in me, the works that I do, he shall do also, and greater than these shall he do: because I go to the Father.*
13 *Because I go to the Father, and whatsoever you shall ask the Father in my name, that will I do: that the Father may be glorified in the Son.*
14 *If you shall ask me any thing in my name, that I will do.*
15 *If you love me, keep my commandments.*
16 *And I will ask the Father, and he shall give you another Paraclete, that he may abide with you for ever.*
17 *The spirit of truth, whom the world cannot receive, because it seeth him not nor knoweth him: but you shall know him; because he shall abide with you, and shall be in you.*
18 *I will not leave you orphans: I will come to you.*
19 *Yet a little while: and the world seeth me no more. But you see me: because I live, and you shall live.*
20 *In that day you shall know that I am in my Father, and you in me, and I in you.*

21 *He that hath my commandments, and keepeth them: he it is that loveth me. And he that loveth me shall be loved of my Father: and I will love him, and will manifest myself to him.*

22 *Judas saith to him, not the Iscariot: Lord, how is it, that thou wilt manifest thyself to us, and not to the world?*

23 *Jesus answered, and said to him: If any one love me, he will keep my word, and my Father will love him, and we will come to him, and will make our abode with him:*

24 *He that loveth me not, keepeth not my words. And the word which you have heard is not mine; but the Father's who sent me.*

25 *These things have I spoken to you, abiding with you.*

26 *But the Paraclete, the Holy Ghost, whom the Father will send in my name, he will teach you all things, and bring all things to your mind, whatsoever I shall have said to you.*

27 *Peace I leave with you, my peace I give unto you: not as the world giveth, do I give unto you. Let not your heart be troubled, nor let it be afraid.*

28 *You have heard that I said to you: I go away and I come unto you. If you loved me, you would indeed be glad: because I go to the Father: For the Father is greater than I.*

29 *And now I have told you before it come to pass: that when it shall come to pass, you may believe.*

30 *I will not now speak many things with you. For the prince of this world cometh, and in me he hath not any thing.*

31 *But that the world may know that I love the Father: and as the Father hath given me commandment, so do I: Arise, let us go hence.*

CAPUT XIV.

1 *Non turbetur cor vestrum. Creditis in Deum, et in me credite.*

2 *In domo Patris mei mansiones multæ sunt. Si quo minus, dixissem vobis: Quia vado parare vobis locum.*

3 *Et si abiero, et præparavero vobis locum: iterum venio, et accipiam vos ad meipsum, ut ubi sum ego, et vos sitis.*

4 *Et quo ego vado scitis, et viam scitis.*

5 *Dicit ei Thomas: Domine, nescimus quo vadis: et quomodo possumus viam scire?*

6 *Dicit ei Jesus: Ego sum via, et veritas, et vita. Nemo venit ad Patrem, nisi per me.*

7 *Si cognovissetis me, et Patrem meum utique cognovissetis: et amodo cognoscetis eum, et vidistis eum.*

8 *Dicit ei Philippus: Domine, ostende nobis Patrem, et sufficit nobis.*

9 *Dicit ei Jesus: Tanto tempore vobiscum sum, et non cognovistis me? Philippe, qui videt me, videt et Patrem. Quomodo tu dicis: Ostende nobis Patrem?*

10 *Non creditis quia ego in Patre, et Pater in me est? Verba, quæ ego loquor vobis, a meipso non loquor. Pater autem in me manens, ipse facit opera.*

11 *Non creditis quia ego in Patre, et Pater in me est?*

12 *Alioquin propter opera ipsa credite. Amen, amen dico vobis, qui credit in me, opera quæ ego facio, et ipse faciet, et majora horum faciet: quia ego ad Patrem vado.*

13 *Et quodcumque petieritis Patrem in nomine meo, hoc faciam: ut glorificetur Pater in Filio.*

14 *Si quid petieritis me in nomine meo, hoc faciam.*

15 *Si diligitis me, mandata mea servate.*

16 *Et ego rogabo Patrem, et alium Paraclitum dabit vobis, ut maneat vobiscum in æternum.*

17 *Spiritum veritatis, quem mundus non potest accipere, quia non videt eum, nec scit eum. Vos autem cognoscetis cum: quia apud vos manebit, et in vobis erit.*

18 *Non relinquam vos orphanos: veniam ad vos.*

19 *Adhuc modicum: et mundus me jam non videt. Vos autem videtis me: quia ego vivo, et vos vivetis.*

20 *In illo die vos cognoscetis quia ego sum in Patre meo, et vos in me, et ego in vobis.*

21 *Qui habet mandata mea, et servat ea: ille est, qui diligit me. Qui autem diligit me, diligetur a Patre meo: et ego diligam eum, et manifestabo ei meipsum.*

22 *Dicit ei Judas, non ille Iscariotes: Domine, quid factum est, quia manifestaturus es nobis teipsum, et non mundo?*

23 *Respondit Jesus, et dixit ei: Si quis diligit me, sermonem meum servabit, et Pater meus diliget eum, et ad eum veniemus, et mansionem apud eum faciemus:*

24 *Qui non diligit me, sermones meos non servat. Et sermonem quem audistis, non est meus: sed ejus, qui misit me, Patris.*

25 *Hæc locutus sum vobis, apud vos manens.*

26 *Paraclitus autem Spiritus sanctus, quem mittet Pater in nomine meo, ille vos docebit omnia, et suggeret vobis omnia, quæcumque dixero vobis.*

27 *Pacem relinquo vobis, pacem meam do vobis: non quomodo mundus dat, ego do vobis. Non turbetur cor vestrum, neque formidet.*

28 *Audistis quia ego dixi vobis: Vado, et venio ad vos. Si diligeretis me, gauderetis utique, quia vado ad Patrem: quia Pater major me est.*

29 *Et nunc dixi vobis prius quam fiat: ut cum factum fuerit, credatis.*

30 *Jam non multa loquar vobiscum. Venit enim princeps mundi hujus, et in me non habet quidquam.*

31 *Sed ut cognoscat mundus quia diligo Patrem, et sicut mandatum dedit mihi Pater, sic facio. Surgite, eamus hinc.*

ANALYSIS.

In this chapter, which contains the commencement of our Lord's discourse, after the Last Supper, He consoles the Apostles, who were saddened at the prospect of His near departure, by pointing to the mansions of bliss He was about preparing for them; and He informs them that He is Himself the way, by which they were to reach the Father—the term of their journey—in whose bosom they were to find everlasting happiness (1–10). He asserts His identity with His Father, and among other proofs, refers to His miracles wrought in attestation of it (10–13). He holds out great promises in favour of prayer, offered up to the Father and to Himself with proper dispositions (13, 14). He points to the observance of the commandments, as the true test of His love (15). He consoles them with a promise of the Paraclete, who was to abide with them for ever (16–18). He again refers to the observance of His commandments, and the spiritual fruits resulting therefrom (20–25). He again promises to send down the Paraclete (26). He leaves them His peace, as a pledge of all spiritual blessings (27). He says, that far from being saddened, they should rather rejoice at His departure and death, which would secure Him greater glory (28). He tells them all beforehand, in order that seeing His predictions verified, their faith may be strengthened (29–31).

Text.

1. *Let not your heart be troubled. You believe in God, believe also in me.*

1. *Non turbetur cor vestrum. Creditis in Deum, et in me credite.*

2. *In my Father's house there are many mansions. If not, I would have told you: because I go to prepare a place for you;*

2. *In domo Patris mei mansiones multæ sunt. Si quo minus, dixissem vobis: Quia vado parare vobis locum.*

Commentary.

1. Our Lord perceived, that owing to His prediction regarding His near departure and death, to be brought about by the treason of Judas, and His denial by Peter, their head and bravest among the Apostles, which should make each one to tremble for himself, the disciples were in a state of great distress and consternation. On this account, He sets about consoling them. "*Let not your hearts be troubled, you believe in God*"—as the law of Moses inculcated—"*believe also in Me.*" The law of Moses inculcated belief in the true God. Some read the words, "*you believe in God,*" imperatively, "*believe in God.*" This the Greek admits. The Vulgate reading, however, is preferable. The particle of comparison seems to be implied, "As *you believe in God,*" who cannot deceive or be deceived, "so, *also believe in Me.*" Have faith in Me, as God; believe all I say; and have that confidence in Me, which that faith inspires. My Providence shall watch over you and help you to come forth victorious in all your conflicts. Although departed from you, I shall be ever present with you, to secure victory in all your conflicts; and, finally, bring you to Myself, to share in My kingdom.

2. "*In My Father's house,*" etc. In that heavenly mansion whither I am about to go, there is room for you all—a place proportioned to each one's merits. So you need have no fear of being excluded, and of not following Me hereafter.

"*If not, I would have told you that I go to prepare a place for you.*" In the Greek, the particle "*that,*" is omitted, and according to this Greek reading, the sense is easier and more natural. If there were not many mansions in My Father's heavenly palace, which you all expect, one day to reach, I would have told you so;

Commentary.

and not be buoying you up and deluding you with vain hopes. "*I go to prepare a place for you.*" In leaving you for a time, I go to get ready for you one of those blissful mansions, for which, from eternity you were predestined. By My death, I shall throw open the gates of this heavenly palace, hitherto closed against men, and shall send down My spirit of grace to render you fit, in due time, for taking possession of it. Others, retaining the Greek (ὅτι), *that*, read the words interrogatively, thus: "If it were not so, would I have said, I would go to prepare a place for you?" (Beelen, Corlui, etc.)

3. "*And if I shall go and prepare a place for you*"—(already destined for you)—"*I will come again and take you to Myself.*" This is understood by some, of His final coming to judgment, when the felicity of the elect, in their union with their glorified bodies, will be consummated. Others, of His coming at death, when, at particular judgment, the fate of each shall be decided. Very likely, it refers to both; for, general judgment virtually takes place at death, as it is only a ratification of particular judgment.

"*That where I am.*" The word, "*am*," refers to our Lord's presence, at the time, in heaven in virtue of His Divinity, where *I am* now, in My Divine nature, Omnipresent, as God, you would be. In His *human* nature, He was on earth with them. But, at a future day, they shall dwell in these heavenly courts, where He was, at the very time, dwelling as to His omnipresent *Divinity*, by which He fills the heavens and the earth. The separation, then, is only temporary. They are to be for ever blessed hereafter with His society in heaven.

4. "*And whither I go you know.*" I frequently told you that I was to go to My Father in heaven, and enter into His glory. "*And the way you know,*" from My repeated declarations on the subject, to be My Passion and death (Matthew xvi. 21; Luke ix. 22; xviii. 31–33). The Apostles ought to have known all from our Saviour's several allusions and declarations. They knew it, in a general way. However, being slow of apprehension, they did not clearly see it, although they *might and ought*. The words, then mean, *you might and ought* to know whither I go, as I so often spoke of going to My Father; and the way, too, which I so often explained, to be My Death and Passion.

5. Thomas, whose slowness of apprehension was shown on another occasion also (xx. 25), here says, probably with a view of eliciting more definite knowledge from our Lord, they did not know whither He was going. Of this they had not a distinct knowledge or recollection at the time, being "*slow of heart*" (Luke xxiv. 25), and tardy of apprehension.

Text.

3. *And if I shall go, and prepare a place for you: I will come again, and will take you to myself, that where I am, you also may be.*

3. *Et si abiero, et præparavero vobis locum: iterum venio, et accipiam vos ad meipsum, ut ubi sum ego, et vos sitis.*

4. *And whither I go you know, and the way you know.*

4. *Et quo ego vado scitis, et viam scitis.*

5. *Thomas saith to him: Lord, we know not whither thou goest; and how can we know the way?*

5. *Dicit ei Thomas: Domine, nescimus quo vadis: et quo modo possumus viam scire?*

Text.

6. *Jesus saith to him: I am the way, and the truth, and the life. No man cometh to the Father, but by me.*

6. *Dicit ei Jesus: Ego sum via, et veritas, et vita. Nemo venit ad Patrem, nisi per me.*

Commentary.

6. Our Lord gives a distinct and explicit reply to the implied request of St. Thomas who, in saying, "*how can we know the way?*" impliedly conveys a request, that our Lord would point it out.

In this verse, He points to *Himself* as the *way;* the *term* of this way, whither He was going, He points out to be the *Father.*

"*I am the way*," about which you question Me; "*the way*" through which alone you will reach the Father, the term of your journey; to whom I am going, so that you may, hereafter, follow Me, and reach to the same, and in Him find eternal happiness and rest. "*I am the way*," because, through My blood and merits this way, hitherto inaccessible to mankind, is thrown open (Heb. x. 20).

"*And the truth and the life.*" "*And*," means, *because.* Our Lord explains how He is "*the way*," because, He is "*the truth*," that is, the source and fountain of *faith*, freeing men from all error, and by His holy doctrines pointing out the road to heaven. "*And the life*," the source of supernatural life, viz., of sanctifying and actual grace, inspiring them with faith and grace, enriching them with merits, whereby, as so many ways, you tend to heaven. Wherefore, be not disturbed, by the prospect of My death, as well as your own, which will soon follow; rather believe and hope in Me, who will one day raise both Myself and you to a glorious life and conduct you to heaven. (A. Lapide, Corlui.)

Some Commentators understand the words, "*the truth and the life*," adjectively, or, in the abstract, to mean, the *true* and life-giving way. He is "*the way*," in His *Divine* Person, manifested in His Incarnation; in His *office*, as mediator with God; in His *sacrifice*, as our great High Priest for ever; in His intercession, as our advocate with the Father, giving us access with confidence to the throne of grace; "*leaving us an example, that we should walk in His footsteps*" (1 Peter xi. 21).

He is "*the truth*," essentially so, the source and fountain of all truth, "*the life*," being "*the Resurrection and the life*," through whom alone we can come to the Father, through His life-giving Spirit.

"*No one cometh to the Father,*" etc. He is Himself the only way for arriving at the destined term which is the Father, who is life eternal in Himself, giving life and happiness to all others.

7. *If you had known me, you would without doubt have known my Father also: and from henceforth you shall know him, and you have seen him.*

7. He answers the other part of Philip's interrogation, "*we know not whither Thou goest,*" or the term, to which you conduct us. They knew it not, because, they did not know Himself, who, appearing in His *human nature*, is, in His *Divine nature*, identical with the Father. They knew and believed Him to be the Son of God. But they did not distinctly apprehend His consubstantiality

Commentary

with the Father, and identity of nature, till after the descent of the Holy Ghost, at Pentecost.

"*And from henceforth, you shall know Him,*" when I shall send My Spirit to enlighten you.

"*And you have seen Him,*" veiled in Me, who am one with Him, in the wonderful works I have performed.

8. Philip fancying our Lord spoke of the Father as visible under some external corporeal appearance, says, with some degree of eagerness, "*Lord, show us*"—under some visible outward appearance—"*the Father,*" of whom you speak, as seen by us. Philip may possibly wish for some vision of God, such as he read was vouchsafed to some of the ancient Prophets.

"*And it is enough for us.*" We will ask no more questions, as to the many mansions in your Father's house reserved for us; or about your death, to be followed by glory or about any other reasons whereby you may be pleased to console us.

9. "*So long a time.*" For the space of three years, "*have I been with you,*" teaching and instructing you, by word and example, proving My Divinity by miracles of the highest order. "*And you have not known Me,*" as *God,* consubstantial with the Father, possessing with Him the same identical, indivisible, essence; as *man,* you have acknowledged Me to be His Son, His legate. This request to show you the Father, arises from your not duly apprehending My *Divinity,* as if the Father and I were not the same, possessing the same identical nature.

"*Philip, he that seeth Me seeth the Father also.*" He that seeth Me in My visible, human form, seeth My Divinity implicitly, as in My *human* and *Divine* nature, I have but *one person,* the Divine Person of the Son of God. He "*seeth My Father also,*" since "*My Father and I are one,*" having one nature, "*one,*" and three distinct persons.

"*Since the Father and I are* "*one,*" "*how sayest thou, show us the Father?*" With a due apprehension of My Divinity concealed beneath My humanity, by seeing My Divinity under these veils, thou seest My Father also, who is *one* in *nature* with Me, though distinct as to person. "*Seeth Me, seeth the Father also,*" points to distinction of persons.

10. "*Do you not believe.*" The Greek is in the singular, *dost thou* not believe?—addressing Philip—"*that I am in the Father and the Father in Me?*" on account of the identity of nature.

This He proves from the effects. For, "*the words which I speak,*" viz., declaring that I am in the Father and the Father in Me. "*I speak not of Myself,*" without the Father. "*But the Father abiding in Me,*" speaks them, and not only speaks what I say in

Text

7. *Si cognovissetis me, et Patrem meum utique cognovissetis: et amodo cognoscetis eum, et vidistis eum.*

8. *Philip saith to him: Lord, shew us the Father, and it is enough for us.*

8. *Dicit ei Philippus: Domine, ostende nobis Patrem, et sufficit nobis.*

9. *Jesus saith to him: So long a time have I been with you; and have you not known me? Philip, he that seeth me, seeth the Father also. How sayest thou, shew us the Father?*

9. *Dicit ei Jesus: Tanto tempore vobiscum sum, et non cognovistis me? Philippe, qui videt me, videt et Patrem. Quomodo tu dicis: Ostende nobis Patrem?*

10. *Do you not believe, that I am in the Father, and the Father in me? The words that I speak to you, I speak not of myself. But the Father who abideth in me, he doth the works.*

Text.

10. *Non creditis quia ego in Patre, et Pater in me est? Verba, quæ ego loquor vobis, a me ipso non loquor, Pater autem in me manens, ipse facit opera.*

11. *Believe you not that I am in the Father, and the Father in me?*

11. *Non creditis quia ego in Patre, et Pater in me est?*

12. *Otherwise believe for the very works' sake. Amen, amen I say to you, he that believeth in me, the works that I do, he also shall do, and greater than these shall he do.*

12. *Alioquin propter opera ipsa credite. Amen, amen dico vobis, qui credit in me, opera quæ ego facio, et ipse faciet, et majora horum faciet: quia ego ad Patrem vado.*

Commentary.

common with Me, but also works with Me, the great miracles you saw Me perform; thus giving proof that we are one; and He thus manifests His Divine nature through My humanity. Works of power are by appropriation, like all manifestations of Omnipotence, attributed to the Father, though common to the two other Persons of the Trinity.

11. He repeats the same, for greater emphasis' sake.

12. If you believe not on account of My words, asserting My identity with the Father, believe Me on account of the great stupendous miracles I performed in proof of this assertion—miracles both as to *substance*, variety and magnitude, also in regard to the *mode* of operation, altogether Divine. These prove to demonstration the truth of My assertion, that the Father is in Me, operating these miracles, and I in Him, operating them also with Him.

"*He that believeth in Me*," in the plenitude of My Divinity, believeth that I am in the Father, and the Father in Me. "*The works that I do, He shall also do.*" Such as the miracles of healing the sick, raising the dead to life, etc. This is not meant for every believer; but for some, such as the Apostles, and Apostolic men; this power is given them, in order to furnish an assurance of the truth of their mission. It is a gift left by our Lord to His Church, and to His followers, without stating that all His followers would do such works. It is meant as a motive of consolation to the Apostles. It also shows the merit and efficacy of faith.

"*And greater than these*," etc. These words are understood by many, not of the intrinsic nature of the works themselves, as evidences of Divine power; since, no works could be a greater proof of Divine power than the raising of the dead. But, if not "*greater*" in *themselves*, they are greater in their *effects*. They had been attended with greater results. They effected the conversion of more sinners; they were not confined to Judea, but they were performed throughout the entire world, the conversion of which they brought about.

Others understand the words, of the works in themselves. For instance, the shadow of Peter cured the sick, which did not happen in our Lord's time. All they did, however, was not from themselves, but through His power, derived from Him. He humbly concealed His power beneath the veils of human nature. But being now in the glory of God the Father, He displays it in all its effulgence through His ministers, who derive all their power from Him.

Commentary.

"*Because I go to the Father.*" I shall in My glorified state display the fulness of My power through My ministers, and when I am in my glory, I shall also send down on the Church the Spirit of power and of truth.

13. "*And whatsoever you shall ask . . . in My name,*" through My merits and powerful intercession. "*Whatsoever,*" without exception, especially in regard to matters connected with the manifestation of His Divinity and the truth of His doctrine. Of course, the object must be good, as the words, "*in My name,*" imply, and the required dispositions must be present.

"*That I will do.*" This shows the unity of nature; since, the Son grants what is asked from His Father.

"*That the Father may be glorified in the Son,*" who with the Father grants the objects of the petitions preferred to them in His Son's name; and thus receives glory through His Son, on whose account, He grants their requests.

14. "*If you ask* ME," etc. "ME," is not in the Greek, but it is supported by the best authorities. Not only will He grant what is asked of the Father through His merits; but also what may be asked directly of Himself, through His own merits and intercession. This He will grant, as being in power and nature equal to the Father and identical with Him. Some understand the preceding verse of petitions having reference to the greater miracles which He promises, especially as regards the spreading of the Gospel; they understand this verse of particular petitions in the several necessities of life.

15. The true test of their love for Him was, not the external expression of grief at His departure; but obedience to His will in all things, and the observance of His commandments. "*The proof of love,*" says St. Gregory, "*is exhibited in work.*"

16. "*And*"—if you observe My commandments—"*I*," as man, as mediator of God and man, "*will ask the Father.*" This shows the distinction of Persons—"*and He will give you another Paraclete,*" or Comforter. "*Another,*" to replace Me on My departure from you. This conveys, that He was a *Paraclete* also.

"*That He may remain with you,*" and with your successors, and the entire Church, not for a time, as happens Me, in My visible stay among you, but, "*for ever,*" to the end of all time, to console you and all My faithful followers in their difficulties and perplexities.

17. "*The Spirit of truth,*" the source and author of all truth, who teaches all truth necessary for salvation, and preserves and frees us from all errors (xvi. 13), "*whom the world,*" the kingdom

Text.

13. *Because I go to the Father, and whatsoever you shall ask the Father in my name, that will I do: that the Father may be glorified in the Son.*

13. *Et quodcumque petieritis Patrem in nomine meo, hoc faciam: ut glorificetur Pater in Filio.*

14. *If you shall ask me any thing in my name, that I will do.*

14. *Si quid petieritis me in nomine meo, hoc faciam.*

15. *If you love me, keep my commandments.*

15. *Si diligitis me, mandata mea servate.*

16. *And I will ask the Father, and he shall give you another Paraclete, that he may abide with you for ever.*

16. *Et ego rogabo Patrem, et alium Paracletum dabit vobis, ut maneat vobiscum in æternum,*

17. *The spirit of truth, whom the world cannot receive, because it seeth him not nor*

Text.

knoweth him: but you shall know him; because he shall abide with you, and shall be in you.

17. *Spiritum veritatis, quem mundus non potest accipere, quia non videt eum, nec scit eum. Vos autem cognoscetis eum: quia apud vos manebit, et in vobis erit.*

18. *I will not leave you orphans: I will come to you.*

18. *Non relinquam vos orphanos: veniam ad vos.*

19. *Yet a little while: and the world seeth me no more. But you see me: because I live, and you shall live.*

19. *Adhuc modicum et mundus me jam non videt. Vos autem videtis me: quia ego vivo, et vos vivetis.*

20. *In that day you shall know that I am in my Father, and you in me, and I in you.*

Commentary.

of Satan, "*the father of lies*" (viii. 14), "*cannot receive*" whilst it remains in its present perverse condition.

"*The world,*" means worldly, carnal, corrupt men, bent on pleasure, and engrossed with the things of earth. "*Cannot receive, because, it seeth Him not,*" etc. Worldly, carnal men, are devoid of the necessary dispositions for receiving the Holy Ghost. They want the necessary intellectual and supernatural vision and knowledge, which comes through the light of faith. This class walk by sight, and not by faith. "*The sensual man perceives not what is of the Spirit of God.*" (1 Cor. ii.) "*Knoweth,*" signifies, besides an act of the intellect, an operation of the will. They *love* not the Holy Ghost or His operations. Hence, they are in no disposition for receiving Him. They neither understand nor care about heavenly things.

"*But you shall know Him.*" The Greek is in the present, "*you know Him,*" by sanctifying grace.

"*And He shall abide with you,*" showing His presence by exerting His influence and power.

"*And shall be in you,*" dwelling in you, in a special manner, as, in His temples, in a manner quite different from the way in which I visibly show Myself to you.

18. Although I go from you to My Father, to send you another Comforter in My place; still, I shall not Myself personally desert you who are My beloved children (xiii. 33), nor leave you comfortless in the destitute condition of children deprived of a parent.

"*I will come to you.*" I will return and console you in My glorious state, after my Resurrection.

19. "*Yet a little while,*" after a short interval of a few hours, "*and the world,*" worldly-minded men, "*shall see Me no more.*" My visible presence shall cease for them at My death, which takes place in a few hours. I shall, after that, be visible to My disciples only; worldly-minded men shall not see Me either visibly or by faith.

"*But you see Me.*" I shall show Myself to you, "*because I live,*" shall be resuscitated to a new and immortal life. I have essential life in my Divinity, "*and you shall live.*" This may mean: you shall not soon be subjected, like Me, to death, and shall continue in life, so that you may be able to see Me. Or, it may refer to their future resuscitation, when they shall see Him in glory and share in His happiness.

20. "*In that day,*" during My stay with you, after My Resurrection, including the time when I shall send down My Spirit at Pentecost, "*you shall know*" these leading mysteries of faith and understand them, viz., "*that I am in the Father,*" consubstantial

Commentary.

with Him, having the same indivisible Divine nature with Him—you shall also know, "*that you are in Me*," by My Incarnation, assuming your nature—as the members connected with the Head—"*and I in you*," imparting to you My Spirit, the great gift of sanctification. "*I in you*," as the vine in the branches, imparting life to you, as the vine imparts it to the branches, that are engrafted on it. "*You in Me*," as the branches in the vine. "*I in you*," as the vine in the branches, communicating the life-giving influence of Divine grace. From this passage are inferred, the mysteries of the *Trinity, Incarnation,* and *Sanctification*.

21. The above favours are not confined to the Apostles alone. They extend to all the faithful. "*He that hath My commandments*," bears them in mind, "*and keepeth them.*" It won't do, to believe and retain them in mind. It is necessary to observe them in deed. "*He it is that loveth Me.*" The observance of My commandments is the true test of love. "*And he that loveth Me will be loved by My Father.*" My commandments are the commandments I received of My Father. He, then, who keeps them, loves My Father, and shall be loved by Him in turn, and shall receive from Him abundant proofs of His love in the great blessings He shall bestow. "*And I shall love him*," not only as *God*, but as *man*, and shall bestow on him great gifts here and hereafter.

"*And will manifest Myself to him*," in this life, by a clearer revelation of Myself, by a practical knowledge and feeling of love, such as My Saints experience when they taste and see how good God is; and in the life to come, when he shall see Me face to face.

22. Judas Iscariot had left, the Evangelist, therefore, who had already stated that he had left, here guards against any mistake. The Judas here referred to was Thaddeus, the brother of James, the Less. He was the author of the Catholic Epistle.

"*How is it, that Thou wilt manifest?*" etc. He refers to verses 19–21. He could not understand how our Lord, in His glorious manifestation after death, would conceal Himself from worldly men, while showing Himself to His disciples.

23. Our Lord, replying in very general terms, says, that He will manifest Himself to more than His apostles, that "*if any one*"—no matter who—"*love Him*," and—in proof of his love—"*keep his word*," His "*Father will love him*," in turn, and so will the Son also, as is conveyed in the plural form in next words, "*and We will come*," Father and Son; the Holy Ghost also comes, "*and make our abode with him*," as guests, in the house of our friend. He will speedily manifest Himself, in His glorified body, to His Apostles after His Resurrection, and He will also specially

Text.

20. *In illo die vos cognoscetis quia ego sum in Patre meo, et vos in me, et ego in vobis.*

21. *He that hath my commandments, and keepeth them: he it is that loveth me. And he that loveth me shall be loved by my Father: and I will love him, and will manifest myself to him.*

21. *Qui habet mandata mea, et servat ea: ille est, qui diligit me. qui autem diligit me, diligetur a Patre meo: et ego diligam eum, et manifestabo ei me ipsum.*

22. *Judas saith to him, not the Iscariot: Lord, how is it, that thou wilt manifest thyself to us, and not to the world?*

22. *Dicit ei Judas, non ille Iscariotes: Domine, quid factum est, quia manifestaturus es nobis teipsum, et non mundo?*

23. *Jesus answered, and said to him: If any one love me, he will keep my word, and my Father will love him, and we will come to him, and will make our abode with him.*

23. *Respondit Jesus, et dixit ei: Si quis diligit me, sermonem*

Text.

meum servabit, et Pater meus diliget eum, et ad eum veniemus, et mansionem apud eum faciemus:

24. *He that loveth me not, keepeth not my words. And the word which you have heard is not mine; but the Father's who sent me.*

24. *Qui non diligit me, sermones meos non servat. Et sermonem, quem audistis, non est meus : sed ejus, qui misit me, Patris.*

25. *These things have I spoken to you, abiding with you.*

25. *Hæc locutus sum vobis apud vos manens.*

26. *But the Paraclete, the Holy Ghost, whom the Father will send in my name, he will teach you all things, and bring all things to your mind, whatsoever I shall have said to you.*

26. *Paraclitus autem Spiritus sanctus, quem mittet Pater in nomine meo, ille vos docebit omnia, et suggeret vobis omnia quæcumque dixero vobis.*

27. *Peace I leave with you, my peace I give unto you: not as the world giveth, do I give unto you. Let not your heart be troubled, nor let it be afraid.*

27. *Pacem relinquo vobis, pacem meam do vobis: non quomodo mundus dat, ego do vobis. Non turbetur cor vestrum, neque formidet.*

Commentary.

manifest Himself to all the faithful, during life, by indwelling in them by His grace and communication of heavenly, spiritual and interior gifts. In this verse it is implied, that it is because worldly men do not love Him nor keep His commandments, He does not manifest Himself to them.

24. He here conveys, that many keep not His commandments, because they do not love Him. And to add greater importance to His commandments, and assert the honour of His Father, as is His invariable custom, He says these commandments are not His, "*is not Mine*," independently of His Father, who, in communicating His Divine nature, to His Son in His eternal generation, communicated also all knowledge. "*In Him were shut up all the treasures of knowledge and wisdom*" (Ser. c. vii. 16). Hence, neither the Father nor the Son love the world, nor shall They manifest themselves to it.

25. "*Remaining with you.*" Conversing in My mortal state with you, who understand the sublimity, as well as the novelty of My doctrines only imperfectly, on account of your rude state of mind.

26. "*But the Paraclete,*" the *Consoler,* to whom I referred already (verse 16), "*the Holy Ghost,*" He now mentions who that Paraclete is, "*whom the Father will send in My name*" (*i.e.*), at My entreaty; or on account of My merits. It may also mean, in My place, who am soon to leave you. "*He will teach you all things,*" causing you to understand clearly what, owing to your rude and imperfect state, you now can hardly understand or apprehend, "*and bring to your minds,*" on all befitting occasions, in the hour of trial and temptation, He *will bring to your mind,* what you might forget and lose sight of, and not even apprehend, in order to strengthen and console you. "*All things whatever*"—pertaining to salvation—"*I have said to you,*" while remaining here with you, in My visible, mortal state.

27. In this valedictory or leave-taking address, our Lord uses the form of benediction in use among the Jews, when using salutations and leave-taking. "*Peace be with you.*" This form of words embraced the abundance of all temporal and spiritual blessings. Our Redeemer, in leaving His Apostles peace, gives a never-failing promise of all blessings, especially tranquillity of soul, and holy resignation in the midst of the trials in store for them, and especially in the midst of their sorrows at His approaching death, and departure from them. In these words our Lord employs the general form in use. In the next words, He specially applies and emphasizes it. "My *peace, I give you,*"

Commentary

a solid, abiding, never-ending peace, both to themselves and their successors. His peace embraces reconciliation and friendship with God, tranquillity of conscience, interior joy in one's self and concord with our brethren. This He bequeaths as His undying inheritance. "*Not as the world giveth.*" The professions of friendship on the part of worldlings are vain, hollow, and insincere, ever changing and changeable. Worldlings may wish us blessings, but, they cannot confer them; and these blessings, such as wealth, pleasures, enjoyment, are brief and changeable. His *peace* is solid, enduring, and ever fruitful of priceless blessings, giving grace and help here, which will lead to eternal happiness hereafter.

"*Let not your heart be troubled,*" etc., at my departure, bearing in mind the many motives of consolation I have proposed to you, and the unfailing promises of support and peace I make you in the midst of tribulations.

This is a repetition of the consolatory affectionate language addressed to them (*v.* 1).

28. "*You have heard that I said to you, I go away*" (*v.* 3), "*and I come to you*" (*v.* 18, 19). This He said, because, He saw them sorrowful at the prospect of His approaching death, as if they would be left destitute, as children without a father, sheep without a shepherd, exposed to the fury of the Jews.

"*I go away*"—owing to My death—"*and I come to you again,*" and shall show Myself visibly, *after* My resurrection, and also by the manifest protection I shall extend to you in all your trials, from My throne of glory in heaven.

"*If you loved Me,*" with sincere love, unmixed with selfishness, putting your entire trust in Me. He knew they loved Him; still, it was a love mixed with selfishness; nor did they fully understand whither He was going, or the result of it.

"*You would indeed be glad, because I go to the Father.*" True love rejoices at the prosperity and advancement of the object loved. They should, therefore, rejoice at seeing Him return to His throne of glory in the bosom of His Father. This would also tend to their benefit, owing to the blessings He would confer on them by establishing the spiritual kingdom of His Church for ever, and delivering His people from their spiritual foes.

"*For the Father is greater than I,*" as man. This is clear if we consider our Lord's human nature, which was to be glorified by His Father. In this sense, He might say, "*I,*" considered in My Divine *Person,* am greater than Myself, considered according to My *humanity.* "*For*"—as St. Augustine expresses it—"*the form of God which He did not lose, is greater than the form of man, which he assumed.*" It is of His *humanity* he speaks; for, in His Divine nature, He is equal to God (Philip. ii.), and it is only in relation

Text

28. *You have heard that I said to you: I go away and I come unto you. If you loved me, you would indeed be glad: because I go to the Father: for the Father is greater than I.*

28. *Audistis quia ego dixi vobis: Vado, et venio ad vos. Si diligeretis me, gauderetis utique, quia vado ad Patrem: quia Pater major me est.*

Text.	Commentary.

to it, He could say, "*I go to the Father,*" and he does not institute a comparison precisely between His Divine nature and that of the Father; but, between His present *lowly* condition, in which He was soon to suffer; and the state of glory, He was to resume, when returning to the bosom of His Father. This should be for them, rather a cause of joy than otherwise.

29. *And now I have told you before it come to pass: that when it shall come to pass, you may believe.*

29. *Et nunc dixi vobis priusquam fiat: ut cum factum fuerit, credatis.*

29. "*And now I have told you before it come to pass.*" I have told you all regarding My death, Resurrection, Ascension, and sending down of the Holy Ghost, not only for the purpose of consoling you; but, also with a view to strengthen and confirm your faith, "*that when it shall come to pass,*" when you shall see all these events which I predicted beforehand, accomplished—which shows I have the faculty of predicting future events—and demonstrated by miracles and works of power,

"*You may believe,*" your faith, which you have in Me already, may be confirmed; and you may see I am truly what I proclaimed Myself to be, viz., Christ, the Son of the living God.

30. *I will not now speak many things with you. For the prince of this world cometh, and in me he hath not any thing.*

30. *Jam non multa loquar vobiscum. venit enim princeps mundi hujus, et in me non habet quidquam.*

30. "*I will not now speak many things with you,*" in explanation of My former teaching, upon which you require to be more fully enlightened. This is no time for lengthened discussions. My last hour is just at hand, My enemy is near.

"*For, the prince of this world.*" The devil, who rules over sinners and lovers of this world, through whose instigation, Judas is to betray Me, and the Jews to put Me to death, "*cometh.*" It is he that impels Judas, into whom he has entered, to approach with an armed band, to apprehend Me. Why the devil is called "*prince of this world*" (see c. xii. 31).

"*And in Me he hath nothing.*" As I am wholly free from sin, in punishment of which death could be justly inflicted. Hence, Satan has no power over Me to put Me to death. Hence, he will act injustly in instigating others to put Me to death. But this will end in his own thorough discomfiture (Rom. viii. 3; Heb. ii. 14). I will cheerfully submit to death, of My own free accord, to destroy his dominion, and rescue My people from his grasp, by fully ransoming them in My blood. Or, the words may mean, understood in a future tense, he *will* not prevail over Me, since My death shall lead to My glory. Or, he *will* have no power over Me, so as to frustrate the plan of Redemption now marked out by Me, in voluntarily submitting to a cruel death.

31. *But that the world may know that I love the Father: and as the Father hath given me commandment, so do I: Arise, let us go hence.*

31. "*But that the world may know that I love the Father,*" and I give the same proof of love that I exact from others, viz., the observance of God's commandments. "*And as the Father has given Me commandment,*" viz., to die for the Redemption of mankind, "*so I do,*" cheerfully, of My own free will. In order to

Commentary.

carry out My obedience in this matter. "*Arise,*" they were reclining on couches at the Last Supper. Then, He tells them to "*arise,*" "*let us go hence,*" to meet the traitor and his satellites, who accompany him for the purpose of violently apprehending Me.

Some Commentators (among them Jansenius) say, the sentence should be transposed, and these words placed first in the sentence, "*Arise, let us go hence,*" "*that the world may know that I love the Father,*" and show this love by observing His commandments. Others supplement the words thus, "*But* (I deliver myself to His power), *that the world may know,*" etc. (Corlui.)

It is a subject of controversy whether the disciples rose up at once, and accompanying our Lord, proceeded with Him on His way to the Garden of Olives. Some hold they did. It is supposed in this opinion, that while on their way He delivered the following discourse (xv., xvi.), and uttered the prayer to His Father (xvii.). Or, whether having risen from the table, they remained in the room, from a reluctance to depart from their beloved Lord, and that while they lingered in the room the following discourse and prayer were uttered. The latter opinion is grounded on the following reasons :—

1. The Evangelist does not state that they left immediately.

2. It would be difficult and inconvenient for the disciples proceeding in a body, to hear all our Lord says up to c. xviii.

3. St. John says (xviii. 1), *it was " when He said these things, He went forth with His disciples,"* etc.

4. The other Evangelists (Matthew and Mark) say, when they left, it was a hymn they sung. They make no allusion to a discourse (A Lapide). The former opinion is regarded as probable, and adopted by many able Commentators, among them, Toletus. These maintain, that our Lord and His disciples, suiting the action to the words, arose at once from the table, and proceeding in the stillness and darkness of the night, along the solitary road towards the place, where He was to be captured and betrayed by Judas, our Lord delivered the following discourse, standing at times, or walking, as best suited the occasion ; and, then, having finished the discourse (xv., xvi.) and the prayer being addressed to His Father (xviii.), He went forth beyond the Cedron, and entered the Garden of Gethsemani.

Text.

31. *Sed ut cognoscat mundus quia diligo Patrem, et sicut mandatum dedit mihi Pater, sic facio. Surgite, eamus hinc.*

CHAPTER XV.

1 *I am the true vine ; and my Father is the husbandman.*

2 *Every branch in me, that beareth not fruit, he will take away: and every one that beareth fruit he will purge it, that it may bring forth more fruit.*

3 *Now you are clean by reason of the word, which I have spoken to you.*

4 *Abide in me: and I in you. As the branch cannot bear fruit of itself, unless it abide in the vine, so neither can you, unless you abide in me.*

5 *I am the vine ; you the branches : he that abideth in me, and I in him, the same beareth much fruit : for without me you can do nothing.*

6 *If any one abide not in me : he shall be cast forth as a branch, and shall wither, and they shall gather him up, and cast him into the fire, and he burneth.*

7 *If you abide in me, and my words abide in you, you shall ask whatever you will, and it shall be done unto you.*

8 *In this is my Father glorified ; that you bring forth very much fruit, and become my disciples.*

9 *As the Father hath loved me, I also have loved you. Abide in my love.*

10 *If you keep my commandments, you shall abide in my love ; as I also have kept my Father's commandments, and do abide in his love.*

11 *These things I have spoken to you, that my joy may be in you, and your joy may be filled.*

12 *This is my commandment, that you love one another, as I have loved you.*

13 *Greater love than this no man hath, that a man lay down his life for his friends.*

14 *You are my friends, if you do the things that I command you.*

15 *I will not now call you servants : for the servant knoweth not what his lord doth. But I have called you friends : because all things whatsoever I have heard of my Father, I have made known to you.*

16 *You have not chosen me : but I have chosen you ; and have appointed you, that you should go, and should bring forth fruit : and your fruit should remain : that whatsoever you shall ask of the Father in my name, he may give it you.*

17 *These things I command you, that you love one another.*

18 *If the world hate you, know you that it hath hated me before you.*

19 *If you had been of the world ; the world would love its own : but because you are not of the world, but I have chosen you out of the world, therefore the world hateth you.*

20 *Remember my word that I said to you: The servant is not greater than his master. If they have persecuted me, they will also persecute you : if they have kept my word, they will keep yours also.*

21 *But all these things they will do to you for my name's sake : because they know not him that sent me.*

22 *If I had not come, and spoken to them, they would not have sin : but now they have no excuse for their sin.*

23 *He that hateth me, hateth my Father also.*

24 *If I had not done among them the works that no other man hath done, they would not have sin: but now they have both seen and hated both me and my Father.*

25 *But that the word may be fulfilled which is written in their law:* They have hated me without cause.

26 *But when the Paraclete cometh, whom I will send you from the Father, the Spirit of truth, who proceedeth from the Father, he shall give testimony of me:*

27 *And you shall give testimony, because you are with me from the beginning.*

CAPUT XV.

1 *Ego sum vitis vera: et Pater meus agricola est.*

2 *Omnem palmitem in me non ferentem fructum, tollet eum: et omnem, qui fert fructum, purgabit eum, ut fructum plus afferat.*

3 *Jam vos mundi estis propter sermonem, quem locutus sum vobis.*

4 *Manete in me: et ego in vobis. Sicut palmes non potest ferre fructum a semetipso, nisi manserit in vite: sic nec vos, nisi in me manseritis.*

5 *Ego sum vitis, vos palmites: qui manet in me, et ego in eo, hic fert fructum multum: quia sine me nihil potestis facere.*

6 *Si quis in me non manserit: mittetur foras sicut palmes, et arescet, et colligent eum, et in ignem mittent, et ardet.*

7 *Si manseritis in me, et verba mea in vobis manserint: quodcumque volueritis petetis, et fiet vobis.*

8 *In hoc clarificatus est Pater meus, ut fructum plurimum afferatis, et efficiamini mei discipuli.*

9 *Sicut dilexit me Pater, et ego dilexi vos. Manete in dilectione mea.*

10 *Si præcepta mea servaveritis, manebitis in dilectione mea, sicut et ego Patris mei præcepta servavi, et maneo in ejus dilectione.*

11 *Hæc locutus sum vobis: ut gaudium meum in vobis sit, et gaudium vestrum impleatur.*

12 *Hoc est præceptum meum ut diligatis invicem, sicut dilexi vos:*

13 *Majorem hac dilectionem nemo habet, ut animam suam ponat quis pro amicis suis.*

14 *Vos amici mei estis, si feceritis quæ ego præcipio vobis.*

15 *Jam non dicam vos servos: quia servus nescit quid faciat dominus ejus. Vos autem dixi amicos: quia omnia quæcumque audivi a Patre meo, nota feci vobis.*

16 *Non vos me elegistis: sed ego elegi vos, et posui vos ut eatis, et fructum afferatis: et fructus vester maneat: ut quodcumque petieritis Patrem in nomine meo, det vobis.*

17 *Hæc mando vobis, ut diligatis invicem.*

18 *Si mundus vos odit; scitote quia me priorem vobis odio habuit.*

19 *Si de mundo fuissetis: mundus quod suum erat diligeret: quia vero de mundo non estis, sed ego elegi vos de mundo, propterea odit vos mundus.*

20 *Mementote sermonis mei, quem ego dixi vobis: Non est servus major domino suo. Si me persecuti sunt, et vos persequentur: si sermonem meum servaverunt, et vestrum servabunt.*

21 *Sed hæc omnia facient vobis propter nomen meum: quia nesciunt eum, qui misit me.*

22 *Si non venissem, et locutus fuissem eis, peccatum non haberent: nunc autem excusationem non habent de peccato suo.*
23 *Qui me odit: et Patrem meum odit.*
24 *Si opera non fecissem in eis, quæ nemo alius fecit, peccatum non haberent: nunc autem et viderunt, et oderunt et me, et Patrem meum.*
25 *Sed ut adimpleatur sermo, qui in lege eorum scriptus est: Quia odio habuerunt me gratis.*
26 *Cum autem venerit Paraclitus, quem ego mittam vobis a Patre spiritum veritatis, qui a Patre procedit, ille testimonium perhibebit de me:*
27 *Et vos testimonium perhibebitis, quia ab initio mecum estis.*

ANALYSIS.

In this chapter, our Lord gives the parable of the vine and the branches (1–4). Application of the parable (5).

Necessity of union with Him, the true vine, in order to be able to do good and avoid eternal tortures (6).

He inculcates a mutual and unselfish self-sacrificing love for one another, of which the love He has shown us, should be the model (12–17).

He fortifies them against the hatred the world would manifest in their regard, and He assigns several reasons why they should pay no heed to such hatred (18–25).

He promises to send down upon them, the Paraclete, the Spirit of truth (26, 27).

Text.

1. *I am the true vine: and my Father is the husbandman.*

1. *Ego sum vitis vera: et Pater meus agricola est.*

Commentary.

1. In the preceding chapter, our Lord had been consoling His Apostles, who were saddened at the prospect of His near departure, and exhorting them to adhere to Him by charity, shown in the observance of His commandments, even under the pressure of trial and persecution. He now continues to inculcate the same, and under the similitude of the vine and its branches, He continues to show, that His followers should be always united with Him, deriving from Him their spiritual nutriment and support—as the branches derive nutriment, vigour and life from the vine-stock—He in turn, engaging, as far as in Him lies, to sustain and nourish them by His abundant graces, if they closely adhere to Him by faith and good works; thus, placing no obstacle to the operations of His grace.

"*I am the true vine,*" "*true,*" in the real spiritual effects I produce. The words are metaphorically put, just as He is called, "*the true light,*" because, He really enlightens men spiritually, better than the material sun does in the natural order. "*A vine,*" by similitude, "*true,*" on account of producing in the members united with Him, in a higher and more exalted spiritual sense, the effects produced by the natural vine in its branches, unlike the false vine, that only produces wild grapes. "*True,*" may also mean, *super-excellent.*

He is the "*vine,*" in His *humanity,* in which the branches of the same nature are united with Him. But it is from His *Divinity,*

Commentary.

the branches derive the spiritual and life-giving influence that lead to eternal happiness.

In the similitude, the words, "*And men united with Me are branches,*" would seem to be understood, in order to complete the similitude.

"*My Father is the husbandman,*" who planted me as a vine upon the earth; and unites to Me My Apostles and faithful followers, whom He tends and cultivates, in a manner, analogous to the process of natural pruning, that they may produce greater fruit. He Himself also, as *God*, is the husbandman. But as it would not suit the similitude, were He to call Himself the husbandman and the vine, at the same time, He attributes this quality of husbandman, to His Father, to whom the operations of Providence are ascribed, by appropriation.

2. In order to derive profit from their union with Him, they should produce the fruits of good works. "*Every branch in Me,*" ingrafted on Me, by baptism and faith, "*that beareth not fruit,*" not producing the fruit of good works, in accordance with the teaching of their faith, "*He will take away,*" His Father will lop off, sometimes by excluding such from the society of the faithful in His Church, as happens in some public scandalous cases, and lately, in the case of the apostate Judas; but, more generally, by depriving them of the life-giving influence of His grace, of which, by their negligence, they make themselves unworthy; and finally, by excluding them from His heavenly kingdom, verifying in their regard the curse inflicted on the barren fig tree, "*Pluck it up, why any longer encumber the ground!*" In this, our Lord, inculcates on His Apostles and all His followers, to bring forth the fruit of good works, by a faithful correspondence with grace.

"*He will purge it,*" by removing all obstacles to the operation of grace, by sending crosses, afflictions and temporal calamities calculated to wean men from the things of earth, and by other means at the disposal of His gracious Providence, such as terrors and alarms in regard to their ultimate destiny. He will thus prepare them for a more abundant infusion of His heavenly graces, and enable them to bring forth a more abundant crop of good works.

3. Applying this general similitude to those present, He says, they were branches inserted in the mystical vine, members of His mystical body, purged from all defilement. The pruning knife employed was His discourse spoken to them in the two preceding chapters. Thomas (xiv. 6, 7), and Philip (*v.* 9), were freed from ignorance regarding Him; the rest from unreasonable sadness; (xiv. 1). Peter, from vain confidence (xiii. 36), etc. From this, to verse 12, He employs several motives and considerations to make them persevere in His love.

Text.

2. *Every branch in me that beareth not fruit, he will take away: and every one that beareth fruit he will purge it, that it may bring forth more fruit.*

2. *Omnem palmitem in me non ferentem fructum, tollet eum: et omnem, qui fert fructum, purgabit eum, ut fructum plus afferat.*

3. *Now you are clean by reason of the word which I have spoken to you.*

3. *Jam vos mundi estis propter sermonem, quem locutus sum vobis.*

Text.

4. Abide in me: and I in you. As the branch cannot bear fruit of itself, unless it abide in the vine, so neither can you, unless you abide in me.

4. Manete in me: et ego in vobis. Sicut palmes non potest ferre fructum a semetipso nisi manserit in vite: sic nec vos, nisi in me manseritis.

5. I am the vine; you the branches; he that abideth in me, and I in him, the same beareth much fruit: for without me you can do nothing.

5. Ego sum vitis, vos palmites: qui manet in me, et ego in eo, hic fert fructum multum: quia sine me nihil potestis facere.

6. If any one abide not in me: he shall be cast forth as a branch, and shall wither, and they shall gather him up, and cast him into the fire, and he burneth.

6. Si quis in me non manserit: mittetur foras sicut palmes, et arescet, et colligent eum, et in ignem mittent, et ardet.

7. If you abide in me, and my words abide in you, you shall ask whatever you will and it shall be done unto you.

Commentary.

4. "*Abide in Me.*" Although now freed from faults, they must persevere in union with Him, by faith, love and good works. For, the purged branches may, possibly, be separated from the vine. "*And I in you.*" I shall, in turn, abide in you, and enliven you by the influx of My graces, "*for, God does not desert us, till He is first deserted*" (St. Augustine, Lib. de Natura et Gratia, c. 46). He shows the necessity of this persevering union. As it is only by persevering in the vine, the branch can bear fruit—it cannot, unless it be united to the vine, and draw nutriment from it—so, neither can you, unless you are united to Me, by faith and love, exhibited in good works. The first condition for obtaining eternal life is adhesion to Christ by faith and love.

5. "*I am the vine,*" etc. Our Lord here applies the similitude to Himself, and accommodates it to His disciples. "*He that abideth in Me and I in him,*" in whom I abide, enlivening him by the abundant influx of My grace, "*the same beareth much fruit.*" Although no one can abide in the vine without the vine abiding in Him; still, our Lord employs these latter words to point out their intimate connexion, and also to show, that it is by the influx of the vine, in giving nutriment to the branches, the branches produce fruit.

It is only the man that abides in the vine, that can produce fruit, "*for, without Me,*" that is, My grace and supernatural assistance, "*you can do nothing,*" nothing meritorious, nothing conducive to salvation. Without God's preventing and co-operating actual grace, independently of habitual grace residing in the soul, we cannot do even the beginning of a good work, "*we can do nothing,*" no work, great or small, in the supernatural order. Man, by his free will, freely assents to or rejects the influence of preventing and co-operating grace. But this assent is effected by grace.

6. As a further motive to cling to Him and remain united with Him, He points out the fate and final punishment of the man who is not united to Him, by faith and love.

"*If any man abide not in Me,*" by faith and love, "*he shall be cast out,*" deprived of the society of Christ and His saints, deprived of the saving influence of grace here, and the inheritance of God hereafter. His end, eternal fire, never ending torture.

7. Another motive to cling to Him, "*if you abide in Me,*" by persevering in My love and grace, "*and My words abide in you,*" by your faithfully observing My commandments—the surest test of love—then, you shall obtain all the blessings arising from your union and connexion with the vine. But, the means you must

Commentary.

adopt to secure such, is prayer. "*You shall ask whatever you will,*" and, provided it be with the proper dispositions, as your union with the vine implies, "*it shall be done unto you*" (see 1 John v. 14, Commentary on). Instead of mentioning the blessings in detail, our Lord points out the source whence they are to come—prayer.

8. Another motive for them to adhere to Him by faith and love—they will, thus, advance the glory of God. The word, "*glorified*," in the *past*, is put for the *present*.

"*That you bring forth much fruit,*" both in yourselves, by advancing in perfection and sanctification; and in others, by the conversion of the world to embrace the Gospel. This is more fully explained in the words; "*So let your light shine before men,*" etc. (Matthew v. 16).

"*That you bring forth,*" etc. "*That,*" is put for "*if.*" "*If you bring forth,*" etc., "*and become My disciples,*" or followers, showing yourselves to be faithful imitators and followers of Me, by advancing more and more in perfection, through the continued performance of good works, especially by your zeal in preaching the Gospel and bringing about the conversion of the world.

9. Another motive for adhering to Him. "*As the Father hath loved Me,*" in an intense degree, conferring on My human nature, the sublime privilege of personal and hypostatic union with the Eternal Word, constituting Me the Redeemer of the human race,—"*As,*" implies, not equality, but similarity—

"*I also have loved you,*" with a similar love, choosing you, of My own gratuitous goodness, out of the rest of mankind to the exalted dignity of the Apostleship; thus, becoming my representatives, sharers in my power, in preaching the Gospel to the entire earth, making Jews and Gentiles, partakers of salvation.

Show, then, your gratitude and love for Me, by "*abiding in My love,*" persevering in the performance of good works; so that, in turn, My love may abide in you. Similar are the words of St. John, "*because He loved us first, and sent His Son to be a propitiation for our sins*" (1 John iv. 10). "*Let us, therefore, love God, because God first hath loved us*" (1 John iv. 19).

Some Expositors (among them Maldonatus), say, that the words, "*abide in My love,*" instead of being a practical conclusion derived from the two foregoing sentences, "*as the Father hath loved Me, I also have loved you, therefore abide in My love,*" form rather the second member of the comparison, thus, "*As the Father hath loved Me, and as, I also love you; so, do you abide in My love.*"

10. "*If you keep My commandments.*" If we, aided by God's grace, observe His commandments, which is the surest test of our

Text.

7. *Si manseritis in me, et verba mea in vobis manserint: quodcumque volueritis petetis, et fiet vobis.*

8. *In this is my Father glorified; that you bring forth very much fruit, and become my disciples.*

8. *In hoc clarificatus est Pater meus, ut fructum plurimum afferatis, et efficiamini mei discipuli.*

9. *As the Father hath loved me, I also have loved you. Abide in my love.*

9. *Sicut dilexit me Pater, et ego dilexi vos. Manete in dilectione mea.*

10. *If you keep my commandments, you shall abide in my love;*

Text.	Commentary.
as I also have kept my Father's commandments, and do abide in his love.	love for Him, we shall secure a continuance of His abiding love for us as, by faithfully observing His Father's commandments, our Lord secured a continuance of the love He shows Him as man.

10. *Si præcepta mea servaveritis, manebitis in dilectione mea, sicut et ego Patris mei præcepta servavi, et maneo in ejus dilectione.*

11. *These things I have spoken to you, that my joy may be in you, and your joy may be filled.*	11. Another motive for them to persevere in His love and the observance of His commandments. "*That My joy be in you,*" that the joy you cause Me, in seeing you as obedient, loving children, observe My commandments—thus, proving your love for Me—may continue, by your persevering in the observance of the same.
11. *Hæc locutus sum vobis: ut gaudium meum in vobis sit, et gaudium vestrum impleatur.*	

"*And your joy,*" at having so good a parent and such a benign, heavenly master, "*may be fulfilled,*" may merit its final consummation in eternal happiness. As branches would have cause to rejoice in being inserted in the vine, and in producing fruit on account of the aliment and vitality, the present stock imparts; so, the vine, in turn, would have cause to rejoice at seeing the abundant fruits produced, through its vivifying influence, by the branches.

Others understand the words thus: that the joy I feel from the prospect of the advancement of My Father's glory and the salvation of man, through My instrumentality, "*may be in you,*" transfused and communicated to you, My Apostles, and co-operators in the ministry.

"*And your joy,*" the joy imparted to you by Me, thus becoming "YOUR JOY," "*may be filled,*" increased and strengthened in this life, amidst your sufferings and afflictions, and receive its full completion in the life to come.

12. *This is my commandment, that you love one another, as I have loved you.*	12. Having spoken of the observance of His commandments, which He made the test of His love, and their abiding in His love (v. 10), He specifies one commandment peculiarly His own, viz., that they should "*love one another.*" He calls it "MY commandment," having already termed it a "*new commandment*" (xiii. 34).
12. *Hoc est præceptum meum ut diligatis invicem, sicut dilexi vos.*	

"*As I have loved you.*" Having inculcated love of one another, He points to His own example, as having Himself first done what He asks others to do; and thus, shows one leading characteristic of their mutual love. It should resemble His love for us, both as to the *end*, viz.: the enjoyment of God; the *mode*, involving the sacrifice of life itself for their salvation; a love, therefore, of unselfish disinterestedness, of self-sacrifice, not even excepting the sacrifice of life. The Apostles, therefore, and their successors, as well as all Christians, should exhibit this spirit of sacrifice. Their mutual co-operation would be their firmest support amidst trials and difficulties, and help them to overcome all obstacles. Hence,

Commentary.

we are told (Proverbs xviii. 19), "*a brother that is helped by a brother is like a strong city*," also (Ecclesiastes iv. 12), "*a threefold cord is not easily broken.*"

13. He describes in general terms, with an implied special application to His own case, His love for them, referred to above, a love exhibiting self-sacrifice and disinterestedness in the highest degree, even involving the sacrifice of life for His friends. The greatest proof of love one friend can show for another is to die for him. Our Lord thus implicitly exhorts them to follow His example by being ready to sacrifice their lives, if necessary, for the salvation of their brethren.

St. Paul, in a special manner, extols the excessive charity of Christ in dying for us, when we were His enemies. That hardly comes in here; nor does our Lord intend the comparison to extend to death for our enemies. He is only speaking of the death of a friend for a friend, in which relation he here considers His Apostles. Our Lord died, no doubt, for His enemies; however, He rendered them friends by the effusion of His blood, and died for them as such. The Apostles, too, should be prepared, if they loved, as He did—so should all Christians—to sacrifice their temporal life for the eternal salvation of the souls of their brethren. Some understand the word, "*friends*," of those *loved by us*, although they may not love us in turn, and may be, in a certain sense, our enemies.

14. When speaking of dying for friends, 'I refer to you, for whom as My friends I am about to sacrifice My life. But, in order to continue in My friendship permanently, I require it as a condition, that you return love for love, and persevere in the performance of "*the things which I command you*," especially with reference to fraternal charity.

15. "*I will not now*," on the eve of My departure from you, when I am disposed to show you special tenderness and affection, "*call you servants.*" The Greek is in the present, "I DO *not call you*," or treat you as servants. "*For the servant knoweth not what his master doth.*" Servants are not usually made the depositaries of their masters' secrets or designs. "*What his master doth.*" The master does not *ordinarily*—there may be exceptions—communicate to his servants his secret counsels, nor the end he may have in view in the performance of his actions. Not so, however, with Me, in your regard.

"*But, I have called you friends.*" I have treated you as friends, I have made you fully acquainted with My secret designs, made you My confidants. "*All things whatever I have heard of My Father, I have made known to you.*" All the counsels of God that

Text.

13. *Greater love than this no man hath, that a man lay down his life for his friends.*

13. *Majorem hac dilectionem nemo habet, ut animam suam ponat quis pro amicis suis.*

14. *You are my friends, if you do the things that I command you.*

14. *Vos amici mei estis, si feceritis quæ ego præcipio vobis.*

15. *I will not now call you servants: for the servant knoweth not what his Lord doth. But I have called you friends: because all things whatsoever I have heard of my Father, I have made known to you.*

15. *Jam non dicam vos servos: quia servus nescit quid faciat dominus ejus. Vos autem dixi amicos: quia omnia quæcumque audivi a Patre meo, nota feci vobis.*

Text.

Commentary.

are known to Me I have communicated to you, as far as was expedient, or as far as you were capable of receiving them and profiting by them. Although by nature and condition you are My servants; still, I treated you as My intimate friends, making known to you what I heard as ambassador from My Father, and not to the crowds or to the Scribes and Pharisees.

Our Lord told His Apostles, afterwards (xvi. 12), there were some things they could not hear so as to profit by them. "*I have many things to say to you; but you cannot bear them now.*" Hence, there would seem to be an apparent contradiction in saying here: "*All things whatever I heard of My Father, I have made known,*" etc. Some explain it, "*all things,*" expedient and profitable for you to know; "*all things,*" according to the measure of your capacity, or, which you could "*bear.*" Others, give the words a future signification. *I shall make* known to you, after a few days, when I shall send you the plenitude of My Spirit at Pentecost. Maldonatus interprets the words, "*I have made known,*" to mean, *I have decreed* to make known, just as it is said here, "*the servant knoweth not what his master does,*" (*i.e.*), is *resolved* on doing.

16. *You have not chosen me: but I have chosen you; and have appointed you, that you should go, and should bring forth fruit: and your fruit should remain: that whatsoever you shall ask of the Father in my name, he may give it you,*

16. *Non vos me elegistis: sed ego elegi vos, et posui vos ut eatis, et fructum afferatis: et fructus vester maneat: ut quodcumque petieritis Patrem in nomine meo, det vobis.*

16. In order to point out the utter gratuitousness of their call to the high dignity of chosen friends and Apostles, and thus elicit their gratitude, and, perhaps, inspire them with due feelings of humility on account of the utter gratuitousness of their call, independently of any claim or merit on their part; He tells them.

"*You have not chosen Me*" (first), to be your friend and master; "*but, I have chosen you.*" I, first, by My preventing grace inspired you and enabled you to become My followers; and this of My own gratuitous free will and choice, "*and have appointed you,*" have firmly placed and immovably constituted you in your Apostolic office with authority of which no power can deprive you; "*that you should go,*" forth into the entire world to preach My Gospel, "*and should bring forth fruit,*" in your own sanctification and the conversion of the world. "*And your fruit should remain,*" in the successful conversion of the world and the sanctification of men, in this life, till the end of time; and in the life to come, in the enjoyment of everlasting happiness. He, thus, shows His love; and wishes, by placing before them the contemplation of the lofty dignity, to which He gratuitously raised them, to stimulate them to labour hard for the salvation of His people; as the fruit of their labour is to endure for ever.

"*That whatsoever you shall ask of the Father.*" "*That,*" expresses not the *cause*, since it was not for the purpose of obtaining requests, they were chosen, but the *consequence*. The consequence of their labouring so hard in His service will be, that they will be inspired with a firm confidence of obtaining from God, whatever they may ask "*in My name,*" that is to say, with the

Commentary.

proper dispositions. It is to the grace of God, secured by prayer, that the success of their labours must be attributed. They may plant and may water; but He alone gives the increase (1 Cor. iii. 6).

"*He may give it you.*" The Greek, δῶ, may be in the first person. "I may give," as in (xiv. 13) that I will do.

17. "*These things,*" etc., may mean, all My preceding mandates are summed up in this, "*that you should love one another.*" Or, My object in giving you the preceding instructions is not to upbraid you with want of love of Myself; but, simply to stimulate you to love one another, by submitting to all hardships and sacrifices for the salvation of your brethren, as I show My love for you.

18. Having inculcated mutual love for one another, which would stand as a powerful wall of defence against privations and trials, He now arms them against hatred and persecutions from the world. In the hatred and persecutions from the world now before them, He consoles them with the thought, that He, their chief and captain, had to endure similar trials. "*The world,*" the selfish l·vers of the world, Jews and Gentiles, "*hated Me before you.*"

19. He consoles them with the further reflexion, that this hatred on the part of the world should be a source of joy and honour to them, since, it is a testimony, that in their lives, they conform not to the corrupt ways and maxims of the world. . "*The world would have loved its own.*" Similarity of manners and of love is the cause of affection; *dissimilarity*, the cause of hatred and aversion (Aristotle in Ethics, St. Augustine and others).

"*But, because you are not of the world.*" Far from embracing and acting on the leading maxims of the world, viz., the *concupiscence of the flesh*, the *concupiscence of the eyes, and the pride of life*. Far from loving riches, honours, and forbidden pleasures, you show the contrary.

"*But I have chosen you out of the world,*" calling you to My Faith and Apostleship, segregating you from the world, giving you grace and strength to trample under foot all that the world loves, and to value only the never-ending goods of the world to come. My spirit, My teaching, are opposed to the world. "*Therefore, the world hateth you,*" because opposed to their works. "*Circumveniamus justum . . . contrarius est operibus nostris*" (Wisdom xi. 12).

20. "*Remember My word that I spoke to you*" (xiii. 16; also, Matthew x. 24, 25). "*The servant is not greater than his master,*" and must be, therefore, prepared to endure the same treatment.

Text.

17. *These things I command you, that you love one another.*

17. *Hæc mando vobis, ut diligatis invicem.*

18. *If the world hate you, know ye that it hath hated me before you.*

18. *Si mundus vos odit: scitote quia me priorem vobis odio habuit.*

19. *If you had been of the world; the world would love its own: but because you are not of the world, but I have chosen you out of the world, therefore the world hateth you.*

19. *Si de mundo fuissetis: mundus quod suum erat diligeret: quia vero de mundo non estis, sed ego elegi vos de mundo, propterea odit vos mundus.*

20. *Remember my word that I said to you: The servant is not greater than his*

Text.	Commentary.
master. *If they have persecuted me, they will also persecute you: if they have kept my word, they will keep yours also.*	"*If they persecuted Me,*" as they have done, "*they will,*" etc. You must be prepared for the same unworthy treatment. "*If they kept My word,*" by simply trampling it under foot, as you know they did ; "*they will keep yours also.*" They will treat your instructions with similar indignity.

20. *Mementote sermonis mei, quem ego dixi vobis ; Non est servus major domino suo. Si me persecuti sunt, et vos persequentur : si sermonem meum servaverunt, et vestrum servabunt.*

21. *But all these things they will do to you for my name's sake : because they know not him that sent me.* 21. *Sed hæc omnia ficient vobis propter nomen meum : quia nesciunt eum, qui misit me.*	21. Rejoice that it is on My account, "*for My name's sake ;*" because you are My disciples and faithful, loving followers, you are thus treated. They treat you and Me thus, "*because*"—through their own fault and wilful blindness—"*they knew not Him who sent Me.*" They know not that I am the Son of the Eternal Father who sent Me into the world, though they should know it, from the many proofs I gave them. In persecuting you, therefore, and Me, they are warring against My Heavenly Father, at the same time.
22. *If I had not come, and spoken to them, they would not have sin : but now they have no excuse for their sin.* 22. *Si non venissem, et locutus fuissem eis, peccatum non haberent : nunc autem excusationem non habent de peccato suo.*	22. Their incredulity is inexcusable. "*Had I not come and spoken to them,*" giving so many proofs of My Divinity and My mission from My Father, "*they would not have sin*"—that is, the sin of incredulity, although they might have other sins to answer for. The Pharisees and the Scribes *before our Lord's coming* had faith in God and in the coming of Christ. But, *after He came* and gave so many proofs of His Divinity ; they, by obstinately refusing to receive Him, wilfully closing their eyes against all evidence, lost the faith, owing to their obstinate incredulity. "*Now, they have no excuse for their sin,*" of incredulity, while blindly and obstinately rejecting Me, even the pretext of ignorance being taken away from them.
23. *He that hateth me, hateth my Father also.* 23. *Qui me odit : et Patrem meum odit.*	23. "*He that hateth Me,*" by rejecting My works, My doctrine, "*hateth My Father also,*" who sent Me. It is His words, His works, they reject ; since we work in common, the Father and I being one. The contumely offered to the Legate is offered to Him whose Legate He is.
24. *If I had not done among them the works that no other man hath done, they would not have sin : but now they have both seen and hated both me and my Father.* 24. *Si opera non fecissem in eis, quæ nemo alius fecit, peccatum non haberent : nunc autem et viderunt, et oderunt et me, et Patrem meum.*	24. Having shown that they were inexcusable for not believing His words, He now shows how much more inexcusable they were for rejecting His Divine works. "*If I had not done among them,*" in their very presence, "*the works which no other man hath done,*" both as to quality and number, done by My own innate power ; such as none of the Prophets laid claim to, and this not unfrequently in attestation of My Divine power and equality with My Father ; works, too, predicted Me by the ancient Prophets (Isaias xxxv. 3). "*They would not have sin,*" the sin of incredulity and black ingratitude.

Commentary.

"*But now they have both seen.*" The words, "*My Father and Me,*" are understood, and to be added. They have seen Me in the flesh, proving by stupendous miracles, that I am the Son of God. They have seen My Father also, since they should know that no one could perform the works I performed unless God were with him.

"*And hated both Me and My Father,*" by rejecting all faith in us, and shutting their eyes against the miracles wrought by us.

25. "*But,*" they hated us, so that as a consequence the words contained in their own inspired Scriptures are verified in their regard. "*They hated Me without cause*" (Psa. 34, 19). These words were spoken by David of himself, in the first instance. But, in this he represented our Lord, respecting whom, these words, were verified in the person of David, as describing beforehand the hatred shown our Lord by the Jews. He wishes to convey, that their own inspired Scriptures had beforehand reproached the Jews with their gratuitous causeless hatred of Christ.

26. "*But when the Paraclete cometh,*" to be your comforter under all tribulations. He adds this, to let them know that, however the Jews may endeavour to palliate their hatred of Him (which hatred was predicted by the Prophet), under the plea of zeal for God, this mendacious pretext will not be allowed to pass. In due time, it shall be exposed and refuted.

"*Whom I will send to you*"—as proceeding from Me—"*from the Father,*" from whom, as well as from Me, jointly, He proceeds. "*The Spirit of truth,*" whose testimony, therefore, is beyond all doubt or question.

"*Who proceedeth from the Father,*" the great original fountain of the Divinity, who begot His Son equal to Him, in all things, by an *eternal generation;* the Holy Ghost equal in all things to the Father and the Son, proceeding from both by a *common active spiration.*

To the words "*Who proceedeth from the Father,*" our Lord omits adding *and from Me;* because, He was referring to the testimony of the Holy Ghost in favour of Himself. Hence, to avoid all suspicion, or rather, lest He might weaken His argument, He omits all mention of the procession of the Holy Ghost from *Himself,* as well as from the Father, though this procession is clearly contained in the words, "*I will send.*"

The error of the Greeks regarding the procession of the Holy Ghost from the Father only, receives no confirmation from this passage. For, the words, "*whom I shall send you,*" show, that He proceeds from the Son also.

"*He will give testimony,*" regarding My innocence, My Divinity. He will testify that I have given no cause of hatred to the Jews.

Text.

25. But that the word may be fulfilled, which is written in their law: They have hated me without cause.

25. Sed ut adimpleatur sermo, qui in lege eorum scriptus est: quia odio habuerunt me gratis.

26. But when the Paraclete cometh whom I will send you from the Father, the Spirit of truth, who proceedeth from the Father, he shall give testimony of me:

26. Cum autem venerit Paraclitus, quem ego mittam vobis a Patre spiritum veritatis. qui a Patre procedit, ille testimonium perhibebit de me:

Text.	Commentary.
	"*Of Me*," as the Messiah, just and veracious, as consubstantial with the Father. This testimony He will bear by His miraculous descent on the Apostles, by the wonderful gifts to be bestowed on the infant Church, by the prodigies to be wrought by the Apostles and faithful men, at all ages of the Church.
27. *And you shall give testimony, because you are with me from the beginning.*	27. "*And you*"—filled with the Holy Ghost—"*will give testimony*," of My Divinity. The Greek for, "*you will give*," will also bear an Imperative construction, thus: "*Do you give testimony*," etc. The future Indicative is equivalent to the Imperative.
27. *Et vos testimonium perhibebitis, quia ab initio mecum estis.*	"*Because, you are with Me from the beginning*," witnesses of My coming in and going out (Acts i. 21), and, therefore, entitled to all belief.

CHAPTER XVI.

1 *These things have I spoken to you, that you may not be scandalized.*

2 *They will put you out of the synagogues: yea, the hour cometh, that whosoever killeth you, will think that he doth a service to God.*

3 *And these things will they do to you, because they have not known the Father, nor me.*

4 *But these things I have told you: that when the hour shall come, you may remember that I told you of them.*

5 *But I told you not these things from the beginning, because I was with you: And now I go to him that sent me: and none of you asketh me: Whither goest thou?*

6 *But because I have spoken these things to you, sorrow hath filled your heart.*

7 *But I tell you the truth: it is expedient for you that I go: for if I go not, the Paraclete will not come to you: but if I go, I will send him to you.*

8 *And when he shall come, he will convince the world of sin, and of justice, and of judgment.*

9 *Of sin indeed: because they have not believed in me.*

10 *And of justice: because I go to the Father: and you shall see me no longer:*

11 *And of judgment: because the prince of this world is already judged.*

12 *I have yet many things to say to you: but you cannot bear them now.*

13 *But when he, the Spirit of truth, shall come, he will teach you all truth: for he shall not speak of himself: but what things soever he shall hear, he shall speak: and the things that are to come, he will show you.*

14 *He shall glorify me: because he shall receive of mine, and will declare it to you.*

15 *All things whatsoever the Father hath are mine. Therefore, I said, that he shall receive of mine, and will declare it to you.*

16 *A little while, and now you shall not see me: and again a little while, and you shall see me: because I go to the Father.*

17 *Then some of his disciples said one to another: What is this that he saith to us: A little while, and you shall not see me: and again a little while, and you shall see me: and because I go to the Father?*

18 *They said, therefore: What is this that he saith, A little while? we know not what he speaketh.*

19 *And Jesus knew that they were desirous to ask him: and he said to them: Of this do you inquire among yourselves, because I said: A little while, and you shall not see me; and again a little while, and you shall see me.*

20 *Amen, amen, I say to you, that you shall lament and weep, but the world shall rejoice: and you shall be sorrowful, but your sorrow shall be turned into joy.*

21 *A woman, when she is in labour, hath sorrow, because her hour is come: but when she hath brought forth the child, she remembereth no more the anguish, for joy that a man is born into the world.*

22 *So also you now indeed have sorrow, but I will see you again, and your heart shall rejoice: and your joy no man shall take from you.*

23 *And in that day you shall not ask me anything. Amen, amen, I say to you: if you ask the Father any thing in my name, he will give it you.*

24 *Hitherto you have not asked any thing in my name: Ask, and you shall receive: that your joy may be full.*

25 *These things I have spoken to you in proverbs. The hour cometh when I will no more speak to you in proverbs, but will show you plainly of the Father.*

26 *In that day you shall ask in my name: and I say not to you, that I will ask the Father for you.*

27 *For the Father himself loveth you, because you have loved me, and have believed that I came forth from God.*

28 *I came forth from the Father, and am come into the world: again I leave the world, and I go to the Father.*

29 *His disciples say to him: Behold now thou speakest plainly, and speakest no proverb.*

30 *Now we know that thou knowest all things, and that for thee it is not needful that any man ask thee: in this we believe, that thou camest forth from God.*

31 *Jesus answered them: Now do you believe?*

32 *Behold the hour cometh, and is now come, that you shall be dispersed, every man to his own, and shall leave me alone: and yet I am not alone, because the Father is with me.*

33 *These things I have spoken to you, that in me you may have peace. In the world you shall have distress: but have confidence, I have overcome the world.*

CAPUT XVI.

1 *Hæc locutus sum vobis, ut non scandalizemini.*

2 *Absque synagogis facient vos: sed venit hora, ut omnis qui interficit vos, arbitretur obsequium se præstare Deo.*

3 *Et hæc facient vobis, quia non noverunt Patrem, neque me.*

4 *Sed hæc locutus sum vobis: ut cum venerit hora, eorum reminiscamini, quia ego dixi vobis.*

5 *Hæc autem vobis ab initio non dixi, quia vobiscum eram: Et nunc vado ad eum, qui misit me; et nemo ex vobis interrogat me, Quo vadis?*

6 *Sed quia hæc locutus sum vobis, tristitia implevit cor vestrum.*

7 *Sed ego veritatem dico vobis: expedit vobis ut ego vadam: si enim non abiero, Paraclitus non veniet ad vos: si autem abiero, mittam eum ad vos.*
8 *Et cum venerit ille, arguet mundum de peccato, et de justitia, et de judicio.*
9 *De peccato quidem: quia non crediderunt in me:*
10 *De justitia vero, quia ad Patrem vado: et jam non videbitis me:*
11 *De judicio autem: quia princeps hujus mundi jam judicatus est.*
12 *Adhuc multa habeo vobis dicere: sed non potestis portare modo.*
13 *Cum autem venerit ille Spiritus veritatis, docebit vos omnem veritatem: non enim loquetur a semetipso: sed quæcumque audiet loquetur, et quæ ventura sunt annunciabit vobis.*
14 *Ille me clarificabit: quia de meo accipiet, et annunciabit vobis.*
15 *Omnia quæcumque habet Pater, mea sunt. Propterea dixi: quia de meo accipiet, et annunciabit vobis.*
16 *Modicum, et jam non videbitis me: et iterum modicum, et videbitis me: quia vado ad Patrem.*
17 *Dixerunt ergo ex discipulis ejus ad invicem: Quid est hoc, quod dicit nobis: Modicum, et non videbitis me: et iterum modicum, et videbitis me, et quia vado ad Patrem?*
18 *Dicebant ergo: Quid est hoc, quod dicit, Modicum? nescimus quid loquitur.*
19 *Cognovit autem Jesus, quia volebant eum interrogare, et dixit eis: De hoc quæritis inter vos quia dixi: Modicum, et non videbitis me: et iterum modicum, et videbitis me.*
20 *Amen, amen dico vobis: quia plorabitis, et flebitis vos, mundus autem gaudebit: vos autem contristabimini, sed tristitia vestra vertetur in gaudium.*
21 *Mulier cum parit, tristitiam habet, quia venit hora ejus: cum autem pepererit puerum, jam non meminit pressuræ propter gaudium: quia natus est homo in mundum.*
22 *Et vos igitur nunc quidem tristitiam habetis, iterum autem videbo vos, et gaudebit cor vestrum: et gaudium vestrum nemo tollet a vobis.*
23 *Et in illo die me non rogabitis quidquam. Amen, amen dico vobis: si quid petieritis Patrem in nomine meo, dabit vobis.*
24 *Usque modo non petistis quidquam in nomine meo: Petite, et accipietis, ut gaudium vestrum sit plenum.*
25 *Hæc in proverbiis locutus sum vobis. Venit hora cum jam non in proverbiis loquar vobis, sed palam de Patre annunciabo vobis.*
26 *In illo die in nomine meo petetis: et non dico vobis quia ego rogabo Patrem de vobis:*
27 *Ipse enim Pater amat vos, quia vos me amastis, et credidistis, quia ego a Deo exivi.*
28 *Exivi a Patre, et veni in mundum: iterum relinquo mundum, et vado ad Patrem.*
29 *Dicunt ei discipuli ejus: Ecce nunc palam loqueris, et proverbium nullum dicis.*
30 *Nunc scimus quia scis omnia, et non opus est tibi ut quis te interroget: in hoc credimus quia a Deo existi.*
31 *Respondit eis Jesus: Modo creditis?*
32 *Ecce venit hora, et jam venit, ut dispergamini unusquisque in propria, et me solum relinquatis: et non sum solus, quia Pater mecum est.*
33 *Hæc locutus sum vobis, ut in me pacem habeatis. In mundo pressuram habebitis: sed confidite, ego vici mundum.*

ANALYSIS.

In this chapter, our Lord forewarns His followers of the sufferings and persecutions in store for them, on account of their steady adhesion to Him. These things He predicts, in order to strengthen their faith, on witnessing the accomplishment of His predictions (1–8).

The effects of the coming of the promised Paraclete in regard to the world, and the sin of which He will convict them (8–12).

The results of His coming in regard to our Lord Himself and His disciples (12–15). While forewarning them of passing sorrow arising from His departure, He promises them lasting joy which is to succeed it (22). He encourages them to present their petitions to His Father in His own name, with the assurance of obtaining their requests. The great love of His Father for them (23–25).

Their profession of faith in Him which was confirmed by His words (29–31).

He guards them against vain glory, by telling them that in a short time their firmness will yield to fear, when each of them will provide, as best He can, for his own safety, leaving Him alone in the hands of His enemies.

He assures them that after sufferings and persecutions from the world, they will come off with Him victorious over the world (33).

Commentary.	Text.
1. "*These things have I spoken to you,*" etc. I have forewarned you of the persecutions shortly to befall you, and of the coming of the Holy Ghost, "*that you may not be scandalized,*" so that, when they come; being forewarned, you may be prepared for them, and be aware, that these things were your portion as My followers; and that, therefore, they may not have the effect of turning you aside from the right path, or cause you to stumble on your direct way to heaven; especially, when you may expect My Spirit, the Spirit of truth, to strengthen and console you.	1. *These things have I spoken to you, that you may not be scandalized.* 1. *Hæc locutus sum vobis, ut non scandalizemini.*
2. You shall be subjected to the greatest indignities. "*They shall,*" ignominiously, "*cast you out of their Synagogues,*" and subject you to excommunication (see ix. 22. "*Synagogue,*" see Matthew iv. 23). Not content with insults, they shall proceed to grievous bodily harm, and inflict on you the greatest bodily injury, nay, even death; and shall fancy that by so doing, they are only worshipping God, offering Him a most pleasing act of sacrifice and religious service, and only displaying their zeal in the cause and defence of His holy law, of which you are supposed to be the enemies. Of this, St. Paul furnishes a practical illustration in his persecution of the Christians.	2. *They will put you out of the synagogues: yea, the hour cometh, that whosoever killeth you, will think that he doth a service to God.* 2. *Absque synagogis facient vos: sed venit hora, ut omnis qui interficit vos, arbitretur obsequium se præstare Deo.*
3. Far from excusing the gross, affected ignorance of the Jews, which rather aggravated their guilt, He tells the Apostles, that it is because "*they knew not,*" nor wished to know, what He demonstrated by the clearest evidence of miracles, viz., that God was His Father; and that He was the Eternal Son of God, they acted thus. He thus consoles the Apostles by suggesting to them, that	3. *And these things will they do to you, because they have not known the Father, nor me.* 3. *Et hæc facient vobis, quia non noverunt Patrem, neque me.*

Text.

4. *But these things I have told you: that when the hour shall come, you may remember that I told you of them.*

4. *Sed hæc locutus sum vobis: ut cum venerit hora, eorum, reminiscamini, quia ego dixi vobis.*

5. *But I told you not these things from the beginning, because I was with you. And now I go to him that sent me, and none of you asketh me: Whither goest thou?*

5. *Hæc autem vobis ab initio non dixi quia vobiscum eram: Et nunc vado ad eum, qui misit me; et nemo ex vobis interrogat me, Quo vadis?*

6. *But because I have spoken these things to you, sorrow hath filled your heart.*

6. *Sed quia hæc locutus sum vobis, tristitia implevit cor vestrum.*

7. *But I tell you the truth: it is expedient to you that I go: for if I go not, the*

Commentary.

they had the knowledge which their persecutors rejected; and that it was a source of glory for them to suffer, on account of unalterably embracing this knowledge and suffering for it. This was afterwards realized (Acts v. 41).

4. You will have to endure great suffering, "*but these things I have told you,*" beforehand, to show My Divine prescience, so that the fulfilment of My prediction may confirm you further in the belief in My Divinity, and arm you with strength to undervalue these sufferings that when you are enduring them, "*you may remember that I forewarned you.*" This will have the effect of increasing your confidence in Me, your Lord and Master, who might prevent them if I pleased. I shall be myself a spectator of your combat, strengthening you, so as to secure for you the crown of eternal life.

5. "*These things I told you not, from the beginning,*" of My ministry, of My familiar intercourse with you, when, as My devoted followers and Apostles, you constantly attended Me; because, they would be too servere a trial to your incipient faith; and because, I was Myself present to protect you, "*because I was with you.*" But now, on the point of leaving and returning to My Father to reap, after My death, the fruit of eternal glory, it is not expedient to conceal them from you; and, therefore, I forewarn you. Although our Lord had spoken of persecutions in store for His Apostles and followers (Matthew x. 17; Luke xii. 12; xxi. 12; Mark xiii. 9), still, He did not speak of them in detail, nor as so near, or, so atrocious or persistent as he does here.

"*And now I go* . . . and *none of you asketh Me,*" etc. Our Lord after announcing what is recorded above, is supposed to be silent for a moment, waiting to see if any of them would interrogate Him as to the nature and circumstances of His departure, or the glory that He had in store for their fidelity and heroism in suffering for His sake. They had asked Him already through Thomas (c. xiv. 5); but *now*, He says, as if surprised at their silence, "*none of you asketh Me,*" on the eve of My departure, as is usual between friends, "*whither goest Thou?*"

6. "*But,*" overwhelmed with sorrow, on account of My having spoken of My near departure, you have omitted questioning Me about what would assuage that sorrow, and should be a source of joy on account of the blessings of which My departure will be productive. He reproaches them mildly for their untimely sorrow and cowardice.

7. "*It is expedient,*" etc. He already spoke of the advantage it would bring *Him* to depart (xiv. 28). Here, He spoke of the advantage it would bring *them*.

Commentary.

To dispel their sorrow, He announces to them a consoling truth, which would dissipate their erroneous ideas regarding His departure, and the bereavement it would cause them, which, as emanating from Him, they should believe. This truth was, that far from being an evil, as regards them, His departure, on the contrary, would be to them a source of blessings.

"*For, if I go not, the Paraclete.*" This sweet Comforter, so often promised you, to console you and teach you all truth—"*will not come.*" My departure by death, and by glorification in the bosom of My Father, is a necessary condition for the coming of this Paraclete—a necessary step to wean My followers from too much attachment to Me personally, and thus render them fit for the reception of the Holy Spirit, and the full participation in the blessings of His coming.

"*But, if I go, I will send Him to you.*" This shows the Holy Ghost proceeds from the Son as well as from the Father; and also the distinction of persons. The person *sending* is distinct from the person *sent*.

8. The public and palpable effect of His coming will be, this: "*He will convince,*" clearly and undeniably exhibit to the gaze of the universe, the crimes of "*the world,*" perverse worldly-minded men, and bring home to their doors, "*convince them,*" "*of sin, justice,*" etc.

9. "*Of sin,*" consisting in the great damning sin of infidelity and stubborn unbelief—the chief source of their spiritual and eternal misery; "*because,*" with the clearest evidence of My Divinity, "*they believed not in Me,*" nor in the teaching and miracles of the Apostles which emanated from the Holy Ghost, whom they received.

10. "*Of justice.*" They shall be convicted of the *want* of true justice bestowed on sincere believers, the foundation and root of which is faith, "*the evidence of things which appear not*" (Heb. xi. 1).

"*Because I,*" withdrawing My visible presence, "*go to the Father,*" to enjoy His glory, and by being invisible to the world, shall become a prominent object of faith. By not believing in Me, whom they no longer see, they are bereft of true justice (see end of next verse).

11. "*And of judgment,*" of a heavy judgment of well-merited condemnation. For, its head, "*the prince of this world,*" who tyrannically rules over the children of unbelief, the enemy of man's salvation, "*is already judged,*" already condemned, deprived of his dominion over men, through My Passion, as he unjustly assailed Me. (The past, "*is judged,*" is put for the near future.) He

Text.

Paraclete will not come to you: but if I go, I will send him to you.

7. *Sed ego veritatem dico vobis: expedit vobis ut ego vadam: si enim non abiero, Paraclitus non veniet ad vos: si autem abiero, mittam eum ad vos.*

8. *And when he is come, he will convince the world of sin, and of justice, and of judgment.*

8. *Et cum venerit ille, arguet mundum de peccato, et de justitia, et de judicio.*

9. *Of sin: because they believed not in me.*

9. *De peccato quidem: quia non crediderunt in me.*

10. *And of justice: because I go to the Father; and you shall see me no longer.*

10. *De justitia vero, quia ad Patrem vado: et jam non videbitis me:*

11. *And of judgment: because the prince of this world is already judged.*

11. *De judicio autem: quia princeps hujus mundi jam judicatus est.*

Text.	Commentary.

shall be driven out of the bodies of men, out of pagan temples by My Apostles, at the invocation of My name. This condemnation will be rendered still more manifest in the ruin of idolatry, and the cure of Energumenists, through My Apostles, strengthened by the Holy Ghost. All the members of whom Satan is head, viz., the wicked, shall share in his fate, being condemned in this world and the next.

Others understand "*justice*," of the justice and innocence of Christ. The Holy Ghost will prove to the world, that Christ is just and innocent, the source of true justice in all.

"*Because I go to the Father*," in the very same flesh I had here. Hence, they have now no pretext, as heretofore, for not believing in Him and regarding Him as just and innocent, now that He shall have risen glorious from the dead, to prove His Divinity and shall have ascended to His Father (St. Chrysostom). The reason assigned for His convicting the world, "*of justice*," viz., "*because I go to the Father*," would render this opinion probable, as it seems that it has some reference to our Lord, "*because I go*," etc.; or, He shall convict the world, Jew and Gentile, of their false justice, which they boasted of as grounded on the works of the law, or moral works; whereas, through Me only can true justice come, by faith. "*Because I go to the Father*." Hitherto, they were scandalized at My preaching, and My humble, infirm condition. But I shall be fully vindicated when, after My death and Resurrection, I ascend in glory to My Father, and send down My Spirit, who will sanctify and justify My faithful, and make it clear to the world, that I am not a mere man; but, a Man-God.

"*And you shall see Me no longer.*" I shall be invisible to all men.

12. *I have yet many things to say to you but you cannot bear them now.*

12. *Adhuc multa habeo vobis dicere: sed non potestis portare modo.*

12. "*I have yet many things to say to you*," many explanations regarding the profound points of doctrine I delivered to you; many additional matters beyond those spoken of already, probably, relating to the mysteries of faith, the conversion of the Gentiles, the government of the Church.

"*But you cannot bear them now.*" You are too rude, in point of intellect, and too imperfect in spiritual knowledge, not to speak of the sadness with which you are overwhelmed, "*to bear them*," to profit by them. But the Holy Ghost shall fully teach you. Hence, He inspires them with a longing desire for the descent of the Holy Ghost.

13. *But when he, the Spirit of truth, is come, he will teach you all truth. For he shall not speak of himself: but what things soever he shall hear,*

13. "*But when He*"—the Paraclete—"*the Spirit of truth*," who is, by essence, truth itself, and the source of all truth, "*is come*," already promised to you, by Me (xv. 26), "*He will teach you*," without ambiguity, in the infused gifts of wisdom and knowledge, "*all truth*," necessary and expedient for you to know in this life,

Commentary

for your own sanctification, and for teaching all nations. He will lead you into a knowledge of all the truth, which I refrain from laying fully before you on account of your inability to profit by it at present. He will supplement what I am obliged now to omit. This He will do gradually as the occasion may require, and not all at once on His descent at Pentecost. Later on, He disclosed to Peter (Acts x.), the preaching of the Gospel to the Gentiles; and also that the Gentiles were not to be circumcised according to the law of Moses. (Acts xv., etc.)

The knowledge "*of all truth*," without exception, is not imparted to us by the Holy Ghost, in this life. It is reserved for us, in heaven.

The Greek for "*teach*," ὁδηγησει, means, to conduct or guide straightway, that is, He will give you to understand and know all truth, which you cannot now bear. This is substantially expressed by the words, "*to teach all truth.*"

"*For He shall not speak of Himself.*" Some understand this to mean, He shall speak the truth and nothing else, as He shall not speak from Himself. Others say, it is meant to inform them that the Holy Ghost will teach them the truths, which our Lord did not think it right to lay before them now, on account of their incapacity. And not being from Himself, but proceeding from the Father and the Son, the Holy Ghost shall not speak from Himself.

"*But what things soever He shall hear, He shall speak.*" This our Lord adds, to obviate any false notion, that the Holy Spirit, who was to teach all things, was greater than the Son, or, would teach anything not in perfect accordance with His teaching. "*Shall hear,*" as legate. These things He shall speak, and nothing else.

This knowledge, which is the same as His essence and existence, was communicated to the Holy Ghost in His *eternal procession* from the Father and the Son, from whom He proceeded from all eternity. This argues no inferiority in the Holy Ghost, any more than it would argue inferiority in the Son, who speaks what is communicated to Him by His Father, who begot Him by an eternal generation (xii. 49, 50; xiv. 10; xv. 15). So also the Holy Ghost speaks what was communicated to Him in His *Eternal Procession*, by the Father and the Son.

"*And the things that are to come, He shall show you.*" He will not only impart a knowledge of things past, but also of things to come. He shall endow them with a spirit of prophecy, and a foreknowledge, especially of what is necessary for them to know, in teaching the nations, in founding His Church, and ruling in it in their own day, and through their successors in future ages. "*The testimony of Jesus is the spirit of prophecy*" (Apoc. xix. 10). The Apostles exercised this gift of prophecy (Acts xi. 28; xx. 29).

Text

he shall speak: and the things that are to come he shall shew you.

13. Cum autem venerit ille Spiritus veritatis, docebit vos omnem veritatem: non enim loquetur a semetipso; sed quæcumque audiet loquetur, et quæ ventura sunt annuntiabit vobis.

Text.

14. *He shall glorify me; because he shall receive of mine, and shall shew it to you.*

14. *Ille me clarificabit: quia de meo accipiet, et annunciabit vobis.*

15. *All things whatsoever the Father hath, are mine. Therefore I said, that he shall receive of mine, and shew it to you.*

15. *Omnia quæcumque habet Pater, mea sunt. Propterea dixi: quia de meo accipiet, et annunciabit vobis.*

16. *A little while, and now you shall not see me: and again a little while, and you shall see me: because I go to the Father.*

16. *Modicum, et jam non videbitis me: et iterum modicum, et videbitis me: quia vado ad Patrem.*

Commentary.

14. "*He shall glorify Me.*" He shall reveal to the world, through the preaching of the Apostles, the Divinity of Christ, and make known His Attributes, His infinite justice, mercy, etc., thus rendering His holy name celebrated and glorious throughout the earth.

"*Because He shall receive of Mine.*" All this knowledge He shall receive, or has already received, in His *Eternal Procession* from the Father and Me; from the fulness of My knowledge and wisdom, which is the same as that of My Father (*v.* 15). "*And shall show it to you.*" Our Lord here shows that the Holy Ghost is Consubstantial with Himself, by receiving from Him that knowledge of future things, which is essential to Him and belongs to His Divinity, since it belongs to God alone to predict future events. He speaks in the future tense. For, this knowledge, although communicated from eternity, has reference here to its communication, at a *future* period, to the Apostles and the faithful; and He speaks of the Holy Ghost, as if it were made known to Him only when He imparted it to the Apostles and the believers. From this verse, the Fathers generally and the Council of Florence (SS. 25) proved the Divinity of Christ and the Procession of the Holy Ghost, from the Son as well as from the Father.

15. Lest it might be imagined from His saying, "*He shall receive of Mine,*" that the Son had this from Himself, and might detract from His Father's glory, he adds, that whatever the Son hath, the Attributes of Power, Wisdom, etc., these He received from the Father. These, which were essentially His, were communicated to Him, with His essential existence in His eternal generation from His Father. All these essential Attributes of the Divine nature they have equally and in common; and hence, "*I said, He shall receive of Mine,*" which are the Father's also The Holy Ghost had these communicated to Him in His *Eternal Procession* from us both, Father and Son. They were possessed equally and in common by three Divine Persons, who are perfectly equal in all things.

From this is proved the *Procession* of the Holy Ghost from the Father and Son. The Son was begotten of the Father by an eternal generation. The Holy Ghost proceeded from both by a common active *spiration*.

16. "*A little while,*" after a short interval of a few hours, between this and My death, "*and you shall not see Me.*" I shall be invisible during the short time My body shall be committed to the grave, after dying on the cross in indescribable torture.

"*And again a little while,*" after being confined for a short time to the tomb.

"*And you shall see Me,*" when I shall appear glorious to you after My Resurrection, to strengthen and console you. The first

Commentary.

"*little while*" embraced the interval between the time He spoke and His death; the second "*little while*," the interval between His death and Resurrection.

"*Because I go to the Father.*" This was why they would not see Him; because, by His Father's ordinance, He was to die and thus become invisible; and afterwards rise again from the grave, and then, and not *till* then, He was to return to the Father, from whose bosom He descended by assuming human nature, in order to redeem the human race.

Others interpret it thus, "*A little while.*" After a short time of forty days, which intervenes between this and My Ascension, "*you shall not see Me.*"

But after "*a little while*," again, "*you shall see Me*," coming at the end of the world, in glory to judge mankind. "*Because I go to the Father*," to enjoy the glory which I merited by My Passion, and then return, after a short interval, at the end of the world. The time between His Ascension and the General Judgment is, in the computation of God, but a mere point.

17, 18. Very likely, our Lord spoke in an obscure enigmatical way, in order to invite His Apostles to put Him some questions for explanation, the answers to which would arrest their attention, and make things more clear and intelligible to them. This would serve to strengthen and console them in their depressed state of sorrow.

19. Our Lord, in virtue of His Divine prescience, knew their inmost thoughts and their secret desires to be enlightened as to the meaning of His words. He anticipates their questions, and shows Himself to be God, the searcher of hearts, which God alone can be.

Instead of directly answering their questions as to the meaning of a "*little while*," or, its duration, or what would happen them, He describes the effect of the sorrow which they would feel during the "*little while*" He was invisible in His death and sepulture; and of their joy during the short period of His manifestation to them.

20. "*Amen, amen*," a form which accompanies or precedes solemn asseveration.

Text.

17. Then some of his disciples said one to another: What is this that he saith to us: A little while, and you shall not see me: and again a little while, and you shall see me, and because I go to the Father?

17. Dixerunt ergo ex discipulis ejus ad invicem: Quid est hoc, quod dicit nobis: Modicum, et non videbitis me: et iterum modicum, et videbitis me, et quia vado ad Patrem?

18. They said therefore: What is this that he saith, A little while? we know not what he speaketh.

18. Dicebant ergo: Quid est hoc, quod dicit, Modicum? nescimus quid loquitur.

19. And Jesus knew that they had a mind to ask him; and he said to them: Of this do you enquire among yourselves, because I said: A little while, and you shall not see me: and again a little while, and you shall see me.

19. Cognovit autem Jesus, quia volebant eum interrogare, et dixit eis: De hoc quaeritis inter vos quia dixi: Modicum, et non videbitis me: et iterum modicum, et videbitis me.

20. Amen, amen I say to you, that you shall lament and weep,

Text.

but the world shall rejoice: and you shall be made sorrowful, but your sorrow shall be turned into joy.

20. *Amen, amen dico vobis: quia plorabitis, et flebitis vos, mundus autem gaudebit: vos autem contristabimini, sed tristitia vestra vertetur in gaudium.*

21. *A woman, when she is in labour, hath sorrow, because her hour is come: but when she hath brought forth the child, she remembereth no more the anguish, for joy that a man is born into the world,*

21. *Mulier cum parit, tristitiam habet, quia venit hora ejus: cum autem pepererit puerum, jam non meminit pressuræ propter gaudium: quia natus est homo in mundum.*

22. *So also you now indeed have sorrow, but I will see you again, and your heart shall rejoice; and your joy no man shall take from you.*

22. *Et vos igitur nunc quidem tristitiam habetis, iterum autem videbo vos, et gaudebit cor vestrum: et gaudium vestrum nemo tollet a vobis.*

23. *And in that day you shall not ask me anything. Amen, amen I say to you: if you ask the Father any thing in my name, he will give it you.*

23. *Et in illo die me non rogabitis quidquam. Amen, amen*

Commentary.

"*You shall lament and weep,*" after the first "*little while,*" when I shall be taken away from you by death.

"*But the world*"—the Jews and the votaries of this world, My murderers—shall rejoice over My death, and this rejoicing shall add to your sorrow.

"*And you shall be made sorrowful,*" plunged in sorrow, while they are rejoicing. But this, your sorrow, shall be only passing and temporary; it shall be succeeded by never ending joy, "*turned into joy.*"

21. He illustrates their passing sorrow and the abiding joy that is to succeed it by describing the feelings of passing sorrow and subsequent permanent joy, on the part of a mother during parturition, and after it.

22. "*So, now also,*" etc. This is the application of the foregoing parable. There is an implied comparison; hence, the particle, *as*, is understood in the preceding verse, thus; *as* "*a woman in labour,*" etc.

"*So also you now,*" etc. They will have sorrow on account of His death and departure, and in the course of life, they and their followers shall suffer sorrow and persecutions. "*But I will see you,*" etc., after My Resurrection, to console you for your passing bereavement, "*and your heart shall rejoice,*" at My resuscitation from the grave, "*and your joy no one shall take from you.*" It will be permanent, not liable to be taken away from you, like human joy. Your spiritual joy at My glory and Resurrection, and your union with Me and the certainty of eternal rewards, can never cease; because, I shall continue in My glorified state, never again to die; and I shall uphold your union with Me, and shall afford you, by My efficacious grace, every security, consistent with the exercise of human liberty, for reaping the never ending rewards stored up for you.

23. "*And in that day,*" when I shall render Myself visible to you in My glorified state, after My Resurrection, "*you shall not ask Me anything.*" The Greek word for "*ask,*" means, to *interrogate*. Hence, our Lord means to convey, that on that day of rejoicing, they shall not require to put any questions similar to those they had now in their minds, as to asking about His stay among them; because, then they shall fully see, from experience, what the meaning of a "*little while*" in both instances is. Or,

Commentary.

the words, "*in that day*," may embrace the whole time after His Resurrection, with special reference to the mystery of Pentecost. Then, enlightened partly by His own teaching, and partly by the Holy Ghost, they will not require to ask any questions about the matter, regarding which they were anxious to receive information now, before His death and the descent of the Holy Ghost.

"*Amen, amen*," etc. From the subject of asking questions, our Lord proceeds, for their further consolation, to the subject of *preferring requests, asking favours*, which, He assures them, will be granted, if properly petitioned for.

"*If you ask the Father*," after the withdrawal of My bodily presence, "*any thing in My name*," through My merits, as *Redeemer*, which are impetratory to a boundless degree, and which our Lord transfers to us, so that we address the Father, as it were, in the person of Christ; through Me, as *Mediator*, now sitting at My Father's right hand, to make intercession for you; through Me, as your *head*, who regards as received by Himself, whatever we, as His members, receive. Hence, the Church concludes her prayers with the words, "*Per Dominum Nostrum Jesum Christum,*" etc.

Every word is emphatic. "*Amen, amen*," conveying a solemn asseveration, "*I say to you*," "*I*"—whose promises cannot be frustrated—"*say to you*"—solemnly promise you as My friends, and all My faithful followers to the end of time, "*if you ask the Father any thing*," which may be conducive to your eternal happiness, any thing not unworthy of God to grant.

"*In My name*" (see above). In this, it is also implied that it be asked with the dispositions He prescribes (see 1 John v. 14, Commentary).

"*He will give it to you.*" Hence, some require, as a condition, in order that our prayers be infallibly impetratory, that they be presented for ourselves, "*to you.*" If offered for others, they may place an obstacle to their receiving them.

If our petitions are not heard, the reason is because, "*we ask amiss*" (James v. 3). We want the necessary dispositions.

24. "*Hitherto,*" owing to His personal presence among them, they asked and obtained everything of Himself, and He obtained everything from the Father for them. They had not, as yet, recourse to His Father to obtain petitions through our Lord, as *Redeemer, Mediator* and *Head*, "*in My name.*" Now, on His departure from them, they need not be saddened; because, by having recourse directly to the Father, through His Son's merits, they will receive from the Father all they want; so that, as a consequence, the joy they felt at His glorious Resurrection would be fully completed in every respect. "*Your joy may be full,*" by obtaining in this life, the full effect of their petitions in regard to

Text.

dico vobis: si quid petieritis Patrem in nomine meo, dabit vobis.

24. *Hitherto you have not asked any thing in my name. Ask and you shall receive; that your joy may be full.*

24. *Usque modo non petistis quidquam in nomine meo: Petite, et accipietis, ut gaudium vestrum sit plenum.*

Text.	Commentary.
	sanctification; and in the next, everlasting glory. "*Gratiam et gloriam dabit Dominus.*" (Psa. lxxxiii.)
25. *These things I have spoken to you in proverbs. The hour cometh when I will no more speak to you in proverbs, but will shew you plainly of the Father.*	25. "*These things,*" of which I spoke already regarding the "*little while,*" also regarding My departure, the coming of the Holy Spirit, prayer in My name, etc., "*I spoke to you in proverbs,*" in an obscure, enigmatical manner. It was expedient to do so in regard to them, considering their prejudices, and their unwillingness to believe, that He would die. "*The hour cometh.*"
25. *Hæc in proverbiis locutus sum vobis. Venit hora cum jam non in proverbiis loquar vobis sed palam de Patre annunciabo vobis.*	The hour of My glorious life is now at hand, when I shall no longer speak to you in this manner, but, "*plainly of the Father.*" As a source of consolation to you, I shall, during the forty days of My converse with you, after My Resurrection, and especially through My Holy Spirit, whom I shall send down upon you, speak in a plain, intelligible style, "*of the Father,*" of His perfections, of the mysteries of faith, the Trinity, Incarnation, economy of Redemption, and the other leading truths, which you are destined to promulgate to the world.
26. *In that day you shall ask in my name: and I say not to you, that I will ask the Father for you.*	26. "*In that day,*" when I shall be seated glorious at the right hand of My Father, after having previously instructed you plainly regarding Him. "*You shall ask in My name,*" through My merits, according to the form of petition, to be henceforth adopted by the Church. "*Per Dominum Nostrum,*" etc.
26. *In illo die in nomine meo petetis: et non dico vobis quia ego rogabo Patrem de vobis:*	"*And I say not, that I will ask the Father,*" etc. You shall be heard by Him without any intervention on My part. Our Lord by the expression, "*I do not say,*" etc., does not mean to convey, that He will cease to pray to the Father for us. For, "*He is always making intercession for us*" (Heb. vii. 25; ix. 24). He asks the Father for us (xiv. 16; xvii. 9). He only means to convey, that He *need not* do so; as the Father will hear the Apostles and the rest of the faithful directly and immediately without the intervention of His Son. This is what is termed, *præteritio*, not, *exclusio*.
27. *For the Father himself loveth you, because you have loved me, and have believed that I came out from God.*	27. "*For the Father Himself loveth you,*" and anticipates the desires of your heart. By His preventing and concomitant graces, He enables you to be His friends and to earn His love. "*He loveth you because you have loved Me,*" His grace enabling you to do so, and you have believed, owing to the sweet influence of the same grace—"*that I come out from God,*" that I am the Son of God, that I descended from His bosom, from His throne in heaven, to assume human nature for the redemption of the human race. The Father, therefore, Himself loves you, and is desirous to shower down His blessings on you. For this, however, He requires, as a condition, that we earnestly pray for them. It is only by asking, "*we shall receive.*" As regards the efficacy of prayer. (See Matth. vi. 8, Commentary on.)
27. *Ipse enim Pater amat vos, quia vos me amastis, et credidistis, quia ego a Deo exivi.*	

Commentary.

28. "*I came forth from the Father,*" being born of Him, as His Son, by an eternal generation; I go forth again from Him. "*I am come into the world,*" by assuming human nature in the Virgin's womb.

"*Again I leave the world,*" withdrawing My bodily and visible presence at My Ascension, "*and go to the Father.*" I return to Him, in my human nature, which He shall glorify, in reward for My humiliation and exalted merits.

29. "*Thou speakest plainly, and no proverb,*" without obscurity or ambiguity. By saying, "*I go to the Father,*" He explains what "*a little while*" meant.

30. "*Now we know,*" from experience, "*that Thou knowest all things,*" even the thoughts of the heart, Thou dost anticipate us by answering (v. 19), "*and Thou needest not that any man should ask Thee,*" to know the thoughts that are passing in our minds, since Thou dost anticipate our desires, and, of Thyself, dost explain away all our doubts.

"*By this we believe that Thou comest forth from God.*" On account of this knowledge of the secret thoughts of our hearts, "*we believe,*" more firmly still, than we hitherto believed in Thy Divinity.

Or, "*by this.*" This alone, if all other motives of credibility were wanting, is a sufficient reason for us to believe in your Divinity and Divine mission; since to God alone, it belongs to search the secrets of hearts.

31. "*Do you now believe?*" By which He insinuates, that, however confident they may seem to be; still, their faith, which He does not question, is not as firm as they may suppose, as was shortly afterwards proved, by their conduct and cowardice in circumstances of danger.

32. "*And now is come,*" just at hand, as Judas and his cohort were approaching. Not only will they fly, but they shall be scattered; each one providing as best he could for his own personal safety. Verifying the words, "*percutiam pastorem et dispergentur oves*" (Zach. xiii. 7).

"*And shall leave Me alone,*" in the hands of My enemies, thus fulfilling the prophecy recorded (Matthew xxvi. 56). He shows the weakness of their faith and the absence of all manly courage in defence of it.

"*And yet I am not alone,*" etc., as if He said, I speak not thus not on my own account, but yours; since, inseparably and indis-

Text.

28. *I came forth from the Father, and am come into the world: again I leave the world, and I go to the Father.*

28. *Exivi a Patre et veni in mundum iterum relinquo mundum, et vado ad Patrem.*

29. *His disciples say to him: Behold now thou speakest plainly, and speakest no proverb.*

29. *Dicunt ei discipuli ejus: Ecce nunc palam loqueris, et proverbium nullum dicis.*

30. *Now we know that thou knowest all things, and thou needest not that any man should ask thee. By this we believe that thou comest forth from God.*

30. *Nunc scimus quia scis omnia, et non opus est tibi ut quis te interroget: in hoc credimus quia a Deo existi.*

31. *Jesus answered them: Do you now believe?*

31. *Respondit eis Jesus: Modo creditis?*

32. *Behold the hour cometh, and it is now come, that you shall be scattered every man to his own, and shall leave me alone: and yet I am not alone, because the Father is with me.*

32. *Ecce venit hora, et jam venit, ut dispergamini unusquisque in propria, et me solum relinquatis: et non sum solus, quia Pater mecum est.*

Text.

33. *These things I have spoken to you, that in me you may have peace. In the world you shall have distress; but have confidence, I have overcome the world.*

33. *Hæc locutus sum vobis, ut in me pacem habeatis. In mundo pressuram habebitis: sed confidite, ego vici mundum.*

Commentary.

solubly united with My Father, I have His Omnipotence ever present to protect Me in every tribulation.

33. "*These things*" (xiv., xv., xvi.), "*I have spoken to you,*" I reminded you beforehand of your weakness; and informed you of the hatred which the world bears you, and its consequent persecution of you, so that by believing and loving Me, you may be prepared for them. Sensible of My paternal concern for you, you will retain "*peace*" and tranquillity of mind. In the midst of persecutions, by calling to mind My predictions and never failing promises of support, you will pass unmoved through the storms that may assail you in your passage through the world.

"*In the world you will have distress.*" Fancy not, that in the midst of that peace which I promised you, you will be free from tribulations and persecutions from the powers of this corrupt "*world,*" which hates and detests you.

"*But, have confidence.*" If your enemies are strong, He on whom you lean for support is stronger; nay, the conqueror of the world, which He overcame for your sakes also (1 John v. 4, 5). "*I have overcome,*" is said by anticipation, as it has reference to His future Passion, whereby He is sure to overcome the world. As I, the captain of your warfare, triumphed; so shall you, by adhering to Me, fighting manfully under my banners, and invoking My help against all your enemies, surely triumph over them, and give them a signal overthrow.

CHAPTER XVII.

1 *These things Jesus spoke, and lifting up his eyes to heaven, he said: Father, the hour is come, glorify thy Son, that thy Son may glorify thee.*

2 *As thou hast given him power over all flesh, that he may give life everlasting to all whom thou hast given him.*

3 *And this is life everlasting: that they may know thee, the only true God, and Jesus Christ, whom thou hast sent.*

4 *I have glorified thee upon the earth: I have finished the work which thou gavest me to do:*

5 *And now glorify thou me, O Father, with thyself, with the glory which I had with thee, before the world was.*

6 *I have manifested thy name to the men whom thou has given me out of the world. Thine they were, and to me thou gavest them: and they have kept thy word.*

7 *Now they have known that all things which thou hast given me are from thee.*

8 *Because the words which thou gavest me, I have given to them: and they have received them, and have known for certain that I came forth from thee, and they have believed that thou didst send me.*

9 *I pray for them: I pray not for the world, but for them whom thou hast given me: because they are thine:*

10 *And all mine are thine, and thine are mine: and I am glorified in them.*

11 *And now I am no more in the world, and these are in the world, and I come to thee. Holy Father, keep them in thy name, whom thou hast given me: that they may be one, as we also are.*

12 *While I was with them, I kept them in thy name. Those whom thou gavest me, I have kept: and none of them hath perished, except the son of perdition, that the Scripture may be fulfilled.*

13 *And now I come to thee: and these things I speak in the world, that they may have my joy filled in themselves.*

14 *I have given them thy word, and the world hath hated them, because they are not of the world: as I also am not of the world.*

15 *I do not ask that thou take them away out of the world, but that thou preserve them from evil.*

16 *They are not of the world: as I also am not of the world.*

17 *Sanctify them in truth. Thy word is truth.*

18 *As thou hast sent me into the world, I also have sent them into the world.*

19 *And for them I do sanctify myself: that they also may be sanctified in truth.*

20 *And not for them only do I pray, but for those also who through their word shall believe in me.*

21 *That they all may be one, as thou, Father, in me, and I in thee, that they also may be one in us: that the world may believe that thou hast sent me.*

22 *And the glory which thou hast given me, I have given to them: that they may be one, as we also are one.*

23 *I in them, and thou in me: that they may be made perfect in one: and that the world may know that thou hast sent me, and hast loved them, as thou hast also loved me.*

24 *Father, I will that where I am, they also whom thou hast give me, may be with me: that they may see my glory, which thou hast given me: because thou hast loved me before the foundation of the world.*

25 *Just Father, the world hath not known thee: but I have known thee: and these have known, that thou hast sent me.*

26 *And I have made known thy name to them, and will make it known: that the love wherewith thou hast loved me, may be in them, and I in them.*

CAPUT XVII.

1 *Hæc locutus est Jesus: et sublevatis oculis in cœlum, dixit: Pater, venit hora, clarifica filium tuum, ut filius tuus clarificet te:*

2 *Sicut dedisti ei potestatem omnis carnis, ut omne, quod dedisti ei, det eis vitam æternam.*

3 *Hæc est autem vita æterna: Ut cognoscant te, solum Deum verum, et quem misisti Jesum Christum.*

4 *Ego te clarificavi super terram: opus consummavi, quod dedisti mihi ut faciam.*

5 *Et nunc clarifica me tu Pater apud temetipsum, claritate, quam habui prius quam mundus esset, apud te.*

6 *Manifestavi nomen tuum hominibus, quos dedisti mihi de mundo. Tui erant, et mihi eos dedisti: et sermonem tuum servaverunt.*

7 *Nunc cognoverunt, quia omnia quæ dedisti mihi, abs te sunt:*

8 *Quia verba, quæ dedisti mihi, dedi eis: et ipsi acceperunt, et cognoverunt vere quia a te exivi, et crediderunt quia tu me misisti.*

9 *Ego pro eis rogo: Non pro mundo rogo, sed pro his, quos dedisti mihi: quia tui sunt:*

10 *Et mea omnia tua sunt, et tua mea sunt: et clarificatus sum in eis.*

11 *Et jam non sum in mundo, et hi in mundo sunt, et ego ad te venio. Pater sancte, serva eos in nomine tuo, quos dedisti mihi: ut sint unum, sicut et nos.*

12 *Cum essem cum eis, ego servabam eos in nomine tuo. Quos dedisti mihi, custodivi: et nemo ex eis periit, nisi filius perditionis, ut Scriptura impleatur.*

13 *Nunc autem ad te venio: et hæc loquor in mundo, ut habeant gaudium meum impletum in semetipsis.*

14 *Ego dedi eis sermonem tuum, et mundus eos odio habuit, quia non sunt de mundo, sicut et ego non sum de mundo.*

15 *Non rogo ut tollas eos de mundo, sed ut serves eos a malo.*

16 *De mundo non sunt, sicut et ego non sum de mundo.*

17 *Sanctifica eos in veritate. Sermo tuus veritas est.*

18 *Sicut tu me misisti in mundum, et ego misi eos in mundum.*

19 *Et pro eis ego sanctifico meipsum: ut sint et ipsi sanctificati in veritate.*

20 *Non pro eis autem rogo tantum, sed et pro eis, qui credituri sunt per verbum eorum in me:*

21 *Ut omnes unum sint, sicut tu Pater in me, et ego in te, ut et ipsi in nobis unum sint: ut credat mundus, quia tu me misisti.*

22 *Et ego claritatem, quam dedisti mihi, dedi eis: ut sint unum, sicut et nos unum sumus.*

23 *Ego in eis, et tu in me: ut sint consummati in unum: et cognoscat mundus quia tu me misisti, et dilexisti eos, sicut et me dilexisti.*

24 *Pater quos dedisti mihi, volo ut ubi sum ego, et illi sint mecum: ut videant claritatem meam, quam dedisti mihi: quia dilexisti me ante constitutionem mundi.*

25 *Pater juste, mundus te non cognovit, ego autem te cognovi: et hi cognoverunt, quia tu me misisti.*

26 *Et notum feci eis nomen tuum, et notum faciam: ut dilectio, qua dilexisti me, in ipsis sit, et ego in ipsis.*

ANALYSIS.

In this chapter, we have the solemn prayer addressed to His heavenly Father, by our Lord when about to enter on His Sacred Passion. 1st. For *Himself*, to receive due glory in compensation for His humiliations, and in return for the glory He had given His Father (1–5). 2ndly. For *His disciples*, to obtain for them perseverance in faith, preservation from evil, and sanctification in truth (6–19). 3rdly. For the *faithful*, who are to receive the faith through the preaching of the Apostles (20). Finally, He prays *for all together;* He asks for the entire Church, the gift of perfect union among themselves, similar to the union existing among the Persons of the Adorable Trinity, and the ineffable blessings of eternal happiness (21–26).

Commentary.

1. "*These things Jesus spoke,*" viz., the discourse contained in the preceding chapters. The following sublime prayer—the longest, as far as the Gospel records them, uttered by our Lord—derives additional interest from the solemn circumstances, in which it was delivered. Jesus, on the eve of His death, commends His disciples, towards whom He was after expressing His love and tenderest affection, to the protection of His heavenly Father, showing us by His example, as St. Thomas remarks, that we should aid by our prayers those, whom we instruct by word. It was uttered, according to some, before leaving the supper hall; according to others, in the open air, on their way to Gethsemane.

"*And lifting up His eyes to heaven.*" Our Lord in this ordinary attitude of prayer, wishes, as our teacher, to show us, that in circumstances of difficulty and trial, our entire confidence is to be placed in God, from whom alone can we hope for strength to overcome our enemies.

"*Father.*" Every word is *emphatic*. As *man*, and as *Man*-God, He appeals to that Father, of whom He was eternally begotten, and who proclaimed, that in His beloved Son, He was always well pleased. What could such a Father refuse to such a Son?

"*The hour is come,*" the long expected time of trial and

Text.

1. *Thesethings Jesus spoke, and lifting up his eyes to heaven, he said: Father, the hour is come, glorify thy Son, that thy Son may glorify thee.*

1. *Hæc locutus est Jesus: et sublevatis oculis in cælum, dixit: Pater venit hora clarifica filium tuum, ut filius tuus clarificet te:*

| Text. | Commentary. |

conflict, when handed over to the fury of My enemies and calumniators, the glory of My Divinity shall be clouded, and I most need help and grace.

"*Glorify Thy Son.*" Make manifest the glory of My name, now that I am to be branded as an impostor and malefactor, so that the world may acknowledge Me, owing to the wonders Thou shalt work in my favour, as Thy Eternal Son, and believing in Me, may be justified and saved.

These wonders took place at His death, and forced men to exclaim, "*Truly, this is the Son of God.*"

"*That thy Son may glorify Thee.*" I ask for this glorious manifestation of My name, as Thy Eternal Son, not so much on My own account, as for your honour; that it may redound to Thy glory, by displaying Thy Infinite Justice, Mercy, Wisdom and Omnipotence, who art the great Author and original source of all good. The spread of the Gospel and the conversion of a sinful world, would redound to the glory of God.

2. *As thou hast given him power over all flesh, that he may give eternal life to all, whom thou hast given him.*

2. *Sicut dedisti ei potestatem omnis carnis, ut omne, quod dedisti ei, det eis vitam æternam.*

2. "*Since Thou hast granted power over all flesh,*" all mankind, without exception, without distinction of Jew or Gentile.

"*Given Him,*" as God, in His birth from eternity, at His Incarnation, and in the glory of His Resurrection, "*Ego hodie genui te*" (Psa.), "*Postula a me et dabo tibi gentes hereditatem tuam,*" etc., and hast, therefore, given Him the power of vivifying all men; it is but meet that He to whom such power was given, should grant to all who believe in Him, life everlasting. Our Lord, so far as He was concerned, has provided the necessary means of salvation for all men. To the elect, He has offered *efficacious* graces; to all, *sufficient* graces.

3. *Now this is eternal life: That they may know thee, the only true God, and Jesus Christ, whom thou hast sent.*

3. *Hæc est autem vita æterna: Ut cognoscant te, solum Deum verum, et quem misisti Jesum Christum.*

3. "*Now this is eternal life.*" This is the source of eternal life, the road, the *means* to it. The effect, "*eternal life,*" is put for its cause, viz., "*that they*" (men), "*may know Thee,*" by faith, "*the only true God,*" that is, to be Him, who is the only true God, with whom are united the Son and the Holy Ghost, who equally participate in the same Divine nature of the true Godhead. "*Only,*" is not the *subject*, but the *attribute* of the proposition affecting "*thee,*" as its attribute, as is clear from the Greek, σε τον μονον αληθινον Θεον. It, therefore, excludes false gods and idols only; but not the other Divine persons, who partake equally of the same Divine nature.

"*Eternal life.*" For obtaining eternal life, this is the foundation. However, it alone will not secure eternal life; other things are indispensable, viz., hope, love of God, and in general, the observance of the commandments.

"*And Jesus Christ whom thou hast sent,*" may know that Jesus,

Commentary.

whom "*Thou hast sent*, is *the Christ*," the promised Redeemer of the world, who, by His merits, bestows eternal life.

Some Expositors connect these latter words with the preceding, so as to make them with the word, "*thee*," the subject of the proposition, and explain them, thus: "This is true life, that they may know Thee, and Him whom Thou hast sent, Jesus Christ, to be the only true God." The Greek will admit of this construction, and is regarded by many, as probable. This is the idea conveyed by St. John (1 John v. 20). Our Lord exhibits Himself in the entire context, as the Son of God. He emphatically asserts His own Divinity in propounding the Divinity of the Father; and declares, in the most explicit way, the necessity of believing in Him, not only as the consubstantial Son of the Father; but also, as Man-God, who assumed human nature for the redemption of mankind.

In this passage, it is conveyed that two things are indispensable for eternal life, viz., the knowledge of the one true God, in which is included a knowledge of and firm belief in the adorable Mystery of the Trinity; and of Jesus Christ as our Mediator and Redeemer of mankind, or, a firm belief in the Mystery of the Incarnation.

Our Redeemer omits all mention of the Holy Ghost, His object here being, to inculcate faith in Himself as God, the only begotten Son of God, God-Man. This was the foundation of faith, and once believed, the faith in the Holy Ghost followed, as a matter of course; since, He had declared that the Holy Spirit proceeded from Himself, and was to be sent by Him.

4. "*I have glorified Thee on earth*," by My life, teaching and preaching; by manifesting Thy goodness and justice in My Passion soon at hand.

"*I have finished the work which Thou gavest me to do.*" He refers to His Passion near at hand, as if it were accomplished and had occurred, on account of the certainty of its accomplishment, as also to the preaching of the Gospel through His Apostles. This is the work which His Father gave Him to do, when He sent Him, as His legate, into this world, by investing Him with human nature.

5. "*And, now, Father*," since I have accomplished the end of My mission, humbling Myself for the love of Thee, and subjecting Myself to the ignominy of the cross, and glorified Thee on *earth*, do Thou glorify Me in *heaven*, "*with Thyself*" in Thy heavenly kingdom, by bestowing on My *humanity*, in My glorious Resurrection, and in My being placed at Thy right hand, a share in that glory—of course, in a limited, but supereminent degree—which I had from eternity in My Divine nature, as My innate, essential right, as *God*. Make the world see, that I am Thy Eternal Son, God as well as Man, by

Text.

4. I have glorified thee on the earth: I have finished the work which thou gavest me to do:

4. Ego te clarificavi super terram: opus consummavi, quod dedisti mihi ut faciam:

5. And now glorify thou me, O Father, with thyself, with the glory which I had, before the world was, with thee.

5. Et nunc clarifica me tu Pater apud temetipsum, claritate, quam habui prius quam mundus esset, apud te.

Text.

Commentary.

communicating to My glorified humanity, at Thy right hand, the fullest participation—of course, in a finite degree—in that glory which I had in the unity of the Divine nature, from eternity. This glory was, to some extent, obscured and laid aside externally in His humbly assuming human nature and in His sufferings. He now prays for its resumption. God heard His prayer by compensating Him for His humiliations and sufferings afterwards (Philip. ii. 9) in the glorious name, above every other name, which He gave Him.

"*Which I had with Thee before the world was.*" This clearly shows the pre-existence of Christ. He existed "*before the world was*," or before any thing else created existed, He was from eternity.

6. *I have manifested thy name to the men whom thou hast given me out of the world. Thine they were, and to me thou gavest them: and they have kept thy word.*

6. *Manifestavi nomen tuum hominibus, quos dedisti mihi de mundo: Tui erant, et mihi eos dedisti: et sermonem tuum servaverunt.*

6. This is the work which I have accomplished, viz., "*I have manifested Thy name,*" made Thee known as the Eternal Father, in Thy relations with the Son, whom Thou hast begotten, consubstantial with Thee, and sent in human flesh into the world, and the Holy Ghost proceeding from us both, a Blessed *Trinity of Persons in the one nature* of God.

"*To the men whom Thou hast given Me,*" viz., the Apostles and faithful followers, whom Thou hast chosen out of the sinful, condemned mass of mankind, preventing them by Thy sweet consolations, enabling them by actual and co-operating graces, to embrace Thy faith, and devote themselves entirely to Thy service.

"*Thine they were,*" as well by eternal election, and creation as by several other titles, to be disposed of according to Thy Sovereign will. "*And to Me,*" as man and Redeemer, "*Thou hast given them.*" Thy grace has not been given to them in vain. "*They have kept,*" by the faithful observance of its precepts, "*Thy Word,*" which I have preached to them.

7. *Now they have known that all things which thou hast given me are from thee.*

7. *Nunc cognoverunt quia omnia, quæ dedisti mihi, abs te sunt.*

7. "*Now,*" believing in Me, "*they have known that all things,*" etc., that all My words and works have proceeded from Thee, as their Divine principle, and not, as My enemies maliciously assert, from the power of demons. In a word, they know, that I am from Thee, and all My works are Divine. All His Divine perfections were communicated to Him by the Father with the Divine essence, in His eternal generation. All His human perfections from the Father and the Holy Ghost; but attributed to the Father, as the great fountain of the Divinity.

8. *Because the words which thou gavest me, I have given to them: and they have received them, and have known*

8. They have known, that I have come from Thee, for this reason; "*because the words,*" or doctrine, "*which Thou gavest Me,*" in order to be communicated to them, "*I have given to them*" —clearly announcing it as it emanated from Thee, "*and they,*" on

Commentary.

their part, "*have received them,*" with docility and obedience. "*And*"—consequently—"*have known in very deed that I came out from Thee,*" in My Divine nature, by an eternal generation. "*And they have believed, that Thou hast sent Me,*" in My Incarnation, into this world, assuming human nature for the redemption of the entire human race. In a word, they know Me to be true God and true man, one of the chief foundations of all Christian faith.

All that our Lord says, from verse 6 to 16, *directly* regards the Apostles, but *indirectly*, the body of the faithful and the entire Church, at all times, which was to be built on the Apostles, as its foundation.

Our Lord commends the faith and devotedness of His Apostles, in order the more securely to obtain the effects of the petition He is now about to pour forth for them.

9. "*I pray for them*"—what it is He prays for them is mentioned verse 11—"*keep them in Thy name.*" "*I pray not for the world,*" viz., those who, following their concupiscences so much indulged in the world—the votaries of this world, who, owing to their resistance to grace, become reprobate. Our Lord does not say, *absolutely* He prays not for such; since, He prayed for His very enemies, "*dimitte, nesciunt, quid faciunt.*" He provides sufficient graces for all, instituted His sacraments for all, died for all, wishes all to be saved. He does not pray for them *here*, on this occasion. His prayer *here* is specially for His Apostles. It is a farewell prayer, and its object is "*to keep them in His name*" (verse 11), which could not apply to the reprobate, for whom He prays, *elsewhere*.

"*But for them whom Thou hast given Me,*" to be specially My followers. This prayer is intended for them also.

"*Because they are Thine.*" This is a motive for confidence in the efficacy of His prayer, and for commending them to His Father. It is but congruous that His Father should have special care of those who are His own, by gracious choice and election.

10. He explains parenthetically, how they belong to the Father, although given by Him to the Son. The Father does not lose His right over them. For, all things belonging to the Son, belong to the Father. All things the Father gave Him either in His eternal or temporal birth, belong still to the Father, on account of the unity and identity of nature, and all Divine perfections in both, in common with the Holy Ghost. And they belong to the Son; because given by the Father, whose right or claim does not cease, owing to this concession; but, remains still the same, as before.

"*And I am glorified in them,*" as they believe in My Divine Sonship and identity with the Father, whose glory is also promoted

Text.

in very deed that I came out from thee, and they have believed that thou didst send me.

8. *Quia verba, quæ dedisti mihi, dedi eis: et ipsi acceperunt, et cognoverunt vere quia a te exivi, et crediderunt quia tu me misisti.*

9. *I pray for them: I pray not for the world, but for them whom thou hast given me: because they are thine;*

9. *Ego pro eis rogo: Non pro mundo rogo, sed pro his, quos dedisti mihi: quia tui sunt.*

10. *And all my things are thine, and thine are mine: and I am glorified in them.*

10. *Et mea omnia tua sunt: et tua mea sunt: et clarificatus sum in eis:*

Text.

11. *And now I am not in the world, and these are in the world, and I come to thee. Holy Father keep them in thy name, whom thou hast given me: that they may be one, as we also are.*

11. *Et jam non sum in mundo, et hi in mundo sunt, et ego ad te venio. Pater sancte, serva eos in nomine tuo quos dedisti mihi: ut sint unum, sicut et nos.*

12. *While I was with them, I kept them in thy name. Those whom thou gavest me have I kept: and none of them is lost, but the son of perdition, that the scripture may be fulfilled.*

Commentary.

in Mine. Some understand, "*am glorified,*" in a future sense, "*shall be glorified,*" by their zeal in spreading the Gospel, and by their labours and death. Hence, another ground for confidence of obtaining His request. He assigns a twofold reason for praying; viz., because they are Thine; and because I am glorified in them by faith and obedience. Here, our Lord clearly declares Himself to be consubstantial with the Father. His words would be blasphemous, were it otherwise, or were He not so.

11. He gives a reason for praying fervently now, especially for His disciples. "*Now I am not in the world.*" I am shortly to leave this earth and withdraw My visible presence, "*and these are in the world.*" These remain after Me, exposed to all the dangers, temptations, and persecutions, cast in their way by a perverse world, without the aid of My personal advice and protection, "*because I come to Thee.*" I return to Thee by My death and Resurrection. I, therefore, specially commend them to Thee.

"*Holy Father.*" He calls Him "*holy,*" as He was the fountain of holiness and sanctity, which He prayed for on behalf of His disciples.

"*Keep them in Thy name,*" which some interpret, *by Thy grace and power,* preserve them in My love and service. Others, keep them *in the confession of Thy name and truth.* Others, keep them in Thy grace, *for the honour of Thy name.*

"*Whom Thou hast given Me.*" There is a diversity of reading in the Greek. For, "*whom*" (ὄυς) some read (ω) (*which*). The reading adopted by the Vulgate is considered preferable. It is the reading employed next verse (12).

"*That they may be one,*" united in love and affection, in some measure, similar to the union that essentially and inseparably exists between the Persons of the Godhead. The essential unity of the Godhead is incommunicable. What He prays for here is the most perfect supernatural union that can exist among men, modelled, in a finite and limited degree on the unity of the Divine nature, unity of *intellect, or faith,* unity of *will,* or *supernatural charity,* unity of *subordination* in the entire Church between pastors and people. This is a comparison and no more, since the unity of the Godhead is incommunicable. It is a *similarity* of union, in a limited degree. Man can never attain the Divine unity.

12. "*While I was with them,*" visibly and corporally conversing with them. In the Greek, is added "*in the world.*" "*I kept them in Thy name,*" by Thy power and authority, attached to Me as Thy Legate. I kept them in Thy service and in the *confession* of Thy name.

"*Those whom Thou gavest Me,*" as My disciples and chosen

Commentary.

followers, "*have I kept*" firm in Thy love and service, and preserved them from all harm, either in regard to soul or body.

"*And none of them is lost*" eternally, or has sustained bodily harm, "*but*" (except) traitorous Judas, "*the son of perdition*," who is irrecoverably doomed, through his own perversity, to eternal perdition ; so "*that*," as a consequence of his previous obstinacy and ingratitude, "*the Scripture*," or Divine prediction regarding him, "*may be fulfilled*" (Psa. cviii. 8). "*Dum judicatur exeat condemnatus, Episcopatum ejus accipiat alter.*" This passage, St. Peter (Acts, i. 20), applies literally to Judas.

13. "*And now*," leaving them, "*I come to Thee.*" I return to Thee, after My death and Resurrection. Deprived of My presence, instruction and personal protection, I earnestly commend them to Thee, to watch over them and specially guard them.

"*And these things I speak in the world.*" These words I address to Thee in their behalf, while I am yet "*in the world.*"

"*So that they may have My joy*," which the knowledge of their union and charity causes Me, "*filled in themselves.*" Fully shared in by themselves, by witnessing My Resurrection, Ascension, and sending down the Holy Ghost—a subject of great joy—and also by the firm hope of hereafter following Me and participating in My joys, in My heavenly kingdom.

14. "*I have given them Thy word*," preached to them Thy doctrines, meant by Thee for the world. They have faithfully attended to them (verse 8).

"*And the world hath hated them, because they are not of this world*," their affections, pursuits, aims and morals are quite dissimilar. "*As I am not of this world*," and hence, for a like reason, hated by them (xx. 18, 19).

15. "*I pray not, that Thou wouldst take them out of the world*," by a holy death, and transfer them at once, to Thy kingdom. This would not be expedient, or, in accordance with Thy Providence, by which it is arranged, that they would battle with the world, suffer persecution, and thus spread the Gospel, and by the exhibition of Christian virtues, and by bravely enduring death for Thy sake, promote the glory of Thy name.

But that "*Thou wouldst keep them,*" whilst conversing in the world, "*from evil,*" by which some understand the *evil one*, the devil, the prince of this world. Others, understand it of evil *in general*, especially sin, and departure from the true faith.

Text.

12. *Cum essem cum eis, ego servabam eos in nomine tuo. Quos dedisti mihi, custodivi: et nemo ex eis periit, nisi filius perditionis, ut Scriptura impleatur.*

13. *And now I come to thee: and these things I speak in the world, that they may have my joy filled in themselves.*

13. *Nunc autem ad te venio: et hæc loquor in mundo, ut habeant gaudium meum impletum in semetipsis.*

14. *I have given them thy word, and the world hath hated them, because they are not of the world; as I also am not of the world.*

14. *Ego dedi eis sermonem tuum, et mundus eos odio habuit, quia non sunt de mundo, sicut et ego non sum de mundo.*

15. *I pray not that thou shouldst take them out of the world, but that thou shouldst keep them from evil.*

15. *Non rogo ut tollas eos de mundo, sed ut serves eos a malo.*

Text.	Commentary.
16. *They are not of the world: as I also am not of the world.*	16. He repeats what He said in verse 14, as a motive for obtaining the following request, as neither He nor they are of the world.
16. *De mundo non sunt, sicut et ego non sum de mundo.*	
17. *Sanctify them in truth. Thy word is truth.*	17. Therefore, "*sanctify them in truth.*" "*Sanctify*" may mean, to confirm them in sanctity and increase the sanctity they already possess; infuse into them by the Holy Ghost, perfect evangelical truth, so that, replete with sanctity and wisdom, they may become teachers of the world, breathing sanctity in every word and act.
17. *Sanctifica eos in veritate. Sermo tuus veritas est.*	Others, by "*sanctify,*" understand, to *set them apart* for the ministry of preaching Thy Gospel, "*in truth,*" in the doctrine of truth, which I delivered to them in Thy name, and which they are to teach others. "*In truth,*" as preachers of Thy word. For, "*Thy word is truth,*" without the least admixture of error. It is the *true*, real fulfilment of the types and empty figures of the old law. Likely, both meanings are intended, viz., that God would bestow on them an increase of interior sanctity and set them apart for His ministry.
18. *As thou hast sent me into the world I also have sent them into the world.*	18. "*As Thou hast sent Me into the world,*" to save souls by dispensing doctrine and grace; to repair and sanctify a world lost in sin.
18. *Sicut tu me misisti in mundum, et ego misi eos in mundum.*	"*I also have sent them,*" etc., for the same object, to be achieved by the same means. Therefore, prepare them for it, lest they fall away either on account of blandishments or the force of persecution.
19. *And for them do I sanctify myself: that they also may be sanctified in truth.*	19. "*And for them,*" in order to sanctify and consecrate them irrevocably for Thy service.
19. *Et pro eis ego sanctifico meipsum: ut sint et ipsi sanctificati in veritate.*	"*I sanctify Myself,*" consecrating and offering Myself up to God, in a few hours, as a victim of atonement on the altar of the cross, holy, pleasing in all things.
	"*That they also may be sanctified in truth,*" that through the merits of My death, of My immolation in sacrifice, they also may be consecrated and set apart, and by advancing still more in real, internal sanctity, may be rendered fit to preach the Gospel of truth, throughout the earth, and by their evangelical labours and final sufferings, be themselves victims agreeable in Thy sight.
20. *And not for them only do I pray, but for them also who through their word shall believe in me:*	20. He now prays for all the believers to the end of the world. "*And not for them only,*" the Apostles here present, "*do I pray.*" "*But for them also who through their word,*" and the words of truth uttered by their successors to the end of time, "*shall believe in Me.*" Our Lord here prays for the entire Church or the congregation of believers, to the end of time.
20. *Non pro eis autem rogo tantum, sed et pro eis, qui credituri sunt per verbum eorum in me.*	
21. *That they all may be one, as thou, Father, in me, and I*	21. "*That they all may be one.*" He asks for *all*, for the entire Church, the same blessing of unity that He had already asked for

Commentary.

the Apostles (v. 11). Here, He prays only for the faithful; elsewhere, as on the cross, He prays for His enemies and unbelievers (v. 9–11). "*All one,*" united in the bonds of faith, hope, charity concord and subordination, in a manner similar, though unequal, to the essential union of the Divine nature. The union of will and love which exists in us, "*as Thou, Father, in Me,*" and that this perfect union may be forwarded and accomplished by their union with us in sanctifying grace, and supernatural love of charity, which makes us, as it were, partakers of the Divine nature.

"*May be one in us, as Thou,*" etc. "*As,*" can only convey a *similarity* of union in some respects; but, not *equality*. For creatures could never attain the adorable union that exists in the Godhead. The three Persons in the Godhead are united by the same Divine nature, identical in each. We are united in an analogous or similar way, by concord and charity and subordination, which has its origin and binding power and persevering stability in God's grace, "*one in us,*" and this union our Lord here prays for all the members of His Church.

"*That the world,*" all mankind, believers and unbelievers, "*may believe;*" the believers confirmed in their faith; and the unbelievers brought to embrace it, on beholding this moral miracle of supernatural union, which could come from God alone, between the faithful among themselves, as well as their union with God. "*That Thou hast sent Me,*" and, that My doctrine comes from Thee which was the great theme of His own preaching and that of the Apostles.

22. "*The glory which Thou hast given Me, I have given,*" etc. By "*glory,*" some understand the Divinity, which the Father gave Him in His eternal generation, and is essentially one with the nature of the Father. This glory, consisting in the most perfect union among themselves, of which creatures are capable, consisting also in their union with God, was, in a limited and analogous degree, bestowed on them, so that through His concession and grace, "*they may be one, as we also are one.*" Of course, there is *similarity* of union, but by no means *equality.* Others, understand "*glory*" of the Divinity, conferred on Him by His Father, and, in turn, communicated by Him to the Apostles and His faithful children in the adorable Eucharist, wherein He communicates with His adorable Body and Blood, etc., His Divinity also. In partaking of the Eucharist, they are *one* among themselves, and *one* with Him whom they receive, as their food; thus, becoming identified with them, as food is identified with the receiver (1 Cor. x. 16, 17); John vi. 57, "*remaineth in Me, and I in Him.*"

23. "*I in them.*" By being united to Me, as members of the same body to their head, as branches to the vine, through the

Text.

in thee: that they also may be one in us: that the world may believe that thou hast sent me.

21. *Ut omnes unum sint, sicut tu Pater in me, et ego in te, ut et ipsi in nobis unum sint: ut credat mundus, quia tu me misisti.*

22. *And the glory which thou hast given me, I have given to them; that they may be one, as we also are one.*

22. *Et ego claritatem, quam dedisti mihi, dedi eis: ut sint unum, sicut et nos unum sumus.*

23. *I in them, and thou in me: that they may be made perfect in*

Text.

one; *that the world may know that thou hast sent me, and hast loved them, as thou hast also loved me.*

23. *Ego in eis, et tu in me: ut sint consummati in unum: et cognoscat mundus quia tu me misisti, et dilexisti eos, sicut et me dilexisti.*

24. *Father, I will that where I am, they also whom thou hast given me may be with me: that they may see my glory which thou hast given me because thou hast loved me before the creation of the world.*

24. *Pater, quos dedisti mihi, volo ut ubi sum ego, et illi sint mecum: ut videant claritatem meam, quam dedisti mihi: quia dilexisti me ante constitutionem mundi.*

25. *Just Father, the world hath not known thee: but I have known thee: and these have known, that thou hast sent me.*

25. *Pater juste, mundus te non cognovit ego autem te cognovi et hi cognoverunt, quia tu me misisti.*

Commentary.

influx of sanctifying grace, "*and thou in Me*," in some measure resembling Thy union and indwelling in Me. Or, "*I in them*," by the communication of My Divinity in the Eucharist, as Thou dwellest in Me, by an essential union and identity.

"*That they may be made perfect in one*," that their union of soul and will may thus reach the greatest perfection.

"*And the world may know*," from their perfect concord and union, which no human means could bring about among themselves and with us, "*that Thou hast sent Me*," that all My doctrines are Thine, "*and hast loved them*," making them Thy adopted children and Apostles. "*As Thou hast loved Me*." Communicating Thyself to them through the medium of My flesh, in a manner somewhat similar to the love Thou didst show Me, when Thou didst communicate by an eternal love, the plenitude of Thy Divinity to Me, in My eternal generation.

24. This is His last petition for His disciples and faithful followers, viz., that they may be partakers of His eternal glory in heaven.

He thus stimulates them, in view of the great glory in store for them, to the performance of heroic actions, and to patient suffering for His sake.

"*I will*," I pray "*that where I am*," after my Ascension, sitting at Thy right hand, "*they also may be with Me*," after this mortal life, sharing in My glory.

"*That they may see*," face to face, "*My glory, which Thou hast given Me.*" This shows that their happiness consists in *seeing* Him, that, aided by *the light of glory—the grace of this life* would not suffice—they may enjoy the beatific vision of My Divinity, "*which Thou hast given Me*," in My eternal generation, and the glory of My Deified humanity, united to My Divinity.

"*Because Thou hast loved Me before the creation of the world*," from eternity. This love was shown in My eternal generation; and, as the result of this eternal love, Thou hast decreed to unite in time My humanity to the Second Person of the Adorable Trinity, and render it glorious. To the same eternal love, all the saints are indebted for the graces and glory bestowed on them.

25. "*Just Father*," who dost reward or punish according to men's deserts. This would seem to be the meaning of "*just*," conveying, why those only who believed in Him would be admitted to a share in His bliss; why some men were reprobated by the just judgment of God and deprived of the faith, as the deserved punishment of their pride, obstinacy and perversity.

"*The world hath not known Thee*," and did not wish to know Thee, by blindly shutting their eyes against the light of truth, and

Commentary

refusing to hear My words. They were, therefore, justly rejected and reprobated from grace and glory.

"*But I have known Thee, and these have known that Thou hast sent Me.*" Knowing it, they have embraced Thy truth, and therefore, by Thy just judgment, admitted to a share in Thy glory.

26. "*And I have made known Thy name.*" Their knowledge of Thee is derived from Me. I have made known to them Thy Attributes, especially Thy love for man, Thy infinite goodness and mercy in sending Me into this world to redeem mankind.

"*And will make it known,*" still more, by My preaching for forty days after My Resurrection, when I shall speak to them "*of the Kingdom of God*" (Acts i. 3), and by sending them My Spirit at Pentecost, to teach them all truth, which is to be communicated to their successors, to the end of time.

"*That the love wherewith Thou hast loved Me,*" by bestowing on My assumed nature the most exalted gifts of grace—the result of Thy eternal love—"*may be in them,*" extended to them through Thy gifts of grace, and permanently secured in them. Since, "*I am in them,*" ever present with them, closely united to them, as the vine to its branches, as the head to the members of the body, influencing them; strengthening, supporting them in their Apostolic labours, to be ultimately rewarded with everlasting happiness.

Text

26. *And I have made known thy name to them, and will make it known: that the love wherewith thou hast loved me, may be in them, and I in them.*

26. *Et notum feci eis nomen tuum, et notum faciam: ut dilectio, qua dilexisti me, in ipsis sit, et ego in ipsis.*

CHAPTER XVIII.

1 *When Jesus had said these things, he went forth with his disciples over the brook Cedron, where there was a garden, into which he entered with his disciples.*

2 *Now Judas also, who betrayed him, knew the place: because Jesus had often resorted thither together with his disciples.*

3 *Judas, therefore, having received a band of men, and servants, from the chief priests and the Pharisees, cometh thither with lanterns, and torches, and weapons.*

4 *Jesus, therefore, knowing all things that were to come upon him, went forward, and said to them: Whom seek ye?*

5 *They answered him: Jesus of Nazareth. Jesus saith to them: I am he. And Judas also, who betrayed him, stood with them.*

6 *As soon, then, as he had said to them: I am he: they went backward, and fell to the ground.*

7 *Again, therefore, he asked them: Whom seek ye? And they said: Jesus of Nazareth.*

8 *Jesus answered, I have told you, that I am he: if, therefore, you seek me, let these go their way.*

9 *That the word might be fulfilled which he said: Of them whom thou hast given me, I have not lost any one.*

10 *Then Simon Peter having a sword, drew it, and struck the servant of the high priest, and cut off his right ear. And the name of the servant was Malchus.*

11 *Then Jesus said to Peter: Put up thy sword into the scabbard. The chalice which my Father hath given me, shall I not drink it?*

12 *Then the band, and the tribune, and the servants of the Jews took Jesus and bound him:*

13 *And they led him away to Annas first; for he was father-in-law to Caiphas, who was the high priest of that year.*

14 *Now Caiphas was he, who had given the counsel to the Jews: that it was expedient that one man should die for the people.*

15 *And Simon Peter followed Jesus, and so did another disciple. And that disciple was known to the high priest, and went in with Jesus into the court of the high priest.*

16 *But Peter stood at the door without. Then the other disciple, who was known to the high priest went out and spoke to the portress and brought in Peter.*

17 *And the maid that was portress, said to Peter: Art not thou also one of this man's disciples? He saith: I am not.*

18 *Now the servants and officers stood at a fire of coals, because it was cold, and warmed themselves: and with them was Peter also standing, and warming himself.*

19 *The high priest then asked Jesus of his disciples, and of his doctrine.*

20 *Jesus answered him: I have spoken openly to the world: I have always taught in the synagogue, and in the temple, whither all the Jews resort: and in private I have spoken nothing.*

21 *Why askest thou me? ask them who have heard what I have spoken to them. behold they know what things I have said.*

22 And when he had said these things, one of the officers standing by gave Jesus a blow, saying: Answerest thou the high priest so?

23 Jesus answered him: If I have spoken ill, give testimony of the evil: but if well, why strikest thou me?

24 And Annas sent him bound to Caiphas, the high priest.

25 And Simon Peter was standing, and warming himself. They said, therefore, to him: Art not thou also one of his disciples? He denied it, and said: I am not.

26 One of the servants of the high priest, a kinsman to him whose ear Peter cut off, said to him: Did I not see thee in the garden with him?

27 Then Peter again denied: and immediately the cock crew.

28 Then they led Jesus from Caiphas to the governor's hall. And it was morning: and they went not into the hall, that they might not be defiled, but that they might eat the Pasch.

29 Pilate, therefore, went out to them, and said: What accusation bring you against this man?

30 They answered, and said to him: If he were not a malefactor, we would not have delivered him up to thee.

31 Pilate then said to them: Take him you, and judge him according to your law. The Jews, therefore, said to him: It is not lawful for us to put any one to death.

32 That the word of Jesus might be fulfilled, which he said, signifying what death he should die.

33 Pilate, therefore, went into the hall again, and called Jesus, and said to him: Art thou the king of the Jews?

34 Jesus answered: Sayest thou this thing of thyself, or have others told it thee of me?

35 Pilate answered: Am I a Jew? Thy nation and the chief priests have delivered thee up to me: what hast thou done?

36 Jesus answered: My kingdom is not of this world. If my kingdom were of this world, my servants would certainly strive that I should not be delivered to the Jews: but now my kingdom is not from hence.

37 Pilate, therefore, said to him: Art thou a king then? Jesus answered: Thou sayest that I am a king. For this was I born, and for this came I into the world: that I should give testimony to the truth: every one that is of the truth, heareth my voice.

38 Pilate saith to him: What is truth? And when he had said this, he went forth again to the Jews, and saith to them: I find no cause in him.

39 But you have a custom that I should release one unto you at the Pasch: will you, therefore, that I release unto you the king of the Jews?

40 Then they all cried again, saying: Not this man, but Barabbas. And Barabbas was a robber.

CAPUT XVIII.

1 Hæc cum dixisset Jesus, egressus est cum discipulis suis trans Torrentem Cedron, ubi erat hortus, in quem introivit ipse, et discipuli ejus.

2 Sciebat autem et Judas, qui tradebat eum, locum: quia frequenter Jesus convenerat illuc cum discipulis suis.

3 Judas ergo cum accepisset cohortem, et a Pontificibus, et Pharisæis ministros, venit illuc cum laternis, et facibus, et armis.

4 *Jesus itaque sciens omnia, quæ ventura erant super eum, processit, et dixit eis: Quem quæritis?*

5 *Responderunt ei: Jesum Nazarenum. Dicit eis Jesus: Ego sum. Stabat autem et Judas, qui tradebat eum, cum ipsis.*

6 *Ut ergo dixit eis: Ego sum: abierunt retrorsum, et ceciderunt in terram.*

7 *Iterum ergo interrogavit eos: Quem quæritis? Illi autem dixerunt: Jesum Nazarenum.*

8 *Respondit Jesus: Dixi vobis, quia ego sum: si ergo me quæritis, sinite hos abire.*

9 *Ut impleretur sermo, quem dixit: Quia quos dedisti mihi, non perdidi ex eis quemquam.*

10 *Simon ergo Petrus habens gladium eduxit eum: et percussit pontificis servum: et abscidit auriculam ejus dexteram. Erat autem nomen servo Malchus.*

11 *Dixit ergo Jesus Petro: Mitte gladium tuum in vaginam. Calicem, quem dedit mihi Pater, non bibam illum?*

12 *Cohors ergo, et tribunus, et ministri Judæorum comprehenderunt Jesum, et ligaverunt eum:*

13 *Et adduxerunt eum ad Annam primum, erat enim socer Caiphæ, qui erat pontifex anni illius.*

14 *Erat autem Caiphas, qui consilium dederat Judæis: Quia expedit, unum hominem mori pro populo.*

15 *Sequebatur autem Jesum Simon Petrus, et alius discipulus. Discipulus autem ille erat notus pontifici, et introivit cum Jesu in atrium pontificis.*

16 *Petrus autem stabat ad ostium foris. Exivit ergo discipulus alius, qui erat notus pontifici, et dixit ostiariæ: et introduxit Petrum.*

17 *Dicit ergo Petro ancilla ostiaria: Numquid et tu ex discipulis es hominis istius? Dicit ille: Non sum.*

18 *Stabant autem servi, et ministri ad prunas, quia frigus erat, et calefaciebant se: erat autem cum eis et Petrus stans, et calefaciens se.*

19 *Pontifex ergo interrogavit Jesum de discipulis suis, et de doctrina ejus.*

20 *Respondit ei Jesus: Ego palam locutus sum mundo: ego semper docui in synagoga, et in templo, quo omnes Judæi conveniunt: et in occulto locutus sum nihil.*

21 *Quid me interrogas? interroga eos, qui audierunt quid locutus sim ipsis: ecce hi sciunt quæ dixerim ego.*

22 *Hæc autem cum dixisset, unus assistens ministrorum dedit alapam Jesu, dicens: Sic respondes pontifici?*

23 *Respondit ei Jesus: Si male locutus sum, testimonium perhibe de malo: si autem bene, quid me cædis?*

24 *Et misit eum Annas ligatum ad Caipham pontificem.*

25 *Erat autem Simon Petrus stans, et calefaciens se. Dixerunt ergo ei: Numquid et tu ex discipulis ejus es? Negavit ille, et dixit: Non sum.*

26 *Dicit ei unus ex servis pontificis, cognatus ejus, cujus abscidit Petrus auriculam: Nonne ego te vidi in horto cum illo?*

27 *Iterum ergo negavit Petrus: et statim gallus cantavit.*

28 *Adducunt ergo Jesum a Caipha in prætorium. Erat autem mane: et ipsi non introierunt in prætorium, ut non contaminarentur, sed ut manducarent Pascha.*

29 *Exivit ergo Pilatus ad eos foras, et dixit: Quam accusationem affertis adversus hominem hunc?*

30 *Responderunt, et dixerunt ei: Si non esset hic malefactor, non tibi tradidissemus eum.*

31 *Dixit ergo eis Pilatus: Accipite eum vos, et secundum legem vestram judicate eum. Dixerunt ergo ei Judæi: Nobis non licet interficere quemquam.*

32 *Ut sermo Jesu impleretur, quem dixit, significans qua morte esset moriturus.*

33 *Introivit ergo iterum in prætorium Pilatus, et vocavit Jesum, et dixit ei: Tu es rex Judæorum?*

34 *Respondit Jesus: A temetipso hoc dicis, an alii dixerunt tibi de me?*

35 *Respondit Pilatus: Numquid ego Judæus sum? Gens tua, et pontifices tradiderunt te mihi: quid fecisti?*

36 *Respondit Jesus: Regnum meum non est de hoc mundo: si ex hoc mundo esset regnum meum, ministri mei utique decertarent ut non traderer Judæis: nunc autem regnum meum non est hinc.*

37 *Dixit itaque ei Pilatus: Ergo rex es tu? Respondit Jesus: Tu dicis quia rex sum ego. Ego in hoc natus sum, et ad hoc veni in mundum, ut testimonium perhibeam veritati: omnis, qui est ex veritate, audit vocem meam.*

38 *Dicit ei Pilatus: Quid est veritas? Et cum hoc dixisset: iterum exivit ad Judæos, et dicit eis: Ego nullam invenio in eo causam.*

39 *Est autem consuetudo vobis ut unum dimittam vobis in Pascha: vultis ergo dimittam vobis regem Judæorum.*

40 *Clamaverunt ergo rursum omnes, dicentes: Non hunc, sed Barabbam. Erat autem Barabbas latro.*

ANALYSIS.

This chapter commences with an account of our Lord's entrance into the Garden of Gethsemane, where His Sacred Passion commenced—the approach of the traitor, Judas, with an armed band of soldiers sent to apprehend Him. The display of our Lord's power in prostrating them on the ground on their declaring their errand (1–7). He commands Peter to desist from any attempt at defending Him, as He had ample means of defence, at His command, if necessary (7–11). He is brought bound to Annas—Peter's first denial of Him (12–18). He is next brought to the house of Caiphas, the High Priest, by whom He is interrogated regarding His disciples and His doctrine, and in the course of His trial receives most ignominious treatment at the hands of one of the servants, unchecked by the High Priest. Peter's second and third denial of Him (19–27). He is brought before Pilate, the Roman Governor, with the object of having the sentence of death pronounced by the Sanhedrim ratified by the Governor. Pilate declares Him innocent of the crimes laid to His charge, after minute interrogation (33–38). Barabbas, a murderer and robber, is preferred before Him (39, 40).

Commentary.	Text.
1. "*When Jesus had spoken these words*," recorded in chapters xv., xvi., with the prayer, chapter xvii., He went forth with "*His disciples*," either from the supper room, according to some, or from the spot, on His way to Gethsemane, where, in the stillness of the night, He had concluded His discourse (see Matthew xxvi. 30; John xiv. 30). "*Over the brook Cedron.*" This is not so particularly described by the other Evangelists, who, however, tell us what St. John here	1. *When Jesus had said these things, he went forth with his disciples over the brook Cedron, where there was a garden, into which he entered with his disciples.* 1. *Hæc cum dixisset Jesus, egressus est cum discipulis suis*

Commentary.

trans Torrentem Cedron, ubi erat hortus. in quem introivit ipse, et discipuli ejus.

omits, viz., that the garden or plot of ground, χωριον—was called "*Gethsemane.*"

"*Cedron.*" This is probably allusive to the flight or passage across the same ravine by David, flying from His ungrateful son, Absalom, and his traitorous counsellor, Achitophel (2 Kings xv. 23). It may be a fulfilment of the words of the Psa. cix. 7, "*De torrente in via bibet.*" David's betrayal by Achitophel, prefigured the treason of Judas, whom our Lord now went forth to meet, or to await.

"*Cedron,*" is a Hebrew word, "*Chidron,*" signifying, *dark*, probably, on account of the darkness of the ravine, or the turbid waters of the stream in winter.

"*Brook.*" The Vulgate almost always renders it, "*torrens, Cedron.*" The Greek χειμαρρον, conveys, that it was a small wintry stream, a ravine generally dry, except in winter. It flowed to the east of Jerusalem, till it joined the water of the pool of Siloam, and the water that flowed down on the west side of the city through the valley of Josephat, dividing the city from the Mount of Olives.

The Septuagint has, "*of the Cedars.*" But the reading followed by the Vulgate is regarded as the more probable. Likely, the word is of Hebrew, not of Greek origin.

"*With His disciples.*" Judas had already left them (c. xiii.).

"*Where there was a garden,*" which our Lord was in the habit of resorting to, for the purposes of prayer. Likely, the owner of the villa of Gethsemane, of which the garden formed a part, was a friend of our Lord or one of His followers. Sin began, having been committed, by the *first Adam*, in the Garden of Eden; and so did the reparation also for sin by the *second Adam*, who alone could make satisfaction, begin in the Garden of Gethsemane.

2. And Judas also, who betrayed him, knew the place: because Jesus had often resorted thither together with his disciples.

2. Sciebat autem et Judas, qui tradebat eum, locum: quia frequentur Jesus convenerat illuc cum discipulis suis.

2. St. Luke (xxii. 39; xxi. 37) conveys the same. It was His wont to resort there, at night for prayer, especially during the latter period of His mortal life. He spent the day in preaching and the night in the solitude of Mount Olivet, communing with His heavenly Father in prayer.

3. Judas therefore having received a band of soldiers, and servants from the chief priests and the Pharisees, cometh thither with lanterns and torches and weapons.

3. Judas ergo cum accepisset cohortem et

3. "*Judas, therefore, having received a band of soldiers,*" which probably denoted a Roman cohort consisting of 1,000 or 600 men that garrisioned the fort Antonia, or a detachment of it, which attended on the Sanhedrim by order of the Procurator, on great festivals. This band of men were placed by the Governor at the disposal of the High Priests, who wished some of their own trusted attendants on whom they relied, to accompany them, in

Commentary

order to capture and secure our Lord, whom they were most anxious to arrest and put to death.

This formidable military array, they calculated, would put down any opposition or attempt at rescue or tumult of any kind from whatever quarter it proceeded. It gave the whole transaction a legal appearance, as the soldiers belonged to the ruling authorities, the Romans. "*Judas*" is said to have "*received them,*" because, although given to the High Priests, it was Judas that headed them, leading them to where our Redeemer was.

"*With lanterns and torches,*" lest in the darkness of the night, they might mistake Him whom they were in search of.

"*And weapons,*" to ward off any possible resistance to their designs.

4. St. John, so fond of recording everything, that proves our Lord's Divinity, speaks of His Divine foreknowledge, and the willingness and freedom with which He offered Himself for death. It was with His own free consent He was captured. "*Oblatus, quia ipse voluit*" (Isaias liii.). He at the same time records the display of Divine power (*v.* 6), and shows how fearlessly and intrepidly He comes forward to meet His enemies, without shrinking from danger.

5. Judas probably, at once, on coming up, gave them the preconcerted signal, betraying Him with a kiss, and then, retiring back, joined them.

Notwithstanding this, awed by the majesty of His person, they dared not apprehend Him. Most likely, He struck them with a kind of blindness, as happened the Sodomites (Genesis xix. 11); so that they could not know Him, notwithstanding the kiss of Judas and the knowledge the servants of the High Priests had of Him, whom they often saw and heard. Hence, they said not, we seek *you,* but, Jesus of Nazareth.

6. Their falling to the ground was, according to the Evangelist's description here, the result of our Redeemer's words, "*I am He.*" Does not this sudden prostrating of an armed infuriated soldiery furnish the clearest evidence of the majesty and power of Him, who is the All-powerful God, concealed under the form of weak human nature?

The Greek is, "*I am,*" as in Exodus, "*sum qui sum.*" Does not this show that His surrender was voluntary; and that if He pleased, He might have prevented them from arresting Him *now*, as on a former occasion (viii. 46)? "*What will He do*"—exclaims St. Augustine—"*when He comes to judge who did such things, when taken to be judged?*" "*What will He be able to inflict from His throne, who had this power when about to die?*"

Text

a Pontificibus, et Phariseis ministros, venit illuc cum lanternis, et facibus, et armis.

4. *Jesus therefore knowing all things that should come upon him, went forth, and said to them: Whom seek ye?*

4. *Jesus itaque sciens omnia, quæ ventura erant super eum, processit, et dixit eis: Quem quæritis?*

5. *They answered him: Jesus of Nazareth. Jesus saith to them: I am he. And Judas also, who betrayed him, stood with them.*

5. *Responderunt ei: Jesum Nazarenum. Dicit eis Jesus: Ego sum. Stabat autem et Judas, qui tradebat eum, cum ipsis.*

6. *As soon therefore as he had said to them: I am he; they went backward, and fell to the ground.*

6. *Ut ergo dixit eis: Ego sum: abierunt retrorsum, et ceciderunt in terram.*

Text.

7. *Again therefore he asked them, Whom seek ye? and they said: Jesus of Nazareth.*

7. *Iterum ergo interrogavit eos: Quem quæritis? Illi autem dixerunt: Jesum Nazarenum.*

8. *Jesus answered, I have told you, that I am he. If therefore you seek me, let these go their way.*

8. *Respondit Jesus: Dixi vobis, quia ego sum: si ergo me quæritis, sinite hos abire.*

9. *That the word might be fulfilled which he said: Of them whom thou hast given me, I have not lost any one.*

9. *Ut impleretur sermo, quem dixit: Quia quos dedisti mihi, non perdidi ex eis quemquam.*

10. *Then Simon Peter having a sword, drew it; and struck the servant of the high-priest, and cut off his right ear. And the name of the servant was Malchus.*

10. *Simon ergo Petrus habens gladium eduxit eum: et percussit pontificis servum: et abscidit auriculam ejus dexteram. Erat autem nomen servo Malchus.*

11. *Jesus therefore said to Peter: Put up thy sword into the scabbard. The chalice which my Father hath given me, shall I not drink it?*

11. *Dixit ergo Jesus Petro: Mitte gladium tuum in vaginam. Calicem, quem dedit mihi Pater, non bibam illum?*

12. *Then the band, and the tribune, and the servants of the Jews took Jesus, and bound him:*

12. *Cohors ergo, et tribunus, et ministri Judæorum comprehenderunt Jesum, et ligaverunt eum:*

Commentary.

7. Our Lord, now after they were baffled, and prostrated long enough to feel His power, gives them an opening on regaining their feet, and repeats His question.

8. After Judas, who stepped forward from the midst of his protecting guard, had returned to his companions, it is likely the Apostles gathered round our Lord. He showed His solicitude for them, and by asking His assailants not to harm them, He by this very utterance deprived them of all power to do so. He would not have Apostles arrested or put to death; because He had destined them for the work of the Gospel, to herald the tidings of salvation to the ends of the earth. Moreover, by dying alone, He wished to convey, that the work of Redemption could not be shared in by any other. It was His and His alone.

9. "*The word . . . which He said*" (xvii. 12), "*might be fulfilled.*" "*Of those . . . not lost any one.*" Of course, the exception there made, is understood here also. He speaks of corporal and spiritual loss. If the Apostles had been arrested, they would suffer *bodily* loss, they would be put to death; especially as Peter had resorted to armed force and had offered violence. They would also have been lost spiritually; as, in all probability, being weak in faith, they would be influenced by the threats of the Jews to deny Him, as Peter did, under circumstances of less provocation; and thus they might be lost eternally.

10. (See Matthew xxvi. 51, 52, Commentary on.) St. John alone gives the names of him who smote, viz.; Peter, and of him who was smitten, the servant, Malchus.

11. (See Matthew xxvi. 52–54, Commentary on.)

12. (See Matthew xxvi. 52–57.) "*Tribune,*" χιλιαρχος, means, the captain of a thousand.

Commentary.

13. (See Matthew xxvi. 57.)

Text.

13. *And they led him away to Annas first, for he was father-in-law to Caiphas, who was the high-priest of that year.*

13. *Et adduxerunt eum ad Annam primum, erat enim socer Caiphæ, qui erat pontifex anni illius.*

14. This was added, probably, to convey what little chance of justice our Lord had at the hands of a man, who had already pronounced Him deserving of death, without hearing His cause; (xi. 49, 50), and also, perhaps, as St. Chrysostom observes, to remove any feeling of scandal or offence which some might entertain on seeing our Lord thus captured, by showing He thus submitted to be captured, in order to die for all.

14. *Now Caiphas was he who had given the counsel to the Jews, that it was expedient that one man should die for the people.*
14. *Erat autem Caiphas, qui consilium dederat Judæis: Quia expedit, unum hominem mori pro populo.*

15, 16. (See Matthew xxvi. 58, Commentary.)

15. *And Simon Peter followed Jesus, and so did another disciple. And that disciple was known to the high-priest, and went in with Jesus into the court of the high-priest.*

15. *Sequebatur autem Jesum Simon Petrus, et alius discipulus.* Discipulus autem ille erat notus pontifici, et introivit cum Jesu in atrium pontificis.

16. *But Peter stood at the door without. The other disciple therefore who was known to the high-priest, went out, and spoke to the portress, and brought in Peter.*

16. *Petrus autem stabat ad ostium foris. Exivit ergo discipulus alius, qui erat notus pontifici, et dixit ostiariæ: et introduxit Petrum.*

17, 18. This was the first of Peter's threefold predicted denials of our Lord. That this took place, not at the house of Annas, but of Caiphas, is shown in Commentary (Matthew xxvi. 58), where the reasons in support of this all but certain opinion are fully stated.

The account of Peter's threefold denial is given, Matthew (xxvi. 69–75), Mark (xix. 69–72), Luke (xxii. 54–62), and in this chapter by St. John. These accounts are given in different words by each, and would seem to be contradictory; but in reality they are not. This will be clearly seen, if we bear in mind, that it is quite usual with the Evangelists in their Gospel history, that one would supply what another omits, and so a full account is furnished by the separate narratives of each taken together. Thus, we find St. Matthew speak of a servant maid, whom Mark calls the maid of the High Priest; John, a portress. All harmonizes. Neither is there any contradiction in their account of the language addressed by the maid to Peter and of his reply to her. Nor is there any contradiction in one Evangelist (Matthew), saying that Peter sat *outside* in the court, and another (St. John), saying he was admitted into the house at the request of another disciple; since the *outside* hall in which he sat, was *within* the house, etc., etc.

17. *The maid therefore that was portress, saith to Peter: Art not thou also one of this man's disciples? He saith: I am not.*

17. *Dicit ergo Petro ancilla ostiaria: Numquid et tu ex discipulis es hominis istius? Dicit ille: Non sum.*

18. *Now the servants and ministers stood at the fire of coals, because it was cold, and warmed themselves. And with them was Peter also standing and warming himself.*

18. *Stabant autem servi, et ministri ad prunas: quia frigus erat, et calefaciebant se: erat autem cum eis et Petrus stans, et calefaciens se.*

Text.	Commentary.
	We must always bear in mind, what St. Augustine observes (Lib. ii. De Consen. Evang. c. 12), that it was not unusual with the Evangelists to employ different words, in narrating the same occurrence.
19. *The high-priest therefore asked Jesus of his disciples, and of his doctrine.* 19. *Pontifex ergo interrogavit Jesum de discipulis suis, et de doctrina ejus.*	19. While the temptation and denial of Peter were going on, the trial and interrogation of our Lord was also taking place; and as both events could not be described together by the Evangelist; hence, after referring to Peter's denial, he now describes our Lord's trial, "*regarding His disciples*," how it is He collected them around Him, "*and His doctrine*," concerning what He taught. He is brought forward, a bound criminal; and these iniquitous judges, having no crime wherewith to charge Him personally, turn to treat of His disciples and of His doctrine.
20. *Jesus answered him: I have spoken openly to the world; I have always taught in the synagogue, and in the temple, whither all the Jews resort: and in secret I have spoken nothing.* 20. *Respondit ei Jesus: Ego palam locutus sum mundo: ego semper docui in synagoga, et in templo, quo omnes Judæi conveniunt: et in occulto locutus sum nihil.*	20. Our Redeemer replies to the charge insinuated by the High Priest, viz., that He privately taught His disciples false and seditious doctrines; by saying He spoke publicly, to the entire world; that His doctrines taught in places of public resort, were known to the entire world; that He spoke nothing in private, "*in secret, He spoke nothing*," nothing that was not in thorough accordance with His public and well-known teachings. He had no twofold teaching, one for the public, and the other for His private friends. He says nothing about His disciples, as He did not wish to implicate them at all.
21. *Why askest thou me? ask them who have heard what I have spoken unto them: behold they know what things I have said.* 21. *Quid me interrogas? interroga eos, qui audierunt quid locutus sim ipsis: ecce hi sciunt quæ dixerim ego.*	21. Our Lord shows His confidence in the truth of what He uttered; at the same time, He insinuates that they were disposed to distrust Him, all along showing due respect for the authority of the High Priest. He refers them with confidence in the justice of His cause, to those who heard Him. His judges could not fairly refuse to listen to their testimony. It was not consistent with the order of justice to question the accused when no proof of guilt was alleged against him. "*Behold, they know,*" etc. "*They,*" might be rendered, "*these,*" those present, even, My enemies, who often heard Me, can bear testimony; so, you need not go far in search of witnesses.
22. *And when he had said these things, one of the servants standing by, gave Jesus a blow, saying: Answerest thou the high priest so?* 22. *Hæc autem cum dixisset, unus assistens ministrorum dedit alapam Jesu, dicens: Sic respondes pontifici?*	22. "*One of the servants,*" etc. This insolent official, affecting to think our Lord's reply to the High Priest, wanting in due respect, treats Him most contemptuously. This affront the High Priest should not tolerate. However, his hatred of our Lord blinded him to every sense of decency. We cannot but admire our Lord's wonderful patience, and be horrified at the iniquity of the High Priest, who took no notice of this outrage perpetrated in his presence.

Commentary.

23. Lest our Redeemer's silence under the affront might be misconstrued into a tacit admission that He spoke evil; and also lest the High Priest might justly censure His teaching, He defends Himself and shows, He had not spoken evil. If He had, His assailant should prove it before His judge; if He "*spoke well*," this outrage should not be tolerated from an underling by the judge, whose feelings He was supposed to reflect. Being on His trial, He could justly claim the protection of the court against all illegal violations of His rights. Our Lord did not in the least depart from the counsel or precept given by Himself about turning the other cheek or ear to our assailant (Matthew v. 39). There, He speaks of *private* injury, and a charitable disposition to forgive all *private* and personal affronts (see Commentary on).

How heaven itself must be astonished at the patience of our Lord. *Who* is it that *smote?* Who is it that was *smitten?*

24. This verse should be inserted after verse 13. The verb "*sent*," has a pluperfect sense, "*had sent.*" The Evangelist now reverts to our Lord's being sent to the house of Annas. Passing over what occured there, he at once enters on the treason of Judas (v. 15), the full account of which was interrupted at verse 19, and now the Evangelist reverts to it.

"*Annas*" (I say) "*sent Him bound to Caiphas the High Priest*" (see Matthew xxvi. 58).

The Evangelist parenthetically introduces what he omitted mentioning after verse 13; his design in this parenthesis being, to show that what is recorded from verse 13 to this verse, took place in the house of Caiphas.

25, 26. The Evangelist after briefly recording some of the occurrences that took place before the High Priest in questioning our Lord, now reverts to the history of Peter's denial. Peter, after having first denied our Lord, was in a sitting posture. When he went out into the outer hall, the cock crew, as Mark states (xiv. 68). He then returned to warm himself at the fire. He was in a standing posture at the second and third denial.

"*They said to him,*" etc., and he said, "*I am not.*" This is Peter's *second* denial. St. Luke (xxii. 58), tells us, that Peter in reply to his interrogator, said, "*O man, I am not.*" On this occasion, the maid did not address Peter at all, she only addressed the bystanders, one of whom, as St. Luke records, spoke in the name of all whom the maid addressed. Hence, the plural here, "*They said.*" They spoke through one man. The use of the plural for the singular is not unusual in Scripture.

What St. Matthew says, of his denying with an oath, on this second occasion (xxvi. 72), is omitted by the other Evangelists.

Text.

23. *Jesus answered him: If I have spoken evil, give testimony of the evil: but if well, why strikest thou me?*

23. *Respondit ei Jesus: Si male locutus sum, testimonium perhibe de malo: si autem bene, quid me cædis?*

24. *And Annas sent him bound to Caiphas the high priest*

24. *Et misit eum Annas ligatum ad Caipham pontificem.*

25. *And Simon Peter was standing, and warming himself. They said therefore to him: Art not thou also one of his disciples? He denied it and said: I am not.*

25. *Erat autem Simon Petrus stans. Dixerunt ergo ei: Numquid et tu ex discipulis ejus es? Negavit ille, et dixit: Non sum.*

26. *One of the servants of the high-priest (a kinsman to him whose ear Peter cut of) saith to him: Did not I see thee in the garden with him?*

26. *Dicit ei unus ex servis pontificis, cognatus ejus, cujus abscidit Petrus auriculam: Nonne ego te vidi in horto cum illo?*

Text.	Commentary.

Text.

27. *Again therefore Peter denied: and immediately the cock crew.*

27. *Iterum ergo negavit Petrus : et statim gallus cantavit.*

Commentary.

27. This is Peter's *third* denial. Matthew and Mark say, a short interval elapsed; Luke, an hour. These two accounts harmonize. Luke (xxii.), says, a certain man now charged him with having been with our Lord. St. John here says, the man was a kinsman of Malchus. This harmonizes with the preceding. The two other Evangelists say, many addressed him, very likely after the kinsman of Malchus spoke, and after Peter's denial. Then all present began to urge him, and sought to convict him from his accent. Peter being thus sorely pressed, and fearing the consequence of his violent action, in regard to Malchus, began to swear and anathematize, the more effectually to clear himself, as is recorded by the other Evangelists, Matthew and Mark. The whole narrative is consistent, and fully harmonizes. No one Evangelist describes the whole scene. A portion is given by each. (See Matthew xxvi. 69–75, Commentary.)

Text.

28. *Then they led Jesus from Caiphas to the Governor's hall. And it was morning: and they went not into the hall, that they might not be defiled, but that they might eat the pasch.*

28. *Adducunt ergo Jesum a Caipha in prætorium. Erat autem mane: et ipsi non introierunt in prætorium, ut non contaminarentur, sed ut manducarent Pascha.*

28. "*Then they led Jesus*," etc. "*Then*," as a particle of inference, has reference to what occurred to our Lord, in the house of Caiphas, which St. John omits; because fully recorded by the other Evangelists. These occurrences principally are, the examination of our Lord before Caiphas and the assembled Sanhedrim, at midnight; the final meeting of the Sanhedrim in the morning; His condemnation by the Sanhedrim; His barbarous treatment by the soldiery, etc., etc. The Evangelist passing over all these, now proceeds to describe our Lord's conference with Pilate, His examination by Pilate (33–38). As the Jews had not power to inflict on our Lord the death of which they judged Him guilty—this power now being reserved to the Roman Governor—they, therefore, lead Him to Pilate, to have their sentence of death ratified by him and carried into execution.

"*The Governor's hall.*" Pontius Pilate, as Procurator, governed Judea in the name of the Emperor. In this "*hall*," the Governor sat as judge and decided all cases, whether of a civil or criminal nature. The original for *Governor's Hall, Prætorium*, a word of military origin, bears different significations. Here and throughout the Gospels, it most likely denotes the hall within his official residence, where the Governor held his court, sat as judge, and dispensed justice.

Pilate is said to have gone *out from the Prætorium*, viz., the hall in question, to speak to the Jews. He certainly did not go outside the house into the public street. Nor would the Jews contract defilement by going into the house of Pilate, the Governor, but only by going into the judgment hall, to which reference is made here.

The Roman Governors usually resided at Cæsarea; but, on occasion of great festivals, they resided at Jerusalem, in order to quell seditions (Josephus, Bello Iud. ii. 14–3). During their stay,

Commentary.

they occupied Herod's former palace on Mount Sion. Tradition has it, that Pilate's prætorium was in the Fort Antonia.

"*And it was morning.*" Reference is here made to the time mentioned by St. Matthew (xxvii. 1), viz., the morning after the night on which the Sanhedrim declared our Lord deserving of death.

"*And they went not into the hall*"—but their servants did, and so did the soldiers—"*that they might not be defiled*" by any communication with a Pagan. What consummate hypocrisy. They scruple entering into the hall in which the judge sat to pronounce sentence—a comparatively trivial affair—and they scruple not in the least, to compass the death of an innocent man, "*straining out gnats and swallowing camels*" (Matthew xxiii. 24). "*O impia et stulta cæcitas!*"—exclaims St. Augustine—"*habitaculo, videlicet, contaminantur alieno, et non contaminantur scelere proprio.*"

"*But,*" they acted so, "*that they might eat the Pasch,*" that they might be able, free from all uncleanness, to eat the Pasch. This refers, not to the Paschal lamb, of which they had already very likely partaken (see Matthew xxvi. 2, Commentary), but to the victims that were slain during the festival days succeeding the great day of the Pasch, and that were religiously partaken of by the Jews.

29. "*Therefore,*" because they did not enter the hall of judgment, but remained outside.

"*Pilate went out to them,*" asking them, "*what accusation bring you against this man?*" Justice required that no man could be condemned unheard. This equitable principle was strictly adhered to by the ancient Romans (Acts xxv. 16).

Hence, Pilate, before condemning our Lord, insists on having a formal indictment laid before him, and the case proved.

30. "*A malefactor,*" an evil doer, a trangessor of the law, deserving of death. The Jews fancied that Pilate would at once ratify their sentence, without himself entering into the merits of the case. Hence, possibly, imagining that he was unwilling to interfere at all, they stand on their own fancied dignity, and would have their word or assertion as to our Lord's guilt, taken on their authority alone, as sufficient, without any formal trial on the part of Pilate. They seem tacitly to complain of his distrust in them. Very likely, Pilate, who can hardly be credited with too scrupulous a regard for justice, was overawed by the majestic presence of our Lord; and, owing to several circumstances, among the rest, the rumours regarding His miraculous wonders, the message from Pilate's own wife, etc., etc., was seized with some superstitious dread in dealing with the case.

Text.

29. *Pilate therefore went out to them, and said: What accusation bring you against this man?*

29. *Exivit ergo Pilatus ad eos foras, et dixit: Quam accusationem affertis adversus hominem hunc?*

30. *They answered and said to him: If he were not a malefactor we would not have delivered him up to thee.*

30. *Responderunt, et dixerunt ei: Si non esset hic malefactor, non tibi tradidissemus eum.*

Y

Text.

31. *Pilate therefore said to them: Take him you, and judge him according to your law. The Jews therefore said to him: It is not lawful for us to put any man to death.*

31. *Dixit ergo eis Pilatus: Accipite eum vos, et secundum legem vestram judicate eum. Dixerunt ergo ei Judæi: Nobis non licet interficere quemquam.*

Commentary.

31. Pilate, who was clearly anxious to have nothing to say to the case, and, perhaps, making little of their charge of blasphemy, tells them: "*Take Him you,*" yourselves, which is somewhat emphatic and scornful. As my law, the Roman law, will not admit of punishing a man unheard, take Him yourselves and award Him the punishment allotted by your law, "*and judge Him according to your law.*" The punishment was stoning, in the case of blasphemy (Leviticus xxiv. 16). This would imply, that, according to Pilate's notions, the Jews were not deprived of all power to deal with violations of their own law. On the other hand, their answer, "*It is not lawful for us, to put any man to death,*" would convey, that the power of life and death had been transferred by this time to the Roman Tribunals. Pilate's words to our Lord (xix. 10) would also convey the impression, that he alone could inflct the punishment of death. It is a vexed question, whether the Sanhedrim had at this time the power to inflict capital punishment or not. It is maintained by many, that they had this power in matters of a religious character, or crimes against the Jewish laws, such as blasphemy, etc. (Acts xviii. 15), and could pass sentence of death, subject in regard to execution, to the approval of the Roman Governor. In some cases, they committed acts of violence, during a popular tumult, as in the case of St. Stephen (Acts vii. 58), and in other cases also (Acts xii. 2; xxiii. 27). But these acts of violence could hardly be regarded as in accordance with legal forms. Likely, the Romans overlooked them or dissembled all knowledge of them. In *civil* or political affairs, violations of Roman law, seditions, homicides, etc., the cognizance of such rested solely with the Roman Procurator (Acts xviii. 14).

Seeing that Pilate did not pay much attention to their charge of blasphemy, they, then, charge our Lord with the gravest offences of a civil or political character (Luke xxiii. 2), with which Pilate alone, as representing the Supreme Civil Authority, could deal. The Jews, whatever might have been their powers in regard to capital punishment—these powers of inflicting death they could not carry out during the Pasch (Acts xii. 4)—thought to throw on Pilate the odium of condemning to death an innocent man, and of carrying it into execution during the Pasch, which was not allowed them. (Acts xii.) They dreaded delays as dangerous, considering all our Lord had heretofore done in the way of escape.

Some understand the words, "*It is not lawful for us to put any man to death,*" to mean, in the literal sense of the words, and in their widest acceptation, "power of life and death is taken away from us. Hence, we come to you, to inflict this well-merited punishment on Him." Against this interpretation, it might be urged, that Pilate told them to take Him themselves and inflict on

Commentary.

Him the punishment which their law awarded to blasphemy, viz., stoning. This, however, was not what they wanted. What they wanted, as is clear from what follows, was *crucifixion*, as being the most *humiliating and infamous* kind of death, reserved for the Roman authorities to inflict. Hence, they have recourse to Pilate.

Others understand them to mean, "we have no power to put any man to death during the Paschal solemnity." And, hence, as we dread delay, we have recourse to you, to have it inflicted at once. Others understand the words to refer specially to *crucifixion*, which alone they wanted; and, hence, their application to Pilate to inflict it, as they could not do so themselves.

32. "*That the word might be fulfilled*," etc. Our Lord had frequently predicted that He would be delivered over to the Gentiles to be crucified (Matthew xx. 19; John iii. 14), and that He would be subjected to the ignominious death of the cross (John viii. 28; xii. 32–34).

In saying, "*It is not lawful for us*," etc., it is clear they desired that Pilate, to whom they delivered up our Lord, would inflict on Him the kind of punishment which the Romans inflicted on rebellious, seditious persons. From this, it followed, as a consequence, "*that the word of Jesus might be fulfilled*," which had reference to His being delivered over to the Gentiles, for their peculiar mode of punishment. That was the death by crucifixion, "*signifying what death He should die.*"

33–39. St. John here passes over what is recorded by St. Luke (xxiii.), that seeing Pilate pay but little heed to their assertions regarding our Lord's guilt, as he seemed to regard our Lord's offence as a mere religious affair, a violation of their law, the Jews now bring against Him several political charges of the gravest character, of which Pilate should take cognizance, such as subverting their nation, forbidding to give tribute to Cæsar, claiming to be King, etc. In consequence of these charges made when Pilate went out of the Prætorium to address the Jews, he returned and questioned our Lord as to the chief point of indictment to which the others were subordinate, about His being King (see Matthew xxvii. 11–14, Commentary where the whole history and connexion of the several parts are explained).

Text.

32. *That the word of Jesus might be fulfilled which he said, signifying what death he should die.*

32. *Ut sermo Jesu impleretur, quem dixit significans qua morte esset moriturus.*

33. *Pilate therefore went into the hall again, and called Jesus and said to him: Art thou the king of the Jews?*

33. *Introivit ergo iterum in prætorium Pilatus, et vocavit Jesum, et dixit ei: Tu es rex Judæorum?*

34. *Jesus answered: Sayest thou this thing of thyself, or have others told it thee of me?*

34. *Respondit Jesus: A temetipso hoc dicis, an alii dixerunt tibi de me?*

35. Pilate answered: Am I a Jew? Thy own nation, and the chief priests have delivered thee up to me; what hast thou done?

35. *Respondit Pilatus; Numquid ego Judæus sum? Gens tua, et pontifices tradiderunt te mihi: quid fecisti?*

36. Jesus answered: My kingdom is not of this world. If I were of the world my servants would certainly strive that I should not be delivered to the Jews: but now my kingdom is not from hence.

36. *Respondit Jesus: regnum meum non est de hoc mundo, si ex hoc mundo esset regnum meum, ministri mei utique decertarent ut non traderer Judæis: nunc autem regnum meum non est hinc.*

Text.	Commentary.

37. Pilate therefore said to him: Art thou a king then? Jesus answered: Thou sayest, that I am a king. For this was I born, and for this came I into the world; that I should give testimony to the truth. Every one that is of the truth, heareth my voice.

37. Dixit itaque ei Pilatus: Ergo rex es tu? Respondit Jesus: Tu dicis quia rex sum ego. Ego in hoc natus sum, et ad hoc veni in mundum, ut testimonium perhibeam veritati: omnis, qui est ex veritate, audit vocem meam.

38. Pilate saith to him: What is truth? And when he said this he went out again to the Jews, and saith to them; I find no cause in him.

38. Dicit ei Pilatus: Quid est veritas? Et cum hoc dixisset, iterum exivit ad Judæos, et dicit eis: Ego nullam invenio in eo causam.

39. But you have a custom that I should release one unto you at the pasch: will you therefore that I release unto you the king of the Jews?

39. Est autem consuetudo vobis ut unum dimittam vobis in Pascha: vultis ergo dimittam vobis regem Judæorum?

40. Then cried they all again, saying: Not this man, but Barabbas. Now Barabbas was a robber.	39, 40 (See Matthew xxvii. 13-18, Commentary.)

40. Clamaverunt ergo rursum omnes, dicentes: Non hunc, sed Barabbam. Erat autem Barabbas latro.

CHAPTER XIX.

1 *Then, therefore, Pilate took Jesus, and scourged him.*

2 *And the soldiers platting a crown of thorns, put it upon his head: and about him they put a purple garment.*

3 *And they came to him, and said: Hail king of the Jews: and they gave him blows.*

4 *Pilate, therefore, went forth again, and saith to them: Behold I bring him forth to you, that you may know that I find no cause in him.*

5 *(So Jesus came forth bearing the crown of thorns, and the purple garment.) And he saith to them: Behold the man.*

6 *When the chief priests, therefore, and the officers, had seen him, they cried out, saying: Crucify him, crucify him. Pilate saith to them: Take him you and crucify him; for I find no cause in him.*

7 *The Jews answered him: We have a law; and according to the law he ought to die, because he made himself the Son of God.*

8 *When Pilate, therefore, had heard this saying, he feared the more.*

9 *And he entered into the hall again; and he said to Jesus: Whence art thou? But Jesus gave him no answer.*

10 *Pilate, therefore, said to him: Speakest thou not to me? knowest thou not that I have power to crucify thee, and I have power to release thee?*

11 *Jesus answered: Thou shouldst not have any power against me, unless it were given thee from above. Therefore, he that hath delivered me to thee, hath the greater sin.*

12 *And from thenceforth Pilate sought to release him. But the Jews cried out, saying: If thou release this man, thou art not Cæsar's friend. For whosoever maketh himself a king, speaketh against Cæsar.*

13 *Now when Pilate had heard these words, he brought Jesus forth: and sat down in the judgment-seat, in the place that is called Lithostrotos, and in Hebrew, Gabbatha.*

14 *And it was the Paraseeve of the Pasch, about the sixth hour, and he saith to the Jews: Behold your king.*

15 *But they cried out: Away with him, away with him, crucify him. Pilate saith to them: Shall I crucify your king? The chief priests answered: We have no king but Cæsar.*

16 *Then, therefore, he delivered him to them to be crucified. And they took Jesus, and led him forth.*

17 *And bearing his own cross, he went forth to that place which is called Calvary, but in Hebrew, Golgotha.*

18 *Where they crucified him, and with him two others, one on each side, and Jesus in the midst.*

19 *And Pilate wrote a title also; and he put it upon the cross. And the writing was,* JESUS OF NAZARETH, THE KING OF THE JEWS.

20 *This title, therefore, many of the Jews read; because the place, where Jesus was crucified, was near to the city; and it was written in Hebrew, in Greek, and in Latin.*

21 *Then the chief priests of the Jews said to Pilate: Write not, The king of the Jews: but that he said, I am the king of the Jews.*

22 *Pilate answered: What I have written, I have written.*

23 *Then the soldiers, when they had crucified him, took his garments, (and they made four parts, to every soldier a part,) and also his coat. Now the coat was without seam, woven from the top throughout.*

24 *They said then one to another: Let us not cut it, but let us cast lots for it, whose it shall be; that the Scripture might be fulfilled, saying: They have parted my garments among them: and upon my vesture they have cast lot. And the soldiers indeed did these things.*

25 *Now there stood by the cross of Jesus, his mother, and his mother's sister, Mary of Cleophas, and Mary Magdalene.*

26 *When Jesus, therefore, saw his mother, and the disciple standing, whom he loved, he saith to his mother: Woman, Behold thy son.*

27 *After that, he saith to his disciple: Behold thy mother. And from that hour the disciple took her to his own.*

28 *Afterwards Jesus knowing that all things were now accomplished, that the Scripture might be fulfilled, said: I thirst.*

29 *Now there was a vessel set there full of vinegar. And they putting a sponge full of vinegar about hyssop, offered it to his mouth.*

30 *When Jesus, therefore, had taken the vinegar, he said: It is consummated. And bowing his head, he gave up the ghost.*

31 *Then the Jews, (because it was the Parasceve,) that the bodies might not remain upon the cross on the sabbath day, (for that was a great sabbath day,) besought Pilate that their legs might be broken, and that they might be taken away.*

32 *The soldiers, therefore, came; and they broke the legs of the first, and of the other that was crucified with him.*

33 *But when they came to Jesus, and saw that he was already dead, they did not break his legs.*

34 *But one of the soldiers opened his side with a spear, and immediately there came out blood and water.*

35 *And he that saw it, gave testimony; and his testimony is true. And he knoweth that he saith true; that you also may believe.*

36 *For these things were done, that the Scripture might be fulfilled: You shall not break a bone of him.*

37 *And again another Scripture saith: They shall look on him whom they pierced.*

38 *And after these things, Joseph of Arimathea (because he was a disciple of Jesus, but in private, for fear of the Jews) besought Pilate that he might take away the body of Jesus. And Pilate permitted him. He came, therefore, and took away the body of Jesus.*

39 *And Nicodemus also came; he who at first came to Jesus by night, bringing a mixture of myrrh and aloes, about a hundred pounds.*

40 *They took, therefore, the body of Jesus, and bound it in linen cloths with the spices, as it is the custom with the Jews to bury.*

41 And there was in the place, where he was crucified, a garden ; and in the garden a new sepulchre, wherein no man had yet been laid.

42 There, therefore, by reason of the Parasceve of the Jews, they laid Jesus, because the sepulchre was nigh at hand.

CAPUT XIX.

1 *Tunc ergo apprehendit Pilatus Jesum, et flagellavit.*

2 *Et milites plectentes coronam de spinis, imposuerunt capiti ejus : et veste purpurea circumdederunt eum.*

3 *Et veniebant ad eum, et dicebant : Ave rex Judæorum : et dabant ei alapas.*

4 *Exivit ergo iterum Pilatus foras, et dicit eis : Ecce adduco vobis eum foras, ut cognoscatis quia nullam invenio in eo causam.*

5 *(Exivit ergo Jesus portans coronam spineam, et purpureum vestimentum :) Et dicit eis : Ecce homo.*

6 *Cum ergo vidissent eum Pontifices, et ministri, clamabant dicentes : Crucifige, crucifige eum. Dicit eis Pilatus : Accipite eum vos, et crucifigite : ego enim non invenio in eo causam.*

7 *Responderunt ei Judæi : Nos legem habemus, et secundum legem debet mori, quia filium Dei se fecit.*

8 *Cum ergo audisset Pilatus hunc sermonem, magis timuit.*

9 *Et ingressus est prætorium iterum : et dixit ad Jesum : Unde es tu ? Jesus autem responsum non dedit ei.*

10 *Dicit ergo ei Pilatus : Mihi non loqueris : nescis quia potestatem habeo crucifigere te, et potestatem habeo dimittere te ?*

11 *Respondit Jesus : Non haberes potestatem adversum me ullum, nisi tibi datum esset desuper. Propterea qui me tradidit tibi, majus peccatum habet.*

12 *Et exinde quærebat Pilatus dimittere eum. Judæi autem clamabant dicentes : Si hunc dimittis, non es amicus Cæsaris. Omnis enim, qui se regem facit, contradicit Cæsari.*

13 *Pilatus autem cum audisset hos sermones, adduxit foras Jesum : et sedit pro tribunali, in loco, qui dicitur Lithostrotos, Hebraice autem Gabbatha.*

14 *Erat autem Parasceve Paschæ, hora quasi sexta, et dicit Judæis : Ecce rex vester.*

15 *Illi autem clamabant : Tolle, tolle, crucifige eum. Dicit eis Pilatus : Regem vestrum crucifigam ? Responderunt Pontifices : Non habemus Regem, nisi Cæsarem.*

16 *Tunc ergo tradidit eis illum ut crucifigeretur. Susceperunt autem Jesum, et eduxerunt.*

17 *Et bajulans sibi crucem exivit in eum, qui dicitur Calvariæ locum, Hebraice autem Golgotha :*

18 *Ubi crucifixerunt eum, et cum eo alios duos hinc, medium autem Jesum.*

19 *Scripsit autem et titulum Pilatus : et posuit super crucem. Erat autem scriptum : Jesus Nazarenus, Rex Judæorum.*

20 *Hunc ergo titulum multi Judæorum legerunt : quia prope civitatem erat locus, ubi crucifixus est Jesus : Et erat scriptum Hebraice, Græce, et Latine.*

21 *Dicebant ergo Pilato Pontifices Judæorum: Noli scribere, Rex Judæorum: sed quia ipse dicit: Rex sum Judæorum.*

22 *Respondit Pilatus: Quod scripsi, scripsi.*

23 *Milites ergo cum crucifixissent eum, acceperunt vestimenta ejus, (et fecerunt quatuor partes, unicuique militi partem) et tunicam. Erat autem tunica inconsutilis, desuper contexta per totum.*

24 *Dixerunt ergo ad invicem: Non scindamus eam, sed sortiamur de illa cujus sit. Ut Scriptura impleretur, dicens: Partiti sunt vestimenta mea sibi: et in vestem meam miserunt sortem. Et milites quidem hæc fecerunt.*

25 *Stabant autem juxta crucem Jesu mater ejus, et soror matris ejus, Maria Cleophæ, et Maria Magdalene.*

26 *Cum vidisset ergo Jesus matrem, et discipulum stantem, quem diligebat, dicit matri suæ: Mulier, ecce filius tuus.*

27 *Deinde dicit discipulo: Ecce mater tua. Et ex illa hora accepit eam discipulus in sua.*

28 *Postea sciens Jesus quia omnia consummata sunt, ut consummaretur Scriptura, dixit; Sitio.*

29 *Vas ergo erat positum aceto plenum. Illi autem spongiam plenam aceto, hyssopo circumponentes, obtulerunt ori ejus.*

30 *Cum ergo accepisset Jesus acetum, dixit: Consummatum est. Et inclinato capite tradidit spiritum.*

31 *Judæi ergo, (quoniam parasceve erat) ut non remanerent in cruce corpora sabbato, (erat enim magnus dies ille Sabbati) rogaverunt Pilatum ut frangerentur eorum crura, et tollerentur.*

32 *Venerunt ergo milites: et primi quidem fregerunt crura, et alterius, qui crucifixus est cum eo.*

33 *Ad Jesum autem cum venissent, ut viderunt eum jam mortuum, non fregerunt ejus crura.*

34 *Sed unus militum lancea latus ejus aperuit, et continuo exivit sanguis, et aqua.*

35 *Et qui vidit, testimonium perhibuit: et verum est testimonium ejus. Et ille scit quia vera dicit: ut et vos credatis.*

36 *Facta sunt enim hæc, ut Scriptura impleretur: Os non comminuetis ex eo.*

37 *Et iterum alia Scriptura dicit: Videbunt in quem transfixerunt.*

38 *Post hæc autem rogavit Pilatum Joseph ab Arimathæa, (eo quod esset discipulus Jesu, occultus autem propter metum Judæorum) ut tolleret corpus Jesu. Et permisit Pilatus. Venit ergo, et tulit corpus Jesu.*

39 *Venit autem et Nicodemus, qui venerat ad Jesum nocte primum, ferens mixturam myrrhæ, et aloes, quasi libras centum.*

40 *Acceperunt ergo corpus Jesu, et ligaverunt illud linteis cum aromatibus, sicut mos est Judæis sepelire.*

41 *Erat autem in loco, ubi crucifixus est, hortus: et in horto monumentum novum, in quo nondum quisquam positus erat.*

42 *Ibi ergo propter Parasceven Judæorum, quia juxta erat monumentum, posuerunt Jesum.*

ANALYSIS.

In this chapter, we have an account of the scourging of our Lord by Pilate's orders, in the vain hope that this would appease the fury of the Jews, and cause them to relent at the sight of His pitiable condition; so that they would give over all further demands for punishment; all in vain. After seeing Him scourged, crowned with thorns, and presented in this sad plight, they still loudly call for His crucifixion (1–8). Next, we have an account of Pilate's fears, his interrogation of our Lord, his dread of being accused before Tiberius. This latter consideration tells on his weakness: hence, trampling on conscience and justice, he hands our Lord over to the Jews to be crucified (8–16). Our Lord is crucified between two robbers (16–18).

The superscription on the cross which Pilate refuses to change, although urged to it by the Jews (19–22).

The division of our Lord's garments between the soldiers, thus fulfilling an ancient prophecy (23, 24).

Our Lord beholding His Mother at the foot of the cross with St. John, commends her to his pious care (25–27). Our Lord in His thirst is offered vinegar, thus fulfilling another prophecy. All being consummated, He expires (28–30).

While the legs of the two robbers are broken, His are not, but His side is transfixed with a spear; thus, is a two-fold prophecy fulfilled (31–37).

Joseph, of Arimathea, and Nicodemus, embalm His sacred body, and place it in a new sepulchre, in which no one else had been deposited before (38–42).

Commentary.

1–13. (See Matthew xxvii. 24–31.)

Text.

1. *Then therefore Pilate took Jesus, and scourged him*

1. *Tunc ergo apprehendit Pilatus Jesum, et flagellavit.*

2. *And the soldiers platting a crown of thorns, put it upon his head; and they put on him a purple garment.*

2. *Et milites plectentes coronam de spinis, imposuerunt capiti ejus: et veste purpurea circumdederunt eum.*

3. *And they came to him, and said: Hail, king of the Jews: and they gave him blows.*

3. *Et veniebant ad eum, et dicebant: Ave rex Judæorum: et dabant ei alapas.*

4. *Pilate therefore went forth again, and saith to them: Behold I bring him forth unto you, that you may know that I find no cause in him.*

4. *Exivit ergo iterum Pilatus foras, et dicit eis: Ecce adduco vobis eum foras, ut cognoscatis quia nullam invenio in eo causam.*

5. *(Jesus therefore came forth bearing the crown of thorns, and the purple garment.) And he saith to them; Behold the Man.*

5. *(Exivit ergo Jesus portans coronam spineam, et purpureum vestimentum:) Et dicit eis: Ecce homo.*

6. *When the chief priests therefore and the servants had seen him, they cried out saying; Crucify him, crucify him. Pilate saith to them; Take him you, and crucify him; for I find no cause in him.*

6. *Cum ergo vidissent eum Pontifices, et ministri, clamabant dicentes: Crucifige, crucifige eum. Dicit eis Pilatus: Accipite eum vos, et crucifigite: ego enim non invenio in eo causam.*

7. *The Jews answered him; We have a law; and according to the law he ought to die, because he made himself the Son of God.*

7. *Responderunt ei Judæi: Nos legem habemus, et secundum legem debet mori, quia filium Dei se fecit.*

8. *When Pilate therefore had heard this saying, he feared the more.*

8. *Cum ergo audisset Pilatus hunc sermonem, magis timuit.*

9. *And he entered into the hall again; and he said to Jesus: Whence art thou? But Jesus gave him no answer.*

9. *Et ingressus est prætorium iterum: et dixit ad Jesum: Unde es tu? Jesus autem responsum non dedit ei.*

Text.	Commentary.

10. *Pilate therefore saith to him; Speakest thou not to me? knowest thou not that I have power to crucify thee, and I have power to release thee?*

10. *Dicit ergo ei Pilatus: Mihi non loqueris: nescis quia potestatem habeo dimittere te?*

11. *Jesus answered; Thou shouldst not have any power against me, unless it were given thee from above. Therefore he that hath delivered me to thee, hath the greater sin.*

11. *Respondit Jesus: Non haberes potestatem adversum me ullam, nisi tibi datum esset desuper. Propterea qui me tradidit tibi, majus peccatum habet.*

12. *And from thenceforth Pilate sought to release him. But the Jews cried out, saying: If thou release this man, thou art not Cesar's friend. For whosoever maketh himself a king, speaketh against Cesar.*

12. *Et exinde quærebat Pilatus dimittere eum. Judæi autem clamabant dicentes. Si hunc dimittis, non es amicus Cæsaris. Omnis enim, qui se regem facit, contradicit Cæsari.*

13. *Now when Pilate had heard these words, he brought Jesus forth: and sat down in the judgment seat, in the place that is called Lithostrotos, and in Hebrew Gabbatha.*

13. *Pilatus autem cum audisset hos sermones, adduxit foras. Jesum: et sedit pro tribunali, in loco, qui dicitur Lithostrotos. Hebraice autem Gabbatha.*

---

14. *And it was the parasceve of the pasch, about the sixth hour, and he saith to the Jews: Behold your king!*

14. (See Matthew xxvii. 45.)

14. *Erat autem parasceve Paschæ, hora quasi sexta, et dicit Judæis: Ecce rex vester.*

---

15. *But they cried out: Away with him, away with him, crucify him. Pilate saith to them: Shall I crucify your king? The chief priests answered: We have no king but Cesar.*

15. *Illi autem clamabant: Tolle, tolle, crucifige eum. Dicit eis Pilatus: Regem vestrum crucifigam? Responderunt Pontifices: Non habemus regem, nisi Cæsarem.*

16. *Then therefore he delivered him to them to be crucified. And they took Jesus and led him forth.*

16. *Tunc ergo tradidit eis illum ut crucifigeretur. Susceperunt autem Jesum, et eduxerunt.*

15, 16. (See Matthew xxvii. 30.)

Pilate was seized with alarm at the idea of being reported to Tiberius, whose jealous disposition had inspired all his governors with terror for befriending and protecting any disaffected subject, who might seek to grasp at sovereign power. The Jews knew this to be Pilate's weak point. Hence, this weak, temporizing judge, fully convinced of our Redeemer's innocence, and knowing Him to be "*a just man*," from a feeling of selfish fear, condemns Him to the cruel and ignominious death of the cross. Little did he think, while trampling on the dictates of conscience, that the day was fast approaching, when he himself would be presented for eternal condemnation; before the judgment seat of Him whom he now unjustly condemned, who was constituted the judge of the living and the dead.

The recall of Pilate shortly after this, his humiliation and degradation, his unhappy end, are sadly recorded in History. (See a picture of an unjust judge, Matthew xxvi. 62, Commentary.)

---

17. *And bearing his own cross he went forth to that place which is called Calvary, but in Hebrew Golgotha.*

17, 18, 19-22, 23. (See Matthew xxvii. 33-37.)

17. *Et bajulans sibi crucem exivit in eum, qui dicitur Calvariæ locum, Hebraice autem Golgotha:*

18. *Where they crucified him, and with him two others, one on each side, and Jesus in the midst.*

18. *Ubi crucifixerunt eum, et cum eo alios duos hinc et hinc, medium autem Jesum.*

Commentary. | Text.

19. And Pilate wrote a title also: and he put it upon the cross. And the writing was, JESUS OF NAZARETH THE KING OF THE JEWS.

19. Scripsit autem et titulum Pilatus : et posuit super crucem. Erat autem scriptum : Jesus Nazarenus, Rex Judæorum.

20. This title therefore many of the Jews did read: because the place where Jesus was crucified, was nigh to the city: and it was written in Hebrew, in Greek, and in Latin.

20. Hunc ergo titulum multi Judæorum legerunt: quia prope civitatem erat locus, ubi crucifixus est Jesus: Et erat scriptum Hebraice, Græce, et Latine.

21. Then the chief priests of the Jews said to Pilate: Write not, The king of the Jews; but that he said, I am the king of the Jews.

21. Dicebant ergo Pilato Pontifices Judæorum: Noli scribere, Rex Judæorum: sed quia ipse dixit: Rex sum Judæorum.

22. Pilate answered: What I have written, I have written.

22. Respondit Pilatus: Quod scripsi, scripsi.

23, 24. (See Matthew xxvii. 35.)

23. The soldiers therefore when they had crucified him, took his garments and made four parts, to every soldier a part) and also his coat. Now the coat was without seam, woven from the top throughout.

23. Milites ergo cum crucifixissent eum, acceperunt vestimenta ejus, (et fecerunt quatuor partes: unicuique militi partem) et tunicam. Erat autem tunica inconsutilis, desuper contexta per totum.

24. They said then one to another: Let us not cut it, but let us cast lots for it whose it shall be; that the scripture might be fulfilled, saying: They have parted my garments among them: and upon my vesture they have cast lots. And the soldiers indeed did these things.

24. Dixerunt ergo ad invicem: Non scindamus eam, sed sortiamur de illa cujus sit. Ut Scriptura impleretur, dicens: Partiti sunt vestimenta mea sibi: et in vestem meam miserunt sortem. Et milites quidem hæc fecerunt.

25. "*Now, there stood by the cross of Jesus, His Mother.*" The three other Evangelists make no mention of this affecting incident, this sorrowful scene, which the disciple of love could not leave unrecorded.

"*There stood by the cross.*" This Mother of Dolours, unmoved, witnessed with great dignity this terrible scene, without any of these violent paroxysms, to which in such circumstances less noble minds give way. This the word, "*stood,*" would convey. Hence, the assertion stating that our Blessed Lady fell into violent convulsive fits, on witnessing the agony of her son, is now generally rejected, as unworthy of her calm dignity and total resignation to the adorable will of God. (See Benedict xiv., de Festis B. M. V., Lib. 2, c. 4).

"*There stood by the cross of Jesus, His mother.*" When almost all had fled, Mary remained "*a tower of Ivory*" (Cant. vii. 4), the faithful witness and sorrowful spectator of His barbarous tortures. Every outrage offered His Divine person, every blow, every wound inflicted on His sacred body, penetrated her inmost soul. Now, according to many of the Fathers, was verified in her regard the prophecy of the aged Simeon, "*A sword of sorrow shall pierce thy own soul.*" (Luke xi. 35). Her feelings, as the tenderest of mothers, weeping over her

25. Now there stood by the cross of Jesus, his mother, and his mother's sister, Mary of Cleophas, and Mary Magdalen.

25. Stabant autem juxta crucem Jesu mater ejus, Maria Cleophæ, et soror matris ejus, Maria Magdalene.

Text.

Commentary.

only Son, and that Son she knew and believed to be her Creator and her God, the ingratitude of her own people, on whom He showered down so many signal blessings, who now in return, subject Him to the lash and nail Him to the cross—"*Pro peccatis suæ gentis, vidit Jesum in tormentis, et flagellis subditum*"—their speedy and irreparable ruin, the enormity of the sins of men, and the inefficacy of the tortures of her Divine Son in regard to millions of His creatures, all engulph her in an ocean of sorrow;—"*Magna est enim velut mare contritio tuo*"—(Lam. ii. 13), which was only equalled by the unshaken firmness of her resignation to God's adorable will, and the seraphic ardour of her burning love.

25. "*Mary of Cleophas.*" There is a great diversity of opinion as to who she was. The Greek is, Mary of *Clopas*. It does not determine, whether she was the wife, sister, or daughter of Cleophas. She is called "*the sister*" of the Blessed Virgin. St. Thomas (ad Gal), says she is the same as "*Mary of James,*" Mary, the mother of James, spoken of by the other Evangelists, and also by St. Jerome (Ad Hebid). She is also supposed to be the same as Mary of Alpheus.

She is called "*the sister*" of the Blessed Virgin. It is considered most probable, indeed, quite certain, that she was not her sister, in the strict sense of the word. She was termed such, according to the usage of the time which gave the appellation of *sister*, to a very near relative. Some say, that she was sister to St. Joseph; and so, could be called the sister of our Blessed Lady, or, that Cleophas was brother of St. Joseph (see Matthew xiii. 55–57).

It is said these women stood afar off (Matthew xxvii. 55, 56).

26. *When Jesus therefore, had seen his mother and the disciple standing, whom he loved, he saith to his mother: Woman, behold thy son.*

26. *Cum vidisset ergo Jesus matrem, et discipulum stantem, quem diligebat, dicit matri suæ: Mulier, ecce filius tuus.*

26. From the lofty summit of His cross, Jesus contemplates the sorrows of this dolorous Queen of Martyrs—"*When, therefore, Jesus saw His mother and the disciple standing, whom He loved*"—and in the person of St. John, who, then, according to the teaching of several holy Fathers, represented the human race; or, at least, the sincere followers of our Divine Lord, He gave us over to her, as her children. "*Woman, behold thy Son.*" Are we not, then, the children whom Mary brought forth in sorrow at the foot of the cross, the children recommended to her by her dying first born? If she was spared the maternal throes in Bethlehem, was it not that she might experience them with tenfold intensity, in giving us, the children of sin, birth amidst the glooms of Calvary?

27. *After that, he saith to the disciple: Behold thy Mother. And from that hour the disciple took her to his own.*

27. Then turning to us in the person of St. John, He exclaims, "*Behold thy mother.*" Woe to us, if we ever fail to reverence with special honour, or love with the most intense filial affection of devoted children, or cherish with unbounded confidence, the

Commentary.

mother bequeathed to us, as the last pledge of His love, by her Divine Son, our dying Saviour. Is she not all powerful by grace, in the order of impetration, as Jesus, is all powerful by the Divine nature which He inherits? Is she not the vehicle, in the language of St. Bernard, through whose hands come all the graces which God imparts to the human race? "*Omnia voluit nos habere per Mariam*" (St. Bernard). Has she ever been known to desert any of her children, however unworthy, who had recourse to her, with the proper dispositions? "Point me out a case," cries out her seraphic servant, St. Bernard, "where she ever deserted her clients, and I will cease to invoke her clemency." But no, he exclaims, addressing the Virgin, "*Memorare, O, Piissima Virgo Maria, non auditum fuisse a sæculo, quemquam ad tua currentem præsidia, tua implorantem auxilia, tua petentem suffragia, derelictum fuisse.*"

Is not a true devotion to her reckoned by Divines among the marks of predestination to glory?

Where is the Catholic worthy of the name, who is not convinced, from the very traditional instincts of faith, that in Her, he has a most powerful protector in the dangers, temptations and trials of life; and especially, when standing on the threshold of eternity, when the roaring lion, knowing he has but a short time, will come down in great wrath (Apoc. xii. 12), with redoubled efforts to accomplish his ruin?

Where is the true Catholic who, ever doubts, that among the many abundant, nay, superabundant helps reserved for us in the treasury of God's grace, as so many fruits of redemption, there is none on which we can so *confidently* rely as on the all-powerful mediation of the Blessed Virgin?

If in this belief, which they have sucked in with their mothers' milk, the faithful are deceived, all we can say is, that it is the Catholic Church, which can never err either as regards doctrines or doctrinal devotions, that has deceived them. From her very institution on earth, there is nothing she so strongly inculcates on all her children as a tender filial devotion to the Mother of God. The Fathers and brightest lights of the Catholic Church, in all ages, would have grossly erred, on a most important point of religious teaching.

Is it not deserving of being gratefully recorded, that among the holy Fathers and saints of the Church in all ages, such of them as were most distinguished for solid learning and extensive erudition; such of them, as were most prominent, as the brilliant lights and intellectual leaders of their time, were equally prominent, and distinguished for zeal in promoting devotion to the Mother of God, and proclaiming her praises.

In proof of this we can confidently quote, Saints Bazil, Gregory Nazian. Gregory the Great, St. Ambrose, St. Jerome, St. Augus-

Text.

27. *Deinde dicit discipulo: Ecce mater tua. Et ex illa hora accepit eam discipulus in sua.*

Text	Commentary
	tine, St. Cyril of Jerusalem, St. John Chrysostom, St. Cyril of Alexand. and later on, St. John Damascene, St. Bernard, St. Thomas of Aquin, St. Anthony of Florence, St. Bonaventure, St. Dominic, St. Francis of Assisium, St. Francis de Sales, St. Alphonsus Liguori, who rivals St. Bernard in his seraphic love for his Blessed Mother, which he displays on all occasions, by proclaiming her praises.
	If in our conviction regarding the powerful advocacy of the Blessed Virgin we are deceived ; then all we can say is, that the saints of heaven and the faithful on earth, have gone astray for eighteen hundred years. Happy we, if we err along with them.
	"*And from that hour, the disciple took her to his own.*" (Greek, εις τα ιδια) his own house, or, took her under his special care and protection.
	The probability is, that Joseph was dead ; otherwise, our Lord would have committed His Blessed Mother to Joseph's pious care.
28. *Afterwards Jesus knowing that all things were now accomplished, that the scripture might be fulfilled, said : I thirst.* 28. *Postea sciens Jesus quia omnia consummata sunt, ut consummaretur Scriptura dixit : Sitio.*	28, 29. (See Matthew xxvii. 48.) "*Afterwards,*" at the close of three hours of darkness, and immediately after the loud cry, "*My God, My God, why hast Thou forsaken Me?*" "*That the Scripture might be fulfilled*" (Psa. lxviii. 22).
	"*Said, I thirst,*" and thus gave them an opportunity of giving Him "*vinegar to drink,*" "*Et in siti mea, potaverunt me aceto*" (Psa. lxviii. 22).
29. *Now there was a vessel set there full of vinegar. And they putting a sponge full of vinegar about hyssop, put it to his mouth.* 29. *Vas ergo erat positum aceto plenum. Illi autem spongiam plenam aceto, hyssopo circumponentes, obtulerunt ori ejus.*	
30. *Jesus therefore when he had taken the vinegar, said ; It is consummated. And bowing his head, he gave up the ghost.* 30. *Cum ergo accepisset Jesus acetum, dixit : Consummatum est. Et inclinato capite tradidit spiritum.*	30. "*It is finished.*" The whole work of Redemption assigned to Him by His Father, is now accomplished ; the object of His Incarnation and of His labours on earth now fully secured (see Matthew xxvii. 50). The mysteries connected with His human existence are accomplished, His tortures now all over. The final catastrophe in death alone remains ; and this is now at hand.
31. *Then the Jews (because it was the parasceve) that the bodies might not remain upon the cross on the sabbath-day (for that was a great sabbath-day) besought Pilate that their legs might be broken, and that they might be taken away.* 31. *Judæi ergo, (quoniam Parasceve erat) ut non remanerent in cruce corpora*	31. "*Parasceve*" (see Matthew xxvi. 2, Commentary).
	"*It was a great Sabbath day,*" more solemn than the other Sabbaths, because, falling within the octave of the Pasch (see Matthew xii. 1). The concurrence of the Pasch and of the ordinary Sabbath made it doubly solemn.
	"*That their legs might be broken,*" in order to cause death more speedily, so that the shortening of the time of their suffering was compensated for by the intensity of pain, arising from the breaking of their legs. This dreadful punishment of *crurifraction* was, like crucifixion, inflicted on slaves (*Seneca de ira*), and on others who incurred the wrath of their masters.

Commentary.

The law of Deuteronomy (xxi. 22), commanded that those who were hanged on a gibbet should be buried the same day. *Crucifixion* was unknown when the law of Deuteronomy was enacted. Those who were merely suspended would almost immediately expire. In the punishment of *crucifixion*, life was prolonged for days. The Romans sometimes allowed their victims to remain suspended till devoured by beasts and the birds of the air. The Jews fearing the land might be polluted, if bodies were left suspended during the Sabbath, requested that their legs would be broken. Thus their pains were intensified and life soon extinguished.

32, 33. "*Finding our Lord already dead, they did not break His legs,*" as in His case, it was unnecessary for accelerating death.

32. *Venerunt ergo milites: et primi quidem fregerunt crura; et alterius, qui crucifixus est cum eo.*

33. *But after they were come to Jesus, when they saw that he was already dead, they did not break his legs.*

33. *Ad Jesum autem cum venissent, ut viderunt eum jam mortuum, non fregerunt ejus crura.*

34. "*But one of the soldiers,*" as if doubting the reality of His death, in order to place the matter beyond all question, "*opened His side with a spear.*" The thrust of a spear from the strong arm of a Roman soldier, even if our Lord were alive, would surely cause death. The aperture caused by this thrust must be pretty large, as our Lord afterwards invited Thomas, when in a state of doubt, to thrust his hand into it (xx. 27). St. John dwells on the circumstance of His side having been opened by the spear of a soldier, which should cause instant death, in order to furnish the fullest proof of the reality of His death, and of His subsequent resurrection; and in order to remove all pretext for supposing that on the cross He merely swooned away; and, hence, not being really dead, He could not have really risen from the dead.

"*And immediately there came out blood and water.*" This is said by some to be the natural effect of the piercing of the side. The flowing of the blood and water renders it likely that the spear reached the heart; and this would have caused death, even if He were then alive. Hence, this is decisive evidence of the death of our Lord. This, by anticipation, refutes the errors, regarding the reality of our Lord's death, as also the errors regarding the reality of His mortal flesh, which were propagated by swarms of early Heretics who soon sprung up, as tares in the field of our Lord. These went under the denomination of *Gnostics*.

Others regard the flow as *supernatural*. Without entering into the question as to the *natural* or *supernatural* character of this

Text.

sabbato, (erat enim magnus dies ille Sabbati) rogaverunt Pilatum ut frangerentur eorum crura, et tollerentur.

32. *The soldiers therefore came; and they broke the legs of the first, and of the other that was crucified with him.*

34. *But one of his soldiers with a spear opened his side, and immediately there came out blood and water.*

34. *Sed unus militum lancea latus ejus aperuit, et continuo exivit sanguis, et aqua.*

Text.	Commentary.
	issue of blood and water; we can say that it was intended by St. John, in describing it, to prove this important fact, on which Christianity rests, viz., that *our Lord truly died*. He shows that on the cross our Lord had not suffered a *syncope* or fainting fit; but, had really died. This he establishes, by showing that those who were sent to ascertain if He were dead, *believed* Him to be dead; that the soldier inflicted a wound which surely, in case He were not dead, would have caused His death. Commentators generally remark, that this issue of blood and water from the side of our Redeemer's dead body, symbolized the two great Sacraments of the Church, viz., Baptism, denoted by the water, and the Eucharist, which really contains His sacred blood.
35. *And he that saw it hath given testimony: and his testimony is true. And he knoweth that he saith true; that you also may believe.*	35. The Evangelist modestly refers to himself, as he always does, in the Third Person. For he was close by (*v.* 27). He dwells on this point of the reality of Christ's death, to confirm our faith, of which the real death of Christ was a fundamental article.
35. *Et qui vidit, testimonium perhibuit: et verum est testimonium ejus. Et ille scit quia vera dicit: ut et vos credatis.*	
36. *For these things were done that the scripture might be fulfilled:* You shall not break a bone of him.	36. "*That the Scripture might be fulfilled,*" mystically or allegorically. For, originally, in their literal sense, the words had reference to the Paschal Lamb, a type and emblem of Christ (Exodus xii. 46).
36. *Facta sunt enim hæc ut Scriptura impleretur: Os non comminuetis ex eo.*	Jesus was "*the Lamb that was slain from the beginning of the world.*" In Him was the type remarkably fulfilled (see Matthew xi. 14, Commentary). In Him, who was chiefly in view in this mandate (Exodus xii. 46), were the words verified in a still higher sense. Thus was the Scripture completely fulfilled, both in its type and antitype; and it is the relation of *type* and *antitype* between Christ and the Paschal Lamb that is clearly contemplated by the Evangelist.
37. *And again another scripture saith:* They shall look on him whom they pierced.	37. "*Another Scripture.*" (Zacharias xii. 10), in which the opening of His side is signified and predicted. These prophetical words denote Christ's twofold coming; His *first*, in the words, "*whom they pierced;*" His *second*, in the words, "*they shall look on Him,*" coming in glory in the clouds of heaven, with great power and majesty.
37. *Et iterum alia Scriptura dicit: Videbunt in quem transfixerunt.*	In the original of Zachary (xii. 10), God, speaking of Himself, says: "*They shall look on* ME, *whom they pierced,*" and this is here applied to Christ. Hence, Christ is God. By saying, "*they shall look on Him, whom they pierced,*" it was predicted He was to be transfixed, and they shall look on Him hereafter *in glory*.

ST. JOHN, CHAP. XIX.

Commentary.

38–41. (See Matthew xxvii. 57–61.)

Text.

38. *And after these things Joseph of Arimathæa, (because he was a disciple of Jesus, but secretly for fear of the Jews), besought Pilate that he might take away the body of Jesus, and Pilate gave leave, He came therefore and took away the body of Jesus.*

38. *Post hæc autem rogavit Pilatum Joseph ab Arimathæa, (eo quod esset discipulus Jesu, occultus autem propter metum Judæorum) ut tolleret corpus Jesu. Et permisit Pilatus Venit ergo, et tulit corpus Jesu.*

39. *And Nicodemus also came, he who at the first came to Jesus by night, bringing a mixture of myrrh and aloes, about an hundred pounds weight.*

39. *Venit autem et Nicodemus, qui venerat ad Jesum nocte primum, ferens mixturam myrrhæ, et aloes, quasi libras centum.*

40. *They took therefore the body of Jesus, and bound it in linen cloths with the spices, as the manner of the Jews is to bury.*

40. *Acceperunt ergo corpus Jesu, et ligaverunt illud linteis cum aromatibus, sicut mos est Judæis sepelire.*

41. *Now there was in the place, where he was crucified, a garden : and in the garden a new sepulchre, wherein no man yet had been laid.*

41. *Erat autem in loco, ubi crucifixus est, hortus ; et in horto monumentum novum, in quo nondum quisquam positus erat.*

42. Owing to the approach of sunset, after which they could not bury Him, on account of the Sabbath just at hand, they laid Him down in the nearest and most convenient place, probably with the intention of honouring Him, in due time, with a more befitting monument, and burying Him with greater solemnity, as Euthymius observes.

42. *There therefore because of the parasceve of the Jews, they laid Jesus, because the sepulchre was nigh at hand.*

42. *Ibi ergo propter Parasceven Judæorum, quia juxta erat monumentum, posuerunt Jesum.*

CHAPTER XX.

1 *And on the first day of the week, Mary Magdalene cometh in the morning, it being yet dark, to the sepulchre; and she saw the stone taken away from the sepulchre.*

2 *She ran, therefore, and cometh to Simon Peter, and to the other disciple whom Jesus loved, and saith to them: They have taken away the Lord out of the sepulchre, and we know not where they have laid him.*

3 *Peter, therefore, went out, and that other disciple, and they came to the sepulchre.*

4 *And they both did run together, and that other disciple outran Peter, and came first to the sepulchre.*

5 *And when he stooped down, he saw the linen cloths lying; but yet he went not in.*

6 *Then cometh Simon Peter, following him, and went into the sepulchre, and saw the linen cloths lying.*

7 *And the napkin, that had been about his head, not lying with the linen cloths, but apart, wrapt up into one place.*

8 *Then that other disciple also went in, who came first to the sepulchre: and he saw, and believed.*

9 *For as yet they knew not the Scripture, that he must rise again from the dead.*

10 *So the disciples went away again to their home.*

11 *But Mary stood without at the sepulchre, weeping. Whilst she was there weeping, she stooped down, and looked into the sepulchre:*

12 *And she saw two angels in white, sitting, one at the head, and one at the feet, where the body of Jesus had been laid.*

13 *They say to her: Woman, why weepest thou? She saith to them: Because they have taken away my Lord: and I know not where they have laid him.*

14 *When she had said these words, she turned herself back, and saw Jesus standing: and she knew not that it was Jesus.*

15 *Jesus saith to her: Woman, why weepest thou? whom seekest thou? She thinking that it was the gardener, saith to him: Sir, if thou hast taken him away, tell me where thou hast laid him: and I will take him away.*

16 *Jesus saith to her: Mary. She turning, saith to him; Rabboni, (that is to say, Master).*

17 *Jesus saith to her: Do not touch me, for I have not yet ascended to my Father: but go to my brethren; and say to them: I ascend to my Father and to your Father, to my God and your God.*

18 *Mary Magdalene cometh, telling the disciples: I have seen the Lord, and these things he said to me.*

19 *Now when it was late that same day, being the first day of the week, and the doors were shut, where the disciples were gathered together for fear of the Jews: Jesus came and stood in the midst, and said to them: Peace be to you.*

20 *And when he had said this, he showed them his hands, and his side. The disciples, therefore, were glad, when they saw the Lord.*

21 *And he said to them again: Peace be to you. As the Father hath sent me, I also send you.*

22 *When he had said this, he breathed on them: and he said to them: Receive ye the Holy Ghost.*

23 *Whose sins you shall forgive, they are forgiven them: and whose you shall retain, they are retained.*

24 *Now Thomas, one of the twelve, who is called Didymus, was not with them when Jesus came.*

25 *The other disciples, therefore, said to him: We have seen the Lord. But he said to them: Unless I shall see in his hands the print of the nails, and put my finger into the place of the nails, and put my hand into his side, I will not believe.*

26 *And after eight days, his disciples were again within, and Thomas with them. Jesus cometh, the doors being shut, and stood in the midst, and said: Peace be to you.*

27 *Then he said to Thomas: Put in thy finger hither, and see my hands, and bring hither thy hand, and put it into my side: and be not incredulous, but faithful.*

28 *Thomas answered, and said to him: My Lord, and my God.*

29 *Jesus saith to him: Because thou hast seen me, Thomas, thou hast believed: blessed are they that have not seen, and have believed.*

30 *Many other signs also did Jesus in the sight of his disciples, which are not written in this book.*

31 *But these are written that you may believe that Jesus is the Christ, the Son of God: and that believing you may have life in his name.*

CAPUT XX.

1 *Una autem sabbati, Maria Magdalene venit mane, cum adhuc tenebrae essent, ad monumentum: et vidit lapidem sublatum a monumento.*

2 *Cucurrit ergo, et venit ad Simonem Petrum, et ad alium discipulum, quem amabat Jesus, et dicit illis: Tulerunt Dominum de monumento, et nescimus ubi posuerunt eum.*

3 *Exiit ergo Petrus, et ille alius discipulus, et venerunt ad monumentum.*

4 *Currebant autem duo simul, et ille alius discipulus praecucurrit citius Petro, et venit primus ad monumentum.*

5 *Et cum se inclinasset, vidit posita linteamina, non tamen introivit.*

6 *Venit ergo Simon Petrus sequens eum, et introivit in monumentum, et vidit linteamina posita,*

7 *Et sudarium, quod fuerat super caput ejus, non cum linteaminibus positum, sed separatim involutum in unum locum.*

8 *Tunc ergo introivit et ille discipulus, qui venerat primus ad monumentum: et vidit, et credidit:*

9 *Nondum enim sciebant Scripturam, quia oportebat eum a mortuis resurgere.*

10 *Abierunt ergo iterum discipuli ad semetipsos.*

11 *Maria autem stabat ad monumentum foris, plorans: Dum ergo fleret, inclinavit se, et prospexit in monumentum:*

12 *Et vidit duos angelos in albis, sedentes, unum ad caput, et unum ad pedes, ubi positum fuerat corpus Jesu.*

13 *Dicunt ei illi: Mulier, quid ploras? Dicit eis: Quia tulerunt Dominum meum: et nescio ubi posuerunt eum.*

14 *Hæc cum dixisset, conversa est retrorsum, et vidit Jesum stantem: et non sciebat quia Jesus est.*

15 *Dicit ei Jesus: Mulier, quid ploras? quem quæris? illa existimans quia hortulanus esset, dicit ei: Domine, si tu sustulisti eum, dicito mihi ubi posuisti eum: et ego eum tollam.*

16 *Dicit ei Jesus: Maria. Conversa illa, dicit ei: Rabboni (quod dicitur Magister.)*

17 *Dicit ei Jesus: Noli me tangere, nondum enim ascendi ad Patrem meum: vade autem ad fratres meos, et dic eis: Ascendo ad Patrem meum, et Patrem vestrum, Deum meum, et Deum vestrum.*

18 *Venit Maria Magdalene annuntians discipulis: Quia vidi Dominum, et hæc dixit mihi.*

19 *Cum ergo sero esset die illo, una sabbatorum, et fores essent clausæ, ubi erant discipuli congregati propter metum Judæorum: venit Jesus, et stetit in medio, et dixit eis: Pax vobis.*

20 *Et cum hoc dixisset, ostendit eis manus, et latus. Gavisi sunt ergo discipuli, viso Domino.*

21 *Dixit ergo eis iterum: Pax vobis. Sicut misit me Pater, et ego mitto vos.*

22 *Hæc cum dixisset, insufflavit: et dixit eis: Accipite Spiritum sanctum:*

23 *Quorum remiseritis peccata, remittuntur eis, et quorum retinueritis, retenta sunt.*

24 *Thomas autem unus ex duodecim qui dicitur Didymus, non erat cum eis quando venit Jesus.*

25 *Dixerunt ergo ei alii discipuli: Vidimus Dominum. Ille autem dixit eis: Nisi videro in manibus ejus fixuram clavorum, et mittam digitum meum in locum clavorum, et mittam manum meam in latus ejus, non credam.*

26 *Et post dies octo, iterum erant discipuli ejus intus: et Thomas cum eis. Venit Jesus januis clausis, et stetit in medio, et dixit: Pax vobis.*

27 *Deinde dicit Thomæ: Infer digitum tuum huc, et vide manus meas, et affer manum tuam, et mitte in latus meum: et noli esse incredulus, sed fidelis.*

28 *Respondit Thomas, et dixit ei: Dominus meus, et Deus meus.*

29 *Dixit ei Jesus: Quia vidisti me Thoma, credidisti: beati qui non viderunt, et crediderunt.*

30 *Multa quidem, et alia signa fecit Jesus in conspectu discipulorum suorum, quæ non sunt scripta in libro hoc.*

31 *Hæc autem scripta sunt ut credatis, quia Jesus est Christus Filius Dei: et ut credentes, vitam habeatis in nomine ejus.*

ANALYSIS.

In this chapter, we have an account of Magdalen's arrival at our Lord's sepulchre, at twilight, on the first day of the week; finding the stone removed, she hastens to inform Peter and John (1, 2). They coming in haste, saw from the linen cloths and bandages that were scattered about, that the Resurrection had taken place. John, in consequence, believed in the Resurrection. After that, they retired to their respective homes (3–11).

Magdalen returning to the sepulchre had a vision of angels. She had, moreover, the ineffable happiness of being met by our Lord Himself, who making Himself known to her, addressed her in consoling language, and instructed her to inform His brethren of it, which she faithfully did (11–18).

ST. JOHN, CHAP. XX.

Late, on the evening of the same day, after the disciples had returned from Emmaus, our Lord entering the chamber, where the disciples were gathered together, the doors being shut, communicates His peace, imparts the Holy Ghost, and gives power to remit and retain sins. Thomas was absent, this time (19, 23).

The incredulity of Thomas, which our Lord, at His apparition on the eighth day after the Resurrection, mercifully removes, by condescendingly giving Thomas the proofs he desired of our Lord's real Resurrection (24–28).

Thomas's ardent faith, and profession in our Lord's Divinity and Humanity (28).

Our Lord's commendation of the faith of the simple believers (29).

The Evangelist declares his reason for writing this Gospel (30, 31).

Commentary.

1. "*And on the first day of the week*" (see Matthew xxviii. 1), "*Mary Magdalen*," accompanied by others, whose names are given by the other Evangelists. Magdalen was the principal among them.

"*Cometh early, when it was yet dark*"—in the early twilight—"*to see the sepulchre*," and anoint the body of Jesus, as we are informed by the other Evangelists (Luke xxiv. 1; Mark xvi. 1).

"*And she saw the stone taken away.*" This was done by the angels (Matthew xxviii.), who announced our Lord's Resurrection (see the other Evangelists). This, however, Magdalen understood not, as appears from the following.

2. "*She ran, therefore,*" etc. She and her companions ran to inform *Simon Peter*, whom they knew to be constituted by our Lord the head of the Apostolic College.

"*And to the other disciple,*" etc., whom they naturally supposed to be most solicitous about His Divine Master.

Text.

1. And on the first day of the week Mary Magdalen cometh early, when it was yet dark, unto the sepulchre: and she saw the stone taken away from the sepulchre.

1. Una autem sabbati, Maria Magdalene venit mane, cum adhuc tenebræ essent, ad monumentum: et vidit lapidem sublatum a monumento.

2. She ran therefore and cometh to Simon Peter, and to the other disciple whom Jesus loved, and saith to them: They have taken away the Lord out of the sepulchre, and we know not where they have laid him.

2. Cucurrit ergo, et venit ad Simonem Petrum, et ad alium discipulum, quem amabat Jesus, et dicit illis: Tulerunt Dominum de monumento, et nescimus ubi posuerunt eum.

3, 4. The other disciple, being younger and more active, outran Peter and arrived first.

3. Peter therefore went out, and that other disciple, and they both came to the sepulchre.

3. Exiit ergo Petrus, et ille alius discipulis, et venerunt ad monumentum.

4. And they both ran together, and that other disciple did out run Peter, and came first to the sepulchre.

4. Currebant autem duo simul, et ille alius discipulus præcucurrit citius Petro, et venit primus ad monumentum.

5, 6. "*Went not in,*" out of deference for his senior and superior, he made way for him, to enter first.

"*Went into the sepulchre.*" The terrified guards fled, leaving the place unprotected.

5. And when he stooped down, he saw the linen cloths lying: but yet he went not in.

5. Et cum se inclinasset, vidit posita linteamina, non tamen introivit.

6. Then cometh Simon Peter, following him, and went into the sepulchre and saw the linen cloths lying.

6. Venit ergo Simon Petrus sequens eum, et introivit in monumentum, et vidit linteamina posita.

Text.	Commentary.
7. *And the napkin, that had been about his head, not lying with the linen cloths, but apart, wrapt up into one place.*	
7. *Et sudarium, quod fuerat super caput ejus, non cum linteaminibus positum sed separatim involutum in unum locum.*	
8. *Then that other disciple also went in, who came first to the sepulchre: and he saw, and believed.* 8. *Tunc ergo introivit et ille discipulus, qui venerat primus ad monumentum; et vidit, et credidit:* 9. *For as yet they knew not the scripture, that he must rise again from the dead.* 9. *Nondum enim sciebant Scripturam, quia oportebat eum a mortuis resurgere.*	8, 9. "*Believed,*" in the Resurrection of our Lord. He remembered our Lord's prediction and promises on this head, and now fully understood them. Peter, it seems, was more tardy in his belief. Our Lord mercifully permitted His followers to be thus confused and tardy in their belief, and to entertain misgivings regarding His Resurrection; so that thus every circumstance connected with this fundamental article of Christian belief, which is the chief foundation of Christian faith, should be thoroughly sifted; and no grounds for doubt or cavil left to future generations. "*For, as yet they knew not the Scripture.*" This has reference to the word, "*believed,*" and to the tardiness of others who did not clearly know or understand the Scriptures, which predicted His Resurrection.
10. *The disciples therefore departed again to their home.* 10. *Abierunt ergo iterum discipuli ad semetipsos.*	10, 11. "*They retired to their homes;*" Peter, in a state of admiration; John, believing; Magdalen remaining alone at the sepulchre, lovingly anxious to inquire further about what was done with the body of her Lord, whom she so ardently loved— "*weeping*" over His death, and the loss of His sacred body.
11. *But Mary stood at the sepulchre without, weeping. Now as she was weeping, she stooped down, and looked into the sepulchre.* 11. *Maria autem stabat ad monumentum foris, plorans: Dum ergo fleret, inclinavit se, et prospexit in monumentum:*	
12. *And she saw two angels in white, sitting, one at the head, and one at the feet, where the body of Jesus had been laid.*	12. Although she had already looked into the sepulchre, she did not fail to do so again, out of anxiety, and was favoured with a vision of angels, in reward for her faith and anxiety. Her companions were similarly favoured (Luke xxiv. 4).
12. *Et vidit duos angelos in albis, sedentes, unum ad caput et unum ad pedes, ubi positum fuerat corpus Jesu.*	
13. *They say to her: Woman, why weepest thou? She saith to them: Because they have taken away my Lord, and I know not where they have laid him.*	13. "*Why weepest thou?*" This is no time for weeping, but a time for joy. The reply of Magdalen, "*because, they have taken away,*" etc., would argue weak and confused ideas regarding our Lord's Resurrection.
13. *Dicunt ei illi: Mulier, quid ploras? Dicit eis: Quia tulerunt Dominum meum: et nescio ubi posuerunt eum.*	
14. *When she had thus said, she turned herself back, and saw Jesus standing; and she knew not that it was Jesus.*	14. "*She turned back and saw Jesus standing.*" It may be, as many suppose, that the angels who were before her, showed signs of reverence to our blessed Lord. This made Magdalen look back to see what it meant; or, some noise may have been made, which would cause her to look back.
14. *Hæc cum dixisset, conversa est retrorsum, et vidit Jesum stantem: et non sciebat quia Jesus est.*	

Commentary.

15. Our Lord in His glorified body, presented a different appearance from what He had in His mortal state. Here, He had the appearance of one whom she took for the gardener, in charge of the garden in which the holy sepulchre was placed, from His appearing there at such an early hour. At another time, He had the appearance of a stranger; as when He appeared to the Apostles on their way to Emmaus.

"*And I will take Him away.*" Possibly, Magdalen's eyes were held, like the disciples at Emmaus, so that she could not know Him (Luke xxiv. 16). The excess of her love makes all things possible. On any other principle, it is hard to see how a feeble, weak woman could speak in such a way. It was the excess of holy love.

"*If thou hast taken Him hence.*" She is so taken up with the idea of our Lord, that she can think of nothing else. She fancies nobody could think of any one else; that all are entirely engrossed, like herself, with the one great object of love.

16. "*Mary,*" addressing her in His natural, well-known tone of voice.

"*Rabboni,*" which is understood by some to mean, "*my master;*" by others, "*master,*" like *Rabbi.*" It would seem to be a more august and respectful term than *Rabbi,* applied to our Lord, only after His Resurrection. "*She turning.*" Likely, as our Lord, whom she took for the gardener, gave her no reply, she turned to the angels to inquire who He was; and, then, on hearing His familiar, well-known tone of voice, she turned to Him. Others understand, "*turned,*" recovered from the stupor she was in, like Peter (Acts xxii. 5).

17. Possibly, Magdalen on discovering it to be her loving Lord, in an ecstasy of love, made signs (as St. Gregory infers, Hom. 25), of Her desire to embrace His knees and kiss His feet, and reverently adore Him, as was permitted afterwards (Matthew xxviii. 9). Seeing this, or knowing it, our Lord prohibits her from remaining there. He, therefore, tells her to go at once, and announce to the brethren all she saw.

"*I am not yet ascended,*" etc., as if, to say, a sufficiently long interval will elapse before I ascend to My Father; so that you will have time enough to exhibit due reverence to Me in person. Therefore, delay not in enjoying the spiritual delights and pleasures now communicated to you. But go at once, and inform My brethren, that I am, soon after My Resurrection, to "*ascend to My Father,*" who is *your Father* also, "*to My God,*" who is *your God* also.

This is the common interpretation and connexion of the words, "*Do not touch Me.*"

Text.

15. *Jesus saith to her: Woman, why weepest thou? whom seekest thou? She thinking that it was the gardener, saith to him: Sir, if thou hast taken him hence, tell me where thou hast laid him: and I will take him away.*

15. *Dicit ei Jesus: Mulier, quid ploras? quem quæris? Illa existimans quia hortulanus esset, dicit ei: Domine, si tu sustulisti eum, dicito mihi ubi posuisti eum: et ego eum tollam.*

16. *Jesus saith to her: Mary. She turning saith to him: Rabboni (which is to say Master).*

16. *Dicit ei Jesus: Maria. Conversa illa, dicit ei: Rabboni (quod dicitur Magister.)*

17. *Jesus saith to her: Do not touch me for I am not yet ascended to my Father: but go to my brethren, and say to them, I ascend to my Father and to your Father, to my God and your God.*

17. *Dicit ei Jesus: Noli me tangere, nondum enim ascendi ad Patrem meum: vade autem ad fratres meos, et dic eis: Ascendo ad Patrem meum, et Patrem vestrum, Deum meum, et Deum vestrum.*

Text.	Commentary.
18. *Mary Magdalen cometh and telleth the disciples: I have seen the Lord, and these things he said to me.* 18. *Venit Maria Magdalene annuncians discipulis; Quia vidi Dominum, et haec dixit mihi.*	18. This was Magdalen's *second* journey. In the former, she announced the taking away of the Sacred Body; in this, the glorious tidings of the Resurrection communicated to her by our Lord Himself. The other Evangelists record the two journeys as one. The disciples did not believe Magdalen (Mark xvi. 1), nor the other women (Luke xxiv. 11).
19. *Now when it was late that same day, the first of the week, and the doors were shut, where the disciples were gathered together for fear of the Jews, Jesus came and stood in the midst and said to them: Peace be to you.* 19. *Cum ergo sero esset die illo, una sabbatorum, et fores essent clausae, ubi erant discipuli congregati propter metum Judaeorum: venit Jesus, et stetit in medio, et dixit eis: Pax vobis.*	19. "*Late that same day,*" not at night time, but in the evening of Resurrection day, "*the first of the week,*" after the disciples had, in the evening, returned from Emmaus. There is reference to the same apparition, as in Luke xxiv. 26; Mark xvi. 14. "*And the doors were shut . . . for fear of the Jews.*" Our Lord's disciples still timorous and terrified at the cruel treatment inflicted by the Jews on their Divine Master, were in dread of similar treatment themselves. Hence, "*the doors*" of the apartment in which they were assembled, "*were shut,*" as a security against attack. "*Jesus came,*" entered the apartment, in virtue of the gift of subtility appertaining to His glorified body, "*and stood in their midst, and said to them. Peace be to you.*" This was a form of salutation common among the Jews, implying the plenitude of all benedictions, temporal and spiritual. It was meant here, to inspire the disciples with confidence and consolation, in their present depressed and dejected condition.
20. *And when he had said this, he shewed them his hands, and his side. The disciples therefore were glad, when they saw the Lord.* 20. *Et cum hoc dixisset, ostendit eis manus, et latus. Gavisi sunt ergo discipuli, viso Domino.*	20. "*He showed them His hands and His side,*" as a proof of His identity. The traces and marks of the wounds in His sacred body, would show He was the same whose hands and side were perforated on the cross. Whether they touched His hands and feet, is disputed. "*The disciples, therefore, were glad.*" Joy succeeded sadness, "*when they saw the Lord,*" and had no doubts of His identity. He now fulfils the promise made them on a former occasion, that "*He would again see them, and their sorrow would be turned into joy*" (xvi. 22).
21. *He said therefore to them again: Peace be to you. As the Father hath sent me, I also send you.* 21. *Dixit ergo eis iterum: Pax vobis. Sicut misit me Pater, et ego mitto vos.*	21. "*He said, therefore, to them again. Peace be to you.*" Now being convinced that it was the Lord, they were, therefore, somewhat confused and disturbed at their inconstancy and want of firm faith. Hence, compassionating their weakness, He removes their uneasiness, and addresses them in words of consolation, giving them His peace; thus, remitting their own sins, receiving them back into favour, and preparing them for the great spiritual gift of remitting the sins of others. Also, about to send them into the entire world, He communicates His peace, which they were to impart to a world of unrest and sin.

Commentary.

"*As the Father hath sent Me*," to redeem mankind, to sanctify and save them. He was thus constituted by His Father, an *Apostle*, which means, "*one sent*"—St. Paul terms Him (Heb. iii. 1), "*the Apostle of our Confession*"—"*I also send you*," thus constituting them His Apostles and vicars, with full power to apply the merits of His Redemption, by preaching His Gospel including the precepts of faith and morals, by instituting in His name, or at least, inculcating the necessity of, the Sacraments. They were also to edify the world by the example of good and holy lives. In a word, He sends them to perfect the work of Redemption, achieved by Him, at such sacrifices, privations, and sufferings, including even the ignominious death of the cross; and communicates to them, all the authority in its fulness that the Father gave Him. The parallelism is remarkable in all the words. "*The Father*" (who is God), "*I*" (who also am God), "*sent*," "*send*" (with the fulness and plenitude of authority), "*Me*," "*you*."

Catholic Tradition enables us to specify what amount of the authority here communicated, in regard to the remission of sin, was reserved for the *Bishops*, the successors of the Apostles to the consummation of ages; and what amount for the *priests*, to whom also was communicated the radical power of remitting sin, with some limitations, as to its actual exercise. The word, "*as*," does not express full *equality*; as if the Apostles received the same amount of authority, and in the same way, as He received from His Father; but, only *similarity*, in many respects.

22. "*Breathed on them*." This breathing on the Apostles was an exterior sign of His communicating of the Holy Ghost which He was about giving them—a Spirit who proceeds from the Father and Him. This breathing denotes, that as God, in the *original* creation, breathed into man the soul, which was the principle of natural life; so, the same God, now in the *second* creation and regeneration of man, breathes into him the Holy Spirit, who is the principle of spiritual and everlasting life.

"*Receive ye the Holy Ghost.*" It is quite clear He now actually imparts to them His Holy Spirit. It was, however, for a certain purpose, and in reference to a certain special gift, viz., the remission of sins, the only means for securing peace and reconciliation to sinful man. This gift, although given by the Father also, is attributed by appropriation to our Lord, who died for sin and specially merited this power. The full abundance of all the gifts of the Holy Ghost, the working of miracles, the gift of tongues, etc., etc., was reserved for the day of Pentecost, and not publicly given, until after He ascended to the Father, as He Himself declared (xvi. 7). But here, *although the Apostles had previously received the Holy Ghost in the gift of sanctifying grace*, a special gift was granted which they had not before, viz., the power to remit sin,

Text.

22. *When he had said this, he breathed on them; and he said to them: Receive ye the Holy Ghost:*

22. *Hæc cum dixisset, insufflavit: et dixit eis: Accipite Spiritum sanctum:*

Text

23. *Whose sins you shall forgive, they are forgiven them: and whose sins you shall retain, they are retained.*

23. *Quorum remiseritis peccata, remittuntur eis, et quorum retinueritis, retenta sunt.*

Commentary.

after He Himself had paid a full ransom for sin, on the tree of the cross. It was a *partial* concession at present of the gifts given in their plenitude on Pentecost; just as the Apostles had previously, in receiving sanctifying grace, received the Holy Ghost. This was not *publicly* given, with great external show and display, as on the day of Pentecost. The power to remit sin belonged to God only, who was offended by sin. But this power is communicated by Him to the Apostles. Hence, in receiving it, they are said to "*receive the Holy Ghost.*"

23. "*Whose sins you, shall forgive, they are forgiven.*" The power here given, as to the number or quality of sins is *universal* and without exception. All depends, so far as its efficacious exercise is concerned, on the dispositions and qualities of the subject, as is clear from the words, "*whose sins,*" etc. It is also clear, that they to whom this power is given, to the end of time, do actually remit sin and, not declare them remitted, as the Innovators teach. They remit on earth; and the sins thus remitted by a subordinate, delegated, ministerial exercise of power, are remitted by the sovereign power of God, in the High Court of Heaven. Similar are the words, "*Whatsoever you shall loose on earth, shall be loosed also in heaven*" (Matthew xvii. 18).

Similar is the power given to Peter (Matthew xvi. 19). "*Whatsoever thou shalt loose on earth, it shall be loosed also in heaven.*"

"*And whose sins you shall retain,*" when in the exercise of judicial discretion, you declare the subjects unfit for absolution, undeserving of receiving pardon from God, from want of proper dispositions, wanting contrition, wanting in a sincere desire to make reparation, and the other required conditions.

This two-fold power of remitting and retaining, which was not to be exercised capriciously, but with a just discretion, considering the merits of each case, shows the necessity of the confession of all sins; otherwise the party exercising would not know the *case.* Many grievous sins are occult—there are also sins of wicked thoughts. Neither could the *dispositions* of the sinner be known, save from his own confession. Hence, the necessity of a full and distinct confession of sins for the just exercise of the power here granted by our Lord to His Church (see Matthew iii. 6, Commentary).

The Council of Trent defines, that the words of this verse are to be understood of the power of remitting and retaining sins in the Sacrament of Penance, as the Catholic Church always understood from the beginning; and anathematizes any one who, denying this, would wrest them, contrary to the institution of this Sacrament, to the authority of preaching the Gospel. (SS. xiv. Canon iii.)

They also condemn any one who, confounding the Sacraments,

Commentary.

shall say that Baptism itself is the Sacrament of Penance, as if these two Sacraments were not distinct. (SS. xiv. Canon 2).

Thomas was absent when this power was given (*v.* 24). Some, however, maintain, that although absent, being a member of the Apostolic College, the gifts bestowed on his colleagues, as a body, were communicated to him; just as of old, the spirit of prophecy given through Moses to the Seventy of the Ancients of Israel, was given to Eldad and Medad, who were numbered among them, although absent when the gift of prophecy was given to the Seventy (Numbers xi. 27).

Others, considering Thomas's incredulity at the time, hold that this power of forgiving sins, etc., was given him after he made a full profession of faith (*v.* 28).

From Catholic Tradition we learn that the words, "*receive ye the Holy Ghost, whose sins,*" etc., were confined, from among those present, to the Apostles, to whom He addressed the words, "*as the living Father sent Me,*" etc. From the words thus understood, is proved the Sacrament of Penance and the necessity of confession (as above). The words also prove, that confession of sins with the absolution of the Priests, is the only *ordinary* means for the remission of sins; otherwise, it would not be true to say, "*whose sins you shall retain,*" etc. I say, *ordinary*; because, from other passages of Sacred Scripture, we know that perfect contrition, including perfect love of God, remits sin. But this contrition including the love of God involves a resolution to observe God's commandments. Now, one of God's commandments is, to have recourse, when convenient, to the Priests of the Church for absolution and remission of sin. On the observance of this precept, when practicable, the remission of sins, by means of *contrition,* is dependent and conditional. To it is it subordinate. (See Treatises on Theology, *passim*).

24. "*Thomas, one of the twelve.*" He says, "*one of the twelve,*" although the Apostolic College was *now* reduced to *eleven,* because "*twelve*" was the original number, just as in the case of the "*Decemvirs,*" they would be thus termed, although only *nine* out of the *ten* were present on a particular occasion.

"*Who is called Didymus.*" "*Didymus*" is not a sirname, but, only a Greek rendering of the term, "*Thomas,*" which, in Hebrew, means what Didymus signifies, in Greek, that is to say, "*twin,*" probably, because he was one of two who were born at the same birth.

Some Commentators seem to think Thomas was present; because, St. Luke (xxiv. 33), informs us, that when the disciples returned from Emmaus, they found "*the eleven gathered together*" where our Lord appeared to them. But, as the Apostolic College went by the name of "*the eleven,*" after our Lord's death,

Text.

24. Now Thomas one of the twelve, who is called Didymus. was not with them when Jesus came.

24. Thomas autem unus ex duodecim qui dicitur Didymus, non erat cum eis quando venit Jesus.

Text.

25. *The other disciples therefore said to him: We have seen the Lord. But he said to them: Except I shall see in his hands the print of the nails and put my finger into the place of the nails, and put my hand into his side, I will not believe.*

25. *Dixerunt ergo ei alii discipuli: Vidimus Dominum. Ille autem dixit eis: Nisi videro in manibus ejus fixuram clavorum, et mittam digitum meum in locum clavorum, et mittam manum meam in latus ejus, non credam.*

26. *And after eight days, again his disciples were within, and Thomas with them. Jesus cometh, the doors being shut, and stood in the midst, and said: Peace be to you.*

26. *Et post dies octo, iterum erant discipuli ejus intus: et Thomas cum eis. Venit Jesus januis clausis, et stetit in medio, et dixit: Pax vobis.*

27. *Then he saith to Thomas. Put in thy finger hither, and see my hands, and bring hither thy hand, and put it into my side; and be not faithless, but believing.*

Commentary.

they might be called ("*the eleven,*" even if any of them were absent on any particular occasion. The words of this verse very clearly state that Thomas was absent on this occasion. It may be, he did not return after the flight of the Apostles at our Lord's Passion; or, he may have gone out on some business, and be absent when our Lord appeared. Possibly, the account given by the disciples, who returned that evening from Emmaus, may have been too much for his incredulity; and he may, becoming impatient at their recital, have left the chamber.

25. Our Lord, as we learn from St. Luke (xxiv. 40), showed them His feet also. Hence, not only His hands were each perforated with a rough nail; but, His feet also—"*foderunt manus meas et pedes meos.*" Whether two distinct nails were used for His feet, a nail for each, or only one for both feet, is disputed. In this is displayed the obstinate incredulity of Thomas.

Our Lord mercifully permitted this hesitation on the part of Thomas, in order to strengthen our faith, and remove all doubt on our part, "*Plus enim nobis Thomæ infidelitas ad fidem, quam fides credentium discipulorum profuit. Quia, dum ille ad fidem palpando reducitur, nostra mens omni dubitatione posthabita, in fide solidatur*"—(St. Gregory, Homil. in Evangel. 26).

26. "*The disciples were within.*" It is disputed whether this took place in the same room at Jerusalem, where He appeared before, or in Galilee, whither He ordered them to repair. (Matthew xxviii.) It seems more likely, that it occurred at Jerusalem, as the Apostles, who were well known, and would be closely watched by the persecuting Jews, would hardly venture much out at this time, while the memory of recent events was still fresh in men's minds. Moreover, the uniformity of narrative in regard to this and the preceding apparition would indicate the same place. There was no reason for assembling with closed doors in Galilee. The eighth day was selected, as likely having been assembled on the preceding Sabbath, they did not depart all at once. Our Lord wished to appear when they were together, so that in bestowing the faith on Thomas, He could confirm the faith of all the rest.

27. "*Then He saith to Thomas,*" specially addressing Him, whose infidelity he came to cure. He employs the language of doubt used by Thomas, thereby showing His Divinity and Omniscience, conveying to him, that, although absent when Thomas used the language of *unbelief,* He still knew what he said. Hence, with merciful condescension, He said to him: as you

Commentary.

would not believe unless you saw the prints of the nails in My hands, etc., thus irreverently dictating to Me what proof of My Resurrection I was to adduce, as if I could not bring home conviction by the sole act of My will; come now, do what you said, and, by touching Me, "*see My hands,*" etc.

We cannot but admire the wonderful love and condescension of our Lord in coming to bring about the conversion of His unbelieving Apostle. It is likely, though others think He durst not do it, that Thomas did actually touch our Lord's hands and feet, which, although now glorified, were, by divine dispensation, made sensible to the sense of touch. "*See My hands,*" etc. The sense of *seeing* is made to comprise all the other senses.

"*And be not faithless, but believing,*" as if He said, thou didst say that unless thou hadst seen My perforated hands and side, thou *wouldst not believe*. Now, thou hast seen them; I have done My part, by exhibiting My wounds for your inspection, with the merciful design of curing thy blindness and unbelief. Do thou, therefore, thy part; give up thy incredulity, and become a sincere believer.

St. Thomas, it is thought, was guilty of the sin of disbelieving our Lord's Resurrection. As regards His Divinity, he would seem to have very unsettled and hazy notions. He was guilty of pride, obstinacy and self-conceit, from which his sin of incredulity sprang.

Text.

27. *Deinde dicit Thomæ: Infer digitum tuum huc, et vide manus meas, et affer manum tuam, et mitte in latus meum: et noli esse incredulus, sed fidelis.*

---

28. "*Thomas*"—addressing our Lord—"*said to Him, My Lord,*" etc. This short incisive sentence, clearly expresses Thomas's earnestness. It was a clear confession, on the part of Thomas, of our Lord's *humanity*, through which He accomplished Redemption, and thus became, by purchase, Thomas's "*Lord*" and Master; and of His Divinity, "*my God.*" In these words, Thomas acknowledges our Lord to be Man and God, and, that not only did He rise again, but raised Himself up by His own power.

The attempt on the part of some to evade the force of these words, which, in their plain and literal import, clearly denote faith in our Lord's Divinity and humanity; by saying they were a mere exclamation, "*O, My God,*" as the Pagans used to exclaim, "*Mi Hercle,*" etc., is more deserving of ridicule than refutation, as Patrizzi (*in hunc locum*) observes.

The language is addressed to our Lord Himself. "*Thomas . . . said to Him,*" without reproof from our Lord, who, far from reproving him for this irreverent exclamation, as He would have done were it so; on the contrary, commends His faith, of which these words are the only expression on record.

Moreover, it would have been a shocking profanity on the part of Thomas—a thing held in horror by the Jews—to invoke the

28. *Thomas answered, and said to him: My Lord, and my God.*

28. *Respondit Thomas, et dixit ei: Dominus meus, et Deus meus.*

Text.	Commentary.
	name of God, so inconsiderately. These words are, therefore, an expression of faith on the part of St. Thomas, in our Lord's Divinity, accepted and commended by our Lord as such.
29. *Jesus saith to him: Because thou hast seen me, Thomas, thou hast believed: blessed are they that have not seen, and have believed.* 29. *Dixit ei Jesus: Quia vidisti me Thoma, credidisti: beati qui non viderunt, et crediderunt.*	29. "*Because thou hast seen Me . . . thou hast believed.*" Our Lord clearly commends the faith of Thomas, who, having seen the proofs of His Resurrection, aided by God's grace, believed in His invisible Divinity, and also believed in what he did not see, viz., that His Resurrection was brought about by His own Divine power. This followed from his believing Him to be his "*God.*" Our Lord does not reprimand Thomas's faith, but accepts it. Hence, He accepts his profession, that He was Himself God by nature, and not by participation. He was his "*Lord*" in right of Redemption, thus indicating His human nature. His "*God*," in whom the Divine nature and all the Divine attributes were essentially resplendent.

The words, "*thou hast believed,*" may be understood of faith in our Lord's Resurrection. Thomas did not believe in our Lord's Resurrection, until he had the testimony of the senses and his own experience in proof of it. But, then, having experimental knowledge of the fact, he believed in it, not on account of his knowledge; but, on account of the authority of God revealing it. For His Resurrection proved Him to be God. Our Lord had frequently predicted His own Resurrection. The truth of this Revelation at once dawned on Thomas, and aided by Divine grace, he believed in our Lord's Resurrection. He believed in His Divinity and Humanity, believed in all He revealed and disclosed. While our Lord commends the faith of Thomas, He tacitly reproaches him for his mode of believing, for his tardiness, and for not simply confiding in the narrative of the other Apostles, who declared they saw Him. In contrast with the obstinate tardiness of Thomas, He praises the simple faith of the others.

"*Blessed are they that have not seen.*" Under the *past*, by a Hebrew idiom, often used by the prophets in expressing *future* events in a *past* form, is, as if they had actually occurred, included the *present*, and not the Apostles alone, but, all future believers, such as are referred to, "*who have not seen.*"

"*Blessed,*" is used in a comparative sense, a thing, by no means unusual in Scriptures—*more blessed.* For, Thomas himself was "*blessed,*" in his faith, "*credidisti,*" which faith our Lord commends.

The faith of these simple believers referred to by our Lord, is deserving of higher commendation, who, without waiting for the argument of experience and demonstration, as a motive of credibility, accept the proposed truths at once on competent authority propounding them.

Commentary.

30. "*Many other signs,*" etc. Some understood these words of all the miracles performed by our Lord both during His mortal life and after His Resurrection, of which this is a brief epitome. Others, more probably understand those of the miracles He wrought after His Resurrection in presence of His disciples, in order to confirm their faith in His Resurrection, the foundation of all Christian faith. The miracles performed during His missionary life were performed in presence of others, as well as "*in the sight of His disciples.*" "*Which are not written in the book;*" these are recorded partly by the other Apostles. Hence, it is not necessary to repeat them here; as those already recorded are sufficient to prove His Resurrection.

31. "*But these,*" viz., the things recorded in this Gospel, "*are written,*" not only that you may have a record of them, but also, and chiefly, "*that you may believe, that Jesus,*" the man so called, whose history I have written, "*is the Christ,*" the promised Messias, "*the* (natural) *Son of God;*" and, therefore, consubstantial, and of the same identical Divine nature, with His Father.

"*And that* (thus) *believing, you may have life,*" the supernatural life of grace here, and the eternal life of glory, hereafter. "*In His name,*" through His merits and the redemption wrought by Him. To prove our Lord's Divinity was the whole scope and end St. John had in view in writing this Gospel. With this theme he commenced, and now with the same he almost concludes his Gospel. He also had in view, as he says here, to bring conviction and faith to the minds of all; and thus to secure for them, life eternal. This design is strictly adhered to throughout the entire Gospel. The record of the miraculous works, arguments and discourses of our Blessed Lord had this clearly in view throughout.

Text.

30. *Many other signs also did Jesus in the sight of his disciples, which are not written in this book.*

30. *Multa quidem, et alia signa fecit Jesus in conspectu discipulorum suorum, quæ non sunt scripta in libro hoc.*

31. *But these are written that you may believe that* JESUS *is the* CHRIST *the Son of God; and that believing you may have life in his name.*

31. *Hæc autem scripta sunt ut credatis, quia Jesus est Christus Filius Dei; et ut credentes, vitam habeatis in nomine ejus.*

CHAPTER XXI.

1 *After this Jesus showed himself again to the disciples at the sea of Tiberias. And he showed himself after this manner:*

2 *There were together Simon Peter, and Thomas, who is called Didymus, and Nathanael, who was of Cana, in Galilee, and the sons of Zebedee, and two others of his disciples.*

3 *Simon Peter said to them: I go a fishing. They say to him: We also come with thee. And they went forth and entered into a ship: and that night they caught nothing.*

4 *But when the morning was come, Jesus stood on the shore: yet the disciples knew not that it was Jesus.*

5 *And Jesus saith to them: Children, have you any meat? and they answered him: No.*

6 *He saith to them: Cast the net on the right side of the ship, and you shall find. They cast, therefore: and now they were not able to draw it for the multitude of fishes.*

7 *That disciple, therefore, whom Jesus loved, said to Peter: It is the Lord. Simon Peter, when he heard that it was the Lord, girded his coat about him, (for he was naked,) and cast himself into the sea.*

8 *But the other disciples came in the ship, (for they were not far from the land, but as it were two hundred cubits,) drawing the net with fishes.*

9 *As soon, then, as they came to land, they saw hot coals lying, and a fish laid thereon, and bread.*

10 *Jesus saith to them: Bring hither of the fishes which you have now caught.*

11 *Simon Peter went up, and drew the net to land, full of great fishes, one hundred and fifty-three. And although there were so many, the net was not broken.*

12 *Jesus saith to them: Come, and dine. And none of them who were at meat, durst ask him: Who art thou? knowing that it was the Lord.*

13 *And Jesus cometh and taketh bread, and giveth them, and fish in like manner.*

14 *This is now the third time that Jesus was manifested to his disciples, after he was risen from the dead.*

15 *When, therefore, they had dined, Jesus saith to Simon Peter: Simon, son of John, lovest thou me more than these? He saith to him: Yea, Lord, thou knowest that I love thee. He saith to him: Feed my lambs.*

16 *He saith to him again: Simon, son of John, lovest thou me? He saith to him: Yea, Lord, thou knowest that I love thee. He saith to him: Feed my lambs.*

17 *He saith to him the third time: Simon, son of John, lovest thou me? Peter was grieved, because he said to him the third time, Lovest thou me? And he said to him: Lord, thou knowest all things: thou knowest that I love thee. He said to him: Feed my sheep.*

18 *Amen, amen, I say to thee: when thou wast younger thou didst gird thyself, and didst walk where thou wouldst: But when thou shalt be old, thou shalt stretch forth thy hands, and another shall gird thee, and lead thee whither thou wouldst not.*

19 *And this he said, signifying by what death he should glorify God. And when he had said this, he saith to me: Follow me.*

20 Peter turning about, saw that disciple whom Jesus loved, following, who also leaned on his breast at the supper, and said: Lord, who is he that shall betray thee?

21 Him, therefore, when Peter had seen, he saith to Jesus: Lord, and what shall this man do?

22 Jesus saith to him: So I will have him to remain till I come; what is it to thee? follow thou me.

23 This saying, therefore, went abroad among the brethren, that that disciple dieth not. And Jesus did not say to him: He dieth not: but, So I will have him to remain till I come; what is it to thee?

24 This is that disciple who giveth testimony of these things, and hath written these things: and we know that his testimony is true.

25 But there are also many other things which Jesus did: which if they were written every one, the world itself, I think, would not be able to contain the books that should be written.

CAPUT XXI.

1 Postea manifestavit se iterum Jesus discipulis ad mare Tiberiadis. Manifestavit autem sic:

2 Erant simul Simon Petrus, et Thomas, qui dicitur Didymus, et Nathanael, qui erat a Cana Galilææ, et filii Zebedæi, et alii ex discipulis ejus duo.

3 Dicit eis Simon Petrus: Vado piscari. Dicunt ei: Venimus et nos tecum. Et exierunt, et ascenderunt in navim: et illa nocte nihil prendiderunt.

4 Mane autem facto stetit Jesus in littore: non tamen cognoverunt discipuli quia Jesus est.

5 Dixit ergo eis Jesus: Pueri, numquid pulmentarium habetis? Responderunt ei: Non.

6 Dicit eis: Mittite in dexteram navigii rete, et invenietis. Miserunt ergo: et jam non valebant illud trahere præ multitudine piscium.

7 Dixit ergo discipulus ille, quem diligebat Jesus, Petro: Dominus est. Simon Petrus cum audisset quia Dominus est, tunica succinxit se (erat enim nudus) et misit se in mare.

8 Alii autem discipuli navigio venerunt: (non enim longe erant a terra, sed quasi cubitis ducentis) trahentes rete piscium.

9 Ut ergo descenderunt in terram, viderunt prunas positas, et piscem superpositum, et panem.

10 Dicit ei Jesus: Afferte de piscibus, quos prendidistis nunc.

11 Ascendit Simon Petrus, et traxit rete in terram, plenum magnis piscibus centum quinquaginta tribus. Et cum tanti essent, non est scissum rete.

12 Dicit eis Jesus: Venite, prandete. Et nemo audebat discumbentium interrogare eum: Tu quis es? scientes, quia Dominus est.

13 Et venit Jesus, et accipit panem, et dat eis, et piscem similiter.

14 Hoc jam tertio manifestatus est Jesus discipulis suis cum resurrexisset a mortuis.

15 Cum ergo prandissent, dicit Simoni Petro Jesus: Simon Joannis, diligis me plus his? Dicit ei: Etiam Domine, tu scis quia amo te. Dicit ei. Pasce agnos meos.

16 *Dicit ei iterum: Simon Joannis, diligis me? Ait illi: Etiam Domine, tu scis quia amo te. Dicit ei: Pasce agnos meos.*

17 *Dicit ei tertio? Simon Joannis, amas me? Contristatus est Petrus, quia dixit ei tertio, amas me? et dixit ei: Domine, tu omnia nosti: tu scis quia amo te. Dixit ei: Pasce oves meas.*

18 *Amen, amen dico tibi: cum esses junior, cingebas te, et ambulabas ubi volebas: cum autem senueris, extendes manus tuas, et alius te cinget, et ducet quo tu non vis.*

19 *Hoc autem dixit significans qua morte clarificaturus esset Deum. Et cum hoc dixisset, dicit ei: Sequere me.*

20 *Conversus Petrus vidit illum discipulum, quem diligebat Jesus, sequentem, qui et recubuit in cœna super pectus ejus, et dixit: Domine quis est qui tradet te?*

21 *Hunc ergo cum vidisset Petrus, dixit Jesus: Domine, hic autem quid?*

22 *Dicit ei Jesus? Sic eum volo manere donec veniam, quid ad te? tu me sequere.*

23 *Exiit ergo sermo iste inter fratres, quia discipulus ille non moritur. Et non dixit ei Jesus: Non moritur, sed: Sic eum volo manere donec veniam, quid ad te?*

24 *Hic est discipulus ille, qui testimonium perhibet de his, et scripsit hæc: et scimus, quia verum est testimonium ejus.*

25 *Sunt autem et alia multa, quæ fecit Jesus: quæ si scribantur per singula, nec ipsum arbitror mundum capere posse eos, qui scribendi sunt libros.*

ANALYSIS.

This chapter opens with an account of our Lord's third public apparition to His Apostles, who were fishing on the Sea of Tiberias—the miraculous draught of fishes, where He is recognized by St. John first, and after that by Peter and the rest (1–9).

Our Lord instructs them to prepare food and distributes the fishes that they had prepared at the fire, and also bread among them (10–14).

In reward for Peter's triple profession of love towards His Divine Master, our Lord gives him charge of His entire flock, "lambs and sheep," and thus gives him full jurisdiction to feed and govern His entire Church, pastors and people (15–17).

He predicts Peter's violent death by martyrdom (18, 19).

He represses Peter's curiosity regarding the end in store for St. John, the disciple of love (20–23).

The conclusion (24, 25).

Commentary.

St. John would seem to have concluded his Gospel at verse 31 of preceding chapter. Hence, the *authenticity* of this chapter has been called in question by some, who doubted whether St. John was its author, or whether it may not have emanated from the pen of some other inspired writer. But, as it has been quoted from by the Fathers, and is found in all the codices of St. John's Gospel, it is generally believed as certain and undoubted that St. John was its author, that the entire chapter was from his pen, and that no other inspired writer had a hand in any portion of it. Some say, it was added by him by way of appendix, for special reasons, as he would seem to have closed his Gospel at verse 31, of preceding chapter.

But its inspiration, whoever its author may be, no Catholic can question after the Decree of the Council of Trent, "*De Canonicis Scripturis.*"

Commentary.

1. "*After this*"—after His manifestation to Thomas and others—"*Jesus showed Himself again to the disciples,*" in a body.

"*At the Sea of Tiberias.*" So called from the town of Tiberias, situated on its western shore, built by Herod Antipas in honour of Tiberius Cæsar. It was also called, "*the Lake of Genesareth,*" "*the Sea of Galilee,*" because situated in Galilee. The Jews were wont to call their large inland lakes, by the name of seas. Our Lord promised to meet His Apostles in Galilee, whither they were commanded to go (Matthew xxvi. 32; xxviii. 10; Mark xiv. 28; xvi. 7). Galilee was a retired district, free from danger, where our Lord could conveniently meet them, in order to give them, without fear of molestation, His final instructions before parting from them.

"*He manifested Himself after this manner.*" The Evangelist describes how He manifested Himself, and tells us who were present.

2. "*Nathanael,*" supposed to be Bartholomew. He was one of our Lord's earliest followers (John i. 45).

"*And two others of His disciples.*" Their names are not mentioned, as probably, they were not among our Lord's prominent followers.

2. *Erant simul Simon Petrus, et Thomas, qui dicitur Didymus, et Nathanael, qui erat a Cana Galilææ, et filii Zebedæi, et alii ex discipulis ejus duo.*

3. The Apostles deprived of the presence of their Divine Master, who managed to have their wants supplied, while in His company, have now no means of support, and, in order to procure the necessaries of life, have recourse to their former occupation. So had St. Paul recourse to the tent-making trade.

"*I go a fishing,*" that is, I am resolved on going to fish. This reminds them also of what they should do. They declare their readiness to accompany Him.

"*That night, they caught nothing.*" It was thus providentially arranged, in order to render the following miracle the more remarkable.

4. At an early hour our Lord stood on the shore, but not recognized by His Apostles. It was only in the exercise of His Divine power, that He was recognized.

4. *Mane autem facto stetit Jesus in littore: non tamen cognoverunt discipuli quia Jesus est.*

Text.

1. *After this Jesus showed himself again to the disciples at the sea of Tiberias. And he showed himself after this manner.*

1. *Postea manifestavit se iterum Jesus discipulis ad mare Tiberiadis. Manifestavit autem sic:*

2. *There were together Simon Peter, and Thomas who is called Didymus, and Nathanael who was of Cana in Galilee, and the sons of Zebedee, and two others of his disciples.*

3. *Simon Peter saith to them: I go a fishing. They say to him: We also come with thee. And they went forth and entered into the ship: and that night they caught nothing.*

3. *Dicit eis Simon Petrus: Vado piscari. Dicunt ei: Venimus et nos tecum. Et exierunt, et ascenderunt in navim: et illa nocte nihil prendiderunt.*

4. *But when the morning was come, Jesus stood on the shore: yet the disciples knew not that it was Jesus.*

Text.

5. *Jesus therefore said to them: Children, have you any meat? They answered him; No.*
5. Dixit ergo eis Jesus: Pueri, numquid pulmentarium habetis? Responderunt ei: Non.

Commentary.

5. "*Children,*" a term of kindness and affability used by superiors towards those with whom they converse.

"*Any meat.*" The Greek word means, *relish*, or something to be eaten with bread. It often denotes meat. Here, it means fish. Our Lord's question means, have they any fish?

Text.

6. *He saith to them: Cast the net on the right side of the ship; and you shall find. They cast therefore: and now they were not able to draw it for the multitude of fishes.*
6. Dicit eis: Mittite in dexteram navigii rete: et invenietis. Miserunt ergo: et jam non valebant illud trahere præ multitudine piscium.

Commentary.

6. "*Right side,*" probably, because it was the side nearest the shore, where there was a less probability of catching fish. A certain place is indicated, to show the capture of fish was not accidental. Without recognizing our Lord, they seemed to have some confidence in Him, as one skilled in the fishing business, and acquainted with where fish might be caught.

"*To draw it,*" into the boat. They drew it afterwards after the boat (v. 8).

Text.

7. *That disciple therefore whom Jesus loved, said to Peter: It is the Lord. Simon Peter, when he heard that it was the Lord, girt his coat about him (for he was naked) and cast himself into the sea.*
7. Dixit ergo discipulus ille, quem diligebat Jesus, Petro: Dominus est. Simon Petrus cum audisset quia Dominus est, tunica succinxit se (erat enim nudus) et misit se in mare.

Commentary.

7. "*That disciple, therefore,*" etc. John himself "*said to Peter,*" the recognized head of the Apostolic College.

"*It is the Lord.*" The miraculous draught put it beyond doubt, that it was He.

"*Girt his coat about him*"—a kind of coarse overcoat used by fishermen, which, in order not to be embarrassed by it in fishing, Peter laid by. He now put it on, out of reverence for his Lord, "*and girt it*" round him, lest it might impede his progress.

("*For he was naked.*") He was without his outer coat, having on him merely his tunic or under garments.

"*And cast himself into the sea,*" out of his impetuosity to meet his Lord. Ardour and impetuosity were Peter's leading characteristics.

Text.

8. *But the other disciples came in the ship (for they were not far from the land, but as it were two hundred cubits) dragging the net with fishes.*
8. Alii autem discipuli navigio venerunt: (non enim longe erant a terra, sed quasi cubitis ducentis) trahentes rete piscium.

Commentary.

8. "*Two hundred cubits,*" about three hundred and fifty (350) feet, or about *twenty* rods.

Text.

9. *As soon then as they came to land, they saw hot coals lying, and a fish laid thereon, and bread.*
9. Ut ergo descenderunt in terram, viderunt prunas positas, et piscem superpositum et panem.

Commentary.

9. "*A fire.*" This may have been miraculously provided by our Lord; or, perhaps, left there by some other fishermen, for the purpose of preparing the fish they might have caught.

ST. JOHN, CHAP. XXI.

Commentary.

10, 11. *Peter drew the net to land,"* aided by his companions. He alone could not do it.

"*One hundred and fifty-three,*" *large fishes.* This very unusual number of large fishes is specified, to show that the draught was miraculous.

> 11. Simon Peter *went up*, and drew the net to land, *full of great fishes*, one hundred and fifty-three. And although there were so many, the net was not broken.
>
> 11. *Ascendit Simon Petrus, et traxit rete in terram, plenum magnis piscibus, centum quinquaginta tribus. Et cum tanti essent, non est scissum rete.*

12. "*Come and dine.*" The Greek would denote a meal earlier than dinner, corresponding with our breakfast. It was early in the day when this occurred.

> 12. *Dicit eis Jesus: Venite, prandete. Et nemo audebat discumbentium interrogare eum: tu quis es? scientes, quia Dominus est.*

13. Whether He ate with them Himself is not mentioned here. But it is likely He did so on this, as He did on the occasion of another apparition (Luke xxiv. 43; Acts i. 4).

> 13. *Et venit Jesus, et accipit panem, et dat eis, et piscem similiter.*

14. "*The third time,*" He appeared to them collectively. To such apparitions alone St. John refers here.

> 14. *Hoc jam tertio manifestatus est Jesus discipulis suis cum resurrexisset a mortuis.*

15–17. "*Simon, son of John, lovest thou Me more than these?*" The form is ambiguous in the Greek as well as in the English. It may mean "more than (*Thou lovest*) these," or "more than these" *love Me*. The former construction is simply frivolous. Why ask Peter who so emphatically professed his love for Him formerly, who so ardently sprang through the waters to embrace the knees of his Divine Master when he knew it was He, if he loved Him, the Son of God, more than he loved his fellow-disciples, mere sinful men like himself, who had no claim of gratitude, as his Divine Master had, on him? What merit could there be in this? Our Lord repeats the question three times. But He only says once, and in His first question, "*more than these.*" For, out of modesty, Peter did not say, in his declaration of love, that he loved his Divine Master more than the others loved Him.

It is to be remarked, that in the first two questions, the Greek for "*lovest thou Me,*" ἀγαπᾷς, is different from the Greek word in the answer, "*I love Thee,*" φιλῶ σε. This, however, makes but very little difference as to sense. Also in the Greek, after Peter's reply to the second question, instead of "*Feed My lambs*" (v. 16),

Text.

10. *Jesus saith to them: Bring hither of the fishes which you have now caught.*

10. *Dicit eis Jesus: Afferte de piscibus, quos prendidistis nunc.*

12. *Jesus saith to them; Come, and dine. And none of them who were at meat, durst ask him; Who art thou? knowing that it was the Lord.*

13. *And Jesus cometh and taketh bread, and giveth them and fish in like manner.*

14. *This is now the third time that Jesus was manifested to his disciples after he was risen from the dead.*

15. *When therefore they had dined, Jesus saith to Simon Peter: Simon, son of John, lovest thou me more than these? He saith to him; Yea, Lord, thou knowest that I love thee. He saith to him; Feed my lambs.*

15. *Cum ergo prandissent, dicit Simoni Petro Jesus: Simon Joannis diligis me plus his? Dicit ei Etiam Domine, tu scis quia amo te. Dicit ei: Pasce agnos meos.*

Text.

16. *He saith to him again: Simon son of John, lovest thou me? He saith to him: Yea Lord, thou knowest that I love thee. He saith to him: Feed my lambs.*

16. *Dicit ei iterum: Simon Joannis, diligis me? Ait illi: Etiam Domine, tu scis quia amo te. Dicit ei: Pasce agnos meos.*

Commentary.

as the Vulgate has it, it is, "*Feed My sheep,*" so that instead of having "*feed My lambs*" twice repeated in verses 15, 16, it is, "*Feed My sheep,*" that is twice repeated. This, however, makes no difference as to meaning, since, in each construction, there is reference made to the entire flock or Church of Christ. "*My lambs,*" "*My sheep,*" are the same in sense as "*My Church*" (Matthew xvi. 18). Our Lord's three-fold question to Peter regarding his love for Him corresponds with Peter's three-fold denial, "*redditur*"—(St. Augustine observes—Tract 133)— "*Trinæ negationi trina confessio, ne minus amori lingua serviat, quam timori.*"

It is also to be observed, that our Lord addresses Peter singly, selecting him from his associates. "*Simon, son of Jonas,*" and that any power, privilege or authority conferred now was confined to Peter, "*Do thou feed My lambs,*" "*feed My sheep,*" so that while Peter was also a sharer in all the privileges and prerogatives conferred on the Apostles collectively, the privilege and authority conferred here was conferred on him individually, and not in common, as on other occasions, with his brethren. "*Lovest thou Me more than these love Me?*" Peter, unable to penetrate the heart of man and mindful of his fall and former presumption, when seemingly heedless of the prediction of our Lord relative to his three-fold denial, he presumptuously replied, no matter how others might fail, he, surely, would not, now humbly and modestly appeals to his Divine Master, the Searcher of Hearts, as to the sincerity and intensity of his love, without comparing himself with the others, and answers, "*Yea, Lord, I love You,*" and, as Searcher of Hearts, Thou knowest it. Our Lord, in reward for this confession, says (*v.* 15), "*Feed My lambs,*" and after having repeated the same question (*v.* 16), and received the same declaration, He says again, "*Feed My lambs,*" which in the Greek is, "*Feed My sheep.*" There is, however, no substantial difference of meaning, as, "*My lambs,*" "*My sheep,*" both refer to the entire flock of Christ. They are all "*lambs,*" all "*sheep,*" in relation to Him.

On our Lord's repeating the question a third time, "*Peter was grieved.*" Very likely, mindful of his former fall and presumption, he now fancies our Lord mistrusted his declaration or profession of love, and perhaps fears he may not persevere in His present dispositions.

He again appeals to our Lord's Omniscience, humbly mistrusting himself—in proof of the sincerity of his love. Then, our Lord, a third time, in reward for his triple confession, gives him charge of His entire flock, "*Feed My sheep,*" without exception or limitation. The commission given to Peter here, thrice repeated, to feed and rule the entire flock of Christ, lambs and sheep, proves demonstratively the Primacy of Jurisdiction given him, and him alone, over

Commentary.

the entire flock of Christ. "*My lambs*"—*all*, are His lambs—"*My sheep*"—*all*, are His sheep, including pastors (that is), Apostles, Bishops, Priests—and people, of every rank and degree. The entire flock is said one time to be, "*lambs;*" at another, "*sheep.*" For, they are all such in relation to their Heavenly Pastor. The mode in which our Lord introduces the subject, three times, questioning Peter as to his great love for Himself—(an element so necessary for a pastor of souls, who in tending His flock, should bear in mind that they are the flock of Christ, to be tended and cared for Christ's sake, and not for the personal gain or emolument accruing to the pastor himself)—three times also repeating the commission, makes it the more remarkable.

It is deserving of remark, that the Greek word, used in the second instance, for "*feed*," means, to *rule*, to *govern*, ποιμαινε—a signification which the word frequently bears with sacred and profane authors, and is commonly applied to kings, to supreme rulers and governors of the people. In the two other concessions of privilege, the word used is, Βοσκε, a word signifying, to *supply food*.

It is not without deep design, this twofold form of word, expressing "*feed*," is addressed to St. Peter, as expressive of his office, which, besides obliging him to furnish to the entire flock the wholesome food of sound doctrine, free from any admixture of error, also implies, a governing, ruling, coercive power to be employed when necessary in restraining and punishing. (See Matthew xvi. 18, where the whole question of the Primacy is fully treated; also Luke xxii. 31.)

Our Lord, in order to mark the vast importance of this exalted office of Supreme Pastor, who is visibly to tend his flock, after his own visible power was withdrawn, which office he confers on Peter only, first promises it in the most solemn manner in reward for Peter's ardent faith. (Matthew xvi.) Then, in some measure, confers it on him on the eve of His death (Luke xxii. 31), and now, on the point of leaving this world and ascending to His Father, confers it on him, in the most *solemn manner*, after having three times, exacted from him a profession of ardent love.

Peter, then, being commissioned to feed (rule) the entire flock of Christ, must be invested with supreme spiritual authority over all the members of the Church. He must, therefore, have *full, ordinary, independent, immediate universal* power directly furnished to him by the Son of God—the source of all power in heaven or on earth—whom he visibly represents, to carry on efficiently, without let or hindrance, all that is necessary for the eternal salvation of his flock, and employ all the means conducive thereto. In other words, as supreme pastor of the fold, he must possess all legislative and executive authority, to enact and enforce laws necessary for conducting his sheep to the pastures of salvation,

Text.

17. He said to him the third time: Simon son of John, lovest thou me? Peter was grieved, because he had said to him the third time, lovest thou me? And he said to him: Lord, thou knowest all things: thou knowest that I love thee. He said to him: Feed my sheep.

17. Dicit ei tertio: Simon Joannis, amas me? Contristatus est Petrus, quia dixit ei tertio, Amas me? et dixit ei: Domine tu omnia nosti: tu scis quia amo te. Dixit ei: Pasce oves meas.

Text.	Commentary.
	and for guarding them against noxious and poisonous pastures, and to restrain by due punishment, such as would lead them aside from the true path, whether in the order of faith and morals, and to appoint subordinate pastors to help in accomplishing these ends. In a word, the unlimited commission given him by Christ involves all necessary power to uphold integrity of faith and purity of morals. This power, in spiritual matters, embraces all persons, and is limited only by the nature of things and the unchangeable law of God. What else is this, but primacy over the entire Church? It involves universal legislative, judicial and executive authority to rule, govern and uphold the universal Church, including pastors and people.
18. *Amen, amen, I say to thee: when thou wast younger, thou didst gird thyself, and didst walk where thou wouldst. But when thou shalt be old, thou shalt stretch forth thy hands, and another shall gird thee, and lead thee whither thou wouldst not.* 18. *Amen, amen dico tibi: cum esses junior, cingebas te, et ambulabas ubi volebas; cum autem senueris, extendes manus tuas, et alius te cinget, et ducet quo tu non vis.*	18. After having raised Peter to the most exalted dignity on earth; after appointing him the supreme, divinely constituted Pastor of the Universal Church, our Lord now predicts the end to which this would lead, viz., a violent death. He consoles him, at the same time, by predicting his perseverance in grace, about which the triple interrogation was naturally calculated to make him uneasy, as if his Lord doubted him and feared for him. "*But when thou shalt be old*"—reduced to a state of decrepitude and dependence on the kind offices of others. "*Thou shalt stretch forth thy hands*," to be assisted and clad by others; or, rather, that those extended hands may be fitted and measured for the cross destined for thee—"*and then another shall gird thee*," round your loins—"*and lead thee whither thou wouldst not*," that is, to be nailed to a cross, from which nature instinctively recoils. Peter willingly submitted to the glorious death of the cross, after the example of his Lord. Nature, however, instinctively recoils from such; and it is to this feeling of natural repugnance, the words "*thou wouldst not*," refer. We have it recorded on undoubted historical authority, that when Peter, yielding to the entreaty of some Christians, during the cruel persecution of Nero, was saving himself by flight, he was met by our Lord, at the Sebastian Gate, and on asking, "*Domine, quo vadis,*" received for reply, "*Venio Romam iterum crucifigi,*" which he understood of our Lord being crucified in his (Peter's) person, and then returning, was subjected to crucifixion, as we are told by SS. Ambrose, Augustine, Gregory, Hegesippus.
19. *And this he said, signifying by what death he should glorify God. And when he had said this, he saith to him: Follow me.*	19. St. John, who survived St. Peter, and knew of the manner of death he underwent, now interprets our Lord's words in the preceding verse, as having reference to Peter's martyrdom. Very likely, Peter himself understood Him so at the time. Tradition has it that Peter begged to be crucified with his head downwards,

ST. JOHN, CHAP. XXI.

Commentary.

humbly declining the honour of being crucified like his Lord. By his death for the cause of truth and the faith, Peter contributed to God's glory, and proclaimed His adorable Attributes of Veracity, Justice and Mercy. Peter once promised to follow his Lord and failed; this time his Lord will not allow him to fail. *"Follow Me,"* may mean, in suffering, in taking the cross, through death to glory; follow Me afterwards (xxi. 36), or, *"follow Me,"* imitate Me in zealously tending and watching over My flock.

20, 21. Following our Lord, in the literal sense of the word, together with the other Apostles (though for him, the words conveyed a still more important prophetic intimation, as to the manner of His death), Peter, on looking back and seeing St. John among them, was anxious to know, now that his own ultimate end was definitely predicted, what St. John's destiny would be, whether he, too, the disciple of love, had a violent end in store for him. Very likely, this curiosity in St. Peter regarding John in particular, arose from his special love for St. John, and from the knowledge that he was the disciple whom our Lord specially loved. He had employed John, at the Last Supper, to ask our Lord which of those present was the traitor; and, in return, he asks for John, who, he supposed, did not wish himself to ask, what his destiny was.

21. *Him therefore when Peter had seen, he saith to Jesus: Lord, and what shall this man do?*

21. *Hunc ergo cum vidisset Petrus, dixit Jesu: Domine hic autem quid?*

22. Our Lord, repressing Peter's undue curiosity, administers to him, a mild rebuke, telling him he was not unduly to pry into the designs of God, in reference to others; he should mind his own affairs; and be satisfied with following our Lord himself, according to the admonition given him already.

"So, I will have him to remain." For, *"so,"* the Greek and Syriac Versions and almost all the Greek Commentators, have *"if"* (εαν), *"if I will have him remain."* However, there is very little difference as to meaning, *"so,"* signifying, in a conditional sense, *supposing* or *granted*, *" that I will have him to remain,"* here on earth, in this mortal life.

"Till I come." There is a great diversity of opinion about this coming. Some understand it of our Lord's glorious coming not to final judgment—for, John passed away long before, but, His coming in power to take vengeance on Jerusalem, and bring about its final destruction. John survived this, many years. Others understand it, till I come at the appointed time, to take him out of this world. St. John did not die a violent death. He died peaceably at Ephesus in the third year of Trajan, although

Text.

19. *Hoc autem dixit significans qua morte clarificaturus esset Deum. Et cum dixisset, dicit ei: Sequere me.*

20. *Peter turning about, saw that disciple whom Jesus loved following, who also leaned on his breast at supper, and said: Lord, who is he that shall betray thee?*

20. *Conversus Petrus vidit illum discipulum, quem diligebat Jesus, sequentem, qui et recubuit in cœna super pectus ejus, et dixit: Domine quis est qui tradet te?*

22. *Jesus saith to him: So I will have him to remain till I come, what is it to thee? Follow thou me.*

22. *Dicit ei Jesus: Sic eum volo manere donec veniam, quid ad te? tu me sequere.*

Text	Commentary
	he was subjected to a violent ordeal, having been cast into a cauldron of boiling oil by the order of the Emperor Domitian, whence he miraculously came forth intact, thus verifying our Lord's prediction, that he would "*drink of His chalice*" (Matthew xx. 23). From this circumstance, he has earned the glorious title of Martyr, as the boiling oil would naturally have caused his death, undergone for the faith, if he were not miraculously preserved. He was afterwards banished to the island of Patmos, where he wrote the Apocalypse. Having survived the other Apostles, a rumour was spread abroad, that he was not to die; but, would remain in life till our Lord's final coming. In order to correct this erroneous impression, St John declares our Lord made no such promise.
23. *This saying therefore went abroad among the brethren, that that disciple should not die. And Jesus did not say to him: He should not die: but, So I will have him to remain till I come, what is it to thee?* 23. *Exiit ergo sermo iste inter fratres quia discipulus ille non moritur. Et non dixit ei Jesus, Non moritur. sed: Sic eum volo manere donec veniam, quid ad te?*	23. Our Lord's ambiguous reply possibly, couched, on purpose, in such language suited to repress undue curiosity, gave rise to a false rumour, viz., that John was destined not to die—the refutation of which would seem to be one of his objects in appending this chapter to the foregoing Gospel. The disciples seemed to know only of our Lord's final coming. Very likely, the ripe old age St. John had reached, after all the other Apostles had, through the ordeal of a violent death, gone to their reward, may have confirmed this rumour. St. John informs us that our Lord did not say, that he himself would not die; that He only spoke conditionally, as to God's designs, which it did not concern Peter or others to scrutinize. "*Among the brethren*," among the body of the faithful. The word, "*brethren*," is often distinguished from the Apostles and disciples in several parts of the New Testament (Acts xi. 1–29; xii. 17; xv. 22, 23). The word, probably, refers to the Christians of Asia, of which St. John had special charge.
24. *This is that disciple who giveth testimony of these things, and hath written these things: and we know that his testimony is true.* 24. *Hic est discipulus ille, qui testimonium perhibet de his, et scripsit hæc: et scimus, quia verum est testimonium ejus.*	24. "*This*"—regarding whom the above erroneous persuasion, not warranted by our Lord's words—"*is the disciple who giveth testimony of these things*," viz., these latter events recorded in the Gospel, "*and hath written these things*," contained in the foregoing Gospel. "*And we know*," may refer to John himself, who elsewhere speaks of himself in the plural (1 John i. 5; 3 John 12), or to John and his disciples together; or, it may signify: it is a thing well known and admitted. "*And His testimony is true.*" This is a declaration on the part of St. John regarding his own certainty as to the truth of his testimony.

Commentary.

25. This is an hyperbole, by which is meant to convey to us an exalted idea of the words, discourses, miracles and marvellous actions of our blessed Lord.

This figure of speech is sometimes used in SS. Scripture.

Some Commentators, who never doubt the *inspiration* of these two last verses, question their *authenticity*. They seem to think they were added by a strange hand. But, the common, almost universal, opinion ascribes them to St. John.

Text.

25. *But there are also many other things which Jesus did: which if they were written every one, the world itself, I think, would not be able to contain the books that should be written.*

25. *Sunt autem et alia multa, quæ fecit Jesus: quæ si scribantur per singula, nec ipsum arbitror mundum capere posse eos, qui scribendi sunt libros.*

GENERAL INDEX OF CONTENTS.

Abraham, true children of, 177-186
Adam, *first, second,* 330
Adultery, woman taken in, punishment of, 167
Æons, 7
Alexandrian School, 7
Annas, 335
Apostles, chosen by our Lord, 294, 295

Baptist, 12-17
—— Deputation to, 20, etc.
—— Character of, 22, etc., 101
—— Baptism of, 23
—— His disciples, 62-68
Baptism, Institution of, 52-54
Bethania, or Bethabara, 23, 220, 222
Bethesda, 92
Blind man, cure of, 192
Blindness, spiritual, 200

Caiphas, wicked counsel of, 28, 231, 334, 337
Cana, Marriage Feast, etc., 35-41
Cedron, 330
Christ, died for all, 232, truly died, 352
Charity, towards God and man, 268, 291-295
Circumcision, date of, 151-153
Coming of our Lord, opinions regarding, 377
Communion, under one kind, 127, etc.
Confession, necessity of, 362, 363
Confidence, inculcated, 312
Council of 72, or Sanhedrim, convening of, 230
Creation, 9
Crucifixion, thirst attending it, 350
Crurification, 350

Darkness, light, 11
Dedication, Feast of, 211
Devil, children of
Docate, errors of, 15

Ebion and Cerinthus, 9
Ephraem, desert of, 232-238
Eucharist, remote reference to, 118
—————— Direct reference to, 125-135.
—————— Proof of, 135-137
—————— Objection, 139-141
—————— Illustration, 138
Excommunication among the Jews, effects of, 195

Father (Eternal) and Son, joint action of, 95-97
—— Judgment by, 99, 100
—— Resuscitation by, 100
Fishing by Apostles, 371
Fishes, miraculous draught of, 372

Galilee, sea of, 114
Galilean, 161
Garasim, 76
Gentiles, Greeks, 157

Gethsemane, 330
Gnostics, 7
Gods, meaning of, 214-216
Grace, 16, attraction of, 123

Hireling, description of, 208
Hours, division of, among Jews, 222

Idioms, 57
Incarnation, 15
Incredulity, inexcusable, 296

Jacob's well, John iv. 6
Jehovah, attributed to Christ, 251
Jerome, St., quotation from, 43
John, Evangelist, error regarding his term on earth, 377, 378
Judas, avarice of, 239; betrays our Lord, 330-332
Julian, Apostate, 161

Lamb of God, 24
Lazarus, sick, sisters of, 220-221
—————— Resuscitation of, 229
Life, 10
Logos, origin of, 6
Love of God for man, 58

Manna, John vi.
Manasses, Schismatic, 76
Mansions, different in Heaven, 274
Marriage Feast, Cana, 35
Magdalen, after the Resurrection, 357-359
Mary and Martha, 224-226; Magdalen, 239
Mary ever Virgin, power of, 36, 347-350
—— Dolours of, 348
Moses, serpent, 58
———— Writings and authority of, 107-120
Miracles of our Lord, very numerous, 367

Nathanael, who? Faith of, 29-371
Nazareth, 29
Nicodemus, 51-57, 161, 353

Parable, Proverb, 206
Paraclete, promised, 282, etc.
———— procession of, 297
———— operation of, 303-306
Pasch, 42, 114; of the Jews, 233-240
Passion of our Lord, anticipated, 245; commences, 329
Penance, Sacrament of, 361-363
Peter's denial, 270-333
———— His Primacy, 373-376; his martyrdom, 376
Philo, Plato, 9
Pontius Pilate, 336-346
Prayer, efficacy of, 280-309
———— of our Lord for entire Church, 315-325

Prince of the world, the Devil, 246
Presence of God, 249
Prophet, what, iv. 19
Probatica, miracle at, 91
Purification among Jews, 40
Purim, Feast of, 91

Regeneration, 52, 53
Reprobation, 249, 250
Resurrection, General, 225, 226
———— of our Lord, 46
Ridicule, resorted to by infidels, 161
Ruler, sick son cured, 85
———— his conversion, 86

Sacrifice, 76 ; of the Mass, 79
Samaria, 70
Samaritans, faith of, 83
Samaritan woman, 71-81
Sanaballeth, 76
Sepulchre, place of, 224
Satan entered Judas, 266
Scourging of our Lord, 345
Scriptures, reading of in vulgar tongue, 103-106
Shepherd, emblems of teachers, 205, etc.,
———— Good, 208, etc.
Sheepfold, 205
Siloam, 193
Sinners, heard by God, 197

Son of Man, 247
Sleep represents death, 222
Soldier's spear, 351

Temple, expulsion of profane Triffickers
———— Emblem of human body, 44
———— of Zorobabel, 23
———— Time taken to build, 23
———— Venerated by Kings, 242
Thorns, crown of
Tiberias, why so called, by whom built, 114, 371
Tiberius, 346
Treasury in Temple, 173
Treason of Judas, 265, 266
Title on cross
Thomas, Apostle, incredulity of, 363-366

Vine, Parable of, 288-291
Vision of God, comprehensive, 19
Voice of God, 245

Word, Eternity, Divinity, etc. of, 5-9
———.. Incarnation of, 15
Wine, miraculous change, 10, 11
Washing of disciples' feet, 258-262

Zeal, 44
———— For God's house, 44

www.ingramcontent.com/pod-product-compliance
Lightning Source LLC
Chambersburg PA
CBHW051249300426
44114CB00011B/957